Perspectives on Career Transitioning of Students with Autism Spectrum Disorders

Boitumelo M. Diale
Sol Plaatje University, Kimberley, South Africa

Chiedu Eseadi
https://orcid.org/0000-0003-1711-7558
University of Johannesburg, South Africa

IGI Global
Scientific Publishing
Publishing Tomorrow's Research Today

Vice President of Editorial Melissa Wagner
Director of Acquisitions Mikaela Felty
Director of Book Development Jocelynn Hessler
Production Manager Mike Brehm
Cover Design Jose Rosado

Published in the United States of America by
IGI Global Scientific Publishing
701 East Chocolate Avenue
Hershey, PA, 17033, USA
Tel: 717-533-8845 | Fax: 717-533-7115
Website: https://www.igi-global.com E-mail: cust@igi-global.com

Library of Congress Cataloging-in-Publication Data

LCCN: (CIP Data Pending)
ISBN13: 9781668472606
Isbn13Softcover: 9781668472644
EISBN13: 9781668472613
British Cataloguing in Publication Data
A Cataloguing in Publication record for this book is available from the British Library.

Table of Contents

Preface

INTRODUCTION

Career transition is the dynamic, developmental, and contextually influenced process through which individuals move from education, training, or periods of dependence into meaningful, sustainable, and self-determined participation in the world of work. The process of transition may include exploration, preparation, entry, adjustment, and progression across the lifespan. Furthermore, career transition for individuals with autism spectrum disorders (ASD) encompasses a multidimensional and ongoing process involving career awareness, decision making, skills development, access to opportunities, workplace entry, adaptation, and long-term career progression, that are shaped by individual strengths, support systems, environmental accommodations, and socio-economic contexts. In addition, it relates to the level of preparedness, engagement, and adjustment of students with ASD in moving from either education or dependence toward meaningful participation in employment or vocational pathways. For individuals with autism, this process often begins in adolescence and extends into adulthood due to delayed pathways, late diagnosis and other developmental challenges common among them. To this end, the implications of the findings in this book concerning the career transition of students with ASD cannot be overemphasized.

The findings presented in this book carry important implications for education policy, programme development, and workplace practice. From a policy perspective, the limited influence of demographic variables on transition outcomes underscores the need for system-level approaches rather than individualised or deficit-oriented interventions. Policies should prioritise coherent transition frameworks that are adequately resourced, monitored, and embedded across educational stages. Leadership commitment to inclusion must be accompanied by clear accountability mechanisms and sustained investment in transition infrastructure. Policies should also explicitly recognise families as partners in transition planning. Clear service pathways, coordinated support systems, and family-inclusive planning processes are essential to reducing service navigation burden and supporting family well-being. At the programme level, educational institutions are encouraged to embed theory-informed, reflective transition practices within professional development structures. The evidence shows that when educators and counsellors are supported to engage reflectively with transition theory and practice, transition support becomes more intentional, responsive, and effective. Structured counselling and intervention programmes that enhance work readiness and vocational confidence should be institutionalised rather than offered as isolated initiatives. Ongoing monitoring and feedback are essential to sustaining gains and ensuring that programmes remain responsive to students' evolving needs. Assessment practices should employ strengths-based, ecological tools that recognise transition readiness as relational and context dependent. Such tools support personalised planning while avoiding reductive or deficit-focused interpretations. In the workplace, the findings point to the importance of early and meaningful collaboration between schools and employers. Inclusive employment practices, reasonable accommodations, and neurodiversity-informed supervision contribute to environments in which autistic employees can perform effectively and sustainably. Capability-oriented approaches that value reliability, focus, and task competence benefit both individuals and organisations.

ORGANISATION OF THE BOOK

The book is organised into ten interrelated chapters that examine career transition for students with ASD from multiple stakeholder perspectives. The chapters address parental and teacher experiences, professional roles and theoretical orientations, policy contexts, counselling interventions, institutional supports, assessment tools, perceived barriers, and solution-focused strategies. The chapters present a comprehensive and empirically grounded account of career transition as a relational, ecological, and system-dependent process.

Chapter 1 examines the unique stresses parents face as they navigate their children's transition from school to work. It provides insights into the emotional, financial, and practical challenges parents experience, as well as the ways they adapt and support their children. By focusing on parental stress, this chapter underscores the critical role of family support during the transition process and highlights the need for resources that can alleviate these burdens.

Chapter 2 explores the perspectives of school-based professionals, including special teachers and school counsellors, and their role in preparing students with ASD for career transition. The chapter discusses various theoretical orientations that guide these professionals in their work and how these frameworks influence their approach to supporting students with ASD.

Chapter 3 addresses the importance of policy in shaping the career transition outcomes for students with ASD. Educators highlight the policies that support or hinder the career transition process, offering recommendations for policy reforms that could improve the transition experience. This chapter highlights the systemic changes needed to create more inclusive environments.

Chapter 4 evaluates various counselling techniques and their impact on students' career readiness and outcomes, presenting evidence-based practices that have been shown to improve self-efficacy, social skills, and adaptability.

Chapter 5 argues that educators often experience their own stress when supporting students with ASD through the transition process. This chapter provides insights into the challenges and emotional toll on teachers, discussing the need for institutional support and professional development to help them manage these demands effectively.

Chapter 6 notes that institutional support, both formal and informal, plays a critical role in career transitioning. This chapter examines the types of support available, from structured transition programs to informal mentorship and peer networks. It emphasizes the importance of creating supportive school and community environments that facilitate successful transitions.

Chapter 7 focuses on assessing the reliability of career transition inventory among students with ASD. The Career Transition Inventory (CTI) is an essential tool for assessing students' readiness for career transition. This chapter examines its reliability and effectiveness specifically among students with ASD, offering insights into how assessments can be adapted to better serve neurodivergent populations.

Chapter 8 explores perspectives on career transition counselling services for students with ASD. This chapter explores the unique needs of students with ASD in career counselling, emphasising personalised approaches that address social and communication challenges. It presents models of counselling services tailored to neurodivergent individuals, highlighting the importance of specialised training for counsellors working with this population.

Chapter 9 notes that understanding the barriers to career transition is essential for creating effective interventions. This chapter identifies common obstacles students with ASD face, including social, environmental, and personal factors that can hinder their success. By recognising these barriers, educators and counsellors can develop targeted strategies to help students overcome them.

Chapter 10 is a solution-focused survey of perspectives on career transition strategies for students with ASD. The chapter takes a solution-focused approach to career transition, presenting practical strategies that have been effective in supporting students with ASD. It includes perspectives from stakeholders, offering a holistic view of the approaches that can enhance career outcomes for neurodivergent individuals.

CONTRIBUTIONS

This book contributes to the growing body of knowledge on ASD and career readiness by offering a comprehensive and multifaceted view of the transition process. This book emphasises the need for a coordinated approach, integrating the efforts of families, educators, counsellors, policymakers, and employers to ensure that students with ASD can achieve their career goals and lead fulfilling lives. By addressing the unique challenges faced by this population, the book encourages the development of inclusive policies, targeted support systems, and a broader understanding of neurodiversity in the workforce. As the field of career transition for students with ASD continues to evolve, this book serves as a valuable resource, providing both theoretical insights and practical guidance. Our hope is that it will inspire further research, policy development, and program implementation that prioritise inclusivity and opportunity for all. In this way, we aim to contribute to a more inclusive world where the talents of individuals with ASD are recognised, valued, and nurtured. With the prevalence of ASD increasing and societal awareness of neurodiversity growing, there is a pressing need for structured support to help individuals with ASD achieve their career aspirations. However, despite these advancements, individuals with ASD continue to face disproportionately high unemployment and underemployment rates due to barriers that could be mitigated through targeted interventions. In today's world, there is a greater emphasis on inclusivity and diversity, particularly in workplaces. Companies and educational institutions are beginning to recognise the unique perspectives and strengths that neurodivergent individuals bring, creating a timely opportunity to expand understanding and supportive strategies. Our book addresses this demand for practical, research-based knowledge on career transition for students with ASD. It is situated at the intersection of education, mental health, and workforce development, offering timely contributions to the fields of neurodiversity and inclusive employment practices. This book is written for educators, researchers, school counsellors, employers, policymakers, and families of individuals with ASD. Educators and school-based professionals will find practical insights into how they can support students with ASD in achieving post-graduation success. Families will gain perspectives on how to advocate effectively for their children and support them throughout the transition process. Employers and policymakers will benefit from understanding the types of support and policies that can ease the transition from education to the workforce for neurodivergent individuals. Researchers interested in neurodiversity, career development, and inclusive practices will find this book a valuable resource for understanding the career transition experiences of individuals with ASD.

NOTE FROM THE EDITORS

This volume, *Career Transitioning of Students with Autism Spectrum Disorders*, is grounded in a long-term scholarly interest in advancing meaningful and sustainable career pathways for neurodivergent learners. It originates from a wider research endeavour titled *Perspectives on Career Transitioning of Students with Neurodiversity*, conducted through the URC Senior Postdoctoral Research Fellowship awarded to Dr C Eseadi, with academic mentorship provided by Prof B M Diale in the Department of Educational Psychology, Faculty of Education, University of Johannesburg.

As scholars and practitioners in education and psychology, we view this work as both a professional obligation and an academic opportunity. Career transitioning constitutes a pivotal developmental phase for students with autism spectrum disorders (ASD), influencing access to further education, vocational training, employment, and broader participation in society. Although global discourse on neurodiversity has expanded, students with ASD continue to encounter persistent institutional, social, and structural challenges when moving from school to post school environments, particularly within employment systems that remain inadequately inclusive.

This book addresses an identifiable shortfall in existing scholarship by presenting a rigorous and evidence-based exploration of career transition processes among students with ASD. Using primary data and a range of complementary research approaches, the chapters examine diverse stakeholders' perspectives that interact to shape transition experiences and outcomes of students with ASD. The analyses generated contextually grounded recommendations, alongside policy-informed and practice-focused insights aimed at strengthening transition planning, career guidance, and post-school support mechanisms.

Acknowledging the distinctive ways in which ASD shapes career choice, self-determination, and workplace participation, the book highlights the necessity of responsive supports, enabling environments, and professionally informed interventions. Particular attention is given to the responsibilities of parents, educational institutions, educators, career counsellors, educational psychologists, and related professionals in providing coordinated, timely, and developmentally appropriate transition support. The discussion further engages with contemporary career counselling perspectives, illustrating practical pathways for enhancing accessibility and responsiveness in transition service provision for students with ASD.

This book is designed to serve as both an academic reference and a practical guide for counsellors, educators, higher education institutions, parents, transition specialists, special education trainees, researchers, and policy makers committed to improving career transition outcomes for students with ASD. The volume seeks to contribute to more just, inclusive, and sustainable career futures for neurodivergent learners.

Boitumelo Molebogeng Diale
Sol Plaatje University, Kimberley, South Africa

Chiedu Eseadi
University of Johannesburg, Auckland Park, Johannesburg, South Africa

Acknowledgements

The authors sincerely appreciate the reviewers for their constructive feedback, which significantly enhanced the scholarly rigour, clarity, and overall presentation of the chapters in this volume. The authors also gratefully acknowledge the intellectual support and professional guidance provided by Dr Amos Amedu, Dr Faith Mesagan, and Dr Tobias Chibueze Orji throughout the development and completion of this book.

Boitumelo Molebogeng Diale
Sol Plaatje University, Kimberley, South Africa

Chiedu Eseadi
University of Johannesburg, Auckland Park, Johannesburg, South Africa

Introduction

Career transitioning is a meaningful and formative stage in the lives of students with autism spectrum disorders (ASD). It is a period characterised by growth, anticipation, and increasing engagement with educational, social, and work environments beyond school. During this phase, students with ASD bring with them distinctive strengths, including persistence, attention to detail, reliability, and strong interests, which can be valuable assets in further education, training, and employment contexts (Mirenda et al., 2024; Scott et al., 2019). Challenges that arise during career transition are not inherent to autism itself; rather, they frequently emerge when systems, services, and environments are not sufficiently responsive to neurodivergent ways of learning, communicating, and working (Gwynette et al., 2021; Ruble et al., 2013; Van Hees et al., 2015). This book, Career Transitioning of Students with Autism Spectrum Disorders, is grounded in a broader research programme examining perspectives on career transitioning among neurodivergent learners. The work was undertaken through the URC Senior Postdoctoral Research Fellowship awarded to Dr C Eseadi, under the academic mentorship of Prof B M Diale in the Department of Educational Psychology, Faculty of Education, University of Johannesburg, South Africa. Drawing on multiple empirical studies conducted within Nigerian educational and community contexts (e.g., Azubuike et al., 2024; Eseadi & Diale, 2024; Hill et al., 2024), the volume brings together the voices and experiences of students with ASD, their parents, teachers, school-based professionals, and institutional leaders to offer an integrated understanding of career transition as a shared and relational process.

Across the studies presented in this book, career transition is shown to be shaped by the interaction between individual strengths, family support, professional practice, institutional capacity, and policy environments (Carter & Schutz, 2022; Lee & Carter, 2012; Roberts, 2010; Stampoltzis et al., 2025). While students with ASD may experience differences in communication styles, sensory processing, or executive functioning, these differences only become barriers when environments lack flexibility, predictability, and appropriate support (Butera et al., 2020; Jones et al., 2020; Tamm et al., 2024). The evidence in this volume demonstrates that career transition difficulties are less about individual capability and more about how effectively systems anticipate, accommodate, and value neurodiversity. Families, particularly parents, play a central role in supporting students with ASD during career transition. The findings indicate that parents often take on extensive advocacy and coordination responsibilities, frequently navigating complex and fragmented service systems. High levels of parental stress are reported, especially in relation to service navigation, career planning uncertainty, and financial pressures. These experiences highlight the emotional and relational labour involved in supporting transition and underscore the importance of systems that reduce responsibility to families.

Teachers and school-based professionals are also key contributors to transition support. It was revealed that educators are invested in supporting students with ASD but often operate under conditions of role overload. Transition-related tasks such as planning, counselling, collaboration with families, and engagement with external agencies are commonly added to existing responsibilities without corresponding increases in time, training, or institutional support. Importantly, the evidence shows that effective transition support is most strongly associated with theory-informed and reflective practice, rather than with formal role titles or job descriptions alone. At the institutional level, the book illustrates an uneven landscape of formal and informal transition supports. While many schools report the presence of counselling services, transition planning structures, and supportive practices, their accessibility and impact are frequently constrained by limited resources and inconsistent implementation. Counselling services are generally viewed as personalised and relationally grounded, yet their effectiveness is often limited by infrastructural gaps, staffing shortages, and the absence of systematic outcome monitoring.

The volume also highlights the value of structured interventions and assessment tools that are aligned with ecological and strengths-based perspectives. Evidence from counselling interventions demonstrates meaningful and sustained improvements in work readiness, vocational confidence, self-efficacy, and independence in career planning for students with ASD. Similarly, the development of psychometrically sound assessment instruments illustrates the importance of understanding transition readiness as a dynamic interaction between strategies, self-related factors, support systems, and situational conditions. The chapters position career transition as a process that must be intentionally designed, collaboratively enacted, and ethically sustained. Rather than viewing students with ASD as needing to "fit" existing systems, the book advances a vision of transition support that adapts environments, practices, and policies to enable diverse learners to thrive.

REFERENCES

Azubuike, A. O., Azubuike, P. C., Onyekachi, E. L., Enyam, M. O., Akinreni, T., Abuo, J., Ogbonna, C. K., Timothy, P. N., Uchegbu, E. R., & Adai, G. S. (2024). Experiences and unmet needs among caregivers of children living with autism spectrum disorder in Nigeria: A qualitative study using the socio-ecological model. *Discover Social Science and Health*, *4*(1), 77. Advance online publication. DOI: 10.1007/s44155-024-00141-w

Butera, C., Ring, P., Sideris, J., Jayashankar, A., Kilroy, E., Harrison, L., Cermak, S., & Aziz-Zadeh, L. (2020). Impact of Sensory Processing on School Performance Outcomes in High Functioning Individuals with Autism Spectrum Disorder. *Mind, Brain and Education : the Official Journal of the International Mind, Brain, and Education Society*, *14*(3), 243–254. DOI: 10.1111/mbe.12242 PMID: 34367324

Carter, E. W., & Schutz, M. A. (2022). Addressing Transition Preparation in Middle and High Schools. In Viezel, K. D., Wilczynski, S. M., & Davis, A. S. (Eds.), *Post-secondary Transition for College- or Career-Bound Autistic Students* (pp. 179–200). Springer International Publishing., DOI: 10.1007/978-3-030-93947-2_9

Eseadi, C., & Diale, B. M. (2024). *Perspectives on career transitioning of students with hearing impairments*. IGI Global., DOI: 10.4018/979-8-3693-2631-2

Gwynette, M. F., Marrus, N., & Vasa, R. A. (2021). Transition-age youth with autism spectrum disorder. In Chan, V., & Derenne, J. (Eds.), *Transition-Age Youth Mental Health Care: Bridging the Gap Between Pediatric and Adult Psychiatric Care* (pp. 211–235). Springer International Publishing., DOI: 10.1007/978-3-030-62113-1_11

Hill, D. A., Fayemi, A., & Ostrowski, S. (2024). The Evolution of Services for Children with Autism and Developmental Disabilities in Nigeria. *International Journal of Disability Development and Education*, *71*(7), 1116–1132. DOI: 10.1080/1034912X.2023.2291570

Jones, E. K., Hanley, M., & Riby, D. M. (2020). Distraction, distress and diversity: Exploring the impact of sensory processing differences on learning and school life for pupils with autism spectrum disorders. *Research in Autism Spectrum Disorders*, *72*, 101515. Advance online publication. DOI: 10.1016/j.rasd.2020.101515

Lee, G. K., & Carter, E. W. (2012). Preparing Transition-Age Students with High-Functioning Autism Spectrum Disorders for Meaningful Work. *Psychology in the Schools*, *49*(10), 988–1000. DOI: 10.1002/pits.21651

Mirenda, P., Zaidman-Zait, A., Cost, K. T., Smith, I. M., Zwaigenbaum, L., Duku, E., Kerns, C., Georgiades, S., Vaillancourt, T., Elsabbagh, M., Bennett, T., & Szatmari, P. (2024). Educators Describe the "Best Things" About Students with Autism at School. *Journal of Autism and Developmental Disorders, 54*(1), 1–17. DOI: 10.1007/s10803-022-05761-2 PMID: 36315320

Roberts, K. D. (2010). Topic areas to consider when planning transition from high school to postsecondary education for students with autism spectrum disorders. *Focus on Autism and Other Developmental Disabilities, 25*(3), 158–162. DOI: 10.1177/1088357610371476

Ruble, L. A., Parsons, B. M., McGrew, J. H., & Hoffman, B. (2013). COMPASS Across Settings. In Ruble, L. A., & McGrew, J. H. (Eds.), *Compass and Innovative Education for Students with Autism* (pp. 191–205). Springer International Publishing., DOI: 10.1007/978-3-031-31395-0_9

Scott, M., Milbourn, B., Falkmer, M., Black, M., B lte, S., Halladay, A., Lerner, M., Taylor, J. L., & Girdler, S. (2019). Factors impacting employment for people with autism spectrum disorder: A scoping review. *Autism, 23*(4), 869–901. DOI: 10.1177/1362361318787789 PMID: 30073870

Stampoltzis, A., Peristeri, E., & Kalouri, R. (2025). Career counselors' attitudes about employment-related skills of individuals with autism spectrum disorders in Greece. *Frontiers in Education, 10*, 1662929. Advance online publication. DOI: 10.3389/feduc.2025.1662929

Tamm, L., Risley, S. M., Hamik, E., Combs, A., Jones, L. B., Patronick, J., Yeung, T. S., Zoromski, A. K., & Duncan, A. (2024). Improving academic performance through a school-based intervention targeting academic executive functions–a pilot study. *International Journal of Developmental Disabilities, 70*(3), 549–557. DOI: 10.1080/20473869.2022.2095690 PMID: 38699503

Van Hees, V., Moyson, T., & Roeyers, H. (2015). Higher Education Experiences of Students with Autism Spectrum Disorder: Challenges, Benefits and Support Needs. *Journal of Autism and Developmental Disorders, 45*(6), 1673–1688. DOI: 10.1007/s10803-014-2324-2 PMID: 25448918

Chapter 1
Parental Stress During the Career Transition of Students With ASD

ABSTRACT

This study examined the dimensions of parental stress experienced during the career transition of students with autism spectrum disorders (ASD) in Nigeria. A sample of seventy-six parents completed the Career Transition-Related Parental Stress Questionnaire, which measured stress across six domains, namely, career planning stress, service navigation stress, financial stress, work-family balance stress, emotional stress, and social support stress. Findings revealed high overall stress, with service navigation representing the most intense stressor. Career planning, financial, work-family balance, and social support dimensions also showed high stress levels, while emotional stress was moderate. We did not identify meaningful differences in relation to demographic factors. These findings underscore the need for structured transition support and coordinated services that would address these stressors. Strengthening existing systems of care is crucial for reducing parental stress and improving transition outcomes for students with ASD.

BACKGROUND

Autism spectrum disorders (ASD) are regarded as neurodevelopmental conditions influenced by genetic predispositions and environmental factors (Crowell et al., 2019; Sraboni, 2023; Victor-Aigbodion & Eseadi, 2025). Children who have ASD (CASD) frequently experience concerns in communicating and interacting socially, along with restricted and recurrent patterns of behaviour, which generally appear in the initial years of life(Crowell et al., 2019; Mushambi et al., 2024; Obasi et al.,

DOI: 10.4018/978-1-6684-7260-6.ch001

2019; Shen & Zhang, 2025). Although these characteristics do not originate from parental actions, the social and communication difficulties associated with ASD can place considerable strain on everyday interactions between parents and their children(Crowell et al., 2019; Nguyen et al., 2025). McStay et al. (2014) observed that among the various child characteristics, hyperactivity was the singular factor that notably predicted parental stress, outweighing the ASD severity and the child's overall life quality. This suggests that challenging behaviours have a substantial role in determining parents' stress levels and their perceptions of their own parenting competence than other developmental features that parents may believe they can manage or influence. Sustained parental stress may, over time, influence relational dynamics and contribute to developmental difficulties for the child(Crowell et al., 2019; Karst & Van Hecke, 2012). In essence, chronic parental stress can become a secondary risk factor that shapes how the child develops socially, emotionally, and behaviourally, amplifying existing challenges associated with ASD.

Parental stress encompasses the psychological and physiological responses parents experience when they perceive the demands of parenting as overwhelming and beyond their coping abilities(Abidin et al., 2022; Bochaver et al., 2023). This stress, according to Ríos et al. (2022), is often characterised by an individual's perceived difficulty and inadequacy in managing parenting responsibilities, and is often experienced as a negative emotional response that can undermine positive parenting behaviours and contribute to dysfunctional parenting. Craig et al. (2016) indicated that parenting CASD is linked to greater stress than is observed among parents of neurotypical children. In their study, Ayinla et al. (2019) reported that 64.5 per cent of Nigerian parents whose children have ASD experienced mild to moderate stress, and their overall coping strategies were assessed as fair. The fact that coping strategies were rated as only fair implies that although parents are managing, they still lack access to effective support systems. This points to a gap in interventions, guidance, and resources that could strengthen Nigerian parents' capacity to manage the concerns of parenting CASD. A study by Ng et al. (2021) revealed four main factors which contributed to stress among parents of CASD, which included psychopathological symptoms of parents, cultural factors, problem behaviours displayed by the child, and the overall burden of caregiving. These factors were shown to influence how parents cope with daily demands and had significant implications for the family's overall quality of life. Nevertheless, we would like to emphasise that stress among parents of CASD can be understood through other dimensions, such as career planning stress, service navigation stress, financial stress, work-family balance stress, emotional stress, and social support stress.

Career planning stress refers to the anxiety and uncertainty parents experience when attempting to support their child with ASD in identifying and preparing for an appropriate vocational direction. It encompasses parents' worries about the availability of suitable employment opportunities, their lack of clarity on how to guide career choices, and concerns that their child's current abilities may not meet labour-market expectations. Career planning stress is often influenced by the demanding caregiving roles that parents undertake. In most societies, including African societies, cultural norms and gender stereotypes may exacerbate this stress, as women often possess less voice and visibility, leading to substantial caregiving roles that limit their career opportunities when compared to men(Kehinde et al., 2023). Johnson and Simpson (2013) had earlier documented that fathers were largely absent from the routine care and support of CASD. Furthermore, the authors reported considerable variation in how mothers perceived the level of assistance they could rely on from spouses and other relatives. These expectations differed particularly in relation to sharing domestic duties, managing competing work obligations, supervising children, addressing behaviour-related challenges, and responding to repeated school absences. The findings indicated that mothers of these children often assumed the bulk of caregiving tasks, which increased their vulnerability to social isolation and heightened stress. The challenges in negotiating caregiving roles within the family when paternal participation was limited emerged as a major contributor to maternal stress.

Service navigation stress describes the difficulty parents face in understanding, accessing, and coordinating the services that support career transition (CT) for their child. This includes stress arising from confusion about which programmes are most suitable, challenges in locating reliable information about vocational training, and feeling overwhelmed by the need to schedule and coordinate multiple services. In other words, service navigation stress arises from the challenges parents face in accessing appropriate services for their CASD. In Nigeria, the dearth of essential services and support systems can significantly increase stress levels among parents. Thus, recent research indicates the need for counselling interventions to improve parents' stress management strategies and highlights the significance of professional assistance in navigating autism-related services(Hamidon et al., 2024). This professional assistance is important, given the earlier report by DesChamps et al. (2020), which showed that parents of CASD consistently experienced greater stress than those whose children had other developmental issues or no identified concerns. Their findings further showed that autism-specific challenges were a substantial determinant of parenting stress, even after taking into account other parent and child characteristics known to influence stress levels. According to Jamison et al. (2017), the demands placed on parents of CASD are substantial and have been connected to high levels of parental stress and under-utilisation of mental health support services.

Financial stress reflects the economic strain linked to preparing CASD for a successful CT. It encompasses parents' anxiety about the child's future financial independence and the burden imposed by costs related to assessments, transportation, feeding, and other transition activities. Financial stress is a major issue for parents of

CASD (Stoner & Stoner, 2014). This stress is compounded by the economic issues related to transportation and treatment accessibility, which are faced by families of CASD in Nigeria (Azubuike et al., 2025). In South Africa, mothers reported financial burdens linked to feeding difficulties in CASD, which likely extends to other areas of care and parental stress (Adams et al., 2021). In the United States, findings by Lee and Barger (2024) suggest that parental stress affects both parents of CASD in different ways, and that socioeconomic and demographic factors can either heighten or buffer these health risks. For fathers, higher stress levels were linked to increased likelihood of poor physical health, whereas being a racial or ethnic minority group member or living well above the national poverty threshold was linked to lower odds of poor mental health. Among mothers, child sleep difficulties significantly predicted poorer physical health, and residing in a two-parent household with income at least 400 per cent above the poverty line was linked to reduced likelihood of poor mental health.

Work-family balance stress refers to parents' struggles to fulfil employment demands while remaining actively involved in their child's transition process. This stress dimension reflects concerns about balancing work responsibilities with caregiving roles and feelings of guilt when unable to attend training sessions or appointments. Studies suggest that in Nigeria, work-family balance stress is common among parents who struggle to balance their professional responsibilities with the demanding caregiving roles(Nnubia et al., 2022; Nnubia et al., 2023). As argued by other scholars, the patriarchal dogma in different societies may influence men's involvement in caregiving, placing a disproportionate burden on women, which affects their ability to maintain a work-family balance(Kehinde et al., 2023). Balancing employment with the intensive demands of caregiving creates substantial stress for many parents of CASD. In Nigeria, research by Olubiyi (2022) reported that the employment rate of mothers of CASD dropped to 51.9 per cent, with a further 25.9 per cent leaving their jobs entirely, and these employment disruptions were substantially and independently linked to psychological distress. Sraboni (2023) reported that many parents of CASD struggled to devote sufficient time to their child due to work commitments, yet they continued to make considerable efforts to balance employment and caregiving responsibilities. In Malaysia, Sitimin et al. (2017) found that parents raising CASD struggled to balance their professional obligations with caregiving demands. The authors emphasised that access to autism-friendly childcare and greater employer support would help reduce the work–family tensions these parents experience. In the United States, Matthews et al. (2011) reported that employed parents of CASD often prioritise family responsibilities over work by drawing firm boundaries between the two domains. These parents rely heavily on flexible or unconventional work arrangements to cope with competing demands, but they still encounter substantial work–family conflict and have limited chances to recover from stress. Only a minority felt that their workplaces were supportive of their family needs. Furthermore, Segev et al. (2025) revealed that parents of children who have disabilities frequently struggle to manage the demands of employment, caregiving, and broader family responsibilities. The study noted that fathers, in particular, faced substantial difficulties integrating work and family roles, yet they also identified positive aspects of fatherhood and coping strategies that helped them adjust to these pressures. These findings underscore the heightened vulnerability of fathers in their place of work and the enormous issues they encounter as they attempt to maintain work and family life.

Emotional stress is used to describe the psychological and emotional burden parents experience during their child's CT. It includes feelings of emotional exhaustion, overwhelming uncertainty about the child's future, and doubts about their own emotional capacity to support their child through the transition. Emotional stress is significantly high among parents of CASD due to the unpredictable behaviour and demanding nature of caregiving. Mothers, in particular, experience higher levels of emotional stress compared to fathers, which is influenced by their primary caregiving roles and the emotional concerns linked to parenting CASD (Dijkstra-de Neijs, et al., 2024; Simelane, 2020; Soltanifar et al., 2015). In the United States, Johnson et al. (2011) found that among couples who had CASD, higher levels of caregiving stress reported by female partners were significantly associated with poorer physical health outcomes. Moreover, differences in how family functioning was perceived predicted lower mental health in female partners, accounting for 31 per cent of the variance. For male partners, elevated stress related to personal and family life, along with mismatched perceptions of family functioning, significantly predicted poorer mental health, with the divergence score explaining 35 per cent of the variance. In the Republic of Croatia, Zovko et al. (2024) reported that 19 per cent of mothers of CASD exhibited clinically significant levels of parental stress. Elevated stress was primarily associated with challenging parent–child interactions (34 per cent), the child's demanding behaviour (27 per cent), and difficulties in managing personal emotional responses to parenting (20 per cent). Collectively, the predictors accounted for 42.8 per cent of the variance in overall parental stress, with friend-based social support and the severity of the child's condition emerging as significant individual predictors. In the Netherlands, Dijkstra-de Neijs et al. (2024) examined parents of CASD and found intense degrees of parenting stress rooted in ambivalent feelings toward the child and difficulties in managing daily parenting demands. Mothers reported more stress linked to feeling limited by their caregiving role than fathers, relative to normative parental samples. Both parents showed compromised quality of life. For mothers, strong conflicting emotions predicted poorer psychological well-being, whereas feeling confined in their role was associated with reduced physical well-being. Fathers' conflicting feelings were related to diminished physical and social well-being, and their parenting challenges were associated with lower psychological and environmental well-being. In Iceland, Sigurðardóttir (2017) reported significant high parental stress, with 79 per cent of parents of CASD scoring within the clinical range. This researcher found that, even though most parents showed anxiety and depression levels within normal limits, about 15 per cent experienced severe or extremely severe anxiety, and 20 per cent reported similarly intense depressive symptoms. The researcher further indicated that child behaviour problems and parents' feelings of restriction when discussing their child with a partner, family members, or friends were significant predictors of elevated parenting stress, depression and anxiety. In their Nigerian study, Azubuike et al. (2024) revealed that parents of CASD often experience intense emotional strain, marked by shock, fear, and significant distress, particularly during the initial period following diagnosis.

Social support stress refers to the strain arising from insufficient emotional, informational, or professional support during the transition process of the child. It includes parents' perceptions of limited social support from family, pals, and community networks and inadequate access to professionals who can ease their anxiety about their child's career future. It is influenced by the level of support parents receive from their social networks. In autism care, the lack of adequate social support can exacerbate parental stress. Studies demonstrated that elevated social support is linked to lower stress levels among mothers of CASD (Hartini et al., 2021; Wahab et al., 2022), which emphasises the need for community and family support systems to alleviate stress. According to Alibekova et al. (2022), Kazakhstan parents of CASD who felt that their needs regarding societal acceptance were not adequately met experienced notably greater levels of stress and depression than those who perceived sufficient support. In contrast, being employed and having strong support from friends were linked to reduced symptoms of stress, anxiety, and depression. In the United States, Martinez and Turnage (2022) highlighted that while stress levels are high among Hispanic families raising CASD, access to both formal and informal social support significantly alleviates parenting stress. The authors emphasised the urgent need for culturally tailored support systems in light of the rising prevalence of ASD, arguing that such interventions are essential for enhancing the overall well-being of families. In Pakistan, Nadeem et al. (2024) examined the well-being of parents raising CASD and their findings showed that parents reported substantially compromised psychological health and weak social connectedness when compared with population benchmarks. Stress was widespread, with 78 per cent indicating frequent stress, and the highest levels linked to core autism features (91 per cent), co-occurring behavioural challenges (77 per cent), and additional physical health problems in their children (65 per cent). Their findings also revealed that moderate psychological distress was common, with 60 per cent meeting the threshold suggestive of probable mental disorder. Stress related to caregiving, particularly in response to comorbid behavioural issues, demonstrated meaningful associations with broader emotional strain and declines in both physical and psychological well-being. The study also identified gender-based differences, with mothers reporting significantly poorer psychological health and higher distress than fathers. Interestingly, parents who have younger children reported relatively better outcomes in areas related to social relationships and environmental quality of life.

Given the above expositions, it is obvious that parents encounter considerable difficulties as they support their CASD during CT, yet there is limited empirical knowledge about the distinct stressors that influence their experiences, especially in Nigeria. Previous Nigerian studies (e.g., Ayinla et al., 2019; Azubuike et al., 2024, 2025; Opelusi & Omoruyi, 2021) have mostly focused on general parenting stress linked to diagnosis, daily caregiving, behavioural challenges, or coping responses, without examining the specific demands associated with preparing students with ASD for CT. Addressing this gap is significant because the transition period requires parents to make complex career decisions, navigate poorly coordinated services, manage significant financial pressures, balance employment with demanding caregiving responsibilities, and cope with emotional uncertainty in the absence of clear guidance and structured transition pathways. Although research suggests that parental stress is multidimensional, shaped by career planning pressures, challenges in accessing services, financial difficulties, work and family conflict, emotional strain, and insufficient social support, no Nigerian study has examined these dimensions in an integrated manner or explored how they operate in the CT context. Moreover, despite national policy discussions such as the proposed National Autism Centre Bill of 2025, which highlight growing awareness of systemic gaps (Ogba, 2025; Ugwu, 2025), no empirical studies have mapped how these systemic gaps affect families during the CT of their child. As a result, policymakers, practitioners, and schools do not have sufficient evidence to design targeted interventions, coordinated transition programmes, or support mechanisms that respond to the needs of families of CASD. In other words, the central problem is the lack of comprehensive, multidimensional, transition-focused research on parental stress among Nigerian parents of students who have ASD, creating a substantial gap in understanding the factors that shape parental well-being when promoting transition outcomes for students with ASD.

THEORETICAL FRAMEWORK

The family stress model explains how economic adversity shapes family functioning and child outcomes through a sequence of stress-related processes (Conger et al., 2010; Masarik & Conger, 2017). From this theoretical standpoint, we assume that when external pressures accumulate, parents experience heightened distress that interferes with their ability to meet both work responsibilities and caregiving demands. This distress can manifest in negative parenting practices, including inconsistent or harsh responses, which then influence children's behavioural and socioemotional development(Gard et al., 2020; H. Lee, 2022; Ponnet, 2014). Evidence from Latino families demonstrates this process clearly, where economic pressure was linked to elevated depression in parents, lower parenting confidence, and strained parent-child interactions, which in turn, contributed to increases in child behavioural difficulties(Hurwich-Reiss & Watamura, 2019). This illustrates the wider applicability of the model and highlights how cumulative stress disrupts family relationships and influences developmental outcomes in CASD.

Bioecological systems theory also offers a conceptual lens for comprehending parental stress during the CT of students with ASD in this study. Bronfenbrenner's bioecological systems theory posits that development and daily functioning are shaped by multiple interacting environmental systems that range from immediate settings to broader societal structures(Bronfenbrenner, 1994, 2000). In applying this theory, we argued that each of the six stress dimensions addressed in this study reflects pressures emerging from different ecological levels. Career planning stress reflects processes within the microsystem, where parents interact daily with their child who has ASD while attempting to interpret the child's strengths, limitations, and career readiness. These interactions become stressful when parents lack clarity about their child's employability or when they feel uncertain about the steps needed to support future work pathways. At the mesosystem level, limited communication between schools, therapists, and families can further intensify this stress. Exosystem influences, such as limited career opportunities and the absence of specialised transition services, can increase the uncertainty surrounding career choices.

Service navigation stress is primarily situated within the mesosystem and exosystem. Parents of CASD must navigate educational, health, and community services that often operate independently. Weak collaboration between these systems can leave parents responsible for interpreting inconsistent information, managing scheduling demands, and making decisions without adequate support. Exosystem constraints such as long travel distances, shortages of trained professionals, and limited availability of transition programmes can increase the difficulty of navigating services by parents of CASD. Financial stress reflects exosystem and macrosystem pressures. Families often carry the full financial burden of assessments, transportation, feeding, and activities required for transition. These costs emerge from exosystem shortages in subsidised services and public support structures. Macrosystem factors such as national economic instability, insufficient disability funding, and weak social welfare systems can intensify the financial strain experienced by families of students with ASD. Work-family balance stress arises from interactions between the microsystem and exosystem. At the microsystem level, parents manage daily caregiving demands while attempting to meet employment responsibilities. Exosystem conditions, including rigid workplace policies, limited employer accommodations, and job insecurity, increase the difficulty of fulfilling both roles. This combination of pressures creates conflict that affects parents' capability to participate fully in the transition process.

Emotional stress reflects influences from the microsystem, mesosystem, and chronosystem. At the microsystem level, parents experience emotional exhaustion, worry, and uncertainty as they support their child's transition. Mesosystem relationships, such as communication quality with schools or the involvement of extended family members, either reduce or increase emotional strain. Across time, the chronosystem shapes the cumulative emotional effect of long-term caregiving, particularly as the transition to adulthood marks a critical developmental shift that magnifies concerns about the future. Social support stress reflects limited support across the mesosystem, exosystem, and macrosystem. Weak family networks, limited peer support, and insufficient professional guidance indicate mesosystem gaps that leave parents isolated. Exosystem deficiencies such as the absence of community-based support structures or trained counsellors can constrain available support. Macrosystem influences, including societal stigma, low public awareness of ASD, and cultural expectations regarding caregiving, can reduce the likelihood that parents will receive adequate support during the transition period. Together, these six stress dimensions demonstrate how parental stress emerges from interactions across multiple ecological layers.

POLICY FRAMEWORK

Recent national developments indicate growing recognition of the systemic gaps confronting families of CASD in Nigeria. In 2025, the Senate introduced a bill to create a National Centre for Autism alongside six zonal centres (Abuja, Bauchi, Enugu, Ibadan, Kaduna, and Port Harcourt) across the country, under the sponsorship of Honourable Natasha Akpoti-Uduaghan from the Kogi Central Senatorial Zone (Ogba, 2025; Ugwu, 2025). The proposed legislation aims to create Nigeria's first coordinated federal structure for autism services, focusing on early diagnosis, therapeutic intervention, educational support, and nationwide awareness(Akubo, 2025). The centres are expected to lead research, maintain a national autism registry, train professionals and caregivers, promote inclusion, and counter persistent stigma and misinformation(Folorunsho-Francis, 2025; Ogba, 2025). The bill emphasises that many Nigerian families continue to struggle without clear diagnostic pathways or accessible support services, often facing emotional and financial strain as a result. Framed as both a social justice measure and an investment in human potential, the initiative aligns with Nigeria's obligations under the Sustainable Development Goals 3 and 4, the National Policy on Inclusive Education and the UN Convention on the Rights of Persons with Disabilities (Ogba, 2025). If enacted, the legislation would represent a major shift toward structured, evidence-based autism support and could significantly strengthen the service environment within which parents navigate their children's development and career transition.

RESEARCH OBJECTIVES

This study's main goal is to examine the dimensions of parental stress experienced during the career transition of students with ASD in Nigeria. Its secondary objectives are as follows:

1. To determine the level of career planning-related stress experienced by parents of students with ASD during their child's CT.
2. To assess the extent of service navigation-related stress reported by these parents during their child's CT.
3. To examine the financial stress experienced by these parents during their child's CT.
4. To evaluate the level of work–family balance stress among these parents during their child's CT.
5. To investigate the degree of emotional stress experienced by these parents during their child's CT.
6. To explore the perceived level of social support available to these parents during their child's CT.

RESEARCH QUESTIONS

1. What is the level of career planning-related stress experienced by parents of students with ASD during their child's CT?
2. How much service navigation-related stress do these parents report during their child's CT?
3. To what extent do these parents experience financial stress during their child's CT?
4. What is the level of work–family balance stress experienced by these parents during their child's CT?
5. To what extent do these parents experience emotional stress during their child's CT?

6. What is the perceived level of social support among these parents during their child's CT?

METHODOLOGY

Ethical Considerations

Ethical approval for the study was obtained from the Faculty of Education Research Ethics Committee at the University of Johannesburg. The ethical clearance number is Sem 2-2020-057. We adhered to the ethical guidelines for research involving human participants(Sales & Folkman, 2000). Each parent received a participant information sheet explaining the aims of the research project, the nature of risk, and assurances of confidentiality. Parents were duly informed that they could revoke consent at any time without consequence and that participating in the project is voluntary. We obtained written informed consent from participating parents before they completed the questionnaire. We trained two postgraduate research assistants who assisted with data collection to be culturally sensitive when conversing with parents and ensured that parents were approached respectfully and that their time was valued. We trained the research assistants on the study aims, ethical standards, confidentiality procedures, and the correct administration of the questionnaire.

Research Approach

We adopted a quantitative research approach to examine parental stress associated with the CT of students with ASD in Southeast Nigeria. This approach enabled us to measure stress across well-defined domains using numerical indicators that could be analysed systematically. Quantitative approach was considered suitable because our research required the assessment of measurable indices rather than the exploration of personal narratives(Buchholz, 2021; England, 2022). The approach also ensured uniform data collection across all respondents and allowed us to produce findings that can be compared across contexts and used for evidence-based decision-making in educational and community settings.

Research Design

We used a cross-sectional survey design, which allowed us to gather data from parents at one point in time(Lau, 2017), reflecting their stress experiences during CT of their CASD. A cross-sectional design was appropriate because transitions into adulthood often create immediate and time-bound pressures for families, and a one-time assessment captured these experiences as they occurred. This design was efficient across geographically dispersed communities in Abia and Anambra States and reduced the burden on parents who already face time constraints.

Research Paradigm and Philosophy

The positivist paradigm, which notes that reality can be objectively measured and comprehended through systematic inquiry and quantitative analysis(Park et al., 2020; Sharma, 2025), underpinned this research study. This research paradigm guided our utilisation of a structured questionnaire and the decision to systematically obtain, validate and analyse empirical data on parental stress to understand the factors influencing the stress of parents of students with ASD in the Nigerian context. In relation to this study, the philosophical components within the positivist paradigm were ontology, epistemology, axiology and methodology(Park et al., 2020). In terms of ontology, the positivist's view holds that reality is objective, stable, and independent of human perception(Sharma, 2025). In this study, the stress experienced by parents of students with ASD during CT is considered a real, concrete phenomenon that can be systematically measured and analysed. With regard to epistemology, the positivist view believes that knowledge is gained and assessed through one's sensory experience(Sharma, 2025). This study is based on quantifiable data obtained from parents to establish relationships between variables such as financial stress, emotional stress, and social support stress that contribute to parental stress. For axiology, the positivist view believes in researcher neutrality by preserving a clear separation between the knower and what is being studied, with the intention of minimising bias throughout the inquiry (Park et al., 2020; Sharma, 2025). Consequently, standardised instruments and statistical methods were used in the study to ensure objectivity in the collection and interpretation of data regarding parental stress. With respect to methodology, we aligned with positivist principles by following a quantitative research design that uses a survey to gather data that can be subjected to statistical analysis to identify generalisable trends regarding stress experiences among parents.

Population and Sample

In this research study, the study population comprised parents of students who have ASD in Abia and Anambra States of Nigeria. Parents were central to the study because they manage their children's transition processes, negotiate service access, and coordinate educational and vocational planning. We focused on parents whose children fell within the age of fifteen to twenty-five years, as this age group typically experiences the shift from school-based learning to post-school pathways.

We used a multi-stage sampling technique to ensure efficient access to respondents across two states. Researchers often use multistage sampling in survey studies where no full sampling frame exists or where the population is spread across large and diverse areas(Chauvet, 2015). According to Lee (2025), multi-stage sampling is an advanced form of cluster sampling that is commonly applied when the target population is widely dispersed or when a complete sampling frame cannot be obtained. It involves selecting samples across several stages, which improves efficiency and reduces the overall cost of data collection. In this study, we first purposively selected Abia and Anambra because of the existence of urban, semi-urban, and rural areas in these states and because they also have schools and centres that support students with neurodevelopmental learning needs, including those with ASD. Second, we identified inclusive schools, special needs education centres, therapy facilities, and local support groups that work with students and young people with ASD and their families. These institutions formed the sampling frame. Third, we used convenience and purposive sampling to recruit eligible parents. Convenience sampling was necessary because diagnosis records are not publicly available, while purposive sampling ensured that only parents with children in transition processes were included. Seventy-six parents participated in this research study. This sample size was appropriate for group comparisons and reflected the number of eligible parents who could be reached within the study period. It also represented a diverse cross-section of communities and service settings in both states.

Data Collection Instrument

We used the Career Transition-Related Parental Stress Questionnaire (CT-ParSQ), documented in the appendix section (see Table 4). The instrument measured stress across six domains: career planning stress, service navigation stress, financial stress, work-family balance stress, emotional stress, and social support stress. It consisted of fifteen items with good factor loadings and satisfactory reliability indices, including Cronbach's alpha and omega coefficients across all subscales. CT-ParSQ utilises a Likert scale of five options [Strongly Disagree (1) to Strongly Agree (5)]. We used this self-developed instrument because it offered a multidimensional, empirically grounded assessment of parental stress that corresponds with the tasks and pressures associated with CT. The items were concise and easy for parents to respond to, which was important for maintaining completion rates among parents with substantial daily responsibilities. The instrument's structure made it appropriate for quantitative analysis and compatible with our overall research design.

Data Collection Procedures

Data were collected over eight weeks by the research assistants who approached parents during school visits, therapy appointments, and parent group meetings. Parents had the opportunity to complete the questionnaire on site or at home. The questionnaires were retrieved by the research assistants within agreed-upon timelines and were checked for completeness. All questionnaires were stored securely and processed using a password-protected database for analysis.

Data Analysis Procedure

We analysed the study data by making use of descriptive and inferential statistics. Descriptive statistics allowed us to offer insights into the respondents' demographic information and stress levels across the six domains. These statistics examined the research questions by indicating the extent and distribution of parental stress. Inferential analysis involved independent samples t-tests and one-way analyses of variance. These procedures enabled us to examine whether stress levels differed across demographic factors. In this research study, a significance threshold of $p < .05$ was employed for all analyses. The main research data analysis was carried out using IBM SPSS Statistics 24.0, and the results were organised in Tables. Charts were created with Microsoft Excel. The statistical procedures aligned with our goals of determining whether demographic variables were linked to higher or lower levels of stress among the parents.

RESULTS

This section presents the findings of the study in accordance with six research questions and the demographic characteristics of the respondents. It contains descriptive statistics analysis of the domains of parental stress, a graphic illustration of the stress levels, and a general stress scores analysis based on the possible confounding factors, all of which were interpreted in relation to the data in Tables 1-3 and Figure 1.

Table 1. Demographic characteristics of respondents

Variables	N	%
Gender Male Female	20 56	26.3 73.3
Age*	45.2±8.69	
Location Urban Semi-urban Rural	24 34 18	31.6 44.7 23.7
Employment Status Unemployed Entrepreneur Employed	21 33 22	27.6 43.4 28.9
Educational level Primary Secondary Post-secondary	25 25 26	32.9 32.9 34.2
Income Level Poor Lower class Middle class Others	29 23 16 8	38.2 30.3 21.1 10.1

*Mean age and standard deviation of respondents

Table 1 reveals the demographic characteristics of the respondents. Respondents consisted of seventy-six parents. As shown in Table 1, twenty respondents were male (26.3 percent) and fifty-six were female (73.3 percent). The mean age of respondents was 45.2 years (SD = 8.69). With regard to residential location, twenty-four parents lived in urban areas (31.6 percent), thirty-four resided in semi-urban locations (44.7 percent), and eighteen were from rural communities (23.7 percent). Employment status included twenty-one unemployed parents (27.6 percent), thirty-three entrepreneurs (43.4 percent), and twenty-two employed respondents (28.9 percent). Educational attainment was distributed across primary (n = 25, 32.9 percent), secondary (n = 25, 32.9 percent), and post-secondary levels (n = 26, 34.2 percent). Income level classifications included twenty-nine parents in the poor category (38.2 percent), twenty-three in the lower class (30.3 percent), sixteen in the middle class (21.1 percent), and eight in the other category (10.1 percent).

Table 2. Mean scores of stress parents face during students' CT

S/No	Stress dimensions	Mean	SD	95% Confidence Interval		Remark
				Lower Limit	Upper Limit	
1	Career Planning Stress	13.46	2.97	12.78	14.14	High Parental Stress
2	Service Navigation Stress	14.00	2.12	13.52	14.48	Very High Parental Stress
3	Financial Stress	9.32	1.47	8.99	9.65	High Parental Stress
4	Work-Family Balance Stress	8.20	1.79	7.79	8.61	High Parental Stress
5	Emotional Stress	9.12	2.94	8.45	9.79	Moderate Parental Stress
6	Social Support Stress	9.08	1.53	8.73	9.43	High Parental Stress
7	Overall Stress	63.17	6.88	61.60	64.74	High Parental Stress

The descriptive statistics for the six stress dimensions and overall parental stress are presented in Table 2. As shown in Table 2, parents reported high stress related to career planning, with a mean score of 13.46 (SD = 2.97, 95 percent CI = 12.78 to 14.14). Service navigation stress demonstrated the highest mean value among all stress dimensions (M = 14.00, SD = 2.12, 95 percent CI = 13.52 to 14.48). Financial stress also reflected high levels, with a mean of 9.32 (SD = 1.47, 95 percent CI = 8.99 to 9.65). Work-family balance stress produced a mean score of 8.20 (SD = 1.79, 95 percent CI = 7.79 to 8.61), which was categorised as high stress in the table. Emotional stress yielded a mean value of 9.12 (SD = 2.94, 95 percent CI = 8.45 to 9.79) and was identified as moderate stress. Social support stress was classified as high, with a mean of 9.08 (SD = 1.53, 95 percent CI = 8.73 to 9.43). Overall stress demonstrated a high mean score of 63.17 (SD = 6.88, 95 percent CI = 61.60 to 64.74).

Figure 1. A bar chart showing the level of stress parents face during students' CT

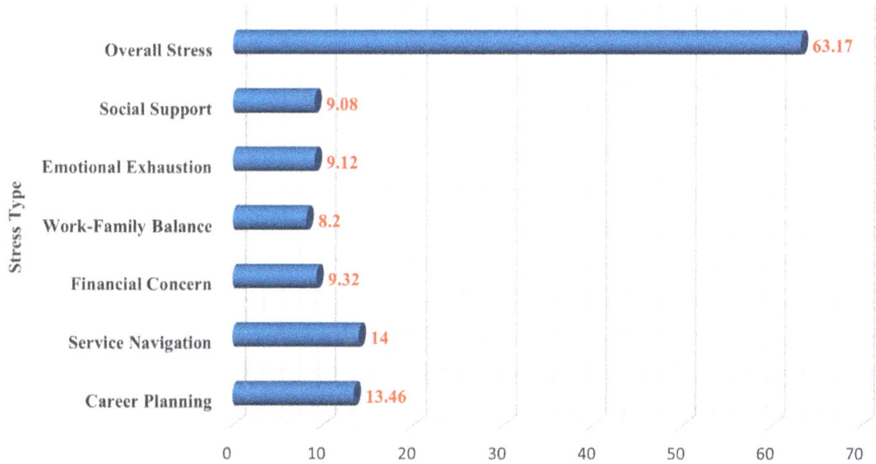

Figure 1 is a graphical representation of the mean stress scores of parents across the six dimensions. As illustrated in Figure 1, service navigation stress had the highest mean score, followed by career planning stress. Financial stress, work-family balance stress, emotional stress, and social support stress appeared in descending order of mean values. The bar chart in Figure 1 visually corroborates the descriptive statistics shown in Table 2. The height of each bar reflects the magnitude of stress reported in each dimension, with the tallest bar corresponding to service navigation stress.

Table 3. Overall stress scores across potential confounders showing the level of stress parents face during students' CT

Confounders	Categories	N	Mean	SD	*P*	95% CI
Gender	Male Female	20 56	64.25 62.79	6.93 6.88	.417	61.60- 64.74
Age*		76	63.17	6.88	.453	58.90- 78.59
Location	Urban Semi-urban Rural	24 34 18	62.50 62.74 64.89	6.32 7.61 6.17	.481	61.82- 67.96
Employment Status	Unemployed Entrepreneur Employed	21 33 22	61.43 64.39 63.00	6.84 6.65 7.18	.304	61.59- 64.74

continued on following page

Table 3. Continued

Confounders	Categories	N	Mean	SD	*P*	95% CI
Educational level	Primary Secondary Post-secondary	25 25 26	64.20 64.24 61.15	6.53 5.98 7.75	.184	58.02- 64.29
Income Level	Poor Lower class Middle class Others	29 23 16 8	62.21 64.87 61.13 65.88	7.26 6.21 6.80 6.66	.202	57.50- 71.45

Table 3 shows the mean parental stress scores and standard deviations across potential confounding variables. No statistically significant differences were observed across any demographic categories. Gender was not associated with significant differences in mean overall stress scores, with males reporting a mean of 64.25 (SD = 6.93) and females reporting a mean of 62.79 (SD = 6.88) (P=.417). Age as a continuous variable also demonstrated no significant relation to overall stress (P = .453).

With regard to residential location, parents from urban areas reported a mean overall stress score of 62.50 (SD = 6.32), those from semi-urban areas reported 62.74 (SD = 7.61), and those from rural locations reported 64.89 (SD = 6.17). These differences were not statistically significant (P = .481). Employment status produced similar findings. Unemployed parents reported a mean stress score of 61.43 (SD = 6.84), entrepreneurs reported 64.39 (SD = 6.65), and employed respondents reported 63.00 (SD = 7.18). No significant differences were found among these groups (P = .304).

Educational level did not yield significant differences in overall stress. Parents with primary education reported a mean score of 64.20 (SD = 6.53), those with secondary education reported 64.24 (SD = 5.98), and those with post-secondary education reported 61.15 (SD = 7.75). These differences were not significant (P = .184). Income level categories similarly demonstrated no significant group differences. Parents classified as poor reported a mean stress score of 62.21 (SD = 7.26), those in the lower class category reported 64.87 (SD = 6.21), those in the middle class reported 61.13 (SD = 6.80), and parents in the other category reported 65.88 (SD = 6.66). These group differences were nonsignificant (P = .202).

DISCUSSION

The findings of this study demonstrate that parents of students with ASD in Nigeria experience considerable stress as they support their children through CT. The overall stress score fell within the high range, indicating that transition planning constitutes a significant psychosocial burden for families irrespective of demographic variables. This aligns with previous studies indicating that these parents are vulnerable to persistent stress because of the intensive and complex demands associated with caregiving(Anyanwu et al., 2019; Dijkstra-de Neijs et al., 2024; Sigurðardóttir, 2017; Wang et al., 2013). This finding also aligns with Nguyen et al. (2025), who reported that more than half of these parents in their Vietnamese study experienced quite frequent or elevated levels of stress. In their study, the most commonly reported symptoms involved physical strain, including fatigue alongside cognitive signs such as persistent worry and heightened fear. Their study also showed a strong link between the stress of parents and autism-related challenges in their children, particularly difficulties with social engagement and communication. Nikmat et al. (2008) revealed that in their study, Malaysian parents of CASD experienced substantial stress, with 90.4 per cent showing significant parenting stress. In our study, the demographic profile showed that most respondents were mothers in their mid-forties who were navigating caregiving responsibilities alongside work demands and household management. This finding is consistent with many autism-related family studies, where women frequently represent the larger proportion of respondents due to their perceived role in daily caregiving (Johnson & Simpson, 2013; Zovko et al., 2024). In a previous Nigerian autism-focused study on parental stress, the study sample was predominantly female, as 71.4% of the participating parents were mothers, while only 28.6% were fathers(Obasi et al., 2019). Our gender distribution aligns with findings from another Nigerian study, where women also represented the majority of participants, with mothers and fathers accounting for 76.1% and 23.9% of the sample, correspondingly(Oduyemi et al., 2021).

In the present study, stress levels did not significantly differ across gender, age, residence, employment status, education, or income, suggesting that transition-related stress is widespread and not confined to specific social groups. This aligns with bioecological perspectives, which emphasise that systemic and environmental factors often exert stronger influence than individual characteristics. Unlike the results reported by Ayinla et al. (2019) in Lagos, where mothers of CASD were found to be more vulnerable to elevated parenting stress than other relatives, our study did not identify gender differences in stress levels. Additionally, our result diverges from earlier research suggesting that mothers experience greater parenting stress than fathers, which could have been influenced by differences in caregiving roles and expectations(Dijkstra-de Neijs et al., 2024; Johnson et al., 2011; Johnson & Simpson, 2013; Kehinde et al., 2023). Moreover, there is also a finding that fathers of CASD experience higher stress than mothers, with parental stress being related to the child's age, cognitive ability, severity of ASD symptoms, and adaptive behaviour, and only fathers' stress being predicted by the severity of ASD features and the child's gender(Rivard et al., 2014). Interestingly, emerging evidence suggests that family dynamics in Nigeria are gradually shifting(Akanle & Nwaobiala, 2019). Urbanisation, greater female participation in paid work, economic pressures on dual-income households, and slow but noticeable changes in traditional gender roles are altering how caregiving is distributed(Akanle & Nwaobiala, 2019; Nnubia et al., 2020, 2024). As patriarchal structures become less rigid, particularly in urban and semi-urban settings, fathers are increasingly involved in childcare and educational responsibilities. These changes may help explain why, in this study, stress levels did not differ significantly between female and male parents. More egalitarian ways of parenting, increased exposure to advocacy around shared caregiving, and the growing awareness of ASD may have contributed to a broader recognition of caregiving demands across both parents. Consequently, the parental stress levels in this study reflect a more shared experience within the Nigerian households.

Service navigation emerged as the most intense stressor, exceeding all other domains. Parents consistently reported difficulty accessing coordinated services, obtaining specialist input, and managing uneven pathways across education, health, and community settings. This is consistent with current research showing that Nigerian families face the complexity of accessing appropriate services and support, which can be overwhelming(Azubuike et al., 2025). As highlighted by previous and recent studies, the need for specialised interventions and the difficulty in navigating healthcare systems contribute to parental stress(Hamidon et al., 2024; Jamison et al., 2017; Zovko et al., 2024). The level of service navigation stress reinforces bioecological systems theory, indicating that mesosystem and exosystem disruptions, such as inconsistent interagency communication and insufficient service infrastructure, could significantly heighten parental stress(Ulofoshio, 2017). This finding also supports Masarik and Conger's (2017) extension of the family stress model, indicating that when institutional demands accumulate and families lack access to stable support systems, parents experience heightened psychological pressure that spills into other domains of family functioning.

Career planning stress was also substantially elevated among parents of CASD. Parents expressed uncertainty about vocational opportunities, employability prospects, and their child's readiness for adult roles. Applying transition theory perspectives (George, 1993; Goodman et al., 2006) to our findings, the high levels of career planning stress reported by parents can be understood as a response to the ambiguity and limited structured pathways within the Nigerian school system for the CT of students with ASD. Because there are limited, clearly established procedures, expectations, or coordinated support guiding families through career decision-making, parents are left to navigate a highly uncertain landscape with their children. This situation creates confusion about the roles parents must play and the actions required to support their child's movement towards adulthood. Consistent with transition theory, this structural ambiguity contributes to heightened parental anxiety and reinforces feelings of being unprepared for the decisions and responsibilities associated with CT. The findings, therefore, highlight the need for clearer, system-level transition frameworks to reduce ambiguity and support parental confidence in CT planning for their child who has ASD. This partly aligns with a previous Turkish study, in which parents noted that supporting CASD had significant implications for their own career progression and goals (Ozdemir & Koç, 2023). In this previous study, parents reported that effective career planning demanded increased time, income, and adaptability, as well as coping strategies informed by their child's needs. As a result, some postponed or relinquished previous career goals, altered what they envisioned for their professional future, and had limited space for self-directed career exploration(Ozdemir & Koç, 2023).

Financial stress was found to be high among parents of CASD. While our finding is consistent with research showing that financial pressures constitute a substantial source of stress for parents raising CASD (Adams et al., 2021; J. Lee & Barger, 2024), we would like to emphasise that these pressures are further exacerbated in Nigeria due to a lack of financial backing from the national and state governments, the predominance of out-of-pocket expenses and the enormous financial burden of caring for the CASD(Bakare et al., 2009, 2019). It is possible that parents of CASD spend a huge amount on travelling to specialist centres or on purchasing medications, and some may take loans or reduce basic household spending to meet the costs of autism care. Opelusi and Omoruyi (2021) observed that the financial costs linked to parenting CASD can be up to three times higher than those incurred by families of typically developing children in Nigeria. Besides, Anyanwu et al. (2019) had argued that family support only partially alleviates financial stress and that urban families of CASD often have even fewer sources of extended help. Recent research also indicates that the demands associated with supporting CASD often create a substantial financial burden for Nigerian families, which often affects their overall economic well-being (Azubuike et al., 2025). This aligns strongly with the early stages of the family stress model in which financial adversity generates daily economic pressures, such as difficulty balancing expenses or affording basic needs. These pressures, in turn, increase parental psychological distress, setting the stage for broader family strain(Masarik & Conger, 2017). The high financial burden reported by parents in this study demonstrates this pathway clearly, emphasising that economic pressure may compound other stressors and intensify the overall strain families experience during the CT of students with ASD.

Work-family balance stress was also substantial, reflecting the difficulty of combining caregiving, transition-related responsibilities, and employment among parents of CASD. The demanding nature of caregiving responsibilities can interfere with professional obligations, leading to conflicts between work and family roles(Calderwood et al., 2022). Our finding corresponds with research showing that parents of CASD frequently adjust or discontinue career goals and career plans. The finding corresponds with evidence from Nigeria, indicating that parents of CASD frequently report difficulty managing the competing demands of caregiving, work responsibilities, and personal obligations(Azubuike et al., 2025). Another study suggests that parents of CASD, particularly mothers, often undertake intense caregiving roles, which intensifies conflict between work and household responsibilities (Kehinde et al., 2023). According to the family stress model, psychological distress created by accumulated strain can disrupt parental functioning, compromise work productivity, and increase emotional exhaustion (Masarik & Conger, 2017). This study is consistent with the findings of Karahan et al. (2022), who reported that employed parents of CASD, especially mothers, often viewed their work and family lives negatively, experiencing emotional turmoil and perceiving inadequate support. On the other hand, Lien et al. (2021) reported that fathers of CASD juggle financial provision with direct caregiving, adopting diverse approaches such as maintaining conventional breadwinner roles, combining earning with caregiving, sharing responsibilities with partners in a tag-team manner, or taking on the main caregiving role themselves. Their study showed that work served as financial security, a pathway to information and brief respite, yet also a source of stress that could evoke guilt, emotional discomfort, and depressive feelings. Pettey (2015) also observed that parents of children with disabilities face heightened demands within the home due to intensive caregiving responsibilities, which often disrupt their ability to balance work and family roles, and that these difficulties are especially pronounced for parents of CASD. Our study supports Balachandran and Bhuvaneswari (2024), who found that working parents of CASD faced intersecting pressures from work, family responsibilities, and caregiving demands, with many experiencing physical and emotional exhaustion that affected functioning across all three domains.

Emotional stress was moderate rather than high, suggesting some degree of adaptation or resilience to the prolonged demands of caregiving. This finding aligns with current evidence, which demonstrates that Nigerian parents often experience emotional strain and a cycle of intense emotions while supporting their CASD across daily and long-term needs (Azubuike et al., 2025; John, 2024). Other studies have also demonstrated that parents of CASD face considerable emotional burden due to the intricacies of their children's behavioural and developmental needs(Dijkstra-de Neijs et al., 2024; Nikmat et al., 2008). Furthermore, our finding aligns closely with Wang et al. (2013), who reported that parenting stress was closely linked to parents' levels of depression and anxiety and their child's behavioural symptoms. Similarly, Bitsika and Sharpley (2004) highlighted high rates of severe anxiety and clinical depression among parents of CASD, noting that these emotional difficulties were shaped by parental health, the adequacy of family support, and confidence in professional expertise. Nikmat et al. (2008) reported that more than half (53.8 per cent) of the parents of CASD presented clinical levels of psychological disturbance and that gender and occupation were significantly associated with psychological well-being. Taken together, the literature suggests that while moderate emotional stress in our sample may reflect some degree of coping, it remains a critical indicator of the psychological vulnerability associated with raising CASD and underscores the need for formal emotional support systems for parents.

Social support stress was high, indicating that parents might have limited access to supportive networks and often manage transition tasks in isolation. The results emphasise the necessity for social supportive services to reduce parental burden and improve transition outcomes for students with ASD. This aligns with the family stress model, in which social support acts as a protective factor that can buffer families against the negative effects of financial strain and psychological distress(Masarik & Conger, 2017). The lack of such support in this context may leave parents more vulnerable to stress, according to a recent Nigerian study(Azubuike et al., 2025). Surprisingly, a previous Nigerian study demonstrated no meaningful difference in stress levels between parents who reported high perceived social support and those who reported low support(Obasi et al., 2019), implying that the buffering effect of social support may be less influential for parents of CASD than typically assumed.

To this end, we believe that transition support for students with ASD within Nigerian schools must be strengthened through structured programmes that include vocational assessment, collaborative planning, and clear timelines in order to reduce parental stress. Better coordination between educational institutions, healthcare providers, and vocational services is needed to address service fragmentation. Expanded and subsidised community-based vocational training could reduce financial stress. Psychoeducational support and parent peer networks would help mitigate emotional and social support stress, while public awareness initiatives may help build community support. Theoretically, our findings reinforce the value of bioecological and family stress perspectives. Interventions should target structural constraints affecting families rather than focusing solely on parental coping. Policies should strengthen mesosystem-level relationships among schools, health systems, and vocational agencies, while the family stress model should guide the design of programmes that reduce economic pressure and improve family resilience. Transition theory should inform the development of predictable, clearly defined pathways that lessen uncertainty for families.

This research study is not without certain limitations. The sample was quite small, and the study itself was restricted to one geopolitical zone, which may limit generalisability. The use of a self-report questionnaire, that is, CT-ParSQ, may result in bias, while the cross-sectional study design we employed could not capture stress fluctuations or causal pathways. Important factors such as ASD severity, extended family involvement, or access to services were not examined but may shape stress experiences. In this regard, qualitative research may offer us deeper insight into the lived experiences of parents, illuminating the emotional and sociocultural factors underlying each stress dimension. Future work should examine the effectiveness of specific transition interventions in reducing parental stress, as well as the influence of policy implementation on family outcomes. Comparative research across regions or African countries may also reveal contextual variations that shape stress experiences of families and inform culturally responsive transition models. Further studies should investigate variables that may buffer the effects of transition-related stress, such as coping strategies, support networks, or cultural beliefs. Longitudinal research is needed to track how parental stress evolves across different transition stages and to explore its long-term impact on vocational outcomes for students with ASD. Research should also examine regional differences within Nigeria to identify context-specific barriers and inform targeted solutions.

CONCLUSIONS

This study demonstrates that parents of students with ASD in Nigeria experience considerable stress as they support their children through the CT process. The findings show that stress is common and multifaceted, cutting across career planning pressures, difficulties navigating services, financial strain, work and family conflict, emotional burden, and limited social support. These stressors were not significantly associated with demographic factors, indicating that transition-related stress is influenced more by systemic and structural conditions than by individual family characteristics. The findings on service navigation stress highlight persistent gaps in service coordination, interagency collaboration, and accessible information. Elevated career planning stress also reflects the absence of structured transition pathways and limited vocational opportunities for students with ASD. Financial pressures and work and family conflict further reveal the extent to which parents absorb the cost of transition in a context where formal support systems are weak. Although emotional stress was moderate, it is a noteworthy burden, especially in the absence of strong social support networks. All of these findings point to the urgent need for coordinated transition frameworks, strengthened services, and policies that support families. Addressing systemic limitations is essential for improving parental well-being and enhancing CT outcomes for students with ASD in Nigeria.

REFERENCES

Abidin, R. R., Smith, L. T., & Kim, H. (2022). Parenting Stress. *WikiJournal of Medicine*, *9*(1), 3. Advance online publication. DOI: 10.15347/WJM/2022.003

Adams, S. N., Dadabhay, A., & Neille, J. (2021). An Exploration into Mothers' Experiences of Feeding Children with Autism Spectrum Disorder in South Africa. *Folia Phoniatrica et Logopaedica*, *73*(3), 164–173. DOI: 10.1159/000507928 PMID: 32645696

Akanle, O., & Nwaobiala, U. R. (2019). Changing but Fragile: Female Breadwinning and Family Stability in Nigeria. *Journal of Asian and African Studies*, *55*(3), 398–411. DOI: 10.1177/0021909619880283

Akubo, J. (2025, October 30). Senator Natasha pushes autism bill. *The Guardian Nigeria*. https://guardian.ng/news/senator-natasha-pushes-autism-bill/

Alibekova, R., Kai Chan, C., Crape, B., Kadyrzhanuly, K., Gusmanov, A., An, S., Bulekbayeva, S., Akhmetzhanova, Z., Ainabekova, A., Yerubayev, Z., Yessimkulova, F., Bekisheva, A., Ospanova, Z., & Rakhimova, M. (2022). Stress, anxiety and depression in parents of children with autism spectrum disorders in Kazakhstan: Prevalence and associated factors. *Global Mental Health (Cambridge, England)*, *9*, 472–482. DOI: 10.1017/gmh.2022.51 PMID: 36618742

Anyanwu, J. I., Onuigbo, L. N., Obiyo, N. O., Eze, U. N., Akaneme, I. N., Aye, E. N., Enyi, C., Oforka, T. O., Chigbu, B. C., Ezenwaji, I. O., Ogbuabor, S. E., & Adimora, E. D. (2019). Parenting Stress in Families of Children With Autism Spectrum Disorder: The Roles of the Extended Family. *Global Journal of Health Science*, *11*(8), 51. DOI: 10.5539/gjhs.v11n8p51

Ayinla, I., Chang, H.-J., & Ayodele, K., & Olanrewaju. (2019). African Parents' Perceptions, Stress and Coping Strategy. *European Journal of Scientific Research*, *153*(4), 434–447.

Azubuike, A. O., Azubuike, P. C., Afape, A. O., Enyam, M. O., Akinreni, T., Imo, U. F., Nwadiche, M., Ogbonna, C. K., Timothy, P. N., Uchegbu, E. R., & Adai, G. S. (2025). Caregiving for autistic children in Nigeria: Experiences and challenges. *Discover Mental Health*, *5*(1), 32. DOI: 10.1007/s44192-025-00159-9 PMID: 40063222

Azubuike, A. O., Azubuike, P. C., Onyekachi, E. L., Enyam, M. O., Akinreni, T., Abuo, J., Ogbonna, C. K., Timothy, P. N., Uchegbu, E. R., & Adai, G. S. (2024). Experiences and unmet needs among caregivers of children living with autism spectrum disorder in Nigeria: A qualitative study using the socio-ecological model. *Discover Social Science and Health*, *4*(1), 77. Advance online publication. DOI: 10.1007/s44155-024-00141-w

Bakare, M. O., Ebigbo, P. O., Agomoh, A. O., Eaton, J., Onyeama, G. M., Okonkwo, K. O., Onwukwe, J. U., Igwe, M. N., Orovwigho, A. O., & Aguocha, C. M. (2009). Knowledge about childhood autism and opinion among healthcare workers on availability of facilities and law caring for the needs and rights of children with childhood autism and other developmental disorders in Nigeria. *BMC Pediatrics*, *9*(1), 12. DOI: 10.1186/1471-2431-9-12 PMID: 19216754

Bakare, M. O., Taiwo, O. G., Bello-Mojeed, M. A., & Munir, K. M. (2019). Autism Spectrum Disorders in Nigeria: A Scoping Review of Literature and Opinion on Future Research and Social Policy Directions. *Journal of Health Care for the Poor and Underserved*, *30*(3), 899–909. DOI: 10.1353/hpu.2019.0063 PMID: 31422978

Balachandran, K. P., & Bhuvaneswari, M. (2024). 'I may have to give up on my career.' Breadwinners or caregivers? Exploring the complexities of work-family conflict among parents of children with neurodevelopmental disabilities. *International Journal of Developmental Disabilities*, *0*(0), 1–18. DOI: 10.1080/20473869.2024.2394733

Bitsika, V., & Sharpley, C. F. (2004). Stress, Anxiety and Depression Among Parents of Children With Autism Spectrum Disorder. *Australian Journal of Guidance & Counselling*, *14*(2), 151–161. DOI: 10.1017/S1037291100002466

Bochaver, A. A., Akhmedjanova, D. R., Bayramyan, R. M., & Fomicheva, E. V. (2023). Initial psychometric properties of the Parental Stress Scale examined using a sample of Russian mothers. *Frontiers in Psychology*, *14*, 1202401. Advance online publication. DOI: 10.3389/fpsyg.2023.1202401 PMID: 37731869

Bronfenbrenner, U. (1994). Ecological models of human development. *International Encyclopedia of Education, 3*(2), 37–43.

Bronfenbrenner, U. (2000). *Ecological systems theory.* American Psychological Association. https://psycnet.apa.org/record/2004-12701-046

Buchholz, S. W. (2021). Quantitative designs for practice scholarship. In B. A. Staffileno, M. P. Murphy, & S. W. Buchholz (Eds.), *Research for Advanced Practice Nurses, Fourth Edition: From Evidence to Practice* (pp. 143–172). Springer Publishing Company. DOI: 10.1891/9780826151339.0009

Calderwood, C., Breaux, R., ten Brummelhuis, L. L., Mitropoulos, T., & Swanson, C. S. (2022). When daily challenges become too much during COVID-19: Implications of family and work demands for work–life balance among parents of children with special needs. *Journal of Occupational Health Psychology*, *27*(5), 516–527. DOI: 10.1037/ocp0000333 PMID: 35901404

Chauvet, G. (2015). Coupling methods for multistage sampling. *Annals of Statistics*, *43*(6), 2484–2506. DOI: 10.1214/15-AOS1348

Conger, R. D., Conger, K. J., & Martin, M. J. (2010). Socioeconomic Status, Family Processes,and Individual Development. *Journal of Marriage and Family*, *72*(3), 685–704. DOI: 10.1111/j.1741-3737.2010.00725.x PMID: 20676350

Craig, F., Operto, F. F., De Giacomo, A., Margari, L., Frolli, A., Conson, M., Ivagnes, S., Monaco, M., & Margari, F. (2016). Parenting stress among parents of children with Neurodevelopmental Disorders. *Psychiatry Research*, *242*, 121–129. DOI: 10.1016/j.psychres.2016.05.016 PMID: 27280521

Crowell, J. A., Keluskar, J., & Gorecki, A. (2019). Parenting behavior and the development of children with autism spectrum disorder. *Comprehensive Psychiatry*, *90*, 21–29. DOI: 10.1016/j.comppsych.2018.11.007 PMID: 30658339

DesChamps, T. D., Ibañez, L. V., Edmunds, S. R., Dick, C. C., & Stone, W. L. (2020). Parenting stress in caregivers of young children with ASD concerns prior to a formal diagnosis. *Autism Research*, *13*(1), 82–92. DOI: 10.1002/aur.2213 PMID: 31593362

Dijkstra-de Neijs, L., Boeke, D. B., Van Berckelaer-Onnes, I. A., Swaab, H., & Ester, W. A. (2024). Parental Stress and Quality of Life in Parents of Young Children with Autism. *Child Psychiatry and Human Development*. Advance online publication. DOI: 10.1007/s10578-024-01693-3 PMID: 38724870

Dijkstra-de Neijs, L., Boeke, D. B., van Berckelaer-Onnes, I. A., Swaab, H., & Ester, W. A. (2024). Parental Stress and Quality of Life in Parents of Young Children with Autism. *Child Psychiatry and Human Development*. Advance online publication. DOI: 10.1007/s10578-024-01693-3 PMID: 38724870

England, A. (2022). Quantitative and qualitative research methods. In E. Seeram, R. Davidson, A. England, & M. F. McEntee (Eds.), *Research for Medical Imaging and Radiation Sciences* (pp. 71–96). Springer International Publishing. DOI: 10.1007/978-3-030-79956-4_5

Folorunsho-Francis, A. (2025, October 31). Senate pushes for regional autism centres. *The Punch Newspaper*. https://punchng.com/senate-pushes-for-regional-autism-centres/

Gard, A. M., McLoyd, V. C., Mitchell, C., & Hyde, L. W. (2020). Evaluation of a longitudinal family stress model in a population-based cohort. *Social Development, 29*(4), 1155–1175. DOI: 10.1111/sode.12446 PMID: 33953492

George, L. K. (1993). Sociological Perspectives on Life Transitions. *Annual Review of Sociology, 19*(1), 353–373. DOI: 10.1146/annurev.so.19.080193.002033

Goodman, J., Schlossberg, N. K., & Anderson, M. L. (2006). *Counseling adults in transition: Linking practice with theory, 3rd ed* (pp. xvii, 334). Springer Publishing Company.

Hamidon, N. A., Anuar, N. I. S. M., Sharoni, S. K. A., & Isa, N. A. M. (2024). Parental Stress among Family Caregivers of Children with Autism in a Teaching Hospital. [MJN]. *The Malaysian Journal of Nursing, 15*(4), 139–149. DOI: 10.31674/mjn.2024.v15i04.016

Hartini, S., Simanjuntak, S. R., & Sutomo, R. (2021). Factors correlating with parenting stress among mothers of children with Autistic Spectrum Disorder (ASD). *Enfermeria Clinica, 31*, 505–510. DOI: 10.1016/j.enfcli.2020.10.042

Hurwich-Reiss, E., & Watamura, S. E. (2019). Family processes among Latino Early Head Start families: Understanding the role of caregiver acculturation. *Journal of Community Psychology, 47*(6), 1433–1448. DOI: 10.1002/jcop.22198 PMID: 31066922

Jamison, J. M., Fourie, E., Siper, P. M., Trelles, M. P., George-Jones, J., Buxbaum Grice, A., Krata, J., Holl, E., Shaoul, J., Hernandez, B., Mitchell, L., McKay, M. M., Buxbaum, J. D., & Kolevzon, A. (2017). Examining the Efficacy of a Family Peer Advocate Model for Black and Hispanic Caregivers of Children with Autism Spectrum Disorder. *Journal of Autism and Developmental Disorders, 47*(5), 1314–1322. DOI: 10.1007/s10803-017-3045-0 PMID: 28168677

John, B. (2024). Parental Perceptions and Experiences of Children with Autism and their Educational Needs in Nigeria: An Interpretative Phenomenological Analysis [PhD Thesis, Leeds Beckett University]. https://figshare.leedsbeckett.ac.uk/articles/thesis/Parental_Perceptions_and_Experiences_of_Children_with_Autism_and_their_Educational_Needs_in_Nigeria_An_Interpretative_Phenomenological_Analysis/26370169/1

Johnson, N., Frenn, M., Feetham, S., & Simpson, P. (2011). Autism Spectrum Disorder: Parenting Stress, Family Functioning and Health-Related Quality of Life. *Families, Systems & Health, 29*(3), 232–252. DOI: 10.1037/a0025341 PMID: 21928891

Johnson, N. L., & Simpson, P. M. (2013). Lack of father involvement in research on children with autism spectrum disorder: Maternal parenting stress and family functioning. *Issues in Mental Health Nursing*, *34*(4), 220–228. DOI: 10.3109/01612840.2012.745177 PMID: 23566184

Karahan, S., Parlak, Ş. Y., & Hacıfazlıoğlu, Ö. (2022). The Experiences of Mothers of Children with Autism Spectrum Disorder in Searching for Balance Between Work and Family Life. *Education in Science*, *47*(212), 103–120. DOI: 10.15390/EB.2022.10970

Karst, J. S., & Van Hecke, A. V. (2012). Parent and family impact of autism spectrum disorders: A review and proposed model for intervention evaluation. *Clinical Child and Family Psychology Review*, *15*(3), 247–277. DOI: 10.1007/s10567-012-0119-6 PMID: 22869324

Kehinde, O. A., Lindly, O. J., Ntombela, B., & Hermann, C. (2023). Brief Report: Gender-Based Stereotypical Roles of Parents Caring for Autistic Children in Nigeria and South Africa. *Journal of Autism and Developmental Disorders*, *53*(12), 4917–4928. DOI: 10.1007/s10803-022-05582-3 PMID: 35581506

Lau, F. (2017). Methods for Correlational Studies. In *Handbook of eHealth Evaluation: An Evidence-based Approach* [Internet]. University of Victoria., https://www.ncbi.nlm.nih.gov/books/NBK481614/

Lee, H. (2022). Family economic hardship and children's behavioral and socioemotional outcomes in middle childhood: Direct and indirect pathways. *Children and Youth Services Review*, *138*, 106527. Advance online publication. DOI: 10.1016/j.childyouth.2022.106527

Lee, J., & Barger, B. (2024). Factors Predicting Poor Mental and Physical Health in Parents of Children with Autism Spectrum Disorder: Results from 2016 to 2019 National Survey of Children's Health. *Journal of Autism and Developmental Disorders*, *54*(3), 915–930. DOI: 10.1007/s10803-022-05870-y PMID: 36562931

Lee, S. (2025, May 15). *Multi-Stage Sampling: Principles & Methods*. Number-Analytics. https://www.numberanalytics.com/blog/multi-stage-sampling-principles-methods

Lien, K., Lashewicz, B., Mitchell, J., & Boettcher, N. (2021). Blending Traditional and Nurturing Fathering: Fathers of Children With Autism Managing Work and Family. *Family Relations*, *70*(1), 264–281. DOI: 10.1111/fare.12472

Martinez, V. C., & Turnage, D. (2022). Social Support and Parenting Stress in Hispanic Parents of Children with Autism Spectrum Disorder. *Issues in Mental Health Nursing*, *43*(11), 1030–1040. DOI: 10.1080/01612840.2022.2100949 PMID: 35849744

Masarik, A. S., & Conger, R. D. (2017). Stress and child development: A review of the Family Stress Model. *Current Opinion in Psychology*, *13*, 85–90. DOI: 10.1016/j.copsyc.2016.05.008 PMID: 28813301

Matthews, R. A., Booth, S. M., Taylor, C. F., & Martin, T. (2011). A qualitative examination of the work–family interface: Parents of children with autism spectrum disorder. *Journal of Vocational Behavior*, *79*(3), 625–639. DOI: 10.1016/j.jvb.2011.04.010

McStay, R. L., Dissanayake, C., Scheeren, A., Koot, H. M., & Begeer, S. (2014). Parenting stress and autism: The role of age, autism severity, quality of life and problem behaviour of children and adolescents with autism. *Autism*, *18*(5), 502–510. DOI: 10.1177/1362361313485163 PMID: 24104515

Mushambi, C., Diale, B., Sefotho, M. M., & Eseadi, C. (2024). Exploring obstacles experienced by learners with high-functioning autism in pursuing careers in sports. *Bulletin of Counseling and Psychotherapy*, *6*(1). Advance online publication. https://journal.kurasinstitute.com/index.php/bocp/article/view/630. DOI: 10.51214/00202406630000

Nadeem, N. J., Afzal, S., Dogar, I. A., Smith, J. G., Shah, T., Noreen, M., & Ali, A. (2024). The impact of having an autisTic child on parental mental health and well-being in pakistan. *Research in Autism Spectrum Disorders*, *115*, 102423. Advance online publication. DOI: 10.1016/j.rasd.2024.102423

Ng, C. S. M., Fang, Y., Wang, Z., & Zhang, M. (2021). Potential Factors of Parenting Stress in Chinese Parents of Children With Autism Spectrum Disorder: A Systematic Review. *Focus on Autism and Other Developmental Disabilities*, *36*(4), 237–248. DOI: 10.1177/10883576211012599

Nguyen, T. M. H., Khuu, D. T., Nguyen, T. A. N., & Nguyen, T. P. (2025). Understanding the link between parental stress and child autism spectrum disorder symptoms: Insights from Vietnam. *Research in Autism*, *125*, 202627. Advance online publication. DOI: 10.1016/j.reia.2025.202627

Nikmat, A. W., Ahmad, M., Oon, N. L., & Razali, S. (2008). Stress and psychological wellbeing among parents of children with autism spectrum disorder. *ASEAN Journal of Psychiatry*, *9*(2), 65–72.

Nnubia, U., Ibeanu, V., & Okechukwu, F. (2022). Socio-economic and household characteristics associated with work-family conflict among female primary school teachers in Enugu State, Nigeria. *African Journal of Teacher Education, 11*(1), 143–165. DOI: 10.21083/ajote.v11i1.6995

Nnubia, U. I., Ibeanu, V. N., & Okechukwu, F. O. (2020). Characterizing female breadwinners among Nigerian primary school teachers. *Community Work & Family, 25*(4), 508–522. DOI: 10.1080/13668803.2020.1797634

Nnubia, U. I., Ibeanu, V. N., & Okechukwu, F. O. (2023). Marital structure and domestic gender role practice: Implications for subjective well-being of working mothers teaching in Nigerian primary schools. *Community Work & Family, 28*(2), 209–232. DOI: 10.1080/13668803.2023.2230347

Nnubia, U. I., Ibeanu, V. N., & Okechukwu, F. O. (2024). Gender role shift: Implications for balancing work and family responsibilities among female primary school teachers in Nigeria. *Journal of Family Studies, 31*(1), 35–53. DOI: 10.1080/13229400.2024.2405106

Obasi, C. C., Ishola, A. A., & Fashola, T. M. (2019). Perceived social support as a predictor of parenting stress among parents of children with autism in Lagos, Nigeria. *African Journal for the Psychological Study of Social Issues, 22*(1), 58–66.

Oduyemi, A. Y., Okafor, I. P., Eze, U. T., Akodu, B. A., & Roberts, A. A. (2021). Internalization of stigma among parents of children with autism spectrum disorder in Nigeria: A mixed method study. *BMC Psychology, 9*(1), 182. Advance online publication. DOI: 10.1186/s40359-021-00687-3 PMID: 34802470

Ogba, O. (2025, October 30). Senate Moves to Establish National Autism Centers across Nigeria [Government]. *National Assembly Library Trust Fund.* https://naltf.gov.ng/senate-moves-to-establish-national-autism-centers-across-nigeria/

Olubiyi, S. (2022). Psychosocial Burden of Mothers' Care of Children with Autism Attending Federal Neuro-Psychiatric Hospital Yaba Nigeria. *TEXILA INTERNATIONAL JOURNAL OF NURSING, 8*(1), 9–17. DOI: 10.21522/TIJNR.2015.08.01.Art002

Opelusi, O. I., & Omoruyi, O. L. (2021). Adoptable coping strategies of parents with autistic school children in tender brain remedial centre, Oredo local government area, Benin city, Edo state. *Sapientia Global Journal of Arts, Humanities and Development Studies, 4*(1). https://www.sgojahds.com/index.php/SGOJAHDS/article/view/160

Ozdemir, N. K., & Koç, M. (2023). Career adaptability of parents of children with autism spectrum disorder. *Current Psychology (New Brunswick, N.J.), 42*(17), 14320–14333. DOI: 10.1007/s12144-021-02649-9 PMID: 35103038

Park, Y. S., Konge, L., & Artino, A. R. J. (2020). The Positivism Paradigm of Research. *Academic Medicine*, *95*(5), 690–694. DOI: 10.1097/ACM.0000000000003093 PMID: 31789841

Pettey, A. (2015). *Examining work-family conflict and parenting stress for parents of children with autism spectrum disorder through the lens of boundary and conservations of resources theories* [Master's Thesis, California State University]. https://scholarworks.lib.csusb.edu/etd/231

Ponnet, K. (2014). Financial Stress, Parent Functioning and Adolescent Problem Behavior: An Actor–Partner Interdependence Approach to Family Stress Processes in Low-, Middle-, and High-Income Families. *Journal of Youth and Adolescence*, *43*(10), 1752–1769. DOI: 10.1007/s10964-014-0159-y PMID: 25053382

Ríos, M., Zekri, S., Alonso-Esteban, Y., & Navarro-Pardo, E. (2022). Parental stress assessment with the parenting stress index (PSI): A systematic review of its psychometric properties. *Children (Basel, Switzerland)*, *9*(11), 1649. DOI: 10.3390/children9111649 PMID: 36360377

Rivard, M., Terroux, A., Parent-Boursier, C., & Mercier, C. (2014). Determinants of stress in parents of children with autism spectrum disorders. *Journal of Autism and Developmental Disorders*, *44*(7), 1609–1620. DOI: 10.1007/s10803-013-2028-z PMID: 24384673

Sales, B. D., & Folkman, S. E. (2000). *Ethics in research with human participants.* American Psychological Association. https://psycnet.apa.org/record/2000-07971-000

Segev, E., Gadot, L., & Fine, M. (2025). Between a "ball and chain" and a "half-full glass": Work–family balance experiences of fathers to children with disabilities. *The American Journal of Orthopsychiatry*. Advance online publication. DOI: 10.1037/ort0000868 PMID: 40587314

Sharma, A. (2025). Positivism. In Jahn, B., & Schindler, S. (Eds.), *Elgar Encyclopedia of International Relations* (pp. 302–303). Edward Elgar Publishing Ltd., DOI: 10.4337/9781035312283.000138

Shen, L., & Zhang, L. (2025). Linking Healthcare, Family, and Work Systems: The Roles of Family-Centered Care, Family Resilience, and Caregiving-to-Work Conflict in Psychological Well-being among Parents of Children with Autism Spectrum Disorder. *Applied Research in Quality of Life*, *20*(5), 2099–2117. Advance online publication. DOI: 10.1007/s11482-025-10515-0

Sigurðardóttir, Á. (2017). *Stress, anxiety, depression and social constraints in parents of children with autism* [BSc Thesis, Reykjavik University]. https://skemman.is/handle/1946/28355

Simelane, A. P. (2020). Understanding daily parenting stresses in caring for children with autism spectrum disorders. *SAJCH : the South African Journal of Child Health, 14*(3), 115. DOI: 10.7196/SAJCH.2020.v14i3.1596

Sitimin, S. A., Fikry, A., Ismail, Z., & Hussein, N. (2017). Work-family conflict among working parents of children with autism in Malaysia. *Procedia Computer Science, 105*, 345–352. DOI: 10.1016/j.procs.2017.01.232

Soltanifar, A., Akbarzadeh, F., Moharreri, F., Soltanifar, A., Ebrahimi, A., Mokhber, N., Minoocherhr, A., & Naqvi, S. S. A. (2015). Comparison of parental stress among mothers and fathers of children with autistic spectrum disorder in Iran. *Iranian Journal of Nursing and Midwifery Research, 20*(1), 93–98. PMID: 25709697

Sraboni, S. A. (2023). *Experience of Child Rearing in Balance with Work-Life of Employed Parents who have a Child with Autism Spectrum Disorder* [PhD Thesis, Bangladesh Health Professions Institute, Faculty of Medicine, the University …]. http://library.crp-bangladesh.org:8080/xmlui/handle/123456789/1060

Stoner, C. R., & Stoner, J. B. (2014). How can we make this work? Understanding and responding to working parents of children with autism. *Business Horizons, 57*(1), 85–95. DOI: 10.1016/j.bushor.2013.10.002

Ugwu, J. (2025, October 30). Senate begins consideration of bill to establish autism centres nationwide. *The Cable*. https://www.thecable.ng/senate-advances-bill-to-set-up-autism-centres-for-early-diagnosis-care/

Ulofoshio, J. I. (2017). *Lived experiences of mothers raising children with autism spectrum disorder in Nigeria* [Doctoral dissertation]. Walden University. https://scholarworks.waldenu.edu/cgi/viewcontent.cgi?article=5982&context=dissertations

Victor-Aigbodion, V., & Eseadi, C. (2025). Effect of purpose-based career coaching on career transition self-efficacy among college students with autism spectrum disorder. *EDULEARN25 Proceedings*, 8088–8101. https://library.iated.org/view/VICTORAIGBODION2025EFF

Wahab, R., Fahmy, K. A. M. F. M., Ibrahim, S. A. S., & Philip, W. (2022). Social support and stress among parents with autism spectrum disorder children. *Environment-Behaviour Proceedings Journal, 7*(20), 449–454. DOI: 10.21834/ebpj.v7i20.3409

Wang, J., Hu, Y., Wang, Y., Qin, X., Xia, W., Sun, C., Wu, L., & Wang, J. (2013). Parenting stress in Chinese mothers of children with autism spectrum disorders. *Social Psychiatry and Psychiatric Epidemiology*, *48*(4), 575–582. DOI: 10.1007/s00127-012-0569-7 PMID: 22968576

Zovko, M., Šimleša, S., & Olujić Tomazin, M. (2024). Parenting stress, coping strategies and social support for mothers of preschool children with autism spectrum disorder in the Republic of Croatia. *Clinical Child Psychology and Psychiatry*, *29*(2), 674–686. DOI: 10.1177/13591045231191802 PMID: 37491211

APPENDIX

Table 4. Career Transition-Related Parental Stress Questionnaire (CT-ParSQ)

S/No	Items	Factor Loading	Cronbach's α	Omega ω
	Career Planning Stress			
1	I worry about finding suitable employment opportunities for my child.	0.94		
2	I feel uncertain about how to guide my child in choosing a career direction.	0.96	0.89	0.90
3	I am concerned that my child's skills may not match job market expectations.	0.67		
	Service Navigation Stress			
4	It is stressful to understand which services or programmes best support my child's transition.	0.69		
5	I find it difficult to access reliable information about vocational training for my child.	0.96	0.83	0.86
6	Scheduling and coordinating my child's transition support services is overwhelming for me.	0.69		
	Financial Stress			
7	I feel anxious about my child's future financial independence.	0.75	0.74	0.68
8	Career transition costs (e.g., feeding, assessments, transport) create a financial burden for our family.	0.67		
	Work-Family Balance Stress			
9	I worry about balancing work and caregiving during transition period for my child.	0.44	0.70	0.62
10	I feel guilty if I cannot be present for my child's training or appointments due to work schedules.	0.83		
	Emotional Stress			
11	I often feel emotionally drained by the entire career transition process for my child.	0.79		
12	I feel overwhelmed by the uncertainty of what lies ahead for my child.	0.75	0.77	0.76
13	I lack confidence in my ability to support my child emotionally during this change.	0.68		
	Social Support Stress			
14	I feel I have enough social support (friends, family, groups) to help manage this stress.	0.69	0.78	0.73
15	I have access to professionals who help alleviate my anxiety about my child's career future.	0.71		

Chapter 2
School-Based Professionals' Roles and Theoretical Orientations in Promoting the Career Transition of Students With ASD

ABSTRACT

This paper explored the roles and theoretical orientations of school-based professionals (SBPs) in promoting the career transition (CT) of students with autism spectrum disorders (SASD). The data analysed included one hundred and twenty SBPs who were chosen via a multi-stage sampling process. We co-designed the measures that assessed the role clarity, role conflict, role efficacy, role breadth, theory-based transition support, theory-based reflective practice, and CT involvement of the SBPs. The role-related variables had weak and no significant relationships with the CT of SASD. In contrast, theory-informed transition support and, in particular, theory-informed reflective practice were important predictors of CT of SASD, and the model accounted for 52.6 per cent of the variance. The results show the importance of theoretically underpinned reflective practices in improving CT practices in Nigerian schools.

DOI: 10.4018/978-1-6684-7260-6.ch002

BACKGROUND

School-Based Professionals (SBPs) encompass a multidisciplinary group of trained personnel operating within educational settings whose roles are crucial in promoting academic, behavioural, and socio-emotional development of students. These professionals, such as special educators, educational psychologists, school counsellors, and social workers, are instrumental in addressing the needs of students with autism spectrum disorders (SASD) throughout the career transition (CT) process (Teresa Rani et al., 2025; Carter & Schutz, 2022; Challenger et al., 2025). They are responsible for transition assessments, designing individualised transition plans, guiding career-related instruction, facilitating vocational and community-based learning, and coordinating transition activities with families and external agencies (Lairson, 2022; Phelps & Hanley-Maxwell, 1997). SBPs perform a variety of interconnected functions that are grounded in professional expertise and collaborative practices and within dynamic institutional frameworks where roles as theorised by Biddle (1979) shape their engagement in inclusive support services. Special educators are often at the forefront of CT support due to their foundational training in improving social communication and adaptive skills (Teresa Rani et al., 2025). They work with families, schools, and community organisations in order to develop individualised transition plans that consider the strengths and needs of students (Lee & Park, 2020). They build essential life skills such as self-advocacy, social competence, vocational readiness, and negotiate accommodations and services necessary for post-school integration of these students (Barrio, 2022; Almalky & Alqahtani, 2021). School counsellors, grounded in a multi-tiered system of support (MTSS), collaborate with transition specialists to individualise postsecondary planning (Challenger et al., 2025). They contribute meaningfully to the Individualised Education Plan (IEP) by aligning it with the student's needs, strengths, and aspirations (Laghi & Trimarco, 2020). Through tailored support, they help to mitigate developmental delays in career planning (Dipeolu et al., 2015).

Educational psychologists are designated to appraise the academic, behavioural and social achievements of SASD. Their activities involve the identification of strengths and the areas that need reinforcement, which is critical in the development of effective transition plans and design of the IEP, which contains transition goals which are founded on the exclusive needs of the SASD (Laghi & Trimarco, 2020). Their engagement with special educators, speech-language therapists, and occupational therapists creates an interdisciplinary model that ensures a holistic CT ecosystem (Perryman et al., 2020; Sansosti & Sansosti, 2013). Social workers, in turn, anchor CT by facilitating work readiness and intersectoral collaboration. Their interventions include strengths-based transition plans, early work exposure, and family-centred counselling to foster resilience and self-esteem(Dente & Parkinson Coles, 2012;

Olaitan & Olaitan, 2022; Nicholas et al., 2019; Schoen & Valdez, 2023). In the Nigerian context, SBPs remain indispensable in tailoring curricula, guiding psychosocial development, identifying career-fit pathways, and fostering multi-systemic engagement(Olagunju et al., 2021; Adigun et al., 2021). Educational psychologists evaluate cognitive and emotional requirements, provide behavioural interventions, and mentor other professionals in managing SASD-related concerns(Bakare et al., 2022). Their expert assessments guide the selection of career pathways aligned with individual strengths. Social workers act as critical liaisons among school, home, and community systems, connecting students to needed services and strengthening the CT ecosystem (Busack et al., 2021). Through sustained engagement with students and families, school counsellors identify career goals, build socio-emotional competence, and reduce transition-related anxiety (Rosenkoetter et al., 2007; Victor-Aigbodion & Eseadi, 2025). Despite these contributions, the efficacy of SBPs in Nigeria is frequently undermined by systemic limitations. In the Southeast region, inconsistencies in role definitions, insufficient training, poor theoretical grounding, and weak interprofessional collaboration have resulted in uneven CT practices. These circumstances necessitate a critical exploration of how SBPs interpret and enact their roles, and how their theoretical orientations influence the quality and scope of transition support they provide.

Recent and prior research underscores some of the progress and challenges in CT practices of SBPs. Arora et al. (2025) found that educators expressed dissatisfaction with practicum preparation for transition services and identified minimal student input in planning. Inter-staff collaboration and parental engagement were also found lacking. The educators had serious problems connecting with the rest of the school staff and community providers, and the challenges that students experience when trying to be the best advocates for themselves. The educators demanded more parental contribution and collaboration between school personnel. In Korea, Lee and Park (2020) revealed that a collaboration system was established with various community organisations for employment and career exploration for SASD. In addition, it found that there are difficulties of collaboration, which are specific to student-focused opportunities, limited to a formal framework, and the boundaries of informal work duties. Furthermore, Sansosti and Sansosti (2013) revealed that both the instructors and specialists are involved in several evidence-based assessment and intervention practices. However, the study identified several areas of improvement, aspects of weakness in the training programmes and the gap between the training that students are given and the real practice that school psychologist performs in their day-to-day work. Challenger et al. (2025) revealed that school counsellors know how to collaborate with stakeholders within and outside of the school to achieve the outcomes of their programme. Nigerian studies by Victor-Aigbodion and Eseadi (2025) confirmed that purpose-driven intervention enhanced CT efficacy and career purpose in SASD, while Otu and Sefotho (2024) revealed the low predictive strength of employability skills for CT among neurodivergent youth. These findings suggest the need for clearer professional role construction and deeper theoretical embedding among Nigerian SBPs. Consequently, our study examined the degree to which SBPs' role variables and theoretical orientations predict their involvement in the CT of SASD.

CONCEPTUALISING AND CONTEXTUALISING SCHOOL-BASED PROFESSIONALS' ROLES

Although SBPs play vital and distinct roles in facilitating the CT of SASD, their ability to effectively support SASD may be determined by role clarity, role conflict, role efficacy, and role breadth, among other factors.

Role Clarity

Role clarity refers to the extent to which SBPs have a well-defined understanding of their responsibilities in CT planning. Clear role definitions allow SBPs to deliver targeted services such as career assessments, vocational training, social-emotional support, or agency coordination (Lee & Carter, 2012; Kucharczyk et al., 2022). The presence of ambiguity in professional roles and duties may cause conflicts and have an adverse effect on the transition process (Kester et al., 2019). The Nigerian support systems for SASD are currently being developed, and it is imperative to create a clear definition of the professional roles. Ambiguity in SBP roles persists due to inadequate training structures, resulting in overlap or neglect of duties. Teachers often assume transition roles without proper capacity, while counsellors and psychologists may lack the tools for career-specific interventions (Deardorff et al., 2021). With the increasing need to be professionally developed in the area of ASD transition planning, clear role definitions would result in the establishment of a more structured and well-organised system of support (Challenger et al., 2025).

Role Conflict

Role conflict refers to the strain experienced by SBPs when competing professional demands interfere with their capability to carry out CT-related duties. High role conflict scores indicate difficulty in balancing overlapping responsibilities and role expectations, a sense of being pulled in multiple directions, or perceived organisational pressure that hinders SBPs' capability to offer CT support effectively. Lower ratings by SBPs indicate greater alignment across responsibilities and reduced interference from competing demands. Role conflict arises when the objectives, expectations, or approaches of SBPs diverge, creating barriers to cohesive transition planning and service delivery (Kim et al., 2017). For instance, a teacher may prioritise behavioural interventions, while a counsellor may focus on socio-emotional development, leading to misalignment in strategies. Similarly, special educators may emphasise individualised behaviour management, whereas career counsellors might advocate broader skill acquisition. These mismatches can result in communication breakdowns, uncoordinated efforts, and planning inefficiencies, ultimately hindering the transition process for SASD (Wiedman, 2023). In Nigeria, these tensions are exacerbated by limited training, unclear role definitions, and a lack of structured transition frameworks, making collaboration more difficult. The situation underscores the critical need for sustained interprofessional dialogue and shared professional development to harmonise practices and prioritise student needs (Carolan & Slattery, 2025; Ogundeji et al., 2023).

Role Efficacy

Role efficacy refers to the confidence that SBPs have in their ability to guide SASD in career planning and preparation. It also includes self-judgements of competence, adequacy of training, and perceived capability in facilitating autonomy, exploration, and goal setting. SBPs with high role efficacy believe they possess the skillset to promote career readiness and provide meaningful support. Low role efficacy reflects SBPs' doubt, hesitation, or uncertainty about their knowledge or proficiency in transition support. When professionals believe in their ability to perform these tasks, they are more likely to engage in proactive and effective transition planning and support (Plotner et al., 2012). Critical components of transition support include teaching problem-solving and executive functioning skills, which are foundational for successful transitions (Snell-Rood et al., 2020). Effective transition planning demands individualised approaches that centre on student needs and promote their participation in designing transition pathways (Roitsch, 2024; Yakubova & Zeleke, 2016). However, many SBPs lack the specialised training necessary to support SASD through this critical phase. Gaps in preparation for CT planning and ASD-specific pedagogy often prevent them from delivering meaningful guidance (Kester et al., 2019). Strengthening professional role efficacy through targeted development is essential to equipping SBPs with the capacity to address the complex challenges of CT for SASD(Corona et al., 2017).

Role Breadth

Role breadth indicates the extent to which professionals extend their responsibilities beyond traditional or narrowly defined job boundaries in order to meet the complex needs of SASD. High role breadth indicates willingness to collaborate with other personnel, coordinate interdisciplinary efforts, and adapt one's professional identity as the students progress toward adulthood. SBPs with broader role involvement may engage with counsellors, therapists, families, or employers to support CT goals. Lower scores suggest a restricted interpretation of one's role or limited engagement outside core instructional duties. In other words, role breadth reflects the extent to which SBPs engage a diverse range of stakeholders, including students, parents, teachers, and allied professionals, in developing a comprehensive transition plan (Bruck et al., 2022; Roitsch, 2024). Broader involvement in the transition process enables professionals to anticipate barriers early and implement responsive strategies.

In contrast, a narrow focus on isolated aspects such as academics or behavioural management often proves insufficient for supporting successful transitions in SASD. A more integrative approach involves collaboration across multiple domains, including vocational training, emotional support, family engagement, and community partnerships, to ensure a rounded support system (Oertle & Trach, 2007). Crucial to this process is effective communication and coordinated planning among all actors. When these components are lacking (as often seen in the Nigerian context), transition efforts become fragmented and less effective (Brooks et al., 2009). The isolation of SBPs and limited interprofessional cooperation hinder outcomes for SASD (Numisi et al., 2020). Nonetheless, enhancing cross-functional collaboration can significantly improve the quality and impact of transition support.

CONCEPTUALISING AND CONTEXTUALISING THEORY-INFORMED TRANSITION SUPPORT AND THEORY-INFORMED REFLECTIVE PRACTICE

Theory-Informed Transition Support

Theory-informed transition support refers to the extent to which SBPs rely on established conceptual frameworks to guide assessment, planning, and implementation of CT services for SASD. SBPs who rate highly on this construct tend to anchor their practice on evidence-based models which emphasise contextual influences, skill development, environmental adaptation, and self-advocacy rather than intuition when addressing the transition needs of SASD. These SBPs often use theoretical frameworks as practical tools for organising transition tasks, structuring goals, and aligning interventions with evidence-based principles. The integration of theory into daily practice has been shown to enhance the quality, consistency, and sustainability of transition support for neurodivergent students like SASD, whose developmental and behavioural needs require systematic planning(McMahon & Cullinan, 2016; Victor-Aigbodion & Eseadi, 2025). Conversely, reduced reliance on theory-informed approaches often leads to fragmented practices where decisions depend on intuition, personal beliefs, or informal experience. Such unstructured approaches may overlook essential domains of transition planning, including independent living, vocational preparation, community participation, and self-determination skills, all of which are critical for the long-term outcomes of SASD (Chandroo et al., 2018; Chen et al., 2019; Hendricks & Wehman, 2009). Studies across contexts suggest that SBPs who lack training in theoretical models tend to focus narrowly on academic support while neglecting the broader ecological, behavioural, and vocational needs required for successful CT (Dinamarca-Aravena, 2024; LaPoint et al., 2025; Sasere & Makhasane, 2023). This knowledge gap aligns with literature demonstrating that inadequate theoretical grounding is one of the primary barriers to implementing high-quality transition services in many low and middle-income countries (Wong et al., 2021).

Evidence-informed transition frameworks also contribute to improved planning and decision-making by helping SBPs coordinate interagency support, engage families, and map long-term trajectories for students with complex needs. For instance, the Taxonomy for Transition Programming 2.0 highlights structured evidence-based components such as student-focused planning, interagency collaboration, and programme structures that are strongly associated with improved employment and educational outcomes for youths with ASD (Cumming et al., 2020; Knudson, 2024; McDonough & Revell, 2010). This framework and some other evidence-based frameworks offer SBPs a coherent framework for identifying barriers, structuring interventions, and monitoring progress over time. In the African context, educators who receive training in inclusive education frameworks demonstrate greater confidence and competence in supporting learners with disabilities, suggesting that theoretical orientation significantly shapes professional behaviour (Chitiyo et al., 2026; Kelly et al., 2024). Teachers familiar with ecological and rights-based theories of inclusion could be more likely to implement structured transition practices, collaborate with families, and advocate for school-level adaptations (Amponteng et al., 2025; Hervie, 2023; Mohammed & Hlalele, 2025). Teachers with theoretical preparation may also rate higher in transition-related competencies than those relying on informal experience or methods (Kariuki et al., 2019; Wawire, 2021). These expositions reinforce the notion that theory-informed practice is essential for consistent and equitable transition planning, especially in contexts where resources are limited and policy frameworks are still evolving. Thus, theory-informed transition support is seen as a practical necessity for effective transition planning for students who have ASD. When SBPs operate from a strong theoretical base, they are better positioned to develop comprehensive, developmentally appropriate, and context-sensitive transition programmes that align with global best practices. In contrast, when theoretical orientation is weak or absent, transition planning becomes inconsistent and dependent on individual discretion, thereby limiting the capacity of schools to prepare SASD for meaningful adult participation. These expositions, therefore, underscore the need for ongoing professional development, pre-service training, and policy alignment that explicitly promote the use of theory-based frameworks in CT support.

Theory-Informed Reflective Practice

Theory-informed reflective practice refers to the extent to which SBPs continually analyse their own actions, evaluate the effectiveness of their approaches, and seek feedback in relation to theoretical principles. It further refers to the disciplined process through which SBPs evaluate their judgments, interactions, and intervention choices in light of established professional knowledge and evidence-based guidelines. In other words, reflection informed by theory involves deliberate examination of one's practices to refine them over time. High ratings on this construct by SBPs indicate openness to feedback, professional self-scrutiny, and ongoing adjustment to improve transition support. Lower levels by SBPs indicate routine practice lacking in critical evaluation or theoretical improvement.

In the context of CT support for students who have ASD, reflective practice enables professionals to question habitual routines, interrogate the assumptions guiding their decisions, and modify their approaches in response to student needs and empirical insight. Rather than relying solely on experience or intuition, reflective practitioners consistently revisit the rationale behind their interventions and assess whether their actions align with best practice principles and demonstrated transition outcomes. This reflective orientation creates a feedback loop, where students provide feedback to peers and then reflect on the feedback received, fostering deeper reflective learning as well as encouraging students to critically assess their own and others' work, resulting in more intentional and thoughtful practice (Mauri & Neiva de Figueiredo, 2025). Across diverse educational contexts, reflective practice has been associated with improved professional judgment, greater confidence in supporting learners with disabilities, and more consistent implementation of inclusive practices (ElSayary et al., 2025a; Garcia & Campbell, 2023). For transition planning specifically, reflective SBPs tend to engage in deeper appraisal of career readiness indicators, environmental barriers, and student preferences. They also demonstrate a higher likelihood of modifying transition strategies when previous approaches fail to yield adequate progress. Educators who engage in routine reflection are more effective in differentiating support, collaborating with families, and documenting transition progress in structured ways that align with evidence-based guidelines (Clarà et al., 2019; ElSayary et al., 2025).

Continuous Professional Development (CPD) forms a critical foundation for sustaining this reflective stance. High-quality CPD strengthens professionals' capacity to engage in analytic reflection, update their knowledge base, and refine the skills needed for specialist support. Empirical evidence across Africa indicates that CPD programmes that incorporate modelling, guided reflection, and collaborative inquiry significantly improve teachers' competence and confidence in supporting learners with disabilities (Goodyear, 2017; Kempen & Steyn, 2016; Mavuso, 2022; Nzimande, 2025). In Nigeria, blended CPD models have demonstrated measurable improvements in professionals' knowledge, reflective decision making, and practical application of inclusive strategies, suggesting that structured professional learning is essential for strengthening transition planning in contexts with limited specialist training opportunities (Haruna et al., 2025; Shikuku et al., 2024). Frameworks such as the Multi-tiered System of Support (MTSS) further reinforce reflective processes by requiring educators to critically analyse student data, determine the adequacy of universal supports, and identify students who require targeted or intensive interventions. MTSS depends on continuous decision cycles in which professionals interpret assessment results, examine student responses to intervention, and adjust their strategies accordingly. MTSS enhances collaboration, improves documentation of student needs, and increases equitable access to support when implemented reflectively (Ahmed et al., 2025; Hughes, 2025; Leonard et al., 2019; Porter, 2021). Within transition planning for SASD, MTSS helps SBPs differentiate between career readiness needs that can be addressed through whole school programmes and those requiring targeted coaching, community-based experiences, or one-to-one intervention.

Reflective practice also requires SBPs to examine contextual influences that affect CT outcomes. Through ecological reflection, which implies considering the multiple settings that shape a student's development, SBPs can enhance students' sense of belonging, which is crucial for their overall development and academic success. By assessing interactions among home, school, community, and service systems, reflective practitioners are better able to anticipate barriers, coordinate supports, and advocate for environmental adjustments that facilitate successful transition to adulthood (El Zaatari & Maalouf, 2022). Furthermore, reflective practice is closely tied to the enhancement of self-efficacy, agency, and goal setting for SASD (McGuinness & Shankar, 2019; Trede & Smith, 2012). When practitioners reflect on whether transition activities genuinely foster autonomy, skill mastery, and goal clarity, students demonstrate greater engagement in career exploration and improved long-term outcomes (Admiraal et al., 2024; Molloy & Keating, 2011; Vinson et al., 2010). Reflective SBPs monitor whether their interventions build confidence, provide appropriate scaffolding, and reinforce realistic yet optimistic expectations regarding post-school possibilities. This kind of reflection ensures that transition planning moves beyond completing mandated tasks to cultivating the capacities that enable SASD to navigate complex adult environments. To this end, theory-informed reflective practice can strengthen the quality, intentionality, and coherence of transition planning. Overall, strengthening reflective competence through CPD, mentoring, and structured planning tools is essential for improving the CT outcomes of SASD, particularly in contexts where specialist training is scarce and interagency infrastructure is still emerging.

RESEARCH OBJECTIVES

The study's primary objective was to examine how SBPs' roles and theoretical orientations influence the CT of SASD. The specific objectives of the study are to:

1. To determine the association between SBPs' roles and their involvement in facilitating CT for SASD.
2. To assess how SBPs' theoretical orientations relate to the CT of SASD.
3. To compare male and female SBPs on their roles and theoretical orientations in facilitating CT for SASD.
4. To determine the combined predictive power of SBPs' roles and theoretical orientations on the CT of SASD.

RESEARCH QUESTIONS

1. What is the relationship between SBPs' roles and their involvement in facilitating CT for SASD?
2. How does SBP's theoretical orientation relate to their involvement in CT for SASD?
3. Are there gender differences in SBPs' roles and theoretical orientations in facilitating CT for SASD?
4. To what extent do SBPs' roles and theoretical orientations jointly predict CT outcomes for SASD?

THEORETICAL FRAMEWORK

This study is grounded in Biddle's role theory, which explains professional behaviour as the enactment of socially defined expectations for organisational roles, with misfit manifesting as role conflict and ambiguity that shape outcomes (Biddle, 1979). Role conflict, role efficacy, role clarity, and role overload are the main tenets of the theory (Karkkola et al., 2019). Role theory provides a valuable framework for comprehending how SBPs organise their duties, interact with others, and influence the CT of SASD. When applying role theory, the SBP reflects on the expectations associated with their position, the behaviours required to fulfil those expectations, and the ways these expectations shape collaboration within the school and the broader transition system. A research report revealed a statistically significant difference in ratings of the level of transition-specific competencies between practice, experience and professional role levels (Kester et al., 2019). SBPs evaluate how school practices, family participation, and community resources shape students' transition experiences (Lindsay et al., 2018). Role clarity is extremely helpful in preventing duplication of duties and ensures tasks associated with the transition are executed in a structural and planned manner. Role theory places great importance on role clarity. However, it also introduces the problem of role conflict that may have serious implications for SBPs, particularly those dealing with SASD (Moss, 2015). Role conflict is a situation in whereby an individual conflicts with the demands or expectations of various roles that they hold (Nir & Eyal, 2003). In the case of SBPs, this may arise when their main role (i.e., educator, counsellor, or therapist) is in conflict with other roles or the requirements of students and families. In most of the schools in Nigeria, the professionals are faced with various responsibilities; hence, there is a likelihood of tension between the academic responsibilities and transition planning. With the help of role theory, the professional can recognise these conflicts in time and find support or cooperation to balance conflicting expectations (Bredeson, 1993). Role theory also emphasised the important of self-efficacy in performing a task. High self-efficacy is related to better job performance, while low self-efficacy has a high likelihood of seeking additional training to enhance their competence (Eltantawy & Fouad, 2025; Neale & Griffin, 2006). Role theory further emphasised the significance of working in interprofessional teams, which include families, cooperating with the community agencies, and facilitating inclusive opportunities (MacNaughton et al., 2013).

POLICY FRAMEWORK

Nigeria's National Policy on Inclusive Education provides a central foundation for interpreting the obligations of SBPs who work with students with disabilities(Federal Ministry of Education, 2023). The policy frames inclusive education (IE) as a whole-system educational approach aimed at ensuring that all students, despite their disability, background, or circumstance, can access meaningful learning opportunities. The policy's emphasis on removing barriers and promoting equal participation establishes a conceptual pathway for how schools should support the CT of SASD. Within the policy framework, IE is understood as an active response to student diversity, in which individual differences are viewed as valuable sources of enrichment for the learning process rather than obstacles to be corrected. A central commitment of the policy is that genuine inclusion can only be achieved when curriculum, school culture, and organisational practices are intentionally restructured to place students' needs at the centre of educational provision. This principle has direct implications for transition planning, as it positions schools as proactive environments that identify and meet students' developmental and vocational needs. The policy stresses the importance of early identification and timely assistance. For SASD, early identification extends beyond academic performance and includes interests, autonomy skills, sensory profiles, communication patterns, and vocational inclinations. These components form the foundation of transition planning and require SBPs to approach students from a strengths-based rather than deficit-based perspective. The policy is grounded in the social understanding of disability, which argues that learning barriers are largely produced by environmental and structural constraints rather than by the student's impairment (Ezewuzie et al., 2025). This orientation fundamentally encourages SBPs to adopt theoretical perspectives that emphasise contextual adaptation and systemic support rather than attempts to fix the child. This position aligns closely with bioecological and social cognitive models of transition, which view future vocational success as dependent on skill development, supportive relationships, and accessible environments (Arubayi & Akobo, 2018; Dente & Parkinson Coles, 2012).

METHODOLOGY

Research Approach, Paradigm and Design

This study used a quantitative approach to empirical inquiry in which a cross-sectional, predictive correlational design was employed to study the associations between the roles of SBPs, their theoretical orientation, and their involvement in facilitating CT for SASD. A quantitative approach was chosen because it is conducive to the identification of systematic patterns across several dimensions of the professional role and the estimation of their predictive strength (Velec & Huang, 2014; Fadele & Rocha, 2025). In addition, a cross-sectional, predictive correlational design was considered crucial because we were not interested in simply describing these constructs, but rather in gaining insight into their collective ability to predict professional involvement in CT activities. The cross-sectional design was also embraced since the data were gathered at one point in various schools that were involved in the study area (Hajra et al., 2025; Setia, 2016). This design allows a structured evaluation of the interplay of variables in real school environments without influencing ongoing practices.

The research was based on a positivist paradigm, with assumptions that the constructs in question can be measured reliably, and that the answers given by the participants are reliable indicators of underlying professional behaviours and beliefs. The positivist paradigm is a philosophy of research that states that knowledge is founded upon objective, measurable observations and quantitative data (Karupiah, 2022; Park et al., 2020). The chosen paradigm of research allows us to adopt a quantitative research questionnaire and statistically analyse the relationship between role clarity, role conflict, role efficacy, role breadth, and theoretically based practices related to CT support of SASD.

Sample and Sampling Method

A multi-stage sampling procedure was utilised to obtain a sample that was both contextually representative and practically accessible. This approach was appropriate for the present study because the population of SBPs who work with SASD in Southeast Nigeria is unevenly distributed across schools and locations, making single-stage sampling neither feasible nor methodologically sound. Multi-stage sampling allowed us to organise the population into meaningful units and draw participants in a structured sequence that aligned with the administrative and geographical realities of the research setting (Puerta et al., 2019). The first stage involved identifying schools in Ebonyi and Enugu States in Southeast Nigeria that enrol SASD. These states were purposively included because they contain a concentration of schools with emerging inclusion programmes and staff who actively participate in transition support activities. This ensured that the study targeted SBPs with direct experience relevant to the research questions. In the second stage, schools were stratified by ownership type and geographical location. Inclusive public and private secondary schools located in urban, semi-urban, and rural areas were selected. This stratification increased the representativeness of the final sample by ensuring that participants reflected the diverse contexts in which transition support occurs. The third stage involved selecting SBPs within participating schools. We utilised the school staff registers provided by each school's administrative heads to identify teachers, counsellors, learning support staff, and other personnel who work directly with SASD and other special educational needs. The participants were then recruited through simple random selection from these lists. This step ensured that each eligible professional had an equal chance of selection while maintaining alignment with the study's focus. The final sample for this research study included one hundred and twenty professionals, thirty-four males and eighty-six females. Age, years of experience and educational backgrounds were diverse in the sample, reflecting the diversity of Nigerian school systems. The goal was not proportional representation by profession but conceptual representation of those who are actively involved in decisions and activities relating to CT within the school system.

Instruments

Two instruments were used in gathering the research data, namely, School School-Based Professionals Role and Theoretical Orientations Questionnaire (SPRTOQ) (see Table 5) and the CT Support for SASD Questionnaire, School-Based Professionals' Version (CTS-SPV) (see Table 6). Both instruments have been developed by us to be used in the Nigerian school context. They were designed to reflect professional experiences, theoretical dispositions and transition support practices that are relevant to educational settings in Southeast Nigeria.

The SPRTOQ assesses six areas: role clarity, role conflict, role efficacy, role breadth, theory-informed transition support, and theory-informed reflective practice. These domains were chosen to represent the major dimensions of professional functioning that affect transition work. Role clarity measures the extent to which professionals know what their role is in supporting CT activities. Role conflict investigates the extent to which competing demands are challenging for effective practice relating to CT transition support. Role efficacy is the confidence in performing transition-related tasks. Role breadth reflects involvement in a broader set of CT responsibilities outside of traditional role boundaries. Theory-informed transition support assesses the degree to which professionals use recognised theoretical frameworks in CT support. Theory-informed reflective practice assists in quantifying the extent to which professionals engage in systematic reflection while supporting SASD during CT. The questionnaire items were organised on a five-point Likert scale from one being strongly disagree to five being strongly agree. This response structure helped participants to indicate different degrees of agreement with each statement (see Figure 1). Higher scores suggest a greater level of endorsement of the construct being measured.

The second one, CTS-SPV, measures the degree of professional involvement in specific transition-related practices. These include planning, working with parents, working with community agencies, preparing students for the workplace demands, and monitoring student readiness. This instrument also uses a five-point Likert scale ranging from strongly disagree to strongly agree. Higher scores reflect a greater level of endorsement of the construct being assessed. Items were developed to represent individual practitioner responsibilities as well as school-wide structures that have an impact on CT. The questionnaire is aligned to recognised frameworks for transition support and was adapted to the context of Nigerian schools, where transition services are still in an emergent stage.

The two instruments were developed using a process of item generation, expert review, and pilot testing. Reliability testing during pilot administration of these instruments showed acceptable internal consistency across all subscales, showing that the constructs were measured coherently (see Table 5 and Table 6). The use of these instruments together provides support for a comprehensive appraisal of the predictors of professional involvement in the CT of SASD.

Data Collection and Ethical Considerations

The data collection procedures complied with recognised ethical and scientific standards for research involving human participants. Prior to fieldwork, we obtained formal approval from the Faculty of Education Research Ethics Committee at the University of Johannesburg (Sem-2-2020-057). We also received administrative permission from school authorities before approaching potential participants. Data collection was done using in-person administration of questionnaires. We chose a paper-based format because many schools in the region have limited digital access and inconsistent connectivity, which will compromise participation and data completeness. The face-to-face format allowed for uniform instructions to be maintained, participant queries to be clarified, and missing responses to be reduced. These advantages were crucial to gathering reliable data that could be used for predictive analysis.

Two postgraduate research assistants assisted in the data collection process. They were trained in research ethics, questionnaire administration protocols and communication procedures. Their involvement allowed multiple schools to be covered at the same time and increased the reliability of data recording across sites. This decentralised structure was important because of travel constraints, time limitations and institutional schedules. Each questionnaire administration session started with an explanation of the objectives of the study, the voluntary nature of participation, and the confidential handling of responses. Participants were given an information sheet summarising these details. The initial part leading to the questionnaire contained an informed consent section, and participants signed the consent form before they moved on to the items. This process ensured that participation was on the basis of awareness and free choice.

Participants took the questionnaires individually, while the research assistants were available to clarify procedural questions, but they did not have an impact on responses. On average, it took twenty minutes to complete the questionnaires. Once completed, the questionnaires were checked for missing responses, then sealed in labelled envelopes. This immediate screening minimised data loss and guaranteed usable data sets for analysis.

All the questionnaire packets were transported to a secure location for storage. Digital versions were made by manually entering responses into an encrypted database. This two-stage storage process ensured confidentiality and ease of later analysis. Identifying information was not gathered, and responses were anonymised. Schools were not identified in reporting in order to protect participant identities further.

Data Analysis

Before the analysis commenced, data were checked for completeness, accuracy and conformity to statistical assumptions. Missing values were minimal and were solved by simple imputation techniques suitable for cross-sectional educational data. Outliers were checked to verify if they were real responses. Most were kept in place because they reflected the diversity inherent in professional roles and orientations. The analytical strategy offered a coherent assessment of the relationships that underpin SBPs' involvement in CT support.

The analysis of data was carried out using the IBM Statistical Package for the Social Sciences. The analytical strategy we employed included steps towards evaluating the reliability of the instruments, analysing the participants' demographics, analysing the associations between the variables, and the predictive relationships. This strategy enabled us to address the research questions systematically. Before undertaking substantive analyses, we examined the internal consistency of each of the subscales from the two instruments. We used Cronbach's α and Omega ω to assess the reliability of role clarity, role conflict, role efficacy, role breadth, theory-informed transition support, theory-informed reflective practice, and the CT support scale. Reliability coefficients were above acceptable thresholds for research purposes, suggesting that each construct was showing adequate internal consistency.

We calculated descriptive statistics to summarise each study variable. These statistics presented an ordered picture of how participants viewed themselves in terms of their demographics, roles and orientations in CT support. The results pertaining to means, standard deviations, and confidence intervals were documented in this research. Descriptive results also aided in comparing between subscales and helped put correlational and regression results into context.

The associations between our study variables were examined through the use of Pearson correlation coefficients. This analysis evaluated the direction and strength of relationships between the role dimensions, theoretical orientation variables, and CT support. Correlation coefficients also informed the development of the regression models because they identified which constructs showed meaningful associations with the outcome variable. Multiple regression analysis was the main analytical method. This model allowed us to estimate the extent to which the role and theoretical orientation variables predicted involvement of professionals in CT practices. Standardised coefficients (β) were interpreted for each predictor. This approach provided an accurate picture of the professional characteristics that were most closely related to transition support.

RESULTS

Table 1. Biodata of participants

Variables	N	%
Gender Male Female	34 86	71.7 28.3
Age*	44.34±8.68	
Location Urban Semi-urban Rural	36 56 28	30.0 46.7 23.3
School Type Private Public	47 73	39.2 60.8
Educational Qualification Bachelors Masters Ph.D.	84 26 10	70.0 21.7 8.3

*Mean age & standard deviation of respondents

Table 1 indicates the demographic features of the one hundred and twenty SBPs who participated in the study. As indicated in the table, the group consisted largely of female professionals (71.7 per cent), with males comprising just over one quarter (28.3 per cent). The average age of the respondents was 44.34 years (SD = 8.68), which suggests that the sample contained practitioners who were predominantly in mid-career stages. The age range indicates a reasonable spread across younger and older professionals.

In relation to geographical distribution, nearly half of the sample worked in semi-urban settings (46.7 per cent), followed by those in urban (30 per cent) and rural locations (23.3 per cent). This distribution reflects the diverse contexts in which the respondents carry out their work. More than half of the respondents were employed in public schools (60.8 per cent), while the remaining group worked in private schools (39.2 per cent). A substantial proportion of respondents held bachelor's degrees (70 per cent), whereas smaller proportions had attained master's degrees (21.7 per cent) or doctoral qualifications (8.3 per cent).

Table 2. Bivariate correlation of the study variables

	Variables	1	2	3	4	5	6	7
1	Role Clarity	1						
2	Role Conflict	.057	1					
3	Role Efficacy	-.079	.092	1				
4	Role Breadth	-.096	.090	-.084	1			
5	Theory-Informed Transition Support	-.055	.136	-.002	.093	1		
6	Theory-Informed Reflective Practice	-.017	.053	.047	.195*	.108	1	
7	Overall Professionals' Roles and Theoretical Orientations	.445**	.555**	.411**	.445**	.349**	.377**	1
8	Career transition for SASD	-.050	.147	.079	.137	.205*	.705**	.343**

**. Significant at the 0.01 level
*. Significant at the 0.05 level

The findings in Table 2 show that the role-related variables, which include role clarity, role conflict, role efficacy, and role breadth, were only minimally associated with CT involvement. Role clarity demonstrated a small negative correlation with CT involvement ($r = -.050$), indicating that clearer role definitions did not necessarily translate into greater participation in transition-related activities. The correlation between role conflict and CT involvement was small and positive ($r =$

.147), suggesting that experiencing competing demands did not strongly affect transition involvement in either direction. Role efficacy also exhibited a small positive relationship ($r = .079$), indicating that higher confidence in performing role tasks was only weakly linked to levels of involvement. Similarly, role breadth demonstrated a small correlation ($r = .137$), pointing to a limited association between having a wider role scope and participating in transition support.

Theory-informed transition support demonstrated a significant positive association with CT involvement ($r = .205, p < .05$), reflecting a meaningful connection between theory and practice. Although the effect size was small, the data suggest that professionals who grounded their decisions in theoretical principles were more likely to take part in transition-related activities. Another result was observed for theory-informed reflective practice, which showed a strong association with CT involvement ($r = .705, p < .001$), representing a large effect size. The strength of this association indicates that reflective practice grounded in theoretical understanding plays a major role in shaping professional engagement in the CT of SASD. Professionals who regularly use theoretical concepts to interpret student needs, reflect on their practices, and adjust their approaches could be substantially more involved in transition activities. The composite index of overall roles and theoretical orientations also showed a significant association with transition involvement ($r = .343, p < .01$). This reinforces the idea that theoretically grounded reflective engagement, rather than structural aspects of roles, is more central to understanding variation in professionals' involvement in transition activities.

Table 3. Descriptive statistics for SBPs' roles and theoretical orientations in facilitating CT for SASD

	Group	N	Mean	SD	SE	Coefficient of Variation	95% Confidence Interval	
							Lower	Upper
Role Clarity	Male Female	32 92	13.09 13.41	4.01 4.12	.709 .429	.306 .307	11.65 12.56	14.54 14.27
Role Conflict	Male Female	32 92	13.67 12.88	3.12 3.16	.551 .329	.228 .245	11.75 13.02	13.99 14.33
Role Efficacy	Male Female	32 92	11.87 11.47	3.68 3.41	.651 .356	.310 .297	10.14 11.16	12.80 12.58
Role Breadth	Male Female	32 92	11.03 12.25	3.03 3.44	.535 .358	.275 .281	11.16 10.32	13.34 11.74
Theory-Informed Transition Support	Male Female	32 92	5.54 5.72	1.95 2.08	.346 .217	.352 .364	5.01 5.11	6.42 5.97

continued on following page

Table 3. Continued

	Group	N	Mean	SD	SE	Coefficient of Variation	95% Confidence Interval	
							Lower	Upper
Theory-Informed Reflective Practice	Male Female	32 92	6.34 6.78	1.81 1.85	.320 .193	.285 .274	6.13 5.95	7.43 6.72
Overall Professionals' Roles	Male Female	32 92	61.87 62.19	8.09 7.87	1.43 .821	.131 .127	59.27 60.24	65.11 63.50
Career transition for SASD	Male Female	32 92	27.08 27.84	6.27 6.62	1.11 .691	.232 .238	25.58 25.70	30.10 28.45

Gender factor was examined through the descriptive statistics presented in Table 3. Across most variables, the mean values for male and female professionals were closely aligned, suggesting substantial similarity in perceptions and practices. For role clarity, male respondents reported a mean of 13.09 (SD = 4.01), while female respondents reported a mean of 13.41 (SD = 4.12). Role conflict also presented only a minor difference, with males scoring 13.67 (SD = 3.12) and females scoring 12.88 (SD = 3.16). These results point to what can be described as a parallel role perception profile, characterised by highly similar role-related experiences across genders. A similar result appeared for role efficacy and role breadth. The differences between male and female means were small and fell within overlapping confidence intervals, indicating no substantial differences.

For theoretical orientation variables, female respondents showed slightly higher means for theory-informed transition support (M = 5.72, SD = 2.08) compared to males (M = 5.54, SD = 1.95). A comparable pattern was observed for theory-informed reflective practice, where females reported 6.78 (SD = 1.85), and males reported 6.34 (SD = 1.81). Although these differences suggest a slightly elevated theoretical engagement profile among females, the effect sizes were small and do not indicate meaningful divergence. The overall professional roles in CT were quite similar. Females reported a mean transition involvement score of 27.84 (SD = 6.62) compared to 27.08 (SD = 6.27) among males. These scores collectively indicate that gender was not a significant determinant of role perceptions, theoretical orientation, or involvement in transition activities.

Table 4. Regression analysis of SBPs' roles and theoretical orientations in facilitating CT for SASD

Regression Models	β	Std. Error	t	Sig.
Role Clarity → Career transition	-.050	.145	-.556	.579
Role Conflict → Career transition	.147	.185	1.639	.104
Role Efficacy →Career transition	.079	.169	.879	.381
Role Breadth → Career transition	.137	.174	1.525	.130
Theory-Informed Transition Support→ Career transition	.205	.283	2.314	.022
Theory-Informed Reflective Practice →Career transition	.705	.227	10.988	.000
Overall → Career transition	.343	.070	4.036	.000

R = 725; R^2 = .526; R^2 change = .502; Adjusted R^2 = .526

The regression results in Table 4 showed three predictive patterns. The role-related variables did not make significant contributions to explaining CT involvement. Role clarity (β = −.050, p = .579), role conflict (β = .147, p = .104), role efficacy (β = .079, p = .381), and role breadth (β = .137, p = .130) showed small effect sizes and nonsignificant associations. This reflects a non-predictive structural role profile, consistent with the earlier correlational findings. In contrast, theory-informed transition support contributed significantly to the prediction of transition involvement (β = .205, p = .022). Although the effect size was modest, the significance suggests that professionals who apply theoretical principles when engaging in transition work tend to be more involved. This can be described as a moderately predictive theoretical support profile.

Theory-informed reflective practice emerged as the strongest predictor in the model. Given the significant regression coefficient (β = .705, p < .001), theory-informed reflective practice had a strong influence on transition involvement. The large effect size shows that reflective practice guided by theoretical knowledge is a critical factor in shaping SBPs' participation in transition activities for SASD. This result constitutes a strong theoretical reflexivity predictor profile. The composite index also significantly predicted CT involvement (β = .343, p < .001). Overall, the model accounted for 52.6 per cent of the variance in transition involvement (R = .725, R^2 = .526), showing strong explanatory capacity.

DISCUSSION

The results demonstrated that role clarity, role conflict, role efficacy and role breadth of SBP had very weak and nonsignificant associations with their involvement in promoting the CT of SASD. Practically, the reduction of conflict and responsibilities, roles, and increased confidence did not translate into more CT participation. This is expected in the Nigerian context as many schools, and particularly the ones located in rural and semi-urban areas, do not have formalised transition models and clearly defined interprofessional coordination frameworks. It is common that educators, counsellors, psychologists and social workers perform various roles at the same time, leading to the lack of boundary demarcation. Even the simple explanation of functions or the widening of duties will not always help the transition engagement in these environments, as the systemic arrangements, training possibilities, and institutional culture do not focus on the transition planning of SASD (Knudson, 2024; Elias et al., 2019). This finding supports the results of Hill et al. (2024), which indicated that a lack of standardised training and effective programmes limits SASD's access to individualised educational programmes, and some of these programmes do not reach rural areas. On the other hand, another study reported that a significant association was found between self-efficacy, confidence, and overall performance in different kinds of educators' roles (Bitsika et al., 2017).

This finding that these role-related variables were weakly and nonsignificantly correlated with the involvement of SBP in CT among SASD seemingly goes against expectations by Biddle's role theory. Rather than having role expectations and role clarity to inform behaviour, the findings indicate that other forces may have more influence, including theoretical grounding and reflective practice. It suggests that contextual or cognitive aspects, such as the way professionals own, comprehend and practise theory, can supersede structural role definition to influence CT practices in inclusive education settings.

There was a significant impact of the SBPs' theoretical orientation on CT of SASD. It was found that theory-informed transition support had a small yet significant positive relationship, which means that professionals who use theoretical principles will be more involved in transition activities. The theory-informed reflective practice of the SBP was most associated with and the most powerful predictor of the CT of SASD in the regression model. This demonstrates that an active involvement in CT among SASD is based on professional reflective engagement that relies on theory. This implies that the more the SBPs base their decisions on behavioural, developmental, social cognitive or ecological principles, the more likely they are to interpret the needs of the students and apply systematic strategies in the process of transition planning in the Nigerian context. The power of reflection practice is that it underlines the need to engage in constant learning, self-reflection, and translation of theory to the local context, particularly in a country where ASD specific training is scarce (Klefbeck, 2023). This suggests that effective transition support is a result of professional expertise, not a result of formal role structures. This study is consistent with the findings of Humpal (2023), whose research highlighted the importance of continual professional growth of middle school educators to enhance the background of knowledge and application of transition services to SASD. Also, this study supports the findings of Ndlovu (2024), which revealed that the facilitating role of the SBPs in the CT of high-functional learners with ASD involves developing the learners' independence, finding particular employment for the learners, collaborating among themselves as professionals, reasonable accommodations and imparting skills to enhance work preparedness.

The findings showed that there were no significant gender differences in all role variables and measures of theoretical orientations. Role clarity, role conflict, role efficacy, role breadth, theory-informed support, and theory-informed reflective practice had male and female professionals with close aligned mean scores and overlapping confidence intervals. These small differences suggest that gender does not have a significant impact on school-based professional roles and theoretical orientation in assisting the CT of SASD. This implies that there is an equal distribution of training, institutional, and resource differences between the genders in Nigeria. Irrespective of gender, all professionals seem to have equal amounts of role clarity, conflict, confidence, and theoretical engagement. This homogeneity is probably caused by the fact that the system does not provide all professionals with formal preparation on ASD transition assistance, which leads to the perceptions and practices being similar. This finding confirmed the report of Almughyiri (2024), which indicated that both male and female teachers reported above-average knowledge of transition skills. Furthermore, this finding affirmed the findings of Kester et al. (2019), which revealed that professional competencies and training needs may be more affected by experience and role rather than gender. However, the findings of this study contradict the findings of Okurame (2007), who reported that female mentors provide more psychosocial support than their male counterparts.

The composite model accounted for 52.6 per cent variance in the CT of SASD due to school-based professional roles and theoretical orientations, which showed a high level of explanation. But the only theoretical variables had a significant contribution. Role clarity, conflict, efficacy, and breadth were not significant predictors and theory-informed transition support and theory-informed reflective practice, in particular, were significant factors. It implies that theoretical grounding, especially reflective practice, plays a significant role in predicting the role of professionals in the CT of SASD as compared to structural role variables. This is an indication that effective transition work is more motivated by competence, reflective ability and theoretical grounding in the context of Nigerian circumstances than positional responsibilities. The explanatory power of the reflective practice shaped by the theory underlines the necessity of the ongoing process of professional growth, mentoring, and training that will provide the professionals with the theoretical instruments that can be used to address the needs of ASD learners. These results are consistent with the results of Li (2025), which revealed that the reflective practice can play a significant role in the development of critical pedagogical skills and in the promotion of a better comprehension of the teaching methods and in increasing the ability of pre-service teachers in implementing these strategies in various learning environments. This revelation authenticated the report of Kim et al. (2024), which revealed that theory-informed systemic practices enable school counsellors to offer the platform on which sustainable, long-term change toward a more just society can be established.

There are a few limitations that have to be admitted concerning the results of this research. To begin with, the study was based on self-report questionnaires by SBP, which can create response bias because of the social desirability or lack of insight into actual practices in transition. The Nigerian context, which is a sensitive area when it comes to the aspects of professional competence, led to the respondents either exaggerating or downplaying their part in the transition activities. Second, the research was centred on professionals in Southeast Nigeria, and this might not be as representative of education systems in other geopolitical regions of Nigeria, which could have a significant difference in resources, educational structures, and cultural perceptions of ASD. Even in more rural or underserved schools, the constraints might be even higher than those in the sample. Third, the study does not allow drawing a causal connection between theoretical orientations, role variables and involvement in transitions, due to its cross-sectional design. Although reflective practice and theory-informed support were found to be important predictors, longitudinal research is required to establish whether theoretical competence increases can produce lasting transition engagement effects. Fourth, institutional variables of administrative support, school culture, or community partnerships were not evaluated in the study, and they may have a significant influence on the capacity of professionals to participate in the transition planning process of SASD. Such contextual factors could have been included, which could have enhanced the explanatory power of the model. Lastly, the research lacked observational or qualitative information that would have given greater information on how theoretical orientations are operationalised in actual school practices.

CONCLUSIONS

This paper explored the roles and theoretical orientations of SBP in promoting the CT of SASD in Southeast Nigeria. The results revealed that role clarity, role conflict, role efficacy, and role breadth had very little predictive power and did not significantly affect the involvement of the professionals in the transition activities. These outcomes indicate the systemic factors in the Nigerian school system, in which role systems are not fixed, transitions are not formalised, and the boundaries between the professions are not well delineated. Therefore, structural role characteristics by themselves cannot be converted into any meaningful involvement in the transition planning. Furthermore, theory-informed reflective practice, as the variable of theoretical orientation, appeared to be a powerful and meaningful predictor of the CT of SASD. Critical engagement of professionals in theoretical principles and reflective processes led to a significant involvement in transition-related tasks. This highlighted the significance of professionally sound judgment based on theory, where formal systems of transition are still in their formative stages. The conspicuousness of reflective practice implies that competence, interpretive skill, and the use of theory to understand complicated realities in schools are primary forces in transition support. Generally, the research demonstrates that specific professional development that builds theoretical competence, reflective capacity, and evidence-based decision-making is required to improve the outcome of transitions of SASD in Nigeria.

REFERENCES

Adigun, O. T., Tijani, F. A., Nzima, D. R., & Vivekanantharasa, R. (2021). Perceived Stress of Special Education Teachers in the Context of the Person-Environment Relationship. *The Open Psychology Journal, 14*(1), 300–309. DOI: 10.2174/1874350102114010300

Admiraal, W., Post, L., Kester, L., Louws, M., & Lockhorst, D. (2024). Learning labs in a secondary school in the Netherlands: Effects of teachers' autonomy support on student learning motivation and achievement. *Educational Studies, 50*(5), 939–956. DOI: 10.1080/03055698.2021.2023473

Ahmed, Y., Mesa, M. P., Zucker, T. A., Fumero, K., Clay, M., & Duran, S. O. (2025). The role of artificial intelligence in modernising multi-tiered systems of support. *Theory into Practice, 64*(4), 448–464. DOI: 10.1080/00405841.2025.2528541

Almalky, H. A., & Alqahtani, S. S. (2021). Special education teachers' reflections on school transition practices that support partnerships with businesses to prepare students with disabilities for employment in Saudi Arabia. *Children and Youth Services Review, 120*, 105813. Advance online publication. DOI: 10.1016/j.childyouth.2020.105813

Amponteng, M., Tracey, D., & Nketsia, W. (2025). Exploring teachers' concerns and recommendations regarding inclusive education in Ghana: An application of the ecological systems theory. *International Journal of Inclusive Education*, 1–18. Advance online publication. DOI: 10.1080/13603116.2025.2541910

Arora, D., Berman, M., Snider, L. A., Segall, M., & South, M. (2025). Educators' knowledge about strategies and supports for autistic students in the transition from school to adulthood. *Research in Autism, 126*, 202648. Advance online publication. DOI: 10.1016/j.reia.2025.202648

Arubayi, D. O., & Akobo, L. A. (2018). The capability approach and national development in Nigeria: Towards a youth transition model. *Human Resource Development International, 21*(5), 463–492. DOI: 10.1080/13678868.2018.1468588

Bakare, M. O., Frazier, T. W., Karpur, A., Abubakar, A., Nyongesa, M. K., Mwangi, P. M., Dixon, P., Khaliq, I., Gase, N. K., Sandstrom, J., Okidegbe, N., Rosanoff, M., Munir, K. M., & Shih, A. (2022). Brief report: Validity and reliability of the Nigerian Autism Screening Questionnaire. *Autism, 26*(6), 1581–1590. DOI: 10.1177/13623613221080250 PMID: 35261274

Biddle, B. J. (1979). *Role Theory: Expectations, Identities, and Behaviors. Elsevier*. Academic Press., DOI: 10.1016/C2009-0-03121-3

Bitsika, V., Warren, A. C., & Sharpley, C. F. (2017). An evaluation of a professional development programme in functional behavior assessment for educators in Australia. *International Journal of Special Education, 32*(3), 630–641.

Bredeson, P. V. (1993). Letting Go of Outlived Professional Identities: A Study of Role Transition and Role Strain for Principals in Restructured Schools. *Educational Administration Quarterly, 29*(1), 34–68. DOI: 10.1177/0013161X93029001004

Brooks, F., Bunn, F., & Morgan, J. (2009). Transition for adolescents with long-term conditions: Event to process. *British Journal of Community Nursing, 14*(7), 301–304. DOI: 10.12968/bjcn.2009.14.7.43078 PMID: 19597382

Bruck, S., Webster, A. A., & Clark, T. (2022). Transition support for students on the autism spectrum: A multiple stakeholder perspective. *Journal of Research in Special Educational Needs, 22*(1), 3–17. DOI: 10.1111/1471-3802.12509

Busack, J., Payton, C., & Hudson, C. (2021). Harnessing Community Resources to Enhance Student Learning and Development. In Cox, T., Fitzgerald, T., & Alvarez, M. E. (Eds.), *The Art of Becoming Indispensable: What School Social Workers Need to Know in Their First Three Years of Practice* (pp. 75–84). Oxford University Press., DOI: 10.1093/oso/9780197585160.003.0008

Carolan, M., & Slattery, Ó. M. (2025). The nature of collaboration in transition planning for autistic students moving into further education and training from the perspectives of post-primary teachers in Ireland. *Irish Educational Studies*, 1–23. Advance online publication. DOI: 10.1080/03323315.2025.2509522

Carter, E. W., & Schutz, M. A. (2022). Addressing Transition Preparation in Middle and High Schools. In Viezel, K. D., Wilczynski, S. M., & Davis, A. S. (Eds.), *Post-secondary Transition for College- or Career-Bound Autistic Students* (pp. 179–200). Springer International Publishing., DOI: 10.1007/978-3-030-93947-2_9

Challenger, C. D., Lombardi, A. R., Duquette, K., Espositio, C., & DeJesus, J. (2025). Strategies to Increase Collaboration Between School Counselors and Transition Specialists: A Multi-Tiered Approach to College and Career Readiness. *Journal of Education, 205*(2), 153–165. DOI: 10.1177/00220574241309103

Chandroo, R., Strnadová, I., & Cumming, T. M. (2018). A systematic review of the involvement of students with autism spectrum disorder in the transition planning process: Need for voice and empowerment. *Research in Developmental Disabilities, 83*, 8–17. DOI: 10.1016/j.ridd.2018.07.011 PMID: 30086472

Chen, J., Cohn, E. S., & Orsmond, G. I. (2019). Parents' future visions for their autistic transition-age youth: Hopes and expectations. *Autism*, *23*(6), 1363–1372. DOI: 10.1177/1362361318812141 PMID: 30445828

Chitiyo, J., Simone, K., Taole, M., & Motitswe, J. M. (2026). An examination of South African teachers' competency in inclusive education: A case of Limpopo. *Journal of Research in Special Educational Needs*, *26*(1), e70046. Advance online publication. DOI: 10.1111/1471-3802.70046

Clarà, M., Mauri, T., Colomina, R., & Onrubia, J. (2019). Supporting collaborative reflection in teacher education: A case study. *European Journal of Teacher Education*, *42*(2), 175–191. DOI: 10.1080/02619768.2019.1576626

Corona, L. L., Christodulu, K. V., & Rinaldi, M. L. (2017). Investigation of School Professionals' Self-Efficacy for Working With Students With ASD: Impact of Prior Experience, Knowledge, and Training. *Journal of Positive Behavior Interventions*, *19*(2), 90–101. DOI: 10.1177/1098300716667604

Cumming, T. M., Strnadová, I., & Danker, J. (2020). Transitions of Students with Autism and Intellectual Disabilities in Inclusive Settings: The Nexus Between Recommended and Actual Practice. *Australasian Journal of Special and Inclusive Education*, *44*(1), 28–45. DOI: 10.1017/jsi.2020.1

Deardorff, M. E., Peltier, C., Choiseul-Praslin, B., Williams-Diehm, K., & Wicker, M. (2021). Teacher Knowledge in Transition Planning: Does Locale Matter? *Rural Special Education Quarterly*, *40*(3), 132–142. DOI: 10.1177/87568705211027982

Dente, C. L., & Parkinson Coles, K. (2012). Ecological approaches to transition planning for students with autism and asperger's syndrome. *Children & Schools*, *34*(1), 27–36. DOI: 10.1093/cs/cdr002

Dinamarca-Aravena, K. A. (2024). Professional training of health professionals to work in schools with school integration programmes in Chile: A mixed-methods analysis. *Professional Development in Education*, *50*(2), 263–278. DOI: 10.1080/19415257.2023.2203721

Dipeolu, A. O., Storlie, C., & Johnson, C. (2015). College Students with High-Functioning Autism Spectrum Disorder: Best Practices for Successful Transition to the World of Work. *Journal of College Counseling*, *18*(2), 175–190. DOI: 10.1002/jocc.12013

El Zaatari, W., & Maalouf, I. (2022). How the Bronfenbrenner Bio-ecological System Theory Explains the Development of Students' Sense of Belonging to School? *SAGE Open, 12*(4), 21582440221134089. Advance online publication. DOI: 10.1177/21582440221134089

Elias, R., Muskett, A. E., & White, S. W. (2019). Educator perspectives on the post-secondary transition difficulties of students with autism. *Autism, 23*(1), 260–264. DOI: 10.1177/1362361317726246 PMID: 29034690

ElSayary, A., Karaki, S., & Ahmed, R. (2025). Exploring Reflective Practices In Blended Learning: A Deep Dive Into Educators' In-Action And On-Action Perspectives In Interdisciplinary Courses. *Journal of Information Technology Education, 24*, 019. Advance online publication. DOI: 10.28945/5553

ElSayary, A., Karaki, S., & Ahmed, R. (2025b). Exploring reflective practices in blended learning: A deep dive into educators' in-action and on-action perspectives in interdisciplinary courses. *Journal of Information Technology Education, 24*, 019. Advance online publication. DOI: 10.28945/5553

Eltantawy, M. M., & Fouad, B. O. E. (2025). The Effectiveness of a Training Program in Equipping Teachers of Students with Intellectual Disabilities with Competencies for Implementing Transition Plans and Enhancing Their Teaching Self-Efficacy. Journal of Intellectual Disability - Diagnosis and Treatment, 13(2), 108–119. DOI: 10.6000/2292-2598.2025.13.02.1

Ezewuzie, S. O. Patricia Amaka Udeogu, & Okoli, H. N. (2025). Assessment of educational policies and reforms in nigeria: challenges and prospects. Chukwuemeka odumegwu ojukwu university journal of arts and social science education, 4(1). https://cooujoasse.org/index.php/cooujoasse/article/view/32

Fadele, A. A., & Rocha, A. (2025). The Art and Science of Quantitative Research. In Studies in Systems, Decision and Control (Vol. 599, pp. 1–188). Springer Science and Business Media Deutschland GmbH. DOI: 10.1007/978-3-031-91431-7

Federal Ministry of Education. (2023). Revised National Policy on Inclusive Education in Nigeria. Federal Ministry of Education Abuja. https://tafafrica.co/publication/Inclusive%20Education.pdf

Garcia, N. A., & Campbell, S. E. (2023). Co-creating spaces for reflective practice in teacher education. In Adams, S. R., & Breidenstein, A. (Eds.), *Exploring Meaningful and Sustainable Intentional Learning Communities for P-20 Educators* (pp. 94–119). IGI Global., DOI: 10.4018/978-1-6684-7270-5.ch005

Goodyear, V. A. (2017). Sustained Professional Development on Cooperative Learning: Impact on Six Teachers' Practices and Students' Learning. *Research Quarterly for Exercise and Sport*, *88*(1), 83–94. DOI: 10.1080/02701367.2016.1263381 PMID: 28001911

Hajra, A., Ghosh, B., & Bhowmik, S. (2025). Cross-sectional studies. In Eltorai, A. E. M., Bakal, J. A., & Gibson, C. M. (Eds.), *Translational Cardiology* (pp. 221–225). Elsevier., DOI: 10.1016/B978-0-323-91790-2.00099-X

Haruna, H. H., Iftikhar, S., Isa, S. M., & Hasan, M. (2025). Effect of Professional Development, Collaborative Learning, and Technology Integration on Teachers' Self-Access Support Competence. *SiSal Journal*, *16*(3), 526–565. DOI: 10.37237/160304

Hendricks, D. R., & Wehman, P. (2009). Transition from school to adulthood for youth with autism spectrum disorders: Review and recommendations. *Focus on Autism and Other Developmental Disabilities*, *24*(2), 77–88. DOI: 10.1177/1088357608329827

Hervie, V. M. (2023). Social inclusion of children with intellectual disabilities in Accra, Ghana: Views of parents/guardians and teachers. *Children and Youth Services Review*, *147*, 106845. Advance online publication. DOI: 10.1016/j.childyouth.2023.106845

Hill, D. A., Fayemi, A., & Ostrowski, S. (2024). The Evolution of Services for Children with Autism and Developmental Disabilities in Nigeria. *International Journal of Disability Development and Education*, *71*(7), 1116–1132. DOI: 10.1080/1034912X.2023.2291570

Hughes, C. E. (2025). MTSS and Twice-Exceptional Learners: Problem-Solving and Possibility-Finding. *Gifted Child Today*, *48*(3), 190–197. DOI: 10.1177/10762175251330325

Kariuki, L. W., Njoka, J. N., & Mbugua, Z. K. (2019). Influence of Teachers Preparedness on Performance of Pupils in Mathematics in Lower Primary Schools in Aberdares Region of Kenya. *European Journal of STEM Education*, *4*(1). Advance online publication. DOI: 10.20897/ejsteme/3931

Karkkola, P., Kuittinen, M., & Hintsa, T. (2019). Role clarity, role conflict, and vitality at work: The role of the basic needs. *Scandinavian Journal of Psychology*, *60*(5), 456–463. DOI: 10.1111/sjop.12550 PMID: 31124156

Karupiah, P. (2022). Positivism. In Islam, M. R., Khan, N. A., & Baikady, R. (Eds.), *Principles of Social Research Methodology* (pp. 73–82). Springer Nature., DOI: 10.1007/978-981-19-5441-2_6

Kelly, J., Mckenzie, J., Watermeyer, B., Vergunst, R., Karisa, A., & Samuels, C. (2024). 'We Need to Go Back to Our Schools, and We Need to Make that Change We Wish to See': Empowering Teachers for Disability Inclusion. *International Journal of Disability Development and Education, 71*(4), 633–649. DOI: 10.1080/1034912X.2022.2141696

Kempen, M., & Steyn, G. M. (2016). Proposing a continuous professional development model to support and enhance professional learning of teachers in special schools in South Africa. *International Journal of Special Education, 31*(1), 32–45.

Kester, J., Beveridge, S., Flanagan, M., & Stella, J. (2019). Interdisciplinary professional development needs of transition professionals serving youth with autism spectrum disorders. *Journal of Rehabilitation, 85*(1), 53–63.

Kim, H., Molina, C. E., Watkinson, J. S., Leigh-Osroosh, K. T., & Li, D. (2024). Theory-informed school counseling: Increasing efficacy through prevention-focused practice and outcome research. *Journal of Counseling and Development, 102*(2), 226–238. DOI: 10.1002/jcad.12507

Kim, S., Bochatay, N., Relyea-Chew, A., Buttrick, E., Amdahl, C., Kim, L., Frans, E., Mossanen, M., Khandekar, A., Fehr, R., & Lee, Y.-M. (2017). Individual, interpersonal, and organisational factors of healthcare conflict: A scoping review. *Journal of Interprofessional Care, 31*(3), 282–290. DOI: 10.1080/13561820.2016.1272558 PMID: 28276847

Klefbeck, K. (2023). Navigating Self-Reflection for Aspiring Special Education Teachers: A Scoping Review on Inclusive Educational Practices and Their Insights for Autism Education. *Education Sciences, 13*(12), 1182. Advance online publication. DOI: 10.3390/educsci13121182

Knudson, S. (2024). Transition planning and perceptions of support in an autism spectrum disorder resource program. *Preventing School Failure, 68*(3), 220–230. DOI: 10.1080/1045988X.2023.2207482

Kucharczyk, S., Szidon, K., & Hall, L. J. (2022). Coaching in Complexity: Lessons Learned Investigating Implementation of Interventions in High Schools. *Career Development and Transition for Exceptional Individuals, 45*(2), 99–113. DOI: 10.1177/21651434211041909

Laghi, F., & Trimarco, B. (2020). Individual planning starts at school. Tools and practices promoting autonomy and supporting transition to work for adolescents with autism spectrum disorder. *Annali dell'Istituto Superiore di Sanita, 56*(2), 222–229. DOI: 10.4415/ANN_20_02_12 PMID: 32567572

Lairson, J. D. (2022). Educator and Community Transition-Service Provider Beliefs Regarding Student Outcomes as a Result of Participation in Work-Readiness Training Opportunities: A Qualitative Study [Ed.D., Northcentral University]. https://www.proquest.com/docview/2729063995/abstract/73074ECD5FC14611PQ/1

LaPoint, S. C., Kim, S. Y., & Bottema-Beutel, K. (2025). Barriers to Providing Transitional Supports for Autistic Students: Insights of School Professionals. *Journal of Autism and Developmental Disorders*, *55*(8), 2807–2819. DOI: 10.1007/s10803-024-06375-6 PMID: 38773033

Lee, G. K., & Carter, E. W. (2012). Preparing Transition-Age Students with High-Functioning Autism Spectrum Disorders for Meaningful Work. *Psychology in the Schools*, *49*(10), 988–1000. DOI: 10.1002/pits.21651

Lee, H., & Park, K.-O. (2020). Analysis of experiences of secondary special educators on interagency collaboration in transition education. Korean Journal of Physical. *Multiple and Health Disabilities*, *63*(4), 75–100. DOI: 10.20971/kcpmd.2020.63.4.75

Leonard, K. M., Coyne, M. D., Oldham, A. C., Burns, D., & Gillis, M. B. (2019). Implementing MTSS in Beginning Reading: Tools and Systems to Support Schools and Teachers. *Learning Disabilities Research & Practice*, *34*(2), 110–117. DOI: 10.1111/ldrp.12192

Li, H. (2025). Reflective Practice for Pre-Service Teachers' Professional Development. *SAGE Open*, *15*(3), 21582440251363136. Advance online publication. DOI: 10.1177/21582440251363136

Lindsay, S., Duncanson, M., Niles-Campbell, N., McDougall, C., Diederichs, S., & Menna-Dack, D. (2018). Applying an ecological framework to understand transition pathways to postsecondary education for youth with physical disabilities. *Disability and Rehabilitation*, *40*(3), 277–286. DOI: 10.1080/09638288.2016.1250171 PMID: 27868448

MacNaughton, K., Chreim, S., & Bourgeault, I. L. (2013). Role construction and boundaries in interprofessional primary health care teams: A qualitative study. *BMC Health Services Research*, *13*(1), 486. DOI: 10.1186/1472-6963-13-486 PMID: 24267663

Mauri, A. J., & Neiva de Figueiredo, J. (2025). Multi-stage Team Projects in the Management Classroom: Using a Double-loop Peer Presentation Feedback to Cultivate Reflective Learning. *Journal of Management Education*, *49*(2), 236–268. DOI: 10.1177/10525629241313196

Mavuso, M. F. (2022). Exploring Senior Phase teachers' competencies in supporting learners with specific learning difficulties: Implications for inclusive education. *African Journal of Disability*, *11*. Advance online publication. DOI: 10.4102/ajod.v11i0.901 PMID: 36092477

McDonough, J. T., & Revell, G. (2010). Accessing employment supports in the adult system for transitioning youth with autism spectrum disorders. *Journal of Vocational Rehabilitation*, *32*(2), 89–100. DOI: 10.3233/JVR-2010-0498

McGuinness, C., & Shankar, K. (2019). Supporting reflection in the MLIS through a Professionally-Oriented capstone module. *Education for Information*, *35*(2), 173–178. DOI: 10.3233/EFI-190256

McMahon, J., & Cullinan, V. (2016). Exploring Eclecticism: The impact of educational theory on the development and implementation of comprehensive education programmes (CEP's) for young children with Autism Spectrum Disorder (ASD). *Research in Autism Spectrum Disorders*, *32*, 1–12. DOI: 10.1016/j.rasd.2016.07.005

Mohammed, A. S., & Hlalele, D. (2025). Inclusion in Early Childhood Education in Ghana. In Sustainable Development Goals Series: Vol. Part F1175 (pp. 255–271). Springer. DOI: 10.1007/978-3-032-05453-1_18

Molloy, E., & Keating, J. (2011). Targeted Preparation for Clinical Practice. In Professional and Practice-based Learning (Vol. 7, pp. 59–82). Springer Nature. DOI: 10.1007/978-90-481-3937-8_4

Moss, C. (2015). Role Conflict and Role Ambiguity as Predictors of Burnout in Special and General Education Co-teachers [Ph.D., Walden University]. https://www.proquest.com/docview/1637727036/abstract/FE142CB37B154B8FPQ/1

Neale, M., & Griffin, M. A. (2006). A model of self-held work roles and role transitions. *Human Performance*, *19*(1), 23–41. DOI: 10.1207/s15327043hup1901_2

Nicholas, D. B., Mitchell, W., Zulla, R., Solomatin, E., & Qi, S. (2019). A Review of CommunityWorks Canada®: Toward Employability Among High School–Age Youth With Autism Spectrum Disorder. *Global Pediatric Health*, *6*, 2333794X19885542. Advance online publication. DOI: 10.1177/2333794X19885542 PMID: 31700949

Nir, A. E., & Eyal, O. (2003). School-based management and the role conflict of the school superintendent. *Journal of Educational Administration*, *41*(5), 547–564. DOI: 10.1108/09578230310489362

Numisi, S., Themane, M., Nel, K., & Govender, I. (2020). Parent-teacher collaboration in children with autism spectrum disorder in Limpopo Province, South Africa. *Journal of Human Ecology (Delhi, India)*, *69*(1–3), 117–126. DOI: 10.31901/24566608.2020/69.1-3.3208

Nzimande, N. G. (2025). Exploring the Impact of Formal Continuous Professional Development Activities on Foundation Phase Mathematics Teachers' Instructional Quality. International Journal of Learning. *Teaching and Educational Research*, *24*(5), 497–516. DOI: 10.26803/ijlter.24.5.26

Oertle, K. M., & Trach, J. S. (2007). Interagency collaboration: The importance of rehabilitation professionals' involvement in transition. *Journal of Rehabilitation*, *73*(3), 36–44.

Ogundeji, Y. K., Tinuoye, O., Bharali, I., Mao, W., Ohiri, K., Ogbuoji, O., Orji, N., & Yamey, G. (2023). Is Nigeria on course to achieve universal health coverage in the context of its epidemiological and financing transition? A knowledge, capacity and policy gap analysis (a qualitative study). *BMJ Open*, *13*(3), e064710. Advance online publication. DOI: 10.1136/bmjopen-2022-064710 PMID: 36898742

Okurame, D. E. (2007). Perceived mentoring functions: Does mentor's gender matter? *Women in Management Review*, *22*(5), 418–427. DOI: 10.1108/09649420710761473

Olagunju, A. T., Akinola, M. A., Fadipe, B., Jagun, O. O., Olagunju, T. O., Akinola, O. O., Ogunnubi, O. P., Olusile, O. J., Oluyemi, O. Y., & Chaimowitz, G. A. (2021). Psychosocial Wellbeing of Nigerian Teachers in Special Education Schools. *Journal of Autism and Developmental Disorders*, *51*(4), 1131–1141. DOI: 10.1007/s10803-020-04606-0 PMID: 32666197

Park, Y. S., Konge, L., & Artino, A. R. (2020). The Positivism Paradigm of Research. *Academic Medicine*, *95*(5), 690–694. DOI: 10.1097/ACM.0000000000003093 PMID: 31789841

Phelps, L. A., & Hanley-Maxwell, C. (1997). School-to-Work Transitions for Youth With Disabilities: A Review of Outcomes and Practices. *Review of Educational Research*, *67*(2), 197–226. DOI: 10.3102/00346543067002197

Plotner, A. J., Trach, J. S., & Strauser, D. R. (2012). Vocational Rehabilitation Counselors' Identified Transition Competencies: Perceived Importance, Frequency, and Preparedness. *Rehabilitation Counseling Bulletin*, *55*(3), 135–143. DOI: 10.1177/0034355211427950

Porter, S. G. (2021). It takes a well-organised village: Implementing RTI/MTSS models in secondary schools. In *Research Anthology on Inclusive Practices for Educators and Administrators in Special Education* (pp. 339–368). IGI Global., DOI: 10.4018/978-1-6684-3670-7.ch020

Puerta, P., Ciannelli, L., & Johnson, B. (2019). A simulation framework for evaluating multi-stage sampling designs in populations with spatially structured traits. PeerJ, 2019(2). DOI: 10.7717/peerj.6471

Roitsch, J. (2024). Transitioning from High School to Adulthood: Optimising Outcomes for Students with Autism Spectrum Disorder. In Volkmar, F. R., Reichow, B., & McPartland, J. C. (Eds.), *Adolescents and Adults with Autism Spectrum Disorders* (2nd ed., pp. 55–74). Springer International Publishing., DOI: 10.1007/978-3-031-46463-8_3

Rosenkoetter, S. E., Hains, A. H., & Dogaru, C. (2007). Successful transitions for young children with disabilities and their families: Roles of school social workers. *Children & Schools*, *29*(1), 25–34. DOI: 10.1093/cs/29.1.25

Sansosti, F. J., & Sansosti, J. M. (2013). Effective School-Based Service Delivery For Students With Autism Spectrum Disorders: Where We Are And Where We Need To Go. *Psychology in the Schools*, *50*(3), 229–244. DOI: 10.1002/pits.21669

Sasere, O. B., & Makhasane, S. D. (2023). School-Based Teacher Professional Development Framework (SBTPDF): A Blueprint for School Principals in Nigeria. International Journal of Learning. *Teaching and Educational Research*, *22*(8), 391–414. DOI: 10.26803/ijlter.22.8.21

Schoen, S. A., & Valdez, A. (2023). Preliminary efficacy of a transition training program for autistic adolescents. *Research in Autism Spectrum Disorders*, *109*, 102281. Advance online publication. DOI: 10.1016/j.rasd.2023.102281

Setia, M. S. (2016). Methodology series module 3: Cross-sectional studies. *Indian Journal of Dermatology*, *61*(3), 261–264. DOI: 10.4103/0019-5154.182410 PMID: 27293245

Shikuku, D. N., Mohammed, H., Mwanzia, L., Ladur, A. N., Nandikove, P., Uyara, A., Waigwe, C., Nyaga, L., Bashir, I., Ndirangu, E., Bedwell, C., Bar-Zeev, S., & Ameh, C. (2024). Evaluation of the feasibility of a midwifery educator continuous professional development (CPD) programme in Kenya and Nigeria: A mixed methods study. *BMC Medical Education*, *24*(1), 534. Advance online publication. DOI: 10.1186/s12909-024-05524-w PMID: 38745243

Snell-Rood, C., Ruble, L., Kleinert, H., McGrew, J. H., Adams, M., Rodgers, A., Odom, J., Wong, W. H., & Yu, Y. (2020). Stakeholder perspectives on transition planning, implementation, and outcomes for students with autism spectrum disorder. *Autism, 24*(5), 1164–1176. DOI: 10.1177/1362361319894827 PMID: 31957461

Teresa Rani, V. S., Mpm, P. K., & Kareem, J. (2025). Understanding the disconnect: A study on competency of special educators in autism education in India. *Support for Learning*, *40*(4), 334–342. DOI: 10.1111/1467-9604.70013

Trede, F., & Smith, M. (2012). Teaching reflective practice in practice settings: Students' perceptions of their clinical educators. *Teaching in Higher Education*, *17*(5), 615–627. DOI: 10.1080/13562517.2012.658558

Velec, M., & Huang, S. H. (2014). Quantitative methodologies and analysis. In Gillan, C., Di Prospero, L., Harnett, N., & Holden, L. (Eds.), *Research for the Radiation Therapist: From Question to Culture* (pp. 87–126). Apple Academic Press. DOI: 10.1201/b16449-8

Victor-Aigbodion, V., & Eseadi, C. (2025). Effect of purpose-based career coaching on career transition self-efficacy among college students with autism spectrum disorder. EDULEARN25 Proceedings, 8088–8101. https://library.iated.org/view/VICTORAIGBODION2025EFF

Vinson, D., Nixon, S., Walsh, B., Walker, C., Mitchell, E., & Zaitseva, E. (2010). Investigating the relationship between student engagement and transition. *Active Learning in Higher Education*, *11*(2), 131–143. DOI: 10.1177/1469787410365658

Wawire, B. A. (2021). Promoting effective early grade reading: The case study of primary teachers' preparation programmes in Kenya. *Curriculum Journal*, *32*(2), 247–268. DOI: 10.1002/curj.69

Wiedman, C. (2023). Navigating role conflict: One professional's journey as a new clinician leader. *BMJ Leader*, *8*(1), 6–8. DOI: 10.1136/leader-2022-000715 PMID: 37339846

Wong, J., Coster, W. J., Cohn, E. S., & Orsmond, G. I. (2021). Identifying School-Based Factors that Predict Employment Outcomes for Transition-Age Youth with Autism Spectrum Disorder. *Journal of Autism and Developmental Disorders*, *51*(1), 60–74. DOI: 10.1007/s10803-020-04515-2 PMID: 32356081

Yakubova, G., & Zeleke, W. A. (2016). A Problem-Solving Intervention Using iPads to Improve Transition-Related Task Performance of Students With Autism Spectrum Disorder. *Journal of Special Education Technology*, *31*(2), 77–86. DOI: 10.1177/0162643416650023

APPENDIX

Table 5. School-Based Professionals' Role and Theoretical Orientations Questionnaire (SPRTOQ)

N	Items	Factor Loading	Cronbach's α	Omega ω
	Role Clarity			
1	I have a clear understanding of what is expected of me in supporting SASD's career transition.	0.756	0.85	0.85
2	My school role description includes responsibilities related to ASD career planning.	0.774		
3	I receive ambiguous instructions about my role in the transition process.	0.762		
4	I am confident I know how my role contributes to students' successful transitions.	0.849		
	Role Conflict			
5	I experience conflicting demands between teaching and transition-support duties.	0.479	0.73	0.73
6	I am pulled in different directions when juggling administrative and transitional tasks.	0.664		
7	Time constraints rarely keep me from fulfilling my transition-related responsibilities.	0.782		
8	I feel supported by leadership when role demands overlap.	0.724		
	Role Efficacy			
9	I feel capable and effective when guiding SASD in career exploration.	0.694	0.75	0.76
10	I have received sufficient training to support SASD in planning their careers.	0.977		
11	I often doubt my skillset to foster career readiness in SASD.	0.722		
12	I can confidently facilitate self-advocacy and goal-setting for SASD.	0.834		
	Role Breadth			

continued on following page

Table 5. Continued

N	Items	Factor Loading	Cronbach's α	Omega ω
	Role Clarity			
13	I actively collaborate with counsellors, therapists, and employers in transition planning.	0.815	0.71	0.73
14	I proactively seek interdisciplinary input for ASD career preparation.	0.915		
15	I work alone without consulting colleagues in transition planning.	0.727		
16	I adapt my professional role as students move through different transition stages.	0.834		
	Theory-Informed Transition Support			
17	I rely on guiding theoretical frameworks when planning career transitions for SASD.	0.905	0.75	0.74
18	I use evidence-based theories to underpin my approach to meeting SASD's career transition needs.	0.670		
	Theory-Informed Reflective Practice			
19	I regularly reflect on my counselling techniques in facilitating career transition readiness of SASD.	0.749	0.77	0.77
20	I seek continuous feedback on my counselling practices and theoretical approaches to improve support for SASD during their career transitions.	0.951		

SASD=Students with Autism Spectrum Disorders

Figure 1. Scree Plot for School-Based Professionals' Role and Theoretical Orientations Questionnaire (SPRTOQ)

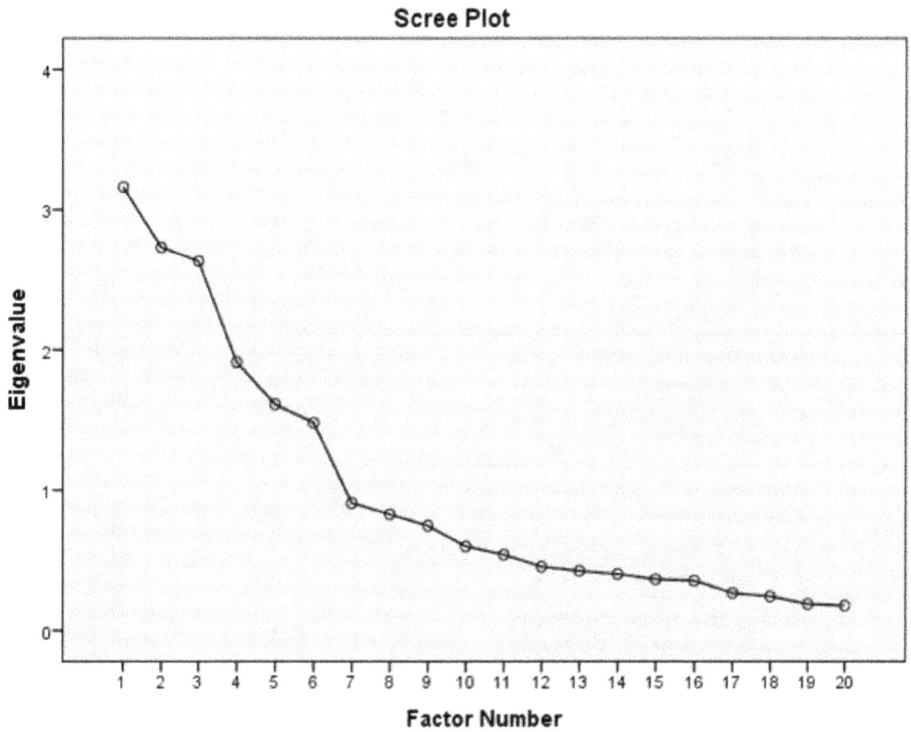

Table 6. Career Transition Support for SASD Questionnaire – School-based Professionals' Version (CTS-SPV)

N	Item	Factor Loading	Cronbach's α	Omega ω
1	Individualised transition plans are developed for each student with ASD.	0.78	0.92	0.90
2	I collaborate effectively with other professionals and external agencies in transition planning.	0.83		
3	SASD are provided with training in employment and daily living skills.	0.66		
4	Families are actively engaged in the career transition process for SASD.	0.79		
5	Transition goals are regularly reviewed and updated for each student.	0.78		
6	SASD are given opportunities for workplace visits, internships, or job sampling.	0.56		
7	I have access to information and resources that help me support students' career transitions.	0.57		
8	We provide support for students to develop self-advocacy and communication skills.	0.77		
9	Community agencies and resources are integrated into our transition planning.	0.83		
10	Our school provides effective support for the career transition of SASD.	0.66		

Chapter 3
Policy Matters Concerning the Career Transition of Students With ASD

ABSTRACT

This study examined the policy matters that influence the career transition of students who have autism spectrum disorders (ASD). The objectives were threefold: (1) to determine the levels of principals' and proprietors' ratings across six policy dimensions; (2) to assess the extent to which demographic characteristics predict variations in these policy practices; and (3) to analyse the results and identify areas for policy improvement that would better support students who have ASD in readiness for adult life. A quantitative, survey-based approach was used, involving the administration of a self-developed questionnaire to school leaders. The major findings indicate strong endorsement of leadership vision, staff training and inclusive structures, although data-driven practice and family engagement remained low. Regression analysis showed a limited predictive influence of demographic factors. Targeted leadership development, strengthened collaboration, and improved accountability systems are essential for effective transition policy implementation.

BACKGROUND

Policy Defined

A policy includes a formal and intentional set of codes, principles, norms or directives adopted by a government or organisation to guide decisions, regulate

DOI: 10.4018/978-1-6684-7260-6.ch003

behaviour, and allocate resources toward achieving specific objectives(Eseadi & Diale, 2025; Gillies, 2024). Policies that support the career transition of students who have ASD (autism spectrum disorders) vary across regions due to differences in political will, resource availability, cultural interpretations of disability, and the growing recognition of inclusive education (IE). While there is a growing appreciation of the need to prepare individuals who have ASD for adult life, the degree to which countries translate policy commitments into effective transition pathways differs generally.

International Policy Context

North America, particularly the United States, has one of the most developed policy environments regarding transition for students who have disabilities (SWD), such as students who have ASD. The Individuals with Disabilities Education Act mandates the inclusion of transition planning within the Individualised Education Programme from age sixteen (or younger, if suitable)(Office of Special Education and Rehabilitative Services U.S. Department of Education, 2000; Stone-MacDonald et al., 2016). This planning must include measurable post-school goals, coordinated activities, and linkages to employment or further education (Office of Special Education and Rehabilitative Services U.S. Department of Education, 2000). Other legislation, such as the United States' Workforce Innovation and Opportunity Act (WIOA), which serves as a key federal framework for developing the workforce and reinforces interagency collaboration between schools and vocational services(Employment and Training Administration U.S. Department of Labour, 2016; Espinoza, 2018). The WIOA came into effect as a law on the 22nd of July 2014. The WIOA seeks to improve individuals' access to jobs, training opportunities, educational pathways, and support services. Its broader goal is to strengthen the alignment between workforce needs and employer demands within the global economy(Employment and Training Administration U.S. Department of Labour, 2016; Espinoza, 2018). WIOA also continues the mandate of the Rehabilitation Act of 1973, which is specifically aimed at supporting people with disabilities (PWD) in obtaining suitable employment. The Rehabilitation Act, updated through Public Law 114–95 in 2015, serves as the principal federal statute guiding vocational rehabilitation (VR) services in the United States. It replaces earlier VR legislation and renews federal grant provisions that help states deliver employment-related support to PWD, with particular attention to PWD who have the most considerable needs. The Act broadens the federal government's role by strengthening research, training, and specialised responsibilities aimed at improving outcomes for PWD. It also establishes a formal relation between state VR programmes and the national workforce development system created under Title I of the Workforce Investment Act of 1998 (Senate and

House of Representatives of the United States of America in Congress, 2016). The Rehabilitation Act significantly influenced subsequent disability rights legislation, most notably serving as a foundational model for the Americans with Disabilities Act (ADA) of 1990. The ADA extends protections beyond federal agencies to the private sector by prohibiting employment prejudice against suitably qualified PWD (Americans with Disabilities Act, 1990; U.S. Equal Employment Opportunity Commission, 2023).

In Canada, both federal and provincial governments share key responsibilities in delivering transition supports to PWD. This shared role is reflected in the 2022 Disability Inclusion Action Plan, a national framework centred on employment, financial security, and inclusive communities(Government of Canada, 2022). The Action Plan serves as the federal government's strategic guide for integrating disability considerations across its programs and systems. Although it addresses federal areas of responsibility, its implementation depends on continued collaboration with provincial and territorial governments, disability organisations, and PWD(Government of Canada, 2022). In Ontario, the Provincial Transition Planning Framework for Young People with Developmental Disabilities mandates early planning (age 14 onward) and collaborative protocols to support youth who have developmental disabilities (DD) towards successful transition to adulthood. The framework promotes a more organised, coordinated, and transparent system for assisting youth who have DD as they move toward adulthood. It ensures that planning is structured and that these individuals can access the services and supports offered through adult developmental service programmes when needed(Ministry of Community and Social Services, Ontario & Ministry of Children and Youth Services, Ontario, 2011). Ontario's Supported Employment Programme Guidelines also stand out as one of the provincial programme guidelines aimed at offering tailored services such as job matching, coaching, retention supports and pathways into employment to PWD (Ministry of Labour, Immigration, Training and Skills Development, 2018). Canada's Services and Supports to Promote the Social Inclusion of Persons with Developmental Disabilities Act of 2008, amended June 2023, establishes the formal procedures that adults who have DD must follow when seeking government-funded supports(Government of Canada, 2023). The Act's provisions governing the new application process came into force on July 1, 2011. Although the Act frames service delivery around assessed need, it clearly notes that access to support is constrained by available resources. The Act also permits the use of waiting lists and offers no guarantee that requested services will be provided, reflecting ongoing limitations in service capacity across jurisdictions(Ministry of Community and Social Services, Ontario, & Ministry of Children and Youth Services, Ontario, 2011).

Europe has advanced policy structures that emphasise rights-based approaches. The European Union promotes transition through directives on equal treatment, IE, and employment access for PWD. Many European countries include transition planning in their national frameworks, supported by social services systems. Northern European nations such as Sweden, Denmark, and the Netherlands have vocational support models that emphasise supported employment, personalised planning, and coordinated health education services. Southern European countries like Italy have made progress but continue to address gaps in implementation due to economic and administrative constraints. The European Agency for Special Needs and Inclusive Education acts as a coordinating body that supports member countries to align their policies with the UN Convention on the Rights of Persons with Disabilities and the European Education Area, providing guidance, country reviews and comparative data on IE and transition (European Agency for Special Needs and Inclusive Education, 2024). The Country Policy Development Support (CPDS) framework plays a central role in the Agency's mandate to promote policy transformation in IE. By enabling countries to examine their existing policy frameworks and implementation practices, the CPDS framework provides structured guidance that helps them strengthen their approaches. Its primary purpose is to meet countries where they are in the policy process and support them in advancing IE more effectively(European Agency for Special Needs and Inclusive Education, 2024). PWD are afforded protection against workplace discrimination under EU legislation. The EU Strategy for the Rights of Persons with Disabilities 2021–2030 clearly obligates the Union and its member states to promote more IE practices and facilitate better transitions into employment for PWD. This encompasses raising the number of PWD in the workforce and reducing the gaps in employment rates between these individuals and those who do not have disabilities (European Commission, 2023). The EU Charter of Fundamental Rights, under Article 26, upholds the rights of PWD to receive support aimed at strengthening their independence, improving their social and occupational inclusion, and enabling them to contribute meaningfully to the community(European Union, 2012). The Employment Equality Directive forbids prejudicial treatment in the workplace and vocational training based on disability and mandates reasonable accommodations, which form the foundation for supported employment and transition initiatives in member states (European Union, 2000).

In Sweden, the transition policy for individuals with intellectual disabilities is closely associated with upper secondary special schools and vocational education(European Agency for Special Needs and Inclusive Education, 2023). The Swedish Education Act (Skollag 2010:800) ensures equal educational value throughout the nation and affirms the right to tailored compulsory and upper secondary education for students with intellectual disabilities (SID) ((Ministry of Education and Research Sweden, 2010). The Workplace-Based Learning (WBL) is one of the significant transition initiatives within national programmes for upper secondary SID, in which students are required to engage in a minimum of 22 weeks of mandatory work-based learning, designed to connect classroom instruction with practical workplace experience and enhance career transition(Ineland et al., 2021). The Sweden's National Agency for Special Needs Education and Schools' responsibility is to ensure that children, youth, and adults, irrespective of their disabilities, have equitable access to learning and developmental opportunities comparable to those available to all members of society(National Agency for Special Needs Education and Schools, 2019; Sweden Sverige & Swedish Institute, 2025). Recent reforms to vocational curricula for SID, set to take effect in 2025, specifically aim to bolster connections to the labour market and improve transition outcomes by revising programme content and fostering closer collaboration between educational institutions and employers(European Centre for the Development of Vocational Training, 2025).

In Denmark, there is a structured national guidance system designed to support educational and career transitions for young people, including PWD. The Act on Guidance in Relation to Choice of Education, Training and Career, originally approved in 2003 and later amended in 2006 and 2007, sets out the system's framework and seven national targets for guidance(European Agency for Special Needs and Inclusive Education, 2025). Oversight and continuous development of the system fall under the Ministry of Education. The Act primarily targets individuals up to age 25 but also extends to adults seeking entry into higher education. Guidance provision is organised through two distinct types of centres. Youth guidance centres, operating at the municipal level, support transitions from compulsory schooling to youth education, with particular emphasis on young people who have not completed a programme or who require specialised guidance. Regional guidance centres handle transitions from youth education to higher education and training (European Agency for Special Needs and Inclusive Education, 2025; Ministry of Education, 2003). These centres offer coordinated support for decisions related to further study, vocational pathways, and labour-market entry, functioning as key mechanisms for managing the transition period.

In the Netherlands, transition from school to further education and training (FET), vocational preparation and employment is supported by a broad legislative and policy environment that places the needs and rights of the student at the centre of educational planning. Transition is given structure through the Appropriate Education (passend onderwijs) policy, which establishes a clear duty on schools to provide each student with an educational space suited to their needs(Ministry of Education, Culture and Science, Government of the Netherlands, 2014). Schools must organise additional support for SWD and prepare an individual development plan that outlines the student's goals and the assistance required to move towards those goals. Regional partnerships coordinate support, arrange placements when a mainstream school cannot meet a student's needs, and ensure that planning remains consistent as students move through primary and secondary stages(European Agency for Special Needs and Inclusive Education, 2019). These arrangements give early attention to long-term destinations, such as vocational education, further study or work, and ensure that families are involved in decision-making. Special education also contributes directly to transition through developmental perspective plans that set expected long-term outcomes, including pathways towards continued education, future employment or independent living. The curriculum in special schools is aligned as closely as possible with the curriculum in mainstream education, with adaptations based on the student's profile. This alignment supports later integration into vocational routes, including the system of upper secondary vocational colleges, where strong links with employers help students gain experience in real work environments. The Dutch system further promotes equitable transition through funding mechanisms that direct additional resources to schools serving students who face educational disadvantage, as well as through anti-discrimination legislation that extends equal treatment for PWD into primary and secondary education. These measures help ensure that SWD do not experience barriers when choosing educational programmes that lead to employment. On the employment side, the Participation Act (Participatiewet) strengthens the bridge between schooling and work by encouraging employers and local authorities to create adapted jobs and provide workplace support(European Agency for Special Needs and Inclusive Education, 2019). Young people with significant disabilities can receive guidance and income support through dedicated schemes that promote gradual entry into employment while maintaining financial security.

In Italy, a long-standing inclusion framework is anchored in Law 104 of 1992, the country's primary disability legislation, which secures essential rights, promotes full social participation and ensures comprehensive support for PWD across education as well as employment(European Agency for Special Needs and Inclusive Education, 2021). Transition planning is further reinforced through Law 328 of 2000, which introduces the Individual Life Project, collaboratively designed by families, social services and health authorities to facilitate meaningful inclusion in family and community life, with a particular focus on the pathway from schooling into adulthood, work and civic engagement(European Agency for Special Needs and Inclusive Education, 2021). Inclusive schooling is implemented by integrating almost all SWD into mainstream settings, supported through individual education plans, specialised teachers and coordinated social-health services, forming a stable foundation for long-term transition processes.

Asia is characterised by significant policy diversity. Countries such as Japan, Singapore, India, and South Korea have transition systems that emphasise life skills education, vocational preparation, and collaboration between schools and community-based programmes. In Japan, the Act to Facilitate the Employment of Persons with Disabilities (Act No. 123 of 1960, revised in 2019) establishes the core policy framework for disability employment, including VR centres, job-placement support and anti-discrimination protections(Ministry of Justice Japan, 2019). The Act recognises Japan's emphasis on life-skills development, vocational education, and structured school-to-work transition for PWD. Japan's emphasis on ASD support is also reflected in its special needs schools and community planning systems. In Singapore, the School-to-Work Transition Programme is jointly led by the Ministry of Education, SG Enable and the Ministry of Social and Family Development to assist graduates of special education schools to transition successfully to employment through tailored training pathways, internships, job referrals, and job matching (Enabling Guide, 2025). The Enabling Masterplan 2030 further strengthens these efforts by prioritising school-to-employment transitions and broader community participation for PWD (Ministry of Social and Family Development Singapore, 2021). These initiatives demonstrate a systematised transition pathway supported through coordinated partnerships for SWD, including those with ASD in Singapore. In India, the Rights of Persons with Disabilities Act 2016 (RPwD Act) (*see* Government of India, 2016; Jose & Muthulakshmi, 2022) and IE under the Samagra Shiksha framework provide a legal foundation for supporting students who have ASD in mainstream schools (Ministry of Education Government of India, 2025). A 2025 statement from the Ministry of Education announced strengthened assistance for students with ASD through Block Resource Centres (Ministry of Education Government of India, 2025). However, implementation of coordinated school-to-work transition pathways remains uneven due to gaps in teacher preparation, limited resources and inconsistent multisectoral collaboration(Teachers Institute, 2023). In South Korea, the Welfare Law for Persons with Disabilities (Law No. 4179, 1989) mandates public authorities to implement policies for vocational guidance, training and employment. Article 13 specifies that national and local governments must ensure access to suitable jobs based on individual abilities and aptitudes(Ministry of Health and Welfare Republic of Korea, 1989). The Korea Employment Agency for Persons with Disabilities (KEAD) expands on this mandate through customised vocational programmes for people and students who have specific types of disabilities by focusing on career planning consultations and employment preparation services tailored to their specific strengths, needs and abilities (Economic and Social Commission for Asia and the Pacific United Nations, 2023; Korea Employment Agency for Persons with Disabilities, 2023).

In Australia, there is a strong legislative basis for transition planning, supported by the Disability Standards for Education (DSE) (Disability Standards for Education, 2005) and the National Disability Insurance Scheme (NDIS) Act (National Disability Insurance Scheme Act, 2013). Schools are required to support individualised planning, while vocational and employment supports are provided through national disability employment services. The 2005 DSE clarify the obligations of educational institutions to provide students with disability, including planning for key transition points(Disability Standards for Education, 2005). The 2013 NDIS Act provides funding for employment support, thus customising plans for young PWD to include transition from school into employment(National Disability Insurance Scheme Act, 2013). The DSE toolkit "milestones and transitions" released by the Australian Government Department of Education highlights transition planning from secondary school to further training or work for SWD(Australian Department of Education, 2022). The transition policy is reinforced by person-centred planning models and interagency collaboration between education, health, and employment sectors.

In New Zealand, IE frameworks emphasise supported transitions, and young people who have ASD have access to school-based and community-based vocational pathways. However, service availability in rural regions remains an ongoing challenge across the continent. The New Zealand Disability Strategy 2016-2026 sets out outcome areas, including education and employment, and aims to ensure a successful transition from the school context to workplace for PWD (Ministry of Education Government of New Zealand, 2016). The Employment and Transition Services provided by Autism New Zealand (AutismNZ) are designed to help senior secondary students with autism spectrum disorder move successfully into employment or community-based roles(Autism New Zealand & Ministry of Social Development, 2025). The programme offers support such as transition planning, work exposure, pre-employment skills coaching and sustained workplace assistance targeting both employees and employers. Its central focus is to match students with employment that is appropriate, meaningful and sustainable, while promoting further skill growth. Participants are guided through a structured process that includes identifying realistic career possibilities, developing personalised employment action plans, constructing curriculum vitae and cover letters, and acquiring job-search and application skills(Autism New Zealand & Ministry of Social Development, 2025). The service also assists with approaching potential employers, rehearsing interviews, receiving on-the-job coaching and providing autism-awareness training to workplaces. In addition, those already employed but facing challenges can access on-site support. Expected outcomes include readiness for employment, job placement and up to twelve months of follow-through support, with additional in-work assistance available beyond this period when necessary(Autism New Zealand & Ministry of Social Development, 2025). The newly established Ministry of Disabled People (Whaikaha) also provides system stewardship for disability policy across education, employment and community services, emphasising inter-agency alignment (Ministry of Disabled People, 2025).

Policy concerning career transition for students who have ASD in South America is evolving. Countries such as Brazil, Chile, and Argentina have national laws guaranteeing IE and the rights of PWD. Brazil's Law on the Inclusion of Persons with Disabilities (Lei Brasileira de Inclusão-LBI 13.146/2015) guarantees IE, promotes supported employment, and obliges public authorities to provide accessibility, vocational preparation, and professional inclusion for PWD, but the execution of structured transition planning varies across regions(Federal Republic of Brazil, 2015). It requires private and public educational institutions to provide accommodations, learning support, and life-skills preparation. Chile's disability and inclusion laws (Law 20.422 and Law 20.845) emphasise access to vocational preparation and community-based services. The Law 20.845 establishes non-discrimination, access to inclusive classrooms, and equal opportunity in education(Ministry of Education Chile, 2015). Law 20.422 defines national disability policy and creates the National Disability Service (SENADIS), which has programmes for vocational pathways and community inclusion. SENADIS also provides transition support, including job coaching and community-based vocational programmes(Ministry of Planning Chile, 2010). In Argentina, the Comprehensive Protection Law for the Rights of Persons with Disabilities (Ley 22.431) guarantees inclusive schooling, employment rights, vocational training, and workplace accommodations. The National Disability Act (Ley 27.043 on Autism Spectrum Disorders) mandates coverage for diagnosis, specialised intervention, and therapeutic services for individuals with ASD, promoting cross-sector responsibility. Most South American countries are still grappling with the challenges of developing effective teacher training programmes, early intervention services, and intersectoral collaboration mechanisms to support career transition for PWD.

Across Africa, policy on career transition for students who have ASD remains the least formalised, although notable progress has been made in recent years. Countries such as South Africa, Kenya, Ghana, and Nigeria have IE policies and disability legislation that provide a foundation for transition support. South Africa's White Paper 6 emphasises full inclusion and community-based support(Department of Education, 2001), but transition programmes vary widely between schools. South Africa's White Paper 6 positions IE as a national strategy for transforming the education system so that all students, including SWD, participate meaningfully in learning and life opportunities(Department of Education, 2001). The policy rejects segregated models and instead promotes a flexible system that adapts to student diversity through early identification, targeted support, and curriculum differentiation. It acknowledges that barriers to learning arise mainly from social and systemic factors, and schools must therefore restructure their cultures, teaching practices, and support mechanisms to become responsive environments. In relation to school-to-work transition, the White Paper 6 emphasises the development of functional, vocational, and independent living skills as integral components of inclusive schooling. It calls for coordinated support from teachers, therapists, parents, and community partners to prepare SWD for adulthood. The policy recognises that transition planning must begin early, with schools offering accessible pathways into further education, training, and employment. It also highlights the need for inter-sectoral collaboration between education, social development, and labour sectors to ensure continuity of support beyond schooling(Department of Education, 2001). The policy positions inclusion and transition as complementary processes aimed at expanding participation, autonomy, and lifelong opportunities for all students. Kenya has strengthened its disability rights legislation and promotes vocational training for young PWD through its 2025 Persons with Disabilities Act(Republic of Kenya, 2025). Kenya's Persons with Disabilities Act 4 of 2025, which was ratified on 8th May, introduces a renewed national commitment to the rights, full participation and rehabilitation of PWD (Republic of Kenya, 2025; Wagacha et al., 2025), including those who have ASD. The Act, which replaces the earlier 2003 legislation and aligns with the mandate of Article 54 of Kenya's 2010 Constitution, establishes a modern framework that requires public and private institutions to uphold equality, dignity, and meaningful inclusion in everyday life (Republic of Kenya, 2025; Wagacha et al., 2025). A central aspect of the Act is its strengthened focus on IE and the creation of the National Council for Persons with Disabilities. In line with the Act, schools are expected to provide accessible learning environments, make reasonable adjustments, and supply appropriate supports so that SWD can learn alongside their peers and progress without discrimination. This includes attention to curriculum adaptation, teacher preparedness, and the availability of assistive resources. Kenya's Persons with Disabilities National Policy also highlights the importance of preparing young PWD for adult life. It encourages access to vocational training, community-based learning opportunities, and pathways into employment, reflecting a clear commitment to improving the school-to-work transition (Ministry of Labour and Social Protection, Kenya, 2024). Both the new Act and national policy positions inclusion as a shared societal responsibility and offer a strengthened legal foundation for building responsive educational systems and equitable transition opportunities for PWD in Kenya. Ghana's IE Policy positions inclusion as a national commitment towards ensuring that all children, which encompasses those with disabilities and other special educational needs, access quality learning in welcoming, student-friendly environments(Ministry of Education Government of Ghana, 2015). The policy recognises that many SWD were historically excluded and therefore mandates early identification, targeted support, teacher training, community involvement, and system-wide reforms to remove barriers to participation. With respect to the school-to-work transition of PWD, the policy links inclusive schooling with later vocational readiness. It commits the state to guarantee equal access to basic and secondary education as well as vocational training, lifelong learning and adult education as required by the UN Convention on the Rights of Persons with Disabilities (United

Nations, 2008). It further requires capacity building for teachers, resource personnel, psychologists and careers advisors to guide students with special educational needs (SEN) through transitions, including preparation for future employment opportunities.

The Nigerian Policy Context

Nigeria has, over the past four decades, developed a range of education and disability policies that provide an important backdrop for understanding the school-to-work transition of students who have ASD. The National Policy on Education recognises the right of all children to basic education and includes provisions for students with SEN, emphasising access, equity, and functional education that prepares young people for life and work(Nigerian Educational Research and Development Council, 2013). Building on this, Nigeria's National Policy on Special Needs Education sets out principles such as the zero rejection, least restrictive environment, diversifying services outside the school environment, including home and hospital-based provisions (Federal Ministry of Education, 2015). These policy commitments create a formal mandate for schools to respond to the needs of schoolchildren with developmental conditions, including ASD, and to ensure that education supports their transition into adult roles. More recently, federal efforts to promote inclusion have become more explicit. The National Policy on Inclusive Education, first introduced in 2017 and revised in 2023, seeks to guarantee that all schoolchildren, irrespective of disability or background, can access quality education in regular schools(Federal Ministry of Education, 2023). The policy calls for the development of teacher capacity, the offering of reasonable accommodation, and the creation of environments where no student is excluded. These provisions are directly relevant to students who have ASD, whose career transition depends on early exposure to inclusive classrooms, adapted curricula, and supportive school cultures. Although the policy does not always single out ASD as a distinct category, the broader commitment to disability IE provides a normative basis for transition planning, work-related learning, and linkages to post-school opportunities. There are also legal frameworks that further reinforce these educational commitments. The Discrimination Against Persons with Disabilities Prohibition Act, signed into law in 2018, prohibits discrimination in education and employment and mandates full integration of PWD into society and created the National Commission for Persons with Disabilities(Federal Republic of Nigeria, 2018). The Act guarantees free education for SWD up to at least secondary level and affirms the right to work on a parallel footing with others. It also requires public institutions and employers to remove barriers and to provide accessible environments, while setting a target that PWD should constitute a proportion of the workforce(Federal Republic of Nigeria, 2018). For students who have ASD, this legal framework offers a formal bridge between schooling and employment, implying that schools, training institutions, and employers share responsibility for enabling effective transition. However, the translation of these policies and legal provisions into concrete support for career transition has been uneven.

Studies of IE implementation in Nigeria highlight persistent gaps between policy statements and school-level realities, with limited resources, low parental involvement and attitudes, inadequate teacher preparation/qualified teaching staff, a dearth of infrastructure, societal stigma towards PWD, funding, and weak monitoring systems often constraining practice(Angwaomaodoko, 2023b, 2023a; Cornelius-Ukpepi & Opuwari, 2019; Garuba, 2003; Osagiobare & Ekwukoma, 2025; Torgbenu et al., 2021). Further analyses point to challenges such as overcrowded classrooms, insufficient specialist personnel, and limited exposure of SWD to structured vocational guidance or work-based learning(Diale & Eseadi, 2025; Eseadi & Diale, 2025). These systemic constraints have particular implications for students who have ASD, whose transition to further education, vocational preparation, or work may require tailored support, individual planning, and collaboration between schools, families, and community-based services. While Nigeria's national frameworks affirm the right to inclusion, the significance of functional skills, and the obligation to remove barriers in both education and employment sectors for PWD, there is limited guidance on how schools should design transition programmes for students who have ASD, how interagency collaboration should operate in practice, or how data on post-school outcomes should be collected and used to refine policy priorities. Research on transition for SWD in Nigeria actually points to a need for stronger institutional capacity, clearer standards for transition planning, and intentional support for movement from secondary school into tertiary education, technical and vocational programmes, and supported employment(Diale & Eseadi, 2025; Eseadi & Diale, 2025). For school principals and proprietors, the Nigerian policy environment creates both responsibilities and opportunities for fostering the school-to-work transition of students who have ASD. They are expected to interpret national policies in ways that shape school-level practices, to establish inclusive structures and allocate resources, and to encourage staff training that equips teachers to assist students who have ASD in readiness for adulthood(Test et al., 2014). They are also positioned to foster interagency partnerships with ministries, training agencies, non-governmental organisations, and employers, so that students can encounter coordinated transition pathways. Without clear operational guidelines that focus specifically on ASD and career transition, school leaders often rely on their own initiative and understanding of policies to design local frameworks to support these students. Consequently, examining policy matters concerning the career transition of students who have ASD in Nigeria requires attention to how these policies are interpreted and enacted by those who lead schools. Understanding the extent to which principals and proprietors develop policy vision, build staff capacity, establish inclusive structures, engage in interagency collaboration, use data, and involve families and communities can provide crucial insight into how the national commitment to inclusive and disability education is being realised for students who have ASD as they move towards adult life.

POLICY FRAMEWORK

International policy perspectives have increasingly recognised school-to-work transition as a critical dimension of IE for SWD, including those who have ASD. Across regions, policy systems that prioritise structured transition planning, coordinated support between education and social sectors, sustained teacher preparation, and clear accountability mechanisms tend to demonstrate more coherent pathways for guiding SWD into adulthood. On the other hand, settings with limited investment, fragmented services, and inadequate professional development frequently struggle to offer meaningful transition support to these students. These global variabilities suggest that the quality of transition outcomes may be strongly influenced by the strength of the policy environment and the extent to which schools operate within well-resourced and coordinated transition systems. The Convention on the Rights of Persons with Disabilities (CRPD) provides the most significant international policy framework shaping these developments. The CRPD positions IE as a human right and requires states to remove barriers, ensure accessibility, and facilitate participation in education, employment, and community life(Bacakova et al., 2025; United Nations, 2008). Nigeria ratified the Convention on the 30th day of March 2007 and subsequently ratified the Optional Protocol, thereby committing to implement education and transition practices that uphold autonomy, equality, and social inclusion for PWD. Under Article 24, the Convention requires states to support SWD in acquiring life skills, vocational skills, and workplace readiness, and to ensure access to tertiary education, lifelong learning, and employment preparation on an equivalent criterion with others(Robinson & Fisher, 2023; United Nations, 2008). These obligations establish a binding expectation that school systems must provide structured, personalised, and well-resourced support for the transition into adult life. When viewed through this lens, national policies such as Nigeria's National Policy on Inclusive Education (Federal Ministry of Education, 2023) derive their legitimacy from the CRPD and serve as instruments for translating international commitments into school-based practice.

THEORETICAL FRAMEWORK

Career Transition Policy Ecosystem Theory

Louis (1980) described career transition as "the period during which an individual is either changing roles (taking on a different objective role) or changing orientation to a role already held (altering a subjective state)" (p. 330). This definition emphasises that career transition involves both structural role changes and shifts in how individuals perceive or enact their existing roles. Career transition can be seen as a lifelong developmental process through which individuals with autism navigate education to work pathways with the goal of achieving meaningful and sustainable participation in employment. In this research study, we theorise that career transition outcomes for students who have ASD are shaped by the interaction of policy vision and leadership, staff training and capacity, inclusive structures and resources, interagency collaboration, data and accountability (evidence governance), and family and community engagement (social engagement). Each domain serves a distinct yet interdependent function within a multi-layered policy ecosystem. The theory is grounded in four assumptions that explain how this ecosystem functions. First, policy is ecological, meaning that it operates simultaneously at leadership, human capital, structural, relational, and community levels. As a result, policy influence flows through a network of interconnected systems. Second, implementation is capacity dependent in that the success of a school-to-work transition policy for SWD is influenced by the human and material resources that schools can mobilise. Without adequate training, staffing, tools, and infrastructure, even well-intentioned transition policies would not materialise. Third, effective transition requires cross-sector cooperation. Schools alone cannot prepare students who have ASD for adulthood; as such, meaningful collaboration with external agencies is crucial. Fourth, sustainable transition outcomes depend on effective feedback. This is important because data-driven decision-making, monitoring processes, and accountability structures enable schools to learn from experience, adjust practices, and improve outcomes over time. These assumptions together provide the conceptual lens for comprehending career transition policy as an integrated ecosystem shaped by several layers of influence, as shown in Figure 1.

Figure 1. Career transition policy ecosystem

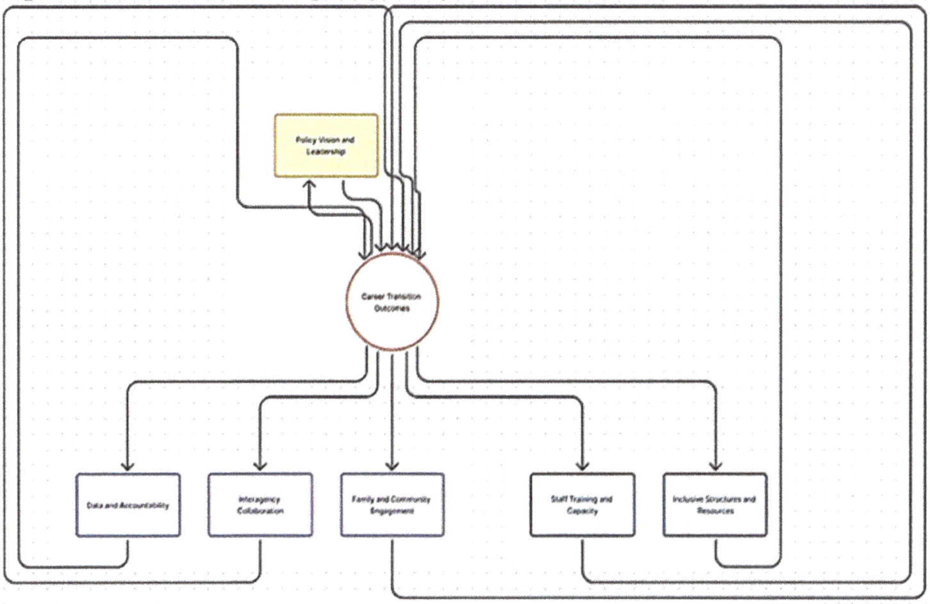

Policy Vision and Leadership

This policy domain refers to the clarity, coherence, and strategic direction that school leaders establish for supporting the career transition of students who have ASD. It captures the extent to which a school has a formally stated transition vision, whether leaders communicate this vision to stakeholders, and whether policy documents explicitly include transition outcomes for students who have ASD. It also reflects leadership commitment through the allocation of budget, time, and institutional support for transition-related initiatives. In essence, this domain encompasses the strength of leadership intentions and strategic guidance that shape transition planning within the school.

Staff Training and Capacity

This policy domain describes the extent to which school personnel have the knowledge, proficiencies, and professional preparation required to care for students who have ASD during their transition to post-school life. It includes continuous training, professional development in inclusive frameworks like Universal Design for Learning, structured induction for new staff, and periodic evaluation of training effectiveness. This domain reflects the capacity of the workforce to deliver evidence-informed transition activities and ensure that staff members are adequately supported to implement policy expectations.

Inclusive Structures and Resources

This policy domain describes the organisational systems, physical spaces, time allocations, and material resources that enable effective transition planning. It captures the presence of transition coordinators or materials, dedicated scheduling for career readiness activities, environmental adaptations that accommodate sensory or functional needs, and policies that guarantee access to vocational or work-based learning experiences. It also considers whether accessibility requirements are integrated into transition policy planning. This domain, therefore, assesses how well the school environment is structured to support meaningful and inclusive transition pathways for students who have ASD.

Interagency Collaboration

This policy domain refers to the partnerships that schools establish with external organisations such as employers, VR agencies, disability services, and community programmes. It entails the presence of formal agreements, joint planning activities, regular interagency meetings, and policy frameworks that promote shared responsibility. Effective interagency collaboration ensures that students who have ASD receive coordinated transition support across sectors. This domain captures the extent to which schools operate within a wider ecosystem of support that links education to employment, training, and community opportunities.

Data and Accountability (Evidence Governance)

This policy domain concerns the systematic use of information to guide transition planning and evaluate outcomes. It includes the collection of transition-related data, such as post-school employment or enrolment in training programmes, the presence of measurable targets in transition policies, and the routine review of data to refine practices. This domain emphasises the importance of evidence-based decision-making and organisational accountability, recognising that transition policies function effectively when progress is monitored and outcomes are used to inform continuous improvement.

Family and Community Engagement (Social Engagement)

This policy domain refers to the extent to which families, community stakeholders, and students who have ASD themselves participate in transition policy processes. It measures family involvement in policy formulation, collaboration with community partners such as employers or disability services, and the gathering and use of feedback from SWD, community partners and their families. This domain also highlights the relational and participatory dimensions of transition planning, acknowledging that strong partnerships beyond the school are essential for preparing students who have ASD for post-school life.

RESEARCH OBJECTIVES

The main objective of our research was to examine the policy matters that influence the career transition of students who have ASD by assessing principals' and proprietors' ratings across key policy dimensions and determining how demographic characteristics predict these policy practices. Secondary objectives are as follows:

1. To ascertain the levels of principals' and proprietors' ratings on policy matters that concern the career transition of students who have ASD across six core dimensions.
2. To examine the extent to which demographic predictors such as position, school type, work experience, school location, and educational qualification influence each policy dimension of career transition for students who have ASD.
3. To identify which demographic factors significantly predict variations in principals' and proprietors' policy practices related to career transition support for students who have ASD.

RESEARCH QUESTIONS

1. What are the levels of principals' and proprietors' ratings on policy matters that concern the career transition of students who have ASD across the six core dimensions?
2. To what extent do demographic predictors such as position, school type, work experience, school location, and educational qualification influence each policy dimension of career transition for students who have ASD?

3. Which demographic factors significantly predict variations in principals' and proprietors' policy practices related to career transition support for students who have ASD?

METHODOLOGY

Research Approach

This research project employed a quantitative approach in order to generate systematic evidence on the policy matters that influence the career transition of students who have ASD within the educational systems of Imo and Abia States. A quantitative approach was considered most suitable because our primary research goal was to engage in measurable assessments (England, 2022; Holton & Burnett, 2005) of principals and proprietors' responses across policy dimensions and to examine the extent to which demographic factors predict variations in these assessments. The intent of our study was not to explore personal meanings or subjective interpretations but to assess the extent to which policy provisions are implemented and to determine the predictive influence of demographic variables such as position, school type, experience, geographical location, and academic qualification. These variables are inherently measurable and lend themselves to statistical analysis. Consequently, the quantitative approach aligns with our aim of arriving at findings that can be generalised to similar educational settings that work with students who have ASD.

Research Design

The cross-sectional, predictive correlation research design was utilised for this investigation. This study design requires gathering research data from respondents at one time point and facilitates examination of relationships among variables of interest without the need for repeated observations(Devi et al., 2022; Hunziker & Blankenagel, 2024; Kumari, 2025). Moreover, cross-sectional design is often utilised in research studies that aim to describe current practices, compare groups, or identify predictors of particular outcomes. In this case, the design provided a coherent structure for documenting the present state of policy implementation related to the career transition of students who have ASD within the selected states. The decision to utilise a cross-sectional design was further informed by the nature of the population we engaged with. Principals and proprietors often have demanding administrative schedules, making prolonged or repeated data collection difficult to maintain. A single administration of the instrument therefore provided a practical and non-intrusive means of obtaining reliable information. The design also enabled us to approach a sufficient number of respondents to perform the statistical analyses required to address the research questions without placing undue burden on respondents. Additionally, the design supports the identification of associations between demographic characteristics and policy ratings, which aligns with our objective of determining predictors of policy implementation.

Research Paradigm

The paradigm for this research study is the positivist research paradigm, which lends itself to the premise that social phenomena can be studied objectively through the systematic measurement of observable variables and quantifiable indicators(Ali, 2024; Diale & Eseadi, 2025; Karupiah, 2022; Park et al., 2020; Sharma, 2025). Within this research paradigm, evidence-based knowledge is created through empiricism and independently of individual experiences. This philosophical stance is consistent with our intention to explore how school leaders implement policy matters that influence the transition of students who have ASD. The assumptions align well with the self-developed instrument employed in the study, which measures policy implementation across six defined domains. A positivist stance also supports the utilisation of statistical tests in order to comprehend the predictive influence of demographic variables. The use of regression analysis, descriptive statistics and confidence intervals to analyse the research data conforms to the positivist perspectives. This paradigm allowed us to treat policy implementation as an observable and quantifiable phenomenon that can be meaningfully compared across individuals and contexts.

Population and Sample

The target population in this research comprised principals and proprietors of schools that provide services to students who have ASD in Imo and Abia States, which are located in Southeast Nigeria. These states were selected due to the presence of a wide range of public and private secondary schools that serve SWD, including students who have ASD. Principals and proprietors play a central role in policy implementation, especially during career transition planning, which requires coordination across multiple systems, allocation of resources, and alignment of school structures with the career transition needs of students who have ASD. Principals and proprietors, therefore, represent the most appropriate population for this study. The multi-stage sampling procedure was utilised in this research study. Multi-stage sampling allows for a structured selection of respondents when the population is geographically dispersed or organised into hierarchical units(Chen et al., 2022; Maas & Hox, 2004). In the first stage, we identified major education zones within

Imo and Abia States. In the second stage, we selected schools within these zones that provide services to students who have ASD. In the final stage, principals and proprietors within the selected schools were invited to take part in the research study. This sampling procedure was considered appropriate because it ensured that the sample included respondents from diverse geographical locations, school types, and administrative contexts. The sampling procedure also allowed us to manage the logistical challenges associated with accessing school leaders who work in different local government areas. The total sample consisted of 44 school leaders, comprising 34 principals and 10 proprietors. Table 1 shows that 31 respondents were drawn from public schools and 13 from private schools. The locations of the schools were also diverse, with 15 respondents from urban areas, 20 from semi-urban areas, and nine from rural areas. The respondents varied in terms of work experience, with representation across early career, mid-career, and highly experienced school leaders.

Data Collection Instrument

Data collection was made possible by utilising a self-developed questionnaire titled the Policy Matters Concerning Career Transition Questionnaire (PolMCTQ). The instrument was designed to assess policy implementation across six key dimensions that are relevant to the career transition of students who have ASD. These dimensions include policy vision and leadership, staff training and capacity, inclusive structures and resources, interagency collaboration, data and accountability, and family and community engagement. The items within each dimension were developed based on a review of relevant literature on special education policy, IE, and transition planning. The instrument consisted of multiple items developed within a five-point Likert scale response system, where one stood for strongly disagree, and five stood for strongly agree. This rating scale was chosen since it allowed the respondents to express different levels of agreement with each item statement. The instrument demonstrated strong reliability based on the evidence presented in the appendix (*see* Table 4, Table 5 and Figure 2). Cronbach's α values ranged from 0.81 to 0.91 across the dimensions, while the omega coefficients ranged from 0.78 to 0.89. These reliability coefficients were well beyond the minimum acceptable threshold of 0.70 and indicate that the items within each domain measured their respective constructs consistently(Gabio & Cajandig, 2025).

Data Collection Procedures

Data collection was implemented with the support of two trained postgraduate research assistants. Before the start of fieldwork, we held a briefing session with the research assistants to ensure they had a vivid comprehension of the study's main goal, the ethical underpinnings, and the procedures to be followed within each school. These assistants were trained on modalities for administering the PolMCTQ consistently and to maintain confidentiality at all times. The data collection process included visiting the selected schools and engaging with principals and proprietors at times that were convenient for them. Upon arrival at each school, the research assistants introduced themselves. They provided respondents with an information sheet with the informed consent form. Respondents were then provided with the questionnaire, which they completed independently. The questionnaires were collected immediately after they were completed by respondents to prevent loss and/ or unauthorised access. The use of trained assistants made it possible for us to ensure that the process of data gathering was systematic and that respondents were given clear instructions. This approach also improved response accuracy and gave respondents opportunities to seek clarification if necessary. Moreover, the data collection was carried out in school premises, which promoted convenience to the respondents and enhanced the response rate.

Data Analysis Procedure

Data analysis was implemented using descriptive and inferential statistical procedures that are consistent with the objectives of the study. Descriptive statistics, encompassing means, standard deviations, standard errors and coefficients of variation, were used to summarise respondent ratings of each policy dimension. These statistics gave an insight into central tendencies and variances in perceptions in the six domains of policy implementation. To answer the research questions pertaining to the predictive effect of demographic variables, multiple regression analysis was used. Regression analysis allowed us to estimate the degree to which each predictor contributes to variations in the dependent variables. In this case, the dependent variables were the six policy dimensions and the independent variables were position, school type, work experience, school location and educational qualifications. Regression analysis was chosen because it enables testing of multiple predictors simultaneously and offers estimates of effect size, statistical significance, and proportion of variance accounted for by the model(Bhattacharya et al., 2017; Shrepnek, 2005; Silva et al., 2014). The decision to use regression analysis was also based on the type of data, which satisfied the assumptions for parametric testing.

Ethical Considerations

Ethical certification for the current research project (Sem-2-2020-057) was from the Faculty of Education Research Ethics Committee, University of Johannesburg(*see* Diale & Eseadi, 2025; Eseadi & Diale, 2025) and the Faculty of Education Research

Ethics Committee, University of Nigeria. This approval ensured that the research was carried out in alignment with the ethical guidelines for research involving human participants. Throughout the data collection phase, we adhered to established ethical protocols, which included securing informed consent, ensuring that participation was entirely voluntary, and upholding both confidentiality and anonymity for all respondents. All respondents received information about the goal of the research, procedures involved, potential benefits of participation, and their rights to decline from participating in the research at any stage without consequences. As a result, we ensured that participation was by volunteering and that there were no incentives or coercive mechanisms used to obtain consent. The confidentiality requirement was upheld by ensuring that questionnaires did not contain identifying information, and completed ones were saved securely in a platform accessible only to the researchers. By following these ethical requirements, we were able to ensure that the rights and dignity of respondents were protected throughout the research process.

RESULTS

Table 1. Respondents' demographic characteristics

Variables	N	%
Position Principal Proprietor	34 10	77.3 22.7
School Type Private Secondary School Public Secondary School	13 31	29.5 70.5
Location Urban Semi-urban Rural	15 20 9	34.1 45.5 20.5
Experience < 5 years 6 – 10 years >10 years	15 11 18	34.1 25.0 40.9
Qualification Bachelors Secondary Post-secondary	32 7 5	72.7 15.9 11.4

The sample for this study comprised a total of 44 school leaders, including principals and proprietors who were responsible for overseeing educational programmes that serve students who have ASD. As shown in Table 1, the distribution of respondents indicated that 34 individuals (77.3 percent) served in principal roles, whereas the remaining 10 respondents (22.7 percent) were proprietors. With regard to school type, 31 respondents (70.5 percent) were from public schools and 13 respondents (29.5 percent) represented private schools. The location of the schools varied, with 15 respondents (34.1 percent) working in urban areas, 20 (45.5 percent) in semi-urban contexts, and 9 (20.5 percent) situated in rural communities.

In terms of work experience, 15 respondents (34.1 percent) had less than five years of experience, 11 (25.0 percent) reported six to ten years of experience, and 18 (40.9 percent) had more than ten years of experience in their roles. This distribution suggests that the sample included a mix of early-career, mid-career, and more experienced school leaders. Regarding educational qualifications, the majority of the respondents held a bachelor's degree (n = 32, 72.7 percent), while 7 (15.9 percent) reported post-secondary qualifications and 5 (11.4 percent) had secondary level qualifications. Accordingly, the results revealed a diverse sample in terms of position, school type, geographical location, professional experience, and educational background, in a way that provides a holistic representation of school leadership profiles within the context of career transition for students who have ASD.

Table 2. Mean scores of principals and proprietors on policy matters concerning the career transition of students who have ASD

N	Policy Dimensions	Mean	SD	SE	Coefficient of variation	95% Confidence Interval	
						Lower Limit	Upper Limit
1	Policy vision and leadership	17.91	3.26	.491	.182	16.92	18.90
2	Staff training and capacity	17.59	2.57	.388	.146	16.80	18.37
3	Inclusive structures and resources	18.18	4.68	.705	.257	16.76	19.60
4	Interagency collaboration	15.70	3.63	.547	.231	14.60	16.81
5	Data and accountability	11.52	3.28	.495	.285	10.53	12.52
6	Family and community engagement	12.00	2.38	.359	.199	11.28	12.72
7	Overall Stress	92.90	8.48		.091	90.33	95.48

Table 2 reveals the mean scores of principals and proprietors on a range of policy matters that concern the career transition of students who have ASD. The results show that policy vision and leadership had a mean score of 17.91 (SD = 3.26), with a relatively narrow confidence interval of 16.92 to 18.90, indicating stable perceptions among the respondents. Staff training and capacity dimension yielded a mean of 17.59 (SD = 2.57), which showed consistent agreement on the significance of equipping staff members with the relevant skills for supporting students who have ASD during their career transition. The confidence interval for this dimension ranged from 16.80 to 18.37, further reflecting a high level of convergence in respondents' views.

The highest mean score across the six dimensions was found for inclusive structures and resources, with a mean of 18.18 (SD = 4.68). While this dimension showed stronger endorsement, the wider confidence interval (16.76-19.60) and higher coefficient of variation suggest greater variability in respondents' responses. The interagency collaboration dimension had a lower mean score of 15.70 (SD = 3.63), implying that collaboration between schools and other agencies may be less developed or experienced differently across settings. The confidence interval for this dimension, ranging from 14.60 to 16.81, reflects a moderate level of variability in perceptions.

Data and accountability dimension had one of the lowest mean ratings at 11.52 (SD = 3.28), with a coefficient of variation of .285, indicating both lower endorsement and greater relative variability across respondents. Family and community engagement also reflected relatively lower agreement, with a mean of 12.00 (SD = 2.38) and a confidence interval ranging from 11.28 to 12.72. Taken together, these results suggest that while school leaders express stronger alignment on dimensions such as policy vision, staff capacity, and inclusive resources, there remains considerable variation and lower overall emphasis on data accountability and active family or community involvement in the career transition of students who have ASD. The overall stress score (M = 92.90, SD = 8.48) further indicates the cumulative pressure perceived across policy domains during the transition process.

Table 3. Regression analysis of predictors on policy matters concerning the career transition of students who have ASD

Models	Predictors	Beta	SE	Adjusted R-square	F-change	t	Sig
Policy vision and leadership	(Constant)	18.055	3.023	-.020	.833	5.972	.000
	Position	.131	3.023			.105	.917
	School type	-.883	1.255			-.787	.436
	Work experience	-.146	1.122			-.203	.840
	Location of school	-.257	.723			-.356	.724
	Educational qualification	1.416	.722			1.868	.069
Staff training and capacity	(Constant)	20.615	1.848	.387	6.438	11.15	.000
	Position	.050	.767			.065	.949
	School type	1.192	.686			1.738	.090
	Work experience	-.600	.442			-1.358	.182
	Location of school	-.500	.441			-1.133	.264
	Educational qualification	-2.173	.463			-4.689	.000
Inclusive structures and resources	(Constant)	26.885	4.116	.080	1.749	6.531	.000
	Position	.070	1.709			.041	.967
	School type	-1.903	1.528			-1.246	.221
	Work experience	-.485	.984			-.493	.625
	Location of school	-1.933	.983			-1.967	.057
	Educational qualification	-.718	1.032			-.696	.491
Interagency collaboration	(Constant)	20.375	3.364	-.023	.809	6.056	.000
	Position	-1.132	1.397			-.810	.423
	School type	-1.802	1.249			-1.443	.157
	Work experience	-.156	.804			-.194	.848
	Location of school	-.352	.803			-.438	.664
	Educational qualification	.542	.844			.642	.525

continued on following page

Table 3. Continued

Models	Predictors	Beta	SE	Adjusted R-square	F-change	t	Sig
Data and accountability	(Constant)	12.252	3.089	-.052	.574	3.967	.000
	Position	.372	1.282			.290	.773
	School type	-.462	1.146			-.403	.689
	Work experience	-.941	.738			- 1.274	.210
	Location of school	.865	.738			1.173	.248
	Educational qualification	-.125	.775			-.161	.873
Family and community engagement	(Constant)	12.419	1.994	.168	2.738	6.229	.000
	Position	1.403	.828			1.694	.098
	School type	-.155	.740			-.210	.835
	Work experience	.403	.477			.846	.403
	Location of school	-.526	.476			- 1.105	.276
	Educational qualification	-1.213	.500			- 2.427	.020

As shown in Table 3, we conducted regression analyses to allow us to ascertain the extent to which demographic predictors accounted for variations in each policy dimension concerning the career transition of students who have ASD. In our data analysis, five demographic variables were included as predictors in each model, namely position, school type, work experience, location of school, and educational qualification. Across the models, the adjusted R-squared values ranged from negative values to modest positive values, indicating that the demographic variables explained limited proportions of variance in respondents' ratings of the policy dimensions.

For the policy vision and leadership dimension, none of the demographic predictors were statistically significant. The adjusted R-squared for this model was negative, which suggests that the set of demographic factors did not meaningfully improve the prediction of respondents' ratings beyond the mean. Although educational qualification demonstrated a relatively higher t value ($t = 1.868$, $p = .069$), this effect did not reach statistical significance. This finding suggests that respondents' views on policy vision and leadership were largely stable across demographic categories.

In the model predicting staff training and capacity, the overall adjusted R-squared was .387, indicating a stronger explanatory capacity compared to the other models. The results showed that educational qualification was a statistically significant predictor of this policy dimension ($\beta = -2.173$, $t = -4.689$, $p < .001$). This result suggests that respondents with different levels of educational attainment varied significantly in how they evaluated staff training and capacity. School type approached significance ($p = .090$), although it did not meet the conventional threshold. The remaining predictors did not yield significant contributions.

The model for inclusive structures and resources yielded an adjusted R-squared of .080. In our results, none of the demographic variables reached statistical significance, although the predictor for school location approached significance with a t value of -1.967 ($p = .057$). This result indicates that while there were slight differences in perceptions based on geographical context, these differences did not reach statistical levels of importance. The broad confidence intervals observed in Table 2 may partially explain the limited predictive power of demographic factors in this model.

The regression model predicting interagency collaboration produced an adjusted R-squared of -.023, indicating that the predictors did not account for meaningful variance in respondents' ratings. All demographic variables had non-significant t values, with school type showing the largest magnitude ($t = -1.443$, $p = .157$). These results suggest that respondents shared generally similar views on the level of interagency collaboration irrespective of their demographic backgrounds.

For data and accountability, the adjusted R-squared was -.052, again indicating a lack of predictive strength. As our results revealed, none of the demographic factors significantly contributed to the model, with the highest t value observed for the location of school ($t = 1.173$, $p = .248$). The limited variation in responses, as indicated in Table 2, may have contributed to the weak predictive capacity of the model.

In the model predicting family and community engagement, educational qualification was the only statistically significant predictor ($\beta = -1.213$, $t = -2.427$, $p = .020$). This finding suggests that respondents' educational backgrounds resulted in meaningful differences in their perceptions of family and community involvement in the career transition of students who have ASD. Position showed a trend towards significance ($t = 1.694$, $p = .098$), but this effect remained non-significant. The adjusted R-squared for this model was .168, indicating a modest level of explanatory power.

Overall, the regression analyses in Table 3 indicate that the demographic predictors examined in this study accounted for limited variation across most policy dimensions. Only educational qualification demonstrated consistent predictive value, particularly for staff training and capacity and for family and community engagement dimensions. The findings suggest that school leaders' views on policy matters concerning career transition are generally stable across demographic categories. However, educational background may influence how they perceive capacity-building needs and family engagement practices.

DISCUSSION

Our study aimed to explore how principals and proprietors in Imo and Abia States interpret and implement policies related to career transition for students who have ASD, and to examine whether demographic characteristics predict variation in these interpretations. One of the key findings was that policy vision, leadership commitment, staff training, and inclusive structures received relatively strong endorsement from school leaders. This suggests that many school leaders recognise the value of aligning institutional policy with the needs of students who have ASD and are taking steps to strengthen internal processes. These results support evidence that school leaders, especially principals who adopt distributed leadership practices, help improve the professionalism of teachers and school success (Galdames-Calderón, 2023). A recent study acknowledges that school leaders function as change agents and influence the extent of inclusion in schools(Alnuaimi et al., 2025). In this regard, another study contends that the implementation of inclusion, particularly for SWD, is significantly influenced by leadership in that inclusive school leaders have the obligation of facilitating the alignment of inclusive structures, fostering a culture of inclusive learning, and coordinating professional development to enhance IE (Black & Simon, 2014; de Oliveira Bernardo, 2025). Also, recent articles emphasise that internal school culture and collaborative relationships are essential prerequisites for effective inclusion and transition preparation(Diale & Eseadi, 2025; Poirier et al., 2022; Uttayotha & Scheef, 2021). The results also support evidence from other contexts, where educators working with students who have ASD adopted inclusive pedagogical strategies such as differentiation, visual supports, and collaborative planning, thereby demonstrating commitment to IE (Nthibeli et al., 2022). Thus, we are of the view that support for staff training opportunities by school leaders is crucial for educators to improve their knowledge and use of inclusive pedagogical strategies when working with students who have ASD.

Our study revealed weaker ratings for data and accountability systems, and family and community engagement, highlighting substantial gaps in transition practice. This is critical because international research emphasises that successful school-to-adult transitions for students who have ASD often depend on structured transition planning and intervention, robust interagency collaboration, family involvement, and systematic tracking of progress(Diale & Eseadi, 2025; Onyishi et al., 2023; Victor-Aigbodion & Eseadi, 2025). The absence of data-informed practice may limit the ability of schools to monitor students' post-school outcomes, adjust transition plans, or coordinate effectively with external agencies. The weak endorsement of the family and community engagement dimension further suggests that schools may struggle to involve key stakeholders whose participation is vital for sustainable post-school success. The study by Jung and Sheldon (2020) suggests that transformational and collaborative leadership by school leaders relates to the quality of school–family collaboration programmes and the extent of engagement with families. Smith et al. (2021) also indicated a meaningful nexus between school principals' leadership and increased engagement with families. Although interagency collaboration received moderate endorsement among leaders, our regression analyses showed that demographic variables did not predict variation in this domain. This implies that collaboration challenges may be structural rather than individual. In contexts where state policy does not mandate formal transition coordination, reliance may fall on informal networks or individual initiative, often leading to inconsistent provision. This outcome echoes findings from transition research in other contexts, wherein interagency collaboration is widely recognised as a critical component for post-school success for SASD, but it remains one of the least consistently implemented components(Poirier et al., 2022).

In our study, neither position (principal vs proprietor), years of experience, nor school type explained meaningful differences in policy implementation. This finding suggests a shared professional culture or similar exposure to inclusion training across schools, but may also reflect systemic constraints that limit variation. Interestingly, educational qualification emerged as the only significant demographic predictor, particularly for staff training and family/community engagement. Our findings support existing research suggesting that school leaders play a critical role in fostering IE, especially when they are aware of IE principles and their actions and attitudes are seen as significantly impactful on the effective inclusion of students with SEN (Khaleel et al., 2021; Romasanta, 2025). According to Crosbie et al. (2024), transition outcomes for SWD can be strengthened when additional structures and supports are embedded across schools, post-school education settings, and disability employment services. Furthermore, these authors observed that when students and their families are encouraged to begin considering future employment pathways early, they are more likely to access a wider range of work-related experiences during the later years of schooling and into early adulthood.

Nevertheless, even where leaders had strong qualifications, the limited variance in location effects implies that environmental constraints such as funding shortages, lack of formal transition frameworks, and inadequate specialist support may overshadow individual leader capacity. This result aligns with evidence showing that even well-intentioned school leaders can struggle to implement comprehensive transition services in under-resourced systems(Diale & Eseadi, 2025; Eseadi & Diale, 2025). Viewed in a broader context, our findings reflect challenges in other countries where IE policy is relatively mature, yet transition systems remain insufficiently developed(Groce, 2004; Pandey & Agarwal, 2013; Pearson et al., 2021; Winn & Hay, 2009). A previous study indicates that many youths who have ASD experience persistently poor post-school outcomes in postsecondary education, independent living and employment (Shattuck et al., 2012). A study on employment outcomes for individuals who have ASD likewise highlights ongoing difficulties in obtaining and maintaining meaningful work, even when services and supports exist(Chen et al., 2015). The endorsement of inclusive structures and leadership vision among Nigerian school leaders is encouraging, but the gaps in data systems, accountability, and stakeholder engagement highlight the urgent need for stronger, system-wide policy mechanisms. Unless transition policy is supported by formal guidelines, resources, interagency coordination, and stakeholder participation, the best intentions at the institutional level may not translate into tangible post-school achievement for students with ASD.

The findings of our research study demonstrate some implications for educational policy and practice. First, the absence of strong data and accountability systems suggests the need for state-level guidelines that require schools to collect, analyse, and report transition-related data. Such systems would enable the identification of transition barriers, guide resource allocation, and enhance post-school outcomes. Second, the persistent weakness in family and community engagement underscores the need for culturally responsive strategies that involve families in transition planning. Schools may require structured tools, training modules, and community outreach frameworks to ensure that families understand their roles and can contribute meaningfully to the transition process. Third, the finding that educational qualification predicts transition-related practices suggests a need for targeted professional development for school leaders. Leadership training should include ASD specific content, transition planning frameworks, and strategies for building interagency partnerships. This could be incorporated into state leadership institutes or continuing education programmes. Finally, the moderate endorsement of interagency collaboration highlights an opportunity for state authorities to develop formal partnerships with health, youth development, vocational training, and employment agencies. Establishing clear referral pathways and service coordination systems would reduce the fragmentation currently experienced by schools and improve the continuity of support for students who have ASD.

Although the research offered critical insights, some of its limitations must be highlighted. The sample was limited to two states and relied on a self-rating scale, which may be subject to social desirability or restricted by the subjective interpretation of items. Future research could employ mixed methods, incorporating interviews or observations to capture the nuances of transition policy implementation. Additionally, broader samples across multiple Nigerian states or regions could provide a more comprehensive understanding of national trends. Further studies are required to examine the role of systemic factors such as funding, teacher training policies, and state-level coordination mechanisms. Investigating how parents, students, and external agencies perceive transition processes would also deepen the understanding of how current policies operate in practice. Comparative studies across African countries may highlight promising models that could be adapted to the Nigerian context

CONCLUSIONS

School leaders demonstrated commitment to internal structures and inclusive leadership, but significant gaps still exist in collaborative practices, family engagement, and data-driven decision-making. The limited influence of demographic variables suggests that broader systemic reforms are needed to strengthen transition practices. The role of educational qualification highlights the importance of leadership development. As Nigeria continues to foster IE, targeted policy interventions that support schools in developing comprehensive career transition programmes will be essential for improving the outcomes of students who have ASD.

REFERENCES

Ali, I. M. (2024). A guide for positivist research paradigm: From philosophy to methodology. *Idealogy Journal, 9*(2). https://www.idealogyjournal.com/ojs/index.php/idealogy/article/view/596

Alnuaimi, A., Opoku, M. P., & Nketsia, W. (2025). Assessment of school leadership and quality of inclusive practices in early childhood education in the United Arab Emirates. *Educational Management Administration & Leadership, 17411432251319999*, 17411432251319999. Advance online publication. DOI: 10.1177/17411432251319999

Americans with Disabilities Act. (1990). *Americans with Disabilities Act of 1990, As Amended.* https://www.ada.gov/law-and-regs/ada/

Angwaomaodoko, E. A. (2023a). A Critique of Inclusive Education Policy and the Extent of Its Implementation in Nigeria. *Traektoriâ Nauki, 9*(11), 2001–2008. DOI: 10.22178/pos.98-4

Angwaomaodoko, E. A. (2023b). The challenges and opportunities of inclusive education in Nigeria. *Traektoriâ Nauki, 9*(7), 1001–1009. DOI: 10.22178/pos.94-1

Australian Department of Education. (2022, July). *Milestones and transitions*. Australian Department of Education. https://www.education.gov.au/download/13621/milestones-and-transitions/28292/milestones-and-transitions/pdf

Autism New Zealand, & Ministry of Social Development. (2025). *Employment and Transition Services Support for gaining employment or to transition from school into work and general life.* AutismNZ. https://autismnz.org.nz/employment-transition-service

Bacakova, M., Veck, W., & Wharton, J. (Eds.). (2025). *Forced Migration, Disability and Education: Inclusion and Exclusion at the Intersection of Displacement and Disablement*. Routledge., DOI: 10.4324/9781003590422

Bhattacharya, S., Sethi, M., Behl, A., & Venkatesh, V. G. (2017). *12. Regression techniques and their application in the corporate social responsibility domain: An overview. Handbook of Research Methods in Corporate Social Responsibility*. Elgar Online., DOI: 10.4337/9781784710927.00019

Black, W. R., & Simon, M. D. (2014). Leadership for all students: Planning for more inclusive school practices. *The International Journal of Educational Leadership Preparation, 9*(2), 153–172.

Chen, J. L., Leader, G., Sung, C., & Leahy, M. (2015). Trends in Employment for Individuals with Autism Spectrum Disorder: A Review of the Research Literature. *Review Journal of Autism and Developmental Disorders*, *2*(2), 115–127. DOI: 10.1007/s40489-014-0041-6

Chen, S., Haziza, D., & Mashreghi, Z. (2022). A Comparison of Existing Bootstrap Algorithms for Multi-Stage Sampling Designs. *Stats*, *5*(2), 521–537. DOI: 10.3390/stats5020031 PMID: 38737922

Cornelius-Ukpepi, B. U., & Opuwari, O. S. (2019). Determinants of effective implementation of inclusive education at the basic education level in Nigeria. *Brock Journal of Education*, *7*(8), 34–44.

Crosbie, J., Wilson, E., Davis, H., & Campain, R. (2024). *School to work transition for young people with disability, the current ecosystem, and the Ticket to Work approach.* https://figshare.swinburne.edu.au/articles/report/School_to_work_transition_for_young_people_with_disability_the_current_ecosystem_and_the_Ticket_to_Work_approach/28646756

de Oliveira Bernardo, N. (2025). *Promoting a Fully Inclusive School Culture* [PhD Thesis, Grand Canyon University]. https://search.proquest.com/openview/0ac571050860c1d08c2899c64c92cf6c/1?pq-origsite=gscholar&cbl=18750&diss=y

Department of Education. (2001, July). *Education White Paper 6, Special Needs Education: Building an inclusive education and training system.* Department of Education, South Africa. https://www.gov.za/sites/default/files/gcis_document/201409/educ61.pdf

Devi, B., Lepcha, N., & Basnet, S. (2022). Application of correlational research design in nursing and medical research. *Journal of Xi'an Shiyou University. Natural Sciences Education*, *65*(11), 60–69.

Diale, B. M., & Eseadi, C. (2025). *Perspectives on career transitioning of students with attention deficit hyperactivity disorder (ADHD).* IGI Global.

Disability Standards for Education. (2005). *Disability Standards for Education 2005.* Attorney-General's Department Australia. https://www.legislation.gov.au/F2005L00767/latest/text

Economic and Social Commission for Asia and the Pacific United Nations. (2023). *Harmonization of national laws with the convention on the rights of persons with disabilities: Country case study Republic of Korea.* United Nations Bangkok. https://www.unescap.org/sites/default/d8files/2023-07/ESCAP-2023-RP-Harmonization-National-Laws-Convention-Rights-Person-Disability-korea-Case-study.pdf

Employment and Training Administration U.S. Department of Labour. (2016). Workforce Innovation and Opportunity Act. *Federal Register, 81*(161), 56072–56469.

Enabling Guide. (2025). *School-To-Work (S2W) Transition Programme*. SG Enable. https://www.enablingguide.sg/im-looking-for-disability-support/training-employment/school-to-work-%28s2w%29-transition-programme

England, A. (2022). Quantitative and qualitative research methods. In E. Seeram, R. Davidson, A. England, & M. F. McEntee (Eds.), *Research for Medical Imaging and Radiation Sciences* (pp. 71–96). Springer International Publishing. DOI: 10.1007/978-3-030-79956-4_5

Eseadi, C., & Diale, B. M. (2025). *Perspectives on Career Transitioning of Students with Hearing Impairments*. IGI Global.

Espinoza, J. G. R. (2018). *Workfare Factors in the US: An Analysis of Employment Attainment by TANF Job Seekers in the US Workforce Development System* [PhD Thesis, California Baptist University].

European Agency for Special Needs and Inclusive Education. (2019, November 27). *Country information for Netherlands—Legislation and policy*. European Agency for Special Needs and Inclusive Education. https://www.european-agency.org/country-information/netherlands/legislation-and-policy

European Agency for Special Needs and Inclusive Education. (2021, April 5). *Country information for Italy—Legislation and policy*. European Agency for Special Needs and Inclusive Education. https://www.european-agency.org/country-information/italy/legislation-and-policy

European Agency for Special Needs and Inclusive Education. (2023, March 13). *Country information for Sweden—Legislation and policy*. European Agency for Special Needs and Inclusive Education. https://www.european-agency.org/country-information/sweden/legislation-and-policy

European Agency for Special Needs and Inclusive Education. (2024). *Country Policy Development Support – Framework*. https://www.european-agency.org/resources/publications/CPDS-framework

European Agency for Special Needs and Inclusive Education. (2025, May 4). *Country information for Denmark—Legislation and policy*. European Agency for Special Needs and Inclusive Education. https://www.european-agency.org/country-information/denmark/legislation-and-policy

European Centre for the Development of Vocational Training. (2025, May 2). *Sweden: Reformed VET curricula for learners with intellectual disabilities.* European Centre for the Development of Vocational Training. https://www.cedefop.europa.eu/en/news/sweden-reformed-vet-curricula-learners-intellectual-disabilities

European Commission. (2023, August 30). *Together for inclusive education and work opportunities.* European Commission. https://employment-social-affairs.ec.europa.eu/together-inclusive-education-and-work-opportunities_en

European Union. (2000). *Council Directive 2000/78/EC of 27 November 2000 establishing a general framework for equal treatment in employment and occupation.* EUR-Lex: Official Journal of the European Union, L 303/16-L 303/22. https://eur-lex.europa.eu/legal-content/EN/TXT/PDF/?uri=CELEX:32000L0078

European Union. (2012). *Charter of Fundamental Rights of the European Union.* EUR-Lex: Official Journal of the European Union, C 326/391-C 326/407. https://eur-lex.europa.eu/legal-content/EN/TXT/PDF/?uri=CELEX:12012P/TXT

Federal Ministry of Education. (2015). *National Policy on Special Needs Education in Nigeria.* Federal Ministry of Education Abuja. https://www.rodra.co.za/images/countries/nigeria/policy/National%20Policy%20on%20Special%20Needs%20Education.pdf

Federal Ministry of Education. (2023). *Revised National Policy on Inclusive Education in Nigeria.* Federal Ministry of Education Abuja. https://tafafrica.co/publication/Inclusive%20Education.pdf

Federal Republic of Brazil. (2015, July 6). *The Brazilian Law for the Inclusion of Persons with Disabilities (Statute of Persons with Disabilities). Law No. 13,146, of July 6, 2015.* https://planalto.gov.br/ccivil_03/_Ato2015-2018/2015/Lei/L13146.htm

Federal Republic of Nigeria. (2018). *Discrimination Against Persons with Disabilities Prohibition Act, 2018.* https://www.un.org/development/desa/disabilities/wp-content/uploads/sites/15/2019/11/Nigeria_Discrimination-Against-Persons-with-Disabilities-Prohibition-Act-2018.pdf

Gabio, J. A., & Cajandig, A. J. S. (2025). College of Teacher Education Students' Mastery of Statistical Concepts: Basis for Proposed Enhancement Program. *International Journal of Research and Innovation in Social Science, 9*(3), 2269–2284. DOI: 10.47772/IJRISS.2025.90300179

Galdames-Calderón, M. (2023). Distributed Leadership: School Principals' Practices to Promote Teachers' Professional Development for School Improvement. *Education Sciences, 13*(7), 715. DOI: 10.3390/educsci13070715

Garuba, A. (2003). Inclusive education in the 21st century: Challenges and opportunities for Nigeria. *Asia Pacific Disability Rehabilitation Journal, 14*(2), 191–200.

Gillies, A. (2024). *Healthcare Management: Global Perspectives.* Routledge., DOI: 10.4324/9781003478874

Government of Canada. (2022). *Canada's Disability Inclusion Action Plan, 2022.* Government of Canada. https://www.canada.ca/en/employment-social-development/programs/disability-inclusion-action-plan/action-plan-2022.html

Government of Canada. (2023). *Services and Supports to Promote the Social Inclusion of Persons with Developmental Disabilities Act, 2008.* https://www.ontario.ca/laws/statute/08s14

Government of India. (2016). *The Rights of Persons with Disabilities Act 2016.* https://www.indiacode.nic.in/bitstream/123456789/15939/1/the_rights_of_persons_with_disabilities_act%2C_2016.pdf

Groce, N. E. (2004). Adolescents and youth with disability: Issues and challenges. *Asia Pacific Disability Rehabilitation Journal, 15*(2), 13–32.

Holton, E. F., & Burnett, M. F. (2005). The basics of quantitative research. *Research in Organizations: Foundations and Methods of Inquiry*, 29–44.

Hunziker, S., & Blankenagel, M. (2024). Cross-Sectional Research Design. In S. Hunziker & M. Blankenagel, *Research Design in Business and Management* (pp. 187–199). Springer Fachmedien Wiesbaden. DOI: 10.1007/978-3-658-42739-9_10

Ineland, J., Karhina, K., & Vikström, L. (2021). School-to-work Transitions for Students with Intellectual Disabilities: Teachers' Perceptions and Experiences of a Recent Workplace-Based Reform in Sweden. *Journal of the International Special Needs Education, 24*(2), 86–96. DOI: 10.9782/JISNE-D-20-00012

Jose, B., & Muthulakshmi, S. (2022). Institutional Framework for the Rehabilitation of Differently Abled Persons in India. *Cuestiones de Fisioterapia, 51*(3), 280–287. DOI: 10.48047/qvyrpp57

Jung, S. B., & Sheldon, S. (2020). Connecting Dimensions of School Leadership for Partnerships with School and Teacher Practices of Family Engagement. *School Community Journal, 30*(1), 9–32.

Karupiah, P. (2022). Positivism. In Islam, M. R., Khan, N. A., & Baikady, R. (Eds.), *Principles of Social Research Methodology* (pp. 73–82). Springer Nature., DOI: 10.1007/978-981-19-5441-2_6

Khaleel, N., Alhosani, M., & Duyar, I. (2021). The Role of School Principals in Promoting Inclusive Schools: A Teachers' Perspective. *Frontiers in Education, 6*, 603241. Advance online publication. DOI: 10.3389/feduc.2021.603241

Korea Employment Agency for Persons with Disabilities. (2023). *Employment Support Service for PWDs*. KEAD. https://www.kead.or.kr/en/empsus/cntntsPage.do?menuId=MENU1461

Kumari, K. (2025). *Employee Retention Strategies in Ireland's Hospitality Industry* [PhD Thesis, Dublin, National College of Ireland]. https://norma.ncirl.ie/8996/

Louis, M. R. (1980). Career Transitions: Varieties and Commonalities. *Academy of Management Review, 5*(3), 329–340. DOI: 10.5465/amr.1980.4288836

Maas, C. J. M., & Hox, J. J. (2004). Robustness issues in multilevel regression analysis. *Statistica Neerlandica, 58*(2), 127–137. DOI: 10.1046/j.0039-0402.2003.00252.x

Ministry of Community and Social Services. Ontario & Ministry of Children and Youth Services, Ontario. (2011, May). *Provincial Transition Planning Framework for Young People with Developmental Disabilities*. https://coordinatedaccess.ca/wp-content/uploads/2015/07/Transition-Planning-Framework-Final-English.pdf?

Ministry of Disabled People. (2025, May 12). *Strategic Intentions Tauākī Whakamaunga Atu: 1 July 2025 to 30 June 2028*. Ministry of Disabled People. https://www.strategicintentions.whaikaha.govt.nz/

Ministry of Education. (2003, October 21). *The Folkeskole (Consolidation) Act*. https://media.unesco.org/sites/default/files/webform/r2e002/db4e18f1f260d4ef8ea9ca6e1d4e08d4532fc083.pdf

Ministry of Education and Research Sweden. (2010). *Skollag (2010:800) [Swedish Education Act, 2010)*. https://www.riksdagen.se/sv/dokument-och-lagar/dokument/svensk-forfattningssamling/skollag-2010800_sfs-2010-800/

Ministry of Education Chile. (2015, May 29). *LEY NÚM. 20.845 De inclusión escolar que regula la admisión de los y las estudiantes, elimina el financiamiento compartido y prohíbe el lucro en establecimientos educacionales que reciben aportes del estado*. Ministry of Education Chile. https://www.bcn.cl/leychile/navegar?idNorma=1078172

Ministry of Education, Culture and Science, Government of the Netherlands. (2014, August). *Appropriate Education Act, 2014*. Ministry of Education, Culture and Science. https://www.government.nl/topics/appropriate-education

Ministry of Education Government of Ghana. (2015). *Inclusive Education Policy*. Ministry of Education Government of Ghana. https://sapghana.com/data/documents/Inclusive-Education-Policy-official-document.pdf

Ministry of Education Government of India. (2025, April 2). *Ministry of Education reaffirms its commitment to inclusive education by strengthening support systems for children with autism spectrum disorder in schools*. https://dsel.education.gov.in/sites/default/files/update/PIB2117857.pdf

Ministry of Education Government of New Zealand. (2016, November 25). *New Zealand Disability Strategy 2016-2026*. Ministry of Education Government of New Zealand. https://ieag.org.nz/assets/Uploads/NZ-Disability-Strategy.pdf

Ministry of Health and Welfare Republic of Korea. (1989). *A. The Welfare Law for Persons with Disabilities (Amended as Law No. 4179, Promulgated on December 30th 1989)*. Ministry of Health and Welfare Republic of Korea. https://www.dinf.ne.jp/doc/english/intl/z15/z15007le/z1500746.html

Ministry of Justice Japan. (2019). *Act to Facilitate the Employment of Persons with Disabilities(Act No. 123 of July 25, 1960). Updated Act No. 36 of 2019*. https://www.japaneselawtranslation.go.jp/en/laws/view/3845/en

Ministry of Labour. Immigration, Training and Skills Development. (2018, February 7). *Supported Employment Program Guidelines*. Ministry of Labour, Immigration, Training and Skills Development, Ontario. https://eopg.labour.gov.on.ca/wp-content/uploads/2025/04/se-guidelines-program-en.pdf?

Ministry of Labour and Social Protection. Kenya. (2024, May). *Persons with Disabilities National Policy*. Ministry of Labour and Social Protection, Kenya. https://socialprotection.go.ke/sites/default/files/Downloads/FINAL%20PERSONS%20WITH%20DISABILITIES%20NATIONAL%20POLICY%20-%20LAKE%20NAIVASHA%20RESORT%20v2-%2030TH%20APRIL%202024.pdf

Ministry of Planning Chile. (2010, February 3). *LEY NÚM. 20.422 Establece normas sobre igualdad de oportunidades e inclusión social de personas con discapacidad*. https://www.bcn.cl/leychile/navegar?idNorma=1010903

Ministry of Social and Family Development Singapore. (2021). *Enabling Masterplan 2030*. https://www.msf.gov.sg/docs/default-source/enabling-masterplan/emp2030-report-%28final2%29.pdf

National Agency for Special Needs Education and Schools. (2019, November 13). *Our mission and role*. National Agency for Special Needs Education and Schools (SPSM in Sweden). https://www.spsm.se/om-oss/other-languages/english/our-mission/

National Disability Insurance Scheme Act. (2013). *National Disability Insurance Scheme Act 2013*. Department of Health, Disability and Ageing Department of the Treasury. https://www.legislation.gov.au/C2013A00020/latest/text

Nigerian Educational Research and Development Council. (2013). *National Policy on Education (6th Edition)*. Nigerian Educational Research and Development Council. https://education.gov.ng/wp-content/uploads/2020/06/NATIONAL-POLICY-ON-EDUCATION.pdf

Nthibeli, M., Griffiths, D., & Bekker, T. (2022). Teaching learners with autism in the South African inclusive classroom: Pedagogic strategies and possibilities. *African Journal of Disability*, *11*(0), 12. DOI: 10.4102/ajod.v11i0.979 PMID: 35812767

Office of Special Education and Rehabilitative Services U.S. Department of Education. (2000, July). *A Guide to the Individualized Education Program*. Office of Special Education and Rehabilitative Services U.S. Department of Education. https://www.ed.gov/sites/ed/files/parents/needs/speced/iepguide/iepguide.pdf

Onyishi, C. N., Sefotho, M. M., & Victor-Aibodion, V. (2023). Psychological distress among parents of children with autism spectrum disorders: A randomized control trial of cognitive behavioural therapy. *Research in Autism Spectrum Disorders*, *100*, 102070. Advance online publication. DOI: 10.1016/j.rasd.2022.102070

Osagiobare, E. O., & Ekwukoma, V. (2025). Perceived Challenges of Implementing the National Policy on Inclusive Education in Nigeria. *Revue Plurilingue: Études Des Langues. Littératures et Cultures*, *9*(1), 79–88. DOI: 10.46325/ellic.v9i1.164

Pandey, S., & Agarwal, S. (2013). Transition to adulthood for youth with disability: Issues for the disabled child and family. *IOSR Journal of Humanities and Social Science (IOSR-JHSS)*, *17*(3), 41–45.

Park, Y. S., Konge, L., & Artino, A. R. J. (2020). The Positivism Paradigm of Research. *Academic Medicine*, *95*(5), 690–694. DOI: 10.1097/ACM.0000000000003093 PMID: 31789841

Pearson, C., Watson, N., Gangneux, J., & Norberg, I. (2021). Transition to where and to what? Exploring the experiences of transitions to adulthood for young disabled people. *Journal of Youth Studies*, *24*(10), 1291–1307. DOI: 10.1080/13676261.2020.1820972

Poirier, S.-È., St-Pierre, M.-C., Julien-Gauthier, F., Flamand, V., Martin-Roy, S., & Desmarais, C. (2022). Inter-Agency Collaboration in the Transition from School to Adulthood of Students with Disabilities: A Narrative Review of the Literature. *International Journal of Disability Development and Education*, *69*(4), 1249–1256. DOI: 10.1080/1034912X.2020.1779915

Republic of Kenya. (2025, May 13). *The Persons With Disabilities Act, 2025*. Kenya Gazette Supplement No 69 (Acts No 4). Government Printer, Nairobi. https://ncpwd.go.ke/download/personswithdisabilitiesact-pdf/?ind=1747986120993&filename=The%20Persons%20with%20Disabilities%20Act%202025.pdf&wpdmdl=640&refresh=693557689954e1765103464

Robinson, S., & Fisher, K. R. (2023). *Research handbook on disability policy*. Edward Elgar Publishing. DOI: 10.4337/9781800373655

Romasanta, J. M. (2025). Integrating Organizational Culture and Leadership Competence for Effective School-Based Management: Inputs for School Improvement Plan. *International Journal of Multidisciplinary Research and Publications*, *8*(1), 519–542.

Senate and House of Representatives of the United States of America in Congress. (2016, January 7). *Rehabilitation Act of 1973 [As Amended Through P.L. 114–95, Enacted December 10, 2015]*. https://assets.section508.gov/assets/files/rehabilitation-act-of-1973-amended-by-wioa.pdf

Sharma, A. (2025). Positivism. In Jahn, B., & Schindler, S. (Eds.), *Elgar Encyclopedia of International Relations* (pp. 302–303). Edward Elgar Publishing Ltd., DOI: 10.4337/9781035312283.000138

Shattuck, P. T., Narendorf, S. C., Cooper, B., Sterzing, P. R., Wagner, M., & Taylor, J. L. (2012). Postsecondary Education and Employment Among Youth With an Autism Spectrum Disorder. *Pediatrics*, *129*(6), 1042–1049. DOI: 10.1542/peds.2011-2864 PMID: 22585766

Shrepnek, G. K. (2005). Regression methods in the empiric analysis of health care data. *Journal of Managed Care Pharmacy : JMCP*, *11*(3), 240–251. DOI: 10.18553/jmcp.2005.11.3.240 PMID: 15804208

Silva, R. C., Corona, C. C., & Galdeano, J. L. V. (2014). Solving regression analysis by fuzzy quadratic programming. *Studies in Computational Intelligence*, *537*, 139–147. DOI: 10.1007/978-3-642-53737-0_9

Smith, T. E., Reinke, W. M., Herman, K. C., & Sebastian, J. (2021). Exploring the link between principal leadership and family engagement across elementary and middle school. *Journal of School Psychology*, *84*, 49–62. DOI: 10.1016/j.jsp.2020.12.006 PMID: 33581770

Stone-MacDonald, A., Cihak, D. F., & Zager, D. (Eds.). (2016). *Autism Spectrum Disorders: Identification, Education, and Treatment* (4th ed.). Routledge., DOI: 10.4324/9781315794181

Sweden Sverige, & Swedish Institute. (2025, November 3). *The Swedish school system*. https://sweden.se/life/society/the-swedish-school-system

Teachers Institute. (2023, December 27). *Advancing Inclusive Education for Children with Disabilities in India*. https://teachers.institute/alternative-education/inclusive-education-children-disabilities-india/

Test, D. W., Smith, L. E., & Carter, E. W. (2014). Equipping Youth With Autism Spectrum Disorders for Adulthood: Promoting Rigor, Relevance, and Relationships. *Remedial and Special Education*, *35*(2), 80–90. DOI: 10.1177/0741932513514857

Torgbenu, E. L., Oginni, O. S., Opoku, M. P., Nketsia, W., & Agyei-Okyere, E. (2021). Inclusive education in Nigeria: Exploring parental attitude, knowledge and perceived social norms influencing implementation. *International Journal of Inclusive Education*, *25*(3), 377–393. DOI: 10.1080/13603116.2018.1554715

United Nations. (2008, May 3). *Convention on the Rights of Persons with Disabilities*. United Nations Human Rights Office of the High Commissioner. https://www.ohchr.org/en/instruments-mechanisms/instruments/convention-rights-persons-disabilities

U.S. Equal Employment Opportunity Commission. (2023). *Employment protections under the Rehabilitation Act of 1973: 50 years of protecting Americans with disabilities in the workplace*. https://www.eeoc.gov/employment-protections-under-rehabilitation-act-1973-50-years-protecting-americans-disabilities

Uttayotha, S., & Scheef, A. R. (2021). Partnerships to promote inclusive education for students with disabilities in Thailand. *Journal of Global Education and Research*, *5*(1), 85–95. DOI: 10.5038/2577-509X.5.1.1102

Victor-Aigbodion, V., & Eseadi, C. (2025). Effect of purpose-based career coaching on career transition self-efficacy among college students with autism spectrum disorder. *EDULEARN25 Proceedings*, 8088–8101. https://library.iated.org/view/VICTORAIGBODION2025EFF

Wagacha, N., Mutisya, A., & Ounoi, I. (2025, October 15). *A landmark shift in rights, compliance and inclusion with Kenya's new Persons with Disabilities Act*. CDH. https://www.cliffedekkerhofmeyr.com/en/news/publications/2025/Practice/Corporate-Commercial/corporate-and-commercial-alert-15-october-A-landmark-shift-in-rights-compliance-and-inclusion-with-Kenyas-new-Persons-with-Disabilities-Act

Winn, S., & Hay, I. (2009). Transition from school for youths with a disability: Issues and challenges. *Disability & Society*, *24*(1), 103–115. DOI: 10.1080/09687590802535725

APPENDIX

Table 4. Policy Matters Concerning Career Transition Questionnaire (PolMCTQ)

N	Items	Factor Loading	Cronbach's α	Omega ω
	Policy Vision and Leadership			
1	Our school has a clear, formally stated vision for supporting ASD students in career transition.	0.901	0.90	0.88
2	I actively communicate this vision to all stakeholders (staff, families, community).	0.829		
3	Policies explicitly include career transition outcomes for ASD students.	0.796		
4	Budget and time are allocated for inclusive transition initiatives.	0.806		
	Staff Training and Capacity			
5	Our school provides ongoing training in ASD-inclusive career transition practices.	0.655	0.81	0.78
6	Professional development includes Universal Design for Learning (UDL) or similar inclusive frameworks.	0.973		
7	I ensure new staff receive policy induction on ASD transition strategies.	0.643		
8	Evaluation of staff training effectiveness is conducted regularly.	0.525		
	Inclusive Structures and Resources			
9	We have dedicated resources (e.g., transition coordinators, materials) for ASD career planning.	0.847	0.91	0.89
10	Scheduling allows structured career-readiness activities for ASD students.	0.804		
11	Physical and virtual spaces are adapted to support ASD students' transition work.	0.889		
12	Policies ensure access to external vocational or work-based learning opportunities.	0.822		
13	Accessibility needs are considered in all transition policy planning.	0.761		
	Interagency Collaboration			

continued on following page

Table 4. Continued

N	Items	Factor Loading	Cronbach's α	Omega ω
	Policy Vision and Leadership			
14	We collaborate with vocational rehab, employers, and community programs in transition planning.	0.818	0.84	0.85
15	Formal agreements (MOUs) guide external partnerships for career transition.	0.527		
16	Our school routinely holds interagency meetings to coordinate transition support.	0.927		
17	Policy frameworks support shared responsibility across school and external partners.	0.826		
	Data and Accountability			
18	We collect and use data (e.g., post-school employment, training enrolment) to monitor ASD students' outcomes.	0.858	0.88	0.86
19	Transition policies include measurable targets for ASD students.	0.786		
20	Data is regularly reviewed to improve inclusive transition practices.	0.926		
	Family and Community Engagement			
21	We actively involve families in policy-making and implementation for career transition.	0.918	0.87	0.83
22	Community stakeholders (e.g., employers, disability services) are engaged in policy discussions.	0.887		
23	Feedback from ASD students and families is formally collected and acted upon.	0.800		

Table 5. Factor Loadings for Policy Matters Concerning Career Transition Questionnaire (PolMCTQ)

	Factor 1	Factor 2	Factor 3	Factor 4	Factor 5	Factor 6	Uniqueness
Inclusion3	**0.889**						**0.222**
Inclusion1	0.847						0.198
Inclusion4	0.822						0.271
Inclusion2	0.804						0.365
Inclusion5	0.761						0.431
Policy1		0.901					0.135
Policy2		0.829					0.383
Policy4		0.806					0.213

continued on following page

Table 5. Continued

	Factor 1	Factor 2	Factor 3	Factor 4	Factor 5	Factor 6	Uniqueness
Inclusion3	**0.889**						**0.222**
Policy3		0.796					0.122
Stafft1		0.472				0.655	0.286
Family1			0.918				0.112
Family2			0.887				0.308
Family3			0.800				0.310
Stafft4			0.525				0.392
Stafft3			0.407			0.643	0.139
Interagency3				0.927			0.294
Interagency4				0.826			0.258
Interagency1				0.818			0.257
Interagency2				0.527			0.632
Data3					0.926		0.189
Data1					0.858		0.170
Data2					0.786		0.276
Stafft2						0.973	0.106

Note. Applied rotation method is promax.

Figure 2. Scree Plot for Policy Matters Concerning Career Transition Questionnaire (PolMCTQ)

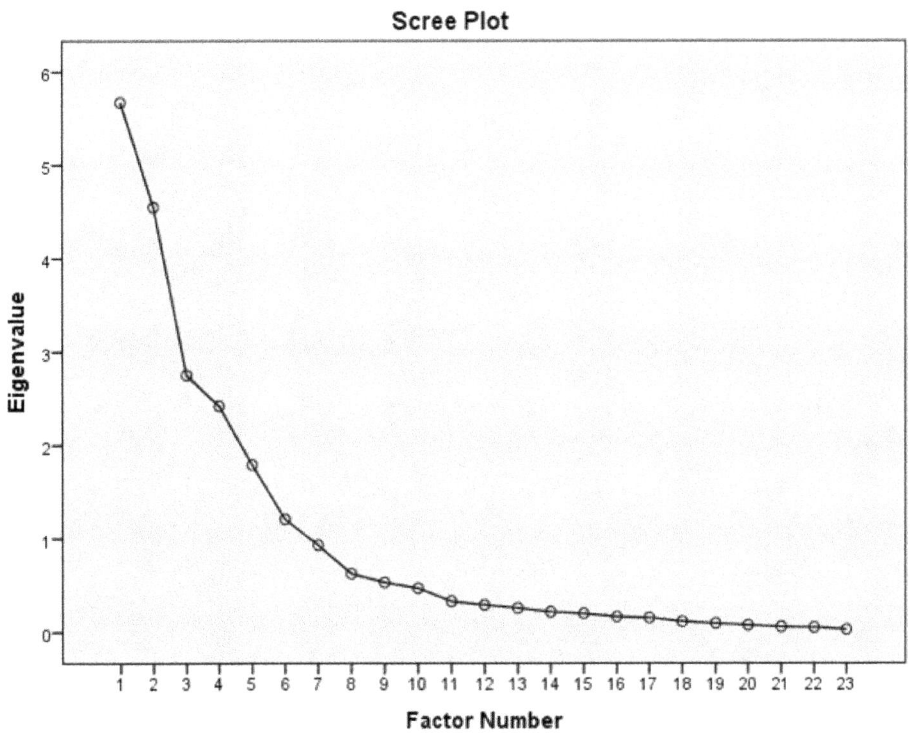

Chapter 4
Effects of Counselling Intervention on Career Transition Outcomes Among Students With ASD

ABSTRACT

This paper investigated the effects of a structured counselling intervention on the career transition process of students with autism spectrum disorders (SASD). The quantitative one-group pretest-posttest design was used, and eight adolescents with high-functioning autism were engaged to undergo a six-week counselling programme. Paired samples t-test results showed a statistically significant improvement between pretest and posttest, as well as a sustained improvement in the work readiness, vocational confidence, and independence in career planning among SASD.

BACKGROUND

The transition between education and employment is an important phase for students with autism spectrum disorders (SASD) (Schall et al., 2012; Wehman et al., 2014). Efficient career transition not only holds great importance in personal health and autonomy, but also enlivens society in terms of diversity in the workforce and economic roles (Tomlinson et al., 2018). However, SASD encounters poor outcomes in the areas of independence, occupation, and higher education (Wehman et al., 2014). These experiences require counselling interventions. Counselling intervention is a school-based professional practice designed to provide assistance

DOI: 10.4018/978-1-6684-7260-6.ch004

and guidance to individuals facing various psychological, emotional, or situational challenges (Fabris et al., 2010). Counselling intervention encompasses a structured process where a counsellor utilises specific skills to communicate effectively and build a therapeutic relationship with clients (Fabris et al., 2009, 2010). Career counselling interventions could be of great importance in closing these gaps, as well as enabling SASD to improve their critical work-readiness skills, increase their job confidence, find placements, and be engaged in vocational life over the long term. Contextually, counselling interventions refer to purposeful, theory-informed and ethically guided professional actions used by counselling professionals to support individuals in comprehending themselves, dealing with socioemotional and psychological concerns, and developing the confidence, skills and strategies needed to cope with life transitions and decisions. In the context of career transition, counselling interventions include activities such as emotional support, career guidance, skills development, decision-making facilitation, goal setting, problem solving, and strengthening self-efficacy. These interventions are grounded in established counselling and career development theories and are tailored to the individual's developmental stage, abilities, cultural context, and support needs, particularly for people with disability (Eseadi, 2023a; Eseadi, 2023b).

Career transition outcomes are the measurable and experiential results that occur following engagement in career transition processes and supports, including counselling interventions. These outcomes reflect how successfully an individual adapts to, navigates, and settles into a new career-related role, pathway or identity. These outcomes may be reflected in improved career clarity, increased confidence and readiness for work or further training, enhanced employability skills, emotional adjustment, sustained participation in education or employment, and overall life satisfaction (Eseadi & Diale, 2024; Diale & Eseadi, 2024; Hanif et al., 2017; Otu & Sefotho, 2024; Schutz & Carter, 2022). Career transition outcomes include both objective indicators, such as employment or training placement, and subjective indicators, such as perceived competence, well-being, and sense of purpose (Alwell & Cobb, 2009; Ma et al., 2020; Murray & Doren, 2013; Schutz & Carter, 2022; Sheftel, Lindstrom & McWhirter, 2014). In the present study, the dimensions of career transition outcomes examined include work readiness skills, job and vocational confidence, engagement in work-based learning experiences, placement success, sustained vocational involvement, preparedness for career-related challenges, and increased independence in career planning and decision making.

Work readiness skills interventions are organised programmes that aim to provide individuals, especially those who have disabilities such as autism spectrum disorder (ASD), with the required skills to be successful in the work environment. Such interventions are usually targeting both technical and non-technical (soft) skills, in order to enhance employability and job performance. The work readiness skills interventions play a paramount part in promoting the employment of SASD (Athamanah & Cushing, 2019a). Nevertheless, these skills are not well developed in the Nigerian educational and vocational environment (Bakare et al., 2019). Work readiness skills interventions in the context of career counselling aim at addressing these areas, giving students the tools and strategies to acquire the needed work readiness competencies. Some of the work readiness skills interventions include literacy-based behavioural intervention (LBBIs), which involves the use of pictures and behavioural rehearsal to implement job-related skills (Honsberger et al., 2019a), Peer-Mediated Interventions (PMI), which are designed for peers in the learning process (Athamanah & Cushing, 2019b), Constant Time Delay (CTD) and eCoaching, which entail real-time feedback and have been found helpful in improving vocational skills and social interactions (Horn et al., 2020), Direct Skills Teaching (DST), which deals with breaking skills into small units and is impactful for implementing soft skills abilities (Herrick et al., 2022) and Video-Based Intervention (VBIs), which deals with improving job performance and social communication skills (Munandar et al., 2020).

Empirical findings have established the significance of these work readiness skills interventions. For instance, a study has shown that LBBIs enhanced secondary school SASD accuracy in the work routine and maintained after the intervention (Honsberger et al., 2019b). Also, PMT has been found to enhance the independent work of all three SASD in occupational skills and communal interactions in secondary schools' work-based learning environment (Honsberger et al., 2019b). Similarly, CTD with eCoaching, which involves real-time feedback, has been found to be impactful in facilitation rapid skill acquisition and generalisation among SASD (Horn et al., 2020). The effectiveness of the DST has indicated the possibility of using the soft-skills training to instil the work-related conversational skills in job-seeking youths with ASD (Herrick et al., 2022). There is evidence of a potential gap in the implementation of counselling intervention programmes for SASD in Nigeria. Therefore, this study addressed how a structured counselling intervention can be useful in building work-readiness skills in SASD, and whether such an intervention can be useful to enhance the major skills needed for successful career transition. Vocational confidence intervention for SASD is another crucial variable of this study, which aims at the development of career self-efficacy, real-world skills, and supportive environments to facilitate the school-to-employment or school-to-higher-education transition (Taylor et al., 2012a). Vocational confidence is directly related to career self-efficacy, that is, students' belief in their capacity to explore, acquire and maintain a job or to continue their education. In the case of SASD, confidence can be boosted when they feel successful in work related to the real world, when provided with feedback, and when there is a good match of their strengths with the conditions of a job. This intervention's best application involves combining organised work placements, skills development and individualised counselling based on the potentials and needs of SASD (Di Rezze et al., 2023).

Some studies have shown the importance of intervention programmes aimed at boosting the vocational confidence of SASD. Some of these interventions include vocational rehabilitation (VR) interventions designed for occupation search, post, and on-the-job supports (Roux et al., 2021a). Others include Assistive Soft Skills and Employment Training (ASSET), a programme designed to enhance soft skills like communication, professionalism, and teamwork and has been impactful in social functioning, self-efficacy and adaptive behaviour of SASD (Connor et al., 2022). Job-Based Social Skills (JOBSS) is a 15-week intervention programme aimed at enhancing social-programmatic skills essential for employment (Gorenstein et al., 2020). Individual Placement and Support (IPS) is another intervention programme designed to enhance competitive employment of people with severe mental disorders (McLaren et al., 2017). These interventions are crucial for supporting transition-aged youth with ASD. In the literature, the term "transition-aged youth" refers to young people in the developmental period bridging late adolescence and early adulthood, during which they face significant educational, vocational, and psychosocial transitions that shape long-term well-being and independence (Chan et al., 2019; Khetarpal et al., 2022). Although definitions vary somewhat across disciplines and systems of care, the age range of approximately 15 to 25 years is frequently used (15–26 years in some mental health research) (*see* Chan et al., 2019; Khetarpal et al., 2022). This age range captures the developmental phase where individuals move from child- and youth-oriented systems (such as school or paediatric services) to adult-oriented systems (such as employment, postsecondary education, and adult healthcare). This life stage is characterised by a convergence of biological, psychological, social, and systemic transitions (Chan et al., 2019). Biologically, brain and executive-function maturation continue well into the early twenties. For example, research indicated that neurodevelopment, particularly in regions governing impulse control, planning, and decision-making, extends into young adulthood (Chan et al., 2019). Psychosocially, youth engage in identity formation, the exploration of intimate relationships, educational and vocational transitions, and increasing autonomy in living arrangements (Khetarpal et al., 2022). From a service systems perspective (in mental health or health care), transition-aged youth often face critical handoffs between child/adolescent-oriented systems and adult services. These handoffs may result in gaps, discontinuity, or mismatches in services because many adult-oriented systems are not configured for the specific developmental needs of 15-25-year-olds (Fegert et al., 2016). Thus, describing transition-aged youth as 15 to 25 years emphasises a developmental epoch characterised by significant change and vulnerability, that is, youth are moving from dependence toward independence, shifting social roles and responsibilities, and navigating complex educational/work and health-service transitions.

A prior study's findings show that the rate of employment among transition-aged SASD can be enhanced with a deliberate provision of employment-related services (Roux et al., 2021a). Another study found that SASD exposed to the ASSETS programme had significant improvement in social functioning, self-efficacy, and adaptive behaviour (Connor et al., 2022). JOBSS has been shown to be impactful in the improvement of social cognition, as well as successful in securing employment (Gorenstein et al., 2020). The IPS programme promoted individuals to achieve competitive jobs, increased autonomy, and general psychosocial benefits (McLaren et al., 2017). One of the most effective interventions to enhance career-transition outcomes among students with disabilities and SASD in particular is work-based learning experience (WBLEs) due to the fact that it offers real job exposure, skill practice and employer contact to the students prior to schooling (Bellman et al., 2014). Such experiences are always associated with increased likelihood of employment in future, improved qualities of employment and more focus on what to do after school (Griffiths et al., 2023). Work-based learning experiences that comprise internships and job shadowing are an important resource to SASD since they prepare students to enter the workforce (Chen et al., 2015a). Internships and job shadowing enable SASD to practice their skills in the real world, which is vital in their vocational development. In addition, paid employment at an early stage in high school can provide students with pertinent occupational, communicative, and interpersonal skills. According to a research study, it was found that around 24.4 per cent of adolescents with ASD reported having undergone some paid work experience in high school at least once in the last year (Qian et al., 2021).

Furthermore, hands-on experiences provide students with an understanding of the professional requirements and the workings of the workplace. Work-based learning interventions, supported by simulation-based training, are augmented reality (AR) and virtual reality (VR), which have been discovered to be useful among the trainees with autism, as they allow them to become more self-sufficient at work (Pagano et al., 2026). Also, work-based learning seeks to enhance the confidence needed in SASD to enable them to find work. Programmes that include intensive internship and work between school and adult services, such as Project SEARCH, have been proven to help youths with ASD earn competitive jobs (Wehman et al., 2013). PMIs are effective in improving vocational skills and social interactions (Athamanah & Cushing, 2019c). A combination of video modelling and feedback has been successful in the instruction of vocational social skills in the classroom, which can be applied to community-based work experience (McLucas & Gonçalves, 2025). Work-based learning can be helpful to a SASD when they receive counselling interventions. Such students tend to have difficulties with comprehending social norms and expectations in the workplace, which may cause reluctance to take opportunities beyond the comfort zone of the educational environment. This current research looked into the possibility of counselling interventions enhancing career transition outcomes in SASD.

Career-related tasks completion is also one of the indicators and predictors of career transition outcome for SASD, as it demonstrates the capacities of SASD to perform and generalise particular work skills required to secure a post-school job (Lee et al., 2022). Career-related task completion is generally described as the extent to which a student can complete particular job or pre-employment tasks autonomously, properly and steadily through tasks such as adhering to multi-step directions, using work instruments, matching productivity criteria, and switching activities (Lee et al., 2022). Some assessment tools have been designed to measure career task completions. These assessment tools include the Kitchen Task Assessment (KTA), which was created to assess executive, organisational, planning, and judgment abilities using a group of tasks performed in the kitchen, thus targeted at the population with neurocognitive disorders. This instrument can be scaled in other workplace situations to evaluate the accomplishment of work based on the same aspects of cognition (Baum, 2024). Another assessment tool for career-related tasks completion is a metric for assessing task implementation in the operating room (OR). This tool evaluates the accomplishment of major OR tasks with essential attention to safety and efficiency, and includes real-time observations and professional opinion to confirm tasks that can be modified to other tasks that involve career evaluation (Russ et al., 2013). Furthermore, task accuracy and independence focus on how correctly and independency students perform job-related steps (Russ et al., 2013). A higher independence score is linked with the probability of competitive continued employment (DeMatteo & Arter, 2015). Work style and adaptability measures how reliable, punctual, response to feedback and adjustment to feedback SASD display (Lee et al., 2022). Students who exhibit higher work style skills predict better employment quality and stability. Task initiation and transitions entail beginning tasks at the appropriate time and shifting between tasks without excessive support among SASD (Lee et al., 2022).

Unlike career-related tasks completion, secured placement is an outcome which implies that the SASD has gained a successful acquisition of a real job or a vocational/practicum placement in the community or a pertinent setting by the programme or school year conclusion (Roux et al., 2021b). Social integration and independence are other areas where getting a job is a measure of success for SASD, not just in the employment sector. The effective work placements of SASD are commonly linked to meticulous workplace preparation, focusing on the connection with their strengths and interests, and the development of work-related competency (Lee et al., 2019). Job search services, employment placement services, and on-the-job training are all employment-related services that significantly influence the likelihood of achieving successful employment outcomes within SASD (Roux et al., 2021b). However, these services are usually not delivered to SASD with equal intensity as to their peers, which means that there is a necessity to make the provision of such services more conscious. As a result, intervention models have been designed to ensure that SASD secure jobs. One of the promising interventions is the Self-Determined Career Design Model (SDCDM). This model has demonstrated statistically significant improvements in goal achievement and work performance among youths with ASD, which indicates its potential to improve transition outcomes (Dean et al., 2022). Moreover, Vocational Rehabilitation (VR) Services, which aim at gender-specific and tailored interventions, such as on-the-job assistance and job placement, help to enhance employment results. This intervention is more impactful when tailored towards the unique desires of SASD (Sung et al., 2015). Research studies further showed that virtual reality enabled job placements and offered on-the-job assistance to both sexes, but counselling, guidance, and job search help were especially beneficial to the male population (Sung et al., 2015). Similarly, another study found that participants who had been trained through the state-federal VR programme had a high tendency to attain competitive employment when compared to the participants who had not received such services (Kaya et al., 2016).

Similar to secured placement, prolonged engagement in work or vocational training interventions has a powerful, beneficial effect on career transition among students and young adults with ASD, particularly when the engagement is intensive, sustained and integrated in a real or realistic work environment (Taylor et al., 2014). The more extended engagement is associated with the increased employment rates, enhanced job stability, as well as the increase in behaviour and everyday living abilities (Taylor et al., 2012b). Continuing involvement helps students build a work history and networks with employers and service providers, which supports later job placement and advancement. Prolonged and sustained work or vocational training also enables repetition of specific and general skills (e.g., adherence to instructions, time management, and social interaction), to the extent that skills become more automatic and transferable to new environments. Some interventions for sustained involvement in work have been identified, which include VR, high-quality transition services for high-functioning SASD, and vocational skills training programmes (Lee & Carter, 2012a; Chen & Yakubova, 2023). Taylor et al. (2012b) revealed that youths with ASD exposed to intensive vocational training and supported employment studies have found very high competitive employment (approximately 90%) and high job maintenance 12 months post-training, compared with very low rates in control groups, which have not received such training. Another study revealed that vocational and work-related services (job coaching, work-based learning, employer-based programmes), offered before graduation, make individuals more likely to obtain paid work, to work more hours, and receive a higher wage in the first years after school exiting (Cimera et al., 2013).

Readiness to career challenges is a significant predictor of young adults' success in career transitions, as well as a predictor of successful career transition outcomes in SASD. Those youths and students better furnished to meet the demands of the real world will have a higher chance of employment, working more hours, retaining their employment, and reporting improved vocational adjustments (Westbrook et al., 2013). Career interventions focus on developing the skills, attitudes and confidence that enable SASD to manage the demands of real-world jobs, and these interventions have been linked to better results in career transition outcomes, which include increased employment rates, work readiness and independence (Fong et al., 2021). This is very crucial since studies by different researchers have revealed that individuals with ASD are linked to joblessness owing to difficulties in behaviour and socialisation, unlike failure to perform the duties bestowed upon them (Chen et al., 2015***b***; Frank et al., 2018). Individualised and strengths-based service, which entails tailoring transition services to the students' strengths and needs, can significantly enhance career outcomes, especially those with ASD (Lee & Carter, 2012b). In addition, providing SASD with early work experiences and promoting positive career development, as well as impactful collaboration, interagency involvement, encouraging self-determination, and independency can assist them in building the necessary potential for employment (Eastman et al., 2021a; Roberts, 2010). Vocational programmes also incorporate work skills courses, collaborating with different agencies, and building portfolios of students (Eastman et al., 2021b), and behavioural skills training that promotes instruction and individualised approaches in job interview skills (Kahng et al., 2023).

To enhance the career outcome of SASD, greater independent in career planning is needed. Greater independent in career planning entails that SASD actively participate in the self-directed process of learning about themselves, considering the options and making their own decisions about their future education and employment without depending on others instructions. It has a strong connection with self-determination ability, such as achieving personal goals, choice, problem-solving and self-advocacy (Tomaszewski et al., 2022). The higher the independent of daily living activities, the higher the vocational outcomes. This is an indication that encouraging independent in the daily activities of SASD can have a positive effect on their career transition (Taylor & Mailick, 2014). Self-monitoring, video modelling and individual work systems are some of the interventions that have also proven effective in enhancing independence as they transfer control, which is under continuous adult care, to other stimuli (Hume et al., 2009; Sreckovic et al., 2020). Similarly, the Boost-A programme, which is domiciled online, has shown preliminary evidence of promoting career outcomes, particularly in career exploration and transition-specific self-determination (Hatfield et al., 2017). These intervention programmes should be tailored towards individualised and strength-based support for SASD, focusing on their early work experiences and meaningful collaboration. This current study explored counselling interventions on SASD career transition outcomes.

RESEARCH OBJECTIVES

The main aim of this study was to investigate the effectiveness of a counselling intervention in promoting the career transition outcomes of SASD while also evaluating the reliability and agreement of counsellor and teacher ratings in assessing students' progress. The specific objectives are to:

1. To determine the changes in students' career transition outcome scores before and after counselling intervention, and across 3-month and 6-month follow-up assessments.
2. To assess the statistical significance of the differences between pretest, posttest, 3-month, and 6-month follow-up scores.
3. To evaluate the inter-rater reliability among counsellors in rating students' career transition outcomes using the Intraclass Correlation Coefficient.
4. To examine the inter-rater reliability among teachers in evaluating students' career transition progress using similar reliability indices.

RESEARCH QUESTIONS

1. What is the level of students' career transition outcomes before and after the counselling intervention, and at the 3-month and 6-month follow-up periods?
2. Are there statistically significant differences in career transition outcome scores between pretest and subsequent assessments following the counselling intervention?
3. What is the degree of inter-rater reliability among counsellors in assessing students' career transition outcomes?
4. What is the degree of inter-rater reliability among teachers in evaluating students' career transition outcomes?

THEORETICAL FRAMEWORK

This study is anchored on the theory of Social Cognitive Career Theory (SCCT) (Lent et al., 1999). This theory is useful in understanding how counselling interventions impact the career transition process of SASD. According to SCCT, self-efficacy beliefs, outcome expectations, and goal-setting behaviours influence career development, and there is a reciprocal interaction. In the case of SASD, where socio-communication challenges and low self-confidence in their vocational competencies tend to limit career path opportunities, SCCT provides a valuable solution to the issue of how counselling interventions may facilitate perceived competence (Lindley, 2005). According to the theory, when students engage in organised interventions, which include guiding practice in work-readiness, exposure to work-related tasks, and counsellor feedback, their self-efficacy will rise, and they will have more positive outcome prospects and proactively pursue career-related behaviour (Chan et al., 2018). In this way, enhanced work readiness, vocational confidence, readiness to challenges and independence in career planning can be regarded as behavioural reflections of enhanced SCCT processes.

POLICY FRAMEWORK

The relevance of Sustainable Development Goals (SDGs) to the career transition of SASD is amplified in Nigeria because of the national efforts to transform education, enhance access to vocation, and promote the involvement of persons with disabilities. Nigeria is a signatory to the 2030 SGD Agenda, but policy undertakings and practice still have been limited (Ilesanmi, 2016). SDG 4, which demands inclusive, equitable, and quality education, is especially important. The goals 4.3, 4.4, and 4.5 stress on boosting access to technical and vocational education, developing employability, and removing inequalities that impact students with disabilities, which includes SASD (Adekunle, 2021). These priorities are in line with the National Policy on Special Needs Education and the Discrimination against Persons with Disabilities (Prohibition) Act, which both require better access, accommodations, and skill development for young people with disabilities (Amucheazi & Nwankwo, 2020). Nigerian SASD still experience impediments in the form of insufficient diagnostic services, untrained educators, scarce career opportunities, and societal stigma (Karim et al., 2014a; Onyishi et al., 2025; Ihenagwam et al., 2024). Regarding employment, SDG 8 supports the goals of Nigeria to establish inclusive labour markets and decrease the unemployment of young people. This is applicable since young Nigerians with ASD are disproportionately being locked out of vocational programmes and paid work experience (Folorunso, 2025). Goals 8.5 and 8.6, which require productive labour of persons with disabilities and reduced youth disengagement, are essential in a nation where the unemployment rates are deemed to be high among the youths, including those with developmental disability cases (Oleribe & Taylor-Robinson, 2016). Although the economic diversification agenda in Nigeria aims at generating employment opportunities in technology, agriculture and manufacturing industries, inclusion of disability such as ASD in these sectors remains in its infancy and career transition counselling has not been a full systematic approach to school- or community-based programmes.

The incorporation of counselling interventions into the policy environment of Nigeria thus becomes a need. These interventions can act as a connector between SDG goals and the realities of SASD by reinforcing the employability skills, increasing vocational confidence, and offering a systematic way of accessing work-based learning and placements. Counselling-based transition programmes are a cost-effective, scalable approach to developing national commitments to inclusive education and decent work in a context that is characterised by limited infrastructure and resources. The interventions can be aligned with the SDG principles to provide Nigeria with a consistent policy direction to enhance the results of transitions, increase access to vocational services, and ensure the social and economic integration of SASD.

METHODOLOGY

Research Approach

This study followed the quantitative research approach to determine the effects of a counselling intervention on the career transition outcomes of SASD in Southeast Nigeria. For us, the quantitative research approach was suitable for this study because our interest was in examining measurable patterns of change across time and determining the statistical significance of differences across pretest, posttest, and follow-up assessments (Fischer et al., 2023). The approach allowed us to evaluate the effectiveness of the intervention through systematic procedures that generate numerical evidence. This quantitative approach guided variable operationalisation, data collection procedures, sampling, and analytic decisions. For instance, the data collection instruments were constructed with clear scoring protocols and rating options that made it possible to do statistical analysis. The counselling intervention was also delivered in a structured manner that enabled quantitative assessment. As such, the quantitative approach provided a strong methodological foundation for achieving the study objectives.

Research Paradigm

We underpinned this research study within the positivist research paradigm, which assumes that social phenomena can be ascertained objectively and knowledge can be created through empirical observation, quantitative measurement, and statistical analysis (Park et al., 2020). Within this paradigm, researchers maintain some level of distance from the participants, adopt standardised instruments, and apply procedures that allow results to be generalised or replicated. These expectations align well with the design of the present study.

Research Design

The study employed a quasi-experimental study design that incorporated a one-group pretest-posttest design, and in this case, we were able to determine the intervention effect of the counselling intervention on SASD in the same group at different time periods (Maggin, 2022). In this design, a single intact group participated in the intervention and was assessed at four intervals: pretest, posttest, three-month follow-up, and six-month follow-up. This design enabled us to observe changes that occurred after exposure to the intervention and to determine whether these changes were sustained over time.

The one-group pretest-posttest design was selected because random assignments to treatment and control groups were neither ethical nor feasible with SASD, who required support related to career transition. Providing the intervention to all eligible students helped us to ensure that no participant was denied a potentially beneficial counselling programme. The design also strengthened the study by allowing each participant to act as their own baseline comparator. By observing repeated measures within the same group, the design helped to control for individual differences in ability, developmental profiles, and prior exposure to career readiness experiences. Overall, this quasi-experimental design provided an appropriate methodological platform for evaluating the effectiveness of the counselling intervention and for analysing the stability of personal and behavioural changes across medium and longer-term follow-up assessments.

Study Area

The study was conducted in Anambra and Ebonyi States, situated in Southeast Nigeria. These states were selected for both contextual and pragmatic reasons. Anambra State is one of the most economically vibrant states in the region, with a growing number of inclusive secondary schools and vocational training centres that are gradually incorporating services for students with neurodevelopmental learning needs. Its school systems and vocational training agenda represent a setting where interventions for SASD are increasingly needed due to rising identification rates. Ebonyi State, on the other hand, is a rapidly developing state with an expanding education sector. Many schools and vocational training centres in the state have limited specialised support services for SASD, making it an important setting for examining the value of structured interventions.

From a geographical standpoint, Anambra is located in the central part of the Southeast region and is characterised by urban, semi-urban, and rural communities. This diversity allowed us to reach students from different backgrounds and schooling contexts. Ebonyi is located in the eastern part of the region, with a range of rural and peri-urban communities. This distribution enabled us to include participants who had limited exposure to formalised career transition services. Together, the two states provided a representative picture of the experiences of SASD in typical Southeast Nigerian educational settings. The selection of these states was further justified because both have witnessed an increase in advocacy for inclusive education and support for neurodivergent students. Conducting the study in these contexts allowed us to contribute evidence that can guide programme development in settings where the need for specialised counselling and transition support is becoming more pronounced. The states also offered logistical feasibility, as we worked with school and centre authorities who supported the delivery of the intervention and allowed our postgraduate research assistants to access the students.

Population and Sample

The population of interest comprised SASD who were enrolled in secondary schools and vocational training centres in Anambra and Ebonyi States, Nigeria. These students represent transition-aged youth (15-25 years), which is a group that often face challenges in career decision-making, job readiness, adaptation to new environments, and maintenance of vocational placements. Their inclusion was essential because the intervention was developed to strengthen their career transition outcomes. We used a multi-stage sampling procedure to select the sample. Multi-stage sampling was adopted because it allowed us to systematically narrow down the sampling frame from the state level to the student level while accounting for administrative boundaries and school classifications. At the first stage, two states were selected for the reasons discussed earlier. At the second stage, schools and vocational training centres within the states that had SASD were identified. At the third stage, schools and vocational training centres that agreed to collaborate were included. At the fourth stage, students who met the inclusion criteria were identified through school counsellors, teachers, and parents. Finally, students whose parents consented and who assented to the study were included.

This multi-stage technique was crucial for multiple reasons. First, the number of schools and vocational training centres that serve SASD in these states is limited, and the students are distributed across different school types and centres. Second, given the ethical requirements involved in working with SASD, it was essential to involve schools and families at multiple stages. Third, the technique helped manage logistical and administrative coordination across multiple sites.

A total of eight students were included in the intervention phase and participated in all four assessments: pretest, posttest, three-month follow-up, and six-month follow-up. Although the sample size is small, it is consistent with repeated measures intervention studies involving SASD, especially in contexts where specialised programmes are scarce. The student participants in this study were adolescents with high-functioning autism. These students possessed average to above-average cognitive abilities and were able to communicate verbally, follow instructions, and participate meaningfully in guided learning activities. They were able to engage with the counselling sessions, complete career-related tasks, and respond to the brief scale used in this study. Their functional learning abilities made them a suitable sample for a career transition counselling programme that required reflection, practice, and increasing levels of independence.

Data Collection Instruments

Data were collected using two self-developed instruments. The first was the Career Transition Outcome Scale–Student Rating (CTOS-SR), which was completed by the students at each assessment point. The second was the Career Transition Observation Scale, Teacher/Counsellor Rating (CTOS-T/CR), which was completed independently by teachers and counsellors who observed the students during the intervention.

Career Transition Outcome Scale – Student Rating (CTOS-SR)

The student version of the scale consisted of eight items designed to assess core aspects of career transition readiness (see Table 11). The items captured practical work readiness skills, confidence in applying for jobs or vocational programmes, completion of career-related tasks, participation in work-based learning experiences, securing placement, sustained involvement in work or training, preparedness for challenges, and independence in planning. The scale had a five-point Likert response format (Strongly Disagree to Strongly Agree). Higher scores reflected higher levels of career transition readiness. The scale demonstrated a Cronbach's alpha reliability coefficient of 0.70. This value indicates acceptable internal consistency for a short scale used with a neurodivergent population. The reliability scores if an item was deleted ranged from 0.53 to 0.76, suggesting that no single item significantly reduced the scale's reliability.

Career Transition Observation Scale – Teacher/ Counsellor Rating (CTOS-T/CR)

The teacher and counsellor ratings of career transition outcomes assessed similar domains but relied on behavioural observation rather than self-report. Each dimension was based on a 5-point scale, with descriptions ranging from no evidence of the behaviour to strong evidence of the behaviour (see Table 12). The scale was designed to capture observable progress across multiple counselling sessions and real-world tasks. The use of the teacher/counsellor rating scale was essential for examining inter-rater reliability. The reliability coefficients from ICC, Cohen's kappa, Fleiss's kappa, and Krippendorff's alpha showed moderate agreement across raters in this research study and reflected shared observations of student behaviour and progress.

Data Collection Procedures

Our data collection process followed a set of procedures. Before commencement, we sought and obtained formal authorisation from the participating schools and vocational training centres. We also secured the cooperation of class teachers, school counsellors, and parents who were responsible for SASD. Two trained postgraduate research assistants worked with us throughout the data collection period. They received a 3-day training on the intervention delivery, study objectives, administration of the scales, ethical protocols, and procedures for managing sensitive information from us. Their involvement was necessary because of the intensive nature of the repeated assessments and the need for consistent administration.

At the pretest stage, students completed the self-rating scale under the guidance of our assistants. Teachers and counsellors also completed their initial observational ratings. After the pretest, the career transition counselling intervention commenced. The intervention comprised activities designed to strengthen the work readiness, career planning abilities, and vocational confidence of SASD. The programme was designed to increase independence in career planning, improve communication and adaptability, and support sustained involvement in work or vocational activities. The intervention used direct instruction, modelling, guided practice, and role play to help students develop key transition-related skills. Students were supported to complete career tasks, participate in simple work-based activities, explore vocational interests, and build confidence in handling workplace concerns. Each session commenced with a short review of prior tasks, followed by step-by-step intervention activities, practical exercises, and guided discussions. This skills-based approach helped the students to gradually strengthen their behaviours and knowledge required for a successful career transition. The intervention continued for six weeks. The career transition counselling intervention was delivered by the two postgraduate research assistants who had prior training in special needs education and educational psychology. Each assistant had accumulated up to five years of practical experience working with neurodivergent students and youths in school and community settings. The sessions were implemented under the observation of the teachers and school counsellors, who monitored the process and ensured that the delivery aligned with the support plans within the schools and vocational training centres. At the posttest stage, students again completed the self-rating scale, and teachers and counsellors rated their observed behaviours. The 3-month and 6-month follow-ups took a similar procedure for completing the rating scales. Uniformity in the administration process was ensured by the use of the same assistants, the administration of instruments in quiet classrooms within the school/centre premises, and the use of the same briefing scripts. All completed instruments were checked for accuracy, coded and entered into secure electronic files. The data were then processed for analysis.

Data Analysis Procedure

Data analysis process was completed using statistical software (IBM SPSS) that enabled the computation of descriptive statistics, paired sample t tests, and inter-rater reliability indices. The analysis started with data cleaning, during which we checked for missing values and coding errors. Once the dataset was verified, we computed mean scores with the standard deviations and coefficients of variation for each measurement point. To analyse how the counselling intervention affected the scores of students, we conducted paired samples t-tests in order to compare the student scores pretest with those at the posttest and three months and six months follow-up. Cohen's d was used to calculate the effects of this study in order to determine the magnitude of the change. To provide answers to the research questions connected with the inter-rater reliability, we have calculated the intraclass correlation coefficients according to a one-way random effects model. This model was appropriate because the raters represented a sample of possible professionals who could evaluate student performance. Cohen's kappa statistics were computed for pairwise comparisons between raters, while Fleiss's kappa was used to assess overall agreement among the group of raters. Krippendorff's alpha was also calculated because it is suitable for nominal and ordinal data and accommodates missing values. Interpretations of all reliability coefficients were based on established benchmarks, including those proposed by Shrout and Fleiss (1979) for ICC and by Landis and Koch (1977) for kappa values. These analyses provided a holistic view of the consistency and dependability of the teacher and counsellor ratings.

Ethical Considerations

The Faculty of Education Research Ethics Committee of the University of Johannesburg gave ethical approval to this project (Sem 2-2020-057). Following this ethical clearance, we complied with the ethical requirements for carrying out the study with human participants, especially vulnerable groups (SASD). The parents and guardians of these students provided written informed consent. The students provided assent. Participants were informed of the aims of the study, the nature of the counselling intervention, the procedures involved, and their right to withdraw at any time without repercussion. All information obtained from the participants was kept anonymous and stored securely. Identifying details were avoided, and coded identifiers were used for analysis. The involvement of the postgraduate research assistants was managed ethically. They signed confidentiality agreements and received instructions on maintaining privacy and respecting the dignity of the students, teachers and counsellors. All counselling sessions and data collection procedures were conducted in ways that ensured comfort, safety, and respect for the research participants.

RESULTS

Table 1. Descriptive statistics for student sample (SASD)

	N	Mean	SD	SE	Coefficient of variation
CTOS_SRT	**8**	**11.875**	**1.727**	**0.611**	**0.145**
CTOS_SRPT	8	28.625	4.373	1.546	0.153
CTOS_SRFT	8	27.750	2.964	1.048	0.107
CTOS_SRFFT	8	28.125	2.167	0.766	0.077

Career Transition Outcome Scale (CTOS-SR) – Student Rating. CTOS_SRT Total for Pretest. CTOS_SRPT=Total for Posttest. CTOS_SRFT=Total for 3 months Follow-up. CTOS_SRFFT= Total for 6 months follow-up

In Table 1, we show the descriptive statistics for the Career Transition Outcome Scale-Student Rating (CTOS-SR) across four time points: pretest (CTOS_SRT), posttest (CTOS_SRPT), three-month follow-up (CTOS_SRFT), and six-month follow-up (CTOS_SRFFT). The results show clear evidence of progressive improvement in students' career transition outcomes following the counselling intervention. At pretest, the SASD had a mean of 11.88 (SD = 1.73), which demonstrates a low initial level of career transition readiness before the intervention exposure. Following the counselling sessions, the posttest mean increased sharply to 28.63 (SD = 4.37), reflecting substantial gains in career-related self-understanding, planning, and confidence. As can be seen, the three-month follow-up mean of 27.75 (SD = 2.96) indicated a stable retention of intervention gains, whereas the six-month follow-up mean of 28.13 (SD = 2.17) confirmed the persistence of positive outcomes over time. As per our results, the relatively small standard errors (SE range = 0.61-1.55) and low coefficients of variation (CV range = 0.08-0.15) across the four measurements demonstrate consistency and reliability in students' self-ratings. The results have shown that the counselling intervention was effective and maintained over the follow-up assessments. The slight variation between posttest and later follow-ups may point to the natural adjustment effects as students applied learned coping and planning strategies in real-world contexts.

Table 2. Paired samples t-test for student sample (SASD)

Measure 1		Measure 2	T	df	p	Cohen's d	SE Cohen's d
CTOS_SRT	-	CTOS_SRPT	-10.117	7	< .001	-3.577	1.352
CTOS_SRT	-	CTOS_SRFT	-13.376	7	< .001	-4.729	1.702
CTOS_SRT	-	CTOS_SRFFT	-13.813	7	< .001	-4.884	2.167
CTOS_SRPT	-	CTOS_SRFT	0.431	7	0.679	0.152	0.550
CTOS_SRPT	-	CTOS_SRFFT	0.378	7	0.717	0.134	0.349
CTOS_SRFT	-	CTOS_SRFFT	-0.299	7	0.773	-0.106	0.483

Career Transition Outcome Scale (CTOS-SR) – Student Rating. CTOS_SRT Total for Pretest. CTOS_SRPT=Total for Posttest. CTOS_SRFT=Total for 3 months Follow-up. CTOS_SRFFT= Total for 6 months follow-up

In Table 2, the paired samples t-test results aimed at comparing mean scores across the different measurement periods are shown. There was statistical evidence that the counselling intervention significantly improved students' career transition outcomes. We also observed a significant mean difference between the pretest and posttest scores ($t(7) = -10.12$, $p < .001$, Cohen's $d = -3.58$), indicating a large practical effect of the counselling sessions on enhancing students' readiness for transition. The improvement continued to be statistically significant when comparing the pretest with the three-month follow-up ($t(7) = -13.38$, $p < .001$, Cohen's $d = -4.73$) and the six-month follow-up ($t(7) = -13.81$, $p < .001$, Cohen's $d = -4.88$). These very large effect sizes suggest a powerful and sustained impact of the intervention on participants' transition-related knowledge, self-efficacy, and adaptability. Comparisons among the posttest, three-month, and six-month follow-ups were not statistically significant ($p > .05$). Specifically, the posttest and three-month follow-up ($t(7) = 0.43$, $p = .68$) and posttest and six-month follow-up ($t(7) = 0.38$, $p = .72$) were not significant. The stability implies that once students achieved improvement at posttest, their skills and attitudes remained relatively constant through subsequent months.

Table 3. Intraclass correlation rater agreement for counsellors

Type	PE	L 95% CI	U 95% CI
ICC1,1	**0.631**	**0.447**	**0.782**

Note: PE=Point Estimate; L=Lower; U=Upper

Table 3 illustrates the intraclass correlation coefficient (ICC) of the ratings given by counsellors of the outcomes in career transitions among students. ICC(1, 1) point estimate was found to be 0.63 with a confidence interval of 0.45 to 0.78. According to the results by Shrout and Fleiss (1979), this figure indicates a moderate level of consistency between the three counsellors. In terms of the lower bound of the confidence interval, agreement occasionally fell below moderate levels, while the upper bound indicates that at times the counsellors demonstrated stronger consistency. Overall, Table 3 suggests that the counsellors shared a reasonable level of agreement in their interpretation of the students' career transition behaviours.

Table 4. Cohen's Kappa rater agreement for counsellors

			95% CI	
Ratings	**kappa**	**SE**	**L**	**U**
Average kappa	**0.484**			
Counselor1 - Counselor2	0.350	0.260	-0.161	0.861
Counselor1 - Counselor3	0.253	0.251	-0.238	0.744
Counselor2 - Counselor3	0.849	0.142	0.570	1.000

			95% CI	
Ratings	FK	SE	L	U
Counselor1	0.541	0.160	0.227	0.855
Counselor2	0.423	0.160	0.109	0.737
Counselor3	0.528	0.160	0.214	0.842

Note. FK=Fleiss Kappa

In Table 5, we showed Fleiss's kappa values on the overall agreement among multiple raters. The values, which ranged from 0.42 to 0.54, suggest moderate agreement across counsellors. Counsellor 1 showed the highest level of agreement (kappa = 0.54), while Counsellor 2 showed slightly lower consistency (kappa = 0.42). These findings indicate that, when considered collectively, counsellors demonstrated moderate reliability in their assessments of students' career transition outcomes.

Table 5. Krippendorff's alpha rater agreement for counsellors

			95% CI	
Method	**K.A**	**SE**	**L**	**U**
Nominal	**0.497**	**0.195**	**0.062**	**0.830**

Note. KA=Krippendorff's alpha

Table 5 analyses Krippendorff alpha, which offers a more flexible measure of agreement across raters. The alpha value of 0.50 reflects moderate agreement among counsellors. The confidence interval, which ranges from 0.06 to 0.83, shows that agreement varied widely across rating categories. Although the point estimate supports moderate reliability, the wider interval implies that some items generated difficulty in achieving consistent ratings. Overall, the results show that counsellors demonstrated a moderate level of shared judgement when evaluating students' transition outcomes.

Table 6. Intraclass correlation rater agreement for teachers

Type	Point Estimate	Lower 95% CI	Upper 95% CI
ICC1,1	**0.631**	**0.447**	**0.782**

Note. 3 raters/measurements. ICC type as referenced by Shrout & Fleiss (1979).

Table 6 shows ICC values for teachers, with a point estimate of 0.63 and a confidence interval from 0.45 to 0.78. The results suggest a moderate level of agreement among teachers. The moderate agreement reflects a common understanding of the scale criteria used to rate career transition outcomes. The similarity between teachers' and counsellors' ICC findings suggests that both groups generally applied comparable levels of consistency in evaluating student behaviour and performance.

Table 7. Cohen's kappa rater agreement for teachers

		95% CI	
Ratings	**Kappa**	**SE**	**L**	**U**
Average kappa	**0.470**			
Teacher1 - Teacher2	0.342	0.196	-0.042	0.727
Teacher1 - Teacher3	0.694	0.149	0.402	0.987
Teacher2 - Teacher3	0.373	0.162	0.056	0.689

Note. 3 raters/measurements. Confidence intervals are asymptotic.

Table 7 shows pairwise Cohen's kappa results for the teachers. The average kappa value was 0.47, indicating moderate agreement. As can be seen, the agreement between Teacher 1 and Teacher 2 was 0.34, suggesting fair to moderate agreement, whereas the agreement between Teacher 1 and Teacher 3 was higher at 0.69, suggesting substantial shared judgment. Teacher 2 and Teacher 3 demonstrated moderate agreeent (kappa = 0.37). These results show that, similar to counsellors, teacher agreement varied across pairs, with some pairings demonstrating stronger alignment.

Table 8. Fleiss' kappa rater agreement for teachers

			95% CI	
Ratings	F K	SE	L	U
Teacher1	0.455	0.144	0.172	0.738
Teacher2	0.395	0.144	0.112	0.678
Teacher3	0.577	0.144	0.294	0.860

Note. 3 raters/measurements. Confidence intervals are asymptotic.

Table 8 revealed the Fleiss kappa results, with values ranging from 0.39 to 0.58, indicating moderate agreement. Teacher 3 demonstrated the highest agreement (kappa = 0.58), whereas Teacher 2 showed lower consistency (kappa = 0.39). This result suggests that while teachers generally agreed on the application of the rating scale, some variation in interpretation persisted.

Table 9. Krippendorff's alpha rater agreement for teachers

			95% CI	
Method	**Krippendorff's alpha**	**SE**	**Lower**	**Upper**
Nominal	**0.479**	**0.132**	**0.206**	**0.722**

Note. 3 raters/measurements.

Table 9 shows the Krippendorff alpha for teacher ratings. The alpha value of 0.48, with a confidence interval from 0.21 to 0.72, reflects moderate agreement. Although the point estimate is consistent with the other reliability measures, the confidence interval indicates that teachers' agreement was not uniform across all items. Nevertheless, the results also suggest that teachers shared a common interpretation of the students' performance on most of the assessed indicators.

DISCUSSION

In response to the level of students' career transition outcomes before and after the counselling intervention, this study established that the counselling intervention significantly affected the career transition outcomes of SASD. The research results of this study have a great implication on the perceptive awareness of career transition pathways among SASD in Nigeria. The significant and continued positive shift in career transition rates after the counselling intervention points to the fact that the developmental trajectories of SASD in the Nigerian educational environment can be responsibly changed by means of the structured, skill-based, and supportive guidance. As there is a lack of specialised transition programmes, as well as emphasis on employability skills in most Nigerian special and inclusive schools, the scale of the impact of psychological interventions is remarkable (Karim et al., 2014b; Onyishi et al., 2025).

The significant improvements from pretest to posttest, at the 3-month mark, and even after six months, indicate that with appropriate counselling intervention, SASD are capable of responding with strength to the intervention, even in resource-limited contexts. This concurs with prior research in terms of SASD responding positively to explicit instruction, routine, modelling, and repetitive practice (Güleç-Aslan, 2013; Sánchez-Blanchart et al., 2019). In Nigeria, however, no such interventions are available mainly because of the lack of trained counsellors, teacher preparation that is specific to SASD, and little infrastructural support to foster transition (Onyishi et al., 2025; Odunsi et al., 2017a). This finding aligned with the tenet of SCCT, which states that increased self-efficacy leads to greater career motivation, improved expectations of outcome and improved involvement in transition behaviours (Adachi, 2004). Consistency of scores in the study also justifies SCCT since it confirms that once students are empowered through increased self-efficacy, they maintain behaviours that enhance career preparedness, independence and strength. That is, the intervention triggered the processes which SCCT lays emphasis on, that is, belief in ability, belief in the worth of effort, and long-lasting engagement in behaviour (Lent & Brown, 2013; Wendling & Sagas, 2020).

The study revealed that the counselling intervention generated a promising effect on the readiness of SASD for career transition. This is evidenced by the fact that there were no significant differences between the follow-up assessments, which means that improvement was ensured once realised at the posttest. This congrieunt with the reports of David et al. (2022) who revealed that career guidance intervention played a significant role in enhancing the knowledge and skills of the students relevant to their career decisions. Similarly, the finding was in line with another report that found PMI encouraged an increase in the level of autonomous engagement in vocational skills and social interactions in the case of SASD (Athamanah & Cushing, 2019). The effect sizes also highlight the significance of skill-based counselling in situations where students do not often receive systematic counselling on work preparedness, vocation exploration or workplace behaviours. The SASD in Nigeria generally do not face occupational assessment, job shadowing, or supported employment services (Hill et al., 2024). Therefore, the intervention was filling a gap that already existed, as the students were provided with the underlying competencies of communication, adaptability, organisation, and self-efficacy that it takes to navigate the labour market needs.

The results of the inter-rater reliability of counsellors are also useful in offering a perception of the extent to which the Nigerian counsellors determine the success in career transition of SASD. This study revealed a moderate level of agreement, which indicates that there was a shared understanding by counsellors in the constructs tested, which is positive because there is limited specialised training in transition in Nigeria (Ryan et al., 2023). This trend is indicative of the potential and constraints of the counselling practice in the Nigerian academic setting, specifically in special needs and transition services (Aluede et al., 2017, Nwokolo, 2023). Many schools have counsellors working with neurodivergent SASD, but do not have general guidelines to follow when assessing them, and do not have the opportunity to develop professionally on evidence-based transition frameworks (Aluede et al., 2017). The study supported the report that stated that reliability was varying in the various domains of the milestone assessment, which were moderate (Montallana et al., 2019). The findings of this study are in agreement with the findings of Zander et al. (2017), who revealed a moderate inter-rater reliability among clinicians' diagnoses of Autism Diagnostic Interview-Revised (ADI-R). The findings of this study support the reports of Odunsi et al. (2017b), who noted that Nigerian teachers demonstrated moderate knowledge of ASD. The finding is equally aligned with a previous study, which revealed that teachers had above-average and uniform knowledge of transitional skills (Almughyiri, 2024). In general, these findings show that with deliberate, systematic counselling support, SASD can successfully make significant and sustainable progress in career readiness. There is a need to enhance professional capacity, standardise assessment practice and clarify modalities for career transition planning in the Nigerian educational and disability policy frameworks.

Despite the fact that the study produced useful evidence, there are a number of limitations that should be noted. First, only eight students were used in the study. Although this level of sample is not abnormal in studies of intensive intervention in SASD, particularly those with restricted access to specialised services, it limits the applicability of the results to other groups of students. The limited number of students also restricted the scope of the analysis of student attributes, including potential moderators of the intervention results. Second, the one-group pretest-posttest quasi-experimental design was not accompanied by a control group. Such a lack of a comparison group does not allow isolating the counselling intervention as the only cause of the noticed improvements. Even though the cause and effect could be established, considering the repeated measurements with time, the chances of maturation effect, outside factors, or normal developmental course could not be completely excluded. Third, the inter-rater reliability results revealed moderate and unstable consistency between counsellors and teachers. The rating pattern was likely to be affected by differences in training, interpretation skills and familiarity with ASD. Fourth, the research was restricted geographically to the states of Anambra and Ebonyi. The two states are typical representatives of the situational context of Southeast Nigeria; however, they are not representative of the entire culture, educational, and infrastructural diversity that exists in Nigeria. The results are, therefore, not likely to be representative of the experiences of the SASD in other places where the school resources, teacher training, or community support may vary. Lastly, the six-month follow up which despite being handy in the evaluation of the medium-term retention of skills, does not give a full picture of the long-term career transition results that would include continuous employment, attendance in vocational programmes or adjustment in the workplace. Research studies in the future should include an extended duration of follow-up and more diverse samples to gain more insight into long-term effects.

CONCLUSION

This study has shown that a counselling intervention approach would play a significant and long-term positive role in enhancing the career transition among SASD. The recorded improvements between pretest and posttest results and the sustainability of the gains at both three and six-month follow-ups testify to the fact that SASD can be taught and facilitated to learn the requisite work readiness skills, vocational confidence, and career planning skills when given clear instructions and facilitation. The effects are especially significant in the context of Nigeria, where specialised transition services are few and where SASD are often confronted by factors associated with a lack of teacher preparation, insufficient exposure to vocation, and the enduring societal beliefs about their potential. The research study adds to an increasing collection of literature which advocates the idea of structured, skill-based interventions which could facilitate the successful integration of neurodivergent learners into vocational tracks.

REFERENCES

Adachi, T. (2004). Career self-efficacy, career outcome expectations and vocational interests among Japanese university students. *Psychological Reports, 95*(1), 89–100. DOI: 10.2466/pr0.95.1.89-100 PMID: 15460362

Adekunle, A. N. (2021). United Nations sustainable development goal 4: Exploring inclusive education of students with developmental disabilities in Lagos State, Nigeria [University of British Columbia]. DOI: 10.14288/1.0406184

Almughyiri, S. (2024). Saudi teachers 'knowledge and implementation of transitional skills and transition planning for students with autism spectrum disorder in Saudi Arabia. *International Journal of Developmental Disabilities*. Advance online publication. DOI: 10.1080/20473869.2024.2327783 PMID: 41624035

Aluede, O., Iyamu, F., Adubale, A., & Oramah, E. U. (2017). Policy, Capacity Building and School-Based Counselling in Nigeria. In Carey, J. C., Harris, B., Lee, S. M., & Aluede, O. (Eds.), *International Handbook for Policy Research on School-Based Counseling* (pp. 239–253). Springer International Publishing., DOI: 10.1007/978-3-319-58179-8_16

Alwell, M., & Cobb, B. (2009). Functional life skills curricular interventions for youth with disabilities: A systematic review. *Career Development for Exceptional Individuals, 32*(2), 82–93. DOI: 10.1177/0885728809336656

Amucheazi, C., & Nwankwo, C. M. (2020). Accessibility to infrastructure and disability rights in Nigeria: An analysis of the potential of the discrimination against persons with disability (prohibition) act 2018. *Commonwealth Law Bulletin, 46*(4), 689–710. DOI: 10.1080/03050718.2020.1781674

Athamanah, L. S., & Cushing, L. S. (2019a). Implementing a peer-mediated intervention in a work-based learning setting for students with autism spectrum disorders. *Education and Training in Autism and Developmental Disabilities, 54*(2), 196–210. DOI: 10.1177/215416471905400209

Athamanah, L. S., & Cushing, L. S. (2019b). Implementing a peer-mediated intervention in a work-based learning setting for students with autism spectrum disorders. *Education and Training in Autism and Developmental Disabilities, 54*(2), 196–210. DOI: 10.1177/215416471905400209

Athamanah, L. S., & Cushing, L. S. (2019c). Implementing a peer-mediated intervention in a work-based learning setting for students with autism spectrum disorders. *Education and Training in Autism and Developmental Disabilities, 54*(2), 196–210. DOI: 10.1177/215416471905400209

Bakare, M. O., Taiwo, O. G., Bello-Mojeed, M. A., & Munir, K. M. (2019). Autism spectrum disorders in Nigeria: A scoping review of literature and opinion on future research and social policy directions. *Journal of Health Care for the Poor and Underserved, 30*(3), 899–909. DOI: 10.1353/hpu.2019.0063 PMID: 31422978

Baum, C. (2024). KITCHEN TASK ASSESSMENT (KTA). In Bortnick, K. (Ed.), *Occupational Therapy Assessments for Older Adults: 100 Instruments for Measuring Occupational Performance* (pp. 250–251). Taylor and Francis., DOI: 10.4324/9781003525288-103

Bellman, S., Burgstahler, S., & Ladner, R. (2014). Work-based learning experiences help students with disabilities transition to careers: A case study of University of Washington projects. *Work (Reading, Mass.), 48*(3), 399–405. DOI: 10.3233/WOR-131780 PMID: 24284672

Chan, C.-C., Chen, S.-C., Lin, Y.-W., Liao, T.-Y., & Lin, Y.-E. (2018). Social Cognitive Perspective on Factors Influencing Taiwanese Sport Management Students' Career Intentions. *Journal of Career Development, 45*(3), 239–252. DOI: 10.1177/0894845316681643

Chan, V., Moore, J., Derenne, J., & Fuchs, D. C. (2019). Transitional age youth and college mental health. *Child and Adolescent Psychiatric Clinics of North America, 28*(3), 363–375. DOI: 10.1016/j.chc.2019.02.008 PMID: 31076114

Chen, B. B., & Yakubova, G. (2023). Evaluating the Effects of Video-Based Intervention to Teach Vocational Skills to Transition-Age Youth with Autism Spectrum Disorder: An Evidence-Based Systematic Review. *Review Journal of Autism and Developmental Disorders, 10*(1), 22–37. DOI: 10.1007/s40489-021-00282-7

Chen, J. L., Leader, G., Sung, C., & Leahy, M. (2015a). Trends in Employment for Individuals with Autism Spectrum Disorder: A Review of the Research Literature. *Review Journal of Autism and Developmental Disorders, 2*(2), 115–127. DOI: 10.1007/s40489-014-0041-6

Chen, J. L., Leader, G., Sung, C., & Leahy, M. (2015b). Trends in Employment for Individuals with Autism Spectrum Disorder: A Review of the Research Literature. *Review Journal of Autism and Developmental Disorders, 2*(2), 115–127. DOI: 10.1007/s40489-014-0041-6

Cimera, R. E., Burgess, S., & Wiley, A. (2013). Does Providing Transition Services Early Enable Students with ASD to Achieve Better Vocational Outcomes as Adults? *Research and Practice for Persons with Severe Disabilities : the Journal of TASH, 38*(2), 88–93. DOI: 10.2511/027494813807714474

Connor, A., Fabrizi, S. E., Nasamran, A., & Sung, C. (2022). Near-Peer Facilitation of a Soft Skills Program for Young Adults With Autism. *The American Journal of Occupational Therapy*, *76*(4), 7604345020. Advance online publication. DOI: 10.5014/ajot.2022.048207 PMID: 35759360

David, L. T., Tru a, C., Cazan, A.-M., Albisser, S., & Keller-Schneider, M. (2022). Exploring the impact of a career guidance intervention program in schools: Effects on knowledge and skills as self-assessed by students. *Current Psychology (New Brunswick, N.J.)*, *41*(7), 4545–4556. DOI: 10.1007/s12144-020-00973-0

Dean, E. E., Hagiwara, M., Shogren, K. A., Wehmeyer, M. L., & Shrum, J. (2022). Promoting Career Design in Youth and Young Adults with ASD: A Feasibility Study. *Journal of Autism and Developmental Disorders*, *52*(6), 2689–2700. DOI: 10.1007/s10803-021-05146-x PMID: 34184143

DeMatteo, F., & Arter, P. S. (2015). When Job Skills Are Not Enough: Transitioning Young Adults with Autism Spectrum Disorder. *Electronic Journal for Inclusive Education*, *3*(3), 6.

Di Rezze, B., O'Connor, I., Georgiades, S., Brennan, R., Honeyman, S., DiFazio, A., Hall, G. B., Chan, L., Steele, R., Fallowfield, E., & Bennett, T. (2023). The Development and Evaluation of a Cross-Context Employment Program for Autistic Adolescents. *Autism in Adulthood: Challenges and Management*, *5*(4), 457–467. DOI: 10.1089/aut.2022.0010 PMID: 38116048

Diale, B. M., & Eseadi, C. (2024). *Perspectives on Career Transitioning of Students with Attention Deficit Hyperactivity Disorder (ADHD)*. IGI Global., DOI: 10.4018/979-8-3693-2635-0

Eastman, K., Zahn, G., Ahnupkana, W., & Havumaki, B. (2021a). Small Town Transition Services Model: Postsecondary Planning for Students With Autism Spectrum Disorder. *Rural Special Education Quarterly*, *40*(3), 157–166. DOI: 10.1177/87568705211027978

Eastman, K., Zahn, G., Ahnupkana, W., & Havumaki, B. (2021b). Small Town Transition Services Model: Postsecondary Planning for Students With Autism Spectrum Disorder. *Rural Special Education Quarterly*, *40*(3), 157–166. DOI: 10.1177/87568705211027978

Eseadi, C. (2023a). Assessing Theories and Strategies Regarding Career Transition for Students with Visual Impairments. *Didaktika: Jurnal Kependidikan*, *12*(4), 803–818.

Eseadi, C. (2023b). Interventions for Supporting Career Transition among Students with Visual Impairments. *Psikoislamika: Jurnal Psikologi dan Psikologi Islam,* 20(2), 698-715.

Eseadi, C., & Diale, B. M. (2024). *Perspectives on Career Transitioning of Students with Hearing Impairments.* IGI Global., DOI: 10.4018/979-8-3693-2631-2

Fabris, C., Coscia, A., Bertino, E., Prete, M., Occhi, L., Giuliani, F., & Quadrino, S. (2009). Counselling in Neonatal Intensive Care Unit (NICU). *Early Human Development, 85*(10, SUPPL.), S47–S48. DOI: 10.1016/j.earlhumdev.2009.08.014 PMID: 19833463

Fabris, C., Coscia, A., Tonetto, P., Bertino, E., & Quadrino, S. (2010). Counselling in neonatal intensive care unit. *Minerva Pediatrica, 62*(3, Suppl 1), 109–111. PMID: 21089730

Fegert, J. M., Hauth, I., Banaschewski, T., & Freyberger, H. J. (2016, June 23). Transition From Adolescence to Adulthood: The Challenges to Establish "Transition Psychiatry.". In *Key Issues Paper by DGKJP and DGPPN.* https://www.escap.eu/events/past-escap-congresses/geneva/duplicate-of-madrid-keynote-and-symposiums/transitions-from-adolescence-to-adulthood-key-issue-paper

Fischer, H. E., Boone, W. J., & Neumann, K. (2023). Quantitative Research Designs and Approaches. In *Handbook of Research on Science Education.* Routledge. DOI: 10.4324/9780367855758-3

Folorunso, A. D. (2025). *Autism Spectrum Disorder Among Nigerian Children Ages 2-17: Prevalence, Awareness, Advocacy and Legislative Action Scoping Review. Research Square.* DOI: 10.21203/rs.3.rs-6735926/v1

Fong, C. J., Taylor, J., Berdyyeva, A., McClelland, A. M., Murphy, K. M., & Westbrook, J. D. (2021). Interventions for improving employment outcomes for persons with autism spectrum disorders: A systematic review update. *Campbell Systematic Reviews, 17*(3), e1185. DOI: 10.1002/cl2.1185 PMID: 37052419

Frank, F., Jablotschkin, M., Arthen, T., Riedel, A., Fangmeier, T., Hölzel, L. P., & Tebartz van Elst, L. (2018). Education and employment status of adults with autism spectrum disorders in Germany – a cross-sectional-survey. *BMC Psychiatry, 18*(1), 75. DOI: 10.1186/s12888-018-1645-7 PMID: 29580218

Gorenstein, M., Giserman-Kiss, I., Feldman, E., Isenstein, E. L., Donnelly, L., Wang, A. T., & Foss-Feig, J. H. (2020). Brief Report: A Job-Based Social Skills Program (JOBSS) for Adults with Autism Spectrum Disorder: A Pilot Randomized Controlled Trial. *Journal of Autism and Developmental Disorders*, *50*(12), 4527–4534. DOI: 10.1007/s10803-020-04482-8 PMID: 32297122

Griffiths, A. J., Hurley-Hanson, A. E., Giannantonio, C. M., Hyde, K., Linstead, E., Wiegand, R., & Brady, J. (2023). Enhancing employment outcomes for autistic youth: Using machine learning to identify strategies for success. *Journal of Vocational Rehabilitation*, *59*(2), 153–168. DOI: 10.3233/JVR-230034

Güleç-Aslan, Y. (2013). A training programme for a teacher working with a student with ASD: An action research. *Educational Sciences: Theory & Practice*, *13*(4), 2229–2246. DOI: 10.12738/estp.2013.4.1738

Hanif, S., Peters, H., McDougall, C., & Lindsay, S. (2017). A systematic review of vocational interventions for youth with physical disabilities. *Factors in studying employment for persons with disability: How the picture can change*, 181-202.: DOI: 10.1108/S1479-354720170000010008

Hatfield, M., Falkmer, M., Falkmer, T., & Ciccarelli, M. (2017). Effectiveness of the BOOST-A™ online transition planning program for adolescents on the autism spectrum: A quasi-randomized controlled trial. *Child and Adolescent Psychiatry and Mental Health*, *11*(1), 54. Advance online publication. DOI: 10.1186/s13034-017-0191-2 PMID: 29051774

Herrick, S. J., Lu, W., Oursler, J., Beninato, J., Gbadamosi, S., Durante, A., & Meyers, E. (2022). Soft skills for success for job seekers with autism spectrum disorder. *Journal of Vocational Rehabilitation*, *57*(2), 113–126. DOI: 10.3233/JVR-221203

Hill, D. A., Fayemi, A., & Ostrowski, S. (2024). The Evolution of Services for Children with Autism and Developmental Disabilities in Nigeria. *International Journal of Disability Development and Education*, *71*(7), 1116–1132. DOI: 10.1080/1034912X.2023.2291570

Honsberger, T. J., Brady, M. P., Honsberger, C. F., & Kearney, K. B. (2019a). Peer-Mediated Literacy-Based Behavioral Interventions: A Job Coaching Strategy for Secondary Students With ASD. *Career Development and Transition for Exceptional Individuals*, *42*(2), 99–110. DOI: 10.1177/2165143418808508

Honsberger, T. J., Brady, M. P., Honsberger, C. F., & Kearney, K. B. (2019b). Peer-Mediated Literacy-Based Behavioral Interventions: A Job Coaching Strategy for Secondary Students With ASD. *Career Development and Transition for Exceptional Individuals*, *42*(2), 99–110. DOI: 10.1177/2165143418808508

Horn, A. L., Gable, R. A., Bobzien, J. L., Tonelson, S. W., & Rock, M. L. (2020). Teaching Young Adults Job Skills Using a Constant Time Delay and eCoaching Intervention Package. *Career Development and Transition for Exceptional Individuals, 43*(1), 29–39. DOI: 10.1177/2165143419828983

Hume, K., Loftin, R., & Lantz, J. (2009). Increasing independence in autism spectrum disorders: A review of three focused interventions. *Journal of Autism and Developmental Disorders, 39*(9), 1329–1338. DOI: 10.1007/s10803-009-0751-2 PMID: 19430897

Ihenagwam, C., Hamrick, J., Wheeler, K., Iwuji, U., Duru, H., & Banda, D. (2024). Parental Perceptions Upon Receiving Diagnosis of Autism Spectrum Disorder and/or Intellectual Developmental Disability for their Child in Nigeria. *International Journal of Special Education, 39*(1), 73–87. DOI: 10.52291/ijse.2024.39.8

Ilesanmi, O. (2016). Stepping up Agenda 2030 for the Attainment of Gender Parity and Sustainable Development in Nigerian Tertiary Institutions: A Case Study. *Asian Research Journal of Arts & Social Sciences, 1*(1), 1–18. DOI: 10.9734/ARJASS/2016/26525

Kahng, S., Butler, C., Kronfli, F. R., Zaki-Scarpa, C., Boragi, B., & Scott, J. (2023). An individualized approach to teaching adults with autism to successfully navigate job interviews via remote instruction. *Journal of Applied Behavior Analysis, 56*(2), 352–364. DOI: 10.1002/jaba.977 PMID: 36759340

Karim, K., Cook, L., & O'Reilly, M. (2014a). Diagnosing autistic spectrum disorder in the age of austerity. *Child: Care, Health and Development, 40*(1), 115–123. DOI: 10.1111/j.1365-2214.2012.01410.x PMID: 22712808

Karim, K., Cook, L., & O'Reilly, M. (2014b). Diagnosing autistic spectrum disorder in the age of austerity. *Child: Care, Health and Development, 40*(1), 115–123. DOI: 10.1111/j.1365-2214.2012.01410.x PMID: 22712808

Kaya, C., Chan, F., Rumrill, P., Hartman, E., Wehman, P., Iwanaga, K., Pai, C.-H., & Avellone, L. (2016). Vocational rehabilitation services and competitive employment for transition-age youth with autism spectrum disorders. *Journal of Vocational Rehabilitation, 45*(1), 73–83. DOI: 10.3233/JVR-160812

Khetarpal, S. K., Auster, L. S., Miller, E., & Goldstein, T. R. (2022). Transition age youth mental health: Addressing the gap with telemedicine. *Child and Adolescent Psychiatry and Mental Health, 16*(1), 8. DOI: 10.1186/s13034-022-00444-3 PMID: 35109881

Landis, J. R., & Koch, G. G. (1977). An application of hierarchical kappa-type statistics in the assessment of majority agreement among multiple observers. *Biometrics, 33*(2), 363–374. DOI: 10.2307/2529786 PMID: 884196

Lee, E. A. L., Black, M. H., Tan, T., Falkmer, T., & Girdler, S. (2019). "I'm Destined to Ace This": Work Experience Placement During High School for Individuals with Autism Spectrum Disorder. *Journal of Autism and Developmental Disorders, 49*(8), 3089–3101. DOI: 10.1007/s10803-019-04024-x PMID: 31049789

Lee, G. K., & Carter, E. W. (2012a). Preparing Transition-Age Students with High-Functioning Autism Spectrum Disorders for Meaningful Work. *Psychology in the Schools, 49*(10), 988–1000. DOI: 10.1002/pits.21651

Lee, G. K., & Carter, E. W. (2012b). Preparing Transition-Age Students with High-Functioning Autism Spectrum Disorders for Meaningful Work. *Psychology in the Schools, 49*(10), 988–1000. DOI: 10.1002/pits.21651

Lee, N. R., McQuaid, G. A., Grosman, H. E., Jayaram, S., & Wallace, G. L. (2022). Vocational Outcomes in ASD: An Examination of Work Readiness Skills as well as Barriers and Facilitators to Employment Identified by Autistic Adults. *Journal of Autism and Developmental Disorders*, •••, 1–14. DOI: 10.1007/s10803-022-05804-8 PMID: 36394783

Lent, R. W., & Brown, S. D. (2013). Social cognitive model of career self-management: Toward a unifying view of adaptive career behavior across the life span. *Journal of Counseling Psychology, 60*(4), 557–568. DOI: 10.1037/a0033446 PMID: 23815631

Lent, R. W., Hackett, G., & Brown, S. D. (1999). A Social Cognitive View of School-to-Work Transition. *The Career Development Quarterly*, *47*(4), 297–311. DOI: 10.1002/j.2161-0045.1999.tb00739.x

Lindley, L. D. (2005). Perceived barriers to career development in the context of social cognitive career theory. *Journal of Career Assessment, 13*(3), 271–287. DOI: 10.1177/1069072705274953

Ma, Z., Dhir, P., Perrier, L., Bayley, M., & Munce, S. (2020). The impact of vocational interventions on vocational outcomes, quality of life, and community integration in adults with childhood onset disabilities: A systematic review. *Journal of Occupational Rehabilitation, 30*(1), 1–21. DOI: 10.1007/s10926-019-09854-1 PMID: 31535267

Maggin, D. M. (2022). Group Experimental and Quasi-Experimental Research Designs for Special Education Intervention Validation. In *Handbook of Special Education Research* (Vol. I). Routledge. DOI: 10.4324/9781003156857-10

McLaren, J., Lichtenstein, J. D., Lynch, D., Becker, D., & Drake, R. (2017). Individual Placement and Support for People with Autism Spectrum Disorders: A Pilot Program. *Administration and Policy in Mental Health, 44*(3), 365–373. DOI: 10.1007/s10488-017-0792-3 PMID: 28176032

McLucas, A. S., & Gonçalves, B. F. (2025). Using Practitioner-Implemented Video Models to Teach Vocational Social Skills in a Rural Public School. *Career Development and Transition for Exceptional Individuals*, 21651434251328271. Advance online publication. DOI: 10.1177/21651434251328271

Montallana, K. L., Gard, B. M., Lotfizadeh, A. D., & Poling, A. (2019). Inter-Rater Agreement for the Milestones and Barriers Assessments of the Verbal Behavior Milestones Assessment and Placement Program (VB-MAPP). *Journal of Autism and Developmental Disorders, 49*(5), 2015–2023. DOI: 10.1007/s10803-019-03879-4 PMID: 30661147

Munandar, V. D., Morningstar, M. E., & Carlson, S. R. (2020). A systematic literature review of video-based interventions to improve integrated competitive employment skills among youth and adults with Autism Spectrum Disorder. *Journal of Vocational Rehabilitation, 53*(1), 29–41. DOI: 10.3233/JVR-201083

Murray, C., & Doren, B. (2013). The effects of working at gaining employment skills on the social and vocational skills of adolescents with disabilities: A school-based intervention. *Rehabilitation Counseling Bulletin, 56*(2), 96–107. DOI: 10.1177/0034355212452614

Nwokolo, E. U. (2023). Screening for Autism and Intellectual Disabilities Amongst the Nigerian Adolescent Population [Ph.D., University of Kent (United Kingdom)]. DOI: 10.22024/UniKent/01.02.102390

Odunsi, R., Preece, D., & Garner, P. (2017a). Nigerian teachers' understanding of autism spectrum disorder: A comparative study of teachers from urban and rural areas of Lagos state. *Disability, CBR and Inclusive Development, 28*(3), 98–114. DOI: 10.5463/dcid.v28i3.637

Odunsi, R., Preece, D., & Garner, P. (2017b). Nigerian teachers' understanding of autism spectrum disorder: A comparative study of teachers from urban and rural areas of Lagos state. *Disability, CBR and Inclusive Development, 28*(3), 98–114. DOI: 10.5463/dcid.v28i3.637

Oleribe, O. O., & Taylor-Robinson, S. D. (2016). Before Sustainable Development Goals (SDG): Why Nigeria failed to achieve the Millennium Development Goals (MDGs). *The Pan African Medical Journal, 24*, 156. DOI: 10.11604/pamj.2016.24.156.8447 PMID: 27795754

Onyishi, C. N., Okpoko, C. C., & Victor-Aigbodion, V. (2025). Teachers' awareness and perceptions of inclusive education for learners with autism: Implications for the campaign against stigma. *Ikenga, 26*(1), 51–80. DOI: 10.53836/ijia/2025/26/1/004

Otu, M., & Sefotho, M. M. (2024). Relationship between employability skills and career transition among neurodivergent individuals. *The International Journal of Interdisciplinary Social and Community Studies, 19*(2), 237–255. DOI: 10.18848/2324-7576/CGP/v19i02/237-255

Pagano, G., Kiwior, M., Gross, J., Reyes, A., Ramos, E., Cumberbatch, I., Latimore, J., Hu-Au, E., Robila, S., & Tuininga, A. R. (2026). Greens Do Good: A Hydroponic Vertical Farm Augmented and Virtual Reality Training Prototype for Autistic Trainees. *Commun. Comput. Info. Sci., 2598 CCIS*, 287–303. DOI: 10.1007/978-3-031-98080-0_18

Park, Y. S., Konge, L., & Artino, A. R. J. (2020). The Positivism Paradigm of Research. *Academic Medicine, 95*(5), 690–694. DOI: 10.1097/ACM.0000000000003093 PMID: 31789841

Qian, X., Johnson, D., & Papay, C. (2021). Exploring Correlates of Paid Early Work Experiences for Youth With Autism Using NLTS2012 Data. *Focus on Autism and Other Developmental Disabilities, 36*(1), 14–24. DOI: 10.1177/1088357620956915

Roberts, K. D. (2010). Topic areas to consider when planning transition from high school to postsecondary education for students with autism spectrum disorders. *Focus on Autism and Other Developmental Disabilities, 25*(3), 158–162. DOI: 10.1177/1088357610371476

Roux, A. M., Rast, J. E., Anderson, K. A., Garfield, T., & Shattuck, P. T. (2021a). Vocational Rehabilitation Service Utilization and Employment Outcomes Among Secondary Students on the Autism Spectrum. *Journal of Autism and Developmental Disorders, 51*(1), 212–226. DOI: 10.1007/s10803-020-04533-0 PMID: 32399821

Roux, A. M., Rast, J. E., Anderson, K. A., Garfield, T., & Shattuck, P. T. (2021b). Vocational Rehabilitation Service Utilization and Employment Outcomes Among Secondary Students on the Autism Spectrum. *Journal of Autism and Developmental Disorders, 51*(1), 212–226. DOI: 10.1007/s10803-020-04533-0 PMID: 32399821

Russ, S., Arora, S., Wharton, R., Wheelock, A., Hull, L., Sharma, E., Darzi, A., Vincent, C., & Sevdalis, N. (2013). Measuring safety and efficiency in the operating room: Development and validation of a metric for evaluating task execution in the operating room. *Journal of the American College of Surgeons, 216*(3), 472–481. DOI: 10.1016/j.jamcollsurg.2012.12.013 PMID: 23357728

Ryan, G., Bhatti, K., Duncan, C., McGinnis, S., Elliott, R., & Cooper, M. (2023). Reliability and validity of an auditing tool for person-centred psychotherapy and counselling for young people: The PCEPS-YP. *Counselling & Psychotherapy Research*, *23*(2), 563–576. DOI: 10.1002/capr.12505

Sánchez-Blanchart, J., Sánchez-Oliva, A., Pastor-Vicedo, J. C., & Martínez-Martínez, J. (2019). Teacher training in the face of the austism spectrum. *Sport TK*, *8*(2), 59–66. DOI: 10.6018/sportk.401121

Schall, C., Wehman, P., & McDonough, J. L. (2012). Transition from School to Work for Students with Autism Spectrum Disorders: Understanding the Process and Achieving Better Outcomes. *Pediatric Clinics of North America*, *59*(1), 189–202. DOI: 10.1016/j.pcl.2011.10.009 PMID: 22284802

Schutz, M. A., & Carter, E. W. (2022). Employment interventions for youth with disabilities: A review of transition practices and partners. *Career Development and Transition for Exceptional Individuals*, *45*(3), 154–169. DOI: 10.1177/21651434221075810

Sheftel, A., Lindstrom, L., & McWhirter, B. (2014). Motivational enhancement career intervention for youth with disabilities. *Advances in School Mental Health Promotion*, *7*(4), 208–224. DOI: 10.1080/1754730X.2014.949061

Shrout, P. E., & Fleiss, J. L. (1979). Intraclass correlations: Uses in assessing rater reliability. *Psychological Bulletin*, *86*(2), 420–428. DOI: 10.1037/0033-2909.86.2.420 PMID: 18839484

Sreckovic, M. A., Hume, K. A., & Regan, T. E. (2020). Use of Work Systems to Increase the Independence of Adolescents With Autism Spectrum Disorder. *Career Development and Transition for Exceptional Individuals*, *43*(4), 240–256. DOI: 10.1177/2165143420948766

Sung, C., Sánchez, J., Kuo, H.-J., Wang, C.-C., & Leahy, M. J. (2015). Gender Differences in Vocational Rehabilitation Service Predictors of Successful Competitive Employment for Transition-Aged Individuals with Autism. *Journal of Autism and Developmental Disorders*, *45*(10), 3204–3218. DOI: 10.1007/s10803-015-2480-z PMID: 26060047

Taylor, J. L., & Mailick, M. R. (2014). A longitudinal examination of 10-year change in vocational and educational activities for adults with autism spectrum disorders. *Developmental Psychology*, *50*(3), 699–708. DOI: 10.1037/a0034297 PMID: 24001150

Taylor, J. L., McPheeters, M. L., Sathe, N. A., Dove, D., Veenstra-VanderWeele, J., & Warren, Z. (2012a). A Systematic Review of Vocational Interventions for Young Adults With Autism Spectrum Disorders. *Pediatrics, 130*(3), 531–538. DOI: 10.1542/peds.2012-0682 PMID: 22926170

Taylor, J. L., McPheeters, M. L., Sathe, N. A., Dove, D., Veenstra-VanderWeele, J., & Warren, Z. (2012b). A Systematic Review of Vocational Interventions for Young Adults With Autism Spectrum Disorders. *Pediatrics, 130*(3), 531–538. DOI: 10.1542/peds.2012-0682 PMID: 22926170

Taylor, J. L., Smith, L. E., & Mailick, M. R. (2014). Engagement in Vocational Activities Promotes Behavioral Development for Adults with Autism Spectrum Disorders. *Journal of Autism and Developmental Disorders, 44*(6), 1447–1460. DOI: 10.1007/s10803-013-2010-9 PMID: 24287880

Tomaszewski, B., Klinger, L., & Pugliese, C. E. (2022). Self-Determination in Autistic Transition-Aged Youth without Intellectual Disability. *Journal of Autism and Developmental Disorders, 52*(9), 4067–4078. DOI: 10.1007/s10803-021-05280-6 PMID: 34536165

Tomlinson, J., Baird, M., Berg, P., & Cooper, R. (2018). Flexible careers across the life course: Advancing theory, research and practice. *Human Relations, 71*(1), 4–22. DOI: 10.1177/0018726717733313

Wehman, P., Schall, C., Carr, S., Targett, P., West, M., & Cifu, G. (2014). Transition From School to Adulthood for Youth With Autism Spectrum Disorder: What We Know and What We Need to Know. *Journal of Disability Policy Studies, 25*(1), 30–40. DOI: 10.1177/1044207313518071

Wehman, P., Schall, C., McDonough, J., Molinelli, A., Riehle, E., Ham, W., & Thiss, W. R. (2013). Project SEARCH for Youth With Autism Spectrum Disorders: Increasing Competitive Employment On Transition From High School. *Journal of Positive Behavior Interventions, 15*(3), 144–155. DOI: 10.1177/1098300712459760

Wendling, E., & Sagas, M. (2020). An Application of the Social Cognitive Career Theory Model of Career Self-Management to College Athletes' Career Planning for Life After Sport. *Frontiers in Psychology, 11*, 9. Advance online publication. DOI: 10.3389/fpsyg.2020.00009 PMID: 32038437

Westbrook, J. D., Fong, C. J., Nye, C., Williams, A., Wendt, O., & Cortopassi, T. (2013). Pre-Graduation Transition Services for Improving Employment Outcomes among Persons with Autism Spectrum Disorders: A Systematic Review. *Campbell Systematic Reviews, 9*(1), 1–70. DOI: 10.4073/csr.2013.11

APPENDIX

Table 10. Career Transition Outcome Scale (CTOS-SR) – Student Rating

N	Item	Strongly Disagree (SD)	Disagree (D)	Neutral (N)	Agree (A)	Strongly Agree (SA)	Cronbach's α if Item Deleted	Cronbach's α
1	I have gained practical work-readiness skills (organization, adaptability, communication).						0.70	0.70
2	I feel prepared to apply for jobs or vocational programs.						0.76	
3	I have completed structured career-related tasks (e.g., writing a resume, practising interviews).						0.70	
4	I have participated in at least one work-based learning experience (e.g., internship, job shadowing).						0.66	
5	I secured a placement (e.g., job, traineeship, volunteer position) since I started receiving this counselling.						0.62	
6	I have maintained involvement in work or vocational training for at least three consecutive months.						0.72	
7	I feel prepared to handle challenges in new career or work environments.						0.53	
8	The transition counselling intervention has increased my independence in planning and managing career steps.						0.55	

Table 11. Career Transition Observation Scale - Teacher/Counsellor Rating (CTOS-T/CR)

N	Dimension	Rating Scale (1-5)	Description
1	Work Readiness Skills	1 = No work-readiness skills observed 2 = Limited work-readiness skills observed 3 = Some work-readiness skills demonstrated 4 = Good work-readiness skills demonstrated 5 = Fully developed work-readiness skills	Assesses the student's development in work-readiness skills, such as organization, adaptability, and communication.
2	Job/Vocational Confidence	1 = No confidence in job applications or vocational programs 2 = Low confidence in job applications or vocational programs 3 = Moderate confidence in job applications or vocational programs 4 = High confidence in applying for jobs or vocational programs 5 = Very confident in applying for jobs or vocational programs	Evaluates the student's confidence in applying for jobs or entering vocational programs.
3	Career-Related Tasks Completion	1 = No career-related tasks completed 2 = Few career-related tasks completed 3 = Some career-related tasks completed 4 = Many career-related tasks completed 5 = Fully completed career-related tasks	Measures the extent to which the student has engaged in career-related tasks such as writing a resume, practicing interviews, and applying for positions.
4	Work-Based Learning Experience	"1 = No work-based learning experience 2 = Limited work-based learning experience 3 = Some work-based learning experience 4 = Significant work-based learning experience 5 = Multiple work-based learning experiences"	"Evaluates the student's exposure to work-based learning experiences like internships, job shadowing, and other practical learning experiences".
5	Placement Secured	1 = No placement secured 2 = Placement in progress or not secured 3 = Secured a temporary or part-time placement 4 = Secured a full-time placement or traineeship 5 = Secured job, traineeship, or volunteer position	Assesses whether the student has secured a work-related placement such as a job, traineeship, or volunteer position.

continued on following page

Table 11. Continued

N	Dimension	Rating Scale (1-5)	Description
6	Sustained Involvement in Work/Vocational Training	1 = No involvement in work or vocational training 2 = Short-term involvement in work or vocational training 3 = Moderate involvement in work or vocational training 4 = Sustained involvement for several months 5 = Involved in work or vocational training for at least 3 consecutive months	Measures the student's ongoing involvement in work or vocational training over an extended period.
7	Preparedness for Career Challenges	1 = Not prepared to handle career challenges 2 = Somewhat unprepared to handle career challenges 3 = Moderately prepared to handle career challenges 4 = Well-prepared to handle career challenges 5 = Fully prepared to handle career challenges in new career environments	Evaluates the student's preparedness to face challenges in new career or work environments.
8	Increased Independence in Career Planning	1 = No increase in independence in career planning 2 = Slight increase in independence in career planning 3 = Moderate increase in independence in career planning 4 = Significant increase in independence in career planning 5 = Significant increase in independence in planning and managing career steps	Measures the extent to which the student has become more independent in managing their career development and planning.

Rate each criterion based on the observed behaviours and outcomes of the student. For each criterion, assign a score from 1 to 5. Each rater (teacher or counsellor) should rate the student independently. The scale should be used to evaluate the student's progress across multiple sessions or milestones within the career counseling intervention. Ratings should be based on observed behaviours and actual outcomes.

Chapter 5
Teacher Stress During the Career Transition of Students With ASD

ABSTRACT

This study examined teacher stress during the career transition of students with autism spectrum disorders (ASD), focusing on role overload, role ambiguity, and role conflict. A quantitative cross-sectional research design was used to explore the teachers' stress and demographic variables that predicted stress. The sample included 140 teachers in both the public and the private secondary schools. The results showed that role overload was the major cause of stress. This study found that teachers experienced moderately levels of stress across all dimensions. Teachers indicated that role overload was their major source of stress, indicating that teachers consistently felt devastated by the magnitude and pace of transition responsibilities. Role ambiguity and role conflict were also reported as factors that contribute to teachers' stressful experiences, but at a lower level.

BACKGROUND

Teacher stress is the physical, emotional, and psychological pressure which teachers experience due to overwhelming occupational demands and which often arouses negative affective responses such as anger, frustration or depression caused by work-related happenings. Teacher stress prevalence in Nigeria differs in studies. However, it constantly indicates high prevalence (between 13.8 per cent. and 72.2 per cent) with respect to location, school type, and measurement instruments (Asa & Lasebikan, 2016; Opara, 2024). One of the important indicators is psychological distress, which impacts 38.1 per cent of all secondary school teachers, including

DOI: 10.4018/978-1-6684-7260-6.ch005

42.7 per cent in the rural and 33.6 per cent in the urban regions (Obimakinde et al., 2022). There are other reports of 32.9% prevalence of psychological problems in Enugu state (Ozoemena et al., 2021), and up to 60.2% distress in recent assessments (Dhungana et al., 2025).

Teacher stress is an important issue that has far-reaching implications for educators and their psychological well-being, teaching efficacy, teaching performance, and commitment to their teaching profession (Asa & Lasebikan, 2016). Available literature has proven that stress is linked to emotional exhaustion, low levels of personal accomplishment, and decision-making impairment (Ozoemena et al., 2021). Chronic stress that teachers experience is responsible for the low quality of support that students with autism spectrum disorders (SASD) receive, which has long-term implications since a successful career transition (CT) for SASD relies on sustained guidance and teachers' involvement (Cappe et al., 2025; Wong et al., 2017). The stress experienced by teachers often manifests from their coordinated efforts that extend beyond the classroom, which are required to promote SASD's CT. Teachers assisting SASD during CT encounter significant psychological and occupational stress as a result of high expectations from society (Nuske et al., 2019). This situation contributes to rising stress within the teaching profession, especially in educational systems with a weak support system and high demand for inclusive education (Vázquez-Cano & Holgueras-González, 2019; Maphal, 2014).

In Southeast Nigeria, teachers experience significant challenges in assisting SASD as they navigate the CT from school to work environments. The region's education system has experienced numerous pressures over the past decade, motivated by population growth, infrastructural constraints, growing inclusive education mandates, and increasing expectations for school accountability (Onyishi et al., 2025; Akanaeme et al., 2021). The scarcity of structured transition frameworks, the deficiency of trained personnel, and systemic resource limitations place considerable pressure on teachers who must consider responsibilities outside traditional academic instruction (Olagunju et al., 2021; Akanaeme et al., 2021). The demand to provide curriculum material in schools lacking adequate resources leads to emotional weariness and a sense of professional ineffectiveness. Teachers of SASD in Nigeria confront an additional burden of stress because these students need individualised instruction and support, functional skills, and special structured preparation for adulthood. The combined effects of systemic weaknesses and autism-associated needs create a heightened risk of stress during transition activities (Akande, 2024; Okpaka & Ajayi, 2025).

Career transition is a necessary developmental stage for SASD, greatly affecting their future opportunities in employment, vocational programmes, tertiary education, apprenticeships, and community contribution (Ayala, 2023; Dipeolu et al., 2015). In Nigeria, students with disabilities frequently confront substantial barriers at the CT stage as a result of limited inclusive institutions for neurodivergent youth, scarcity of teachers eager to provide inclusive opportunities, inadequate social support, and negative societal attitudes (Eseadi & Diale, 2025). Consequently, teachers serve as the main facilitators entrusted with the planning, preparation, and execution of transition activities, even though some of them were not exposed to formal training in areas such as occupational therapy, behavioural analysis, vocational counselling, or supported employment (Michaels & Orentlicher, 2004). The disparity between expected roles and actual practice raises the possibility of experiencing chronic stress. Also, the high expectation that teachers must provide quality instruction while promoting transition planning presents a complicated array of professional obligations that contribute to stress (Nwoko et al., 2024). The unavailability of a harmonised transition system in Nigeria indicates that teachers are always tasked with determining transition prospects, bargaining placements, and collaborating with families repeatedly, without formal guidance.

Even though teachers are significant in the transition activities of SASD, there is a dearth of studies specifically investigating teacher stress at the CT phase of SASD. Most of the studies conducted in Nigeria concentrate on academic performance, the implementation of inclusive education issues, and the challenges experienced by students with learning difficulties. A significant gap exists in the challenges that school professionals, like teachers, experience in rendering assistance to students during their transitions. To address this gap, this study aimed to address teachers' stress during the CT of SASD. It is extremely important to address this lacuna because teachers' stress has a direct detrimental effect on the quality of transition planning, the fidelity of its implementation, the effectiveness of student preparation, and the sustainability of inclusive education. In this study, we explored role overload, role ambiguity, and role conflicts and how they contribute to overall teachers' stress in the context of CT of SASD in Southeast Nigeria.

Role Overload

Role overload is a condition where teachers sense that the volume, pace, and intensity of responsibilities involved in supporting the career transition of SASD exceed their available time, physical energy, and emotional capacity. Secondary school teachers' workloads are frequently high and consist of planning, conducting classes, involvement in extracurricular activities, and administrative activities (Mason, 2019). The trend of an increase complexity of workload and working hours has been observed within the past decades. It has resulted in significant stress and challenges in balancing professional and personal life (Bridges & Searle, 2011). In Nigeria, particularly in the Southeast, overload is prevalent among secondary school teachers working with SASD during the CT period (Uzodinma et al., 2022; Dike et al., 2021). These teachers are involved in many academic responsibilities alongside the peculiar demand associated with SASD that comprises behavioural regulation, communication assistance, sensory management, and organised teaching strategies. The workload of teachers becomes overwhelming and consumes significant time when transition planning is added to their duties in a school with insufficient staffing (Ayeni, 2017; Ojionuka, 2016).

Many schools in Southeast Nigeria lack specialised personnel, which contributes to work overload. Several schools do not employ speech therapists, school psychologists, or occupational therapists, thereby creating more responsibility for teachers (Eseadi & Diale, 2025; Ramos & Alves, 2008). Teachers compensate for the absence of multidisciplinary support by stretching their capacity across multiple roles, such as analysing behaviours, designing individualised behaviour plans, and modifying the classroom environment, despite the fact that these responsibilities fall under therapeutic professionals. Likewise, transition planning for SASD requires teachers to navigate external systems that are poorly developed due to the scarcity of vocational schools that cater for SASD, and few companies are interested in accepting for trial placements and are coupled with insufficient government support. Therefore, teachers are required to seek chances through personal contacts, negotiations, and constantly accompanying students to community exposure activities, which results in overload.

Some related studies have been conducted on the teachers' overload during the CT of SASD. A study conducted in Nigeria on managing job stress of teachers reported that rational emotive occupation health coaching was extremely impactful in reducing stress symptoms among teachers (Ogba et al., 2020). Furthermore, a study found that school teachers encounter challenges such as difficulty in engaging SASD in classroom and common activities, as well as challenges in collaborating with other teachers and educational professionals (Raudeliūnaitė & Steponėnienė, 2020). On the psychological distress of special education teachers, a study reported that psychological burden is prevalent among teachers, with four in every ten teachers having experienced it (Olagunju et al., 2021b). Similarly, a study revealed that unfavourable working environments and insufficient motivation are the major sources of stress to teachers (Adigun et al., 2021). Previous studies have shown that researchers have concentrated on establishing relationships between stress and other variables, the incidence of stress among teachers, and intervention studies to reduce work-related stress. However, none of these studies explored the stress overload peculiar to CT of SASD in Southeast Nigeria.

Role Ambiguity

Role ambiguity is the uncertainty that teachers experience concerning what is expected of them at the CT processes, such as unclear responsibilities, unclear guidance from school administrators, unclear evaluation standards or the distribution of tasks among stakeholders. Role ambiguity is inversely related to job satisfaction and organisational performance of teachers (Pérez et al., 2017; Schwab & Iwanicki, 1982). In Southeast Nigeria, which is characterised by a lack of a formalised transition framework that defines accountability of teachers, role ambiguity is pervasive in the transition process for SASD. Even though inclusive education has been encouraged at the national level, the policy for career transition from school to work is still underdeveloped, leading to substantial uncertainty for teachers.

Teachers are often confused about the appropriate duties to undertake during the transition periods (Sasere, 2023). They display uncertain behaviour with regard to carrying out transition assessments, partnership with other vocational institutions or the arrangement of work placements. Due to a lack of clear directives, teachers usually depend on their own discretion, peers, or administrators to ascertain which responsibilities to prioritise. Role ambiguity prevalence varies among schools and boosts stress levels because teachers worry about neglecting essential tasks. Role ambiguity manifests from insufficient training, as Nigerian teachers rarely undergo training in transitional planning for SASD because educational programmes focus on curriculum delivery, classroom management, and subject pedagogy (Sasere, 2023). Without the procedural knowledge necessary for effective implementation, teachers interpret ambiguous expectations despite the fact that they may not know how to train SASD for workplace expectations and adjust transition activities to their cognitive, behavioural, and sensory profiles.

Role ambiguity also manifests from the lack of collaboration between schools and external agencies, which can shape how teachers perceive their roles and professions (Epp, 2023; Goodson & Ümarik, 2019). Nigerian teachers are often uninformed regarding agencies that offer transition-related services, the process for guiding students, or the individuals responsible for follow-up support. Teacher experiences a lot of inconsistencies in communication and ambiguous procedures, which intensifies uncertainty surrounding their roles in the transition process. Similarly, role ambiguity also emanates from ASASD parents' expectations since some will anticipate that teachers will promote their children's admission into higher institutions. In contrast, others might organise and facilitate job placement training. These conflicting anticipations generate confusion, which heightens teachers' stress.

We are aware of some related studies that have been done on role ambiguity. For instance, Pérez et al. (2017) reported that teachers experience ambiguity in two dimensions, such as in demand and in standard, attributed to insufficient clarity in the guidelines and frameworks governing the assessment of academic achievements. Also, a study revealed that role ambiguity exists between university faculty expectations and the supervisor's expectations, which has resulted in a delay in teaching (Deng et al., 2022). Furthermore, a study found that school principals encounter role ambiguity, which resulted from organisational ambiguity (Tabancalı & Su, 2021). On the teachers' management of stress, Hassan et al. (2020) revealed that a moderate level of stress and a significant relationship between role conflicts, role ambiguity, and role overload.

Role Conflict

Role conflict is the experience of incompatible, competing, or mutually interfering demands imposed on teachers as they try to harmonise their instructional accountabilities with the expectations of parents, administrators, and transition programmes on SASD. Role conflict is a significant contributor to teachers' stress in Southeast Nigeria, especially during the CT of SASD (Ozoemena et al., 2021). The major source of role conflict and stress is the tension between academic instruction and transition planning (Myburgh & van der Vyver, 2022). School teachers are mandated to cover the academic curriculum and organise students for examinations. Another source of stress for teachers in Southeast Nigeria is the conflicting expectations from the school administration and the parents of the students (Nnah & George, 2025). School administrators may expect better achievements, while parents may anticipate meaningful transition supports for career transitions (Dada et al., 2025). Teachers experience stress in an attempt to satisfy these conflicting expectations.

Institutional constraints, such as a lack of tools, infrastructure, and materials necessary for CT of ASD, contribute to role conflicts. The teacher may attempt to provide hands-on vocational training or workplace simulation but is unable to implement these activities due to a lack of facilities. As a result, the teachers experience stress, which manifests in the form of guilt, frustration, and dismay when they cannot provide the level of support they know is necessary for successful transition outcomes. Cultural expectation is another significant source of role conflict teachers encounter in Southeast Nigeria because teachers are viewed as moral guides, counsellors, and community leaders. As a result, during the transition period, families expect teachers to mediate social challenges and take responsibilities that extend well outside educational duties (Dietrich & Salmela-Aro, 2013). These conflicting expectations of culture and professional boundaries contribute significantly to teacher stress.

Some empirical related studies have been done on the role ambiguity of teachers that contributes to their stress. On role ambiguity and role conflict, Myburgh and van der Vyver (2022) revealed that the head of the department experienced significant role ambiguity and conflicts. Teachers expect a great deal from the principal, and the principal expects a great deal from the head of the department. Also, Dada et al. (2025) revealed that role ambiguity and role conflict significantly impacted the performance of lecturers. On the lecturer burnout, Adeboye and Obawole (2019) revealed that role ambiguity substantially predicted job burnout among the participants. These previous empirical studies have shown that the majority of the studies established the association between role conflict and other variables, identified role conflict among participants, and established the association between role conflicts and job burnout. However, none of these studies focused on the role conflicts that induce teachers' stress during CT of SASD in Southeast Nigeria. Therefore, this study explored the teachers' stress during the CT of SASD.

RESEARCH OBJECTIVES

The main objective of this study is to examine the pattern and predictors of teacher stress during the career transition of students with ASD. The specific objectives of this study are:

1. To assess the degree of teacher stress across the three dimensions of stress (role overload, role ambiguity, and role conflict) during the career transition of students diagnosed with ASD.
2. To investigate the differences in teacher stress levels based on gender on the three dimensions of stress.
3. To determine the extent to which demographic and school-related variables serve as predictors of teacher stress within the three dimensions.

RESEARCH QUESTIONS

1. What are the levels of teacher stress in terms of role three dimensions of stress during the career transition of students with ASD?
2. Are there gender differences in the three dimensions of stress during the CT of SASD?
3. To what extent do demographic and school-related factors predict role overload among teachers during the CT of SASD?

THEORETICAL FRAMEWORK

This study adopted Kahn et al.'s Role Stress theory propounded in 1964. The theory illustrates how individuals encounter stress as a result of excessive, unclear, and ambiguous expectations tied to their roles (Kahn et al., 1964). This theory stipulates that members of an organisation fulfil several roles that are associated with the expectations expressed by the stakeholders. Stress occurs when these expectations become excessive, ambiguous, and incompatible, which hinders the effectiveness of the member (Kahn et al., 1964). This theory is relevant to this study, which explores the teachers' stress during CT of SASD in the Nigerian educational landscape, which is characterised by a complex environment marked by insufficient resources, disjointed policies, and competing demands from administrators, parents, and external agencies. In Kahn's theory, role overload entails stakeholders' excessive expectations placed on teachers who are expected to combine instruction with transition planning, behavioural support, documentation, and coordination with vocational or community organisations. Role ambiguity entails the absence of clear guidelines, inconsistent communication from school leadership, and inadequate training, which leaves teachers uncertain about their responsibilities in the transition processes. Role conflict arises when teachers face incompatible expectations, such as the need to balance academic instruction with intensive individualised transition support or to address conflicting demands from parents and administrators (Bredeson, 1993; King & King, 1990; Silvia et al., 2025). Utilising role stress theory enables this study to elucidate the reasons behind the high levels of stress experienced by teachers in Nigeria during the transition of SASD. This theory presents a conceptual framework for understanding how systemic deficiencies, vague policies, and conflicting expectations affect teacher well-being and impact the quality of transition support provided to SASD.

POLICY FRAMEWORK

The present study is based on the National Policy on Special Needs Education in Nigeria, which outlines the background principles of enabling equitable learning opportunities, inclusive education, and specialised support of SASD (Federal Republic of Nigeria, 2015). The policy guides on the least restrictive settings, complete inclusion, a zero-reject, and diversification of services, both in school, home, and hospital settings. These principles put in place the expectations that teachers are core in the identification, support, and preparation of SASD to continue with life after school, including CT. The policy further emphasises the importance of specialised teacher training and retraining by acknowledging that the delivery of effective services needs personnel who have a comprehensive understanding of special needs education and skills to support the behavioural, cognitive and vocational challenges being encountered by SASD (Agunowei & Mayombe, 2024). Even though the policy gives general training duties, it does not offer adequate operational instructions on what teachers should do during the transition planning (Agunowei & Mayombe, 2024). This procedural gap adds to role overload, role ambiguity and role conflict since the transition expectations in the Nigerian schools are usually understood individually without any specific administrative or interagency coordination. Moreover, the policy singles out poor facilities, lack of coordination between the ministries, as well as disjointed service delivery as structural issues that impact special needs education in Nigeria. These weaknesses in structure directly influence the shape of teacher stress, due to restricted access to the support services, overreliance on classroom teachers, as well as uneven communication between the various stakeholders (Umeh & Anyaele, 2024a). Consequently, the National Policy on Special Needs Education provides not only an empowering framework but also a series of situational impositions that greatly affect the experience of teacher stress in the CT of SASD in Nigeria.

METHODOLOGY

Research Approach

This study employed a quantitative research approach to examine the patterns and predictors of teacher stress during the career transition of SASD (Hsueh et al., 2008; Lazaraton, 2005). Quantitative approach was chosen because the study sought to evaluate measurable attributes of teacher stress, test statistical associations among variables, and model predictive relationships using numerical data. Through this approach, we were able to capture variations in stress levels across teachers, compare subgroups such as gender and school type, and determine the extent to which demographic and school-related factors explained differences in stress. The quantitative approach supported our aim of generating objective evidence that could be generalised across similar settings in Southeast Nigeria. Using quantitative measurement tools allowed us to assess teacher stress dimensions and to evaluate relationships among the constructs using inferential analyses. In the context of the career transition of students with ASD, where demographic and organisational factors may influence stress responses, the quantitative approach provides a systematic means of identifying the relative contributions of each factor.

Research Design

We employed a cross-sectional predictive correlational design (Devi et al., 2022). This design allowed us to gather data from teachers at a single point in time and investigate the association between their demographic characteristics, school contextual factors, and their levels of stress across role overload, role ambiguity and role conflict. The cross-sectional perspective provided a snapshot of teacher stress experiences during the transition period, making it possible to analyse patterns of stress that concurrent work conditions may shape. The predictive correlational component of the design made it possible to model how selected predictors, such as age, school type and educational qualification, contributed to teacher stress. Given the structure of the research questions, which aimed to identify both the magnitude of stress and the predictors of stress, the correlational design was suitable. It enabled us to employ regression analyses to evaluate how well the demographic variables predicted the three stress dimensions. By using this design, we were able to establish statistically meaningful associations that shed light on how teacher attributes and school context influence stress during career transition processes for students with ASD.

Research Paradigm

The research was based on the positivist research paradigm, which operates under the assumption that reality is objective, quantifiable, and exists independently of the observer (Park et al., 2020). This stance provided the philosophical foundation for collecting numerical data on teacher stress and analysing the relationships between variables using statistical procedures. From an ontological perspective, the positivist paradigm assumes that phenomena such as teacher stress exist as real and observable constructs that can be measured through structured instruments (Ali, 2024). We treated the stress dimensions of role overload, role ambiguity and role conflict as quantifiable realities that reflect the experiences of teachers supporting career transition for students with ASD. Epistemologically, the positivist paradigm assumes that knowledge is gained through systematic observation, measurement and analysis. In this study, we sought to generate knowledge by capturing teachers' self-reported stress levels through a standardised questionnaire and by subjecting the data to statistical analyses. The use of empirical evidence allowed us to make claims that are grounded in observable patterns rather than subjective interpretations. Axiologically, the positivist paradigm emphasises objectivity and minimisation of researcher influence. In order to affirm our commitment to objectivity, we validated the questionnaire for collecting research data, structured its administration, and used relevant statistical techniques for the data analysis. We also refrained from any form of personal interpretation during data collection and followed the ethical and analytical protocols of the study. The positivist perspective further emphasises the importance of utilising structured questionnaires, statistical tests, and deductive reasoning in research. Our methodological decisions, such as the utilisation of cross-sectional design, validated instrument, and regression modelling, align with these perspectives.

Study Setting

The study was conducted in Southeast Nigeria, specifically in Enugu and Imo States. These states were selected because they reflect diverse educational environments in the region, including urban and rural communities, government and private schools, and schools with different levels of exposure to inclusive education practices. Enugu State, often referred to as the Coal City State, is known for its strong educational infrastructure, a high concentration of secondary schools and a significant presence of trained teachers. It is one of the leading educational hubs in Southeast Nigeria, making it an ideal setting for studies focused on teacher experiences and practices. On the other hand, Imo State has a broad distribution of schools across rural and semi-urban communities. It is known for its community engagement in education and its increasing participation in inclusive schooling initiatives. The presence of schools serving students with neurodevelopmental learning needs, including ASD, made Imo State a relevant context for this research study. The selection of both states presented unique school contexts in terms of teacher training opportunities, resource availability, and school administrative structures, thus enhancing the representativeness of the sample. Carrying out the study across these two states also allowed us to capture experiences from a broader population of teachers involved in transition planning for SASD.

Population and Sample

The population was composed of teachers in public and private secondary schools in Enugu and Imo States who were involved in supporting students with ASD. These teachers were responsible for teaching, guidance, counselling and other transition-related activities. They represented a diverse demographic group with varying levels of experience, age and professional qualifications. We employed a multi-stage sampling procedure to enhance representativeness while ensuring feasibility (Hossan et al., 2023). Multi-stage sampling was appropriate because the study covered large geographical areas across two states and involved multiple school types. The approach allowed us to systematically narrow the sampling frame from states to local government areas, then to schools and finally to individual teachers. In the first stage, we selected local government areas from each state to ensure both urban and rural representation. This step was essential for capturing variations in school environments that might influence teacher stress levels.

In the second stage, we selected secondary schools within the chosen local government areas. Schools were sampled to reflect variation in school type, including government-funded and privately owned institutions. This decision was based on the fact that school type may influence job demands and teacher experiences during career transition support (Fasching, 2014). In the final stage, we purposively selected teachers who directly engaged in transition support for students with ASD. These included classroom teachers, special education teachers, guidance counsellors and teachers who had prior experience with transition planning. Selecting teachers with direct involvement ensured that the data collected were relevant and that the participants could provide informed responses. The final sample included 140 teachers with diverse demographic and professional attributes. The sample size represents the number of teachers who fulfilled the research inclusion criteria and agreed to participate.

Data Collection Instrument

Data were gathered via a self-developed questionnaire, titled the Teacher Stress Questionnaire in Supporting Student Career Transition (TSQ SCT). The instrument was developed to measure the levels of stress teachers experienced while supporting SASD during their CT. The items in the instrument were developed based on theoretical models of occupational stress and empirical literature on teacher stress in inclusive education contexts. The TSQ-SCT consists of three major components reflecting the three stress dimensions measured in the study:

Role Overload – This subscale captures the extent to which teachers feel burdened by excessive responsibilities associated with career transition. This dimension includes items such as the number of transition tasks, time constraints, and the emotional and physical demands of transition support.

Role Ambiguity – This subscale measures the degree to which teachers experience uncertainty about their responsibilities, expectations and evaluation criteria in supporting transition planning. This dimension includes items that assess clarity of role, consistency of communication and understanding of transition processes.

Role Conflict – This subscale measures the tension teachers experience when competing expectations arise from their instructional duties, administrative demands and parental involvement. This dimension captures conflicting instructions, competing priorities and pressure stemming from multiple stakeholders.

The instrument employed a five-point Likert scale where 1 implied Strongly Disagree, 2 implied Disagree, 3 implied Neutral, 4 implied Agree, and 5 implied Strongly Agree. Higher scores on each subscale imply increased levels of teacher stress within that specific dimension. This scale structure is consistent with instruments commonly used to evaluate occupational stress, thus enabling the comparability of results (Lyne et al., 2000). The instrument was subjected to psychometric analysis to ensure the reliability and stability of the scores. As shown in Table 4, the reliability coefficients for the three subscales were acceptable. In our study, the role overload subscale had a Cronbach's α of 0.82 and an Omega ω of 0.81, indicating strong internal consistency. The role ambiguity subscale showed a Cronbach's α of 0.77 and Omega ω of 0.77, which reflects stable measurement. The role conflict subscale had a Cronbach's α of .73 and an Omega ω of 0.79, which also demonstrates acceptable reliability (see Table 4, see also Figure 3). These reliability values confirmed that the instrument measured each construct consistently, making it suitable for this study.

Data Collection Procedures

Data collection started after we received ethical clearance. Two postgraduate research assistants with prior training in special needs education and educational psychology facilitated the data collection process. Their training enabled them to interact sensitively with teachers and navigate school environments effectively. We provided detailed guidance to the assistants on administering the questionnaire to ensure standardisation. The assistants visited selected schools, introduced the study to teachers, obtained informed consent and distributed the questionnaires. Teachers were given time to complete the instrument in a comfortable and non-intrusive environment. Collecting data through trained assistants helped minimise bias and ensured that the presence of the researchers did not influence teachers' responses. The assistants clarified any questions regarding the instrument while avoiding leading explanations that could affect the responses.

Data Analysis Procedure

The research data were examined using both descriptive and inferential statistical methods. Descriptive statistics, including means, standard deviations, and confidence intervals, were employed to illustrate teacher stress across three dimensions. These analyses enabled us to discern overarching trends in stress levels and variations among subgroups, such as gender. Inferential analyses were carried out to address the predictive research inquiries. In particular, multiple regression analyses were utilised to ascertain the degree to which demographic and school-related variables forecasted role overload, role ambiguity, and role conflict. The regression models facilitated the evaluation of both individual and collective impacts of predictors, which encompassed gender, age, school type, school location, and educational qualifications.

Ethical Considerations

Ethical clearance for the research was obtained from the Faculty of Education Research Ethics Committee at the University of Johannesburg (number: Sem-2-2020-057). This clearance verified that the research adhered to recognised ethical guidelines for studies involving human subjects. We made certain that all participants were made aware of the study's objectives, the voluntary aspect of their involvement, their entitlement to withdraw at any point, and the precautions implemented to protect their confidentiality. A written informed consent form was completed and submitted by all participants before the questionnaire was administered. Anonymity was maintained throughout the study. Teachers were not required to provide their names or any identifying details, and the data were analysed and reported in aggregated form. Therefore, the measures taken ensured that participants' responses were confidential and that no individual teacher or school could be identified from the results. Ethical principles guided every stage of the study, from planning to data analysis. Respect for participants, fairness, integrity and responsibility were central to the conduct of the research.

RESULTS

Figure 1 contains the demographic characteristics of the teachers who participated in the study. As shown in the figure, the sample reflects diversity in gender, age categories, educational qualifications, school type, and school location. The respondents' characteristics provide some insights into the demographic composition that may influence how teachers experience stress during the career transition of students with ASD.

Figure 1. Respondents' demographic characteristics

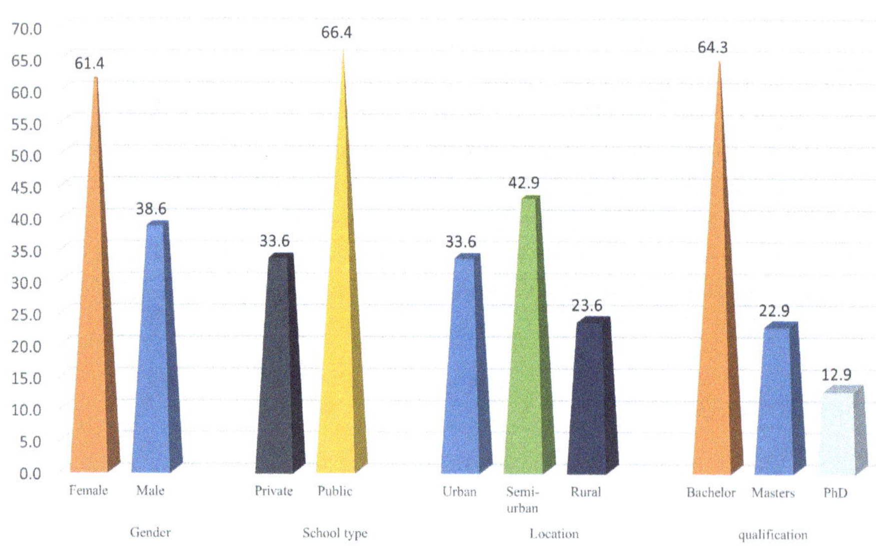

Table 1. Mean scores of teacher stress during the CT of SASD

		N	Mean	SD	SE	Coefficient of variation	95% Confidence Interval	
							Lower Limit	Upper Limit
Role Overload	Female	86	22.15	3.91	.422	.176	21.33	22.98
	Male	54	22.98	3.82	.520	.166	21.96	24.00
Role Ambiguity	Female	86	22.01	3.66	.395	.166	21.24	22.79
	Male	54	21.83	3.91	.532	.179	20.79	22.88
Role Conflict	Female	86	19.92	4.01	.432	.201	19.07	20.77
	Male	54	18.91	3.26	.444	.173	18.04	19.78
Overall	Female	86	64.08	8.77	.945	.137	62.23	65.93
	Male	54	63.72	7.68	1.045	.121	61.67	65.77

Gender differences in teacher stress were considered using the clustered bar chart in Figure 2, along with the descriptive statistics in Table 2. Figure 2 shows only slight variations between male and female teachers across all stress dimensions, and these differences align closely with the means reported in Table 2. For role overload, male teachers displayed marginally higher scores than female teachers, although the difference appears small and is not supported by large differences in variability. For role ambiguity, the scores for both gender groups overlap almost entirely, indicating that ambiguity related to transition duties is experienced at comparable levels.

In role conflict, the differences between gender groups appear slightly more distinct, with female teachers reporting a higher mean score. However, the size of the difference was modest. The overall stress levels also confirm this level of difference, with male and female teachers showing similar levels of total stress in Figure 2. Taken together, the evidence from Figure 2 and Table 1 indicates that gender related differences in stress are minimal, and the distribution suggests that teacher stress during the career transition of SASD is a shared experience that does not differ substantially by gender identity.

Figure 2. Clustered bar chart showing gender differences in teacher stress (role overload, role ambiguity, role conflict, and overall scores)

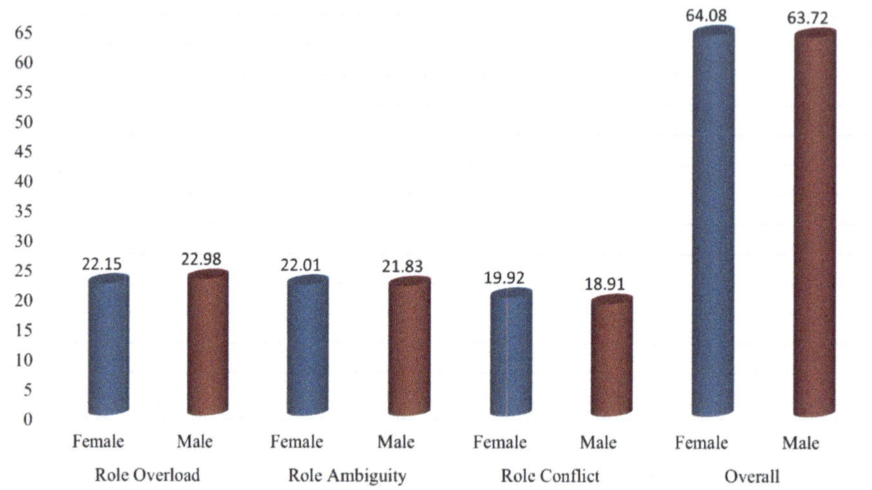

Table 2. Regression analysis of predictors on teacher stress during the CT of SASD

Models	Predictors	Unstandardised coefficients		Adjusted R-square	F-change	T	Sig
		Beta (β)	SE				
Role Overload	(Constant)	13.517	2.622	.072	3.146	5.155	.000
	Gender	.759	.657			1.156	.250
	Age	1.929	.684			2.820	.006
	School type	.099	.035			2.811	.006
	Location of school	.168	.435			.387	.699
	Educational qualification	-.043	.451			-.095	.924
Role Ambiguity	(Constant)	26.695	2.640	-.009	.756	10.112	.000
	Gender	-.232	.661			-.352	.726
	Age	-.553	.688			-.804	.423
	School type	-.059	.035			-1.663	.099
	Location of school	-.365	.438			-.833	.406
	Educational qualification	-.117	.454			-.257	.798

continued on following page

Table 2. Continued

Models	Predictors	Unstandardised coefficients		Adjusted R-square	F-change	T	Sig
		Beta (β)	SE				
Role Conflict	(Constant)	22.783	2.640	-.004	.881	8.629	.000
	Gender	-1.044	.661			-1.580	.116
	Age	.101	.689			.147	.883
	School type	-.042	.035			-1.191	.236
	Location of school	-.208	.438			-.474	.636
	Educational qualification	.209	.454			.461	.645

Table 2 reveals the regression model evaluating demographic and school-related predictors of role overload. The results show that age was a significant predictor of role overload (B = 1.929, SE = .684, p = .006), indicating that older teachers reported higher levels of overload. School type also significantly predicted role overload (B = .099, SE = .035, p = .006), suggesting that teachers in certain school settings experienced greater overload than others. In contrast, gender did not significantly predict role overload (p = .250), consistent with the descriptive findings reported in Table 2 and Figure 2. School location was also not a significant predictor of role overload (p = .699), implying that the geographic context of the school did not meaningfully contribute to overload levels. Educational qualification similarly showed no significant predictive effect (p = .924). The adjusted R-squared value shows that the predictors explained a modest proportion of variance in role overload, implying that although age and school type contribute meaningfully to teachers' experiences of overload, other unmeasured contextual or organisational factors are also likely to influence overload during transition support. These findings reflect the complexity of understanding teacher stress in career transition contexts and suggest that demographic factors alone do not fully account for teachers' experiences.

The predictors of role ambiguity were also examined via the regression model presented in Table 2. The results show that none of the demographic or school-related variables significantly predicted role ambiguity among teachers supporting students with ASD during career transition. Gender was not a significant predictor (B = –.232, SE = .661, p = .726), and age likewise did not contribute meaningfully to the model (B = –.553, SE = .688, p = .423). School type showed a negative but non-significant coefficient (B = –.059, SE = .035, p = .099), indicating an outcome that did not attain statistical significance. School location (p = .406) and educational qualification (p = .798) also failed to predict role ambiguity. The adjusted R-square value for the model was negative, indicating that the included predictors did not explain a meaningful proportion of variance in teachers' experiences of ambiguity in their transition-related responsibilities. The findings suggest that role ambiguity is not shaped by the demographic or institutional characteristics assessed in this study. Instead, ambiguity may arise from broader organisational issues, unclear communication patterns, or inconsistencies in role expectations that extend beyond individual and school-level factors.

In Table 2, the regression model assessing predictors of role conflict showed that none of the demographic or school-related variables significantly predicted teachers' conflict experiences. Gender did not significantly predict role conflict ($B = -1.044$, $SE = .661$, $p = .116$), although the direction of the coefficient suggests that male teachers tended to report slightly lower conflict than female teachers. Age was not a significant predictor ($B = .101$, $SE = .689$, $p = .883$), indicating that conflict levels were experienced similarly across age groups. School type had a small negative coefficient that did not reach significance ($B = -.042$, $SE = .035$, $p = .236$). School location ($p = .636$) and educational qualification ($p = .645$) likewise did not significantly contribute to the model. The adjusted R-squared value was negative, indicating no explanatory value from the included predictors. These findings suggest that teachers' demographic or school-related characteristics do not strongly shape role conflict during student career transition. Instead, conflict may reflect structural or systemic challenges inherent in balancing instructional responsibilities with the additional demands of transition planning. Such conflict may arise from competing expectations placed on teachers across different layers of the school environment rather than from individual characteristics alone.

Across the three regression models, only the role overload model identified significant predictors, with age and school type contributing to teachers' experiences of overload. In contrast, neither role ambiguity nor role conflict was significantly predicted by any of the demographic or school variables. These findings indicate that certain demographic factors may increase the intensity of overload, ambiguity, and conflict stemming from organisational dynamics rather than individual or structural characteristics. Therefore, the findings highlight the multifaceted nature of teacher stress during the career transition of students with ASD and require that workplace interventions aimed at clarifying roles and reducing conflicting expectations should focus on systemic school processes rather than individual teacher attributes.

DISCUSSION

This study investigated the teacher stress during the CT of SASD. This study found that teachers experienced moderately levels of stress across all dimensions. Teachers indicated that role overload was their major source of stress, indicating that teachers consistently felt devastated by the magnitude and pace of transition responsibilities. In Nigerian schools, this finding is not surprising based on the reality on the ground. Large class sizes, insufficient staffing, and limited instructional materials characterise the Nigerian school, which creates a demanding environment even before transition responsibilities are added. Nigerian teachers are responsible for planning and writing lesson notes, assessing and evaluating learners, managing classrooms, and engaging in administrative tasks. Since the implementation of inclusive education, schools have been accommodating students with special needs without subjecting teachers to the suitable training and resources required for the implementation (Ayeni, 2017). This finding is consistent with most of the previous literature. A study conducted in Southeast Nigeria has shown that 40% of teachers revealed encountering emotional exhaustion, 39.4% experienced depersonalisation, and 36.8% indicated a decline in personal attainment. In addition, 32.9% of these teachers confronted psychological distress, and 39.6% experienced low levels of job satisfaction (Okwaraji & Aguwa, 2015). Also, the findings of this study affirmed the report of the previous study, which revealed that role overload has a detrimental impact on teachers' job performance and the pressure resulting from an excessive workload, large class sizes, and extra non-teaching duties contributes to diminished job performance, heightened anxiety, and burnout (Adewale et al., 2017). This study equally authenticated a report from the Northeast Nigeria by Dankade et al. (2016), which indicated that a considerable number of vocational secondary school teachers experienced significant job stress, primarily attributed to excessive workloads, large class sizes, insufficient motivation, and student indiscipline. These factors have been associated with diminished job performance, heightened anxiety, feelings of boredom, and overall exhaustion. This study also aligned with a recent study conducted by Orhero et al (2023), which reported that role overload has a considerable effect on how individuals adapt to their employment. Stressful interactions between people and their environments, which exceed their ability to cope, can result in human stress and jeopardise their long-term health.

Role ambiguity and role conflict were also reported as factors that contribute to teachers' stressful experiences, but at a lower level, reflecting persistent uncertainty and competing demands faced by teachers during transition support. This study revealed that role ambiguity was not associated with the demographic or institutional characteristics assessed, but may arise from broader organisational issues, unclear communication patterns, or inconsistencies in role expectations that extend beyond individual and school-level variables. These findings could be related to the challenges teachers encounter due to organisational and policy challenges. For instance, the National policy on special needs and inclusive education stipulated inclusive objectives but offers insufficient operational guidance concerning transition procedures of teachers in assisting SASD at the time of CT (Chandra, 2024). As a result, teachers are forced to interpret expectations from school, society, and framework objectives based on their knowledge, resulting in variations in the understanding of duties among schools (Umeh & Anyaele, 2024b). This ambiguity that emanates from educational structure promotes an environment where uncertainty is prevalence in the norm rather than the exception.

The communication practices within the schools exacerbate the role ambiguity that teachers experience in the secondary schools in Nigeria, which contributes to teachers' stress (Amu et al., 2025). The flow of information in most secondary schools in Nigeria is inconsistent despite the fact that the decision-making process is centralised (Peretomode, 2006). Teachers often get fragmented instructions from administration, counsellors, special needs units, and this complicates the identification of who is responsible for certain transition activities (Uba-Mbibi, 2013). This inability to communicate increases uncertainty even for an experienced teacher. Additionally, the absence of clearly established interagency coordination systems leaves teachers uncertain concerning their interaction with vocational centres, rehabilitation services or employers (Km & Js, 2007). Since transition activities are also associated with the need for collaboration with different sectors, unclear boundaries between agencies further reinforce role ambiguity. The results of this study aligned with most of the previous literature reports. Also, Peretomode (2006) revealed that most school teachers are deprived of involvement in decision-making, even though the burden of instruction falls on them, while those who are given the opportunity are not satisfied. This finding aligns with the previous findings of Ogharen et al. (2022), which indicated that interpersonal conflicts were mainly attributed to both intergroup and interpersonal relationships.

This study revealed that teachers' demographic or school-related characteristics do not strongly influence role conflict during student career transition. Instead, conflict may reflect structural or systemic challenges inherent in balancing instructional responsibilities with the additional demands of transition planning. Such conflict may arise from competing expectations placed on teachers across different layers of the school environment rather than from individual characteristics alone. The schools in the Nigerian setting have an environment that is characterised by the scarcity of resources, strict curriculum requirements, and a high focus on examination results (Nwagwu, 1997). The teachers are mandated to follow syllabi, prepare learners for high-stakes assessments and provide discipline and while at the same time ensuring transition readiness (Ogu & Chike, 2025). All these conflicting expectations are a result of the various levels of the educational setting, such as administrators who consider academic performance as their main priority, parents who desire individual transition supports, and policymakers who advocate inclusive education without offering operational guidelines. As a result lack of harmonisation of these expectations, teachers often find themselves in a position where one set of expectations makes them compromise with the performance of the other requirement, and this contributes to their stress.

This finding could also be attributed to a lack of a structured transition framework, which intensifies conflicts. Nigeria does not have a definite protocol stipulating the definite responsibilities of teachers in the transition process, leaving schools to interpret them independently (Otegbeye, 2021; Salahu, 2020). Teachers, therefore, have to contend with conflicting directives from principals, counsellors and special needs units. Teachers who work in understaffed schools may be mandated to supervise classrooms while simultaneously organising vocational assessments or community-based learning activities, a circumstance that creates unavoidable conflict (Westheimer, 1998). Furthermore, cultural expectations are a major source that brings about systemic role conflict. Parents tend to perceive teachers as multipurpose support providers and expect them to secure vocational placement opportunities for their children (Fagan et al., 2012). However, teachers do not have the authority or institutional capacity to meet these demands. Role conflict is a product of systemic pressures rather than individual teacher characteristics, stressing the need for coordinated policies, clearer role definitions, and organisational supports within Nigerian schools.

The finding of this study concerning role conflict as a source of teachers' stress experiences in CT of ASD is related to some previous studies. Anazia et al. (2025) reported that there was a disagreement between parents and teachers based on their expectations of teachers, which is beyond their academic responsibilities. Similarly, another study found that role conflicts occur when there is a mismatch between expectations and the real role of the teacher, which results in frustration (Bukhori et al., 2020). Also, another study found that role conflict occurs when teachers struggle to meet both instructional and administrative needs (Ololube, 2013).

This study found that stress levels were largely similar for male and female teachers. However, males revealed marginally higher overload and females reported slightly higher conflict; the differences were small and insignificant. For role ambiguity, it was almost identical irrespective of gender groups. Both male and female teachers revealed that role overload was their major source of stress, indicating that teachers consistently felt devastated by the magnitude and pace of transition responsibilities. Even though males showed significantly more overload and females showed slightly more conflict, which were insignificant. The implication of this is that, irrespective of gender, teacher stress in the process of CT of SASD is a shared experience irrespective of gender. In the Nigerian context, gender does not significantly influence how workload is distributed within schools (Nnubia et al., 2025). In an inclusive school, teaching roles are assigned without gender differentiation (Lindner et al., 2021). Therefore, both males and females are mandated to perform similar tasks such as managing the classroom, engaging in transition planning, and liaising with parents.

Additionally, the Nigerian educational system does not formally differentiate teaching responsibilities by gender, particularly in the government schools (Nakpodia & James, 2012). Both genders have the same working conditions and resource constraints, and administrative expectations. The small differences in gender that were observed in this study reflect the broader egalitarian assignment of duties in the Nigerian schools aligns with the report of the previous study, which revealed that male teachers encountered more emotional exhaustion compared to their female counterparts, who displayed increased job satisfaction (Anastasiou & Belios, 2020). Furthermore, the results of this study contradict the reports of Geng et al. (2022), which revealed that males had higher stress levels than their female counterparts among pre-service teachers. Additionally, a study's report indicated that female teachers experienced higher occupational stress, especially in their interactions with students and colleagues (Antoniou et al., 2006).

This study revealed that age and school type significantly predicted role overload, implying that the stress teachers experience varies based on age and school. However, teachers' gender, school location, and educational qualification did not predict overload. Finally, none of the demographic or school-related variables was a significant predictor of role ambiguity and role conflict, and the models explained little variance. These findings suggest that ambiguity and conflict emanate more from structural and organisational challenges rather than individual teacher attributes. Age and school type significantly predicted role overload, which contributes to teachers' stress experience in CT of SASD. Age of teacher has been a significant predictor, indicating that older teachers experience more overload as a result of increased responsibilities, reduced physical abilities, and the importance of age implies that educators feel the pressure of age more, possibly because of the added responsibilities, decrease in physical capabilities, or additional leadership position (Anastasiou & Belios, 2020). Furthermore, another study revealed that younger teachers encountered higher stress with regard to government support (Antoniou et al., 2006).

The school type as a predictor of teacher stress is indicative of differences in the school systems between the public and private schools. The school classes in public schools tend to be bigger, and there are fewer resources, as well as support services, which makes the workload of the teachers higher. Private schools are commonly known for imposing higher performance expectations on teachers, pressuring them to deliver high-quality outcomes. Both public and private schools provide conditions of role overload, but the type of school influences the nature and extent of the overload. This finding aligns with the previous studies, like Odoh (2020), who revealed that the school environment impacted teachers' commitment to teaching in public and private schools. A similar study indicated that school climate was impactful on the job satisfaction and performance of teachers.

The insignificant of the level of educational qualification in teachers' stress experiences indicates that training does not necessarily provide teachers potential to handle transition tasks effectively. This evidence supports the necessity to change the teacher education Programmes and introduce the modules regarding transition planning and autism support. This finding is indicative of historical lapses in teacher education programmes in the Nigerian context, where the curriculum focuses on general pedagogy and content area, and not on discipline-specific skills, such as disability support, behaviour management and transition planning (Boujut et al., 2016). Many teachers' training programmes offer little in terms of coursework on autism, how to teach functional skills or even collaborate with other agencies, and thus, make their graduates inadequately equipped to face the reality of inclusive practice (Gómez-Marí et al., 2021). In addition, professional development opportunities in the service sector that are focused on the process of transition are either minimal, intermittent or abstract as opposed to practical. As a result, teachers with advanced degrees might be unacquainted with evidence-based transition models or vocational preparedness models. This disjuncture highlights a structural problem in Nigeria, in the teacher development system, in qualifications not being able to be translated into specialised competencies of transition work (Nwamara & Nwakacha, 2025). Another feature of transition support that is highlighted by the findings includes its experiential and contextual nature. The teachers often learn by experience, by working together with others, or by solving problems informally instead of by any formal qualification. In such a way, an educational level fails to distinguish the capacity of teachers to cope with transition tasks, thus highlighting the need to train capacity and implement professional development. The results of this study align with the findings of Kalsoom et al. (2020), which indicated that there was no notable difference in teacher knowledge and awareness when considering their qualifications.

The insignificance of school location suggests that the urban-rural disparity does not affect overload, ambiguity, and conflict roles. Although the urban schools might have better resources, they also have more enrolment and demand from parents. The schools in the rural areas might lack resources, but they might not undergo much administrative pressure (Okpilike Felix, 2010). The location has no impact on these conflicting forces. Despite having relatively high infrastructure in urban schools in Nigeria, they also face increased enrolment, parental expectations, as well as administrative scrutiny (Shernoff et al., 2011). All these factors add to workloads and create conflicting needs that increase the stress levels of teachers despite the increased availability of resources. In contrast, in rural schools, facilities are usually limited, and the quality of trained staff is also lower; however, the teachers working in such institutions can have less administrative stress and fewer parental expectations, which can eliminate the predicted shortcomings (Okpilike Felix, 2010).

The overall finding is that urban and rural settings result in different but equally stressful factors and lead to non-significant differences in role overload, ambiguity, or conflict. This result highlights the structural character of the stress associated with the transition in Nigeria. Regardless of the place, educators must struggle to overcome the vague transitioning policies, insufficient specialist assistance, and conflicting demands of school leaders and families (Ezewuzie et al., 2025). As a result, the lack of locational differences highlights the need to implement national-level changes instead of geographically oriented interventions since teachers in different settings will face similar systemic issues in helping students with autism to handle career transitions.

These findings emerged based on the societal expectation of the teachers to deliver content, manage behavioural challenges, adapt teaching materials, collaborate with parents, and conduct transition planning despite limited support structures in Southeast Nigeria. These multiple sources of burden create an environment for teachers that is pervasive and hard to avoid. The educational situation in Nigeria amplifies the demands associated with career transition responsibilities as a result of ineffective institutional support systems, minimal interagency collaboration, and inadequate special needs training across teacher education programmes.

The CT period is intrinsically complicated for SASD because it demands coordinated teaching in vocational skills, daily living competencies, workplace behaviour, and future planning. In Nigeria, where there is a scarcity of professionals coupled with limited transitional pathways and

Community-based vocational education, teachers serve as the primary facilitators of these outcomes. The teachers' stress patterns revealed in this study depict an expanded set of responsibilities, which extends far beyond traditional teaching duties, validating the need for stronger institutional frameworks where teachers should be trained and guided to reduce stress.

The results of this research authenticated the Role Stress Theory by demonstrating that overload, ambiguity, and conflict significantly contribute to teacher stress within the context of the CT of SASD in Southeast Nigeria. The insignificance of the demographic variables in explaining role ambiguity and role conflict indicates that the two constructs are highly organisational phenomena, which is in line with theoretical assumptions. The findings indicate that teacher stress during transition work for SASD is rooted in systemic and organisational conditions. Policymakers should revise the NPSNIE with specific instructions on the transition planning, the role of the teacher, interagency cooperation, and the necessary resources. Schools are advised to offer structured professional development on transition processes, autism facilitation, as well as behaviour regulation. To manage workload, reducing class sizes and providing teaching assistants should be adopted to alleviate teachers' overload. Ambiguity and conflict would be minimised by having clear channels of communication and descriptions of roles.

Even though this research shed more critical light on teacher stress as SASD transition through their careers in Nigeria, several limitations should be acknowledged. First, the investigations depended on self-reporting scales, which might have been affected by the social desirability or personal perceptions that are not all-inclusive of the diversity of lived experiences of teachers. Second, the cross-sectional design restricts the causal explanations and fails to consider variations in stress levels across time or across the school year. Third, the sample consisted only experienced teachers who have been serving SASD and hence generalisation to other teachers providing support to other types of special needs students is limited. Fourth, the study was carried out over a narrow geopolitical area (even though the sample was diverse in terms of school type and location), and the results might not be applicable to the experiences of teachers in other regions of Nigeria with a different administrative structure or where resources were more abundant. Fifth, the demographic and school-related predictors were studied. Still, no organisational culture, leadership practices, and access to specialist support services were measured, although these aspects may play a crucial role in role overload, ambiguity, and conflict. Lastly, the research failed to include qualitative methodologies that can give a more insightful interpretation of the contextual and emotional aspects of teacher stress in the process of transition planning.

CONCLUSIONS

This research focused on teacher stress in the CT of SASD in Nigeria through role overload, role ambiguity, and role conflict, while exploring the differences in gender and demographic factors as predictors. The results indicate that teachers experience stress are under considerable stress across all dimensions, with role overload emerging as the most significant challenge. This overload is indicative of the stressful realities of the Nigerian educational setting, where teachers must deal with both teaching responsibilities and transition planning responsibilities in a setting that is marked by scarcity of resources, poor staffing, and inconsistency in policy implementation. In the study, gender differences in the level of stress were minimal, which signifies that during CT work is a shared professional burden that surpasses gender identity. Regression outcomes indicated that predictors of role overload were age and type of school, such that some groups of teachers might have increased demands based on institutional factors and the cumulative nature of teacher roles. Conversely, demographic and school variables did not predict role ambiguity or role conflict, which indicates that these challenges originated from systematic and organisational factors. These results demonstrate the importance of extensive policy review, especially the establishment of clear transition models into the National Policy of Special Needs and Inclusive Education. The enhancement of professional development, the definition of teacher roles, the enhancement of communication channels, and greater access to specialist support services are necessary measures in stress reduction and transition outcomes improvement. Addressing systemic barriers is a significant step to improve teacher well-being and to guarantee effective and coordinated transition support to SASD.

REFERENCES

Adeboye, T. A., & Obawole, A. (2019). Pay Satisfaction and Role Ambiguity as Predictors of Job Burnout Among Osun State Civil Servants, Nigeria. *European Scientific Journal, 15*(8), 41–58. DOI: 10.19044/esj.2019.v15n8p41

Adewale, A. S., Ghavifekr, S., & Abdulsalam, I. (2017). Impact of stress on academic staff: Implication for higher education management and leadership. *Malaysian Online Journal of Educational Management, 5*(2), 75–91. DOI: 10.22452/mojem.vol5no2.5

Adigun, O. T., Tijani, F. A., Nzima, D. R., & Vivekanantharasa, R. (2021). Perceived Stress of Special Education Teachers in the Context of the Person-Environment Relationship. *The Open Psychology Journal, 14*(1), 300–309. DOI: 10.2174/1874350102114010300

Agunowei, D. I., & Mayombe, C. (2024). The fate of special needs children in the midst of inclusive education policy in Abuja, Nigeria. In Sánchez-Santamaría, J., & Cervantes, B. B. (Eds.), *Exploring Educational Equity at the Intersection of Policy and Practice* (pp. 264–286). IGI Global., DOI: 10.4018/979-8-3693-1614-6.ch015

Akanaeme, I. N., Ekwealor, F. N., Ifeluni, C. N., Onyishi, C. N., Obikwelu, C. L., Ohia, N. C., Obayi, L. N., Nwaoga, C. T., Okafor, A. E., Victor-Aigbodion, V., Ejiofor, T. E., Afiaenyi, I. C., Ekomaru, C. I., & Dike, I. C. (2021). Managing job stress among teachers of children with autism spectrum disorders: A randomised controlled trial of cognitive behavioral therapy with yoga. *Medicine, 100*(46), E27312. Advance online publication. DOI: 10.1097/MD.0000000000027312 PMID: 34797272

Akande, O. O. (2024). *Exploring the Challenges Faced by Parents of Children With ASD in Rural Nigerian Communities: A Multidimensional Analysis of Support Systems and Intervention* [Ed.D., Houston Baptist University]. https://www.proquest.com/docview/3054424848/abstract/D177D505934E4DEBPQ/1

Ali, I. M. (2024). A Guide for positivist research paradigm: From philosophy to methodology. *Idealogy Journal, 9*(2). Advance online publication. DOI: 10.24191/idealogy.v9i2.596

Amu, S. I., Answem, A. B., & Amu, M. M. (2025). Impact of stress on teacher's performance in business studies at junior secondary schools in Makurdi metropolis. *Open Journal of Educational Development, 6*(1), 29–42. DOI: 10.52417/ojed.v6i1.707

Anastasiou, S., & Belios, E. (2020). Effect of Age on Job Satisfaction and Emotional Exhaustion of Primary School Teachers in Greece. *European Journal of Investigation in Health, Psychology and Education, 10*(2), 644–655. DOI: 10.3390/ejihpe10020047 PMID: 34542525

Anazia, I. U., Skinner, B., & Woods, C. (2025). Home-school partnerships: Values and expectations of rural teachers and parents. *Educational Research, 67*(2), 170–189. DOI: 10.1080/00131881.2025.2492143

Antoniou, A.-S., Polychroni, F., & Vlachakis, A.-N. (2006). Gender and age differences in occupational stress and professional burnout between primary and high-school teachers in Greece. *Journal of Managerial Psychology, 21*(7), 682–690. DOI: 10.1108/02683940610690213

Asa, F. T., & Lasebikan, V. O. (2016). Mental health of teachers: Teachers' stress, anxiety and depression among secondary schools in Nigeria. *International Neuropsychiatric Disease Journal, 7*(4), 1–10. DOI: 10.9734/INDJ/2016/27039

Ayala, K. (2023). LEADERS: A Psychoeducational support group for college-bound high school students with autism spectrum disorder (ASD). *Journal of Applied School Psychology, 39*(4), 397–412. DOI: 10.1080/15377903.2023.2221201

Ayeni, A. J. (2017a). Teachers' Classroom management and Quality Assurance of Students' Learning Outcome in Secondary Schools in Ondo State, Nigeria. *Journal of Social and Administrative Sciences, 4*(2), 166–180. DOI: 10.1453/jsas.v4i2.1312

Ayeni, A. J. (2017b). Teachers' Classroom management and Quality Assurance of Students' Learning Outcome in Secondary Schools in Ondo State, Nigeria. *Journal of Social and Administrative Sciences, 4*(2), 166–180. DOI: 10.1453/jsas.v4i2.1312

Boujut, E., Dean, A., Grouselle, A., & Cappe, E. (2016). Comparative Study of Teachers in Regular Schools and Teachers in Specialized Schools in France, Working with Students with an Autism Spectrum Disorder: Stress, Social Support, Coping Strategies and Burnout. *Journal of Autism and Developmental Disorders, 46*(9), 2874–2889. DOI: 10.1007/s10803-016-2833-2 PMID: 27282858

Bredeson, P. V. (1993). Letting Go of Outlived Professional Identities: A Study of Role Transition and Role Strain for Principals in Restructured Schools. *Educational Administration Quarterly, 29*(1), 34–68. DOI: 10.1177/0013161X93029001004

Bridges, S., & Searle, A. (2011). Changing workloads of primary school teachers: "I seem to live on the edge of chaos.". *School Leadership & Management, 31*(5), 413–433. DOI: 10.1080/13632434.2011.614943

Bukhori, I., Nora, E., & Suputra, I. N. (2020). Role conflict, training, and participative leadership on teachers' performance: Lesson from junior high school in Mojokerto of Indonesia. *International Journal of Scientific and Technology Research, 9*(3), 3264–3266.

Cappe, É., Despax, J., Ridremont, D., & Boujut, E. (2025). Are Stress and Burnout Specific to French Teachers of Autistic Students? A Comparative Study With Attention-Deficit/Hyperactivity Disorder and Conduct Disorder. *Psychology in the Schools*, *62*(5), 1397–1409. DOI: 10.1002/pits.23409

Chandra, S. (Ed.). (2024). *Universal Design for Learning: Addressing the Barriers*. IP Innovative Publication., DOI: 10.18231/978-93-91208-76-9

Dada, J. A., Adesina, S., Obaseki, B. E., Dada, G. O., & Adesina, J. A. (2025). Can Role Ambiguity and Role Conflict Affect Employee's Job Performance in Christian Faith-based University in Nigeria. *Journal of Arts and Sociological Research*. DOI: 10.70382/ajasr.v8i6.033

Dankade, U., Bello, H., & Deba, A. (2016). Analysis of job stress affecting the performance of secondary schools' vocational technical teachers in north east, Nigeria. *Journal of Technical Education and Training*, *8*(1), 43–51.

Deng, Y., Zeng, H., Xu, A., & Chen, Y. (2022). Based on Role Expectation to Discuss Role Ambiguity and Practice of University Teachers in Business Administration. *Frontiers in Psychology*, *13*, 789806. DOI: 10.3389/fpsyg.2022.789806 PMID: 36478930

Devi, B., Lepcha, N., & Basnet, S. (2022). Application of correlational research design in nursing and medical research. *Journal of Xi'an Shiyou University, Natural Sciences Edition, 65*(11), 60-69. https://doi.org/DOI: 10.17605/OSF.IO/YRZ68

Dhungana, P., Joshi, A., Chalise, A., & Paudel, S. (2025). Psychological well-being and occupational stress among public secondary school teachers in Beni Municipality, Nepal: A cross-sectional study. *BMC Public Health*, *25*(1), 3372. DOI: 10.1186/s12889-025-24677-x PMID: 41057805

Dietrich, J., & Salmela-Aro, K. (2013). Parental involvement and adolescents' career goal pursuit during the post-school transition. *Journal of Adolescence*, *36*(1), 121–128. DOI: 10.1016/j.adolescence.2012.10.009 PMID: 23190942

Dike, I. C., Onyishi, C. N., Adimora, D. E., Ugodulunwa, C. A., Adama, G. N., Ugwu, G. C., Eze, U. N., Eze, A., Ogba, F. N., Obiwluozo, P. E., Onu, J. C., Onu, A. O., Omenma, Z. O., Nwaeze, V. C., Ani, C., Ngwu, C. N., Uzodinma, U. E., & Iremeka, F. U. (2021). Yoga complemented cognitive behavioral therapy on job burnout among teachers of children with autism spectrum disorders. *Medicine*, *100*(22), E25801. Advance online publication. DOI: 10.1097/MD.0000000000025801 PMID: 34087823

Dipeolu, A. O., Storlie, C., & Johnson, C. (2015). College Students with High-Functioning Autism Spectrum Disorder: Best Practices for Successful Transition to the World of Work. *Journal of College Counseling*, *18*(2), 175–190. DOI: 10.1002/jocc.12013

Epp, A. (2023). Relations between Professional Action and Biographical Transition Experiences of Teachers' – Dealing with Uncer-tainty as an Intertwined Connection. *Historia Scholastica*, *9*(1), 55–81. DOI: 10.15240/tul/006/2023-1-003

Eseadi, C., & Diale, B. M. (2025). *Perspectives on career transitioning of students with hearing impairments*. IGI Global., DOI: 10.4018/979-8-3693-2631-2

Ezewuzie, S. O. Patricia Amaka Udeogu, & Okoli, H. N. (2025). Assessment of educational policies and reforms in Nigeria: Challenges and prospects. *Chukwuemeka Odumegwu Ojukwu University Journal of Arts and Social Science Education, 4*(1). https://cooujoasse.org/index.php/cooujoasse/article/view/32

Fagan, C., Lyonette, C., Smith, M., & Saldaña-Tejeda, A. (2012). *The influence of working time arrangements on work-life integration or 'balance': A review of the international evidence*. International Labour Organization. https://research.manchester.ac.uk/en/publications/the-influence-of-working-time-arrangements-on-work-life-integrati/

Fasching, H. (2014). Career counselling at school for placement in sheltered workshops? *British Journal of Learning Disabilities*, *42*(1), 50–57. DOI: 10.1111/bld.12009

Federal Republic of Nigeria. (2015). *National Policy on Special Needs Education in Nigeria*. Federal Ministry of Education Abuja.

Gómez-Marí, I., Sanz-Cervera, P., & Tárraga-Mínguez, R. (2021). Teachers' Knowledge Regarding Autism Spectrum Disorder (ASD): A Systematic Review. *Sustainability (Basel)*, *13*(9), 5097. DOI: 10.3390/su13095097

Goodson, I. F., & Ümarik, M. (2019). Changing policy contexts and teachers' work-life narratives: The case of Estonian vocational teachers. *Teachers and Teaching*, *25*(5), 589–602. DOI: 10.1080/13540602.2019.1664300

Hassan, M., Azmat, U., Sarwar, S., Adil, I. H., & Gillani, S. H. M. (2020). Impact of job satisfaction, job stress and motivation on job performance: A case from private universities of karachi. [Kuwait Chapter]. *Arabian Journal of Business and Management Review*, *9*(2), 76–86.

Hossan, D., Mansor, Z. D., & Jaharuddin, N. S. (2023). Research Population and Sampling in Quantitative Study. [IJBT]. *International Journal of Business and Technopreneurship, 13*(3), 209–222. DOI: 10.58915/ijbt.v13i3.263

Hsueh, N.-L., Chu, P.-H., & Chu, W. (2008). A quantitative approach for evaluating the quality of design patterns. *Journal of Systems and Software, 81*(8), 1430–1439. DOI: 10.1016/j.jss.2007.11.724

Kahn, R. L., Wolfe, D. M., Quinn, R. P., Snoek, J. D., & Rosenthal, R. A. (1964). Organizational stress: Studies in role conflict and ambiguity.

King, L. A., & King, D. W. (1990). Role conflict and role ambiguity: A critical assessment of construct validity. *Psychological Bulletin, 107*(1), 48–64. DOI: 10.1037/0033-2909.107.1.48

Km, O., & Js, T. (2007). Interagency collaboration: The importance of rehabilitation professionals' involvement in transition. *Journal of Rehabilitation, 73*(3), 36. https://openurl.ebsco.com/contentitem/gcd:105946890?sid=ebsco:plink:crawler&id=ebsco:gcd:105946890

Lazaraton, A. (2005). Quantitative Research Methods. In *Handbook of Research in Second Language Teaching and Learning*. Routledge.

Lindner, K.-T., Nusser, L., Gehrer, K., & Schwab, S. (2021). Differentiation and Grouping Practices as a Response to Heterogeneity – Teachers' Implementation of Inclusive Teaching Approaches in Regular, Inclusive and Special Classrooms. *Frontiers in Psychology, 12*, 676482. Advance online publication. DOI: 10.3389/fpsyg.2021.676482 PMID: 34566756

Lyne, K. D., Barrett, P. T., Williams, C., & Coaley, K. (2000). A psychometric evaluation of the Occupational Stress Indicator. *Journal of Occupational and Organizational Psychology, 73*(2), 195–220. DOI: 10.1348/096317900166985

Maphal, M. C. (2014). The manifestation of occupational stress in the teaching profession: The unheeded voices of teachers. *Mediterranean Journal of Social Sciences, 5*(1), 77–88. DOI: 10.5901/mjss.2014.v5n1p77

Mason, S. (2019). Teachers, twitter and tackling overwork in Japan. *Issues in Educational Research, 29*(3), 881–898.

Michaels, C. A., & Orentlicher, M. L. (2004). The role of occupational therapy in providing person-centred transition services: Implications for school-based practice. *Occupational Therapy International, 11*(4), 209–228. DOI: 10.1002/oti.212 PMID: 15771211

Myburgh, S., & van der Vyver, C. P. (2022). Role conflict and role ambiguity in mid-level management in primary schools: Challenges and expectations. In L. van Jaarsveld, C. C. Wolhuter, & C. P. van der Vyver (Eds.), *Education leadership: Scoping, perspectives and future trajectory* (pp. 139–159). AOSIS (pty) Ltd. DOI: 10.4102/aosis.2022.BK383.08

Nakpodia, E. D., & James, U. (2012). Gender Discrimination in Nigerian School System. *International Journal of Development and Management Review*, *7*(1). https://www.ajol.info/index.php/ijdmr/article/view/79287

Nnah, M. O., & George, A. (2025). *Tackling Teacher Burnout and Low Morale in Nigerian Secondary Schools through Effective Leadership Strategies. 18(2b)*, 313–333.

Nnubia, U. I., Ibeanu, V. N., & Okechukwu, F. O. (2025). Gender role shift: Implications for balancing work and family responsibilities among female primary school teachers in Nigeria. *Journal of Family Studies*, *31*(1), 35–53. DOI: 10.1080/13229400.2024.2405106

Nuske, H. J., McGhee Hassrick, E., Bronstein, B., Hauptman, L., Aponte, C., Levato, L., Stahmer, A., Mandell, D. S., Mundy, P., Kasari, C., & Smith, T. (2019). Broken bridges—new school transitions for students with autism spectrum disorder: A systematic review on difficulties and strategies for success. *Autism*, *23*(2), 306–325. DOI: 10.1177/1362361318754529 PMID: 29458258

Nwagwu, C. C.NWAGWU. (1997). The Environment of Crises in the Nigerian Education System. *Comparative Education*, *33*(1), 87–96. DOI: 10.1080/03050069728659

Nwamara, E. N., & Nwakacha, C. I. (2025). National Policy on Education: An examination of policy provisions and implications. *Beyond Babel: BU Journal of Language. Literature and Humanities*, *9*(1), 352–360. DOI: 10.5281/zenodo.16273925

Nwoko, J. C., Anderson, E., Adegboye, O., Malau-Aduli, A. E. O., & Malau-Aduli, B. S. (2024). Navigating Teachers' Occupational Well-Being in the Tides of Classroom Processes and School Structures. *Education Sciences*, *14*(11), 1225. DOI: 10.3390/educsci14111225

Obimakinde, A. M., Balogun, M. O., Adeleye, J., Oloruntoba, E., Popoola, O., Adedokun, B., & Omokhodion, F. (2022). Work-related psychological distress among teachers in southwest Nigeria: A rural and urban comparison. *Occupational Health Southern Africa*, *28*(3), 95–100. DOI: 10.10520/ejc-ohsa_v28_n3_a4

Odoh, J. N. (2020). Comparative analysis of school climate and teachers' commitment in public and private secondary schools in Ebonyi state. *National Journal Of Educational Leadership, 5*(1). https://ezenwaohaetorc.org/journals/index.php/NJOEL/article/view/1373

Ogba, F. N., Onyishi, C. N., Victor-Aigbodion, V., Abada, I. M., Eze, U. N., Obiweluozo, P. E., Ugodulunwa, C. N., Igu, N. C. N., Okorie, C. O., Onu, J. C., Eze, A., Ezeani, E. O., Ebizie, E. N., & Onwu, A. O. (2020). Managing job stress in teachers of children with autism: A rational emotive occupational health coaching control trial. *Medicine, 99*(36), e21651. DOI: 10.1097/MD.0000000000021651 PMID: 32898998

Ogharen, B. B., Egbule, E. O., & Joy, A. C. (2022). Management of Interpersonal Conflict Involving Principals and Teachers of Selected Public Secondary Schools in Nigeria. *Journal of Educational and Social Research, 12*(3), 320–336. DOI: 10.36941/jesr-2022-0090

Ogu, E. N., & Chike, O. G. -. (2025). Curriculum Management in Nigerian Secondary School for Sustainable Development: Challenges and Opportunities. *International Journal of Educational Management, Rivers State University., 1*(2), 118–129. https://ijedm.com/index.php/ijedm/article/view/49

Ojionuka, A. N. (2016). *Nigerian Educators' Attention Deficit Hyperactivity Disorder Knowledge and Classroom Behavior Management Practices* [Ph.D., Walden University]. https://www.proquest.com/docview/1783595516/abstract/2FAA5256A138461EPQ/1

Okpaka, O., & Ajayi, O. (2025). *Inclusive Strategies for Students with Autism Spectrum Disorder Within the Framework of Evidence-Based Practices—A Scoping Review* (SSRN Scholarly Paper No. 5119762). Social Science Research Network. DOI: 10.2139/ssrn.5119762

Okpilike Felix, M. E. (2010). Towards coping with the major contemporary challenges of the classroom teacher in Nigeria. *Social Sciences, 5*(6), 565–569. DOI: 10.3923/sscience.2010.565.569

Okwaraji, F. E., & Aguwa, E. N. (2015). Burnout, psychological distress and job satisfaction among secondary school teachers in Enugu, south east Nigeria. *African Journal of Psychiatry (Johannesburg), 18*(1). Advance online publication. DOI: 10.4172/Psychiatry.1000198

Olagunju, A. T., Akinola, M. A., Fadipe, B., Jagun, O. O., Olagunju, T. O., Akinola, O. O., Ogunnubi, O. P., Olusile, O. J., Oluyemi, O. Y., & Chaimowitz, G. A. (2021a). Psychosocial Well-being of Nigerian Teachers in Special Education Schools. *Journal of Autism and Developmental Disorders*, *51*(4), 1131–1141. DOI: 10.1007/s10803-020-04606-0 PMID: 32666197

Olagunju, A. T., Akinola, M. A., Fadipe, B., Jagun, O. O., Olagunju, T. O., Akinola, O. O., Ogunnubi, O. P., Olusile, O. J., Oluyemi, O. Y., & Chaimowitz, G. A. (2021b). Psychosocial Well-being of Nigerian Teachers in Special Education Schools. *Journal of Autism and Developmental Disorders*, *51*(4), 1131–1141. DOI: 10.1007/s10803-020-04606-0 PMID: 32666197

Ololube, N. P. (2013). The problems and approaches to educational planning in Nigeria: A theoretical observation. *Mediterranean Journal of Social Sciences*, *4*(12), 37–48. DOI: 10.5901/mjss.2013.v4n12p37

Onyishi, C. N., Okpoko, C. C., & Victor-Aigbodion, V. (2025). Teachers' awareness and perceptions of inclusive education for learners with autism: Implications for the campaign against stigma. *Ikenga*, *26*(1), 51–80. DOI: 10.53836/ijia/2025/26/1/004

Opara, C. J. (2024). Workplace Stress: A comparison of public and private school teachers in Port Harcourt, Rivers State, Nigeria. *The Nigerian Health Journal*, *24*(2), 1211–1219. DOI: 10.60787/tnhj.v24i2.798

Orhero, A. E., Okereka, O. P., & Okolie, U. C. (2023). Role Stressor and Work Adjustment of University Lecturers in Delta State. *Ianna Journal of Interdisciplinary Studies*, *5*(1), 124–135.

Otegbeye, C. U. (2021). Rethinking Teacher Professionalism and Policy Reforms in the Nigerian Educational Context [Doctoral, UCL (University College London)]. In *Doctoral thesis, UCL (University College London)*. UCL (University College London. https://discovery.ucl.ac.uk/id/eprint/10136626/

Ozoemena, E. L., Agbaje, O. S., Ogundu, L., Ononuju, A. H., Umoke, P. C. I., Iweama, C. N., Kato, G. U., Isabu, A. C., & Obute, A. J. (2021). Psychological distress, burnout, and coping strategies among Nigerian primary school teachers: A school-based cross-sectional study. *BMC Public Health*, *21*(1), 2327. DOI: 10.1186/s12889-021-12397-x PMID: 34969391

Park, Y. S., Konge, L., & Artino, A. R. J. (2020). The Positivism Paradigm of Research. *Academic Medicine*, *95*(5), 690–694. DOI: 10.1097/ACM.0000000000003093 PMID: 31789841

Peretomode, V. F. (2006a). Decisional deprivation, equilibrium and saturation as variables in teacher motivation, job satisfaction and morale in Nigeria. *Academic Leadership*, *4*(1), 111–126.

Peretomode, V. F. (2006b). Decisional deprivation, equilibrium and saturation as variables in teacher motivation, job satisfaction and morale in Nigeria. *Academic Leadership*, *4*(1), 111–126.

Pérez, E. G. S., Medina, D. E. M., & Caraveo, M. del C. S. (. (2017). Indications of role ambiguity in university teachers. *Revista Electrónica de Investigación Educativa*, *19*(1), 73–83. DOI: 10.24320/redie.2017.19.1.889

Ramos, A. de S., & Alves, L. M. (2008). Speech therapy in the interaction between regular primary schools and special education schools in the process of inclusion. *Revista Brasileira de Educação Especial*, *14*(2), 235–250. DOI: 10.1590/S1413-65382008000200007

Raudeliūnaitė, R., & Steponėnienė, E. (2020). Challenges for primary school teachers in ensuring inclusive education for children with autism spectrum disorders. *Pedagogika*, *138*(2), 209–225. DOI: 10.15823/p.2020.138.12

Salahu, M. O. (2020). *Assessment of Educational Policy in Nigeria: A Study of State and Non-state Provision of Basic Education in Kwara State (2009-2019)* [Ph.D., Kwara State University (Nigeria)]. https://www.proquest.com/docview/2447051198/abstract/82A9E457504CB7PQ/1

Sasere, O. B. (2023). *Leadership roles of school administrators in teachers' professional development in Nigeria* [University of the Free State]. http://hdl.handle.net/11660/12404

Schwab, R. L., & Iwanicki, E. F. (1982). Perceived Role Conflict, Role Ambiguity, and Teacher Burnout. *Educational Administration Quarterly*, *18*(1), 60–74. DOI: 10.1177/0013161X82018001005

Shernoff, E. S., Mehta, T. G., Atkins, M. S., Torf, R., & Spencer, J. (2011). A Qualitative Study of the Sources and Impact of Stress Among Urban Teachers. *School Mental Health*, *3*(2), 59–69. DOI: 10.1007/s12310-011-9051-z

Silvia, M., Hadi, S., & Kurniawan, I. S. (2025). The role of role overload, role conflict, and role ambiguity in job stress. *The Fourth International Conference on Government Education Management and Tourism*, *4*, 094–094. https://www.conference.loupiasconference.org/index.php/ICoGEMT-4/article/view/616

Tabancalı, E., & Su, Y. (2021). Role ambiguity of school principals. *Eğitimde Nitel Araştırmalar Dergisi*, *9*(1), 335–359.

Uba-Mbibi, F. O. (2013). Decision making and job satisfaction as correlates of teachers' job performance in junior secondary schools in Abia state, Nigeria. *Mediterranean Journal of Social Sciences, 4*(8), 107–112. DOI: 10.5901/mjss.2013.v4n8p107

Umeh, N. C., & Anyaele, D. O. (2024a). Assessment of the Implementation of Inclusive Education Policy Among Stakeholders in Abia State, Nigeria. In *Ius Gentium* (Vol. 117, pp. 1–19). Springer Science and Business Media B.V., DOI: 10.1007/978-3-031-64549-5_1

Umeh, N. C., & Anyaele, D. O. (2024b). Assessment of the Implementation of Inclusive Education Policy Among Stakeholders in Abia State, Nigeria. In *Ius Gentium* (Vol. 117, pp. 1–19). Springer Science and Business Media B.V., DOI: 10.1007/978-3-031-64549-5_1

Uzodinma, U. E., & Onyishi, N, C., Ngwoke, A. N., Ugwu, J. I., Okorie, C. O., A. Amujiri, B., ... & Akanaeme, I. N. (. (2022). Effectiveness of rational emotive occupational health coaching in reducing burnout symptoms among teachers of children with autism. *Science Progress, 105*(2), 00368504221100907. DOI: 10.1177/00368504221100907 PMID: 35619571

Vázquez-Cano, E., & Holgueras-González, A. I. (2019). Teacher stress factors and performance in high schools in Ecuador. *KEDI Journal of Educational Policy, 16*(2), 21–41.

Westheimer, J. (1998). *Among School Teachers: Community, Autonomy and Ideology in Teachers' Work*. Teachers College Press.

Wong, V. W., Ruble, L. A., Yu, Y., & McGrew, J. H. (2017). Too stressed to teach? Teaching quality, student engagement, and IEP outcomes. *Exceptional Children, 83*(4), 412–427. DOI: 10.1177/0014402917690729 PMID: 30555178

APPENDIX

Table 3. Teacher Stress Questionnaire in Supporting Student Career Transition (TSQ-SCT)

S/No	Items	Factor Loading	Cronbach's α	Omega ω
	Role Overload			
1	The number of tasks related to supporting students' career transition is overwhelming on my side.	0.763	0.82	0.81
2	I often feel I lack the time to properly support students in transition activities.	0.756		
3	I struggle to manage classroom duties alongside mentoring autistic students.	0.610		
4	I frequently work beyond regular hours due to career-transition responsibilities.	0.634		
5	I feel emotionally and physically exhausted by the pace of transition support work.	0.645		
	Role Ambiguity			
6	I am unsure about my specific role in facilitating career transition for students.	0.865	0.77	0.77
7	The expectations for my transition-support role are unclear.	0.824		
8	I receive inconsistent messages from administrators regarding my transition-related duties.	0.512		
9	I find it difficult to understand who is responsible for which aspects of transition planning.	0.524		
10	I am unclear about the criteria used to evaluate my effectiveness in transition support.	0.501		
	Role Conflict			
11	I often experience conflicting instructions when working with parents and school staff.	0.806	0.73	0.79
12	I feel torn between classroom responsibilities and assisting with career transition tasks.	0.803		
13	My professional goals sometimes conflict with expectations from transition Programmes.	0.680		
14	I face pressure to comply with administrative demands that interfere with transition support.	0.486		
15	I find it challenging to balance academic teaching with individualised transition planning.	0.478		

Figure 3. Scree Plot for Teacher Stress Questionnaire in Supporting Student Career Transition (TSQ-SCT)

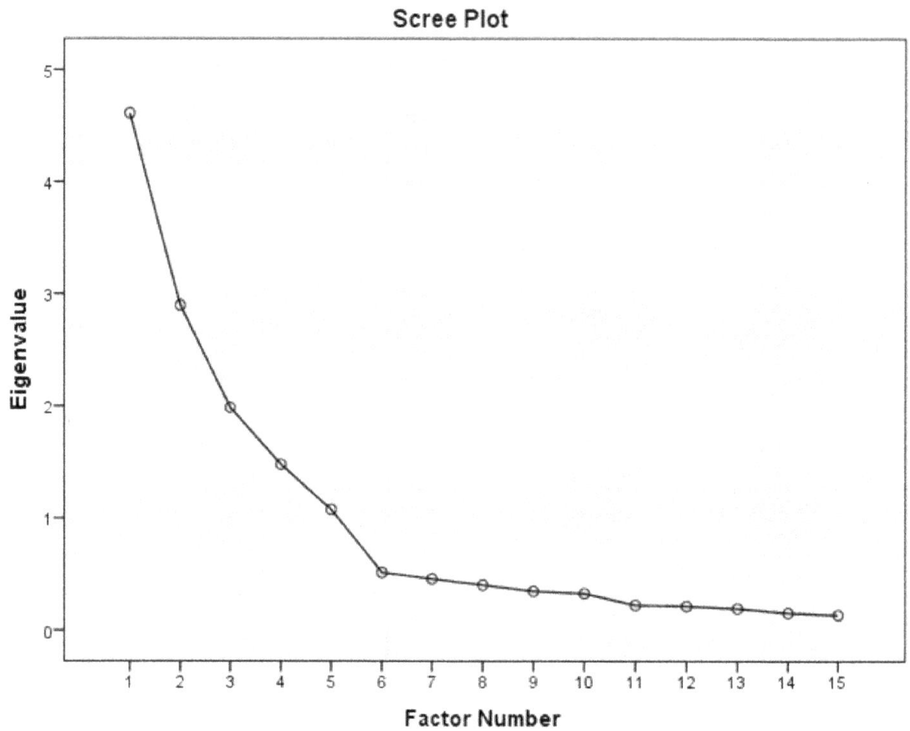

Chapter 6
Formal and Informal Institutional Support for Career Transition Among Students With ASD

ABSTRACT

This study examined the formal institutional and informal supports for the career transition of students with autism spectrum disorders (SASD). Based on the data of 88 teachers and parents in private and public schools of urban, semi-urban, and rural areas, the study evaluated the levels of support, the variation of the levels between the demographic groups, as well as the predictive power of the group, type of school and location. Regression models established that none of the demographic variables predicted support levels, hence indicating that institutional support is influenced by larger system practices. Findings indicate the necessity of enhanced capacity, equal distribution of resources, and inclusive institutional cultures that more effectively support SASD.

BACKGROUND

Autism Spectrum Disorders (ASD) refers to a developmental disorder that is characterised by challenges in social interaction, communication, and behaviour, which can limit the capacity of individuals to cope with career transition challenges. Students with autism spectrum disorders (SASD) face significant challenges in career transition because of these challenges. These challenges significantly hinder their ability to overcome life transitions such as getting and maintaining jobs upon leaving school. Literature has shown that there is a three to fourfold lower proba-

DOI: 10.4018/978-1-6684-7260-6.ch006

bility of adults with ASD being employed compared to adults without a disability (Mpofu et al., 2019), and that unemployment and underemployment are common among SASD after school (Hendricks, 2010; Yarrow et al., 2024). As a result, these students need several support systems to empower their potential at the point of transition from secondary schools. In Nigeria, where educational policies are still being developed to accommodate more students with special needs, there is still a wide discrepancy between formal and informal support systems for the career transitions of SASD. This chapter discusses the formal and informal institutional supports given to SASD in the Nigerian institutions, and how effective they facilitate smooth career transitioning.

Formal institutional support is the structured policy-driven mechanisms and frameworks that are put in place by educational institutions to make sure that SASD are able to bridge the gap between education and employment or subsequent education. Institutional support of SASD entails formal, policy-based processes and structures that are put in place by the learning institutions to ensure the successful career transition of students through education into employment (Davis et al., 2021). These supports are usually institutionalised in policies, procedures and partnerships, and are also designed to meet the unique needs of SASD when it comes to career planning and development. Formal institutional policies guarantee that career transition is prioritised for SASD, and such students are provided with the right support systems. These policies can incorporate an aspect of personalised transition plans, career guidance, and vocational training in order to equip SASD with a job after graduation. A successful transition of SASD needs extensive planning and constant support that targets areas which encompass career exploration, academic goal setting, self-advocacy skills, reasonable accommodations, and interagency cooperation (Roberts, 2010). These policies are in line with wider national and international policies on special education and rights of persons with disabilities (Sefotho & Onyishi, 2021; Nigeria National Policy on Special Needs Education, 2015; Yibakuro, 2025). Schools provide an Individual Education Plan (IEP) for SASD who qualify for the programme. Therefore, parents of the SASD are free to request for free school-based evaluation if their children are qualified for the development of an IEP (Doda et al., 2024).

For the successful implementation of these polices, the institutions with formal institutional support structures usually have a specific office or coordinator that handles the process of career transition among SASD. The role entails the planning, organisation, and execution of career transition programmes, including job shadowing, internships, and placements. The coordinator serves as a point of contact between students, staff, external agencies and families to make sure transition plans are coordinated and implemented (Scheef & Mahfouz, 2020). Some of the professionals at the forefront of coordinating the process are School psychologists. School psychologists are depicted as one of the important stakeholders and collaborators in the provision of quality transition services in schools and districts (Carter & Schutz, 2022). They engage in designing and delivering transition services to prepare students for college, career, and community outcomes. Another vital workforce development partner is also referred to as Speech-Language Pathologists (SLPs), who assist SASD to acquire the necessary skills to succeed in their postsecondary and workplace life, including communication and interaction skills (Perryman et al., 2020).

These professionals need to undergo formal, continuous training on ASD-inclusive transition planning to assist students with ASD effectively. They need training on the best practices of dealing with students with ASD, approaches of promoting independence, career growth and the ways of dealing with the challenges that such students encounter. Frequent training keeps the staff members informed with the required knowledge and skills to facilitate the various needs of the students with ASD as they go through their transitions. Studies have indicated that training opportunities, such as workshops and ongoing educational programmes, are very helpful in enhancing the knowledge and confidence of individuals who handle SASD (Kossewska et al., 2021; Iannuzzi et al., 2019). Some of these trainings involve the evidence-based practices (EBPs) as well as interventions with the specific needs of SASD, which encompasses independent-fostering strategies, social skills training, as well as cognitive-behavioural therapy (Chancel et al., 2022; Reichow et al., 2025). A study has also emphasised that the training must focus on the establishment of functional self-help and daily living abilities that are paramount in the independence of individuals with ASD (Meiring et al., 2016). The leadership of institutions is instrumental in spearheading career transition programmes for SASD. Leadership support, including speeches, policies, and funding, sends a strong message to the staff, students, and external partners that the institution has a strong commitment to inclusive education and career development of SASD. This leadership support programme is extremely crucial for SASD because literature has shown that most of the students who had undergone transition planning did not assume a leadership role in their transition planning. SASD were far less likely than other students to have a leadership position (Shogren & Plotner, 2012). A study has also established that mentorship programmes and other programmes which engage SASD in leadership positions have been found to positively impact in terms of self-advocacy and social skills (Hotez et al., 2018).

Effective career planning for SASD usually involves partnership with external agencies like the vocational rehabilitation services, employers, and disability advocacy organisations. The key aspects of quality transition services to SASD include meaningful collaboration and interagency involvement (Lee & Carter, 2012). Formal association with these agencies facilitates students to have internship opportunities, job placements and career advice outside the institution of education. Such partnerships provide SASD with real-life experiences and professional networks that help them in their adulthood. For instance, Vocational Rehabilitation Services are crucial in assisting SASD secure and retain employment as well as ongoing support, including job customisation, lateral job moves, and career advancement, which are crucial for long-term employment success (Brooke et al., 2018; Nicholas et al., 2018). Moreover, Community organisations that are engaged in vocational rehabilitation and work integration contribute a lot towards preparing SASD to work. They also offer effective methods, like instructional videos, to enable students to learn and carry out job activities efficiently (Bertrand-Ouellet et al., 2025).

Other formal institutional supports, like Formal Assessment and Monitoring of Student Progress, ensure that career transition progress must be evaluated and measured to make sure students with ASD are achieving their transition objectives. It may involve the monitoring of the rates of placements, measurement of the job readiness skills, and the monitoring of employment or further education results. Frequent evaluations allow the institutions to change their transition programmes to address the needs of students and support them where needed in a more specific manner (Yamamoto & Alverson, 2022; Karola et al., 2016). After the assessment, the Schools are expected to periodically document and report the outcomes of their transition programmes on SASD. Such reports could contain the data on the placement rates, stories of success, difficulties, and efficiency of some resources. This kind of documentation assists the institution in determining the effectiveness of its transition programmes and provides effective tips for continuous improvement (Anderson et al., 2018; Wong et al., 2020).

Formal institutions also engage in Memorandums of Understanding (MOUs) or other formal agreements of the institution with external partners that define specific roles and responsibilities of assisting students with ASD in their career transitions. These agreements would guarantee that every party knows their responsibilities, expectations and resources they would put in the agreement to ensure collaboration and accountability. By having specialised support, institutions that have specific career-transition resources for SASD ensure that these students can access such resources, as they need specialised support. Expenses such as career counselling centres staffed with ASD-trained personnel or special areas where students can practice career-related skills could also be regarded as physical resources. Access to career development materials provided through digital resources, including available online platforms or tools, can provide students with flexibility in the way they can access them and at different locations. These tools can be in the form of customised job search sites, workshops, online mentorship tools or job readiness programmes. With the physical and digital opportunities, the institutions will be able to serve the various preferences and enable the closure of the gap that ASD students may face in the traditional environment (Roux et al., 2021; Smyth et al., 2021).

The existence of formal guidelines that define accommodations and supports of career preparation activities plays a key role in providing uniformity and clarity in supporting SASD. These policies must describe particular measures and changes that need to be done to prepare the careers, such as the flexibility of the internship schedule, extra help with the interview preparation, or changes in the work environment that should be made to address sensory sensibility. These guidelines need to be well-documented so that students can be provided with the accommodations that they require to be successful (Accardo et al., 2019). Also, these guidelines must include the cooperation of career services, academic departments, and disability support services to have a comprehensive and integrated approach towards career readiness (Southall, 2013). Also, having well-defined accountability mechanisms, i.e., committees or oversight bodies, is critical to tracking the quality of career transition supports SASD. Career transitions committees or task forces ensure that all the institutional policies and resources are in line with the needs of SASD. These bodies may have the mandate of monitoring the progress of the students, assessing the results, and modifying strategies according to the feedback. It can be assisted by regular reporting and assessments to make sure that the programme is being effective and that the support offered has been on a continuous improvement. The accountability framework must also be open with students, staff, and families knowing who is to be accountable in what part of the transition process and how the success is to be quantified (Snell-Rood et al., 2020; Hume et al., 2018).

For these formal supports to be impactful on the career transition of SASD, it is essential to have a suitable budgetary allocation for the programme. This budgetary allocation is such that it ensures that there are sufficient funds to plan and execute programmes that will address the needs of the SASD application. Such resources include funds tailored towards career counselling services, career training, external collaborations, employee development and career preparation, specific tools and technology (Sharma et al., 2019). Successful implementation of career transition SASD programmes requires an adequate budget. It guarantees in-depth planning, competency building, effective work support, integrated services, and follow-ups. Unless they are sufficiently financed, these programmes may not be sufficient to address the special needs of ASD individuals, which leads to poor post-school outcomes and low employment rates (Knudson, 2024; Von Holzen et al., 2024). To utilise this budget allocation effectively, formal institutions established Standardised Transition protocols, which guarantee that the provision of services to SASD is uniform and well-structured. These protocols establish certain procedures, schedules, and duties of the personnel and students. These may involve processes of personalised evaluation, setting of goals and providing follow-up assistance to check the progress of the students in the transition process. These standardised processes guarantee that all students with ASD are given equal and holistic support. Some of the key elements of standardised protocols are structured transition planning, like the Secondary School Success Checklist and Project FUSE focus on structured planning, which involves career exploration, academic goal development, and preparation for postsecondary life (Hume et al., 2018; Schoen & Valdez, 2023). Such programmes tend to incorporate online programmes and interactive tools to promote planning.

Informal Institutional Support

Informal institutional supports, including family and friends' emotional and informational support, have a major role in promoting resilience in SASD. These supports assist the families to adapt and prosper in the face of adversity, implying that such informal networks may be useful to students during career transitioning (Fong et al., 2021). Informal institutional supports are important because SASD tend to enjoy non-formal services that allow them to have personal contact with other staff. These associations offer them advice and motivation that are essential for their career transition (Accardo et al., 2019). One of the advantages of informal institutional support is easy access to staff support. Informal support plays an important role for SASD because it offers a less intimidating method of getting assistance. Lack of formalities in communication between students and management through an open-door policy enables SASD to seek advice regarding their career issues without necessarily having to make previous appointments, which creates a supportive atmosphere. This informal communication may be especially significant to SASD, who might believe that formal meetings or an organised environment intimidate them. The freedom to openly discuss issues enables SASD to seek advice at the initial stages and pose questions, and receive reassurance as they make career-related choices (ăpuru, 2023). Informal support networks, such as casual conversations, are very important sources of emotional and informational support that are very appreciated by both students and staff (Marsack-Topolewski, 2020).

Information institutional supports also promote mentoring and provide advice for SASD. Informal guidance and support strategies by colleagues and mentors are essential in supporting SASD emotionally and practically. As compared to formal programmes, this form of mentorship is usually less structured, which makes it more friendly to students (Lucas & James, 2018). Mentors can generously give personal experiences, career-oriented insights or practical guidance on how to approach the job market. Regular unofficial check-ins and motivation create a positive environment in which SASD are inspired to work towards career ambitions. Anxiety can be mitigated, and self-efficacy enhanced by having mentors who can offer support and lessons learned (Tomfohrde et al., 2023).

The informal supports that are very effective are peer mentoring programmes. Peer mentoring matches SASD with others who have already made the career transition successfully or who are more familiar with the issues at hand. Peer mentors provide peer support through a sense of belonging and reassurance, as the mentor is a peer. Such systems also enhance social integration, as students can establish contact with people who are exposed to similar experiences or struggles (Nguyen et al., 2020). This peer-to-peer support system improves the process by offering ASD students relatable guidance and emotional support (Siew et al., 2017). Another manifestation of informal institutional support is the availability of staff members to provide discretionary time to assist SASD in the process of their social transition to the career world (Sansosti et al., 2017). The engagement may include impromptu talk, informal encounters or times in which personal career advice is given. The staff members who extend their duties by communicating with SASD informally outside their official duties assist in creating a more inclusive environment where SASD feel appreciated and given a sense of belonging. It also offers the SASD a comfortable environment to raise issues without the strain of propriety.

Similarly, the SASD who have access to informal networks like those offered by the faculty, staff, and alums can access beneficial opportunities in interacting with the members of the community, including potential employees. These informal networks may provide prospects that are not placed using the more formal job boards or career fairs, such as internship placements, job shadowing, or networking events (Margeviča-Grinberga & Kalēja, 2025; Cleveland & Williams, 2022). Through these informal networks, SASD are able to find opportunities which they may not be able to discover in formal channels.

Informal support promotes peer consultations for staff, which is evident when staff feel at ease consulting with their colleagues, where formal structures are not well defined, a collaborative problem-solving atmosphere is created to the benefit of the SASD. This transparency enables staff to exchange resources, strategies, and ideas on the best way to assist SASD, and the informal supports become more detailed and effective. It also makes sure that SASD are given consistent and careful guidance by various members of staff and departments (Dale et al., 2025). Furthermore, professional development of staff can also be achieved through peer feedback and mentoring to enable them to offer higher-quality support and interventions. Peer feedback can be made more effective by using structured feedback mechanisms (scripting and self-monitoring) to increase the engagement of the staff in the consultation process (Lahza et al., 2025; Wang et al., 2023).

Families are also important in the career transition of students with ASD, and the institutions which make the families feel free to discuss career issues, not during formal meetings, offer a valuable form of informal support. Having personnel who are willing to talk to families in an informal manner (e.g., by making phone calls, sending emails, or during informal meetings) will allow the staff to feel a part of the transition process and informed. This relationship can also be useful when making sure that the family members are also supportive of the career development of the SASD to have an extra emotional and logistical support outside of the institution. A report has shown that involvement of their parents is also a central factor in the success of SASD, both under the early intervention programmes and the education programmes during high school and beyond (Dallas et al., 2018; Kristofik & Johnson, 2024).

Informal support equally entails the culture of flexibility and adaptation, which is a great help to SASD in their career transition. Institutions that require the cultivation of a culture in which the individual's needs are honoured and accommodated have students who are better placed to express their issues and explore the support they require (Loubser, 2025). This flexibility might be in the form of non-formal adaptations within career workshops, job placements, or even networking activities that are flexible to the needs of SASD in order to be able to engage in activities that may accommodate their tastes and difficulties (Šilc & Krajnc, 2022). Informal recognition, whether by compliment or encouragement, could be very encouraging to the SASD. Positive reinforcement, which is like recognition in a less formal environment, can be used to gain confidence and will motivate SASD to put more effort towards their career objectives. This kind of recognition fosters a sense of belonging and being validated, a factor that is vital considering that there are SASD who may feel ignored or misunderstood in formal settings (Williams Harryman, 2025; Bialopotocki, 2006).

RESEARCH OBJECTIVES

The main objective of this study is to examine the patterns, differences, and predictors of formal and informal institutional support for the career transition of students with ASD across groups, school types, and geographical locations. The specific objectives include:

1. To determine the levels of formal and informal institutional support for the career transition of students with ASD across different respondent groups, school types, and geographical locations.
2. To examine whether formal and informal institutional support differ significantly across groups, school types, and geographical locations.
3. To determine the extent to which group, school type, and geographical location predict formal and informal institutional support for career transition.

RESEARCH QUESTIONS

1. What are the levels of formal and informal institutional support for the career transition of students with ASD across groups, school types, and geographical locations?
2. Are there significant differences in formal and informal institutional support based on group, school type, and geographical location?
3. To what extent do group, school type, and geographical location predict formal and informal institutional support for the career transition of students with ASD?

THEORETICAL FRAMEWORK

This theoretical framework is based on the Neurodiversity Paradigm, which was proposed by Judy Singer in 1998 (Singer, 1998). The neurodiversity paradigm is a conceptualisation of brain differences that recognises differences in thoughts, sensing and learning as normal variations in human diversity and not as defects to be cured or normalised. It changes the object of concern from what is wrong with this person, to what nature of environments, supports and rights does this person require to thrive. This perspective contradicts the conventional medical approach, which tends to conceptualise ASD as something to be treated or cured (Rodríguez, 2024). The Neurodiversity Paradigm, instead, proposes the understanding of the strengths and potential of individuals with ASD with the concern of their distinctive cognitive, emotional, and sensory experiences (Jing, 2024; Cherewick & Matergia, 2024; Lang, 2025). The Neurodiversity Paradigm within the framework of career transition calls for institutional supports, both formal and informal, that recognise and accommodate the diverse needs of SASD. The paradigm emphasise that SASD are not supposed to fit into one societal norm, and that learning and professional settings ought to be modified to accommodate their diverse modes of processing, interacting, and communicating (Guldberg, 2010). Through an inclusive approach, institutions can develop opportunities that enable SASD to have a successful career transition, where potential is acknowledged, and special needs are addressed so that their strengths are capitalised in the workplace (Aguilera Rodríguez et al., 2024).

POLICY FRAMEWORK

This study's policy framework is informed by the International Labour Organisation Disability Inclusion Strategy 2020-2023, a comprehensive global blueprint for ensuring that persons with disabilities are provided with fair access to education and employment (ILO, 2022; Mitra & Dominik, 2023). The strategy highlights the necessity of inclusive institutional frameworks where the environmental and attitudinal barriers are eliminated and the supportive structures empowering the participation of the workforce are enhanced (Buhari et al., 2025). When applied to the case of SASD in Nigeria, the strategy provides a clear direction as to the co-ordinated support mechanisms to meet both formal and informal aspects of career transition (Lee & Carter, 2012). This framework highlighted four priorities that directly resonate with the focus study. First, it requires mainstream institutions to establish structured accommodations, available career services, and mechanisms of accountability that ensure SASD receive equal preparation for employment. Second, it also facilitates the growth of informal supports such as mentoring, peer networks and community involvement, which are critical in supporting the growth of confidence, social belonging and smoother transition experiences. Third, it emphasises staff and stakeholder capacity building so that they can be made aware of neurodiversity and can respond effectively to the needs of SASD. Moreover, finally, this framework promotes collaboration with families, school administrators, interagency, and community organisations to reinforce career transition pathways and increase opportunities for meaningful work participation (Lukianova et al., 2022; Ligon & McKelvey, 2025; Lovett, 2021). Using the ILO Disability Inclusion Strategy, this paper places the institutional transition supports in a framework that has been recognised internationally, and which has been used to promote inclusive education and employment outcomes.

METHODOLOGY

Research Approach

We adopted a quantitative research approach for this research study. We aimed to examine patterns, differences, and predictors of formal and informal institutional support for the career transition of students with ASD across respondent groups, school types, and geographical locations. These aims are fundamentally concerned with measuring the strength and direction of relationships among variables, estimating group differences, and testing predictive models. A quantitative approach allowed us to work with numerical indicators of institutional support, to summarise trends using descriptive statistics, and to test predictor models through inferential statistics (Alsarmi & Al-Hemyari, 2015). By relying on structured questionnaires and standardised scoring, we were able to minimise subjective bias in measurement and to treat the constructs of interest as variables that can be compared across contexts. This approach also enabled us to address the research questions in a way that permits replication and secondary analysis in other regions of Nigeria or similar low and middle-income contexts.

Research Design

Within the quantitative approach, we employed a cross-sectional predictive correlational design (Rindfleisch et al., 2008). Data were collected once from teachers and parents of students with ASD in selected schools, rather than across several time points. The cross-sectional structure of the design was appropriate because we were interested in the current landscape of institutional support rather than changes over time (Sokratous et al., 2013). This single wave of data collection made it possible to reach a broader range of respondents in different locations with limited resources and within the timeframe of the broader career transition project. The design is predictive and correlational because we examined the extent to which group (teacher or parent), school type (private or public), and location (urban, semi-urban, or rural) are associated with, and predict, levels of formal and informal institutional support. We did not manipulate any variables and did not assign respondents to conditions. Instead, we used naturally occurring differences to estimate statistical associations and predictors. This choice was due to the ethical and practical impossibility of randomly allocating teachers, parents, or schools to demographic categories or institutional conditions. Although a cross-sectional correlational design does not permit firm causal claims, it is well-suited to identifying patterns that can inform policy and targeted interventions. In the context of an emerging field such as career transition for SASD in Nigeria, estimating the direction and magnitude of relationships is a necessary foundation for later experimental or longitudinal work.

Research Paradigm

Our research study lends itself to the positivist research paradigm. Positivist paradigm foregrounds systematic inquiry, measurement, and hypothesis testing as central routes to knowledge. This paradigm aligns with our intention to quantify institutional support, to subject our assumptions to empirical testing, and to draw inferences. From an ontological point of view, we worked with the assumption that institutional support for SASD has an external and structured reality that exists independently of us as researchers. We assumed that there are real patterns in how schools organise policies, resources, and informal practices, and that these patterns can be captured with carefully constructed indicators. This stance guided our emphasis on constructing a scale where items represent recognisable institutional practices such as formal policies, dedicated transition offices, and informal mentoring networks. From an epistemological perspective, we adopted the view that knowledge about institutional support can be approached through objective measurement and the application of statistical techniques. We sought to reduce the influence of our own expectations by using a self-developed but systematically validated instrument, standard administration procedures, and numerical analysis. At the same time, we recognised that full objectivity is an ideal rather than a perfect reality, and we therefore emphasised transparency in reporting our procedures and analytic decisions. Our axiological stance acknowledges that values are present in all research, especially in studies focused on the career transition of a vulnerable group such as SASD. We value inclusive education, equitable access, and evidence-informed policy. These commitments shaped our choice of topic and our concern with both formal structures and informal practices that support the career transition of students with ASD. Moreover, within the positivist orientation, we emphasised these values as far as possible during data collection and analysis by applying the same procedures to all respondents and by interpreting the numerical results before drawing normative conclusions.

Methodologically, the positivist paradigm informed our reliance on a structured questionnaire, probability-oriented sampling strategies, and the statistical techniques we adopted. The adoption of this philosophical stance enabled us to quantify levels of institutional support and to estimate how strongly demographic factors predict these supports.

Setting of the Study

The study took place in the South-South Geopolitical Zone of Nigeria, specifically in Akwa Ibom and Bayelsa States. These states are located in the Niger Delta region and are characterised by a mixture of coastal, riverine, and inland communities. Akwa Ibom is known for its fast-growing urban centres, such as Uyo, as well as numerous semi-urban and rural communities where educational resources are unevenly distributed. Bayelsa is one of the smaller states in Nigeria by land mass and population, with many riverine settlements that are accessible mainly by water. Both states are part of the oil-producing belt and face complex development challenges, including environmental degradation, income inequality, and inequity in access to health and education services. We selected Akwa Ibom and Bayelsa States as the setting for this study for conceptual and practical reasons. Conceptually, the South-South region has a growing network of inclusive and mainstream schools that are beginning to identify and support SASD and other neurodevelopmental needs. Hence, it is a suitable context for examining how formal and informal institutional supports are emerging around career transition. Practically, both states have urban, semi-urban, and rural locations, as reflected in our sample, which allowed us to compare institutional support across different geographical environments. In addition, we had existing professional networks with school administrators and special education officers in these states, which facilitated access and data collection processes.

Population and Sample

The target population for this research comprised teachers and parents of SASD enrolled in selected secondary schools in Akwa Ibom and Bayelsa States. We focused on schools that either practised inclusive education by enrolling SASD alongside their typically developing peers or that had designated special units or classes for students with neurodevelopmental learning disorders. Teachers in these settings are involved in curriculum delivery, classroom management, and transition planning, while parents are central partners in decision-making and advocacy for their children. Our interest in both teachers and parents reflects the understanding that institutional support for career transition is experienced and interpreted from multiple vantage points. Teachers may be more aware of the organisational structures and internal policies that shape transition practices. In contrast, parents may perceive how these structures translate into real support or barriers for their children. Including both groups, therefore, enriched our understanding of formal and informal supports.

We made use of a multi-stage sampling strategy to select the study sample. This approach was chosen to ensure that we obtained a sample that reflected variation in state, location, and school type, while also remaining logistically feasible. In the first stage, we focused on the two states of interest within the South South zone, Akwa Ibom and Bayelsa. In the second stage, within each state, we identified urban, semi-urban, and rural local government areas with a known presence of secondary schools that enrol SASD. In the third stage, we approached both private and public schools within these local government areas, using lists from state education authorities and special education units. Schools were eligible if they had at least one identified SASD at the time of the study and if the school leadership granted permission for data collection. In the final stage, we recruited teachers and parents from the selected schools. Teachers were eligible if they taught students with ASD in any secondary school grade and had at least one year of teaching experience in the current school. Parents were eligible if they had a child or ward with ASD enrolled in one of the participating schools and were willing to complete the questionnaire in English. Within each school, we used a combination of purposive and convenient procedures, guided by the inclusion criteria, to identify and invite teachers and parents who fit these conditions. The total sample consisted of 88 respondents, of whom 38 were teachers and 50 were parents, as shown in the demographic table. Of the 88 respondents, 32 were from private schools and 56 from public schools. With respect to location, 29 respondents were drawn from urban areas, 40 from semi-urban areas, and 19 from rural areas. The multi-stage design helped to enhance sample representativeness within the two states by drawing respondents from a range of schools and locations rather than from a single cluster.

Data Collection Instrument

Data were collected using the Career Transition-Related Formal and Informal Institutional Supports Questionnaire (CTFIISQ), a self-developed scale designed specifically for this project (see Table 4). The instrument was developed after a review of international and Nigerian literature on transition planning, inclusive education, and institutional responses to the needs of students with ASD. We also drew on policy documents related to schools, special needs education and career guidance to ensure that the items reflected realistic practices in school settings.

The CTFIISQ consists of 25 items grouped into two main subscales. The first subscale, Formal Institutional Support, contains 13 items that capture structured, policy-driven, and recognised forms of support. These items include the presence of formal policies that prioritise career transition for SASD, a designated office or coordinator responsible for transition planning, budget allocations for transition programmes, standardised transition protocols, regular training on ASD inclusive transition for professionals, visible leadership support for transition initiatives, official partnerships with external agencies such as vocational rehabilitation centres and employers, systematic monitoring of student progress, documentation of outcomes in institutional reports, formal agreements with partner organisations, dedicated career transition resources, specified guidelines for accommodations, and accountability structures such as committees or oversight mechanisms.

The second subscale, Informal Institutional Support, includes 12 items that capture relational, culture-based, and less formal forms of support. These items address the ease with which SASD can approach staff with career concerns, informal advice and encouragement from colleagues and mentors, peer mentoring or buddy systems, staff time for social support of transition, openness to family discussions outside official meetings, informal networks that link students to community and employer contacts, a culture of flexibility and adaptation to student needs, informal recognition of student efforts, peer consultation among staff when formal structures are unclear, organically arising networking events, casual check in practices that improve support, and informal involvement of community members such as alumni and employers in nurturing students career aspirations.

All items in the CTFIISQ are rated on a five-point Likert scale. Respondents stated the extent to which each statement reflects practices in their institution, using options from 1 (strongly disagree) through 2 (disagree), 3 (uncertain), 4 (agree), to 5 (strongly agree). Higher scores on an item indicate a stronger perception that the specific type of support is present and active in the school. Subscale scores are computed by summing or averaging responses to the relevant items, yielding separate indices for formal and informal institutional support.

We assessed internal consistency reliability for each subscale of the questionnaire. The Formal Institutional Support subscale had a Cronbach alpha coefficient of 0.76 and an omega value of 0.57. In contrast, the Informal Institutional Support subscale had a Cronbach alpha coefficient of 0.72 and an omega value of 0.62. These coefficients indicate acceptable internal consistency for research purposes, especially in a context where the instrument is newly developed and the constructs are multidimensional. In addition, we examined the effect of deleting each Item on the overall alpha values. The analysis showed that no item decreased reliability to an unacceptable extent, and thus all 25 items were retained to preserve content coverage. The content validity of the CTFIISQ was implemented via two expert reviewers who examined the items for clarity, relevance, and cultural appropriateness. Minor wording adjustments were made to ensure that both teachers and parents could understand the Item statements. The decision to use a self-developed instrument instead of an existing international scale was deliberate. Existing measures of institutional support tend to be grounded in high-income settings and may not adequately reflect the realities of Nigerian schools, particularly in the South-South region.

Data Collection Procedures

Data collection occurred after ethical approval and administrative permissions had been secured. We sought and received permission from the principals or proprietors of the participating schools in Akwa Ibom and Bayelsa States. Two postgraduate research assistants assisted in the data collection process. Both assistants had prior training in special needs education and educational psychology, and they were familiar with issues relating to ASD and inclusive schooling. Before entering the field, we conducted a briefing session in which we discussed the goal of the research, the content of the questionnaire, procedures for approaching respondents, and ethical requirements such as informed consent and respect for confidentiality. In each school, the research assistants first met with the school principal or proprietor to confirm the agreed-upon dates and times and to identify suitable spaces for administering the questionnaires. The teachers who met the study's inclusion criteria were invited during staff meetings or through departmental heads. Parents were invited either during scheduled parent-teacher meetings or through written invitations sent home with their children, depending on the communication patterns of the school.

At the point of data collection, the assistants explained the study in clear language, emphasising that participation was voluntary, that there were no penalties for non-participation, and that respondents could withdraw at any time before submitting their questionnaires. All respondents provided written informed consent. For parents who preferred oral explanations, the assistants read the information sheet and consent form aloud before signatures were obtained. Respondents completed the CTFIISQ in paper format in quiet spaces such as the staff room, classroom, or conference room. The assistants remained available to answer questions about item wording but did not influence the responses. Most respondents took between 20 and 30 minutes to complete the instrument. The filled questionnaires were placed in sealed envelopes and retrieved by the assistants, who then transported them to a secure location for data entry. No identifying names were written on the questionnaires; instead, numeric codes were used to distinguish schools and respondent categories.

Data Analysis Procedure

Data were entered into IBM SPSS for cleaning and analysis. We first screened the data for completeness, outliers, and obvious entry errors. Cases with substantial missing responses on the main subscales were excluded from analysis. In contrast, minor missing values were handled using appropriate single imputation or pairwise deletion strategies, depending on the analysis. To address the first research question on levels of formal and informal institutional support, we computed descriptive statistics for each subscale and across respondent groups, school types, and locations. These included means, standard deviations, standard errors, coefficients of variation, and 95 per cent confidence intervals. The descriptive results provided an ordered picture of how teachers and parents perceived formal and informal supports, and they enabled comparison across categories. To address the second research question on differences across groups, school types, and locations, we examined group means and the extent of overlap in their confidence intervals. While the modest sample size limited the power of formal tests for multiple group comparisons, the descriptive patterns and variability indices were sufficient to indicate whether marked differences were likely. For the third research question, we employed multiple regression analysis to estimate the predictive contributions of group, school type, and location to formal and informal institutional support. Each regression model included one support subscale as the dependent variable and the three demographic predictors as independent variables. We inspected unstandardised coefficients, standard errors, t values, significance levels, adjusted R-squared values, and F-change statistics to understand both the overall explanatory power of the models and the contribution of each predictor. The use of regression analysis was helpful because it enabled us to estimate predictive relationships. In this way, we determined whether any demographic factor served as a meaningful predictor of institutional support.

Ethical Considerations

Ethical principles guided all stages of the study. The Faculty of Education Research Ethics Committee at the University of Johannesburg granted ethical clearance for the broader career transition project (Sem-2-2020-057). This approval confirmed that our procedures complied with standards regarding respect for persons, beneficence, and justice. We ensured informed consent by providing respondents with an information sheet that explained the goal of the research, its voluntary nature of participation, the approximate time required, potential benefits and minimal risks, and the ways in which confidentiality would be maintained. Respondents signed the consent form before filling out the questionnaire. They were informed that they could decline to answer any item that made them uncomfortable and that they could withdraw from the study at any point before submitting their responses.

Voluntary participation was further emphasised by assuring teachers and parents that their decision to participate or not would have no consequences for their employment, their relationship with the school, or the educational experiences of their children. We did not collect data directly from students, and no information that could identify individual students with ASD was requested from respondents. Anonymity and confidentiality were protected by assigning codes rather than names to all questionnaires and datasets. The link between school codes and school names was stored in a separate password-protected document accessible only to us. The questionnaires that had been filled in were stored in locked cabinets, and electronic data were saved on a password-protected platform. We presented aggregated results and did not disclose any details that could enable the identification of individual participants or schools. Given the sensitivity of issues surrounding ASD and educational provision in the South-South region, we also took care to present our findings in a way that avoids blaming individuals or specific schools. Instead, we framed the results as evidence that can support systemic improvement in policy and practice. This ethical stance aligns with our broader commitment to promoting inclusive and supportive environments for students with ASD as they navigate career transitions.

RESULTS

Table 1. Demographic distribution of respondents

		N	%	Valid Percent	Cumulative Percent
Group	Teachers	38	43.2	43.2	43.2
	Parents	50	56.8	56.8	100.0
	Total	88	100.0	100.0	
School type	Private	32	36.4	36.4	36.4
	Public	56	63.6	63.6	100.0
	Total	88	100.0	100.0	
Location	Urban	29	33.0	33.0	33.0
	Semi-urban	40	45.5	45.5	78.4
	Rural	19	21.6	21.6	100.0
	Total	88	100.0	100.0	

Table 1 showcases the demographic distribution of the respondents and provides important context for interpreting institutional support patterns. As shown in the table, the sample consisted of 88 respondents, with parents representing the larger proportion at 56.8 per cent, and teachers comprising 43.2 per cent. This distribution is relevant because it indicates that responses reflect slightly more parent perspectives than teacher perspectives. In terms of school type, most respondents were from public schools (63.6 per cent), while private schools accounted for 36.4 per cent. In relation to geographical location, the highest proportion of respondents was drawn from semi-urban areas (45.5 per cent), followed by urban settings (33.0 per cent), and rural locations (21.6 per cent). As a result, reported support levels may be shaped by relatively stronger representation from semi-urban communities and comparatively fewer rural respondents. Overall, these demographic patterns offer an essential background for understanding variations in support levels examined in this research.

Table 2. Descriptive statistics for formal and informal institutional support for career transition for students with ASD

	Group	N	Mean	SD	SE	Coefficient of variation	95% Confidence Interval	
							Lower	Upper
Formal Institutional Support	Teachers		47.66	5.78	.938	.121	45.76	49.56
	Parents		46.48	6.14	.869	.132	44.73	48.23
	Private		47.25	6.34	1.121	.134	44.96	49.54
	Public		46.84	5.82	.778	.124	45.28	48.40
	Urban		48.72	5.07	.942	.104	46.79	50.65
	Semi-urban		46.00	6.30	.996	.137	43.99	48.01
	Rural		46.42	6.30	1.446	.136	43.38	49.46
Informal Institutional Support	Teachers		47.08	7.67	1.244	.163	44.56	49.60
	Parents		47.24	4.89	.691	.103	45.85	48.63
	Private		47.91	5.70	1.008	.119	45.85	49.96
	Public		46.75	6.48	.866	.139	45.01	48.49
	Urban		47.76	6.69	1.243	.140	45.21	50.30
	Semi-urban		46.60	5.91	.934	.127	44.71	48.49
	Rural		47.47	6.27	1.44	.132	44.45	50.49

Table 2 shows descriptive statistics for formal and informal institutional support across groups, school types, and geographical locations. The overall formal support mean scores for both teachers (M = 47.66) and parents (M = 46.48) suggest moderately high perceptions of structured support, with confidence intervals showing overlapping ranges, which suggests similar views between both groups. For school type, private school respondents recorded a mean of 47.25 while public school respondents recorded 46.84, again with overlapping confidence intervals, suggesting minimal practical differences. In relation to location, urban school respondents reported the highest formal support (M = 48.72), while semi-urban and rural school respondents reported lower but comparable means (M = 46.00 and M = 46.42). This result indicates that urban schools may have slightly stronger formal structures aligned with career transition for students with ASD.

For informal support, teacher and parent means were closely aligned (M = 47.08 and M = 47.24), suggesting shared experiences of informal encouragement and interpersonal support systems. In the results, it is shown that private school respondents reported a slightly higher mean (M = 47.91) compared with public school respondents (M = 46.75), although confidence intervals again overlap, suggesting subtle rather than meaningful differences. Informal support across locations revealed similar patterns, with urban school respondents reporting slightly higher support (M = 47.76) compared with semi-urban (M = 46.60) and rural (M = 47.47) school respondents. As such, Table 2 shows that both formal and informal institutional support levels are generally positive across all groups and settings, with only minor fluctuations based on contextual factors.

Figure 1. Clustered bar chart showing institutional support differences for career transition for students with ASD

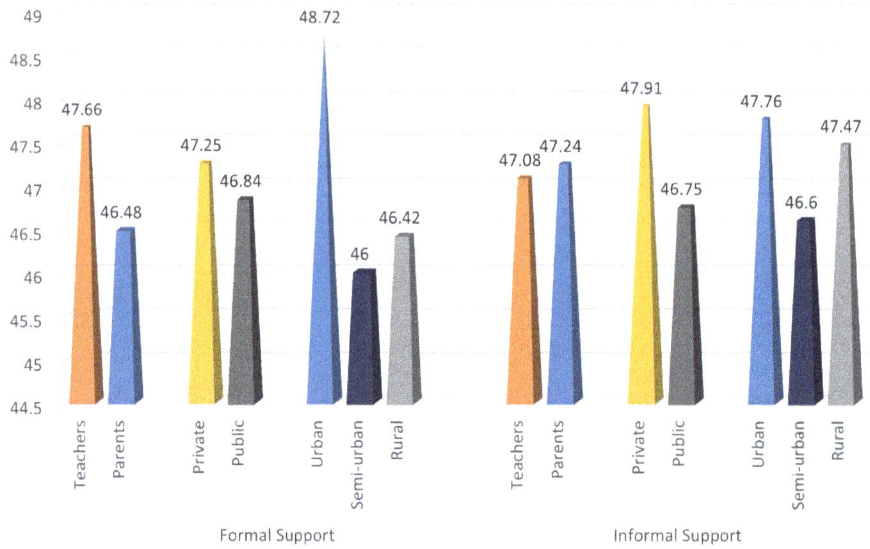

Figure 1 shows the comparative patterns of support across demographic categories. The clustered bars show that formal and informal support levels do not diverge sharply between teachers and parents, echoing the descriptive findings in Table 2. The chart further illustrates that differences between private and public school respondents are relatively small, confirming that both settings offer comparable levels of support. In consonance with geographical location, the bar chart reinforces that urban school respondents consistently reported slightly higher levels of both formal and informal support. Semi-urban and rural locations show more modest levels of support, although the differences were narrow. Therefore, the figure indicates that although variations exist across groups and contexts, they are not pronounced, which aligns with the nonsignificant findings reported in the regression models.

Table 3. Regression analysis of predictors on showing institutional support differences for career transition for students with ASD

Models	Predictors	Unstandardised coefficients		Adjusted R-square	F-change	t	Sig
		Beta (β)	SE				
Formal Institutional Support	(Constant)	52.686	3.762	.003	1.098	14.004	.000
	Group	-1.219	1.308			-.932	.354
	School type	-.808	1.350			-.599	.551
	Location	-1.306	.876			-1.490	.140
Informal Institutional Support	(Constant)	49.759	3.958	-.026	.267	12.573	.000
	Group	-.027	1.376			-.020	.984
	School type	-1.201	1.420			-.846	.400
	Location	-.308	.922			-.334	.739

Table 3 shows the regression results assessing whether the three predictors explain variations in formal and informal institutional support. For formal support, the model shows a very small adjusted R-squared (.003), indicating that group, school type, and location collectively account for less than one per cent of the variance in support levels. None of the predictors were statistically significant, as reflected in their nonsignificant t values and p values greater than .05. For instance, group (t = -.932, p = .354), school type (t = -.599, p = .551), and location (t = -1.490, p = .140) did not meaningfully predict perceived formal support. In the same manner, the model for informal support yielded an adjusted R-squared of -.026, indicating no predictive value. All predictors further showed nonsignificant contributions, including group (t = -.020, p = .984), school type (t = -.846, p = .400), and location (t = -.334, p = .739). These findings suggest that demographic dimensions do not meaningfully influence either formal or informal support levels. Institutional support may therefore be shaped more by broader structural or cultural factors rather than the respondents' demographic categories.

DISCUSSION

The result of the study shows that there is a significant uniformity in the formal and informal institutional support of the career transition of students with ASD in all of the studied demographic categories. The descriptive statistics indicate that teachers and parents had moderately high ratings of formal and informal support, as both the mean scores are similar and their confidence intervals are also similar. This consensus suggests that the views regarding the institutional support are similar within the groups of respondents. Similarly, the comparison of the support levels between the private and public schools reveals similar results with a few differences, which do not have any practical implications. Geographical difference is more prominent: urban schools are characterised by more formal and informal support, semi-urban and rural schools are characterised by less support that is still positive (Aduwa-Ogiegbaen & Iyamu, 2010; Sher, 2019). These results of the research indicate a generally stable trend of institutional support in the career transition of students with ASD in the Nigerian educational context, indicating both the strengths of the system and the contextual constraints (Hill et al., 2024). The broadly average scores of formal and informal support indicated in all respondent groups indicate that Nigeria schools are expanding their understanding of the necessity to establish both formal and relationship-based features to support neurodiverse students when they embark on post-school life trajectories. The consistency of teacher and parent views also reflects the common meaning of the available supports, which points to the increasing culture of cooperation between the key stakeholders engaged in the process of transition.

However, the small geographical differences that are evident underscore contextual differences that characterise the Nigerian education system. Schools in urban areas with slightly higher scores of support are congruent with the long-held urban advantage of access to trained staff, digital equipment, specialised services, and external connections to employers or community agencies (Akin-Fakorede et al., 2025). Although semi-urban and rural schools also show positive levels of support, they use fewer resources, have less exposure to the inclusive models of career development, and have a weaker institutional capacity (Murtadlo et al., 2025). These contextual realities can limit the capacity of the schools towards providing a stronger framework of transition in the case of SASD. The findings of this study resonate with the report of recent studies, which revealed a significant difference in the availability of assistive digital learning tools for SASD students in urban and rural areas (Murtadlo et al., 2025; Akin-Fakorede et al., 2025).

Inferential statistics analysis with respect to the second research question indicated that there were no significant differences in the support levels in relation to the group, type of schools, and geographical location of the school. Although there was a difference in the mean scores, these differences were not significant, meaning that institutional support structures are evenly distributed across the respondent groupings. The lack of statistical significant differences between groups and typological of schools, combined with the non-determining effect of demographic factors, suggests that institutional support is not determined predominantly by categorical differences; instead, it seems to be conditioned by systemic reasons that are beyond the governance frameworks. This observation is in line with the available evidence in Nigeria, where practices in inclusive education are more dependent on school culture, leadership commitment and attitude of teachers than on structural classifications like public and private ownership. It is also indicative of the influence of nation-wide policy directives such as the Discrimination Against Persons with Disabilities Act and the Inclusive Education Policy, which facilitate that support services are implemented in a similar way regardless of the type of school or geographical setting (Umeh & Anyaele, 2024). These findings affirmed the previous research findings, which revealed that the cultural factors of the Nigerian society undermine efforts for inclusive education, and these practices influence the behaviour and attitude of people towards disabilities (Charles, 2019).

With regards to the third research question, the multiple regression analyses showed that group affiliation, school type, and geographic location were not significant predictors of formal and informal institutional support. The adjusted R-squared values (of these models) indicated that these demographic factors explained a very minor share of variance in levels of support. The findings suggest that institutional support of SASD career transition in Nigeria can be explained by the influence of overarching institutional practices, policy implementation, and organisational culture rather than demographics factors, which influence inclusive education and transition. The low predictive power of demographic factors supports the assumption that neither the formal nor informal institutional support in Nigeria would be more susceptible to the overarching organisational practices, institutional readiness, and culture conceptions of disability than it would be to situational or contextual variables. This observation is especially relevant to the context of the Nigerian environment, where the difference in implementation, as opposed to the lack of policy systems, is often the main challenge. Those institutions with supportive beliefs, investment in staff professional development and well-developed family and community partnerships have a higher ability to offer effective transition support regardless of institutional type or geographic location. The findings, in general, outline a new but non-homogeneous occupational transition support landscape of SASD in Nigeria, whereby systemic commitments are evident but contextual disparities persist. Strengthening the institutional capacity of underserved areas, making teacher education more focused on neurodiversity, and expanding communal informal networks will be invaluable in helping to achieve more equitable outcomes in the transition of SASD. The findings of this study contradict the existing report, which revealed that school type can impact the quality and kind of support provided (Dörffer & Bernhard, 2025). Similarly, another study found that institutional type and location substantially affect students' outcomes, indicating that they play a role in the educational outcomes.

The results are aligned with the neurodiversity paradigm, conceptualising SASD as having quality cognitive differences but not deficits. The overall positive scores of both formal and informal support in various groups and environments indicate that institutions are beginning to acknowledge and embrace these various strengths, as Judy Singer posits that the environments should be designed to meet the needs of the neurodivergent individuals, like SASD. The absence of considerable demographic differences also indicates a new turn to a culture of inclusion and no longer selective practices. These results indicate that Nigeria is slowly developing in line with the International Labour Organisation Disability Inclusion Strategy, as it shows a steady institutional backing to SASD. Nevertheless, the thin urban edge and narrow predictive power of the demographic variables point to the necessity of growing the capacity in the whole nation towards the creation of equitable and entirely inclusive transition systems.

This study has some limitations that need to be pointed out when analysing this study. First, the sample size was selected through a random sample in a group, and this reduces the applicability and generalisation to the whole Nigerian population. Since data was collected through questionnaires, which are self-report measures of teachers and parents, there is a probability of biased responses and social desirability effects, and subjectivity interpretations of institutional support. Since there is no administrator or students' voices are restriction on the completeness of the institutional supports. Third, the study design is cross-sectional, which implies that the opinions are taken at one time only, and that the effects of support practice differ between academic sessions and the changes in policy implementation are not considered. A longitudinal study would have provided more information on how the institutional support changes with time. Lastly, the research failed to provide direct observational and document analysis in order to confirm the levels of formal and informal support that had been reported, which limited the possibility of triangulating the results. These limitations do not invalidate the significant contribution it has made to the literature on the career transition of SASD.

CONCLUSIONS

This study examined the formal and informal institutional support for career transition among SASD in Nigeria. The findings of the study highlight the existence of moderate formal and informal institutional supports for the career transition of the SASD in the Nigerian school system. The levels of support were positive across respondent groups, types of schools, and geographical areas, which also means that an institutional commitment to achieve positive transition outcomes of SASD is emerging. In fact, despite slightly higher levels of support in urban schools, the differences between demographic categories were also rather low and statistically insignificant. The regression models also indicated that the group, school type, and geographical location had no significant effect on levels of institutional support;

hence, it can be concluded that larger systemic practices and organisational cultures might be significantly more important than demographic factors in defining levels of support to SASD. Overall, these results indicate that Nigerian educational facilities should leverage the current strengths by developing transition supports in all environments with respect to depth, quality, and consistency. Enhancing the institutional capacity, especially in semi-urban and rural settings, and cultivating a culture based on the principles of neurodiversity and inclusive practice, continue to be critical to enhancing the results of the transition. The research adds to the existing literature on African studies of SASD and career transition supports and strengthens the need to continue policy implementation, teacher training, and community collaboration. Further studies are also needed to examine other institutional and systemic factors that contribute to transition support, so that a more detailed insight into how Nigerian schools could maximise the career transition of SASD would be achieved.

REFERENCES

Accardo, A. L., Kuder, S. J., & Woodruff, J. (2019). Accommodations and support services preferred by college students with autism spectrum disorder. *Autism*, *23*(3), 574–583. DOI: 10.1177/1362361318760490 PMID: 29475372

Aduwa-Ogiegbaen, S. E. O., & Iyamu, E. O. S. (2010). Availability and utilization of classroom computers across urban and rural schools in Southwestern Nigeria. In Tomei, L. (Ed.), *Online Courses and ICT in Education: Emerging Practices and Applications* (pp. 189–202). IGI Global., DOI: 10.4018/978-1-60960-150-8.ch015

Aguilera Rodríguez, G., Márquez González, C. V., Villaseñor-Cabrera, T. J., & Valadez Sierra, M. (2024). University experiences of students and graduates with neurodiversity: Tools for creating a specialized mentoring program related to working life. *Frontiers in Education*, *9*, 1432930. Advance online publication. DOI: 10.3389/feduc.2024.1432930

Akin-Fakorede, O. O., Ironbar, V. E., Inaku, J. F., Ekpo, M. E., Umoh, M. S., Nakanda, E. V., Agbade, O. P., Bessong, C. D., Bessong, N. O., Ayiba, O. R., Odey, M. O., Odok, J. A., Arop, L. O., Eburu, O. S., Egbonyi, E. E., Undie, A. A., & Oko, B. A. (2025). Exploring the use of Assistive Digital Resources in Enhancing Learning for Students with Intellectual Disabilities in Cross River and Akwa Ibom States, Nigeria. *Journal of Intellectual Disability - Diagnosis and Treatment, 13*(2), 161–177. DOI: 10.6000/2292-2598.2025.13.02.5

Alsarmi, A. M., & Al-Hemyari, Z. A. (2015). Quantitative and qualitative statistical indicators to assess the quality of teaching and learning in higher education institutions. *International Journal of Information and Decision Sciences*. https://www.inderscienceonline.com/doi/10.1504/IJIDS.2014.066631

Anderson, K. A., Sosnowy, C., Kuo, A. A., & Shattuck, P. T. (2018). Transition of individuals with autism to adulthood: A review of qualitative studies. *Pediatrics*, *141*(Supplement_4), S318–S327. DOI: 10.1542/peds.2016-4300I PMID: 29610413

Bertrand-Ouellet, J., Vincent, C., Julien-Gauthier, F., Dumont, F., Desmarais, C., Lecours, A., Poulin, V., Kiss, J., Hu, T., & Blouin, L. (2025). Instructional Videos to Familiarize Young Autistic Adults With Grocery Tasks With a View to Vocational Integration: From Design to Practicability. *Journal of Vocational Rehabilitation*, *62*(3), 218–233. DOI: 10.1177/10522263251326017

Bialopotocki, R. N. (2006). *Recognition and Praise Relate to Teachers' Job Satisfaction* [Ph.D., The University of Nebraska - Lincoln]. https://www.proquest.com/docview/305291829/abstract/33DAF7ED8DE43FCPQ/1

Brooke, V., Brooke, A. M., Schall, C., Wehman, P., McDonough, J., Thompson, K., & Smith, J. (2018). Employees with Autism Spectrum Disorder Achieving Long-Term Employment Success: A Retrospective Review of Employment Retention and Intervention. *Research and Practice for Persons with Severe Disabilities : the Journal of TASH*, *43*(3), 181–193. DOI: 10.1177/1540796918783202

Buhari, A. M., Sultan Ibrahim, S. A., & Radhil, N. I. M. (2025). Exploring Factors Influencing Employment Opportunities Among People With Disabilities: A Scoping Review. *Malaysian Journal of Medicine and Health Sciences*, *21*, 253–264. DOI: 10.47836/mjmhs.21.s7.29

Carter, E. W., & Schutz, M. A. (2022). Addressing Transition Preparation in Middle and High Schools. In Viezel, K. D., Wilczynski, S. M., & Davis, A. S. (Eds.), *Post-secondary Transition for College- or Career-Bound Autistic Students* (pp. 179–200). Springer International Publishing., DOI: 10.1007/978-3-030-93947-2_9

Chancel, R., Miot, S., Dellapiazza, F., & Baghdadli, A. (2022). Group-based educational interventions in adolescents and young adults with ASD without ID: A systematic review focusing on the transition to adulthood. *European Child & Adolescent Psychiatry*, *31*(7), 1–21. DOI: 10.1007/s00787-020-01609-1 PMID: 32889578

Charles, O. O. (2019). Cultural factors currently affecting inclusive practice—Africa. In Heck, S., & Block, M. E. (Eds.), *Inclusive Physical Education Around the World: Origins, Cultures, Practices* (pp. 205–213). Taylor and Francis., DOI: 10.4324/9780429026294-14

Cherewick, M., & Matergia, M. (2024). Neurodiversity in Practice: A Conceptual Model of Autistic Strengths and Potential Mechanisms of Change to Support Positive Mental Health and Wellbeing in Autistic Children and Adolescents. *Advances in Neurodevelopmental Disorders*, *8*(3), 408–422. DOI: 10.1007/s41252-023-00348-z

Cleveland, J., & Williams, E. (2022). Considerations for School Psychology University Faculty: Developing and Implementing Services for Students with ASD. In Viezel, K. D., Wilczynski, S. M., & Davis, A. S. (Eds.), *Postsecondary Transition for College- or Career-Bound Autistic Students* (pp. 243–258). Springer International Publishing., DOI: 10.1007/978-3-030-93947-2_12

Dale, B. A., Ogle, L. N., Ruble, L. A., & Azad, G. F. (2025). Dyadic mechanisms of effect in home–school consultation: Evidence from two school-based consultation models. *School Psychology International*, *46*(2), 115–134. DOI: 10.1177/01430343241283025

Dallas, B., Ramisch, J., & Ashmore, A. (2018). How Involved should they be? Students with ASD in postsecondary settings and their family members. *The Qualitative Report*, *23*(5), 1208–1222. DOI: 10.46743/2160-3715/2018.3149

Davis, M. T., Watts, G. W., & López, E. J. (2021). A systematic review of firsthand experiences and supports for students with autism spectrum disorder in higher education. *Research in Autism Spectrum Disorders*, *84*, 101769. Advance online publication. DOI: 10.1016/j.rasd.2021.101769

Doda, V., Kennedy, C., & Kaur, M. (2024). Policies for Individuals With Autism: Gaps, Research, and Recommendations. *Cureus*, *16*(1), e51875. DOI: 10.7759/cureus.51875 PMID: 38327931

Dörffer, N., & Bernhard, N. (2025). Overcoming Obstacles? Institutional Support for the Pathways to Higher Education at German Vocational Schools. *Social Inclusion (Lisboa)*, *13*, 8771. Advance online publication. DOI: 10.17645/si.8771

Fong, V., Gardiner, E., & Iarocci, G. (2021). Satisfaction with informal supports predicts resilience in families of children with autism spectrum disorder. *Autism*, *25*(2), 452–463. DOI: 10.1177/1362361320962677 PMID: 33106025

Guldberg, K. (2010). Educating children on the autism spectrum: Preconditions for inclusion and notions of "best autism practice" in the early years. *British Journal of Special Education*, *37*(4), 168–174. DOI: 10.1111/j.1467-8578.2010.00482.x

Hendricks, D. (2010). Employment and adults with autism spectrum disorders: Challenges and strategies for success. *Journal of Vocational Rehabilitation*, *32*(2), 125–134. DOI: 10.3233/JVR-2010-0502

Hill, D. A., Fayemi, A., & Ostrowski, S. (2024). The Evolution of Services for Children with Autism and Developmental Disabilities in Nigeria. *International Journal of Disability Development and Education*, *71*(7), 1116–1132. DOI: 10.1080/1034912X.2023.2291570

Hotez, E., Shane-Simpson, C., Obeid, R., DeNigris, D., Siller, M., Costikas, C., Pickens, J., Massa, A., Giannola, M., D'Onofrio, J., & Gillespie-Lynch, K. (2018). Designing a summer transition program for incoming and current college students on the autism spectrum: A participatory approach. *Frontiers in Psychology*, *9*(FEB), 46. Advance online publication. DOI: 10.3389/fpsyg.2018.00046 PMID: 29487547

Hume, K., Dykstra Steinbrenner, J., Sideris, J., Smith, L., Kucharczyk, S., & Szidon, K. (2018). Multi-informant assessment of transition-related skills and skill importance in adolescents with autism spectrum disorder. *Autism*, *22*(1), 40–50. DOI: 10.1177/1362361317722029 PMID: 29020804

Iannuzzi, D., Rissmiller, P., Duty, S. M., Feeney, S., Sullivan, M., & Curtin, C. (2019). Addressing a Gap in Healthcare Access for Transition-Age Youth with Autism: A Pilot Educational Intervention for Family Nurse Practitioner Students. *Journal of Autism and Developmental Disorders, 49*(4), 1493–1504. DOI: 10.1007/s10803-018-3846-9 PMID: 30536218

ILO. (2022). *ILO Disability Inclusion Policy and Strategy 2020-23.* https://share.google/B8SQei7sNRjjDkpTR

Jing, J. (2024). Perspectives on the concept of "neurodiversity" in autism spectrum disorder and related evaluation. *Zhongguo Ertong Baojian Zazhi, 32*(7), 709-712and745. DOI: 10.11852/zgetbjzz2024-0645

Karola, D., Julie-Ann, J., & Lyn, M. (2016). School's out Forever: Postsecondary Educational Trajectories of Students with Autism. *Australian Psychologist, 51*(4), 304–315. DOI: 10.1111/ap.12228

Knudson, S. (2024). Transition planning and perceptions of support in an autism spectrum disorder resource program. *Preventing School Failure, 68*(3), 220–230. DOI: 10.1080/1045988X.2023.2207482

Kossewska, J., Bombińska-Domżał, A., Cierpiałowska, T., Lubińska-Kościółek, E., Niemiec, S., Płoszaj, M., & Preece, D. R. (2021). Towards inclusive education of children with Autism Spectrum Disorder. The impact of teachers' autism-specific professional development on their confidence in their professional competences. *International Journal of Special Education, 36*(2), 27–35. DOI: 10.52291/ijse.2021.36.15

Kristofik, A., & Johnson, K. (2024). Opportunities to support the caregivers of children and young adults with ASD as they transition into the workforce and university. In Papaneophytou, N. L., & Das, U. N. (Eds.), *Understanding Autism: Perspectives, Assessment, Interventions, and the Journey Towards Inclusion* (pp. 365–371). Elsevier., DOI: 10.1016/B978-0-443-27366-7.00021-3

Lahza, H. F., Demartini, G., Noroozi, O., Gašević, D., Sadiq, S., & Khosravi, H. (2025). Enhancing peer feedback provision through user interface scaffolding: A comparative examination of scripting and self-monitoring techniques. *Computers & Education, 230*, 105260. Advance online publication. DOI: 10.1016/j.compedu.2025.105260

Lang, H. M. (2025). History of the Autism Diagnosis– How the Perspectives Have Changed. *Health Care Analysis, 33*(4), 337–348. DOI: 10.1007/s10728-025-00527-0 PMID: 40439995

Lee, G. K., & Carter, E. W. (2012). Preparing Transition-Age Students with High-Functioning Autism Spectrum Disorders for Meaningful Work. *Psychology in the Schools*, *49*(10), 988–1000. DOI: 10.1002/pits.21651

Ligon, K., & McKelvey, S. (2025). Effects of a Paid Internship Model on Postschool Outcomes of At-risk Youth with Disabilities. *Journal of Vocational Rehabilitation*, *62*(3), 279–285. DOI: 10.1177/10522263251326495

Loubser, D. (2025). Lecturers as redemptive change agents supporting students with autism spectrum disorder (ASD) at higher educational institutions. *Koers*, *90*(1), 2626. Advance online publication. DOI: 10.19108/KOERS.90.1.2626

Lovett, B. J. (2021). Educational Accommodations for Students With Disabilities: Two Equity-Related Concerns. *Frontiers in Education*, *6*, 795266. Advance online publication. DOI: 10.3389/feduc.2021.795266

Lucas, R., & James, A. I. (2018). An Evaluation of Specialist Mentoring for University Students with Autism Spectrum Disorders and Mental Health Conditions. *Journal of Autism and Developmental Disorders*, *48*(3), 694–707. DOI: 10.1007/s10803-017-3303-1 PMID: 28918532

Lukianova, N. N., Fell, E. V., & Shavlokhova, A. A. (2022). Environmental barriers as a factor affecting the ways in which students with disabilities construct their career design. *Perspektivy Nauki i Obrazovania*, *58*(4), 425–439. DOI: 10.32744/pse.2022.4.25

Margeviča-Grinberga, I., & Kalēja, A. (2025). Job shadowing adults' non-formal education programme through social-emotional learning. *Frontiers in Sociology*, *10*, 1524922. DOI: 10.3389/fsoc.2025.1524922 PMID: 40933785

Marsack-Topolewski, C. N. (2020). A Snapshot of Social Support Networks Among Parental Caregivers of Adults with Autism. *Journal of Autism and Developmental Disorders*, *50*(4), 1111–1122. DOI: 10.1007/s10803-019-04285-6 PMID: 31848797

Meiring, M., Seabi, J., Amod, Z., Vorster, A., & Kern, A. (2016). Transition for adolescents with autism spectrum disorder: South African parent and professional perspectives. *Frontiers in Psychiatry*, *7*(JUN). Advance online publication. DOI: 10.3389/fpsyt.2016.00093 PMID: 27375502

Mitra, G., & Dominik, G. (2023). United Nations Disability Inclusion Strategy: A framework to accelerate transformative change for persons with disabilities in the peace and security pillar. *International Review of the Red Cross*, *105*(922), 459–464. DOI: 10.1017/S1816383122001096

Mpofu, E., Tansey, T., Mpofu, N., Tu, W.-M., & Li, Q. (2019). Employment practices with people with autism spectrum disorder in the digital age. In Potgieter, I. L., Ferreira, N., & Coetzee, M. (Eds.), *Theory, Research and Dynamics of Career Wellbeing: Becoming Fit for the Future* (pp. 309–326). Springer International Publishing., DOI: 10.1007/978-3-030-28180-9_15

Murtadlo, M., Albana, H., Nisa, Y. F., Izazy, N. Q., Sumiati, N. T., Dewi, M. S., Abdullah, H., & Henry, C. (2025). Inclusive education in Africa: Transforming higher education in low-income countries. *Scientific African*, *28*, e02708. Advance online publication. DOI: 10.1016/j.sciaf.2025.e02708

Nguyen, L., Jack, S., Ketelaar, M., Di Rezze, B., Soper, A. K., & Gorter, J. W. (2020). Understanding the essential components and experiences of youth with autism spectrum disorders in peer mentorship programmes during the transition to adulthood: A qualitative meta-ethnography. *Child: Care, Health and Development*, *46*(6), 667–681. DOI: 10.1111/cch.12804 PMID: 32840907

Nicholas, D. B., Zwaigenbaum, L., Zwicker, J., Clarke, M. E., Lamsal, R., Stoddart, K. P., Carroll, C., Muskat, B., Spoelstra, M., & Lowe, K. (2018). Evaluation of employment-support services for adults with autism spectrum disorder. *Autism*, *22*(6), 693–702. DOI: 10.1177/1362361317702507 PMID: 28637355

Perryman, T., Ricks, L., & Cash-Baskett, L. (2020). Meaningful transitions: Enhancing clinician roles in transition planning for adolescents with autism spectrum disorders. *Language, Speech, and Hearing Services in Schools*, *51*(4), 899–913. DOI: 10.1044/2020_LSHSS-19-00048 PMID: 32585119

Reichow, B., Doehring, P., & Volkmar, F. R. (Eds.). (2025). *Handbook of Evidence-Based Practices in Autism Spectrum Disorder*. Springer Nature., DOI: 10.1007/978-3-031-78143-8

Rindfleisch, A., Malter, A. J., Ganesan, S., & Moorman, C. (2008). Cross-Sectional versus Longitudinal Survey Research: Concepts, Findings, and Guidelines. *JMR, Journal of Marketing Research*, *45*(3), 261–279. DOI: 10.1509/jmkr.45.3.261

Roberts, K. D. (2010). Topic areas to consider when planning transition from high school to postsecondary education for students with autism spectrum disorders. *Focus on Autism and Other Developmental Disabilities*, *25*(3), 158–162. DOI: 10.1177/1088357610371476

Rodríguez, Y. Y. (2024). Autism: An Interdisciplinary Analysis from Neuroscience. *Seminars in Medical Writing and Education*, *3*, 615. Advance online publication. DOI: 10.56294/mw2024615

Roux, A. M., Rast, J. E., Anderson, K. A., Garfield, T., & Shattuck, P. T. (2021). Vocational Rehabilitation Service Utilization and Employment Outcomes Among Secondary Students on the Autism Spectrum. *Journal of Autism and Developmental Disorders*, *51*(1), 212–226. DOI: 10.1007/s10803-020-04533-0 PMID: 32399821

Sansosti, F. J., Merchant, D., Koch, L. C., Rumrill, P., & Herrera, A. (2017). Providing supportive transition services to individuals with autism spectrum disorder: Considerations for vocational rehabilitation professionals. *Journal of Vocational Rehabilitation*, *47*(2), 207–222. DOI: 10.3233/JVR-170896

Scheef, A., & Mahfouz, J. (2020). Supporting the post-school goals of youth with disabilities through use of a transition coordinator. *Research in Educational Administration and Leadership*, *5*(1), 43–69. DOI: 10.30828/real/2020.1.2

Schoen, S. A., & Valdez, A. (2023). Preliminary efficacy of a transition training program for autistic adolescents. *Research in Autism Spectrum Disorders*, *109*, 102281. DOI: 10.1016/j.rasd.2023.102281

Sefotho, M. M., & Onyishi, C. N. (2021). Transition to Higher Education for Students with Autism: Challenges and Support Needs. *International Journal of Higher Education*, *10*(1), 201. https://EconPapers.repec.org/RePEc:jfr:ijhe11:v:10:y:2021:i:1:p:201. DOI: 10.5430/ijhe.v10n1p201

Sharma, U., Furlonger, B., & Forlin, C. (2019). The Impact of Funding Models on the Education of Students With Autism Spectrum Disorder. *Australasian Journal of Special and Inclusive Education*, *43*(1), 1–11. DOI: 10.1017/jsi.2019.1

Sher, J. P. (2019). Education in the countryside: Overview of conditions and some conclusions. In Sher, J. P. (Ed.), *Rural Education In Urbanized Nations: Issues and Innovations* (pp. 21–90). Taylor and Francis., DOI: 10.4324/9780429305054-2

Shogren, K. A., & Plotner, A. J. (2012). Transition planning for students with intellectual disability, autism, or other disabilities: Data from the national longitudinal transition study-2. *Intellectual and Developmental Disabilities*, *50*(1), 16–30. DOI: 10.1352/1934-9556-50.1.16 PMID: 22316223

Siew, C. T., Mazzucchelli, T. G., Rooney, R., & Girdler, S. (2017). A specialist peer mentoring program for university students on the autism spectrum: A pilot study. *PLoS One*, *12*(7), e0180854. Advance online publication. DOI: 10.1371/journal.pone.0180854 PMID: 28704446

Šilc, M., & Krajnc, M. S. (2022). Challenges in Educational Inclusion of Students with Autism Disorders in Primary Schools. *Journal of Elementary Education*, *15*(2), 181–198. DOI: 10.18690/rei.15.2.181-198.2022

Singer, J. (1998). *Odd people. The Birth of Community Amongst People on the" Autistic Spectrum.* University of Technology.

Smyth, S., Mc Laughlin, N., Egan, C., Gurrin, C., Quinn, K., McGarrell, M., & Devlin, S. (2021). Study protocol for autism specific transition resources (T-Res Study): Developing a flexible resource package for dealing with the loosening and/ or lifting of COVID-19 related restrictions. *HRB Open Research, 4.* https://doi.org/ DOI: 10.12688/hrbopenres.13155.1

Snell-Rood, C., Ruble, L., Kleinert, H., McGrew, J. H., Adams, M., Rodgers, A., Odom, J., Wong, W. H., & Yu, Y. (2020). Stakeholder perspectives on transition planning, implementation, and outcomes for students with autism spectrum disorder. *Autism, 24*(5), 1164–1176. DOI: 10.1177/1362361319894827 PMID: 31957461

Sokratous, S., Merkouris, A., Middleton, N., & Karanikola, M. (2013). The association between stressful life events and depressive symptoms among Cypriot university students: A cross-sectional descriptive correlational study. *BMC Public Health, 13*(1), 1121. DOI: 10.1186/1471-2458-13-1121 PMID: 24304515

Southall, C. (2013). Use of Technology to Accommodate Differences Associated with Autism Spectrum Disorder in the General Curriculum and Environment. *Journal of Special Education Technology, 28*(1), 23–34. DOI: 10.1177/016264341302800103

ăpuru, I. A. (2023). KNOWLEDGE SHARING THROUGH INFORMAL COMMUNICATION. *eLearning Softw. Educ. Conf., 1*, 433–444. DOI: 10.12753/2066-026X-23-041

Tomfohrde, O., Hudock, R. L., Kremer, K. B., Fatiha, N., & Weiler, L. (2023). Fostering social connectedness among adolescents and adults with autism: A qualitative analysis. *Psychology in the Schools, 60*(1), 23–39. DOI: 10.1002/pits.22759

Umeh, N. C., & Anyaele, D. O. (2024). Assessment of the Implementation of Inclusive Education Policy Among Stakeholders in Abia State, Nigeria. In *Ius Gentium* (Vol. 117, pp. 1–19). Springer Science and Business Media B.V., DOI: 10.1007/978-3-031-64549-5_1

Von Holzen, A. V., Skoning, S. N., Fisher, T. A., Clark, D. M., & Cook, J. A. (2024). Factors of Career Development Impacting Transition for Young Adults with Autism Spectrum Disorder. *Exceptionality Education International, 34*(2), 91–114. DOI: 10.5206/eei.v34i2.17529

Wang, A., Yu, S., Wang, M., Wu, L., Wang, D., & Huang, L. (2023). Promoting meaningful peer feedback among in-service Chinese language teachers in an online lesson study. *System*, *115*, 103055. Advance online publication. DOI: 10.1016/j.system.2023.103055

Williams Harryman, E. (2025). Elementary Teachers' Experiences Supporting the Academic Growth and Development of Students on the Autism Spectrum in Inclusion Classrooms. *Walden Dissertations and Doctoral Studies*. https://scholarworks.waldenu.edu/dissertations/16909

Wong, V., McGrew, J., & Ruble, L. (2020). Predicting the Outcomes of Parents of Transition-Age Youth or Young Adults with ASD. *Journal of Autism and Developmental Disorders*, *50*(8), 2723–2739. DOI: 10.1007/s10803-020-04362-1 PMID: 32030578

Yamamoto, S. H., & Alverson, C. Y. (2022). From high school to postsecondary education, training, and employment: Predicting outcomes for young adults with autism spectrum disorder. *Autism & Developmental Language Impairments*, *7*, 23969415221095019. Advance online publication. DOI: 10.1177/23969415221095019 PMID: 36382083

Yarrow, E., Tereshko, L. M., Weiss, M. J., Gerhardt, P., & Magrauth, M. (2024). Interventions targeting work-related skills in adults with autism spectrum disorders: A comprehensive literature review. *Journal of Vocational Rehabilitation*, *61*(3), 348–370. Advance online publication. DOI: 10.1177/10522263241285204

Yibakuro, E. A. (2025). The Role of Education Law in Supporting Special Needs Students in Nigerian Tertiary Institutions. *International Journal of Educational Management, Rivers State University.*, *1*(2), 372–385. https://ijedm.com/index.php/ijedm/article/view/67

APPENDIX

Table 4. Career Transition-Related Formal and Informal Institutional Supports Questionnaire (CTFIISQ)

S/No	Items	Cronbach's α if Item Deleted	Cronbach's α	Omega ω
	Formal Institutional Support			
1	Our institution has formal policies prioritising career transition for students with ASD.	0.74	0.76	0.57
2	There is a designated office or coordinator responsible for ASD transition planning.	0.74		
3	An adequate budget is allocated specifically for ASD career transition programmes.	0.75		
4	Staff are required to follow standardised transition protocols for ASD students.	0.73		
5	Formal training on ASD-inclusive transition is regularly provided to professionals.	0.75		
6	Institutional leadership publicly supports and champions ASD transition initiatives.	0.76		
7	We have official partnerships with external agencies (e.g., vocational rehab, employers).	0.75		
8	Student progress in transition is formally assessed and monitored (e.g., placement rates).	0.75		
9	Transition outcomes and resources are documented in institutional reports.	0.75		
10	The institution has formal agreements (e.g., MOUs) outlining roles and responsibilities for transition programmes.	0.75		
11	Dedicated physical or digital career-transition resources are available for ASD students.	0.74		
12	Institutional guidelines specify accommodations and supports for career preparation activities.	0.74		
13	Clear accountability structures exist for transition outcomes (e.g., committees, oversight).	0.76		
	Informal Institutional Support			

continued on following page

Table 4. Continued

S/No	Items	Cronbach's α if Item Deleted	Cronbach's α	Omega ω
	Formal Institutional Support			
14	Students with ASD can easily approach staff informally about their career concerns.	0.70	0.72	0.62
15	Colleagues and mentors frequently provide informal advice and encouragement.	0.70		
16	Peer mentoring programmes or buddy systems support ASD students' career efforts.	0.70		
17	Staff discretionary time is available to support student career transition socially.	0.67		
18	Families feel welcomed to discuss career concerns outside official meetings.	0.68		
19	Informal networks connect ASD students to community or employer contacts.	0.69		
20	There is a strong culture of flexibility and adaptation for student needs during transition.	0.69		
21	Informal recognition (e.g., praise, acknowledgment) boosts ASD students' career efforts.	0.69		
22	Staff feel comfortable seeking consult from peers when formal structures are unclear.	0.71		
23	Networking events (e.g., career fairs, visits) arise organically through staff/student initiative.	0.71		
24	Informal feedback loops (e.g., casual check-ins) help improve transition support.	0.70		
25	Community members (e.g., alumni, employers) participate informally in supporting ASD students' career aspirations.	0.72		

Chapter 7
Assessing the Psychometric Properties of a Career Transition Inventory for Students With ASD (CTI–SASD)

ABSTRACT

In the present research, we designed and tested a self-developed Career Transition Inventory for students with autism spectrum disorders (SASD) (CTI-SASD) based on the bioecological systems theory developed by Bronfenbrenner, and incorporates four domains, including strategies, self, support, and situation. Based on a quantitative approach, confirmatory factor analysis and structural equation modelling were employed to examine the instrument's factor structure, reliability, validity, and structural relationships. Results show that a four-factor model with high item loadings was observed and consistent across all domains. The indices of internal consistency, such as Cronbach's alpha and composite reliability, were well above the recommended values. Convergent and discriminatory validities were also defined. Model fit indices revealed an acceptable measurement model. At the same time, path analysis showed meaningful interrelationships among the four constructs, highlighting the dynamic interplay of personal, behavioural, and contextual factors in career transition.

DOI: 10.4018/978-1-6684-7260-6.ch007

BACKGROUND

The career transitioning of students in the bioecological systems perspective of Bronfenbrenner is the process by which students move from school to work due to the continuing interactions between the personal attributes of students and various nested systems within the environment. Career transition among students who have autism spectrum disorders (SASD) is a complex process that requires convergence of individual qualities, social expectations, organisational set-ups, and institutionalisation. Even though its importance has been acknowledged, a considerable number of SASD still face serious challenges. Some of these challenges include psychological and social demands, where students often struggle with anxiety, social relationships, and adapting to new environments (Van Hees et al., 2015; Nuske et al., 2019). The challenges are equally complicated by a lack of communication and social skills, which are essential for workplace success (Dipeolu et al., 2015; Laghi & Trimarco, 2020). Furthermore, the transition services offered by schools might not be adequately individualised to the needs of SASD, thus leading to poor employment placements and unproductive implementation of new skills (Sharpe et al., 2022). Understanding these challenges and developing effective strategies to address them begins with a thorough assessment using psychometric tools. Unfortunately, there is a significant dearth of assessment tools for assessing and understanding the career transition of SASD.

Assessing the career transition of SASD is important. This study aimed to do this by assessing the psychometric properties of a career transition inventory designed for SASD. The inventory captures four core domains that are conceptually grounded in Bronfenbrenner's Bioecological Systems Theory (BBST), which positions individual development as resulting from continuous interactions between a person and their surrounding environments; the four domains are strategies, self, support, and situation (Lee & Carter, 2012). The strategies domain is crucial for the career transition of SASD since it incorporates purposeful, flexible, and sustainable behaviour that assists SASD in progressing towards work-related goals (Lingo et al., 2024). Based on the BBST, the strategies domain constitutes the proximal process, which is the key driver of development. Good proximal processes require frequent, mutual interaction between the individual and their environment, and their effectiveness depends on the quality, consistency and flexibility of the involved behaviours (Henriques et al., 2025). Some of the measurement items in this domain include setting clear goals; reviewing, solving problems, modifying approaches, and seeking advice reflect the degree to which students actively engage in these developmental processes. Setting goals in classrooms effectively helps in acquiring and developing social and emotional learning (SEL) skills, especially for SASD (Sanders et al., 2023). Some SASD demonstrate skills in defining sequential tasks; nonetheless, a large percentage of them are faced with the difficulty of translating abstract career goals into operational action plans, as well as the lack of social and cultural capital necessary for effective career decision-making. This lack is reflected in the behaviour of some of them to avoid planning altogether, which shows their reduced involvement in the process of building preparedness and making adaptation possible (Maietta, 2023).

Also, reviewing progress is important in an educational environment, most especially for SASD, because active engagement in this process through feedback and goal setting can lead to better academic achievement and motivation (Furey & Loftus-Rattan, 2022). Successful transition planning requires systematic assessment of actions and results taken, which should preferably include advice from a professional. However, SASD often have a limited metacognitive awareness that makes it difficult to provide an objective measure of progress. Without continuous review, these SASD demonstrate less ability to observe ineffective strategies or those spheres that have to be changed. Reviewing facilitates students' grit, utility value, help-seeking behaviour, and executive control, which are impactful in problem-solving skills (Rodil, 2024). Students who are not equipped with a systematic approach to resolving learning challenges may experience frustration when learning routines are disrupted. SASD are associated with related rigidity that commonly disrupts their ability to switch strategies when an approach is ineffective. Although the instrument represents flexibility by measuring the readiness to alter methods, the behavioural flexibility is challenging for many students. Furthermore, modifying approaches by students is a vital aspect of strategies through adapting strategies, indicating the alignment of their goals with real situations, emphasising the need for choice selection, and goal significance (Faelasofi et al., 2025). SASD may have a hard time evaluating the effectiveness of a number of strategies, especially when the tasks involve abstract reasoning or general comparative analyses across activities. Poor reflective ability inhibits self-managed learning and prevents SASD from internalising successful behaviours, coupled with the fact that their strategic repertoire is small and inconsistent. However, teachers can encourage SASD to accept their current status and commit to realistic action, acquire new knowledge, skills, and attitudes (Jellicoe & Forsythe, 2024).

Successful transition planning strategies involve taking a proactive role in working with teachers, family members, and professionals. However, a lot of SASD are not just inclined to seek advice unless they are motivated to consult with the mentor, family, and professionals. Challenges related to social communication, fear of unfavourable judgments, or the inability to know whom to address are frequently the causes of these issues. The poor usage of help-seeking minimises the microsystem resources being accessible to the student, which are critical in achieving progress. Therefore, the strategies domain emphasised gaps in goal setting, adaptability, reflection, problem solving, and help seeking, all of which weaken the proximal processes necessary for effective career transition. When these weaknesses are assessed, teachers and other school professionals will be able to design interventions that support strategic behaviour and enhance transition readiness for SASD.

Another significant aspect in this study is the self-domain, which highlights insights into the personal features that influence students' career transition readiness. Self-domain entails the personal characteristics that influence how SASD interpret, engage with and respond to career transition requirements (Shafik, 2025). BBST highlights the significance of personal traits, including dispositions, resources, and demand characteristics, in influencing how individuals, mostly SASD, manage career transitions. In this study, the self-domain includes self-awareness, confidence, emotional preparedness, comprehension of personal limitations, and the resilience needed to maintain involvement in career planning (Kodama, 2017; Shafik, 2025; Lavigna & La Torre, 2024; Patel, 2019). Self-awareness serves as the cornerstone for both personal growth and professional advancement. It encompasses the comprehension of one's thoughts, emotions, behaviours, and personality characteristics, which is essential for regulating emotions and making deliberate choices that are in harmony with individual values and goals. Self-awareness significantly contributes to the effectiveness of leadership and the performance of teams, as it enables SASD to establish connections with themselves and with others (Carden, 2025).

Similarly, emotional preparedness entails the effective management of emotions, a vital component for addressing career-related challenges and preserving mental health. Emotional intelligence (EI), encompassing self-awareness, self-regulation, motivation, empathy, and social skills, is fundamental for career progression and professional achievement (Bansal & Bhattacharya, 2025). Emotional intelligence assists SASD in navigating workshop difficulties, making informed decisions, and building strong interpersonal relationships (Shafik, 2025). Although emotional intelligence reflects confidence in their ability to succeed, anxiety and uncertainty continue to be prevalent emotional characteristics of SASD. The conflict between self-confidence and self-doubt indicates unstable self-perceptions that can hinder consistent engagement. Emotional vulnerabilities, including fear of failure or lack of familiarity with workplace expectations, further diminish readiness. When emotional instability coincides with career transition tasks, students frequently withdraw or exhibit hesitance to engage in new activities. Also, recognising personal limitations is an essential component of self-awareness and career planning. By acknowledging these limitations, SASD can establish realistic goals and formulate effective strategies to address challenges. This understanding fosters a greater appreciation of reality and enhances the effectiveness of career counselling (Bright & Pryor, 2015). This domain reveals vulnerabilities in the manner in which SASD handle their internal limitations. While some exhibit an understanding of their personal challenges, a significant number find it difficult to convert this understanding into effective compensatory strategies.

Furthermore, resilience, which is a vital component of self-domain, refers to the capacity to adjust to changes and rebound from difficulties, which is essential for achieving success in one's career. It encompasses managing challenges, sustaining a positive outlook, and utilising interpersonal skills to handle career-related risks. The development of career resilience can be enhanced through organisational practices, supportive social networks, and an educational atmosphere that encourages relationships conducive to personal growth (Kodama, 2017; Lengelle et al., 2017). Constraint pertains to resilience, which is represented in the inventory by items that indicate emotional strength in the face of career challenges. SASD often exhibit restricted behavioural flexibility and increased sensitivity to stress, both of which diminish resilience. When faced with new environments or unforeseen changes, many SASD encounter emotional overload, resulting in avoidance instead of active participation. Diminished resilience hampers their ability to persevere through intricate transition tasks and restricts their capacity to bounce back from difficulties.

Unlike the self domain, the support domain evaluates how well SASD are able to access, utilise, and depend on the social and relational resources essential for a successful career transition. According to BBST, support is mainly located at the microsystem and mesosystem levels, where interactions with teachers, family members, mentors, peers, and professionals create the immediate developmental environment (Tong & An, 2024). Supports that are individualised and strength-based are critical for effective transition. Lee and Carter (2012) emphasised that transition services should be customised to the unique strengths and requirements of SASD, which encompass individualised career development plans and early work experiences that correspond with their interests and capabilities. Structured, organised support frameworks, including academic coaching, counselling, and mentorship initiatives, are essential because they assist SASD in navigating the challenges associated with higher education and professional environments (Accardo et al., 2019). Similarly, interagency collaboration support for the career transition of SASD requires significant cooperation among educational institutions, families, and outside organisations. This collaboration guarantees a thorough support network that encompasses different facets of the student's life, such as education, job opportunities, and self-sufficiency (Carter & Schutz, 2022). In addition, family support through engagement and backing can greatly affect the success of the transition by offering emotional support and championing the required resources and accommodations (Wong et al., 2021).

A significant drawback is associated with the inconsistency and unpredictability of support provided within schools. Numerous SASD do not receive consistent guidance from teachers or mentors who are aware of SASD's learning profiles or career aspirations (Tong & An, 2024). Insufficient instructional continuity leads to disjointed transition planning, minimal follow-up on skill development, and a lack of exposure to competencies relevant to the workplace (Hetherington et al., 2010). When guidance is lacking, SASD are unable to rely on the microsystem to organise or reinforce their transition behaviours. This inconsistency undermines the stability of proximal processes that Bronfenbrenner considers crucial for ongoing developmental advancement.

A second major weakness is the variability in family support. Some families may not have the resources, knowledge, or time to support the transition activities, while others may only have encouragement (Anderson et al., 2013). Low assistance is associated with families that face financial difficulties, low education level, or lack of knowledge about SASD. The lack of family engagement reduces the emotional stability and access to critical information of the SASD and creates disparities in motivation and readiness. Furthermore, we acknowledge the level of access to professionals who know the needs of the SASD, which results in a gap at the system level. Many SASD interact with counsellors who are not trained in autism planning. The inadequate knowledge on communication differences, sensorial issues, behavioural patterns, or executive functioning problems can make professionals misinterpret behaviours, ignore positive aspects, or prescribe the wrong interventions (Snell-Rood et al., 2020). This impairs the quality of mesosystem interactions, which constrains the coordination among school, healthcare services, and vocational programs.

In addition, SASD's feelings of being unsupported show a psychological barrier with substantial development implications. Hence, they are less likely to seek help and disclose challenges when they cannot rely on one another. This results in less involvement in transition-related tasks, poor adaptive behaviour, and a lack of motivation. The perceived support is as significant as real support since it has a direct effect on the readiness of the SASD to engage in the proximal processes (Snell-Rood et al., 2020). This support domain shows that not all students receive stable emotional reinforcement in the process of transition. Emotional assistance is essential in controlling anxiety, keeping people motivated, and preventing dropouts. In a case of poor emotional support, SASD experience a heightened stress when carrying out unfamiliar tasks, which might result in withdrawal, behavioural rigidity, or non-participation (Córdova et al., 2023).

The situation domain describes the degree to which SASD comprehend, analyse, and act on the contextual factors that influence their career transition, such as the reason behind the transition, when it occurs, the importance of the activities, the barriers involved, and the general expectations within their environment. In the BBST, this situation domain reflects the effect of the exosystem and macrosystem, which affect the way the student interprets the wider social expectation, institutional frameworks, and cultural meanings in relation to the transition (Tong & An, 2024). In spite of the fact that the domain identifies situational awareness as a cornerstone of coherent career planning, the domain unveils some weaknesses that hinder the creation of preparedness among students with ASD.

One of the biggest shortcomings is the lack of clarity provided to students about the purpose and the objectives of the transition. Many students cannot comprehend the main point of their work or education preparation, which is caused by the inconsistency in environmental messages (Dipeolu et al., 2015). Most schools usually do not provide tangible explanations that are consistent with the cognitive profiles of SASD. Due to this, students engage in transition practices without internalising their relevance (Van Hees et al., 2015). Bronfenbrenner suggests that in cases where the meaning is poorly conveyed on the macrosystem level, the proximal processes are not powerful enough to produce development(Young, 1983). Another substantial shortcoming is the poor alignment between transition timing and students' readiness. Most of the students encounter challenges interpreting the appropriateness of the career preparation timing, either as the timing of transition is introduced quickly or because institutional policies impose uniform timelines, which are not consistent with the students' developmental path (Lippold et al., 2013). SASD often require time to prepare, to follow a routine and to be progressively exposed, but the system usually provides inflexible schedules (Spelman, 2025). Such a discrepancy undermines situational support by generating confusion and anxiety, thereby restricting involvement in transition tasks.

The absence of specific and personalised reasons that make sense to SASD weakened situational supports. Most SASD depend on the instructions of adults instead of an internalised purpose, thus reducing their intrinsic motivation (Cohen et al., 2022). The absence of personalised meaning means that the engagement would be passive and reliant on external reinforcement (Benita & Matos, 2021). This, in the form of Bronfenbrenner's theory, indicates breakdown on how exosystem level expectations are communicated and internalised. Furthermore, the inability to manage unexpected challenges is another limitation since SASD are more likely to be under stress in case of changes in routines or when they face unexpected issues. Sudden shift in schedules, poorly defined guidelines or abrupt change of expectations are some of the situations that may cause withdrawal or emotional overload in SASD (Stanton, 2012; Spelman, 2025b). Adaptability is generally weaker in SASD, which means that disruptions in a situation become even more significant. These barriers disrupt the ability of SASD to maintain a transition task engagement and minimise the possibility that they will develop stable transition-related habits.

SASD cannot be fully comprehended in terms of career transition without recognising the dynamic interaction between the individual and the environment and the development processes that bind them together. The subsequent work by Bronfenbrenner on the Process Person Context Time (PPCT) model focuses on the idea that development is a product of interaction between the proximal processes, personal characteristics, contextual systems, and time. When applied in career transition, it can be used to explain how repetitive participation in planning processes, personal traits that include confidence and resiliency, situational factors that encompass family and school support, and the timing of the transition process give rise to the overall readiness (Nelson & Lund, 2017; Strachan et al., 2016; Giri et al., 2024). As an example, student who frequently train their problem-solving approaches in the long run tend to be competent in handling complicated career-related tasks. Likewise, those students whose teachers and counsellors continuously support them have more chances of being confident. The student will also interpret the process based on the contextual clarity of the purpose and the time the transition took place. Consequently, the PPCT model is a comprehensive approach to interpreting the pathways through which career transition readiness develops.

Irrespective of the significance of ecologically grounded transition planning, most instruments that measure career transition do not take into consideration the complex experiences of SASD. Traditional inventories tend to place a lot on the internal qualities like self-determination, motivation or career interests without adequately adding the relational or contextual dimension that are vital for this population (Rumsey, 2020). SASD often need stipulated approaches, situational clarity, and effective support systems to help them go through the process of career transition smoothly. Due to a lack of instruments that can capture such embedded domains of ecological continuity, teachers and other professionals might find it difficult to detect any gaps in readiness, offer suitable interventions or monitor progress. This weakness highlights the necessity of psychometrically competent instruments that can reveal the ecological reality of SASD.

This chapter contributes to the literature by assessing the reliability, validity, and structural characteristics of a career transition inventory that is designed for SASD. Psychometric assessment is important to ensure that the instrument measures the targeted constructs and produces a consistent result. The items of inventory are well constructed to capture the ecological aspects of transition readiness. As an example, the strategies domain is assessed using items to determine whether the student uses goal setting, progress monitoring, reflective practice, and adaptive coping, which are essential to involvement in proximal processes. Self domain items assess personal inclinations, which determine interactions. Support domain items measure connections with the microsystem that affect development. Situation domain items evaluate contextual perceptions, which are used to make meanings. The study offers empirical support for the utilisation of this instrument in both practice and research by reviewing the psychometrics of these domains.

Likewise, the design and appraisal of an instrument based on the bioecological systems theory of Bronfenbrenner contributes to the field by shifting the perspective beyond individual-centred approaches. It underlines the fact that the SASD are placed in the layers of systems that have an impact on their career development (Snell-Rood et al., 2020b; Pinder-Amaker, 2014). This direction aligns with international priorities in inclusive education and labour market preparation that focus on the necessity of a systemic approach to transition planning (Roberts, 2010). It is also consistent with empirical evidence, which has shown that SASD outcomes are better when interventions target both student skills and contextual supports (Gantman et al., 2012; Matthews et al., 2020). Accordingly, validated instruments based on ecological concepts are necessary in the development of interventions and policy, and to guide teachers in providing meaningful transition support for SASD.

In most of the education systems, including those in Sub-Saharan Africa, transition planning for SASD is incomplete, lacks resources, or is inconsistently implemented (Meiring et al., 2016; Strnadová et al., 2016). The death of suitable assessment tools in this context worsens these challenges. The present research addresses these challenges by developing an inventory that includes ecologically significant constructs and can be useful in the formulation of evidence-based interventions. The instrument provides a comprehensive perspective of transition readiness, which is consistent with the complexity of the career transitions among SASD, because it combines internal dispositions, environmental supports, strategic behaviours, and situational knowledge.

RESEARCH OBJECTIVES

This study assesses the psychometric properties of a newly developed Career Transition Inventory for Students with ASD (CTI-SASD), including its factor structure, reliability, construct validity, and overall model fit. Below are the specific objectives.

1. To assess the underlying factor structure of the CTI-SASD using a four-factor model comprising Strategies, Self, Support, and Situation based on BBST
2. To evaluate the internal consistency reliability of each CTI-SASD subscale using Cronbach's alpha, composite reliability, and omega coefficients.
3. To establish convergent and discriminant validity of the CTI-SASD for each subscale.
4. To determine the overall model fit of the CTI-SASD using structural equation modelling indices.
5. To test the structural relationships among the four CTI-SASD constructs as represented in the path analysis model.

RESEARCH QUESTIONS

1. What is the underlying factor structure of the CTI-SASD, and do the items load appropriately onto the four expected dimensions: Strategies, Self, Support, and Situation?
2. What is the level of internal consistency reliability of the CTI-SASD subscales as indicated by Cronbach's alpha, omega, and composite reliability values?
3. Does the CTI-SASD demonstrate acceptable convergent validity and adequate discriminant validity?
4. Does the CTI-SASD measurement model demonstrate good model fit based on SEM indices?
5. What are the structural relationships among the four CTI-SASD constructs in a path analysis model?

THEORETICAL FRAMEWORK

BBST is an inclusive developmental framework for comprehending how individuals grow based on the collaboration of personal features and environmental conditions. Originally known as the Ecological Systems Theory in the 1970s, later extended and elaborated by Bronfenbrenner into the Process Person Context Time (PPCT) model (El Zaatari & Maalouf, 2022a). This revised theory represented a transition from perceiving the environment as a collection of nested structures to highlighting the dynamic, mutual interactions between persons and their ecological contexts (Navarro & Tudge, 2025). The bioecological model has since emerged as part of the considerable powerful theories in developmental psychology, since it describes the process of development as a collective action of individual qualities, interaction processes, systems of contexts, and time. BBST reconceptualised human development as the result of dynamic, reciprocal interactions between individuals and their environments over time. This formulation is operationalised through the PPCT model as the core drivers of development (El Zaatari & Maalouf, 2022a).

The model of PPCT comprises four components that are interrelated (Siraj & Huang, 2020: Henriques et al., 2025). Process is the proximal interactions between the person and the environment that instigate development. Such interactions should be frequent, protracted and increasingly more complicated. Person represents the personal traits of the person, its dispositions, resources, and demand features, which influence the manner in which it undertakes developmental activities. Context entails the microsystem, mesosystem, exosystem, and macrosystem, representing the multiple layers of environmental influence from immediate relationships to broader societal structures. Time is the chronological and situational factors that affect developmental processes such as life transitions and historical conditions.

The theoretical background is related to this study because career transition is an extensive developmental change that requires continuous interaction between the SASD and their environment. The proximal processes are reflected in the behaviours of goal setting, reflection, problem solving, and adaptation, which are represented in the inventory in the strategies domain (Snell-Rood et al., 2020b). Self-domain reflects a person's characteristics, including confidence, knowledge of strengths and emotional preparedness. The contextual influences are found in the support and situation domains, which are the domains that measure the accessibility of guidance, family engagement, peer support and the awareness of the student of their larger transition environment. Time is embedded in the student's perception of transition timing, readiness, and progression toward adulthood. The application of the PPCT model places the assessment inventory on a rigorous developmental framework. It explains that transition readiness for SASD emerges from the interplay of personal attributes, environmental structures, and the quality of interactions that connect them.

The concepts of strategies, self, support, and situation can be meaningfully mapped onto the PPCT model to explain how transition outcomes emerge for SASD. In this context, strategies refer to the adaptive behaviours and actions which SASD develop by proximal career preparation processes. These are goal-setting, self-advocacy, problem-solving, practice of vocational skills, and decision-making. In the case of SASD, the success of these strategies is determined by the frequency, quality, and scaffold of interactions among teachers, counsellors, peers, and working conditions. Once transition-related activities are organised, regular, and reinforced between settings, SASD have a higher likelihood of exhibiting greater engagement and preparedness to take post-school positions (White, McGarry et al., 2025). Strategies are therefore not just those that arise out of an individual capacity but from sustained interaction within supportive contexts.

Self is associated with the Person aspect of the PPCT model and represents the personal attributes, which SASD bring into the transition process. These are cognitive strengths, communication profiles, interests, sensory needs, motivation and self-efficacy. Instead of focusing on individual traits, Bronfenbrenner stressed that the development is influenced by the individual characteristics interacting with the environmental demands. In the process of career transition, SASD who view themselves as competent and have their interests recognised are more inclined to investigate vocational opportunities and remain committed to career-related activities (Kodama, 2017) . In contrast, settings that do not acknowledge individual profiles may hinder the demonstration of abilities, even when potential exists (Shafik, 2025; Lavigna & La Torre, 2024; Patel, 2019).

Support is incorporated into the context dimension of the PPCT model, and it is seen as the interpersonal and institutional resources that the SASD have access to during transition. Support functions at microsystems like the family and school levels, mesosystems between the microsystem and exosystems like labour markets, service agencies, and policy structures. In the case of SASD, interprofessional, family, and community support through coordinated effort has been vital in the sustainability of proximal processes with regard to career development. Research evidence has persistently shown that discontinuous or disjointed support decreases the success of the transitions, and integrated and joint support increases post-school performance (Hetherington et al., 2010).

The situation illustrates both Context and Time within the PPCT model, capturing the wider conditions under which career transitions occur. Situational factors encompass school culture, the availability of vocational programs, community attitudes towards disability, economic circumstances, and the policy frameworks that govern inclusive education and employment. Time holds equal importance, as transition experiences are influenced by developmental timing, the duration of support exposure, and historical changes in policy and practice. For SASD, early and ongoing engagement in transition planning throughout their school years is linked to more stable and meaningful adult outcomes (El Zaatari & Maalouf, 2022b). The PPCT model emphasises that effective career transition for students with ASD arises from the integration of adaptive strategies, a supported self-concept, coordinated assistance, and conducive situational contexts over time. This ecological viewpoint highlights the necessity of treating career transition as a dynamic, system-embedded process that demands continuous interaction across various ecological levels.

POLICY FRAMEWORK

The National Policy on Inclusive Education in Nigeria forms the legal basis of assisting the SASD and other students with diverse needs by ensuring that they have quality access to education (FRN, 2023). The policy is based on the fact that inclusion is a human right and requires that all students, regardless of disability, learn together in settings that eliminate the barriers to participation (Angwaomaodoko, 2023). The policy indicates that the government is committed to equalising educational opportunities and ensuring that all individuals receive appropriate support within inclusive learning environments. The policy emphasised that inclusion is vital for social justice, participation, and full citizenship and is congruent with international policies like the Salamanca Statement and Education for All (FRN, 2023).

In this policy direction, the preparation of SASD in transitioning is positioned as an aspect of their right to equitable learning opportunities that can make them independent and ready to work in the workplace. The policy emphasises that learning structures, flexible teaching methods, and multi-level assistance should be modified to address the diversity of students because it is the duty of the school to address the peculiarities of each student and minimise any barriers to studying and engagement (Orlunga & Alikor, 2023). These instructions explain why psychometrically adequate tools are necessary that help determine the preparedness of SASD to participate in systematic transition procedures.

METHODOLOGY

Study Participants

A total of one hundred and ninety-three students with ASD were initially contacted across a range of secondary schools and transition support programmes in Cross River and Delta States, which form part of the South-South Geopolitical Zone of Nigeria. These states were selected because they include urban centres, semi-urban communities, and rural localities where varying educational opportunities influence the transition experiences of young people with special learning needs. We reached out to schools through special education units, guidance counsellors, and transition support programme coordinators, and informed them of the purpose and relevance of the study. Of the one hundred and ninety-three students who were invited to participate, one hundred and thirty-nine agreed to take part and began the survey. This represented a strong initial willingness to engage with the research. However, not all students were able to complete the questionnaire. In total, one hundred and twenty students completed the entire instrument and were retained for analysis, giving a completion rate of 86.33 percent. The attrition recorded in this study was not surprising. Students with ASD may experience varying levels of cognitive load, fluctuating attention, sensory sensitivities, or difficulty with extended tasks, which may influence their capacity to complete questionnaires. In addition, some schools experienced timetable changes or interruptions that affected the ability of students to complete the survey in full. We considered these contextual realities to be part of the natural variation expected in research involving neurodivergent learners in school environments.

Although our recruitment strategy aimed to ensure a broad reach, our final sample characteristics reflect the nature of voluntary participation in transition-related research within Nigerian school settings. Of the one hundred and twenty students retained in the final analyses, seventy-three identified as female and forty-seven as male. Their ages ranged from fifteen to twenty-five years, with a mean age of 19.42 years and a standard deviation of 3.18. This age range aligns with what is commonly described as the transition period, where learners begin to engage with decisions concerning work, further education, and independent living. Students were drawn from diverse geographical settings: thirty-eight students (31.7 percent) lived in urban areas, forty-two (35 percent) were located in semi-urban settings, and forty (33.3 percent) came from rural communities across both states. This distribution indicates that the sample captured a balanced spread of environmental contexts, which is particularly important for a questionnaire designed to examine planning, support, and situational awareness in career transition. In terms of school type, fifty-nine students were enrolled in public schools, while sixty-one attended private schools. This near equal representation allowed us to observe the instrument's performance across different institutional systems. Public and private schools in Cross River and Delta States may differ in terms of resources, staffing, curriculum emphasis, and the availability of support services. Including students from both sectors was therefore essential to ensuring that the Career Transition Inventory for SASD could be meaningfully applied in a range of educational environments.

Research Approach, Design, and Paradigm

The use of a quantitative approach, cross-sectional survey design and positivist paradigm gave a clear and coherent framework for the examination of the psychometric properties of the CTI-SASD. The quantitative approach was selected because the constructs being investigated were most appropriately expressed as measurable variables (Quick & Hall, 2015). This enabled us to analyse patterns in the students' responses and determine the degree to which the instrument captured behavioural strategies, internal beliefs, perceived support and understanding of the situation relating to career transition. The cross-sectional survey design was appropriate for the aim of determining the structure and reliability of the instrument at one point in time (Hunziker & Blankenagel, 2024). It made it possible to efficiently collect data from students in a wide range of schools in Cross River and Delta States without the need to measure repeatedly. This approach ensured that the dataset was adequate for the factor analyses and reliability assessments required for validation. Grounding the study in a positivist paradigm was a natural fit to the need for objective evaluation of the instrument. Positivism assumes that constructs can be studied by looking at observable indicators and that empirical evidence provides a good basis for evaluating the quality of a scale (Ali, 2024). This philosophical position was used to support our use of statistical criteria such as factor loadings, composite reliability, and model fit indices to determine whether the four-factor model was supported.

Instrument

The Career Transition Inventory for Students with ASD (CTI-SASD) was developed to assess the constructs most relevant to the career transition process for neurodivergent learners in the Nigerian context. Although research on the career transition of students with ASD is growing internationally, there is still limited empirical work in the South-South region of Nigeria that captures the psychological and contextual attributes influencing transition readiness. For this reason, we constructed an instrument grounded in both theoretical insight and the practical realities of local schooling systems.

The initial pool of items was informed by a review of existing literature on transition planning, self-determination, ecological support systems, and the unique challenges faced by students with ASD in preparing for future pathways. The structure of the instrument was guided by Bronfenbrenner's bioecological systems theory, which proposes that the dynamic interaction of personal attributes, immediate social supports, and broader contextual conditions shapes development (El Zaatari & Maalouf, 2022). In line with this framework, items were generated across four domains: Strategies, Self, Support, and Situation. These domains were developed to reflect essential areas of transition competence, including behavioural planning skills, internal beliefs and emotions, perceived support from the environment, and the individual's interpretation of the transition context.

Once the initial pool of items was drafted, we reviewed the statements for clarity, developmental suitability, and conceptual relevance. We ensured that the wording was accessible for students with varied reading skills. The final instrument consisted of twenty-five items distributed across the four subscales. The Strategies subscale contained seven items assessing planning behaviours such as setting goals, reviewing progress, identifying obstacles, and modifying approaches when necessary. The Self subscale included six items capturing confidence, emotional readiness, awareness of strengths and limitations, and resilience. The Support subscale contained six items measuring access to teachers, family members, professionals, peers, and emotional encouragement. The Situation subscale included six items assessing the learners' interpretation of the timing, meaning, and obstacles surrounding the transition.

All items were rated on a five-point Likert scale ranging from one, Strongly Disagree, to five, Strongly Agree. This structure aligned with the Likert conventions described in other psychological instruments and enabled students to express the degree to which each statement described their transition experiences. Higher scores reflected stronger endorsement of the corresponding domain.

Study Procedure

The procedures used in this study were designed to ensure systematic, respectful, and ethically responsible engagement with students with ASD. Data collection was conducted by two postgraduate research assistants with experience in educational psychology and special needs education. Their familiarity with autism characteristics ensured that they were well-positioned to provide appropriate support during administration without influencing participants' responses. The process began with contacting school administrators across selected local government areas in Cross River and Delta States. We provided detailed information about the study, including its purpose, expected duration, and relevance to improving transition practices for students with ASD. Schools that indicated interest were visited by the research assistants, who arranged data collection times that fit within the schools' timetables. On the day of data collection, the research assistants introduced the study to eligible students, explaining its aims in clear, accessible language. Students were reminded that participation was voluntary and that they were free to discontinue at any point. Consent and assent procedures were completed in accordance with ethical guidelines. Once consent was obtained, students were given printed questionnaires in quiet and comfortable classroom spaces to ensure full concentration. The research assistants assisted students who needed support with reading or understanding specific words, but care was taken to avoid influencing the content of their responses. The assistants focused only on rephrasing instructions or clarifying wording when necessary. Students were encouraged to complete the questionnaires at their own pace. Upon completion, the questionnaires were checked for completeness, then stored securely. Although we anticipated a high level of participation, some students were unable to finish the questionnaire due to time constraints, sensory or attention challenges, or unexpected interruptions in the school schedule. These incomplete cases were excluded from analysis in order to preserve the integrity of the data.

Ethical approval for this study was obtained from the Faculty of Education Research Ethics Committee at the University of Johannesburg, South Africa (Sem-2-2020-057). Prior to participation, all students were informed of the nature and aims of the study. They were assured of their right to withdraw and were told that their participation would have no negative consequences for their academic standing or access to school support services. Students who were eighteen years or older provided informed consent independently, while assent was obtained from younger students with corresponding parental or guardian consent.

Data Analysis Plan

This study's analysis was guided by a positivist orientation, which values objective and measurable indicators of psychological constructs. Consistent with this paradigm, the analytical procedures focused on identifying patterns in students' responses and examining how well the CTI-SASD represented the constructs it intended to measure. We began by screening the dataset for issues such as missing values, inconsistent entries, or extreme outliers. Cases that contained significant missing data were removed at this stage. Exploratory statistics were computed to summarise the demographic profile of the sample. These summaries comprised frequencies for gender, school type, and geographical location, as well as means and standard deviations for age.

To analyse the underlying dimensions of the CTI-SASD, factor analysis procedures was used. The factor loadings offered in Table 1 were evaluated to determine the extent to which each item contributed to its designated factor. Following the interpretive guidelines recommended in the measurement literature, loadings above 0.70 were considered satisfactory for supporting item retention. Loadings exceeding point eight illustrated a strong association between the item and its latent construct. Internal consistency reliability was established using Cronbach's alpha, composite reliability, and omega coefficients. All subscales met or exceeded threshold, demonstrating that the CTI-SASD captured stable and coherent patterns of responding.

Convergent validity was assessed through the Average Variance Extracted (AVE) values, which demonstrated whether the items within each subscale shared an adequate proportion of variance. Discriminant validity (DV) was evaluated by contrasting the Average Variance Extracted with the Discriminant Validity index. Values exceeding 0.5 for Average Variance Extracted and higher Discriminant Validity scores than the respective Average Variance Extracted values indicated that each construct preserved its conceptual distinction. The CMIN/DF (Chi-square minimum/degree of freedom index) was also computed. Ultimately, we analysed the overall measurement model utilising structural equation modelling indices. The Comparative Fit Index (CFI), Standardised Root Mean Square Residual (SRMR), Root Mean Square Error of Approximation (RMSEA), and PClose value were examined to evaluate the sufficiency of model fit. The indices indicated that the suggested four-factor solution provided a accurate depiction of the observed data.

RESULTS

Table 1. Psychometric properties of a Career Transition Inventory for Students with ASD (CTI-SASD)

S/No	Items	F 1	F 2	F3	F 4	CR	AVE	DV
	Strategies							
1	I set clear, step-by-step goals for my career tasks.	.828						
2	I regularly review my progress with someone involved.	.713						
3	I use problem-solving strategies when facing obstacles.	.836						
4	I change my approach when something is not working.	.842				0.91	0.62	0.78
5	I seek advice proactively to improve my planning.	.766						
6	I avoid making plans for my career.	.828						
7	I reflect on what strategies work best for me.	.713						
	Self							
8	I am aware of my personal strengths related to work and careers.		.823					
9	I am confident in my abilities to succeed in a job.		.890					
10	I understand my limitations and how to work around them.		.867			0.92	0.65	0.81
11	I see myself as capable of managing this career change.		.805					
12	I feel anxious or unsure about whether I am ready.		.752					
13	I feel resilient when facing challenges in career planning.		.729					
	Support							
14	I can rely on teachers or mentors for guidance during transition.			.790				
15	My family provides encouragement for my career goals.			.855				
16	I have access to professionals who understand my needs.			.741		0.91	0.64	0.79
17	I feel unsupported by the people I rely on.			.768				
18	My peers offer practical help during transition activities.			.808				
19	I feel emotionally supported throughout the process.			.811				
	Situation							
20	I clearly understand why I am preparing for this career transition.				.786			
21	I feel the timing of this career change is appropriate.				.810			
22	My reasons for pursuing career activities are well-defined.				.828	0.93	0.66	0.81
23	I experience unexpected obstacles in starting my transition.				.836			
24	I perceive this as an essential step, not just a suggestion.				.750			
25	I see this transition as a natural progression in my life.				.730			

Note: F = Factor

In Table 1, the factor structure of the CTI-SASD corresponds with the proposed four-dimensional model. Its loading pattern shows that each item clusters meaningfully within its assigned construct, suggesting that students' responses reflect coherent groupings of career transition competences. For the Strategies dimension, all seven items load strongly, with values ranging from .713 to .842, which indicates that behaviours such as setting goals, reviewing progress, problem solving, and reflecting on planning strategies form a unified behavioural domain. The Self dimension also shows robust loadings, between .729 and .890, suggesting that self-knowledge, confidence, awareness of limitations, readiness concerns, and resilience collectively measures a distinct internal attribute domain related to personal agency in transition. The Support dimension indicates similar strength, with loadings between .741 and .855, indicating that students' perceptions of teacher, family, professional, peer, and emotional support form a consistent construct. The Situation dimension also shows stable loadings, ranging from .730 to .836, demonstrating that students' understanding of timing, reasons, obstacles, and transition relevance are captured as a cohesive interpretive domain. The factor loadings confirm a stable four-factor solution, showing that item distribution reflects the intended theoretical structure of career transition experiences among students with ASD.

The confirmatory factor analysis indicated that all items were appropriately associated with their respective constructs—Strategies (.713–.842), Self (.729–.890), Support (.741–.855), and Situation (.730–.836)—thereby affirming a stable and theoretically sound model. Reliability assessments indicated exceptional internal consistency across all subscales, with Cronbach's alpha values ranging from .89 to .91 and composite reliability values between .91 and .93, all of which surpassed the established benchmarks for psychological measurement. Convergent validity was demonstrated by the values of AVE exceeding .50 for each subscale (.62–.66), while discriminant validity was validated through DV values (.78–.81) that exceeded the corresponding AVE values, signifying that the constructs were interrelated yet empirically distinct.Model fit indices from SEM further validated the measurement model. The fit statistics (CMIN/df = 1.447, CFI = .942, SRMR = .08, RMSEA = .06, PClose = .09) indicated an adequately fitting model consistent with recommended psychometric standards. Path analysis revealed meaningful structural relationships among the four constructs, demonstrating that strategies, self attributes, support systems, and situational understanding interact to shape overall transition readiness. Collectively, the results confirm that the CTI-SASD is a psychometrically sound tool for assessing career transition competencies in students with ASD.

Figure 1. Path analysis of a Career Transition Inventory for Students with ASD (CTI-SASD)

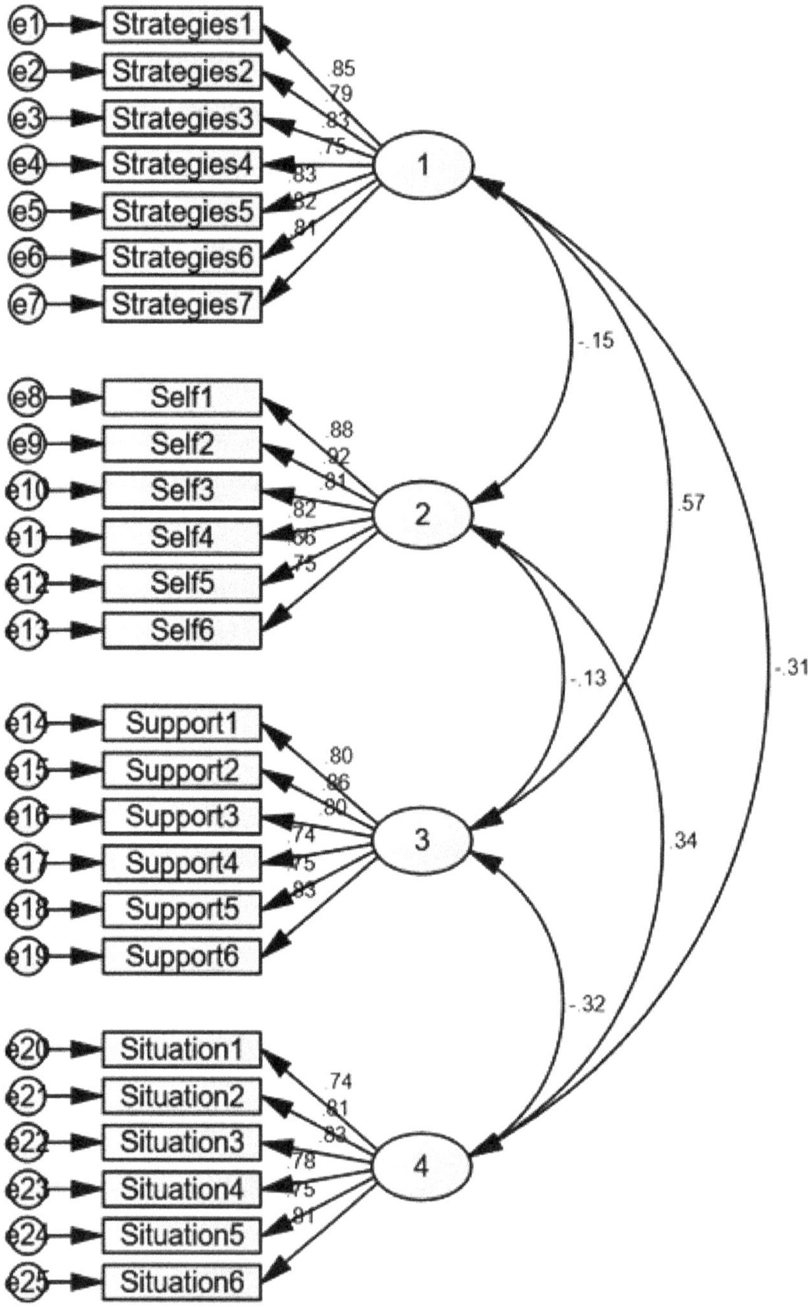

The path analysis in Figure 1 reveals how the four constructs of the CTI-SASD interact within the broader career transition framework. Each of the constructs in the CTI-SASD contributes meaningfully to the overall model. The model shows the interdependence between students' planning strategies, self-beliefs, external support systems, and situational understanding. It shows that a combination of internal factors and the surrounding environment shapes effective career transition for students with ASD. It, therefore, reflects a balanced structure in which personal competence, support opportunities, and contextual conditions work together to influence transition readiness and progression.

Table 2. Model fit Measures and validity Analysis of a Career Transition Inventory for Students with ASD (CTI-SASD)

S/No	Subscales	Cronbach's α	ω	CR	AVE	DV	CMIN/Df	CFI	SRMR	RMSEA	PClose
1	Strategies	0.91		0.91	0.62	0.78	1.447	0.942	0.08	0.06	0.09
2	Self	0.89		0.92	0.65	0.81					
3	Support	0.90		0.91	0.64	0.79					
4	Situation	0.91		0.93	0.66	0.81					

In Table 2, strong internal consistency across all four subscales of the CTI-SASD was found. The Strategies subscale had a Cronbach's alpha of .91 and a composite reliability of .91, which suggests an excellent reliability index. The Self subscale showed similarly high reliability, with an alpha of .89 and a composite reliability of .92. The Support subscale also emerged strongly, with an alpha of .90 and a composite reliability of .91. The Situation subscale follows the same pattern, with an alpha of .91 and a composite reliability of .93. These values exceed the commonly accepted threshold of .70 for adequate reliability in psychological measures. Although omega values are not fully displayed, the consistency observed across alpha and composite reliability suggests that the instrument captures stable and dependable patterns of responding. Overall, the reliability indices indicate that the CTI-SASD subscales function as internally coherent measures of career transition constructs among students with ASD.

Evidence in Tables 1 and 2 shows strong support for convergent and discriminant validity. For convergent validity, all four subscales exceed the .50 criterion for AVE, with values of .62 for Strategies, .65 for Self, .64 for Support, and .66 for Situation. These results imply that each subscale captures a meaningful proportion of variance from its items and that the items within each domain share a common conceptual theme. Discriminant validity (DV) is also supported, with DV values of .78, .81, .79, and .81 across the four subscales. These values surpass the corresponding AVE values, which indicates that each construct retains distinction from the others rather than overlapping excessively. Combined, the AVE and DV values reveal that the CTI-SASD measures four related yet distinct domains of career transition experiences.

Evidence from Table 2 indicates that the overall measurement model attained an acceptable level of fit. The CMIN divided by degrees of freedom is 1.447 (this value falls below the recommended value of 3.0). The CFI is .942, which exceeds the .90 threshold, indicating that the model compares favourably to a baseline model. The SRMR is .08, and this value meets the acceptable standard for residuals. On one hand, the RMSEA value of .06 is considered to be within the acceptable confidence range. On the other hand, the PClose value of .09 indicates that the model fits reasonably within the proposed structural boundaries. In summary, these indices show that the model offers an adequate representation of the observed data and supports the structural validity of the CTI-SASD.

DISCUSSION

The current research assessed the psychometric validity of the Career Transition Inventory for SASD (CTI-SASD), a self-developed tool based on Bronfenbrenner's bioecological systems theory. It aimed at evaluating four theoretically distinct areas that collectively influence career transition readiness: Strategies, Self, Support, and Situation. The findings provide evidence regarding the factor structure, internal consistency, convergent and discriminant validity, overall model fit, and the interrelations of the underlying constructs. These findings not only confirm the psychometric reliability of the CTI-SASD but also underscore significant implications for the conceptualisation and support of career transitions for SASD. Importantly, each domain corresponds with essential elements of the PPCT model within bioecological theory, suggesting that transition preparation embodies the dynamic interaction of individual skills, proximal processes, systemic supports, and broader temporal and contextual factors (Shattuck et al., 2012).

The confirmatory evidence supporting a four-factor structure highlights that career transition readiness in SASD is fundamentally multidimensional, rather than merely unidimensional. The structure of the CTI-SASD strongly aligns with a robust body of literature that clearly demonstrates how successful outcomes after school are the result of interconnected personal abilities, acquired strategies, supportive environments, and contextual awareness. Pioneering reviews of transition predictors reveal that factors such as paid work experience at the high school, social skills, and family expectations are associated with post-school employment and educational involvement, a trend that is consistent with the view of transition as a complex construct (Mazzotti et al., 2021). Likewise, studies using longitudinal data show that youth with ASD fare worse in both postsecondary education and employment participation compared to peers with other learning needs, reinforcing the need to measure multiple dimensions of transition readiness concurrently (Shattuck et al., 2012b)

The clear-cut clustering of items under each of the domains shows that SASD distinguish between internal strategic behaviours, self-related characteristics, social/environmental supports, and situational appraisal to evaluate their readiness to transition. This finding aligns with the ecological perspective that stress developments cannot be reduced to some underlying characteristic but rather to the aggregate outcome of the proximal processes and interactions with personal and contextual conditions in the course of time (Baum et al., 2020; Schiamberg et al., 2019). For instance, strategies like goal setting and adaptive problem-solving are conceptually different and cannot be postulated as the same latent trait.

From a practical perspective, acknowledging multidimensional readiness facilitates the creation of detailed transition plans in which teachers and professionals evaluate particular areas of need instead of depending on overarching assessments. This methodology is reinforced by transition practice frameworks that highlight skill instruction (such as planning and decision-making) and social support scaffolding as distinct yet interconnected components of successful preparation (Carter et al., 2013). The CTI-SASD subscales demonstrated a high level of internal consistency, with reliability coefficients exceeding the accepted standards for psychological evaluation (Cronbach's 0.90 is the approximate value of the existing reliability coefficient). These findings reaffirm the reliability benchmarks commonly referenced in the literature on scale development, indicating that values exceeding .70 are regarded as acceptable, while those surpassing .80 are considered robust for both research and practical applications (Elwyn et al., 2009; Meethal & Thomas, 2024; Li et al., 2020; Zincirli & Polat, 2025).

The robust reliability observed across all four domains suggests that item wording and construct operationalisation effectively captured coherent latent traits. In autism research specifically, achieving high reliability for constructs such as self-perception and strategy use is noteworthy because autistic individuals often present heterogeneous profiles of skills, preferences, and communication styles that can complicate self-report consistency. Evidence from previous work on psychometric assessment in autism had revealed moderate reliability for constructs like job interview skills, highlighting the difficulty in achieving stable measurement in this population (Smith et al., 2023; Genova et al., 2023). Reliable measurement is essential for transition planning, allowing practitioners to differentiate between persistent strengths and areas requiring targeted intervention. For example, consistently high scores on the strategies domain suggest that instruction aimed at enhancing problem-solving or planning could be monitored over time with confidence that changes are reflective of true growth rather than measurement error. This finding aligns with previous studies' reports, which indicated that strength-based assessment offers a balanced view of individual potentials and highlights the value of recognising and leveraging SASD strengths, interests, and unique abilities to improve their quality of life and self-esteem (Chow & Cooper, 2024; Clark & Adams, 2020; Courchesne et al., 2020).

This study revealed that the robust convergent validity indicated by AVE values exceeding the .50 threshold affirms that each domain of the CTI-SASD effectively measures a unified ecological construct. This finding is in agreement with the methodological criteria established by previous researchers, which emphasised that AVE is a crucial measure of significant variance within constructs. In the domains of Strategies, Self, Support, and Situation, elevated AVE values suggest that the items accurately reflect proximal processes, individual variables, contextual factors, and temporally-based evaluations, respectively (dos Santos & Cirillo, 2023; Zulkifli & Zin, 2024; Chen et al., 2019). In a similar vein, discriminant validity, characterised by the square root of AVE surpassing inter-construct correlations, illustrates that each domain addresses a unique ecological aspect rather than indicating a generalised transition readiness factor. This result is consistent with the previous findings, which indicate that autistic adolescents frequently distinguish between their internal capabilities, available resources, and contextual needs when assessing academic or vocational activities (Munsell et al., 2022; White, Brewe et al., 2025). These results contradict the frameworks that treat transition preparedness as a single linear construct or assume that increasing one aspect instantly improves others. Evident from the literature has proven that several aspects of transition readiness encompass domains like self-advocacy, health responsibility, and social supports (Jaipaeng et al., 2025; Hart et al., 2017). The Bronfenbrenner framework supports the idea that career transition is not an isolated event but one that is developed over time (Tong & An, 2023; Darpatova-Hruzewicz et al., 2025). SASD who start planning earlier in their lives tend to have more time to strategise, refine their self-understanding, cultivate supportive relationships, and gain clarity about the situation (Yuliawati & Ardyan, 2022; Evans & Raines, 2017). The items of the instrument measuring perceptions of preparedness, timing, and progression represent developmental processes. The insights enable teachers to recognise when to increase efforts of interventions, when to strengthen the support networks and how to synchronise operations of transition activities with developmental requirements.

The uniqueness of these domains highlights the necessity for meticulously focused intervention planning. Boosting a student's self-confidence (Self) is not equivalent to developing planning abilities (Strategies). In the same vein, enhancing contextual understanding (Situation) should be treated independently from fortifying interpersonal support networks (Support). This precision, specific to each domain, is vital for SASD, who typically gain more from clear instruction and organised scaffolding than from vague or generalised interventions. The CTI-SASD measurement model confirmed strong prevailing fit across multiple indices consistent with accepted SEM thresholds (Hu & Bentler, 1999). These fit indices confirm that the measurement model offers a mathematically articulate representation of the theorised ecological constructs. Attaining a strong model fit is especially significant in autism research, where issues of measurement invariance and response variability frequently present difficulties (Zhong et al., 2023). The strong fit achieved by the CTI-SASD suggests that the items were adequately clear, accessible, and in alignment with the lived experiences and cognitive profiles of SASD. The structural coherence of the model supports the theoretical assumption that the four domains are interdependent but not interchangeable. This finding resonates with applied ecological frameworks that conceptualise development as the outcome of numerous interacting systems operating simultaneously (Read & Szokolszky, 2025; Simon et al., 2014). A robust model fit substantiates the application of the CTI-SASD in research contexts (such as cross-group comparisons and longitudinal modelling) as well as in high-stakes educational decision-making. This finding strengthens the notion that the instrument's structure is not merely a measurement artefact, but rather a substantial reflection of the ecological aspects of career transitions for SASD.

The findings from the path analysis revealed a significant association among the CTI-SASD domains, which align with Bronfenbrenner's PPCT model. The strategies, which comprised proximal processes, were significantly forecasted by both the self and support domains. This suggests that individual characteristics and contextual resources collaboratively promote active participation in transition planning. These results are in agreement with previous research showing that self domains are predictors of increased involvement in career-related activities among autistic youth (Zhong et al., 2023; Turcan et al., 2024). Correspondingly, the impact of support on strategies is congruent with research indicating that supportive microsystems such as family, educators, and peers influence the chances through which proximal processes occur (Kearney & Bookspan, 2023; Buntinx, 2008). Support networks offer modelling, feedback, and strengthening that enable SASD to practise and strengthen strategies like setting goals and adaptive planning. Furthermore, the robust influence of the situation domain emphasised the important role of contextual meaning-making and temporal clarity. SASD mainly depend on the predictability, detailed explanations, and structured expectations. Therefore, when they identify transition as poorly timed, unclear, or externally imposed, engagement typically declines (Mori et al., 2018). Collectively, these pathways illustrate Bronfenbrenner's claim that development does not arise from individual traits alone, but rather from coordinated interactions among individuals, processes, contexts, and time. These results imply that effective support must incorporate internal capacity building, strategy instruction, environmental support, and contextual clarity.

CONCLUSION

This study has illustrated that the CTI-SASD is a psychometrically sound and ecologically relevant tool that effectively captures the essential areas influencing career transition readiness among SASD. By incorporating Bronfenbrenner's PPCT theory with empirical data derived from CFA, SEM, and reliability assessments, the results affirm that the process of transition development is dynamic, influenced by personal, behavioural, relational, and contextual factors. This multidimensional perspective provides a strong basis for creating interventions, enhancing policy alignment, and furthering investigation in the area of autism transition studies.

REFERENCES

Accardo, A. L., Kuder, S. J., & Woodruff, J. (2019). Accommodations and support services preferred by college students with autism spectrum disorder. *Autism, 23*(3), 574–583. DOI: 10.1177/1362361318760490 PMID: 29475372

Ali, I. M. (2024). *A Guide for Positivist Research Paradigm: From Philosophy to Methodology. 187–196*. DOI: 10.24191/idealogy.v9i2.596

Anderson, L. L., Larson, S. A., & McDonald, S. (2013). Unmet needs and quality of support for parents of transition-aged youth: Differences by disability group, age, and household income. *Research in Social Science and Disability, 7*, 63–95. DOI: 10.1108/S1479-3547(2013)0000007006

Angwaomaodoko, E. A. (2023). The Challenges and Opportunities of Inclusive Education in Nigeria. *Traektoriâ Nauki, 9*(07), 1001–1009. https://www.ceeol.com/search/article-detail?id=1264806

Bansal, D., & Bhattacharya, N. (2025). Navigating Success: The Intersection of Emotional Intelligence and Career Development. In Dutta, P. K., Gupta, S., Kashyap, S., Gehlot, A., Karmakar, R., & Bhattacharya, P. (Eds.), *Emotional Intelligence in the Digital Era: Concepts, Frameworks, and Applications* (pp. 141–158). CRC Press., DOI: 10.1201/9781032715377-10

Baum, A., Fleming, R., & Singer, J. E. (2020). Understanding environmental stress: Strategies for conceptual and methodological integration. In A. Baum & J. E. Singer (Eds.), *Advances in Environmental Psychology (Volume 5): Methods and Environmental Psychology* (pp. 185–205). Taylor and Francis. DOI: 10.4324/9781003052944-7

Benita, M., & Matos, L. (2021). Internalization of Mastery Goals: The Differential Effect of Teachers' Autonomy Support and Control. *Frontiers in Psychology, 11*, 599303. DOI: 10.3389/fpsyg.2020.599303 PMID: 33613356

Bright, J. E. H., & Pryor, R. G. L. (2015). Limitation and Creativity: A Chaos Theory of Careers Perspective. In Maree, K., & Di Fabio, A. (Eds.), *Exploring New Horizons in Career Counselling: Turning Challenge into Opportunities* (pp. 131–147). Sense Publishers., DOI: 10.1007/978-94-6300-154-0_8

Buntinx, W. (2008). The logic of relations and the logic of management. *Journal of Intellectual Disability Research, 52*(7), 588–597. DOI: 10.1111/j.1365-2788.2008.01067.x PMID: 18557861

Carden, J. (2025). Self-Awareness. In Laker, B., Soga, L. R., & Bolade-Ogunfodun, Y. (Eds.), *Elgar Encyclopedia of Leadership* (pp. 284–285). Edward Elgar Publishing Ltd., DOI: 10.4337/9781035307074.000123

Carter, E. W., Harvey, M. N., Taylor, J. L., & Gotham, K. (2013). Connecting Youth and Young Adults with Autism Spectrum Disorders to Community Life. *Psychology in the Schools*, *50*(9), 888–898. DOI: 10.1002/pits.21716 PMID: 26236045

Carter, E. W., & Schutz, M. A. (2022). Addressing Transition Preparation in Middle and High Schools. In Viezel, K. D., Wilczynski, S. M., & Davis, A. S. (Eds.), *Post-secondary Transition for College- or Career-Bound Autistic Students* (pp. 179–200). Springer International Publishing., DOI: 10.1007/978-3-030-93947-2_9

Chen, X., Yu, Q., Yu, F., Huang, Y., & Zhang, L. (2019). Psychometric evaluation of the Chinese version of the Snizek-revised Hall's Professionalism Inventory Scale. *The Journal of International Medical Research*, *47*(3), 1154–1168. DOI: 10.1177/0300060518817401 PMID: 30614338

Chow, C., & Cooper, K. (2024). What Are the Lived Experiences of Strengths in Autistic Individuals? A Systematic Review and Thematic Synthesis. *Autism in Adulthood: Challenges and Management*, aut.2023.0172. Advance online publication. DOI: 10.1089/aut.2023.0172

Clark, M., & Adams, D. (2020). The self-identified positive attributes and favourite activities of children on the autism spectrum. *Research in Autism Spectrum Disorders*, *72*, 101512. Advance online publication. DOI: 10.1016/j.rasd.2020.101512

Cohen, R., Katz, I., Aelterman, N., & Vansteenkiste, M. (2022). Understanding shifts in students' academic motivation across a school year: The role of teachers' motivating styles and need-based experiences. *European Journal of Psychology of Education*, •••, 1–26. DOI: 10.1007/s10212-022-00635-8 PMID: 40479431

Córdova, A., Caballero-García, A., Drobnic, F., Roche, E., & Noriega, D. C. (2023). Influence of Stress and Emotions in the Learning Process: The Example of COVID-19 on University Students: A Narrative Review. *Health Care*, *11*(12), 1787. DOI: 10.3390/healthcare11121787 PMID: 37372905

Courchesne, V., Langlois, V., Gregoire, P., St-Denis, A., Bouvet, L., Ostrolenk, A., & Mottron, L. (2020). Interests and Strengths in Autism, Useful but Misunderstood: A Pragmatic Case-Study. *Frontiers in Psychology*, *11*, 569339. Advance online publication. DOI: 10.3389/fpsyg.2020.569339 PMID: 33123051

Darpatova-Hruzewicz, D., Marek, P., & Kaminski, K. (2025). An Ecological Investigation of Polish Olympic Coaches' Career Pathways and Their Experiences of Career Transition to Olympic Coaching Roles. *International Sport Coaching Journal, 12*(1), 79–92. DOI: 10.1123/iscj.2023-0109

Dipeolu, A. O., Storlie, C., & Johnson, C. (2015). College Students with High-Functioning Autism Spectrum Disorder: Best Practices for Successful Transition to the World of Work. *Journal of College Counseling, 18*(2), 175–190. DOI: 10.1002/jocc.12013

dos Santos, P. M., & Cirillo, M. Â. (2023). Construction of the average variance extracted index for construct validation in structural equation models with adaptive regressions. *Communications in Statistics. Simulation and Computation, 52*(4), 1639–1650. DOI: 10.1080/03610918.2021.1888122

El Zaatari, W., & Maalouf, I. (2022). How the Bronfenbrenner Bio-ecological System Theory Explains the Development of Students' Sense of Belonging to School? *SAGE Open, 12*(4), 21582440221134089. DOI: 10.1177/21582440221134089

Elwyn, G., O'Connor, A. M., Bennett, C., Newcombe, R. G., Politi, M., Durand, M.-A., Drake, E., Joseph-Williams, N., Khangura, S., Saarimaki, A., Sivell, S., Stiel, M., Bernstein, S. J., Col, N., Coulter, A., Eden, K., Härter, M., Rovner, M. H., Moumjid, N., & Edwards, A. (2009). Assessing the quality of decision support technologies using the International Patient Decision Aid Standards instrument (IPDASi). *PLoS One, 4*(3), e4705. Advance online publication. DOI: 10.1371/journal.pone.0004705 PMID: 19259269

Evans, T. M., & Raines, L. (2017). Career Planning Quick Guide. In Evans, T. M., Lundsteen, N., & Vanderford, N. L. (Eds.), *ReSearch* (pp. 249–254). Elsevier., DOI: 10.1016/B978-0-12-804297-7.00018-5

Faelasofi, R., Nisa, K., Usman, M., & Yunarti, T. (2025). Application of Confirmatory Factor Analysis and Latent Growth Model to Examines the Goal-Setting Behavior of Students. *Asian Journal of Interdisciplinary Research, 8*(4), 13–25. DOI: 10.54392/ajir2542

FRN. (2023). National Policy on Inclusive Education. In *Nigeria*. Federal Republic of Nigeria.

Furey, J., & Loftus-Rattan, S. M. (2022). Actively Involving Students With Learning Disabilities in Progress Monitoring Practices. *Intervention in School and Clinic, 57*(5), 329–337. DOI: 10.1177/10534512211032618

Gantman, A., Kapp, S. K., Orenski, K., & Laugeson, E. A. (2012). Social skills training for young adults with high-functioning autism spectrum disorders: A randomized controlled pilot study. *Journal of Autism and Developmental Disorders, 42*(6), 1094–1103. DOI: 10.1007/s10803-011-1350-6 PMID: 21915740

Genova, H. M., Kallen, M. A., Sherwood, K. L., DaWalt, L., Bishop, L., Telfer, D., Brown, C., Sanchez, B., & Smith, M. J. (2023). Development and psychometric properties of self-reported job interview skills and job interview anxiety for autistic transition-age youth. *Journal of Vocational Rehabilitation, 58*(2), 199–217. DOI: 10.3233/JVR-230009 PMID: 38974409

Giri, M., Pathak, S., Srivastava, S., & Mukherjee, S. (2024). Exploring the Psychosocial Challenges and Strengths of Indigent Adolescents: A Reflexive Thematic Analysis of Counsellor's Insights. *Journal of Research and Health, 14*(5), 439–448. DOI: 10.32598/JRH.14.5.2424.1

Hart, L. C., Pollock, M., Hill, S., & Maslow, G. (2017). Association of Transition Readiness to Intentional Self-Regulation and Hopeful Future Expectations in Youth With Illness. *Academic Pediatrics, 17*(4), 450–455. DOI: 10.1016/j.acap.2016.12.004 PMID: 27979748

Henriques, C. G. P., Rosa, E. M., & Merçon-Vargas, E. A. (2025). Emotional Violence as an Inverse Proximal Process Under the Perspective of the Bioecological Theory. In L. F. Habigzang, A. S. G. Pessoa, & S. R. Lordello (Eds.), *Violence Against Children: Contributions of the Bioecological Theory of Human Development to Research and Intervention* (pp. 45–63). Springer Science+Business Media. DOI: 10.1007/978-3-031-91786-8_4

Hetherington, S. A., Durant-Jones, L., Johnson, K., Nolan, K., Smith, E., Taylor-Brown, S., & Tuttle, J. (2010). The lived experiences of adolescents with disabilities and their parents in transition planning. *Focus on Autism and Other Developmental Disabilities, 25*(3), 163–172. DOI: 10.1177/1088357610373760

Hu, L., & Bentler, P. M. (1999). Cutoff criteria for fit indexes in covariance structure analysis: Conventional criteria versus new alternatives. *Structural Equation Modeling, 6*(1), 1–55. DOI: 10.1080/10705519909540118

Hunziker, S., & Blankenagel, M. (2024). Cross-Sectional Research Design. In Hunziker, S., & Blankenagel, M. (Eds.), *Research Design in Business and Management: A Practical Guide for Students and Researchers* (pp. 187–199). Springer Fachmedien., DOI: 10.1007/978-3-658-42739-9_10

Jaipaeng, W., Payakkaraung, S., & Witoonsakul, P. (2025). Factors Predicting Transition Readiness in Adolescents with Kidney or Urinary Tract Diseases: A Cross-Sectional Study. *Pacific Rim International Journal of Nursing Research, 29*(4), 748–762. DOI: 10.60099/prijnr.2025.273831

Jellicoe, M., & Forsythe, A. (2024). Goal-setting practices that connect feedback with action in higher education. In Evans, C., & Waring, M. (Eds.), *Research Handbook on Innovations in Assessment and Feedback in Higher Education: Implications for Teaching and Learning* (pp. 38–52). Edward Elgar Publishing Ltd., DOI: 10.4337/9781800881600.00010

Kearney, K., & Bookspan, S. (2023). Increasing family engagement in transition planning. In Musyoka, M. M., & Shen, G. (Eds.), *Meaningful and Active Family Engagement: IEP, Transition and Technology Integration in Special Education* (pp. 222–238). IGI Global., DOI: 10.4018/979-8-3693-1384-8.ch012

Kodama, M. (2017). Functions of Career Resilience Against Reality Shock, Focusing on Full-time Employees During Their First Year of Work. *The Japanese Psychological Research, 59*(4), 255–265. DOI: 10.1111/jpr.12161

Laghi, F., & Trimarco, B. (2020). Individual planning starts at school. Tools and practices promoting autonomy and supporting transition to work for adolescents with autism spectrum disorder. *Annali dell'Istituto Superiore di Sanita, 56*(2), 222–229. DOI: 10.4415/ANN_20_02_12 PMID: 32567572

Lavigna, A., & La Torre, G. (2024). Validation of the Self Awareness Outcome Questionnaire (SAOQ) in the Italian framework. *La Clinica Terapeutica, 175*(4), 234–238. DOI: 10.7417/CT.2024.5069 PMID: 39010807

Lee, G. K., & Carter, E. W. (2012). Preparing Transition-Age Students with High-Functioning Autism Spectrum Disorders for Meaningful Work. *Psychology in the Schools, 49*(10), 988–1000. DOI: 10.1002/pits.21651

Lengelle, R., Van der Heijden, B. I. J. M., & Meijers, F. (2017). The foundations of career resilience. In Maree, K. (Ed.), *Psychology of Career Adaptability, Employability and Resilience* (pp. 29–47). Springer International Publishing., DOI: 10.1007/978-3-319-66954-0_3

Li, P., Fu, N., Li, Q., Wang, G., Gao, L., & Zhang, X. (2020). The Griffiths Development Scales-Chinese (GDS-C): A reliable and valid neurodevelopmental assessment tool in children with ASD aged 3–8 years old in Tianjin, China. *Asian Journal of Psychiatry, 52*, 102144. Advance online publication. DOI: 10.1016/j.ajp.2020.102144 PMID: 32417746

Lingo, M. E., Deardorff, M. E., & Williams-Diehm, K. (2024). Using Applied Behavior Analysis Methodology to Improve Transition to Postsecondary Education and Employment. In Carr, R. N. (Ed.), *Applied Behavior Analysis in Schools: Realistic Implementation of Evidence-Based Interventions by Teachers* (pp. 237–254). Taylor and Francis., DOI: 10.4324/9781003522584-13

Lippold, M. A., Powers, C. J., Syvertsen, A. K., Feinberg, M. E., & Greenberg, M. T. (2013). The Timing of School Transitions and Early Adolescent Problem Behavior. *The Journal of Early Adolescence*, *33*(6), 821–844. DOI: 10.1177/0272431612468317 PMID: 24089584

Maietta, H. (2023). CAREER DEVELOPMENT NEEDS OF FIRST-GENERATION COLLEGE STUDENTS. In Longwell-Grice, R., & Longwell-Grice, H. (Eds.), *At the Intersection: Understanding and Supporting First-Generation Students* (pp. 244–259). Taylor and Francis., DOI: 10.4324/9781003443131-29

Matthews, N. L., Laflin, J., Orr, B. C., Warriner, K., DeCarlo, M., & Smith, C. J. (2020). Brief Report: Effectiveness of an Accelerated Version of the PEERS® Social Skills Intervention for Adolescents. *Journal of Autism and Developmental Disorders*, *50*(6), 2201–2207. DOI: 10.1007/s10803-019-03939-9 PMID: 30825083

Mazzotti, V. L., Rowe, D. A., Kwiatek, S., Voggt, A., Chang, W.-H., Fowler, C. H., Poppen, M., Sinclair, J., & Test, D. W. (2021). Secondary Transition Predictors of Postschool Success: An Update to the Research Base. *Career Development and Transition for Exceptional Individuals*, *44*(1), 47–64. DOI: 10.1177/2165143420959793

Meethal, S. V. K., & Thomas, A. (2024). Construction of a Scale to Measure Correlates of Adoption of Sustainable Domains in On-Farm Testing Interventions. *Indian Journal of Extension Education*, *60*(4), 112–117. DOI: 10.48165/IJEE.2024.604RT1

Meiring, M., Seabi, J., Amod, Z., Vorster, A., & Kern, A. (2016). Transition for adolescents with autism spectrum disorder: South African parent and professional perspectives. *Frontiers in Psychiatry*, *7*(JUN). Advance online publication. DOI: 10.3389/fpsyt.2016.00093 PMID: 27375502

Mori, Y., Downs, J., Wong, K., Heyworth, J., & Leonard, H. (2018). Comparing Parental Well-Being and Its Determinants Across Three Different Genetic Disorders Causing Intellectual Disability. *Journal of Autism and Developmental Disorders*, *48*(5), 1651–1665. DOI: 10.1007/s10803-017-3420-x PMID: 29192378

Munsell, E. G. S., Orsmond, G. I., Fulford, D., & Coster, W. J. (2022). Metacognition Mediates the Effect of Social Communication and Internalizing Behaviors on Self-management of Daily Life Tasks for Diploma-Track Autistic Youth. *Journal of Autism and Developmental Disorders*, *52*(10), 4274–4285. DOI: 10.1007/s10803-021-05306-z PMID: 34611837

Navarro, J. L., & Tudge, J. R. H. (2025). *Understanding and Teaching Bronfenbrenner's Bioecological Theory*. Taylor & Francis. DOI: 10.4324/9781003464860

Nelson, J. R., & Lund, E. M. (2017). Bronfenbrenner's theoretical framework adapted to women with disabilities experiencing intimate partner violence. In Johnson, A. J., Nelson, J. R., & Lund, E. M. (Eds.), *Religion, Disability, and Interpersonal Violence* (pp. 11–23). Springer International Publishing., DOI: 10.1007/978-3-319-56901-7_2

Nuske, H. J., McGhee Hassrick, E., Bronstein, B., Hauptman, L., Aponte, C., Levato, L., Stahmer, A., Mandell, D. S., Mundy, P., Kasari, C., & Smith, T. (2019). Broken bridges—new school transitions for students with autism spectrum disorder: A systematic review on difficulties and strategies for success. *Autism*, *23*(2), 306–325. DOI: 10.1177/1362361318754529 PMID: 29458258

Orlunga, B. G., & Alikor, O. (2023). Inclusive education and policy implementation in Nigeria: An implication for educational development in the 21st century. *European Journal of Education Studies*, *10*(11). Advance online publication. DOI: 10.46827/ejes.v10i11.5076

Patel, T. R. (2019). Confidence and Its Impact on Your Aspiring Career. In M. M. Shoja, A. Arynchyna, M. Loukas, A. V. D'Antoni, S. M. Buerger, M. Karl, & R. S. Tubbs (Eds.), *A Guide to the Scientific Career: Virtues, Communication, Research, and Academic Writing* (pp. 33–44). wiley. DOI: 10.1002/9781118907283.ch5

Pinder-Amaker, S. (2014). Identifying the unmet needs of college students on the autism spectrum. *Harvard Review of Psychiatry*, *22*(2), 125–137. DOI: 10.1097/HRP.0000000000000032 PMID: 24614767

Quick, J., & Hall, S. (2015). Part Three: The Quantitative Approach. *Journal of Perioperative Practice*, *25*(10), 192–196. DOI: 10.1177/175045891502501002 PMID: 26717587

Read, C., & Szokolszky, A. (2025). Developmental Ecological Psychology meets organicist biology: The example of the ecological self. *Frontiers in Psychology*, *16*, 1569356. Advance online publication. DOI: 10.3389/fpsyg.2025.1569356 PMID: 40667396

Roberts, K. D. (2010). Topic areas to consider when planning transition from high school to postsecondary education for students with autism spectrum disorders. *Focus on Autism and Other Developmental Disabilities*, *25*(3), 158–162. DOI: 10.1177/1088357610371476

Rodil, M. S. P. (2024). Gearing towards Efficient Problem Solving: Exploring the Determinants That Influence Success. *Journal of Interdisciplinary Studies in Education*, *13*(2), 120–151. DOI: 10.32674/thv32d10

Rumsey, M. G. (2020). Personality and interests for selection: Theoretical perspectives. *Military Psychology : the Official Journal of the Division of Military Psychology, American Psychological Association*, *32*(1), 7–23. DOI: 10.1080/08995605.2019.1652478 PMID: 38536247

Sanders, S., Rollins, L. H., & McFall, A. (2023). Aiming High: Applying Goal Setting to Social and Emotional Learning Skills in the Elementary Classroom. *Beyond Behavior*, *32*(1), 4–14. DOI: 10.1177/10742956221145692

Schiamberg, L. B., Paulson, S., & Zawacki, K. (2019). An ecological perspective for teaching about the adolescent. In Paul McKinney, J., Schiamberg, L. B., & Shelton, L. G. (Eds.), *Teaching About Adolescence: An Ecological Approach* (pp. 15–38). Taylor and Francis., DOI: 10.4324/9781315861500-2

Shafik, W. (2025). The Role of Emotional Intelligence in Career Development and Career Success. In Dutta, P. K., Gupta, S., Kashyap, S., Gehlot, A., Karmakar, R., & Bhattacharya, P. (Eds.), *Emotional Intelligence in the Digital Era: Concepts, Frameworks, and Applications* (pp. 96–116). CRC Press., DOI: 10.1201/9781032715377-7

Sharpe, M., Hutchinson, C., & Alexander, J. (2022). The Lived Experiences and Perspectives of People with Autism Spectrum Disorder in Mainstream Employment in Australia. *Disabilities*, *2*(2), 164–177. DOI: 10.3390/disabilities2020013

Shattuck, P. T., Narendorf, S. C., Cooper, B., Sterzing, P. R., Wagner, M., & Taylor, J. L. (2012). Postsecondary education and employment among youth with an autism spectrum disorder. *Pediatrics*, *129*(6), 1042–1049. DOI: 10.1542/peds.2011-2864 PMID: 22585766

Simon, D. J., Cruise, T. K., Huber, B. J., Swerdlik, M. E., & Newman, D. S. (2014). Supervision in school psychology: The developmental/ecological/problem-solving model. *Psychology in the Schools*, *51*(6), 636–646. DOI: 10.1002/pits.21772

Siraj, I., & Huang, R. (2020). Operationalizing Bronfenbrenner's PPCT Model in Researching Human Development: Commentary on Xia, Li, and Tudge. *Human Development*, *64*(1), 21–25. https://www.jstor.org/stable/27139590. DOI: 10.1159/000508341

Smith, M. J., Sherwood, K. L., Genova, H. M., Ross, B., DaWalt, L. S., Bishop, L., Telfer, D., Brown, C., Sanchez, B., & Kallen, M. A. (2023). Psychometric properties of the mock interview rating scale for autistic transition-age youth. *Frontiers in Psychiatry*, *14*, 1235056. Advance online publication. DOI: 10.3389/fpsyt.2023.1235056 PMID: 38025460

Snell-Rood, C., Ruble, L., Kleinert, H., McGrew, J. H., Adams, M., Rodgers, A., Odom, J., Wong, W. H., & Yu, Y. (2020). Stakeholder Perspectives on Transition Planning, Implementation, and Outcomes for Students with Autism Spectrum Disorder. *Autism*, *24*(5), 1164–1176. DOI: 10.1177/1362361319894827 PMID: 31957461

Spelman, D. B. (2025). Routine Disruption in Autism. *Private Therapy Clinic*. https://theprivatetherapyclinic.co.uk/blog/autism-and-routine-disruption/

Stanton, A. L. (2012). Regulating Emotions during Stressful Experiences: The Adaptive Utility of Coping through Emotional Approach. In Folkman, S. (Ed.), *The Oxford Handbook of Stress, Health, and Coping*. Oxford University Press., DOI: 10.1093/oxfordhb/9780195375343.013.0018

Strachan, L., Fraser-Thomas, J., & Nelson-Ferguson, K. (2016). An ecological perspective on high performance sport and positive youth development. In N. L. Holt (Ed.), *Positive Youth Development through Sport: Second edition* (pp. 57–68). Taylor and Francis. DOI: 10.4324/9781315709499-6

Strnadová, I., Cumming, T. M., & Danker, J. (2016). Transitions for Students with Intellectual Disability and/or Autism Spectrum Disorder: Carer and Teacher Perspectives. *Australasian Journal of Special Education*, *40*(2), 141–156. DOI: 10.1017/jse.2016.2

Tong, P., & An, I. S. (2023). Review of studies applying Bronfenbrenner's bioecological theory in international and intercultural education research. *Frontiers in Psychology*, *14*, 1233925. Advance online publication. DOI: 10.3389/fpsyg.2023.1233925 PMID: 38259539

Tong, P., & An, I. S. (2024). Review of studies applying Bronfenbrenner's bioecological theory in international and intercultural education research. *Frontiers in Psychology*, *14*, 1233925. DOI: 10.3389/fpsyg.2023.1233925 PMID: 38259539

Turcan, C., Delamain, H., Loke, A., Pender, R., Mandy, W., & Saunders, R. (2024). Measurement invariance of the parent-reported Strengths and Difficulties Questionnaire in autistic adolescents. *Autism*, *28*(10), 2623–2636. DOI: 10.1177/13623613241236805 PMID: 38481018

Van Hees, V., Moyson, T., & Roeyers, H. (2015). Higher Education Experiences of Students with Autism Spectrum Disorder: Challenges, Benefits and Support Needs. *Journal of Autism and Developmental Disorders*, *45*(6), 1673–1688. DOI: 10.1007/s10803-014-2324-2 PMID: 25448918

White, J., McGarry, S., Williams, P. J., & Black, H., M. (. (2025). 'We think differently, we learn differently, but at the end of the day we're not that different': Strengths-based approaches in high school from the perspectives of autistic adolescents. *Autism*, *29*(11), 2804–2817. DOI: 10.1177/13623613251348557 PMID: 40567122

White, S. W., Brewe, A. M., & Powell, N. (2025). Stepped Transition to Employment and Postsecondary Education Success (STEPS) for Adolescents and Adults with Autism: Community Implementation Pilot Trial. *JMIR Formative Research*, *9*, v9i4e70137. Advance online publication. DOI: 10.2196/70137 PMID: 40882612

Wong, J., Coster, W. J., Cohn, E. S., & Orsmond, G. I. (2021). Identifying School-Based Factors that Predict Employment Outcomes for Transition-Age Youth with Autism Spectrum Disorder. *Journal of Autism and Developmental Disorders*, *51*(1), 60–74. DOI: 10.1007/s10803-020-04515-2 PMID: 32356081

Young, R. A. (1983). Career development of adolescents: An ecological perspective. *Journal of Youth and Adolescence*, *12*(5), 401–417. DOI: 10.1007/BF02088723 PMID: 24306360

Yuliawati, L., & Ardyan, E. (2022). The Role of Life Planning in Finding Purpose and Living Out One's Career Calling Among Indonesian Emerging Adults. *Journal of Career Development*, *49*(3), 538–550. DOI: 10.1177/0894845320950834

Zhong, N. H., Grimm, R. P., Kanne, S. M., & Mazurek, M. O. (2023). Measurement invariance of the Autism Impact Measure (AIM) across sex in children with autism spectrum disorder. *Autism Research*, *16*(1), 154–163. DOI: 10.1002/aur.2845 PMID: 36341720

Zincirli, M., & Polat, E. (2025). Development of the Digital Transformation Scale: Assessment of Measurement Invariance. *SAGE Open*, *15*(3), 21582440251378827. Advance online publication. DOI: 10.1177/21582440251378827

Zulkifli, N. R., & Zin, H. M. (2024). The Performance of Regularization Technique in Assessing Reliability and Validity of the Constructs in Structural Equation Modeling: Application in Breast Cancer Awareness Research. *Malaysian Journal of Medicine and Health Sciences*, *20*, 112–118. DOI: 10.47836/mjmhs.20.s8.15

Chapter 8
Perspectives on Career Transition Counselling Services for Students With ASD

ABSTRACT

This study examined perspectives on career transition counselling services for students with autism spectrum disorders (SASD). This study focused specifically on needs assessment and personalisation, counselling processes and techniques, resource availability and accessibility, and outcome monitoring and feedback dimensions. Using a quantitative cross-sectional design, data were collected from 160 teachers and parents. This study revealed that there is a moderate overall evaluation of counselling services, with relatively stronger endorsement of counselling processes and personalisation, and consistently weaker ratings for resource availability and accessibility. Underpinned by the Ubuntu theory, the findings suggest that while counselling practices reflected communal care and engagement, limited resources constrained the realisation of equitable transition outcomes.

BACKGROUND

There is an increasing consensus that effective transition counselling for students with autism spectrum disorders (SASD) should be based on thorough needs assessments and tailored strengths-oriented planning to facilitate successful outcomes at old age (Stampoltzis et al., 2025; Dipeolu et al., 2015; Hannah & Topping, 2013). A comprehensive and individualised need assessment is important for effective support and career transition counselling for SASD. This approach is expected to focus on

DOI: 10.4018/978-1-6684-7260-6.ch008

strengths-based profiling, which incorporates several aspects like cognitive abilities, vocational interests, sensory preferences, communication styles, and contextual supports. Transitional services are expected to be tailored to the individual needs of SASD, highlighting their strengths and potentials rather than dealing with their limitations (Lam et al., 2023; Lee & Carter, 2012; Rashid & Ostermann, 2009). Some individuals with high-functioning autism spectrum disorders may display a sensitive attention to detail; exhibit thoroughness regarding rules, accuracy, and routines; possess a high degree of reliability, conscientiousness, persistence, and technical proficiency; retain extensive, accurate facts; and show remarkable long-term memory (National Autistic Society, 2004). If harnessed effectively, these attributes enable SASD to excel in positions that necessitate specific skills for preparation for employment. The career transition processes offer a crucial framework for identifying the particular services that SASD need for effective preparation for employment. Best practices suggest that SASD should be afforded significant prospects and practice to take on administrative roles (Martin & Williams-Diehm, 2013). Furthermore, empirical evidence from The Learning Academic (TLA) revealed that placing responsibility and accountability on the SASD was extremely impactful (Lam et al., 2023). This denotes that if students comprehend that they have responsibilities and that there are expectations, they will strive to achieve their goals if given the opportunity. Strength-based assessments provide a detail picture of each SASD, promoting their clinical clarity and improving the range of information for planning (Rashid & Ostermann, 2009).

Furthermore, assessment of vocational interest for SASD to understand their unique strengths, challenges, and preferences to tailor supports and interventions is significantly effective for their successful career transitioning. As stated in the National Autism Plan for Children (2003), individuals exhibiting signs of autism spectrum disorders (ASD) ought to undergo assessment that (a) establish their specific health and educational requirements, taking into account differential diagnosis; (b) assess the possible consequences of the condition, enabling the implementation of suitable intervention and support strategies, and (c) cater to their needs within the family setting, fostering the ability of family members to assist each other. Several assessment tools and approaches have been developed and evaluated, including the Work Rehabilitation and Adaptation Profile for ASD (WRAP-ASD), an Excel-based observation grid for evaluation of work functioning of several domains like motivation, attendance, peer relationships, communication, and cognitive skills (Zemrani et al., 2025). In addition, there is the Ready, Set, Work (RSW), a video modelling programme designed to assist individuals with ASD prepare for vocational settings by simulating social dilemmas (Zemrani et al., 2025). Another example is the Pre-vocational Skills Laboratory (PVS-Lab), an online-based learning environment aimed at enhancing pre-vocational and employment skills (Tsiopela & Jimoyiannis,

2017). Others include Concurrent-Chains Preference Assessment (CCPA), used for identification of preferred and non-preferred activities and context for SASD (Vargo & Loflin, 2022) and Basic Work Skills Assessment Tool for measuring work potentials and attitudes, including verbal and non-verbal prompts (Pongsaksri et al., 2017). Empirical evidence has reported that these vocational assessment tools for SASD promote the development of personalised instruction programmes and transition plans that involve the students and their families (Yang et al., 2023; Zemrani et al., 2025). Therefore, frequent assessment of vocational interest and skills of SASD should start early and continue throughout the student's educational journey to ensure effective intervention.

Assessing the sensory preferences of SASD is extremely significant because it influences the daily lives of individual SASD, affecting the various aspects of their functioning and well-being. For instance, SASD prefer predictable and controllable sensory inputs; hence, unpredictable sensations can be seen as unpleasant and lead to sensitive awareness and difficulty filtering extraneous sensory input (Ashburner et al., 2013). In school settings, sensory experiences of SASD affect learning and participation. Literature has revealed that positive sensory experiences can promote engagement if sensory needs are met, while negative sensory experiences can cause distraction, anxiety, and limited participation (Jones et al., 2020). Sensory preferences promote adaptation to the environment and daily activities, which enhance their engagement in learning activities (Hasselbusch & Baumgarten, 2014).

Communication style plays a significant role in the career transition of SASD. As a result, there is a consistent need for a comprehensive assessment that includes caregiver reports, direct assessments, and innovative methods like eye tracking and touch-screen assessments to provide a more holistic picture of a student's communication abilities (Trembath & Iacono, 2016). The instruments selected for evaluations will differ based on their intended use. Considering the significance of prompt identification for timely access to suitable services, both screening and diagnostic tools must possess robust psychometric characteristics, as evidenced by assessments of validity and reliability (American Speech Language and Hearing Association, 2006). Research findings indicate that augmentative and alternative communication methods, such as the implementation of graphic symbols and aided language inputs, have significantly contributed to enabling individuals with severe and complex communication needs to express themselves effectively. This is particularly evident in their use of abstract graphic symbols that represent core vocabulary for making requests, which has been facilitated by educators' emphasis on this aspect of communication (Dorney & Erickson, 2019).

Furthermore, a concise evaluation framework designed to assess the acquisition rates and preferences for various communication modalities has demonstrated that SASD exhibit diverse preferences and learning rates for different communication styles (LaRue et al., 2016). The results suggest that participants cultivated diverse communication methods at different rates and displayed unique inclinations towards various communication styles. In addition, there is evident of a substantial impact of information and communication technologies in enhancing communication, reading comprehension and social interaction (Andaluz-Delgado et al., 2025). A study revealed significant heterogeneity in receptive language abilities across participants and across assessment methods, which included PPVT-4 for assessing receptive lexical knowledge, Vineland Receptive Communication for the receptive aspect of communication, and the Caregiver Vocabulary Checklist for understanding single-word vocabulary in non-laboratory settings (Plesa Skwerer et al., 2016). Evaluating the communication styles of SASD requires an understanding of their distinct verbal and non-verbal communication techniques, the use of thorough and creative assessment instruments, and the application of tailored educational and technological solutions. These approaches are instrumental in tackling the communication difficulties encountered by SASD and promoting their holistic development and integration within educational environments.

The needs assessment of SASD extends beyond conventional psychometric evaluations. Although psychometric instruments play a crucial role in diagnosing SASD and comprehending cognitive capabilities, a thorough needs assessment should take into account a range of additional factors to facilitate the comprehensive development of SASD. For instance, concurrent-chains preference assessment (CCPA) serves as an alternative method for identifying both preferred and non-preferred activities and contexts, thereby assisting in the customisation of educational interventions (Vargo & Loflin, 2022). Similarly, approaches such as semi-structured interviews, diaries, drawings, and focus groups can be used to gather the views of SASD, which is crucial for understanding their needs and preferences (Tyrrell & Woods, 2018). In addition, integration of behavioural investigations into the assessment process can assist in determining the reasons behind challenging behaviours and developing suitable interventions (Bitsika, 2008). The needs assessment emphasised that partnership between parents, teachers, and allied health professionals is essential for aligning educational goals and interventions. This collaboration ensures that the needs of SASD are met comprehensively. The assessment of needs underscores the significance of partnership among parents, educators, and allied health professionals in aligning educational objectives and interventions. Such collaboration guarantees that the requirements of students with special educational needs are addressed in a thorough manner (Azad et al., 2021; Dale et al., 2025). A need assessment framework that is holistic should consider the child's adaptive skills, challenging behaviours, and the needs of the family. This approach assists in building a supportive environment that addresses all aspects of the SASD development (Brown et al., 2010).

It is important for counselling services to actively support students in developing their ability to express preferences and objectives, encompassing those conveyed through unconventional or indirect means of communication. Several counselling processes and techniques have been identified for addressing the unique challenges faced by SASD at the transition period. One of the services counsellors provide is tailoring transition services to align with the unique strengths and requirements of SASD. This strategy aids in establishing practical and attainable career objectives (Lee & Carter, 2012). Career counselling frameworks based on Cognitive Information Processing Theory, Holland's Typological Model, and Social Cognitive Career Theory (SCCT) have shown significant applicability when tailored to meet the requirements of SASD (Wang et al., 2022). Also, the Self-Determined Career Design Model (SDCDM) can improve goal achievement and job performance by emphasising students' interests and their self-determination (Dean et al., 2022; Hagiwara et al., 2019). This study's findings reported that significant improvements were observed in goal achievement and occupational performance, and offer initial evidence that the SDCDM can effectively improve outcomes for youth and young adults with ASD. Counsellor services (example: providing early work experience, assisting SASD in building necessary skills, and confidence for future employment) have been found to be impactful in career transitioning (Lee & Carter, 2012). It involves collaboration among stakeholders such as family, teachers, and vocational rehabilitation services to ensure a comprehensive support system for SASD (Snell-Rood et al., 2020). Involving families of SASD in the career transition process and setting realistic expectations can significantly affect the success of the transition. Family involvement assists in reinforcing the skills and strategies acquired during counselling (Lee & Carter, 2012; Morris et al., 2021). Counsellor services and accommodations offer a range of academic and non-academic support, including extended exam time, coaching, and mentorship from faculty, all of which can help students successfully navigate their transition (Accardo et al., 2019).

Counselling sessions should be modified to meet the sensory and communication requirements of SASD. This entails making changes to the physical environment, adjusting the pace of sessions, utilising visual aids, and allowing for flexibility in communication methods. Research consistently indicates that providing alternative seating options, such as seating that provides deep pressure therapy, can enhance comfort, calmness, and participation for SASD (Wong, 2023; Santosa et al., 2025). Also, counsellors should emphasise counselling techniques that focuses on strengths recognition, incremental goal accomplishment, and reframing of setbacks contribute to the development of these resources, which in turn foster more active engagement in career planning and decision-making. Some of these techniques entail identifying and enhancing the SASD's inherent strengths and potential rather than concentrating on its deficits. Strength-based counselling is specifically effective in building self-efficacy and resilience, which are vital for career planning and decision-making (Harris et al., 2007; Smith, 2006; Smith, 2006). Research evidence has shown that incorporating cultural competence into strength-based counselling ensures acknowledgement of cultural significance and meaningfulness, which promotes engagement and motivation in career planning (Grothaus et al., 2012; Chung, 2006). Counselling technique like incremental goal attainment focuses on special plans that enhance the likelihood of achieving objectives, and maintain flexibility to accommodate alternative opportunities, especially when time is limited (Park et al., 2017; Masicampo & Baumeister, 2012). Career adaptability skills like concern, control, curiosity, and confidence assist individuals in managing their career transitions efficiently (Taber, 2019). Counselling techniques like reframing setbacks through therapeutic reframing assist individuals to see setbacks from a different viewpoint, changing perceived failures into opportunities for growth. This technique can improve resilience and facilitate a more optimistic outlook on career challenges (Atkinson, 2014; Karpetis, 2016; Panichelli, 2013). Another impactful reframing of setbacks is motivational interviewing, which incorporates both client-centred and directive strategies to assist clients in reshaping their narratives, highlighting their strengths and dedication to transformation, which can be beneficial in career counselling (Aaen Maagaard & Nielsen, 2025).

To effectively facilitate the career transition of SASD, access to available resources is very important. SASD repeatedly face hard-to-access career information, which can intensify feelings of uncertainty and hinder proactive planning. Efficient services propose tailored resources, such as job databases, training opportunities, and labour market insights, delivered in formats that cater to various cognitive and sensory preferences (Laghi & Trimarco, 2020; Lee & Carter, 2012). Literature has shown that SASD need a supportive educational environment, which requires additional academic supports, reasonable accommodations, and understanding of their learning styles (Roberts, 2010; Viezel et al., 2022). This support, which extends to providing digital accessibility and training teachers on technological accessibility, is important for the inclusion of SASD at all levels of the education system (Fernández-Batanero et al., 2025). Available resources, such as social and employment-related skills, like skills instruction, are vital for preparing SASD for the workforce (Lee & Carter, 2012). Skills instruction assists SASD and their families in accessing available services and acquiring skills that enhance career outcomes (Viezel et al., 2022), whereas job coaching and community placement have revealed enhanced employment outcomes (Nicholas et al., 2015; Nicholas et al., 2018).

Furthermore, interagency collaboration supports, which involve collaborating with several agencies that offer employment and other related supports, have been found to be impactful (Lee & Carter, 2012). Fostering robust connections between students and essential services, along with facilitating relationships among different service providers within a neighbourhood, can guarantee that the needs and prospects recognised during transition planning are effectively met and provided collaboratively. Gaining a comprehensive understanding of available resources at both the community and state levels, as well as acquiring the skills to network efficiently among these resources, is highlighted as essential for supporting the planning and execution of a successful transition programme for SASD (McDonough & Revell, 2010). This collaboration entails an alliance between schools, community organisations, and vocational rehabilitation services, which is important for successful transition (Lee & Carter, 2012; McDonough & Revell, 2010).

Resource availability and accessibility for SASD career transitioning entail providing work experiences and career exploration opportunities to develop the necessary skills that are very interesting. For SASD, it may be really challenging to keep and advance in a job than other challenges related to job search. Consequently, recognising an appropriate job and obtaining vital on-the-job assistance from the start holds increased importance. A strong correspondence between the key attributes of the workplace, core job responsibilities, and the strengths, interests, and needs of young individuals is expected to improve their job satisfaction and lessen their need for additional support (Lee & Carter, 2012). Vocational rehabilitation services, such as job search assistance, job placement, and on-the-job supports, significantly improve employment outcomes for SASD (Roux et al., 2021; Kaya et al., 2018). Resource accessibility encompasses not only students but also their families and support personnel. Granting parents or mentors access to counselling materials promotes a shared understanding and coordinated support, especially during crucial decision-making times. Educational programmes which involve parent mentors providing ongoing support and education to other parents have been shown to enhance family outcomes, including emotional wellbeing and satisfaction with services (Moody et al., 2019).

Studies have shown that family engagement and robust parent-teacher relationships can immensely aid the educational experience of SASD (Garbacz et al., 2016). The Partners in School and COMPASS methodologies unite parents and caregivers with educators to collaboratively establish goals, guided by a consultant through mutual dyadic processes of influence. These processes encompass shared decision-making, the caregiver-teacher alliance, and consensus on educational objectives (Dale et al., 2025). Furthermore, the availability of counsellors beyond scheduled sessions is another salient factor. Research evidence indicated that extended availability can strengthen the therapeutic alliance between counsellors and SASD, which is crucial for positive therapeutic outcomes (Grover, 2017; Donnell et al., 2004).

Finally, outcome monitoring and feedback are effective for the career transition of SASD. Systematic outcome monitoring is an attribute of career transition counselling services. Monitoring outcomes for career transition among SASD entails the evaluation of employment, educational pursuits, and independent living after high school, utilising surveys, longitudinal studies, and data-informed assessments. For monitoring educational outcomes, literature has shown that the SDCDM has shown promise in promoting goal attainment and occupational performance for SASD (Dean et al., 2022). For employment outcomes, the Vocational Rehabilitation (VR) service has consistently improved employment rates (Roux et al., 2020; Kaya et al., 2018; Ditchman et al., 2018). The impact of VR services on job placement, on-the-job support, and job search significantly correlated with better employment outcomes (Kaya et al., 2018; Ditchman et al., 2018; Nye-Lengerman, 2017). Similarly, scholars (Smith et al., 2024; Sherwood et al., 2023; Smith et al., 2021) revealed that Virtual Interview Training for Transition Age Youth (VIT-TAY) has been found efficient in enhancing job interview skills, reducing anxiety, and increasing employment rates. Finally, for monitoring independent living, Hendrickson et al. (2017) noted that College Adjustment Program Evaluation Scales (CAPES) are impactful in the emotional adjustment and self-advocacy. Therefore, Hagner et al. (2012) disclosed that transition planning interventions that incorporate family training, person-centred planning, and follow-up assistance have led to substantial progress in self-determination and career decision-making abilities.

Feedback concerning career transition services for SASD highlights the importance of consistent team check-ins, immediate input during behavioural skills training, and evaluations to enhance vocational support (Roux et al., 2013; Gillespie-Lynch et al., 2017). These strategies foster self-advocacy, modify interventions according to real-time progress, and integrate insights from students, parents, and educators. Parents of SASD play a substantial role in providing feedback to the counsellor on the effectiveness of some of the intervention programmes. Kirby et al. (2021) reported that parents' feedback on intervention programmes such as the Maximising Adolescent Postsecondary Success (MAPSS) increases parental efficacy and expectations, which in turn positively impact the transition outcomes for their children. Similarly, other researchers (e.g., Hendrickson et al., 2017; Nachman, 2024) have established that SASD are encouraged to develop self-advocacy skills, which are imperative for their career advancement, and that feedback from SASD concerning their experiences in transition programmes provides valuable insights for counsellors. Dean et al. (2022) reported that the SDCDM is impactful in enhancing transition-related outcomes through goal attainment and occupational performance based on the students' feedback. Bambling (2014) revealed that counsellors offering instance feedback to SASD during extend availability sessions help in the identification of cases that are not advancing as anticipated, allowing for timely corrective actions, and are impactful in reducing intervention noncompletion and improving outcomes for clients believed to be intervention resistant.

Despite the increasing disclosure of the significance of career transition counselling for SASD, there are still considerable deficits in the empirical studies. The existing research emphasises employment outcomes while failing to investigate the counselling processes that lead to these outcomes adequately. Furthermore, the viewpoints of students and their families concerning the services are not sufficiently represented. As a result of this significant research gap, this chapter examined perspectives on career transition counselling services for SASD, focusing specifically on needs assessment and personalisation, counselling processes and techniques, resource accessibility, and outcome monitoring.

RESEARCH OBJECTIVES

The main objective of this research study is to examine parents' and teachers' perspectives regarding career transition counselling services for SASD. The specific objectives were:

1. To determine the descriptive patterns of participants' perspectives on the four counselling dimensions (needs assessment and personalisation, counselling process and techniques, resource availability and accessibility, and outcome monitoring and feedback).
2. To assess whether teachers and parents differ significantly in their perspectives on career transition counselling services for SASD.
3. To examine whether gender has a significant influence on participants' perspectives on career transition counselling services for SASD.
4. To determine whether differences in ASD levels significantly affect participants' perspectives on career transition counselling services.
5. To investigate whether there are interaction effects of participant type, gender, and ASD level on perspectives of career transition counselling services.
6. To compare participants' perspectives on counselling services across educational qualification categories.

RESEARCH QUESTIONS

1. What are the descriptive trends of participants' perspectives on the four dimensions of career transition counselling services for SASD?
2. Are there significant differences in the perspectives of teachers and parents regarding career transition counselling services for SASD?

3. Does gender significantly influence participants' perspectives on career transition counselling services for SASD?
4. Are there significant differences in participants' perspectives based on ASD levels?
5. Are there interaction effects among participant type, gender, and ASD level on participants' perspectives regarding career transition counselling services for SASD?
6. Do participants' perspectives differ across levels of educational qualification?

THEORETICAL FRAMEWORK

This study is rooted in the Ubuntu theory of career transitioning as a theoretical framework for understanding perspectives on career transition counselling services for SASD. Ubuntu is an African word that means "I am because we are," perceiving human development and wellbeing as a product of interdependence, mutual cohabitation, care, and shared commitment (Frempong & Kadam, 2025; Shandu-Phetla et al., 2023). Key tenets include affirming humanity through respect for others, prioritising life preservation over wealth, and fostering communal accountability (Ajitoni, 2024). This theory is related to this study because Ubuntu deviate from an individualised-only model of career transition to a community-based transition process in which identity, agency, opportunity, and dignity are co-constructed within social systems to support career transition. Within this framework, career transition counselling for SASD is interpreted as a structured practice of relational enablement. Specifically, the need assessment phase is understood as a community-based knowledge of the strengths, interests, preferences of communication, and support needs of the student, in which meaning is negotiated with the families, mentors, and institutional forces, instead of being drawn out in a deficit-focused testing process. This theory is related to this study since the counselling process and techniques as means of intensifying belonging, self-efficacy, and socially supported autonomy, acknowledging the fact that independence for SASD often depends on steady relational supports and predictable environments (Mpofu & Sefotho, 2025). Ubuntu theory's affirmation of the commitments to inclusion and shared success is evident since the resource availability and accessibility dimensions are framed as collective duties of the institution and its partners. Accessible information, flexible formats, and responsive counsellor availability are crucial for inclusion (Mosala, 2025). The outcome monitoring and feedback are interpreted as evidence of community-expanded engagement to facilitate SASD's career transition process and strengthen social bridges to workplaces and communities (Frempong & Kadam, 2025). Ubuntu theory provides a theoretical foundation based on cultural and African perspectives for exploring whether and how career transition counselling services for SASD cultivate dignity, inclusion, reciprocity, and sustainable community participation.

POLICY FRAMEWORK

The Nigeria National Policy on Special Needs Education forms the policy basis of this study because it establishes a rights and service basis for assisting students with special needs (Federal Republic of Nigeria, 2015). The policy is based on the four key implementation principles, which include the least restrictive environment, zero reject, total inclusion, and diversification of services exceeding the school setting to include home and hospital contexts (Agunowei & Mayombe, 2024; Umeh & Anyaele, 2024). These policy principles are directly important to the career transition of SASD since counsellors see inclusion responsibility as mandatory, which necessitates them to provide services to SASD across settings where transition barriers are experienced (Agunowei & Mayombe, 2024; Hill et al., 2024). The policy acknowledges that prior practice has overemphasised producing graduates without preparing them for life after school. It therefore states that transition programmes should be an essential part of Special Needs Education in Nigeria. This policy affirmed the position of arranging educational programmes or interventions that are tailored to individual needs, such as differentiated curricula, therapy, and planning that are suitable for the needs of SASD's personal development (Umeh & Anyaele, 2024). This policy reemphasised the removal of obstacles that impede learning and support services and promotes access to the support services requirements that are commensurate with the SASD responsive counselling adaptations, accessible resources, and flexible delivery formats. In relation to service infrastructure, the policy provides for service provision centres located in schools (and other settings), which legitimise systematic needs assessment and structured transition planning within secondary schooling. The policy further mandates that education for children with special needs must be provided free of charge at every level, accompanied by suitable training, facilities, and equipment to facilitate effective implementation. The policy offers criteria that this study uses to evaluate whether career transition counselling services for SASD are personalised, accessible, adequately resourced, and accountable through evidence-informed monitoring.

METHODOLOGY

Study Context and Design

This research was carried out in the South-South Geopolitical Zone of Nigeria, specifically concentrating on Edo and Rivers States. Edo State, with Benin City as its administrative centre, combines urban, semi-urban and rural ecologies with long-established school systems. Rivers State is a coastal region, with Port Harcourt as its administrative centre, a major metropolitan hub with diverse populations and varied educational infrastructures. These two states were selected since they host schools that serve SASD and have ongoing efforts to strengthen support services for neurodivergent students. A quantitative, cross-sectional survey design was used. This design was appropriate because we aimed to obtain a structured account of how teachers and parents perceive career transition counselling services for SASD at a single point in time. A cross-sectional design allowed us to investigate overall patterns and to test group differences across gender, participant type, autism severity level of the students under their care, and educational qualification using established statistical procedures.

Research Paradigm

A positivist paradigm guided the study. Within this paradigm, human experiences are approached as measurable constructs that can be represented through observable indicators (Park et al., 2020).

Ontological Position

We assumed that participants hold real, identifiable perceptions about career transition counselling services and that these perceptions can be meaningfully captured through well-constructed items.

Epistemological Position

We approached knowledge generation through systematic measurement and statistical analysis. The use of a standardised questionnaire reflected our view that reliable and valid evidence emerges from controlled data collection procedures.

Axiological Position

Although we value inclusive education and improved services for SASD, we maintained neutrality in instrument design, administration, and analysis. Items were phrased without evaluative language, and all procedures were implemented in a manner that minimised researcher bias.

Methodological Position

Positivism informed our use of quantitative scales, multi-stage sampling, and analysis of variance. The paradigm supports studies that quantify patterns, evaluate statistical significance, and draw inferences from aggregated scores rather than individual narratives.

Population and Sampling

The population was composed of teachers and parents of SASD who were enrolled in schools across Edo and Rivers States. Teachers included class teachers, subject teachers, counsellors, and other instructional staff directly involved in student support. Parents included biological parents, guardians, and caregivers responsible for daily decision-making regarding the child's education. A multi-stage sampling strategy was utilised to obtain the final sample. The first stage involved selecting Edo and Rivers States based on their dense blend of mainstream and inclusive schools and their growing attention to autism-related support. In the second stage, we identified local government areas with schools known to serve SASD. The third stage involved selecting specific schools or service centres with records of admitting or supporting SASD. Finally, within these institutions, we used purposive and convenience procedures to recruit eligible teachers and parents who had recent experience supporting a student with ASD. This approach ensured coverage of diverse school settings while remaining practical in states where school locations are dispersed. A total of 160 participants completed the study. The sample included males and females, and individuals with bachelor's, master's, and doctoral qualifications. Students' autism severity levels were represented across Levels 1, 2, and 3, which enabled us to examine whether the autism severity of students under their care was linked to differences in perceived service quality.

Instrument

Data were collected using the Career Transition Counselling Services Questionnaire - Adults (CTCSQ-A), a self-developed instrument designed to measure participants' perspectives on the core components of career transition counselling for SASD. The questionnaire contains 20 items grouped into four validated dimensions:

Needs Assessment and Personalisation (5 items)

These items assess whether services begin with a structured assessment of strengths and needs, involve families in planning, and recognise communication preferences.

Counselling Process and Techniques (5 items)

Items assess the use of structured career theory frameworks, practical skill-building activities, and strategies for decision-making and self-efficacy.

Resource Availability and Accessibility (5 items)

This particular subscale within the CTCSQ-A measures the availability of career resources, accessibility of tools, support for parents, and flexibility in scheduling.

Outcome Monitoring and Feedback (5 items)

Item statements on this subscale capture the extent to which progress is tracked, feedback is provided, and outcome data are used to improve services.

Each item statement received a rating ranging from one (indicating strong disagreement) to five (indicating strong agreement). Higher scores reflect stronger endorsement of the counselling practices described in each subscale. A psychometric analysis supported the factor structure of the instrument. Factor loadings across items were moderate to high, and reliability indices were strong. Cronbach's alpha values were 0.90 (Needs Assessment and Personalisation), 0.92 (Counselling Process and Techniques), .77 (Resource Availability and Accessibility), and 0.90 (Outcome Monitoring and Feedback). Omega coefficients supported these reliability estimates. These results indicate that CTCSQ-A provides a stable measurement across its four domains.

Data Collection Procedures

The Faculty of Education Research Ethics Committee at the University of Johannesburg provided ethical approval for the study (Sem-2-2020-057) in order to proceed to the data collection phase. School authorities in Edo and Rivers States granted administrative permission. Two postgraduate research assistants assisted with data collection. Both assistants held academic training in special needs education and educational psychology and had practice experience of up to five years. Their training ensured professional interaction with participants and consistent implementation of study procedures.

Before fieldwork began, the assistants received training on the purpose of the research, consent procedures, confidentiality, eligibility criteria, and the correct administration of the questionnaire. They practised standardised instructions to avoid influencing participant responses. Teachers completed the questionnaire during school visits, often during break periods or staff meetings. Parents completed the instrument during scheduled parent sessions, school meetings, or through arranged return visits. All participants got the information sheets and signed informed consent forms before completing the questionnaire. Completed forms were collected in sealed envelopes to protect anonymity and were stored securely.

Data Analysis

Data were input into IBM SPSS, version 24.0. Preliminary assessments confirmed that the presence of missing values and outliers was negligible. Descriptive statistics, such as means, standard deviations, standard errors, coefficients of variation, and confidence intervals, were calculated to respond to the initial research question regarding descriptive trends across the four counselling dimensions. To address subsequent research questions, we made use of analysis of variance. Participant type, gender, and autism severity level of their child were entered as independent variables, and the overall counselling perspective score served as the dependent variable. We tested the model for main effects and interaction effects among these sociodemographic factors. Prior to interpretation, we examined normality and homogeneity of variance assumptions. Statistical significance was ascertained at the .05 level. We used figures in order to provide visual comparisons across teachers and parents, gender groups, autism severity levels of the child under their care, and educational qualification categories.

Ethical Considerations

All procedures adhered to ethical standards for research that includes human participants. Participation in this research study was voluntary, and an informed consent form had to be signed by all participants. The questionnaire contained no identifying information, and all data were stored securely. Participants were told that they could discontinue participating in the study at any point in time without penalisation. We trained the research assistants to respond respectfully and to refer participants back to school counsellors if participation raised concerns or discomfort. Ethical approval provided oversight to ensure participants' safety and data integrity.

RESULTS

Table 1. Demographic distribution of participants

		N	%	Valid Percent	Cumulative Percent
Gender	Female	47	29.4	29.4	29.4
	Male	113	70.6	70.6	100.0
	Total	160	100.0	100.0	
Levels of ASD severity	1	33	20.6	20.6	20.6
	2	45	28.1	28.1	48.8
	3	82	51.3	51.3	100.0
	Total	160	100.0	100.0	
Educational qualifications	Bachelors	92	57.5	57.5	57.5
	Masters	45	28.1	28.1	85.6
	PhD.	23	14.4	14.4	100.0
	Total	160	100.0	100.0	

Table 1 indicates the participants' demographic distribution. The sample consisted of 160 participants, of whom most identified as male (70.6 per cent), while 29.4 per cent identified as female. A large percentage of the SASD receiving support from the participants were categorised as Level 3 in severity (51.3 per cent), followed by Level 2 (28.1 per cent) and Level 1 (20.6 per cent). Educational qualifications of participants also differed, with most of them holding a bachelor's degree (57.5 per cent), followed by a master's degree (28.1 per cent) and a smaller group with doctoral qualifications (14.4 per cent).

Table 2. Descriptive statistics on perspectives of career transition counselling services for SASD

	Group	N	Mean	SD	SE	Coefficient of variation	95% Confidence Interval		
							Lower	Upper	
Needs Assessment and Personalisation	Male	47	11.81	4.38	.639	.371	10.52	13.09	
	Female	113	10.43	4.69	.442	.450	9.55	11.30	
Counselling Process and Techniques	Male	47	12.66	4.71	.687	.372	11.28	14.04	
	Female	113	10.51	4.89	.460	.465	9.60	11.43	

continued on following page

Table 2. Continued

	Group	N	Mean	SD	SE	Coefficient of variation	95% Confidence Interval		
							Lower	Upper	
Resource Availability and Accessibility	Male	47	8.04	2.51	.366	.312	7.31	8.78	
	Female	113	7.79	2.70	.254	.346	7.29	8.30	
Outcome Monitoring and Feedback	Male	47	11.68	4.27	.623	.366	10.43	12.94	
	Female	113	10.71	4.81	.453	.450	9.81	11.61	
Overall Perspective		160	40.84	14.13	1.117	.346	38.63	43.04	

Table 2 shows the mean scores for each of the four dimensions of career transition counselling services. Across all dimensions, male participants consistently reported slightly higher ratings compared to female participants. For needs assessment and personalisation, males recorded a mean of 11.81, while females recorded 10.43. A similar rating was observed for counselling process and techniques, where males (M = 12.66) rated the services higher than females (M = 10.51). Ratings for resource availability and accessibility were relatively low for both groups, indicating that both males and females perceived that resources may not yet be sufficient, although males still scored slightly higher (M = 8.04) than females (M = 7.79). For outcome monitoring and feedback, males again reported higher ratings (M = 11.68) compared to females (M = 10.71). The average perspective score across all participants was 40.84, suggesting a moderate level of perceived service strength across dimensions. These results show that participants generally view the career transition counselling services positively, although resource availability appears to be the area with the lowest endorsement.

Table 3. ANOVA results for differences in perspectives of teachers and parents on career transition counselling services for SASD

Cases	Sum of Squares	*df*	Mean Square	*F*	*p*
Participants	547.820	1	547.820	2.674	.104
Gender	1002.098	1	1002.098	4.892	.029
ASD level	46.163	2	23.082	0.113	.894
Participants Gender	278.448	1	278.448	1.359	.246
Participants ASD level	135.834	2	67.917	0.332	.718
Gender ASD level	55.241	2	27.620	0.135	.874

continued on following page

Table 3. Continued

Cases	Sum of Squares	*df*	Mean Square	*F*	*p*
Participants Gender ASD level	77.590	2	38.795	0.189	.828
Residuals	30318.427	148	204.854		

In Table 3, our results did not demonstrate any notable differences in the perspectives of teachers and parents regarding career transition counselling services for SASD F(1, 148) = 2.67, p = .104. This result is further emphasised in Figure 1, where the mean ratings for teachers and parents appear relatively close with no substantial divergence between the groups. Together, the table and figure show that both teachers and parents share similar views regarding the quality and effectiveness of career transition counselling services for SASD.

Figure 1. Means ratings of teachers and parents (by participant type) on their perspectives on career transition counselling services for SASD

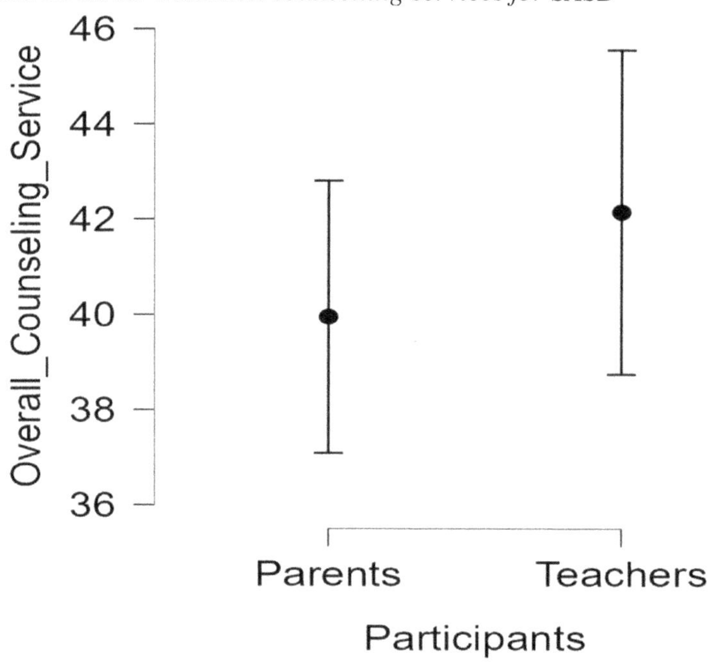

Table 3 further shows that gender had a statistically significant effect on participants' perspectives, F(1, 148) = 4.89, p = .029. As shown in Figure 2, males consistently had higher mean ratings across all dimensions of the career transition counselling services for SASD. Figure 2 further illustrates these results by visualising the difference between male and female respondents. The results suggest that gender is an important characteristic shaping how individuals perceive the availability, quality, and usefulness of career transition counselling services for SASD.

Figure 2. Means ratings of participants on their perspectives on career transition counselling services for SASD by gender

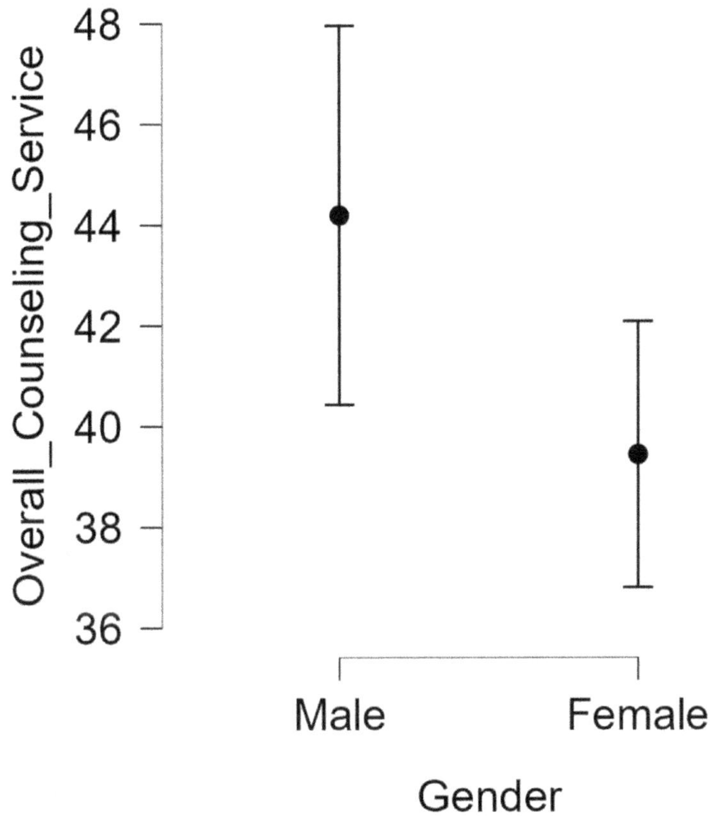

The analysis in Table 3 also shows that autism severity level did not significantly influence participants' perspectives, $F(2, 148) = .113$, $p = .894$. Figure 3 supports this result by showing that the mean ratings for the three levels of autism severity remain closely aligned, with no noticeable separation between the levels. Taken together, the results suggest that regardless of whether the student was categorised as Level 1, Level 2, or Level 3, participants tended to evaluate the counselling services in similar ways. This result indicates that perceptions of service quality were not shaped by the specific autism severity characteristics of the students being supported.

Figure 3. Participants' ratings regarding their views on career transition counseling services for SASD, categorized by levels of ASD

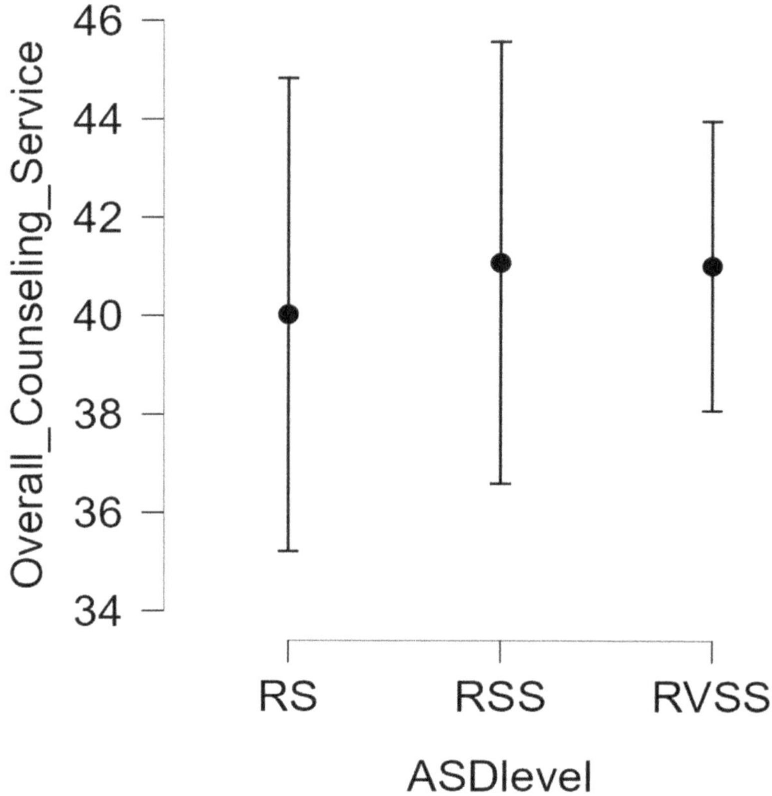

Furthermore, Table 3 indicates that none of the interaction effects among participant type, gender, and autism severity level were statistically significant. As can be seen, the interaction between participant type and gender, F(1, 148) = 1.36, p = .246, was not significant, suggesting that gender did not influence teachers' and parents' perspectives differently. Similarly, the interaction between participant type and autism severity level was not significant, F(2, 148) = .332, p = .718. The results show that the three-way interaction among participant type, gender, and autism severity level was not significant, F(2, 148) = .189, p = .828. These results suggest that each sociodemographic variable operated independently, with no combined effects influencing how participants viewed counselling services.

Figure 4. Means ratings of participants on their perspectives on career transition counselling services for SASD based on educational qualification

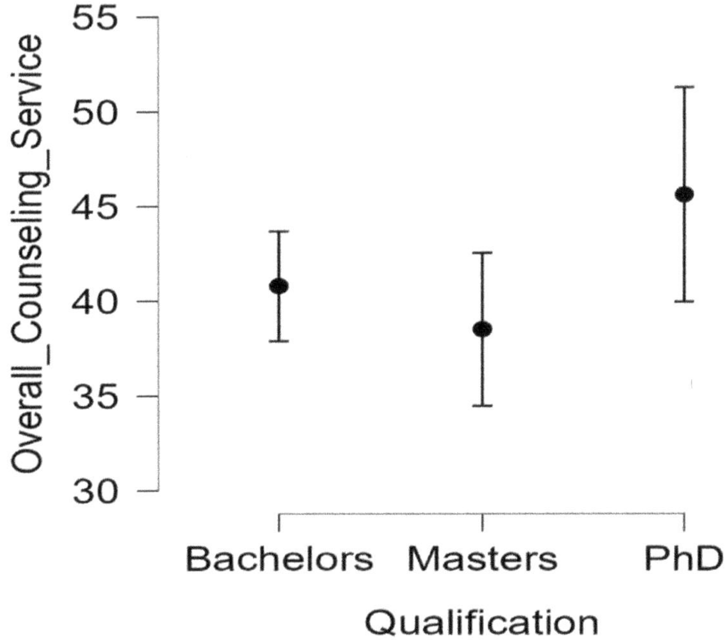

Figure 4 presents a visual comparison of the average ratings among holders of bachelor's, master's, and doctoral degrees. The figure shows relatively similar levels of endorsement across the three qualification groups, with no substantial differences seen in the height of the bars. This result suggests that educational qualification did not substantially influence perceptions of the counselling services. Individuals possessing advanced qualifications exhibited no significant differences in their evaluations of the available services when compared to those holding bachelor's or master's degrees.

DISCUSSION

This research examined perspectives on career transition counselling services for students with autism spectrum disorder (SASD). This study found that participants' perceived need assessment and personalisation as comparatively more substantial components of career transition counselling services for SASD. This suggests that counselling services are focused on recognising individual strengths, interests, and support needs of SASD. This study's finding is attributed to the centrality of individualised transition planning in autism, where a viable pathway relies on identifying SASD strengths, interests, support needs, sensory considerations, communication preferences, and contextual barriers into an actionable plan. This finding aligns with contemporary literature, which revealed that centred that person-centred planning can be effectively utilised for transition-aged youth on the autism spectrum as a tool to enhance their involvement in transition planning (Hagner et al., 2014).

This study showed the SASD severity profile, which entails that many supported SASD require considerable assistance. As a result, personalisation must be extended beyond preference identification into collective environmental adjustment and sustained structure when support needs are high. Previous research has consistently demonstrated the significance of acknowledging and integrating each SASD's strengths, interests, and talents assists in resolving their specific challenges and leveraging their motivations for better outcomes (Lanou et al., 2012; Feather et al., 2025). In the context of Ubuntu theory, need assessment is a relational process because the individual is comprehended as ingrained within a network of associations among students, families, educators, and counsellors that shape identity, opportunity, and agency (Manthalu, 2023; Singha, 2024). This study's report should be interpreted with caution because participants have identified intentional tailoring, despite the fact that the extent to which tailoring translates into accessible pathways depends on resource capacity and interagency coordination.

This study revealed that the counselling process and techniques were rated highest across service domains by the participants, indicating that they were perceived as structured, purposeful, and supportive. This means that structured counselling activities, such as guided discussions, practical skill building and reflective exercises, are perceived as helpful for SASD. In secondary school contexts, such processes are often the most visible aspect of career transition support, occurring within scheduled sessions and facilitated by trained personnel. These findings resonate with previous studies, which suggested that structure counselling services uses practical activities to enhance social communication and emotional regulation among high-functioning youth with ASD (Schweizer et al., 2024, 2024; White et al., 2010). This result indirectly supports the report of Yang and Zhang (2025), which found that intervention incorporating rhythm, interactive singing, and instruments immensely enhanced social communication and emotional regulation among children with ASD. The Ubuntu theory emphasised that enriching social work knowledge, theories, and practice, decolonising and addressing gaps left by Western approaches (Udah et al., 2025). As the participants positively assessed the counselling processes, this suggests that counsellors are able to establish relational connections that foster trust and engagement. This is significant because trust is a prerequisite for effective guidance, particularly for students whose prior educational experiences may include exclusion or misunderstanding.

Ubuntu fosters a sense of connectivity among individuals and integrating the elements within the educational curriculum, pedagogical strategies, and cultural customs fosters comprehensive growth, moral progress, and interconnectivity (Singha, 2024), and that Ubuntu principles can empower students to free themselves from academic and personal barriers used to justify exclusion, oppression and self-promotion over collective good (Duvenage, 2025). While this study has shown that the counselling processes were perceived positively, its influence may be restrained by the limited resources and weak institutional linkages. Counselling efficiency is amplified when integrated within a network system that comprises school, families, employers, and community agencies (Popovic & Jinks, 2013).

This study revealed that resource availability and accessibility were the lowest-rated domains, showing a shared understanding that material and systemic support are insufficient. This finding is significant because resource bridges planning and outcomes. The low rating of resource availability and accessibility means that SASD may be ready for transition without being supported materially for effective transition. This results in symbolic inclusion. From an Ubuntu perspective, studies (Gore, 2023; Ngubane & Makua, 2021; Sabela, 2023) have shown that the lack of material support undermines the dignity of SASD by raising expectations that cannot be met, leading to symbolic rather than substantive inclusion. The theory recommends that the community mobilise tangible resources to support its members, and emphasises that the moral promise of Ubuntu would remain unfulfilled when resources are lacking (Kwembeya et al., 2025). In fact, students who engage in internships in their community often acquire professional skills and intrinsic motivation, which enhance their readiness for the labour market (Thuy & Duong, 2026; Tobin & Rozek, 2025): Chong et al., 2021).

This study revealed that outcome monitoring and feedback were moderately rated among participants, indicating that some mechanisms exist for tracking progress and communicating with SASD and families. The monitoring domain is a vital component of career transition services of counsellors because it provides ongoing modification and ensures that plans remain responsive to changing needs. From the Ubuntu perspective, monitoring is a form of accountability that represents community commitments to remain engaged with SASD's journey instead of terminating support once plans are formulated (Mutema, 2025). Evidence from this study shows that commitment is partially realised. The presence of an insignificant difference among autism severity levels further raises questions about whether monitoring practices are adequately responsive to various support needs. Concentrating barely on task completion may fail to capture the full spectrum of transition success. A holistic approach, as advocated by Ubuntu theory, which includes both skill development (Yi et al., 2025) and broader psychosocial outcomes (Chapados et al., 2023), is essential for meaningful transition monitoring. This approach ensures that individuals have a feeling of inclusion and are supported by their community, leading to a more successful and sustainable transition (Hatendi, 2025; Kwembeya et al., 2025).

This study revealed that there was no significant different in the teachers' and parents' perspectives on career transition counselling services for SASD, suggesting a convergence of stakeholder views regarding the quality and effectiveness of career transition counselling services. This agreement is significant, as teachers and parents typically interact with these services from distinct viewpoints and may possess differing expectations. This denotes that schools and families' communications aligned to produce a shared understanding. This finding aligned with the Ubuntu theory, which indicates that shared perspectives and collective understanding are foundational for collective action in transition planning. Ubuntu emphasises interconnectedness, community-driven engagement, and the importance of empathy, equality, and shared humanity (Obasa, 2024; Taylor, 2014). Thus, effective communication and collaboration between teachers and parents can create a conducive environment that respects individual dignity and promotes collective well-being.

Furthermore, teachers and parents often note that systemic constraints, such as inadequate resources, hinder the effective implementation of educational transitions and support services (Arar et al., 2018; Polovina, 2010). Gonzales et al. (2022) reported that these conditions can manifest in various forms, including inadequate funding, lack of training resources, and inadequate technological infrastructure. Researchers like Makhanya (2022) and Kwembeya et al. (2025) have shown that Ubuntu's emphasis on collective responsibility suggests that stakeholders should work together to overcome systemic constraints through actively seeking solutions to improve the educational system.

This study disclosed that there is evidence of a statistically significant gender effect, even though inconsistencies in group labelling necessitate caution in interpreting directionality. Empirical evidence on counselling service perception always suggests that gender differences constantly indicate variation in role expectations and caregiving responsibilities rather than inherent evaluative tendencies. In the Ubuntu perspective, researchers (Chigangaidze & Chinyenze, 2022; Hofmeyr, 2025; Makhanya, 2022) have reported that Ubuntu theory indicates that emphasising interconnectedness and community reframes gender disparities in service perceptions as indicators of the uneven distribution of relational labour within the community. This means that individuals bearing greater caregiving responsibilities, especially women, could be more critical of service as a result of their heightened role in navigating service gaps. Furthermore, the absence of severity level effects indicated that perceptions of counselling service quality do not vary based on the intensity of students' support needs. This indicates equitable counselling service provision across severity levels, or it may indicate insufficient differentiation of supports. Due to participants' low rating for resource availability, the latter interpretation warrants consideration. Ubuntu calls for proportionate responses to vulnerability, ensuring that resources and support are distributed equitably. This aims to address the needs of vulnerable populations like SASD (Dhai & Kurihara, 2025; Shumbamhini & Chirongoma, 2025). Similarly, evidence of no substantial differences by educational qualification of participants indicates that experiential engagement with counselling services outweighs formal credentials in shaping perceptions. Rosa et al (2025) indicated that educational systems constantly encounter limitations due to insufficient infrastructure and systemic support, which can limit the effectiveness of individual expertise. However, dynamic systems and collective capacity building are essential to overcome these constraints (O'Hara et al., 2019: Farmer et al., 2023).

The study's results have practical implications. First, schools should emphasise available transition resources like structured career information, adapted materials for diverse communication profiles and flexible delivery modes that decrease barriers to participation. Resource availability should include supported access, implying guidance in utilising resources, translation into actionable steps and ongoing follow-up. Second, transition counselling processes should be consolidated as standardised practice since counselling techniques and personalisation are perceived as moderate. As a result, they should be protected through clear service standards; minimum session structures, consistent use of practical skill-building activities, and systematic inclusion of student preferences and strengths. Third, through measurable indicators of transition readiness, monitoring and feedback should be strengthened. For effective monitoring, proximal indicators (skills acquisition and completed action steps) and developmental indicators (self-advocacy growth, confidence, and future planning clarity) should be tracked. Finally, the teachers and parents' alignment can be leveraged for joint transition governance through collaborative planning that encompasses transition meetings, coordinated action plans, and clear role allocation for families and schools of SASD.

CONCLUSIONS

This study investigated the perspectives on career transition of SASD. This study revealed that effective engagement for career transition with SASD entails counselling processes, personalisation, and stakeholder alignment. The constraints for the realisation of inclusive SASD's career transition outcomes are limitations in resource availability and differentiated support. This study was anchored on Ubuntu theory, which offered a robust lens for interpreting these findings, emphasising the ethical imperative of communal responsibility in career transition services. This study recommends advancing career transition counselling services for SASD and also rallying collective resources and sustaining relational commitments beyond the school context.

REFERENCES

Aaen Maagaard, C. A., & Nielsen, A. S. (2025). Motivational interviewing and the reframing of identity: Small stories in first encounters between clients with alcohol use disorders and their therapists. *Text & Talk*, •••, 1–26. DOI: 10.1515/text-2024-0161

Accardo, A. L., Kuder, S. J., & Woodruff, J. (2019). Accommodations and support services preferred by college students with autism spectrum disorder. *Autism*, *23*(3), 574–583. DOI: 10.1177/1362361318760490 PMID: 29475372

Agunowei, D. I., & Mayombe, C. (2024). The fate of special needs children in the midst of inclusive education policy in Abuja, Nigeria. In Sánchez-Santamaría, J., & Cervantes, B. B. (Eds.), *Exploring Educational Equity at the Intersection of Policy and Practice* (pp. 264–286). IGI Global., DOI: 10.4018/979-8-3693-1614-6.ch015

Ajitoni, B. D. (2024). Ubuntu and the philosophy of community in African thought: An exploration of collective identity and social harmony. *Journal of African Studies and Sustainable Development*, *7*(3), 1–15.

Andaluz-Delgado, S., Ordóñez-Olmedo, E., & Gutiérrez-Martín, N. (2025). The 5 Best Educational Apps to Enhance Learning for Students with ASD. *Siglo Cero*, *56*(3), 99–114. DOI: 10.14201/scero.32119

Arar, K., Abu Nasra, M., & Alshafi, H. (2018). Arab teachers' perception of parent involvement (PI): Components and differences. *International Journal of Educational Management*, *32*(3), 326–341. DOI: 10.1108/IJEM-01-2016-0003

Ashburner, J., Bennett, L., Rodger, S., & Ziviani, J. (2013). Understanding the sensory experiences of young people with autism spectrum disorder: A preliminary investigation. *Australian Occupational Therapy Journal*, *60*(3), 171–180. DOI: 10.1111/1440-1630.12025 PMID: 23730782

Atkinson, G. (2014). Suitable for reframing: The myers-briggs type indicator in couples therapy. In Brothers, B. J. (Ed.), *Couples Therapy, Multiple Perspectives: In Search of Universal Threads* (pp. 121–132). Taylor and Francis., DOI: 10.4324/9781315801278

Azad, G. F., Minton, K. E., Mandell, D. S., & Landa, R. J. (2021). Partners in School: An Implementation Strategy to Promote Alignment of Evidence-Based Practices Across Home and School for Children with Autism Spectrum Disorder. *Administration and Policy in Mental Health*, *48*(2), 266–278. DOI: 10.1007/s10488-020-01064-9 PMID: 32653973

Bambling, M. (2014). Creating positive outcomes in clinical supervision. In C. Edward Watkins & D. L. Milne (Eds.), *The Wiley International Handbook of Clinical Supervision* (pp. 445–457). wiley. DOI: 10.1002/9781118846360.ch21

Bitsika, V. (2008). Including an analysis of difficult behaviour in the assessment of children with an autism spectrum disorder: Implications for school psychologists. *Australian Journal of Guidance & Counselling, 18*(1), 1–14. DOI: 10.1375/ajgc.18.1.1

Brown, H. K., Ouellette-Kuntz, H., Hunter, D., & Kelley, E. (2010). Assessing need in school-aged children with an autism spectrum disorder. *Research in Autism Spectrum Disorders, 4*(4), 539–547. DOI: 10.1016/j.rasd.2009.12.009

Chapados, P., Provencher, S., Aramideh, J., Dumont, É., Lugasi, T., Laverdière, C., Sultan, S., & Desjardins, L. (2023). Transition Readiness Assessment Questionnaire: Skill gaps and psychosocial predictors of transition readiness among adolescents and young adults with chronic medical conditions. *Child: Care, Health and Development, 50*(1).1-10. e13156. DOI: 10.1111/cch.13156

Chigangaidze, R. K., & Chinyenze, P. (2022). What it means to say, 'a person is a person through other persons': Ubuntu through humanistic-existential lenses of transactional analysis. *Journal of Religion & Spirituality in Social Work, 41*(3), 280–295. DOI: 10.1080/15426432.2022.2039341

Chong, K., Neo, P. H., Sing, S. H., Krishnan, T., & Choo, K. W. (2021). Enhancing workplace learning through structured internship. *Proc. Int. CDIO. Conf.*, 273–282.

Chung, I. (2006). The use of reframing in clinical practice with Chinese immigrants. *Journal of Immigrant and Refugee Services, 3*(3–4), 1–14. DOI: 10.1300/J191v03n03_01

Dale, B. A., Ogle, L. N., Ruble, L. A., & Azad, G. F. (2025). Dyadic mechanisms of effect in home–school consultation: Evidence from two school-based consultation models. *School Psychology International, 46*(2), 115–134. DOI: 10.1177/01430343241283025

Dean, E. E., Hagiwara, M., Shogren, K. A., Wehmeyer, M. L., & Shrum, J. (2022). Promoting Career Design in Youth and Young Adults with ASD: A Feasibility Study. *Journal of Autism and Developmental Disorders, 52*(6), 2689–2700. DOI: 10.1007/s10803-021-05146-x PMID: 34184143

Dhai, A., & Kurihara, C. (2025). Ubuntu Principles: Solidarity to Include Vulnerable Communities for Equitable Access. In C. Kurihara, D. Greco, & A. Dhai (Eds.), *The 2024 Declaration of Helsinki: Global Efforts Towards the Highest Ethical Standards* (pp. 23–32). Springer Science+Business Media. DOI: 10.1007/978-981-96-9294-1_2

Dipeolu, A. O., Storlie, C., & Johnson, C. (2015). College Students with High-Functioning Autism Spectrum Disorder: Best Practices for Successful Transition to the World of Work. *Journal of College Counseling, 18*(2), 175–190. DOI: 10.1002/jocc.12013

Ditchman, N. M., Miller, J. L., & Easton, A. B. (2018). Vocational Rehabilitation Service Patterns: An Application of Social Network Analysis to Examine Employment Outcomes of Transition-Age Individuals With Autism. *Rehabilitation Counseling Bulletin, 61*(3), 143–153. DOI: 10.1177/0034355217709455

Donnell, C. M., Lustig, D. C., & Strauser, D. R. (2004). The working alliance: Rehabilitation outcomes for persons with severe mental illness. *Journal of Rehabilitation, 70*(2), 12–18.

Dorney, K. E., & Erickson, K. (2019). Transactions within a classroom-based AAC intervention targeting preschool students with autism spectrum disorders: A mixed-methods investigation. *Exceptionality Education International, 29*(2), 42–58. DOI: 10.5206/eei.v29i2.9401

Duvenage, A. (2025). Realising Pedagogical Love Through Ubuntu: Cultivating Inclusion and Undoing Coloniality for Pluriversity. In E. Vanderheiden, C.-H. Mayer, & A. M. F. Barcelos (Eds.), *Pedagogical Love in Adult Education: New Perspectives in Nurturing, Growth and Transformation* (pp. 247–262). Springer Science+Business Media. DOI: 10.1007/978-3-031-82046-5_13

Farmer, S., Ward, C. S., & Cusumano, D. (2023). Implementation science: Foundations and applied practice in educational settings. In Fenning, P. A., & Nellis, L. M. (Eds.), *Systems Consultation and Change in Schools: Integrating Implementation Science into Practice* (pp. 13–34). Springer International Publishing., DOI: 10.1007/978-3-031-21381-6_2

Feather, K. A., Dahl-Jacinto, H., & Clark, M. (2025). Exploring Mental Health Professionals' Experiences With Using Humanistic Counseling for Children With ASD. *The Journal of Humanistic Counseling, 64*(3), 184–192. DOI: 10.1002/johc.70004

Federal Republic of Nigeria. (2015). *National Policy on Special Needs Education in Nigeria*. 1–44.

Fernández-Batanero, J. M., Fernández-Cerero, J., & Montenegro-Rueda, M. (2025). Technological accessibility and Autism. Level of Training of Secondary Education, Baccalaureate and Vocational Training Teachers. *International Journal of Technology and Educational Innovation, 11*(2), 42–58. DOI: 10.24310/ijtei.112.2025.21437

Frempong, G., & Kadam, R. (2025). The Ubuntu Mindset: Learning to Manage and Lead Better Together, the Africentric Way. In Williams, K. S., Mills, A. J., & Weigand, H. (Eds.), *Management Education in Canada: Historical Reflections* (pp. 156–175). Taylor and Francis., DOI: 10.4324/9781003612612-8

Garbacz, S. A., McIntyre, L. L., & Santiago, R. T. (2016). Family involvement and parent-teacher relationships for students with autism spectrum disorders. *School Psychology Quarterly*, *31*(4), 478–490. DOI: 10.1037/spq0000157 PMID: 27929318

Gillespie-Lynch, K., Bublitz, D., Donachie, A., Wong, V., Brooks, P. J., & D'Onofrio, J. (2017). "For a Long Time Our Voices have been Hushed": Using Student Perspectives to Develop Supports for Neurodiverse College Students. *Frontiers in Psychology*, *8*, 544. DOI: 10.3389/fpsyg.2017.00544 PMID: 28458645

Gonzales, G., Costan, F., Suladay, D., Gonzales, R., Enriquez, L., Costan, E., Atibing, N. M., Aro, J. L., Evangelista, S. S., Maturan, F., Selerio, E.Jr, & Ocampo, L. (2022). Fermatean Fuzzy DEMATEL and MMDE Algorithm for Modelling the Barriers of Implementing Education 4.0: Insights from the Philippines. *Applied Sciences (Basel, Switzerland)*, *12*(2), 689. Advance online publication. DOI: 10.3390/app12020689

Gore, O. T. (2023). Disability and inclusion in South African higher education: An Ubuntu philosophical perspective. In Mutanga, O. (Ed.), *Ubuntu Philosophy and Disabilities in Sub-Saharan Africa* (pp. 30–47). Taylor and Francis., DOI: 10.4324/9781003343684-3

Grothaus, T., McAuliffe, G., & Craigen, L. (2012). Infusing cultural competence and advocacy into strength-based counseling. *The Journal of Humanistic Counseling*, *51*(1), 51–65. DOI: 10.1002/j.2161-1939.2012.00005.x

Grover, J. M. (2017). Bonding with your hard of hearing or late-deafened VR client. *Journal of Vocational Rehabilitation*, *47*(1), 47–64. DOI: 10.3233/JVR-170882

Hagiwara, M., Dean, E. E., & Shogren, K. A. (2019). The Self-determined Career Design Model: Supporting Young People with Developmental Disabilities and Their Families in Home and Community Settings. In *Promoting Social Inclusion: Co-Creating Environments that Foster Equity and Belonging* (13, p. 201-220). Emerald Publishing Limited. DOI: 10.1108/S1479-363620190000013016

Hagner, D., Kurtz, A., Cloutier, H., Arakelian, C., Brucker, D. L., & May, J. (2012). Outcomes of a family-centered transition process for students with autism spectrum disorders. *Focus on Autism and Other Developmental Disabilities*, *27*(1), 42–50. DOI: 10.1177/1088357611430841

Hagner, D., Kurtz, A., May, J., & Cloutier, H. (2014). Person-centered planning for transition-aged youth with autism spectrum disorders. *Journal of Rehabilitation, 80*(1), 4–10.

Hannah, E. F., & Topping, K. J. (2013). The transition from primary to secondary school: Perspectives of students with autism spectrum disorder and their parents. *International Journal of Special Education, 28*(1), 145–157.

Harris, A. H. S., Thoresen, C. E., & Lopez, S. J. (2007). Integrating positive psychology into counseling: Why and (when appropriate) how. *Journal of Counseling and Development, 85*(1), 3–13. DOI: 10.1002/j.1556-6678.2007.tb00438.x

Hasselbusch, A., & Baumgarten, A. (2014). Including children with autism in everyday life. *Ergotherapie und Rehabilitation, 53*(1), 14–18.

Hatendi, C. M. (2025). Ubuntu, Diversity and Inclusiveness: Afro-descendants in the United States. In E. Chitando, B. Okyere-Manu, S. Chirongoma, & M. W. Dube (Eds.), *The Palgrave Handbook of Ubuntu, Inequality and Sustainable Development* (pp. 633–646). Springer Science+Business Media. DOI: 10.1007/978-3-031-69573-5_39

Hendrickson, J. M., Woods-Groves, S., Rodgers, D. B., & Datchuk, S. (2017). Perceptions of students with Autism and their parents: The college experience. *Education & Treatment of Children, 40*(4), 571–596. DOI: 10.1353/etc.2017.0025

Hill, D. A., Fayemi, A., & Ostrowski, S. (2024). The Evolution of Services for Children with Autism and Developmental Disabilities in Nigeria. *International Journal of Disability Development and Education, 71*(7), 1116–1132. DOI: 10.1080/1034912X.2023.2291570

Hofmeyr, B. (2025). Reading Ubuntu relationality through a Levinasian lens. *Acta Academica, 57*(1), 53–71. DOI: 10.38140/aa.v57i1.9072

Jones, E. K., Hanley, M., & Riby, D. M. (2020). Distraction, distress and diversity: Exploring the impact of sensory processing differences on learning and school life for pupils with autism spectrum disorders. *Research in Autism Spectrum Disorders, 72*, 101515. Advance online publication. DOI: 10.1016/j.rasd.2020.101515

Karpetis, G. (2016). Evaluating the Effectiveness of the Reframing Technique in Psychodynamic Social Work Practice. *Australian Social Work, 69*(2), 194–205. DOI: 10.1080/0312407X.2015.1069865

Kaya, C., Hanley-Maxwell, C., Chan, F., & Tansey, T. (2018). Differential vocational rehabilitation service patterns and outcomes for transition-age youth with autism. *Journal of Applied Research in Intellectual Disabilities, 31*(5), 862–872. DOI: 10.1111/jar.12443 PMID: 29441662

Kirby, A. V., Feldman, K. J. C., Himle, M. B., Diener, M. L., Wright, C. A., & Hoffman, J. M. (2021). Pilot test of the maximizing adolescent post-secondary-success(mapss) intervention: Supporting parents of autistic youth. *The American Journal of Occupational Therapy*, *75*(3), 7503180070. Advance online publication. DOI: 10.5014/ajot.2021.045815 PMID: 34781348

Kwembeya, M., Munasirei, P., Mutongoreni, N. A., Mandoga, E., & Kwembeya, L. (2025). Ubuntu Philosophical Framework for Inclusive Sustainable Development Goals. In Ro ca, A.-E. (Ed.), *Exploring Multicultural Dimensions of Literary, Linguistic, and Educational Frontiers* (pp. 207–231). IGI Global., DOI: 10.4018/979-8-3693-8196-0.ch009

Laghi, F., & Trimarco, B. (2020). Individual planning starts at school. Tools and practices promoting autonomy and supporting transition to work for adolescents with autism spectrum disorder. *Annali dell'Istituto Superiore di Sanita*, *56*(2), 222–229. DOI: 10.4415/ANN_20_02_12 PMID: 32567572

Lam, G. Y. H., Timmons, J., & Zalewska, A. (2023). Program logic model and impacts perceived by stakeholders in a post-school transition program for autistic young adults. *Research in Autism Spectrum Disorders*, *107*, 102220. Advance online publication. DOI: 10.1016/j.rasd.2023.102220

Lanou, A., Hough, L., & Powell, E. (2012). Case studies on using strengths and interests to address the needs of students with autism spectrum disorders. *Intervention in School and Clinic*, *47*(3), 175–182. DOI: 10.1177/1053451211423819

LaRue, R. H., Pepa, L., Delmolino, L., Sloman, K. N., Fiske, K., Hansford, A., Liebross, S., & Weiss, M. J. (2016). A brief assessment for selecting communication modalities for individuals with Autism Spectrum Disorders. *Evidence-Based Communication Assessment and Intervention*, *10*(1), 32–43. DOI: 10.1080/17489539.2016.1204767

Lee, G. K., & Carter, E. W. (2012). Preparing Transition-Age Students with High-Functioning Autism Spectrum Disorders for Meaningful Work. *Psychology in the Schools*, *49*(10), 988–1000. DOI: 10.1002/pits.21651

Makhanya, T. B. (2022). Azibuyele emasisweni: Exploring the discourse of Ubuntu philosophy in social work education and practice. *African Journal of Social Work*, *12*(6), 136–143.

Manthalu, C. H. (2023). An Ubuntu Philosophy of Higher Education as Justice. In *African Higher Education: Developments and Perspectives* (15, pp. 58–72). Brill Academic Publishers. DOI: 10.1163/9789004543805_005

Martin, J. E., & Williams-Diehm, K. (2013). Student Engagement and Leadership of the Transition Planning Process. *Career Development and Transition for Exceptional Individuals, 36*(1), 43–50. DOI: 10.1177/2165143413476545

Masicampo, E. J., & Baumeister, R. F. (2012). Committed but closed-minded: When making a specific plan for a goal hinders succes. *Social Cognition, 30*(1), 37–55. DOI: 10.1521/soco.2012.30.1.37

McDonough, J. T., & Revell, G. (2010). Accessing employment supports in the adult system for transitioning youth with autism spectrum disorders. *Journal of Vocational Rehabilitation, 32*(2), 89–100. DOI: 10.3233/JVR-2010-0498

Moody, E. J., Kaiser, K., Sharp, D., Kubicek, L. F., Rigles, B., Davis, J., McSwegin, S., D'Abreu, L. C., & Rosenberg, C. R. (2019). Improving Family Functioning Following Diagnosis of ASD: A Randomized Trial of a Parent Mentorship Program. *Journal of Child and Family Studies, 28*(2), 424–435. DOI: 10.1007/s10826-018-1293-z

Morris, P., Weglarz-Ward, J. M., & Love, H. R. (2021). Preparing Families of Young Children With Autism Spectrum Disorder for Formal School Settings. *Intervention in School and Clinic, 57*(2), 126–131. DOI: 10.1177/1053451220928968

Mosala, M. (2025). Promoting Inclusivity Through Ubuntu Philosophy. In Dhakal, R., Davis, W. G., & Heske, K. (Eds.), *Building Collaborative Learning Communities to Drive Student Success* (pp. 237–288). IGI Global., DOI: 10.4018/979-8-3373-0796-1.ch008

Mpofu, J., & Sefotho, M. M. (2025). Embracing Ubuntu: Promoting Inclusion of Learners With Autism Spectrum Disorders in Education. In Phasha, N. T. (Ed.), *Mental Health, Disability, and Combating Marginalization in Education* (pp. 117–144). IGI Global., DOI: 10.4018/979-8-3373-7163-4.ch005

Mutema, G. (2025). Confronting Inequalities in Education: The Symbiosis of Ubuntu and the Nordic Model. In E. Chitando, B. Okyere-Manu, S. Chirongoma, & M. W. Dube (Eds.), *The Palgrave Handbook of Ubuntu, Inequality and Sustainable Development* (pp. 473–482). Springer Science+Business Media. DOI: 10.1007/978-3-031-69573-5_30

Nachman, B. R. (2024). "A little too helicoptery": Reconciling parental involvement during autistic students' transitions into college. *Teachers College Record, 126*(11-12), 32–58. DOI: 10.1177/01614681241311637

Ngubane, N. I., & Makua, M. (2021). Intersection of ubuntu pedagogy and social justice: Transforming south african higher education. *Transformation in Higher Education, 6*, 113. DOI: 10.4102/the.v6i0.113

Nicholas, D. B., Attridge, M., Zwaigenbaum, L., & Clarke, M. (2015). Vocational support approaches in autism spectrum disorder: A synthesis review of the literature. *Autism, 19*(2), 235–245. DOI: 10.1177/1362361313516548 PMID: 24449603

Nicholas, D. B., Zwaigenbaum, L., Zwicker, J., Clarke, M. E., Lamsal, R., Stoddart, K. P., Carroll, C., Muskat, B., Spoelstra, M., & Lowe, K. (2018). Evaluation of employment-support services for adults with autism spectrum disorder. *Autism, 22*(6), 693–702. DOI: 10.1177/1362361317702507 PMID: 28637355

Nye-Lengerman, K. (2017). Vocational rehabilitation service usage and outcomes for individuals with Autism Spectrum Disorder. *Research in Autism Spectrum Disorders, 41–42*, 39–50. DOI: 10.1016/j.rasd.2017.08.003

O'Hara, S., Bookmyer, J., Martin, R., & Newton, R. (2019). Theory of action for resourcing professional growth. *Journal of Professional Capital and Community, 4*(1), 52–65. DOI: 10.1108/JPCC-02-2018-0006

Obasa, A. E. (2024). Large language models through the lens of ubuntu for health research in sub-Saharan Africa. *South African Journal of Science, 120*(5/6). Advance online publication. DOI: 10.17159/sajs.2024/16814

Panichelli, C. (2013). Humor, Joining, and Reframing in Psychotherapy: Resolving the Auto-Double-Bind. *The American Journal of Family Therapy, 41*(5), 437–451. DOI: 10.1080/01926187.2012.755393

Park, J., Lu, F.-C., & Hedgcock, W. M. (2017). Relative Effects of Forward and Backward Planning on Goal Pursuit. *Psychological Science, 28*(11), 1620–1630. DOI: 10.1177/0956797617715510 PMID: 28910234

Park, Y. S., Konge, L., & Artino, A. R. (2020). The Positivism Paradigm of Research. *Academic Medicine, 95*(5), 690–694. DOI: 10.1097/ACM.0000000000003093 PMID: 31789841

Plesa Skwerer, D., Jordan, S. E., Brukilacchio, B. H., & Tager-Flusberg, H. (2016). Comparing methods for assessing receptive language skills in minimally verbal children and adolescents with autism spectrum disorders. *Autism, 20*(5), 591–604. DOI: 10.1177/1362361315600146 PMID: 26408635

Polovina, N. (2010). General beliefs of teachers and students about working and living environment: Implications for mutual cooperation. *Zbornik Instituta za Pedagoska Istrazivanja, 42*(1), 74–91. DOI: 10.2298/ZIPI1001074P

Pongsaksri, M., Lersilp, S., & Suchart, S. (2017). Development and Reliability of the Basic Skill Assessment Tool for Adolescents with Autism Spectrum Disorder. *TheScientificWorldJournal, 2403943*, 1–7. Advance online publication. DOI: 10.1155/2017/2403943 PMID: 28280769

Popovic, N., & Jinks, D. (Eds.). (2013). *Personal consultancy: A model for integrating counselling and coaching*. Taylor and Francis., DOI: 10.4324/9781315882550

Rashid, T., & Ostermann, R. F. (2009). Strength-based assessment in clinical practice. *Journal of Clinical Psychology, 65*(5), 488–498. DOI: 10.1002/jclp.20595 PMID: 19294732

Roberts, K. D. (2010). Topic areas to consider when planning transition from high school to postsecondary education for students with autism spectrum disorders. *Focus on Autism and Other Developmental Disabilities, 25*(3), 158–162. DOI: 10.1177/1088357610371476

Rosa, R. A., Correa, M. V. P., & Bulgacov, S. (2025). RESOURCES IN ACTION: THE DYNAMICS OF RESOURCING IN AN EDUCATIONAL ORGANIZATION. *RAE Revista de Administracao de Empresas, 65*(5). https://doi.org/DOI: 10.1590/S0034-759020250504x

Roux, A. M., Rast, J. E., Anderson, K. A., Garfield, T., & Shattuck, P. T. (2021). Vocational Rehabilitation Service Utilization and Employment Outcomes Among Secondary Students on the Autism Spectrum. *Journal of Autism and Developmental Disorders, 51*(1), 212–226. DOI: 10.1007/s10803-020-04533-0 PMID: 32399821

Roux, A. M., Rast, J. E., & Shattuck, P. T. (2020). State-Level Variation in Vocational Rehabilitation Service Use and Related Outcomes Among Transition-Age Youth on the Autism Spectrum. *Journal of Autism and Developmental Disorders, 50*(7), 2449–2461. DOI: 10.1007/s10803-018-3793-5 PMID: 30357645

Roux, A. M., Shattuck, P. T., Cooper, B. P., Anderson, K. A., Wagner, M., & Narendorf, S. C. (2013). Postsecondary Employment Experiences Among Young Adults With an Autism Spectrum Disorder RH: Employment in Young Adults With Autism. *Journal of the American Academy of Child and Adolescent Psychiatry, 52*(9), 931–939. DOI: 10.1016/j.jaac.2013.05.019 PMID: 23972695

Sabela, P. T. (2023). Inclusive education: Challenging barriers, claiming human rights and social justice. In Maguvhe, M. O., & Masuku, M. M. (Eds.), *Using African Epistemologies in Shaping Inclusive Education Knowledge* (pp. 259–284). Springer., DOI: 10.1007/978-3-031-31115-4_15

Santosa, I., Sakya, K. A., Junaidy, D. W., Rahma, M. S., Mawali, L., & Rangga, S. (2025). Associative Concept Network Analysis-Driven Insights for Developing Adaptive Seating Solutions for Children with Autism Spectrum Disorder. *International Journal of Designed Objects, 19*(2), 21–45. DOI: 10.18848/2325-1379/CGP/v19i02/21-45

Schweizer, T., Endres, D., Dziobek, I., & Tebartz van Elst, L. (2024). Psychosocial therapeutic approaches for high-functioning autistic adults. *Frontiers in Psychiatry, 14*, 1265066. DOI: 10.3389/fpsyt.2023.1265066 PMID: 38274434

Shandu-Phetla, T., Ngubane, S. A., & Adigun, O. T. (2023). Injecting Ubuntu in designing accessible virtual learning for students with disabilities. In Mutanga, O. (Ed.), *Ubuntu Philosophy and Disabilities in Sub-Saharan Africa* (pp. 88–108). Taylor and Francis., DOI: 10.4324/9781003343684-6

Sherwood, K., Smith, M. J., Ross, B., Johnson, J., Harrington, M., Blajeski, S., DaWalt, L., Bishop, L., & Smith, J. D. (2023). Mixed methods implementation evaluation of virtual interview training for transition-age autistic youth in pre-employment transition services. *Journal of Vocational Rehabilitation, 58*(2), 139–154. DOI: 10.3233/JVR-230004 PMID: 38881791

Shumbamhini, M., & Chirongoma, S. (2025). Ubuntu, Gender Equality and Sustainable Development in Africa: An African Feminist Perspective. In E. Chitando, B. Okyere-Manu, S. Chirongoma, & M. W. Dube (Eds.), *The Palgrave Handbook of Ubuntu, Inequality and Sustainable Development* (pp. 781–798). Springer Science+Business Media. DOI: 10.1007/978-3-031-69573-5_47

Singha, R. (2024). Cultivating holistic learning environments in higher education: Mindfulness, compassion, and ubuntu philosophies. In Omona, K., & O'dama, M. K. (Eds.), *Global Perspectives on Micro-Learning and Micro-Credentials in Higher Education* (pp. 174–194). IGI Global., DOI: 10.4018/979-8-3693-0343-6.ch011

Smith, E. J. (2006). The Strength-Based Counseling Model. *The Counseling Psychologist, 34*(1), 13–79. DOI: 10.1177/0011000005277018

Smith, M. J., Merle, J. L., Baker-Ericzén, M., Sherwood, K., Bornheimer, L. A., Ross, B., Harrington, M., Sharma, A., Brown, C., Gordon, T., Telfer, D., Reese, J., Hirst, J., Oulvey, E. A., Dignadice, V., Williams, E.-D., Magaña, S., Hume, K., Sung, C., & Smith, J. D. (2024). A type 1 hybrid multi-site randomized controlled trial protocol for evaluating virtual interview training among autistic transition-age youth. *Contemporary Clinical Trials Communications, 42*, 101384. Advance online publication. DOI: 10.1016/j.conctc.2024.101384 PMID: 39525564

Smith, M. J., Sherwood, K., Ross, B., Smith, J. D., DaWalt, L., Bishop, L., Humm, L., Elkins, J., & Steacy, C. (2021). Virtual interview training for autistic transition age youth: A randomized controlled feasibility and effectiveness trial. *Autism, 25*(6), 1536–1552. DOI: 10.1177/1362361321989928 PMID: 33567883

Snell-Rood, C., Ruble, L., Kleinert, H., McGrew, J. H., Adams, M., Rodgers, A., Odom, J., Wong, W. H., & Yu, Y. (2020). Stakeholder perspectives on transition planning, implementation, and outcomes for students with autism spectrum disorder. *Autism, 24*(5), 1164–1176. DOI: 10.1177/1362361319894827 PMID: 31957461

Stampoltzis, A., Peristeri, E., & Kalouri, R. (2025). Career counselors' attitudes about employment-related skills of individuals with autism spectrum disorders in Greece. *Frontiers in Education, 10*, 1662929. Advance online publication. DOI: 10.3389/feduc.2025.1662929

Taber, B. J. (2019). Career Counselling Interventions to Enhance Career Adaptabilities for Sustainable Employment. In Maree, J. G. (Ed.), *Handbook of Innovative Career Counselling* (pp. 103–115). Springer International Publishing., DOI: 10.1007/978-3-030-22799-9_7

Taylor, D. F. P. (2014). Defining ubuntu for business ethics- A deontological approach. *South African Journal of Philosophy, 33*(3), 331–345. DOI: 10.1080/02580136.2014.948328

Thuy, V. T. T., & Duong, D. P. N. (2026). Can internship experiences bridge the gap between university training and work readiness? Evidence from vietnamese economics students. *Multidisciplinary Science Journal, 8*(4), 2026265. Advance online publication. DOI: 10.31893/multiscience.2026265

Tobin, C. T., & Rozek, E. (2025). Enhancing undergraduate psychology internship by integrating professional core competencies. *Mentoring and Tutoring: Partnership in Learning*. 1-25https://DOI: 10.1080/13611267.2025.2571494

Trembath, D., & Iacono, T. (2016). Standardized Assessment of Prelinguistic Communication. In Keen, D., Meadan, H., Brady, N. C., & Halle, J. W. (Eds.), *Prelinguistic and Minimally Verbal Communicators on the Autism Spectrum* (pp. 75–100). Springer., DOI: 10.1007/978-981-10-0713-2_5

Tsiopela, D., & Jimoyiannis, A. (2017). Using a Web-Based Environment to Enhance Vocational Skills of Students with Autism Spectrum Disorder. In Mikropoulos, T. A. (Ed.), *Research on e-Learning and ICT in Education: Technological, Pedagogical and Instructional Perspectives* (pp. 381–395). Springer International Publishing., DOI: 10.1007/978-3-319-95059-4_23

Tyrrell, B., & Woods, K. (2018). Gathering the views of children and young people with ASD: A systematic literature review. *British Journal of Special Education, 45*(3), 302–328. DOI: 10.1111/1467-8578.12235

Udah, H., Tusasiirwe, S., Mugumbate, R., & Gatwiri, K. (2025). Ubuntu philosophy, values, and principles: An opportunity to do social work differently. *Journal of Social Work : JSW, 25*(4), 433–451. DOI: 10.1177/14680173241312749

Umeh, N. C., & Anyaele, D. O. (2024). Assessment of the Implementation of Inclusive Education Policy Among Stakeholders in Abia State, Nigeria. In *Ius Gentium* (Vol. 117, pp. 1–19). Springer Science and Business Media B.V., DOI: 10.1007/978-3-031-64549-5_1

Vargo, K. K., & Loflin, L. J. (2022). Assessing Preference for Activities and Instructional Contexts. *Intervention in School and Clinic, 58*(1), 31–38. DOI: 10.1177/10534512211047575

Viezel, K. D., Wilczynski, S. M., & Davis, A. S. (Eds.). (2022). *Postsecondary Transition for College- or Career-Bound Autistic Students.* Springer International Publishing., DOI: 10.1007/978-3-030-93947-2

Wang, D., Liu, X., & Deng, H. (2022). The perspectives of social cognitive career theory approach in current times. *Frontiers in Psychology, 13*, 1023994. DOI: 10.3389/fpsyg.2022.1023994 PMID: 36533045

White, S. W., Koenig, K., & Scahill, L. (2010). Group social skills instruction for adolescents with high-functioning autism spectrum disorders. *Focus on Autism and Other Developmental Disabilities, 25*(4), 209–219. DOI: 10.1177/1088357610380595

Wong, L. H. G. (2023). Sensory-Based Interventions for Managing Difficulties of Children with Autism Spectrum Disorder at School. *Current Developmental Disorders Reports, 10*(4), 240–249. DOI: 10.1007/s40474-023-00288-2

Yang, J., & Zhang, R. (2025). Melodic bridges: Music intervention as a catalyst for social skills development in preschool children with autism. *Frontiers in Psychology, 16*, 1542662. DOI: 10.3389/fpsyg.2025.1542662 PMID: 40636053

Yang, L., Pang, F., & Sin, K.-F. (2023). Assessing the Psychometric Properties of the Practice and Product Inventory of Supporting Students with ASD (PPI-SSA): A Concise Assessment Tool for Teachers in Inclusive Classrooms. *Sustainability (Basel), 15*(19), 14576. Advance online publication. DOI: 10.3390/su151914576

Yi, T., Hu, Y., Xia, L., Zhang, Y., Chen, X., & Dong, C. (2025). Instruments to Assess Transition Readiness Among Adolescents With Chronic Disease: A COSMIN Systematic Review of Measurement Properties. *Child: Care, Health and Development, 51*(1), e70017. DOI: 10.1111/cch.70017 PMID: 39629862

Zemrani, C., Vincent, C., Dumont, F. S., Julien-Gauthier, F., Caouette, M., Jolicoeur, E., Letscher, S., Boucher, N., & Mercure, F. (2025). The 'Work Rehabilitation and Adaptation Profile' for Adults with Autism, a Validated French-Canadian Observation Grid. *Journal of Vocational Rehabilitation, 63*(3), 282–298. DOI: 10.1177/10522263251376329

APPENDIX

Table 4. Career Transition Counselling Services Questionnaire-Adults (CTCSQ-A)

N	Items	Factor Loading	Cronbach's A	Omega ω
	Needs Assessment and Personalisation			
1	The service begins with a thorough assessment of each student's strengths, interests, and needs.	.500	0.90	0.90
2	Counsellors adapt their approach based on the student's individual profile.	.633		
3	Students and families are involved in crafting individualised career plans.	.692		
4	Counselling addresses both personal and environmental (e.g., workplace/social) factors.	.571		
5	The service recognises the unique ways ASD students communicate preferences and goals.	.709		
	Counselling Process and Techniques			
6	Counsellors use structured career theory frameworks (e.g., cognitive processing, Holland, SCCT).	.926	0.92	0.92
7	Sessions include practical activities like resume building, interviewing, or informational interviews.	.877		
8	Techniques (e.g., role-play, feedback, self-reflection) are regularly used to build skills.	.966		
9	Counsellors integrate evidence-based strategies for self-efficacy and decision-making.	.850		
10	Sessions accommodate the sensory or communication needs of ASD students.	.886		
	Resource Availability and Accessibility			
11	Career resources (e.g., job posting databases, training info) are readily provided for students.	.832	0.77	0.75
12	Digital or print tools are accessible in user-friendly formats for ASD students.	.649		
13	Parents or support personnel can access resources alongside students.	.668		
14	Flexible scheduling and session formats (e.g., in-person, virtual) are offered.	.393		
15	Counsellors are available for additional support as needed beyond planned sessions.	.857		
	Outcome Monitoring and Feedback			

continued on following page

Table 4. Continued

N	Items	Factor Loading	Cronbach's Α	Omega ω
	Needs Assessment and Personalisation			
16	Transition progress is tracked and discussed regularly with students.	.761	0.90	0.89
17	Objective indicators (e.g., action steps completed, readiness levels) are used to evaluate progress.	.867		
18	Students receive constructive feedback about strengths and areas for growth.	.675		
19	Families are invited to give feedback on service effectiveness.	.928		
20	Data on outcomes (e.g., self-confidence, skills development) are used to improve the service.	.791		

Figure 5. Scree Plot for the Career Transition Counselling Services Questionnaire-Adults (CTCSQ-A)

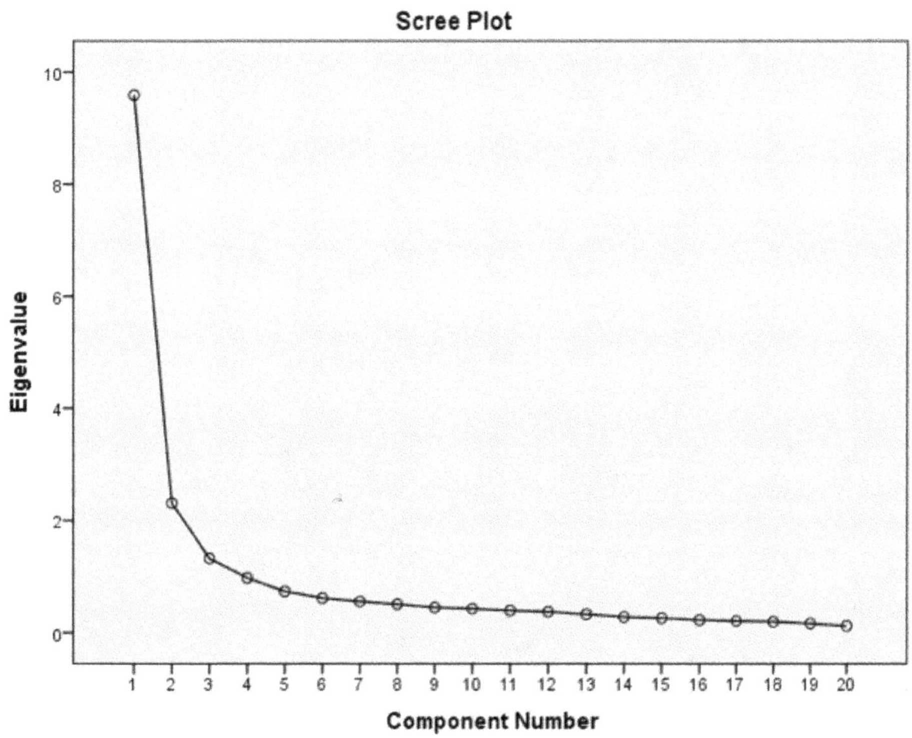

Chapter 9
Recognising Barriers in the Career Transition Process of Students With ASD

ABSTRACT

This research explored the obstacles to career transition of students with autism spectrum disorders (SASD), focusing on both teachers' and parents' responses. The study used a quantitative design to investigate the perceived personal, social, institutional, awareness-related, and resource-related barriers within Nigerian school contexts. Results show that parents recognised significantly higher levels of perceived career transition barriers than teachers, reflecting more exposure to systemic barriers beyond the school environment. The study underscores the need for coordinated transition planning, enhancing professional awareness, and reinforcing resource provision to enhance equitable career transitions for SASD.

BACKGROUND

A barrier refers to a circumstance that hinders, constrains, or limits an individual's potential to reach a transition. Practically, a barrier acts as an obstacle to action, access, or adjustment. Barriers encountered during career transition encompass personal, social, institutional, and structural challenges that hinder an individual's capacity to transition smoothly from one phase of education, training, or employment to another (Luwei & Huimin, 2024; Scott, 2014; Söner & Yılmaz, 2025). Specifically, barriers in career transition denote factors that limit access, preparedness, decision-making, adaptability, or ongoing engagement towards desired career goals, consequently

DOI: 10.4018/978-1-6684-7260-6.ch009

postponing, distorting, or obstructing career advancement. The transition from education to employment for students with autism spectrum disorders (SASD) is characterised by several challenges and systemic barriers. These challenges continually lead to less favourable employment and postsecondary results when compared to neurotypical counterparts.

Traditional transition services usually fall behind in meeting the required standards as a result of a lack of personalisation, a lack of support structure, a deficit in SASD-specific training for professionals, and systemic obstacles like disconnected service delivery and restricted collaboration among stakeholders (Alfawzan & Almulhim, 2024; Chun et al., 2023; Eseadi & Diale, 2024; Ookeditse et al., 2024). Studies have shown that the interaction between individual features, social contexts, and institutional systems plays a significant role in affecting career transition for SASD (Eilenberg et al., 2019; Kim et al., 2023; Lee et al., 2023; Milen & Nicholas, 2017). In this evolving viewpoint, barriers are perceived as dynamic processes, the impact of which is contingent upon recognition, interpretation, and response. Barriers impact outcomes through failures in detection, acknowledgement, and coordinated action. Barrier recognition framework is particularly useful for examining the career transition of SASD, as it highlights the importance of recognising and addressing these barriers effectively (Bross et al., 2021). Barrier recognition focuses on the processes through which obstacles are identified and addressed, instead of the presence of the obstacles. Concerning SASD, some barriers are invisible, contextual, or misattributed. For instance, administrative functioning difficulties may be analysed as a lack of motivation, while communication differences could be framed as mindset problems (Frazier et al., 2022). Some of these misrepresentations prevent suitable support and push the burden onto SASD, who have limited capacity to restructure its environments. Exploring career transition through teachers' and parents' lenses on the barriers that SASD face during the career transition process can provide a more explanatory account and persistent inequalities.

This chapter explored barriers such as personal barriers, social barriers, institutional barriers, awareness and knowledge constraints, and resource constraints. Personal barriers refer to individual-level characteristics and functional challenges that directly interfere with a student's ability to prepare for, enter, and adapt to employment or further education. SASD encounter several personal barriers during their career transition process, which significantly impact their potential to successfully incorporate into the labour force or higher education. For SASD, these barriers commonly include sensory sensitivities that make typical work environments overwhelming; communication difficulties, particularly in interviews, networking, and workplace interactions; anxiety associated with change and unfamiliar settings; and limited self-advocacy skills, which restrict the student's ability to request reasonable accommodations (Arimoro, 2019; Bross et al., 2021; McKnight-Lizotte, 2018).

SASD experience numerous sensory sensitivity challenges, which affect their potential to engage actively in various environments, including workplaces (Bross et al., 2021; Hunter & Hunter, 2022). This experience of sensitivities is associated with distress and distraction, making it difficult to focus on tasks and interact with colleagues. Another significant personal barrier SASD encounters during transition is the struggle with social interaction and communication which are vital for self-advocacy and essential for their career transition from secondary education and beyond (Santhanam & Wilson, 2024). Santhanam and Wilson reported that SASD perceived themselves as substantially lower in self-advocacy than other disabilities. These authors revealed that SASD were more or less likely to report challenges in recognising the need for academic help when compared to their peer groups. In the context of the barrier recognition viewpoint, this indicates a dual failure whereby individual student struggle to identify their own needs and institutions fail to support advocacy development (Eseadi & Diale, 2024).

Furthermore, other personal challenges SASD encounters are communication challenges that have an adverse effect on their job-seeking and early employment experiences, which are evident during job interviews which heavily rely on pragmatic language, nonverbal cues, and impression management (Kahng et al., 2023; McKnight-Lizotte, 2018). SASD exhibition of anxiety at the job interview can lead to reduced job attainment and avoidance of career exploration activities (Kahng et al., 2023; Kumazaki et al., 2019), while a deficit in nonverbal communication skills like eye contact and interpreting body language further disadvantages SASD in interview settings (Kumazaki et al., 2019). Other authors have also indicated that SASD encounter pre-employment difficulties like inadequate job interview skills and a disconnect between their interests and job tasks (Bross et al., 2021; Smith et al., 2024). These studies' results emphasised the significance of recognising communication barriers as interactional defects. In Nigeria, SASD also encounter a lot of emotional distress, which hinders their career transition (Azubuike et al., 2024).

Social barriers arise from interpersonal relationships, cultural norms, and societal attitudes that constrain students' career opportunities and transition experiences (Anderson et al., 2018; Eastman et al., 2021; Wisner-Carlson et al., 2020). For SASD, social barriers often manifest as stigma, misunderstanding, and low expectations from peers, family members, educators, and employers (Underhill et al., 2019; Zainal & Zainodin, 2025). Furthermore, social barriers play a critical role in influencing transition outcomes. Fear is well-documented in SASD literature, which adversely impacts their decision-making process regarding disclosure (Lindsay et al., 2021, 2023). The delay in disclosing SASD status could lead to poor employment outcomes, and in the absence of disclosure, SASD have low chances of receiving workplace accommodation that could help them perform better and integrate more effectively into the work environment (Hendricks, 2010; Lindsay et al., 2021). Despite the short-term benefit of non-disclosure in mitigating immediate stigma, it often raises stress and undermines job sustainability. Furthermore, at the initial stage of employment, misunderstandings between colleagues and supervisors commonly occur. In neurotypical workplace environments, implicit communication and unspoken norms are often favoured, which may not be intuitively understood by SASD. Research findings revealed that these behaviours are commonly misattributed to personality or attitude instead of neurodiversity, resulting in less favourable perceptions and reduced support (Nestorowich et al., 2022; Szechy & O'Donnell, 2025). Scholars (e.g. Fairchild et al., 2020; Nguyen et al., 2020; Thompson et al., 2018) have revealed that barriers SASD encounter encompass limited access to peer mentoring, which provides informal guidance, modelling and emotional reassurance to those who constantly experience social isolation. The unavailability of mentoring support promotes reliance on the formal systems that are frequently fragmented and under-resourced. In addition, family expectations contribute to barriers to career transition trajectory as family resources affect adolescents' career choices through mediators like personal achievements and educational expectations (Popov et al., 2013). Other social barriers experienced by SASD are social perceptions and attitudes towards them, which are constantly influenced by stereotypes and a lack of knowledge (Chen et al., 2015; Wisner-Carlson et al., 2020). As a result, SASD experience stigmatisation and hostile behaviour, further increasing their barriers in social and professional settings (Lesnykh & Zangieva, 2025; Yokota & Tanaka, 2024). For Nigerian SASD, social barriers are commonly exacerbated by cultural beliefs and societal attitudes, which can negatively affect their progress and acceptance (Azubuike et al., 2024; Hill et al., 2024; Tonnsen & Hahn, 2016). These beliefs often lead to misconceptions and marginalisation of SASD (Hill et al., 2024). Stigma and isolation are the social barriers experienced in Nigeria by SASD and families (Azubuike et al., 2024). This stigma can lead to exclusion and limited opportunities for social interaction, which are important for career transition.

Institutional barriers refer to systemic shortcomings within educational institutions, training systems, and workplaces that fail to provide adequate transition support. The failure of school and transition actors to provide accessible guidance, inclusive curriculum supports, and trained personnel relates to institutional barriers (Arimoro, 2019). For SASD, prevalent institutional obstacles often encompass the absence and/or inadequacy of career transition programmes, inadequately trained career counsellors, a deficiency in personalised transition planning, and insufficient collaboration among educational institutions, families, and employers (Hume et al., 2018; Josilowski & Morris, 2019; Stampoltzis et al., 2025). Additionally, inflexible curricula, standardised assessment methods, and learning environments that are not accessible further alienate students whose learning and transition requirements diverge from conventional expectations (Cleary et al., 2024; Waisman et al., 2022).

Moreover, educational institutions often lack autism-specific policies that address the career development needs of SASD, resulting in barriers during their transition from school to employment or further education. Ruble et al. (2013) reported that career transition services are constantly fragmented, lacking integration across school, home, and community settings, which negatively impacts the attainment of both Individualised Education Program and postsecondary goals. Inadequate postsecondary transition plan equally constitutes an institutional barrier that hinders SASD's successful transition planning (Pinder-Amaker, 2014; Von Holzen et al., 2024). Some institution reports a shortage of qualified staff and inadequate autism-specific training, which limits the ability to deliver evidence-based career transition services (Holingue et al., 2022). Poor financing reduces access to specialised staff jobs and autism-informed programmes (Corby-Edwards, 2014; Dillenburger et al., 2016; Hamrick et al., 2025). Inadequate resources characterise the Nigerian educational system, as teachers often report being unprepared and lacking the essential resources to teach and manage SASD (Onyishi, 2022). In addition, there is evidence of inconsistency in inclusive education policy implementation aimed at assisting SASD (Hill et al., 2024).

Awareness and knowledge constraints constitute an under-examined dimension of career transition difficulties for SASD in Nigeria. Awareness and knowledge constraints refer to gaps, distortions, or absences of accurate information and understanding that limit effective career planning, transition decision-making, and support provision. For SASD, these limitations manifest across various levels. On an individual basis, students might possess a restricted understanding of the career options accessible to them, the expectations within the workplace, or the rights and accommodations they are entitled to receive. Iwuji et al. (2024) found high awareness in the knowledge domain but low awareness in the perception domain, indicating a gap in understanding and practical implications for SASD. According to Hill, Fayemi and Ostrowski (2024), the lack of knowledge adversely impacts standardised training and accreditation programmes for teachers, which limits the effectiveness of Individualised Education Programmes and classroom inclusion of SASD. This limited knowledge undermines impactful transition planning as teachers and counsellors underestimate students' potential during career transition.

Furthermore, at the family level, awareness gaps negatively influence career expectations and planning, as parents may lack information about possible career pathways and available support services for SASD. Oduyemi et al. (2021) found that knowledge of SASD among parents is too poor, with many SASD internalising stigma as a result of societal attitudes. In addition, at the employment levels in Nigeria, significant evidence of a lack of awareness and understanding of SASD among employers intensifies rigid recruitment practices and reluctance to offer necessary accommodation (Bakare et al., 2015; Igwe et al., 2010; Odunsi et al.,

2017). The absence of awareness could lead to misinterpretations of communication and behaviour differences as a poor fit instead of recognising them as an aspect of SASD (Odunsi et al., 2017), as well as aggravate exclusionary practices during the hiring process (Bakare et al., 2015).

Resource constraints in the context of career transition encompass insufficient material, human, financial, and structural supports required to facilitate effective career transition. For SASD, resource constraints are evident in limited access to trained specialists, career coaches, job placement services, assistive technologies, and workplace accommodations (Hamrick et al., 2025; Nicholas et al., 2015; Sánchez Amate & Luque De La Rosa, 2025; Waisman-Nitzan et al., 2021). Schools and universities may lack funding for individualised transition planning, supported internships, or employer engagement initiatives. Families often shoulder financial and emotional costs associated with therapy, transport, and transition preparation, which can restrict post-school options (Barrett et al., 2012; Knudson, 2024; Wang et al., 2012; Zhao et al., 2023). Research evidence has shown that many Nigerian school lacks the necessary resources to support inclusive education, including physical accessibility and teaching materials (Onyishi, 2022; Umeh, 2024). These are as a result of underfunding of special educational services and a potential gap in training for inclusive education, resulting in unpreparedness of special educators to handle SASD (Dike et al., 2025; Nwosu et al., 2025). Resource limitations denote that, despite awareness of transition needs, institutions cannot often respond, schools may lack funds to train personnel for programme implementation, and employers may lack guidance and resources to make adjustments. Thus, resource constraints pose a significant barrier to the career transition of SASD.

Based on the available research evidence in the Nigerian context, there is evidence of a lacuna in the empirical studies that focus on career transition processes for SASD within secondary school contexts. The majority of research focuses on inclusion concerning access and participation within the classroom, neglecting the circumstances that arise when students exit the educational system (Azubuike et al., 2024; Hill et al., 2024; Onyishi et al., 2025). There is a scarcity of multidimensional frameworks that classify obstacles into interrelated categories. Consequently, the responses from policy and practice tend to be disjointed rather than being strategic and proactive. Few research studies explored the experiences of students, families, educators, and institutions in relation to transition barriers, which are essential for identification points of intervention programmes (Arimoro, 2019; Coombs et al., 2023; Onyishi et al., 2025). This current chapter explores the perceived barriers that affect SASD's career transition in Nigerian schools. SASD frequently graduate from schools without structured pathways and support despite policy commitments to inclusion. The unavailability of a career transition framework informed by Nigerian realities eternalises exclusion and undermines the potential contributions of

SASD. The justification for the current study is embedded in the need to capture the multidimensional nature of career transition barriers within Nigerian schools. Thus, the study provides an integrated analytical lens that reflects the complexity of transition processes because it captured personal barriers, social barriers, institutional barriers, awareness and knowledge constraints, and resource constraints from the perspectives of parents and teachers.

RESEARCH OBJECTIVES

The main objective of this study is to examine teachers' and parents' perspectives on the barriers that SASD face during the career transition process. The specific objectives are stated below.

1. To assess teachers' and parents' mean ratings of personal, social, institutional, awareness-related, and resource-related barriers faced by SASD during career transition.
2. To determine whether participants' perspectives on career transition barriers significantly differ by gender, residential location, and participant type.
3. To examine whether interaction effects exist among participant type, gender, and residential location in shaping perceptions of career transition barriers.

RESEARCH QUESTIONS

1. What are the mean levels of teachers' and parents' perspectives on personal, social, institutional, awareness-related, and resource-related barriers to career transition for SASD?
2. Do perspectives on barriers to the career transition of SASD significantly differ by gender, residential location, or participant type?
3. Are there interaction effects among participant type, gender, and residential location on participants' perceptions of career transition barriers among SASD?

THEORETICAL FRAMEWORK

The barrier recognition theory (BRT), which offers a structured lens for identifying, categorising, and interpreting the obstacles that constrain successful career transition among students with disabilities, formed the theoretical framework of this study. This theory posits that transition barriers arise from identifiable and recurrent limitations that operate across personal, social, educational, and systemic contexts (Eseadi & Diale, 2024). This theory is based on the Barrier Identification Framework, which describes barriers as clustered limitations that deviate in intensity and persistence across the lifecycle of transition, including preparation, implementation, and post-school adjustment (Yang et al., 2021). Career transition within this framework is seen as a process that is affected by the degree to which barriers are recognised early, accurately interpreted and strategically addressed. Cases such as increased risk of exclusion, misaligned expectations, and poorly designed transition supports are evidence of failure to identify barriers. The theory emphasised the conditions that precede and shape career transition outcomes and the prerequisite for effective intervention and sustainable transition planning being barrier identification. There are four major domains of BRT, which include individual factors, educational environment, social support systems, and societal and policy contexts (Eseadi & Diale, 2024). Conceptually, these domains align with the five dimensions this study explored, which include personal barriers, social barriers, institutional barriers, awareness and knowledge constraints, and resource constraints. The present study conceptualises the career transition of SASD as interconnected constraints that accumulate when recognition and response are inadequate. Therefore, this theory guides the investigation of underestimated barriers within Nigerian school contexts that impede career transition, limit opportunity structures, and weaken transition outcomes for SASD.

POLICY FRAMEWORK

The policy framework for this chapter is guided by Nigeria's Discrimination Against Persons with Disabilities (Prohibition) Act, 2018, which provides a rights-based policy basis for analysing and addressing barriers that deprive the career transition of SASD (Federal Republic of Nigeria, 2018). This study is centred on this Act, because its paramount objective is non-discrimination orientation and anticipation that public systems and service providers withdraw exclusionary conditions that limit individuals with disability, like SASD, from engaging on an equal basis, in both education and employment paths (Mohammed et al., 2025). This Act is adapted as a policy framework for interpreting the five domains of barriers this study explored. Policy implementation gap implicates awareness and knowledge constraints (Azubuike et al., 2025). Resource constraints are embedded in the systematic capacity deficits that weaken compliance, since legal protection is weak when schools lack the personnel, assistive supports, and transition services required to operationalise inclusion (Amucheazi & Nwankwo, 2020).

METHODOLOGY

Research Approach

We adopted a quantitative research approach to address the study aim of examining how teachers and parents make sense of barriers to the career transition of SASD in Nigerian school settings. A quantitative approach was suitable because our core interest was to measure the intensity of perceived barriers across clearly defined domains and to compare these perceptions across demographic groups using standardised numerical indicators. This approach also allowed us to examine response patterns in a relatively large group of participants and to subject observed differences to statistical testing.

Research Design

In order to actualise the goal of this study, we employed a cross-sectional survey design (Van der Stede, 2014). In this regard, all data were collected at a single point in time from teachers and parents who were currently involved in the education and support of SASD. This design was well-suited to mapping participants' current perceptions of personal, social or relational, institutional or structural, awareness-related, and resource-related barriers in the career transition process. The cross-sectional nature of the design meant that we did not seek to infer causal relationships or developmental trajectories. Instead, our purpose was to characterise the nature of barriers as perceived in the South-South region at the time of data collection and to examine whether these perceptions varied across gender, participant type, and residential location. A survey design was chosen over more open-ended qualitative designs because our objectives required comparability of scores, presentation of responses using means and standard deviations, and the use of analysis of variance to test for differences. The design also made it possible to explore interaction effects between participant characteristics, which would have been difficult to quantify in purely qualitative work.

Research Paradigm

The positivist research paradigm guided this research study (Ali, 2024). From this standpoint, we treated barriers to career transition as phenomena that can be approximated through quantitative data collection and measurement. This positivist paradigm was used because our research questions focused on examining whether mean scores on different barrier domains differed significantly by gender or location. Within this perspective, we subscribed to an ontological, epistemological, axiological and methodological stance in this study.

Ontological Stance

Ontologically, we assumed that there is an underlying reality to the barriers experienced by SASD during career transition. In this respect, these barriers may manifest through personal characteristics, social relationships, institutional practices, and contextual constraints. While teachers and parents may differ in individual experience, we assumed that these barriers are sufficiently stable and shared to be captured through aggregated ratings. The use of a factor analysis model in the development of the questionnaire on barriers in career transition of SASD reflects this assumption that common factor structures can be identified beneath observed responses.

Epistemological Stance

Epistemologically, we researched from the assumption that knowledge about barriers can be acquired through careful construction of measurement instruments, standardised data collection procedures, and the application of statistical analysis. We assumed that valid inferences about career transition barriers can be drawn when items display adequate reliability and when samples are systematically selected.

Axiological Stance

Axiologically, we recognised that the study is driven by a value commitment to improving the career transition experiences of SASD and to supporting teachers and parents in inclusive practice. At the same time, within a positivist stance, we sought to minimise personal bias in the production of findings. We did this by using a structured instrument, keeping the wording of items neutral, training assistants to follow standard procedures, and relying on statistical criteria rather than personal narratives to judge the presence or absence of differences. We remained reflexive about our positionality as scholars of inclusive education, and we used this reflexivity to inform the interpretation stage.

Methodological Stance

Methodologically, we followed a predominantly deductive logic that informed the identification of five key domains of career transition barriers. These domains then guided the generation of questionnaire items and analytic procedures. The questionnaire was administered to a defined population, and the resulting data were reported using descriptive statistics, reliability indices, factor analytic evidence, and analysis of variance. In keeping with a positivist viewpoint, we used established thresholds for statistical significance to evaluate our research questions.

Study Setting

The study was carried out in two states (Akwa Ibom and Cross River States) in the South-South Geopolitical Zone of Nigeria. These two coastal states are located in the Niger Delta region and share important socioeconomic and educational features. Akwa Ibom State is known for its oil and gas resources and rapid urbanisation. Urban, semi-urban, and rural communities characterise the state. Cross River State also has coastal and inland areas, with diverse communities that range from relatively urban areas to remote rural settlements. We selected Akwa Ibom and Cross River States for some reasons. First, they host a growing number of mainstream and special schools that have begun to admit students with neurodevelopmental learning needs, including ASD, in line with the national inclusive education agenda. Second, the two states also represent a realistic cross-section of the educational and service challenges in the South-South zone with regard to resource limitations, uneven infrastructure, and varied access to specialist services. Third, the presence of teacher education institutions and active education networks in these states facilitated coordinated access to schools and parent groups.

Population and Sample

The target population comprised teachers and parents who were directly involved in the education and career planning of SASD in selected schools in Akwa Ibom and Cross River States. We focused on teachers and parents of students who were approaching or had reached transition age, that is, those for whom planning for post-school work, training, or further education had become a salient issue. Teachers were drawn from mainstream and special schools, including inclusive schoolteachers, special educators, school counsellors, and other staff involved in transition planning. Parents included biological parents, guardians, or extended family members who played a central role in supporting the student's educational and career decisions. Inclusion criteria required that teacher participants had at least one year of experience in supporting a SASD in the relevant school, and that parents were able to read and respond to the questionnaire in English. Exclusion criteria were minimal but included individuals who had only casual contact with students and were not involved in any aspect of educational or transition planning.

We used a multi-stage sampling strategy to obtain a sample that reflected variation across states, school types, and residential locations, while remaining feasible within the resources of the project. At the first stage, Akwa Ibom and Cross River States were purposively selected from the South-South Geopolitical Zone because of the presence of urban, semi-urban, and rural communities, their commitment to inclusive education, and the presence of schools that admit students with neurodevelopmental learning needs. At the second stage, we identified local government areas within each state that contained a concentration of schools with inclusive or special education programmes. These local government areas were selected purposively to ensure that both urban and less resourced settings were represented.

At the third stage, schools within the selected local government areas were recruited. We approached principals and head teachers at schools that enrolled SASD. From these, schools were included where the leadership indicated that there were active efforts to support career preparation or transition activities, even if such efforts were informal. A combination of purposive and convenience sampling was used at this stage to balance representativeness with access. At the fourth stage, individual participants were recruited within participating schools. Across all stages, ninety-six participants completed the questionnaire. The sample included both teachers and parents, with female and male participants represented, and participants were drawn from urban, semi-urban, and rural residential areas. The distribution across gender and location is shown in Figure 1. The sampling of teachers and parents allowed us to capture school-based and home-based perspectives on the barriers that SASD face during career transition.

Data Collection Instrument

Data were collected using a self-developed instrument, the Questionnaire on Barriers in Career Transition of Students with Autism Spectrum Disorder (QBCT-SA). The development of this tool was informed by an extensive review of previous literature on transition planning and inclusive education. We also drew on policy documents and practitioner reports from Nigeria to ensure contextual relevance.

The QBCTSA was designed to capture perceived barriers in five conceptual domains. The first domain, personal barriers, focuses on characteristics of the student that may hinder career transition, such as sensory sensitivities, self-advocacy, time management, communication difficulties, anxiety about unfamiliar work environments, and limited flexibility in adapting to new routines. The second domain, social or relational barriers, reflects interpersonal and community-level factors, including fear of disclosure of diagnosis, misunderstandings with peers or supervisors, lack of peer mentoring, family uncertainty about career options, insufficient community understanding, and social stigma. The third domain, institutional or structural barriers, taps into features of school and service systems. Items address the presence or absence of policies that accommodate autism-related needs, the tailoring of transition goals, coordination with external agencies and employers, budget constraints, administrative delays, and gaps in staff training. The fourth domain, awareness and problem recognition, captures how far teachers and parents feel able to identify obstacles in students' lives, recognise failed or stalled transition planning, and detect whether personal or institutional issues have not been addressed. The fifth domain, resource and solution constraints, addresses the perceived difficulty of responding to recognised barriers, including feelings of uncertainty about what to do, limited access to autism-informed career resources, restrictive employer policies, and the sense that staff or budget limitations make meaningful planning difficult. The final version of the QBCTSA consists of twenty-six items distributed across these domains. Participants responded using a five-point Likert-type scale of one (strongly disagree) to five (strongly agree). Higher scores indicated stronger recognition of a given barrier. Subscale scores on the QBCTSA were calculated by summing the relevant items for each domain and dividing by the number of items, to yield mean scores that are easier to interpret.

Evidence for internal consistency and construct validity of the questionnaire is presented in the appendix (see Table 3). Cronbach's alpha values for the subscales of the QBCTSA ranged from approximately 0.77 to 0.87, and omega coefficients were in similar ranges, which indicates satisfactory internal consistency. For example, the personal barriers subscale and the institutional or structural barriers subscale both showed alpha values in the low to mid-point eight range. At the same time, awareness and problem recognition and resource and solution constraints also demonstrated acceptable reliability. Exploratory factor analysis using an oblique rotation method supported the underlying structure of the instrument (see Table 4). QBCTSA items relating to personal factors and awareness tended to load on a common factor. QBCTSA items on social and resource constraints formed a second factor. Institutional items clustered on a third factor. Factor loadings were generally moderate to strong, with many above 0.6, and uniqueness values fell within acceptable ranges. Content validity of the QBCTSA was conducted through expert reviews by three educational psychologists whose roles were to examine the items for clarity, cultural appropriateness, and coverage of key aspects of career transition. Based on their feedback, items were reworded, redundant statements were removed, and the ordering of items was adjusted to aid comprehension. Pilot testing with a small group of teachers and parents in a different state helped to refine the layout and instructions.

Data Collection Procedures

Two postgraduate research assistants assisted us with data collection. Both assistants had training in special needs education and educational psychology and had adequate years of experience working with students with disabilities. Before data collection, we provided them with additional training on the study's aims, the content of the questionnaire, ethical procedures, and strategies for engaging in a culturally sensitive manner with teachers and parents. Role play sessions were used to ensure consistency in how they introduced the study and responded to participants' questions. In the participating schools, data collection sessions were scheduled at times that minimised disruption to teaching. For teachers, questionnaires were administered during staff meetings. Teachers then completed the questionnaires individually in an office space where they could reflect on their experiences. The research assistants remained available to clarify the meaning of any items. Once questionnaires were completed, they were kept in sealed envelopes to protect confidentiality and retrieved immediately.

For parents, several pathways were used, depending on the organisation of each school. In some cases, questionnaires were distributed during parent meetings, workshops, or consultation days. After a group explanation, parents who agreed to participate completed the instruments on site and returned them to the research team before leaving. In most rural or semi-urban areas where attendance at meetings was irregular, school staff helped us send the questionnaires home through the students, together with an information sheet and consent form. Parents who chose to participate had to return the completed forms and questionnaire to the school in sealed envelopes, which the research assistants then collected. Throughout data collection, we emphasised that participation was voluntary, that there were no correct or incorrect responses, and that responses would be used only for research and transition planning purposes. No monetary incentives were provided, but school leaders and participants were informed that a summary of findings would be shared to inform local planning.

Data Analysis Procedure

After we finished data collection, questionnaires were checked for completeness and coded with anonymous identification numbers. Data entry was done using IBM SPSS, version 24.0. Double-entry procedures and random checks were employed to minimise errors. Where missing responses occurred on individual items, we examined the pattern and proportion of missingness. Because missing data were minimal and appeared to be random, we used simple imputation or case-wise deletion strategies that preserved the integrity of the dataset. First, we computed the descriptive statistics to show the central tendency and variability of each barrier domain. Means, standard deviations, standard errors, as well as 95% confidence intervals were reported for relevant subgroups, such as female and male participants. These summaries allowed us to address the first research question by identifying which domains of barriers were perceived as more salient and which appeared less prominent. Coefficients of variation were also inspected as indicators of relative variability in perceptions. The reliability indices, including Cronbach's alpha and omega coefficients, were reported to demonstrate the internal consistency of the subscales in the present sample. To address the second and third research questions, we employed analysis of variance models that included participant type, gender, and residential location as between-group factors. The main effects of each factor on perceived barriers were tested, and two-way and three-way interaction effects were also examined. A conventional significance level of 0.05 was used to judge the presence of statistically significant differences.

Ethical Considerations

The study formed part of broader research on career transition and neurodiversity that had received ethical clearance from the Faculty of Education Research Ethics Committee at the University of Johannesburg, South Africa (Sem-2-2020-057). In addition, we obtained permission from relevant education authorities and school leadership in the participating states before approaching potential participants. Informed consent was obtained in writing from all parents and teachers who participated in this study. Information sheets described the research goal, the nature of participation, the voluntary involvement, and the right to decline participation at any point without consequences. We explained that completing and returning the questionnaire would be contingent on completing the informed consent form. For parents who had limited literacy, the research assistants read the information aloud in accessible language before they decided whether to participate. We took care to ensure confidentiality. No names or school identifiers were recorded on the questionnaire. Instead, anonymous codes were used to link responses for data management. Digital datasets were password-protected and accessible only to the researchers. When reporting results, we used aggregated statistics rather than individual profiles, and we avoided describing small subgroups in ways that might make them identifiable.

Given that the topic of barriers in career transition could raise sensitive feelings about unmet needs or frustrations with service systems, participants were encouraged to share any concerns with school counsellors. In addition, we provided contact details for local support services and parent organisations that work with families of SASD.

RESULTS

Figure 1. Demographic characteristics of participants

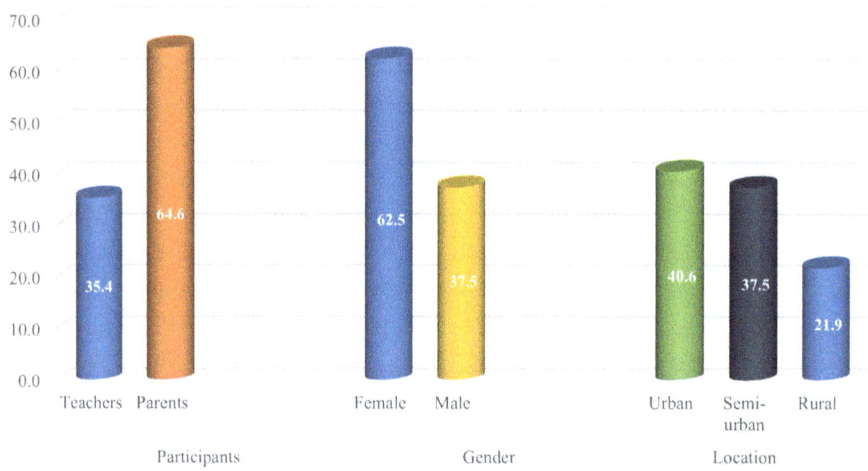

The results presentation in Figure 1 showcases a graphical illustration of participants' demographic characteristics by gender and residential locations. The demographic spread indicates that male and female participants (comprising teachers and parents) from diverse contexts contributed to the understanding of career transition barriers among SASD.

Table 1. Mean perspectives of teachers and parents on barriers to career transition of SASD

	Group	N	Mean	SD	SE	Coefficient of variation	95% Confidence Interval	
							Lower	Upper
Personal Barriers	Female	60	16.833	4.392	0.567	0.261	15.699	17.968
	Male	36	16.028	4.450	0.742	0.278	14.522	17.533
Social Barriers	Female	60	19.617	4.117	0.532	0.210	18.553	20.680
	Male	36	18.583	4.563	0.761	0.246	17.039	20.127
Institutional Barriers	Female	60	17.700	4.411	0.569	0.259	15.860	18.140
	Male	36	18.056	4.804	0.801	0.266	16.430	19.681
Awareness Constraints	Female	60	11.267	3.030	0.391	0.269	10.484	12.049
	Male	36	11.000	3.207	0.535	0.292	9.915	12.085

continued on following page

Table 1. Continued

	Group	N	Mean	SD	SE	Coefficient of variation	95% Confidence Interval	
							Lower	Upper
Resource Constraints	Female	60	11.483	3.306	0.427	0.288	10.629	12.337
	Male	36	10.500	3.158	0.526	0.301	9.432	11.568

Table 1 shows the mean scores and variability estimates for the different categories of barriers reported by participants. These results address research question one by showing how personal, social, institutional, awareness-related, and resource-related barriers were perceived. Across all categories, the means show a consistently moderate level of perceived barriers among both teachers and parents. For personal barriers, female participants reported a slightly higher mean score (M = 16.83, SD = 4.39) compared to male participants (M = 16.03, SD = 4.45). Although both groups fall within a similar range, the scores indicate that personal barriers are viewed as meaningful concerns in the transition process. The confidence intervals also show considerable overlap, which indicates that perceptions between the groups are fairly similar.

For social barriers, participants reported some of the highest mean scores among the barrier categories. Female participants had a mean score of 19.62 (SD = 4.12), while male participants scored a mean of 18.58 (SD = 4.56). The slightly higher female mean score may suggest heightened sensitivity to the social and relational challenges that emerge during transition planning. This inference is consistent with the trend seen in institutional barriers, where male participants scored marginally higher (M = 18.06, SD = 4.80) compared to female participants (M = 17.70, SD = 4.41). Although the difference is small, male participants may perceive institutional barriers as more prominent.

In the area of awareness-related barriers, both female and male participants reported relatively lower mean scores compared to the other categories. Female participants scored a mean of 11.27 (SD = 3.03), while male participants reported a mean of 11.00 (SD = 3.21). This result indicates that although participants are aware of barriers, awareness-related issues are perceived as relatively less severe compared to personal, social, or institutional barriers.

Resource constraints showed that female participants reported a mean score of 11.48 (SD = 3.31), while male participants scored slightly lower (M = 10.50, SD = 3.16). These results suggest that while participants recognise limitations in resources and solutions, these concerns are moderate and do not overshadow the stronger perceptions regarding social, institutional, or personal barriers. As such,

Table 1 shows that social barriers received the highest recognition, followed closely by institutional barriers.

Table 2. ANOVA results on differences in perspectives of teachers and parents on recognising barriers in the career transition process of SASD

Cases	**Sum of Squares**	*Df*	**Mean Square**	*F*	*p*
Participants	6.879	1	6.879	0.033	0.857
Gender	136.589	1	136.589	0.652	0.422
Location	329.990	2	164.995	0.787	0.459
Participants Gender	73.537	1	73.537	0.351	0.555
Participants Location	3.246	2	1.623	0.008	0.992
Gender Location	224.458	2	112.229	0.535	0.587
Participants Gender Location	90.692	2	45.346	0.216	0.806
Residuals	17609.190	84	209.633		

Table 2 addresses research question two by examining whether statistically significant differences exist by gender, participant type, and residential location. The results indicate that none of the main effects were statistically significant. Participant type had an F value of 0.03 ($p = .86$), which indicates no meaningful difference between teachers and parents in how they perceive barriers. Figure 2 shows participants' comparable views regarding the career transition barriers faced by SASD. Similarly, gender did not yield a significant effect ($F = 0.65$, $p = .42$), suggesting that female and male participants hold comparable views regarding the career transition barriers faced by SASD.

Figure 2. Means ratings of teachers and parents on the barriers faced by SASD during career transition

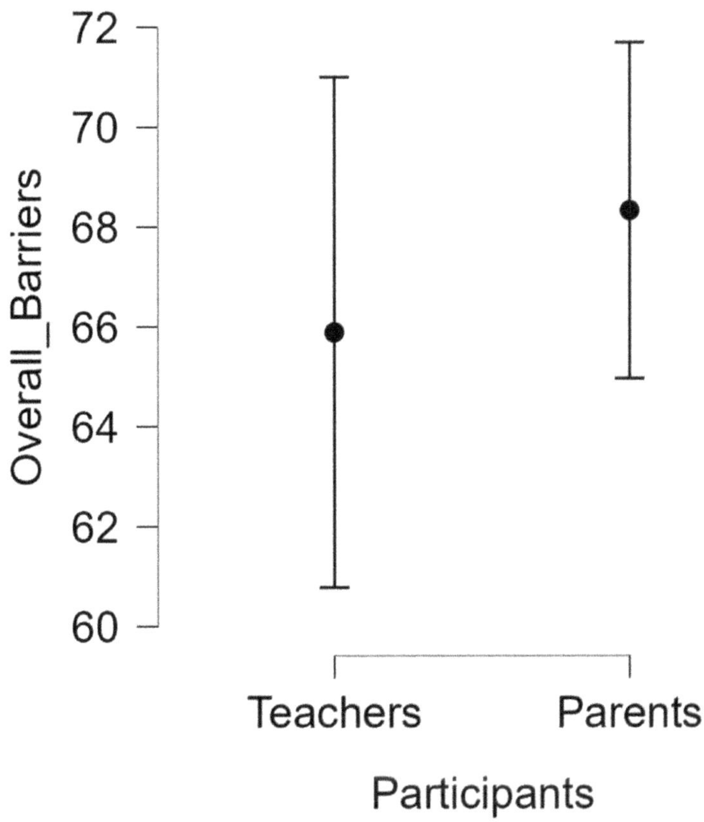

As shown in Table 2, residential location also did not yield a significant effect ($F = 0.79, p = .46$). This result implies that participants from rural, peri-urban, and urban settings reported similar barriers, highlighting a shared recognition of the challenges regardless of living context. Together, these findings show that differences in demographic characteristics do not account for statistical distinctions in perceptions, even though mean variations are descriptively seen.

Table 2 also provides insight into research question three by examining every possible combination of participant type, gender, and residential location. As shown in the results, the interaction effects between participant type and gender ($F = 0.35, p = .56$), participant type and location ($F = 0.01, p = .99$), and gender and location ($F = 0.54, p = .59$) were non-significant. The three-way interaction was also non-significant ($F = 0.22, p = .81$). These results reveal that the combination of demographic factors does not meaningfully influence how teachers and parents perceive the career transition barriers of SASD. The absence of interaction effects suggests that teachers and parents share a largely unified understanding of the barriers faced by SASD during career transition, regardless of gender or place of residence.

Figure 3. Means ratings of participants on the barriers faced by SASD during career transitioning based on gender

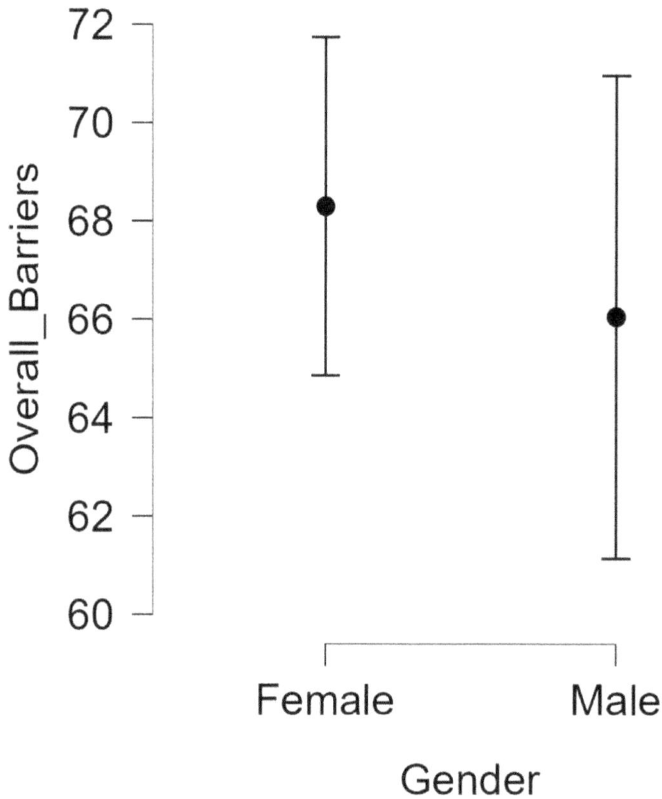

Figure 3 shows gender variations in the perceived barriers. Although the figure shows slight numerical differences between male and female participants across the barrier categories, the overall trends suggest striking similarity. Female participants rated barriers at marginally higher levels, particularly within social/relational and personal barriers. However, these ratings were small and aligned with the ANOVA findings, which show no statistically significant gender differences. The visual evidence supports the interpretation that both genders identify similar types and levels of challenges in the transition process.

Figure 4. Means ratings of participants on the barriers faced by SASD during career transition based on residential location

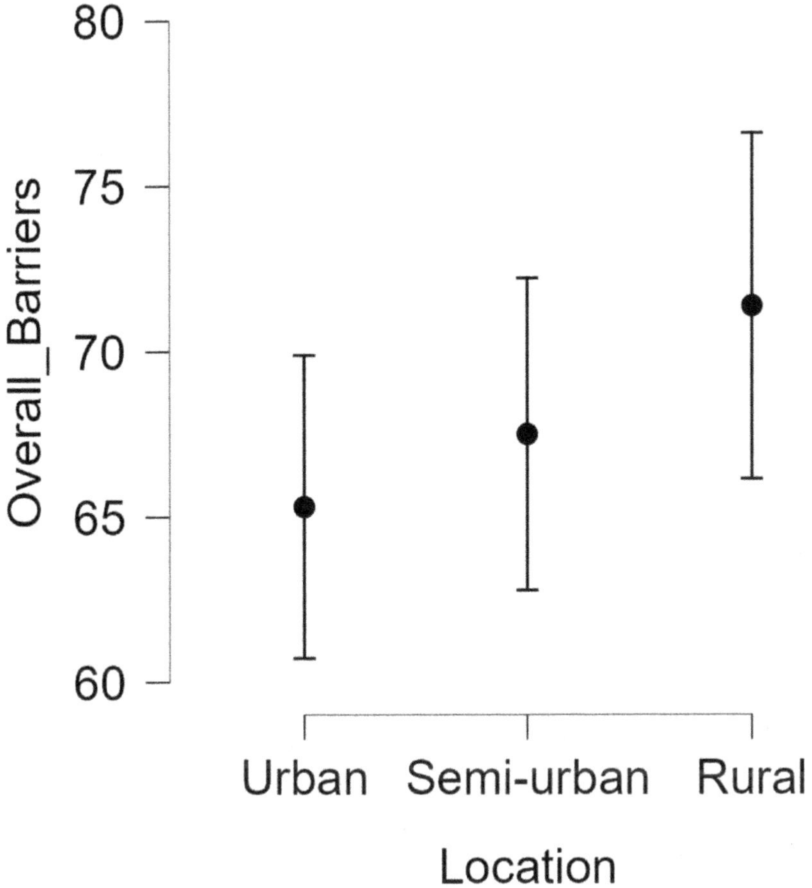

Figure 4 shows participants' mean ratings based on residential location. As seen from the figure, urban, peri-urban, and rural participants follow relatively similar patterns across all barrier categories. Although the mean values fluctuate slightly, the differences are not large enough to indicate any distinct trend or perception pattern based on location. This visual interpretation aligns with the ANOVA results, which show that location does not significantly influence how participants perceive barriers to career transition for SASD.

DISCUSSION

This current study examined the barriers to the career transition of SASD through the perspectives of teachers and parents, with particular attention to personal, social, institutional, awareness, and resource constraints. This study revealed that there was no substantial difference between teachers' and parents' perceived barriers that SASD experienced during transition. Just like teachers, parents are exposed to resource limitations and institutional gaps. These findings resonate with the recent reports that parents are likely to mention barrier-associated school practices and teacher supports (Stephenson et al., 2021). The participants affirmed the personal barriers among those career transition barries SASD experiences in Nigeria. This study has contributed to the growth of the literature with regard to barriers SASD encounter during the transition period, as it emphasised that personal barriers are salient in Nigerian schools and that transition vulnerability is a function of developmental demands. These findings aligned with the previous studies on personal barriers which show that SASD experience issues which affect their emotional regulation and overall well-being (Ayala, 2023; Izuno-Garcia & Pagán, 2024; Wisner-Carlson et al., 2020) as well as experience stress and anxiety, which makes it difficult for them to regulate their emotions (Bross et al., 2021; Kuo et al., 2018). Experiences of communication barriers are prominent among SASD in Nigeria, which aligns with the prior literature, indicating that career aspirations of SASD are often limited by social communication deficits, which manifest as difficulty in expressing interests, understanding social cues, and engaging in job interviews (Waisman-Nitzan et al., 2021; Welch et al., 2023). Challenges of coping with unfamiliar environments among SASD align with previous studies that found that such environments contribute to overwhelming feelings, leading to difficulties in adapting to new settings (Stavrou, 2024; Waisman-Nitzan et al., 2021), and the unavailability of adequate support systems in the new environment makes it challenging for them (Bross et al., 2021; Soeker, 2020). However, BRT warns against seeing personal barriers as intrinsic deficits; rather, the theory frames these challenges as barriers when environments fail to anticipate and support them (Eseadi & Diale, 2024). Therefore, this finding entails that personal barriers could be triggered by inadequate preparatory supports within schools. When structured transition planning is lacking, personal features that could be managed through anticipatory intervention become a strong barrier during school transition.

Participants recognised awareness barriers as among those challenges SASD experience during career transitioning, especially those related to limited knowledge of career pathways, rights and support mechanisms among students, families, educators and employers. Without sufficient knowledge of prospects, SASD and their families may not make informed decisions or receive appropriate support.

This study aligned with the findings of Odunsi et al. (2017), who found that most teachers have limited knowledge about ASD, which adversely affects their support for SASD. BRT emphasised that awareness is a precursor to action since barriers that are not well comprehended cannot be addressed. Identification of awareness constraints for SASD in the Nigerian schools denotes that transition difficulties may be engendered by information deficits. These findings imply that targeted training for educators and employers could enhance transition outcomes by increasing recognition of needs and accommodations.

Social barriers were identified by participants, especially those associated with stigma, peer exclusion, fear of disclosure and limited social networks. These findings are consistent with autism-related transition literature that highlights social misconceptions and negative perspectives as critical determinants of exclusion from employment opportunities (Adams et al., 2017; Barbi et al., 2024; Fisher & Taylor, 2016). The present study adds contextual depth by demonstrating that such social barriers are perceived as equally potent within Nigerian contexts, where cultural interpretations of disability may further intensify stigma. The findings support previous literature that emphasised the prevalent of stigma and isolation for SASD and their families in Nigeria, which results in social exclusion and limited opportunities for social interaction (Azubuike et al., 2024; Hill et al., 2024). BRT highlighted that social barriers are important since they impact how personal attributes are interpreted by others. In a circumstance where social environments are distinguished by low expectations, individual differences are reclassified as incompetence (Underhill et al., 2019). The affirmation of social barriers by the participants denotes that transition challenges are embedded within a relational context instead of confined to individual capability.

This study revealed that the participants perceived the institutional barrier as one of the dominant barriers SASD experience during transition, particularly those related to inadequate career guidance, limited transition programmes, lack of trained personnel and weak school-to-work linkages. These findings could be attributed to the inability of the state and federal governments of Nigeria to maintain public schools and monitor the private schools to provide necessary support for SASD transitions. This finding is consistent with the findings of Hendricks and Wehman (2009), who reported that a lack of career guidance in most schools could lead to poor performance in employment and independent living. Limited transition programmes are part of the institutional barrier that limits smooth career transition since there will be no programme that will be tailored to the unique needs of SASD (Hotez et al., 2018; Martin et al., 2021). Therefore, the link between school and work environment is constantly weak, making it challenging for SASD to transition smoothly into the workforce. This situation is heightened by inadequate interagency and multidisciplinary collaboration required to address the varying levels of need of SASD (Elias et al., 2019; Izuno-Garcia & Pagán, 2024; Kuo et al., 2018). This result supported the key principle of BRT that barriers continue to exist because the structured system has failed to recognise and address them systematically (Eseadi & Diale, 2024). The participants concurred that the schools lacked the equipment to facilitate career transition, which indicated that institutional accountability towards career still not developed.

Participants uniformly converged that resources were also salient, particularly those relating to limited funding, absence of specialised personnel, lack of assistive supports, and scarcity of structured transition services for SASD. Lack of resources affects the households and schools of SASD, which limits the necessary preparation for a successful career transition. This finding could be attributed to the high poverty rate that is ravaging the country. The majority of Nigerian households live below the global threshold of poverty, and this adversely affects their children with ASD in respect to transition (Anthony et al., 2025; Azubuike et al., 2024; Bello-Mojeed et al., 2016). Hill et al. (2024) reported that resource barriers contribute to inadequate infrastructure, which hinders services for SASD, as well as affects the availability and quality of individualised education programmes and classroom inclusion. These findings align with the report of a recent study, which revealed that financial constraints towards SASD complicate access to necessary service and support (Azubuike et al., 2024; Razaq-Shuaib, 2025). BRT sees resource constraints as a structural constraint that converts recognised needs into unmet needs. The findings indicate that Nigerian schools may be operating within systemic constraints that limit their capacity to respond even when barriers are acknowledged (Odunsi et al., 2017). These highlight the importance of policy and investment in translating recognition into action.

Furthermore, there were no significant differences in the responses of the participants based on participants' types, gender, and location. This finding indicates a high level of agreement between teachers and parents in how barriers are perceived in Nigeria. This finding aligned with the previous studies, which revealed that teachers and parents emphasised inadequate resources and support systems as significant barriers for career transition (Ain, 2025; Stephenson et al., 2021; Strnadová et al., 2016). The absence of participant type, gender, and residential location effects suggests that perceived barriers are structurally embedded rather than demographically contingent. This finding resonates with the report, which revealed that structural constraints within the educational and vocational systems create the same challenges for all stakeholders (Strnadová et al., 2016; Von Holzen et al., 2024). Furthermore, this finding is theoretically unique in the sense that it revealed a different view from the existing empirical evidence, which established that teachers and parents hold different views because of their different roles and points of engagement during the career transition of SASD (Ain, 2025; Lambert et al., 2023; Stephenson et al., 2021).

This study revealed that there are no significant interaction effects based on participants' type, gender, and residential location on the perception of career transition barriers for SASD. This finding points to the structural rather than situational nature of transition barriers. This study aligned with the literature, which reported that barriers are interconnected and impact students regardless of specific demographic groups (Thiem & Dasgupta, 2022). The BRT offers a useful explanation for this by highlighting that when barriers are systemic, their identification does not deviate markedly across demographic subgroups (Eseadi & Diale, 2024). However, identified barriers in the Nigerian schools are characteristics of the career transition landscape that SASD often experienced. The lack of interaction effects clearly affirmed that career transition barriers for SASD are embedded within the broader educational and social system.

The combination of the results of all three research questions reveals a coherent trend that supports the main tenets of BRT. First, the barriers to career transition among SASD are multifaceted, comprising personal, social, institutional, awareness-related, and resource-related barriers. Second, these barriers are always recognised by the major stakeholders, which implies that they are not hidden. Third, any differences in recognition do not reflect positioning of the stakeholders, and lastly, the fact that barriers still exist even after recognition highlights systemic inertia.

The findings of this study have both practical and policy implications. First, these findings reinforce the use of BRT as a framework for analysing transition processes in complex contexts. BRT links recognition to accountability. If the career transition barriers for SASD are consistently recognised, accountability changes from individuals to institutions and systems. This reframing is extremely essential in a situation where SASD are expected to adapt to rigid environments without mutual adjustment. In policy terms, the results indicate that to enhance the outcomes of career transition, there is a need to shift between access-based inclusion and outcome-based accountability. Policies requiring inclusive education without defining transition supports risk recreating exclusion during the transition period. The identification of institutional and resource barriers suggest that career guidance, training, transition planning, and employer engagement should be prioritised as the main aspects of inclusion during policy implementation. The educational implications of these findings highlight the need for early and sustained career transition. For the personal barriers to be addressed, it requires embedding self-advocacy, executive functioning, and career exploration within the curriculum. Furthermore, to address the social barriers of SASD for career transition, intentional efforts to challenge stigma, build peer networks, and support safe disclosure are required. The institutional barriers require coordination between schools, vocational providers, and employers to create supported pathways for SASD.

CONCLUSIONS

This chapter analysed barriers to career transition of SASD using the lenses of teachers and parents. The results of this study showed that the barriers of career transition are multidimensional, including personal, social, institutional, awareness-related, and resource-related barriers. These barriers were consistently recognised by key stakeholders, underscoring their visibility and persistence within school contexts. The research adds value to the literature by providing empirical evidence in a Nigerian population, broadens the research about autism-related career transition, and offers a coherent analytical framework through which the barriers to transition can be understood. The results highlight the significance of policy and practice that prioritises the importance of structured transition planning, professional capacity building, and resource allocation. Addressing systemic barriers is critical towards altering career transition from a direction of vulnerability into meaningful participation and inclusion among SASD.

REFERENCE

Adams, R., Bishop, S., & Taylor, J. L. (2017). Negative Peer Experiences in Adolescents With Autism Spectrum Disorders. *International Review of Research in Developmental Disabilities, 52*, 75–107. DOI: 10.1016/bs.irrdd.2017.07.003

Ain, G. (2025). Parental involvement and barriers in transitional services for students with autism spectrum disorder in Saudi schools: A mixed-methods study. *Frontiers in Education, 10*, 1647206. DOI: 10.3389/feduc.2025.1647206

Alfawzan, S., & Almulhim, N. (2024). Barriers and facilitators to implementing transition services for students with intellectual disabilities in the kingdom of Saudi Arabia: A systematic review. *Journal of Intellectual Disabilities*, 17446295241301853. Advance online publication. DOI: 10.1177/17446295241301853

Ali, I. M. (2024). A Guide for Positivist Research Paradigm: From Philosophy to Methodology. *Idealogy Journal, 9*(2), 187–196. DOI: 10.24191/idealogy.v9i2.596

Amucheazi, C., & Nwankwo, C. M. (2020). Accessibility to infrastructure and disability rights in Nigeria: An analysis of the potential of the discrimination against persons with disability (prohibition) act 2018. *Commonwealth Law Bulletin, 46*(4), 689–710. DOI: 10.1080/03050718.2020.1781674

Anderson, K. A., Sosnowy, C., Kuo, A. A., & Shattuck, P. T. (2018). Transition of individuals with autism to adulthood: A review of qualitative studies. *Pediatrics, 141*(Supplement_4), S318–S327. DOI: 10.1542/peds.2016-4300I

Anthony, C. S., Agbo, C. E., Ogieuhi, I. J., Ajekiigbe, V. O., Agu, M. C., Ayomide, J. H., Oyetola, E. O., Adejumo, T. P., Umenzeakor, K. H., Akinmeji, O., Ajimotokan, O. I., Matthew, O. A., & Ikekwere, J. C. (2025). Caregiving for children with autism in africa: A scoping review of socioeconomic impact with a call for intersectoral collaboration. *European Child & Adolescent Psychiatry*. Advance online publication. DOI: 10.1007/s00787-025-02843-1

Arimoro, A. E. (2019). Are they not nigerians? The obligation of the state to end discriminatory practices against persons with disabilities. *International Journal of Discrimination and the Law, 19*(2), 89–109. DOI: 10.1177/1358229119846764

Ayala, K. (2023). LEADERS: A Psychoeducational Support Group for College-Bound High School Students with Autism Spectrum Disorder (ASD). *Journal of Applied School Psychology, 39*(4), 397–412. DOI: 10.1080/15377903.2023.2221201

Azubuike, A. O., Azubuike, P. C., Onyekachi, E. L., Enyam, M. O., Akinreni, T., Abuo, J., Ogbonna, C. K., Timothy, P. N., Uchegbu, E. R., & Adai, G. S. (2024). Experiences and unmet needs among caregivers of children living with autism spectrum disorder in Nigeria: A qualitative study using the socio-ecological model. *Discover Social Science and Health*, *4*(1), 77. Advance online publication. DOI: 10.1007/s44155-024-00141-w

Azubuike, P. C., Akinreni, T., Adai, S. G., Ogbonna, C. K., Abba, M. E., Udofia, M. D., Odo, O. J., Nwadiche, M., & Imo, U. F. (2025). Equity and social justice perspectives on disability inclusion in healthcare services in Nigeria. *Communications Medicine*, *5*(1), 1–7. DOI: 10.1038/s43856-025-01070-8

Bakare, M. O., Tunde-Ayinmode, M. F., Adewuya, A. O., Bello-Mojeed, M. A., Sale, S., James, B. O., Yunusa, M. A., Obindo, J. T., Igwe, M. N., Odinka, P. C., Okafor, C. J., Oshodi, Y. O., Okonoda, K. M., Munir, K. M., & Orovwigho, A. O. (2015). Recognition of Autism Spectrum Disorder (ASD) symptoms and knowledge about some other aspects of ASD among final year medical students in Nigeria, Sub-Saharan Africa. *BMC Research Notes*, *8*(1), 1–8. DOI: 10.1186/s13104-015-1433-0

Barbi, K. B. S., Serralvo, E. R., Pavão, G. M., Bitencort, L. P., Messias, J. C. C., & Labarthe, J. (2024). Challenges of social interaction of people with autism in the job market. *Ciencias Psicológicas (Montevideo)*, *18*(1). Advance online publication. DOI: 10.22235/cp.v18i1.3283

Barrett, B., Byford, S., Sharac, J., Hudry, K., Leadbitter, K., Temple, K., Aldred, C., Slonims, V., Green, J., Bourne, K., Blazey, L., Holt, C., Kapadia, D., MacDonald, W., Pickles, A., White, L., Houghton, T., Taylor, C., Cutress, A., & Charman, T. (2012). Service and wider societal costs of very young children with autism in the UK. *Journal of Autism and Developmental Disorders*, *42*(5), 797–804. DOI: 10.1007/s10803-011-1306-x

Bello-Mojeed, M., Ani, C., Lagunju, I., & Omigbodun, O. (2016). Feasibility of parent-mediated behavioural intervention for behavioural problems in children with Autism Spectrum Disorder in Nigeria: A pilot study. *Child and Adolescent Psychiatry and Mental Health*, *10*(1), 1–8. DOI: 10.1186/s13034-016-0117-4

Bross, L. A., Leko, M., Patry, M. B., & Travers, J. C. (2021). Barriers to competitive integrated employment of young adults with autism spectrum disorder. *Education and Training in Autism and Developmental Disabilities*, *56*(4), 394–408. DOI: 10.1177/215416472105600403

Chen, J. L., Leader, G., Sung, C., & Leahy, M. (2015). Trends in Employment for Individuals with Autism Spectrum Disorder: A Review of the Research Literature. *Review Journal of Autism and Developmental Disorders*, *2*(2), 115–127. DOI: 10.1007/s40489-014-0041-6

Chun, J., Kuo, H. J., Curtiss, S. L., Lee, G. K., Lee, H., & Awadu, J. (2023). The interplay of supports and barriers during the transition to adulthood for youth on the autism spectrum. *Disability and Rehabilitation*, *45*(18), 2879–2889. DOI: 10.1080/09638288.2022.2112097

Cleary, M., West, S., McLean, L., Johnston-Devin, C., Kornhaber, R., & Hungerford, C. (2024). When the Education System and Autism Collide: An Australian Qualitative Study Exploring School Exclusion and the Impact on Parent Mental Health. *Issues in Mental Health Nursing*, *45*(5), 468–476. DOI: 10.1080/01612840.2024.2328251

Coombs, E. C., Vincent, J., McMorris, C. A., & Ames, M. E. (2023). Barriers and facilitators to supporting Canadian autistic postsecondary students: Experiences of accessible learning staff and administrators. *Research in Autism Spectrum Disorders*, *109*, 102260. Advance online publication. DOI: 10.1016/j.rasd.2023.102260

Corby-Edwards, A. K. (2014). The Combating Autism Act: Overview and funding. In D. Harlow (Ed.), *The Combating Autism Act: Elements, Funding and Analyses* (pp. 1–18). Nova Science Publishers, Inc.

Dike, N., D'Ambruoso, L., Morgan, H. M., Skea, Z. C., & Ekpenyong, B. N. (2025). How does the Nigerian health system serve people living with disabilities? A socio-ecological analysis on people living with visual impairment. *Global Health Action*, *18*(1), 1–23. DOI: 10.1080/16549716.2025.2581456

Dillenburger, K., McKerr, L., Jordan, J.-A., & Keenan, M. (2016). Staff training in autism: The one-eyed wo/man…. *International Journal of Environmental Research and Public Health*, *13*(7), 716. DOI: 10.3390/ijerph13070716

Eastman, K., Zahn, G., Ahnupkana, W., & Havumaki, B. (2021). Small Town Transition Services Model: Postsecondary Planning for Students With Autism Spectrum Disorder. *Rural Special Education Quarterly*, *40*(3), 157–166. DOI: 10.1177/87568705211027978

Eilenberg, J. S., Paff, M., Harrison, A. J., & Long, K. A. (2019). Disparities Based on Race, Ethnicity, and Socioeconomic Status Over the Transition to Adulthood Among Adolescents and Young Adults on the Autism Spectrum: A Systematic Review. *Current Psychiatry Reports*, *21*(5), 32. Advance online publication. DOI: 10.1007/s11920-019-1016-1

Elias, R., Muskett, A. E., & White, S. W. (2019). Educator perspectives on the post-secondary transition difficulties of students with autism. *Autism*, *23*(1), 260–264. DOI: 10.1177/1362361317726246

Eseadi, C., & Diale, B. M. (2024). *Perspectives on career transitioning of students with hearing impairments*. IGI Global., DOI: 10.4018/979-8-3693-2631-2

Fairchild, L. A., Powell, M. B., Gadke, D. L., Spencer, J. C., & Stratton, K. K. (2020). Increasing social engagement among college students with autism. *Advances in Autism*, *6*(2), 83–93. DOI: 10.1108/AIA-09-2019-0030

Federal Republic of Nigeria. (2018). *Discrimination Against Persons with Disabilities (Prohibition) Act, 2018.*

Fisher, M. H., & Taylor, J. L. (2016). Let's talk about it: Peer victimization experiences as reported by adolescents with autism spectrum disorder. *Autism*, *20*(4), 402–411. DOI: 10.1177/1362361315585948

Frazier, T. W., Crowley, E., Shih, A., Vasudevan, V., Karpur, A., Uljarevic, M., & Cai, R. Y. (2022). Associations between executive functioning, challenging behavior, and quality of life in children and adolescents with and without neurodevelopmental conditions. *Frontiers in Psychology*, *13*, 1022700. DOI: 10.3389/fpsyg.2022.1022700

Hamrick, J., Prueitt, N., & Favela, A. (2025). Supporting Special Education Practice for Students with ASD in Rural Districts. In *Springer International Handbooks of Education: Vol. Part F910* (pp. 89–124). Springer Nature. DOI: 10.1007/978-3-031-60258-0_5

Hendricks, D. (2010). Employment and adults with autism spectrum disorders: Challenges and strategies for success. *Journal of Vocational Rehabilitation*, *32*(2), 125–134. DOI: 10.3233/JVR-2010-0502

Hill, D. A., Fayemi, A., & Ostrowski, S. (2024). The Evolution of Services for Children with Autism and Developmental Disabilities in Nigeria. *International Journal of Disability Development and Education*, *71*(7), 1116–1132. DOI: 10.1080/1034912X.2023.2291570

Holingue, C., Jang, Y., Azad, G., & Landa, R. (2022). Key Stakeholder Perspectives on Obstacles to an Autism-Specific Medicaid Waiver Service Delivery Model. *Journal of Applied Research in Intellectual Disabilities*, *35*(1), 205–216. DOI: 10.1111/jar.12940

Hotez, E., Shane-Simpson, C., Obeid, R., DeNigris, D., Siller, M., Costikas, C., Pickens, J., Massa, A., Giannola, M., D'Onofrio, J., & Gillespie-Lynch, K. (2018). Designing a summer transition program for incoming and current college students on the autism spectrum: A participatory approach. *Frontiers in Psychology*, *9*(FEB), 46. Advance online publication. DOI: 10.3389/fpsyg.2018.00046

Hume, K., Dykstra Steinbrenner, J., Sideris, J., Smith, L., Kucharczyk, S., & Szidon, K. (2018). Multi-informant assessment of transition-related skills and skill importance in adolescents with autism spectrum disorder. *Autism*, *22*(1), 40–50. DOI: 10.1177/1362361317722029

Hunter, S. T., & Hunter, M. D. (2022). PERFORMANCE MANAGEMENT AND CAREER DEVELOPMENT FOR EMPLOYEES WITH AUTISM: Uncovering Hidden Requirements. In Bruyère, S. M., & Colella, A. (Eds.), *Neurodiversity in the Workplace: Interests, Issues, and Opportunities* (pp. 211–240). Taylor and Francis., DOI: 10.4324/9781003023616-9

Igwe, M. N., Bakare, M. O., Agomoh, A. O., Onyeama, G. M., & Okonkwo, K. O. (2010). Factors influencing knowledge about childhood autism among final year undergraduate Medical, Nursing and Psychology students of University of Nigeria, Enugu State, Nigeria. *Italian Journal of Pediatrics*, *36*(1), 44. DOI: 10.1186/1824-7288-36-44

Iwuji, U., Hamrick, J., Wheeler, K., Ihenagwam, C., Hixson, J., Kelly, D., Duru, H., Ademulegun, T., Banda, D., & Hilbert, S. (2024). Educators' knowledge of and perceptions towards students with autism in Nigeria. *International Journal of Developmental Disabilities*, 1–11. Advance online publication. DOI: 10.1080/20473869.2024.2359137

Izuno-Garcia, A. K., & Pagán, A. F. (2024). Neurodiversity-Affirming Entrepreneurship: Improving Work Experiences for Young Adults on the Spectrum. In Markel, K. S., Hanson, M. E., Giannantonio, C. M., & Hurley-Hanson, A. E. (Eds.), *Neurodiversity and Entrepreneurship* (pp. 123–132). Emerald Publishing., DOI: 10.1108/978-1-83753-798-320241006

Josilowski, C. S., & Morris, W. A. (2019). A Qualitative Exploration of Teachers' Experiences with Students with Autism Spectrum Disorder Transitioning and Adjusting to Inclusion: Impacts of the Home and School Collaboration. *The Qualitative Report*, *24*(6), 1275–1286. DOI: 10.46743/2160-3715/2019.3757

Kahng, S., Butler, C., Kronfli, F. R., Zaki-Scarpa, C., Boragi, B., & Scott, J. (2023). An individualized approach to teaching adults with autism to successfully navigate job interviews via remote instruction. *Journal of Applied Behavior Analysis*, *56*(2), 352–364. DOI: 10.1002/jaba.977

Kim, H., Ruppar, A. L., Baker, D., Kim, S., & Yu, B. (2023). Interweaving disentangled: Korean American students with autism go to college. *Race, Ethnicity and Education*, *26*(7), 892–913. DOI: 10.1080/13613324.2020.1842349

Knudson, S. (2024). Transition planning and perceptions of support in an autism spectrum disorder resource program. *Preventing School Failure*, *68*(3), 220–230. DOI: 10.1080/1045988X.2023.2207482

Kumazaki, H., Muramatsu, T., Yoshikawa, Y., Corbett, B. A., Matsumoto, Y., Higashida, H., Yuhi, T., Ishiguro, H., Mimura, M., & Kikuchi, M. (2019). Job interview training targeting nonverbal communication using an android robot for individuals with autism spectrum disorder. *Autism*, *23*(6), 1586–1595. DOI: 10.1177/1362361319827134

Kuo, A. A., Crapnell, T., Lau, L., Anderson, K. A., & Shattuck, P. (2018). Stakeholder perspectives on research and practice in autism and transition. *Pediatrics*, *141*(Supplement_4), S293–S299. DOI: 10.1542/peds.2016-4300F

Lambert, A., McKelvey, S., Getzel, E. E., Belluscio, T., & Parthemos, C. (2023). Perspectives on the implementation of pre-ETS services: Identification of barriers and facilitators to early career planning for youth with disabilities. *Journal of Vocational Rehabilitation*, *58*(2), 103–114. DOI: 10.3233/JVR-230001

Lee, H., Lee, G. K., Chun, J., Kuo, H.-J., Curtiss, S. L., & Okyere, C. (2023). Perspectives of Autistic Emerging Adults, Parents, and Practitioners on the Transition to Adulthood. *Journal of Child and Family Studies*, *32*(3), 938–950. DOI: 10.1007/s10826-022-02430-x

Lesnykh, K. A., & Zangieva, I. K. (2025). Factors Determining the Perceptions and Attitudes of People with Autism Spectrum Disorder in Russia. *Mir Rossii*, *34*(3), 146–166. DOI: 10.17323/1811-038X-2025-34-3-146-166

Lindsay, S., Cagliostro, E., & Osten, V. (2023). Exploring autistic workplace disability disclosure: Youth and employer perspectives. In Barret, S. B. (Ed.), *People with Disabilities: Perceptions, Stigmas and Stereotypes* (pp. 145–170). Nova Science Publishers, Inc.

Lindsay, S., Osten, V., Rezai, M., & Bui, S. (2021). Disclosure and workplace accommodations for people with autism: A systematic review. *Disability and Rehabilitation*, *43*(5), 597–610. DOI: 10.1080/09638288.2019.1635658

Luwei, W., & Huimin, M. (2024). From jobs to careers: Drivers and barriers to career development in emerging labor markets. *Frontiers in Sociology*, *9*, 1486871. DOI: 10.3389/fsoc.2024.1486871

Martin, T., Dixon, R., Verenikina, I., & Costley, D. (2021). Transitioning primary school students with Autism Spectrum Disorder from a special education setting to a mainstream classroom: Successes and difficulties. *International Journal of Inclusive Education*, *25*(5), 640–655. DOI: 10.1080/13603116.2019.1568597

McKnight-Lizotte, M. (2018). Work-Related Communication Barriers for Individuals with Autism: A Pilot Qualitative Study. *Australian Journal of Rehabilitation Counselling*, *24*(1), 12–26. DOI: 10.1017/jrc.2018.4

Milen, M. T., & Nicholas, D. B. (2017). Examining transitions from youth to adult services for young persons with autism. *Social Work in Health Care*, *56*(7), 636–648. DOI: 10.1080/00981389.2017.1318800

Mohammed, O. O., Ayeni, V. O., & Fowowe, A. I. (2025). A Comparative Analysis of the Discrimination Against Persons with Disabilities (Prohibition) Act 2018, and The United Kingdom Equality Act 2010: Prospects and Challenges. *East African Journal of Law, Policy and Globalization, 2*(1), 24–43. https://journal.kiut.ac.tz/index.php/eajlpg/article/view/192

Nestorowich, D. L., Lupien, S. P., & Madaus Knapp, V. (2022). Perceptions of Behaviors Associated with ASD in Others: Knowledge of the Diagnosis Increases Empathy and Improves Perceptions of Warmth and Competence. *European Journal of Investigation in Health, Psychology and Education*, *12*(11), 1594–1606. DOI: 10.3390/ejihpe12110112

Nguyen, L., Jack, S., Ketelaar, M., Di Rezze, B., Soper, A. K., & Gorter, J. W. (2020). Understanding the essential components and experiences of youth with autism spectrum disorders in peer mentorship programmes during the transition to adulthood: A qualitative meta-ethnography. *Child: Care, Health and Development*, *46*(6), 667–681. DOI: 10.1111/cch.12804

Nicholas, D. B., Attridge, M., Zwaigenbaum, L., & Clarke, M. (2015). Vocational support approaches in autism spectrum disorder: A synthesis review of the literature. *Autism*, *19*(2), 235–245. DOI: 10.1177/1362361313516548

Nwosu, K. C., Letzel-Alt, V., & Pozas, M. (2025). From theory to practice: Exploring Nigerian student teachers' experiences of managing learners with special needs in inclusive classrooms. *British Journal of Special Education, 52*(4), 511–522. DOI: 10.1111/1467-8578.70042

Odunsi, R., Preece, D., & Garner, P. (2017). Nigerian teachers' understanding of autism spectrum disorder: A comparative study of teachers from urban and rural areas of Lagos state. *Disability, CBR and Inclusive Development, 28*(3), 98–114. DOI: 10.5463/dcid.v28i3.637

Oduyemi, A. Y., Okafor, I. P., Eze, U. T., Akodu, B. A., & Roberts, A. A. (2021). Internalization of stigma among parents of children with autism spectrum disorder in Nigeria: A mixed method study. *BMC Psychology, 9*(1), 182. DOI: 10.1186/s40359-021-00687-3

Onyishi, C. N. (2022). Teachers' use of inclusive education practices for learners with neuro-developmental disorders in Enugu State, Nigeria. *Ikenga, 23*(3), 1–16. DOI: 10.53836/ijia/2022/23/3/003

Onyishi, C. N., Okpoko, C. C., & Victor-Aigbodion, V. (2025). Teachers' awareness and perceptions of inclusive education for learners with autism: Implications for the campaign against stigma. *Ikenga, 26*(1), 51–80. DOI: 10.53836/ijia/2025/26/1/004

Ookeditse, G. B., Habulezi, J., Batsalelwang, K. J. P., & Molemane, N. J. (2024). Postsecondary transition barriers for students with disabilities in two neighboring school regions in Botswana. *Preventing School Failure, 68*(1), 37–49. DOI: 10.1080/1045988X.2022.2153784

Pinder-Amaker, S. (2014). Identifying the unmet needs of college students on the autism spectrum. *Harvard Review of Psychiatry, 22*(2), 125–137. DOI: 10.1097/HRP.0000000000000032

Popov, D., Tyumeneva, Y., & Larina, G. (2013). Life after 9th grade: How do personal achievements of students and their family resources influence life trajectories. *Voprosy Obrazovaniya / Educational Studies Moscow, 2013*(4), 310–334. DOI: 10.17323/1814-9545-2013-4-310-334

Razaq-Shuaib, B. (2025). Understanding the Impact of Early Childhood and Primary Education for Children with Neurodevelopmental Disabilities on Parents in Nigeria. *BMJ Paediatrics Open, 9*(1), 1–9. DOI: 10.1136/bmjpo-2025-003909

Ruble, L. A., Parsons, B. M., McGrew, J. H., & Hoffman, B. (2013). COMPASS Across Settings. In Ruble, L. A., & McGrew, J. H. (Eds.), *Compass and Innovative Education for Students with Autism* (pp. 191–205). Springer International Publishing., DOI: 10.1007/978-3-031-31395-0_9

Sánchez Amate, J. J., & Luque De La Rosa, A. (2025). Research on the Inclusion of Students with Autism Spectrum Disorder: Educational Strategies, Attitudes, and Resources from an Integrative Systematic Review. *Journal of Cultural Analysis and Social Change*, *10*(2), 2006–2016. DOI: 10.64753/jcasc.v10i2.1899

Santhanam, S. P., & Wilson, K. (2024). A Comparison of Autistic and Non-Autistic College Students' Perceived Challenges and Engagement in Self-Advocacy. *American Journal of Speech-Language Pathology*, *33*(3), 1471–1484. DOI: 10.1044/2024_AJSLP-22-00381

Scott, R. D. (2014). The treatment barrier. In Walrond-Skinner, S. (Ed.), *Developments in Family Therapy: Theories and Applications since 1948* (pp. 30–59). Taylor and Francis., DOI: 10.4324/9781315814742-13

Smith, M. J., Merle, J. L., Baker-Ericzén, M., Sherwood, K., Bornheimer, L. A., Ross, B., Harrington, M., Sharma, A., Brown, C., Gordon, T., Telfer, D., Reese, J., Hirst, J., Oulvey, E. A., Dignadice, V., Williams, E.-D., Magaña, S., Hume, K., Sung, C., & Smith, J. D. (2024). A type 1 hybrid multi-site randomized controlled trial protocol for evaluating virtual interview training among autistic transition-age youth. *Contemporary Clinical Trials Communications*, *42*, 101384. Advance online publication. DOI: 10.1016/j.conctc.2024.101384

Soeker, M. S. (2020). A descriptive, qualitative study of the challenges that individuals with Autism Spectrum Disorder experience when transitioning from skills training programs into the open labor market in Cape Town, South Africa. *Work (Reading, Mass.)*, *65*(4), 733–747. DOI: 10.3233/WOR-203127

Söner, O., & Yılmaz, O. (2025). Exploring the associations of career transition components with adolescents' career decision-making self-efficacy and anxiety. *BMC Psychology*, *13*(1), 1115. DOI: 10.1186/s40359-025-03479-1

Stampoltzis, A., Peristeri, E., & Kalouri, R. (2025). Career counselors' attitudes about employment-related skills of individuals with autism spectrum disorders in Greece. *Frontiers in Education*, *10*, 1662929. Advance online publication. DOI: 10.3389/feduc.2025.1662929

Stavrou, K. (2024). Independent Living for Individuals With Autism. In Dimitriadou, I., Vasileiadis, I., & Koutras, S. (Eds.), *Tools for Promoting Independent Living Skills in Individuals with Disabilities* (pp. 151–170). IGI Global., DOI: 10.4018/979-8-3693-6026-2.ch008

Stephenson, J., Browne, L., Carter, M., Clark, T., Costley, D., Martin, J., Williams, K., Bruck, S., Davies, L., & Sweller, N. (2021). Facilitators and Barriers to Inclusion of Students With Autism Spectrum Disorder: Parent, Teacher, and Principal Perspectives. *Australasian Journal of Special and Inclusive Education*, *45*(1), 1–17. DOI: 10.1017/jsi.2020.12

Strnadová, I., Cumming, T. M., & Danker, J. (2016). Transitions for Students with Intellectual Disability and/or Autism Spectrum Disorder: Carer and Teacher Perspectives. *Australasian Journal of Special Education*, *40*(2), 141–156. DOI: 10.1017/jse.2016.2

Szechy, K. A., & O'Donnell, L. A. (2025). Autism Knowledge Matters: Perceptions of an Autistic Employee's Competency and Attitudes Toward Workplace Social Inclusion. *Autism in Adulthood: Challenges and Management*, aut.2024.0261. Advance online publication. DOI: 10.1089/aut.2024.0261

Thiem, K. C., & Dasgupta, N. (2022). From Precollege to Career: Barriers Facing Historically Marginalized Students and Evidence-Based Solutions. *Social Issues and Policy Review*, *16*(1), 212–251. DOI: 10.1111/sipr.12085

Thompson, C., Falkmer, T., Evans, K., Bölte, S., & Girdler, S. (2018). A realist evaluation of peer mentoring support for university students with autism. *British Journal of Special Education*, *45*(4), 412–434. DOI: 10.1111/1467-8578.12241

Tonnsen, B. L., & Hahn, E. R. (2016). Middle School Students' Attitudes Toward a Peer with Autism Spectrum Disorder. *Focus on Autism and Other Developmental Disabilities*, *31*(4), 262–274. DOI: 10.1177/1088357614559213

Umeh, N. C. (2024). Access to Inclusive Education for Learners with Disabilities in Nigeria: Discursive Interpretation of Findings. In *Ius Gentium* (Vol. 117, pp. 47–71). Springer Science and Business Media B.V. DOI: 10.1007/978-3-031-64549-5_3

Underhill, J. C., Ledford, V., & Adams, H. (2019). Autism stigma in communication classrooms: Exploring peer attitudes and motivations toward interacting with atypical students. *Communication Education*, *68*(2), 175–192. DOI: 10.1080/03634523.2019.1569247

Van der Stede, W. A. (2014). A manipulationist view of causality in cross-sectional survey research. *Accounting, Organizations and Society*, *39*(7), 567–574. DOI: 10.1016/j.aos.2013.12.001

Von Holzen, A. V., Skoning, S. N., Fisher, T. A., Clark, D. M., & Cook, J. A. (2024). Factors of Career Development Impacting Transition for Young Adults with Autism Spectrum Disorder. *Exceptionality Education International*, *34*(2), 91–114. DOI: 10.5206/eei.v34i2.17529

Waisman, T., Alba, L. A., & Green, S. A. (2022). Barriers to Inclusive Learning for Autistic Individuals. *Pediatrics*, *149*(Suppl 4), e2020049437Q. DOI: 10.1542/peds.2020-049437Q

Waisman-Nitzan, M., Gal, E., & Schreuer, N. (2021). "It's like a ramp for a person in a wheelchair": Workplace accessibility for employees with autism. *Research in Developmental Disabilities*, *114*, 103959. Advance online publication. DOI: 10.1016/j.ridd.2021.103959

Wang, J., Zhou, X., Xia, W., Sun, C.-H., Wu, L.-J., Wang, J.-L., & Tomoda, A. (2012). Parent-reported health care expenditures associated with autism spectrum disorders in Heilongjiang province, China. *BMC Health Services Research*, *12*(1), 1–7. DOI: 10.1186/1472-6963-12-7

Welch, K. C., Pennington, R., Vanaparthy, S., Do, H. M., Narayanan, R., Popa, D., Barnes, G., & Kuravackel, G. (2023). Using Physiological Signals and Machine Learning Algorithms to Measure Attentiveness During Robot-Assisted Social Skills Intervention: A Case Study of Two Children with Autism Spectrum Disorder. *IEEE Instrumentation & Measurement Magazine*, *26*(3), 39–45. DOI: 10.1109/MIM.2023.10121412

Wisner-Carlson, R., Uram, S., & Flis, T. (2020). The Transition to Adulthood for Young People with Autism Spectrum Disorder. *The Psychiatric Clinics of North America*, *43*(4), 673–686. DOI: 10.1016/j.psc.2020.08.005

Yang, J., Yang, L., Quan, H., & Zeng, Y. (2021). Implementation Barriers: A TASKS Framework. *Journal of Integrated Design & Process Science*, *25*(3–4), 134–147. DOI: 10.3233/JID-210011

Yokota, S., & Tanaka, M. (2024). Less Negative Implicit Attitudes Toward Autism Spectrum Disorder in University Students: A Comparison with Physical Disabilities. *Journal of Autism and Developmental Disorders*, *54*(1), 182–192. DOI: 10.1007/s10803-022-05749-y

Zainal, M. S., & Zainodin, N. N. A. W. (2025). Educational and Psychosocial Challenges Among Individuals with High-Functioning Autism: A Systematic Literature Review. *International Journal of Learning. Teaching and Educational Research, 24*(8), 1024–1040. DOI: 10.26803/ijlter.24.8.45

Zhao, Y., Luo, Y., Zhang, R., & Zheng, X. (2023). Direct and indirect costs for families of children with autism spectrum disorder in China. *Autism, 27*(8), 2337–2347. DOI: 10.1177/13623613231158862

APPENDIX

Table 3. Questionnaire on Barriers in Career Transition of Students with ASD (QBCTSA)

S/No	Items	Factor Loading	Cronbach's α	Omega ω
	Personal Barriers			
1	I recognise that sensory sensitivities may impede student job success.	0.748	0.83	0.82
2	Lack of self-advocacy skills is a significant personal barrier for ASD students.	0.803		
3	Time management difficulties pose a real challenge for students during career transition.	0.726		
4	Communication challenges (e.g., interviews) are a key personal obstacle.	0.636		
5	Anxiety about stepping into unfamiliar work environments is a major barrier.	0.427		
6	Students often lack flexibility in adapting to new job routines.	0.520		
	Social Barriers			
7	Students may fear disclosing their ASD, preventing them from seeking accommodations.	0.652	0.80	0.79
8	Misunderstandings with peers or supervisors can derail transition success.	0.881		
9	Limited peer mentoring reduces support during career exploration.	0.682		
10	Family uncertainty about career options restricts transition planning.	0.636		
11	A lack of community understanding toward ASD hinders advancement opportunities.	0.528		
12	Social stigma about neurodiversity creates additional obstacles for students.	0.403		
	Institutional Barriers			

continued on following page

Table 3. Continued

S/No	Items	Factor Loading	Cronbach's α	Omega ω
	Personal Barriers			
13	Institutional policies (or lack thereof) make it hard to accommodate ASD-related career needs.	0.715	0.83	0.84
14	Schools often lack formalised transition goals tailored for students with ASD.	0.807		
15	Coordinating external services (e.g., support agencies, employers) is difficult.	0.755		
16	Restricted budgets limit access to transition staff and programs.	0.592		
17	Administrative delays slow down access to resources needed for transition.	0.613		
18	Insufficient training for staff prevents the timely identification of transition barriers.	0.505		
	Awareness Constraints			
19	I am aware of the obstacles students with ASD face in starting a career.	0.738	0.77	0.76
20	I can identify reasons why transition planning fails to take off.	0.772		
21	I recognise when a student's personal factors are not yet addressed.	0.684		
22	I perceive when institutional systems are causing bottlenecks in career transition.	0.585		
	Resource Constraints			
23	Even when aware of barriers, I feel uncertain about how to address them.	0.627	0.87	0.86
24	Limited access to autism-informed career resources makes barrier-solving difficult.	0.574		
25	External constraints (e.g., employer policies) feel too challenging to overcome.	0.597		
26	Budget and staff limitations make planning career steps seem unachievable.	0.685		

Table 4. Factor Loadings for Questionnaire on Barriers in Career Transition of Students with ASD (QBCTSA)

	Factor 1	Factor 2	Factor 3	Uniqueness
Personal2	**0.803**			**0.372**
Awarenes2	0.772			0.423
Personal1	0.748			0.508
Awarenes1	0.738			0.528
Personal3	0.726			0.394
Awarenes3	0.684			0.465
Personal4	0.636			0.606
Awarenes4	0.585			0.658
Personal5	0.427			0.553
Social2		0.881		0.333
Resource4		0.685		0.406
Social3		0.682		0.576
Social1		0.652		0.568
Social4		0.636		0.649
Resource1		0.627		0.483
Resource3		0.597		0.436
Resource2		0.574		0.436
Social5		0.528		0.726
Personal6		0.520		0.457
Social6		0.403		0.847
Institution2			0.807	0.343
Institution3			0.755	0.421
Institution1			0.715	0.475
Institution5			0.613	0.587
Institution4			0.592	0.576
Institution6			0.505	0.670

Note. Applied rotation method is promax.

Chapter 10
Solution-Focused Perspectives on Career Transition Strategies for Students With ASD

ABSTRACT

This paper examined solution-focused career transition strategies for students with autism spectrum disorders (SASD). The data were gathered using a quantitative cross-sectional design among teachers and parents of SASD. The results demonstrated a great similarity in the perceptions of the stakeholders in all strategy dimensions, and strengths and exceptions were the most strongly supported in the survey. Meanwhile, a future-focused vision was comparatively less highlighted. There were no significant differences between genders, types of participants, or residential area, which means that there is a common perception landscape that is influenced by structural limitations as opposed to personal traits. When viewed through the lens of Hephapreneurship, the findings emphasise the position of capability, meaning-making, and context-responsive pathways for career transition among SASD. This chapter presents a theoretically combined and contextually based framework for enhancing inclusive career transition practices for SASD in Nigeria.

BACKGROUND

Strategy is a thoughtful, consistent course of action that is aimed at attaining a long-term objective in circumstances of limitation and ambiguity. It is the act of making decisions regarding priorities, allocation of scarce resources and choosing what to act on and what to leave unacted to develop an advantage or move forward

DOI: 10.4018/978-1-6684-7260-6.ch010

to a specified outcome. In this study, strategy is contextualised as purposeful approaches individuals or institutions use to navigate change, manage constraints, and move toward desired future outcomes. Career transition strategy is a complex action plan that involves mapping of the past, present, and future, support networks, reskilling, and lifelong learning (Stambulova, 2010). It also entails psychological and social support, personal branding, as well as structured programs based on the individual's needs (Rochat & Borgen, 2023). All these strategies are aimed at assisting individuals in making successful transitions in their career paths and realising their professional development (Coppola & Young, 2022; Malta et al., 2025). The career transition strategies of Students with Autism Spectrum Disorder (SASD) are based on the ability to utilise the positive aspects, like focus and detail orientation, while addressing weaknesses, like communication needs and sensory needs, through structured individual support (Dean et al., 2022; Qian et al., 2021).

This current chapter explored the future-focused, strengths and exceptions, action planning and scaling, and support and reinforcement. Future-focused career transition strategies are the deliberate capacity of SASD to construct a clear and personally meaningful picture of a preferred occupational future and to use that picture to guide present decisions, learning priorities, and help-seeking behaviours. In the transition literature, a future-focused transition strategy is perceived as a functional cognitive asset that reduces uncertainty, enhances objective commitment, and improves participation with preparatory tasks (Malekpour, 2019; Tourais & Videira, 2024). Research findings from scholars (Hazan-Liran & Walter, 2025; Tomaszewski et al., 2020, 2022) strongly support the notion that higher self-determination and goal-directedness are associated with better educational and adult outcomes for transition-aged autistic individuals. Future orientation serves as a practical mechanism to achieve these outcomes, emphasising the need for targeted interventions and supports to enhance self-determination and future planning skills. According to Wehmeyer and Zhao (2020), career development models prioritise self-determination, and future objectives serve as the central organising element that structures choice-making, planning, and ongoing action, especially in unpredictable environments (Wehmeyer & Zhao, 2020). For SASD, with constant high executive functioning load and ambiguous social cues, a future-focused strategy provides ground that makes tasks more intelligible and less emotionally destabilising.

In the school-based transition, future-focused strategies operate through three interlocking processes. The first is preferred future-focused construction, where the SASD are supported in a detailed description of adult working life, encompassing daily routines, workplace sensory conditions, kinds of tasks, supervision styles, and social demands (Webster et al., 2022). This is vital because SASD benefits from aspirations that are specific and have predictable transition plans instead of vague aspirations that are less actionable (Lam et al., 2023; Torres et al., 2024). Second is future to present alignment in transition planning encompasses a comprehensive approach that integrates individualised education plans, skill development, home-school collaboration, and social supports. By focusing on these elements, educators and policymakers can better prepare SASD and intellectual disabilities for successful transitions to postsecondary education, employment, and independent living (Cumming et al., 2020; Shepherd, 2022; Torres et al., 2024). Cumming et al. (2020) indicated that this process should be formalised and individualised through involving students and families to ensure that the plans are tailored to the aspirations of the individual students. The third is anticipatory coping, where future scenarios are used to identify common barriers and to plan adaptation before a crisis occurs. These processes are closely aligned with student-focused planning that involves tailoring transition plans to the individual needs and strengths of students, ensuring they are equipped with the necessary skills and knowledge for future success (Griffiths et al., 2021; Salmela-Aro et al., 2010).

The Nigerian educational environment makes future-focused career transition strategies both important and extremely difficult. Future-focused career transition strategies are important because there is an absence of career advice, guidance and counselling services, limited awareness and resource constraints and inconsistent disability specific transition planning, which indicates that students can graduate from secondary school without a credible pathway narrative (Luft & Reynolds, 2023; Okolie et al., 2020). The future-focused career transition strategies are extremely difficult in Nigeria because the opportunity is constrained by stigma, social marginalisation and isolation, weak linkage between school and work, and lack of readiness among employers to accommodate and support SASD (Onalu et al., 2024; Wolffe et al., 2013). Nigerian teachers constantly reveal low professional knowledge about ASD, which limits their potential to assist SASD. Lack of required knowledge impacts their ability to facilitate future-oriented transition conversations and provide suitable career guidance (Ahmad & Khairuddin, 2025). When teachers are not fully aware of ASD, their default response is always to minimise expectations as well as to avoid complex career transition planning, which leaves future vision formation to families instead of structured school practice.

Furthermore, another career transitional strategy for SASD is the strength and exception. Strengths and exceptions strategies are an important change in how the career transitioning of SASD is understood and supported. Instead of framing transition challenges as a result of deficits that are part and parcel of being autistic, strengths and exceptions approaches anticipate prevailing competencies, adaptive abilities, interests, and past accomplishments as a foundation for future career development. In the context of career transition, strengths mean stable capacities like technical skills, focused interests, persistence, and attention to detail (Akbar et al., 2024; Blokker et al., 2025), while exceptions mean contexts in which expected difficulties were reduced or managed effectively (Greer & Minnis, 2022). Exceptions are concrete evidence of possible successful functioning under specific conditions, which refute the negative perceptions of themselves and external low expectations that frequently characterise their learning experiences.

The applicability of the strengths and exceptions strategies has been especially high in the situation of Nigeria, where the educational systems are typically examination-based and deficit-oriented. The evaluation practices in the Nigerian secondary schools have been more focused on standardised academic performances at the expense of non-academic skills that are very pertinent in employment and vocational achievement. Because of this, SASD are often tested in a very limited way that focuses on the problems with communication, or social dynamics and ignores such aspects of competence as technological skills, visual processing, or task persistence. Research evidence in Nigeria has consistently reported that teachers are unprepared to teach students with learning needs, including SASD, as a result of insufficient training and resources (Nwosu et al., 2025; Onyishi, 2022). This environment reinforces negative identity formation and undermines the development of adaptive career narratives.

Therefore, addressing the strengths and needs of SASD can create a more supportive and effective learning environment, as well as improve engagement (Obadeji et al., 2024), and strengthening vocational education and training can address the skilled shortage, offering students with practical skills that are useful in the job market (Awe et al., 2009). In career transitioning, this entails assisting the SASD to identify what they do well, what they enjoy doing and the conditions under which they have already been successful academically, socially or practically. A case in point is a student who has difficulty working as a group but is very good at formal individual tasks indicates that there is an exception that can be used in future job matching and workplace accommodations. Research indicates that a clear discussion and documentation of exceptions in transition planning can be used to foster more realistic and motivating expectations for postsecondary outcomes when paired with SASD preferences (Harrison et al., 2017; Thompson et al., 2000).

The use of strength and exception strategies in the Nigerian education system is affected by cultural and socioeconomic realities. This is because of limited formal employment opportunities, and many youths transition into informal sectors such as entrepreneurship and family-based occupations. In this circumstance, offer opportunities to leverage on SASD's strengths that are not based on the conventional academic pathways but are nonetheless economically viable. For SASD, the Nigerian context strength-based transitioning entails channelling focused interest with vocational trades, digital skills, or micro-enterprise activities, where appropriate guidance and support are provided (Lee & Carter, 2012). Research evidence from Africa, including Nigeria, has shown that strengths-based interventions lead to positive outcomes, such as improved self-efficacy and reduced anxiety, because they focus on leveraging the unique strengths and interests of SASD to create meaningful and engaging career pathways (Hill et al., 2024; Rumsa et al., 2025; Snyman et al., 2023).

Strength and exception strategies are underrepresented in Nigerian school-based transition practices, irrespective of their promise. There are scarce career guidance services, and little available service rarely integrates individualised strengths mapping or reflective analysis of past successes. In many cases, Nigerian parents constantly become the primary advocates for identifying their children's abilities; however, without institutional reinforcement, these efforts have little impact. This research gap in the Nigerian context emphasised the need for structured, school-mediated approaches that incorporate strengths and exceptions strategies into career transition planning processes for SASD.

The concept of action planning and scaling strategies has gained increased relevance to current descriptions of career transitioning SASD, as it allows the translation of preferred futures into observable behaviour, as well as providing a practical method to track preparedness and progress. In this study, the Action strategy is the systematic breakdown of a transition goal into sequenced tasks that are concrete, time-limited and achievable in the current environment of the SASD. While scaling involves quantitative ratings that are often based on a bounded scale to assist the SASD in estimating the current level, confidence or readiness and finding the next small step that would be considered improvement. Scaling strategies is not an assessment device designed to label ability but a conventional tool employed in schools to enhance SASD self-monitoring, motivation, and identification of workable actions for improvement expectancy and commitment to improvement (Abdulla & Woods, 2023; Dermer, 2014; Taylor, 2019).

The significance of action and scaling strategies for SASD is strongly supported by evidence on executive functioning, self-regulation, and goal-directed behaviour (Kim et al., 2019; McCook et al., 2025; Monteiro, 2022). This is because SASD experience challenges in planning, prioritising, time management, task initiation, and self-monitoring, which directly influence their potential to complete career transition activities like exploring career options, preparing applications, participating in work experience, or sustaining vocational training. Literature has shown that these domains are often affected in autistic development and are associated with everyday functioning at home and school (Gentil-Gutiérrez et al., 2022). Regarding transition, this renders an unstructured approach to career guidance unfair, as the students who most require planning support are the ones least likely to benefit from generic advice. Accessibility mechanisms are therefore action planning and scaling since they externalise cognitive organisation into visible steps, assist in planning and organising their career exploration activities, and managing deadlines (Pugliese et al., 2024; Stark & Lindo, 2023).

Transition guidance also supports the centrality of structured planning and progress monitoring. Evidence-based secondary transition frameworks stress student-directed and person-centred planning where goals are finalised, action plans are developed, and progress and adjust strategies are monitored over time (Childre & Chambers, 2005; Fisher et al., 2025; Maggin & Bruhn, 2018). Goal operationalisation through routines, checklists, timelines, and step-wise tasks can be useful to SASD, especially in environments where even the school environment is unpredictable. The Nigerian environment amplifies both the need and the complexity of action planning and scaling strategies.

In most of the Nigerian secondary schools, career guidance is minimal and is presented in sporadic form, rarely personalised in line with disability related needs. For SASD, this creates a planning gap with transition tasks supposed to be carried out without scaffolded means of implementation. The career transition success relies on the SASD's potential to organise actions and on the family's capacity to offer additional guidance because of the presence of structural constraints such as large classes, a small number of specialised staff, poor school-employer connectivity, and disproportional access to inclusive work experience. The qualitative data available on transition into higher education in Nigeria revealed that SASD face several challenges and that their needs are often unmet, which implies that preschool planning practices would prove protective if incorporated into school practices (M. Sefotho & Onyishi, 2020).

Action planning strategies provide a feasible approach to operating within constraints of the Nigerian setting since they can be incorporated into normal classroom and counselling practices and do not necessitate major infrastructure. An example is when a student has a preferred career direction, action planning will allow teachers and counsellors to state that the SASD should do something each week, like meet with a mentor, take a brief skills course, visit a workplace or practice a work-related routine.

Scaling assists the SASD in having a quantified readiness or confidence in a manner that facilitates conversation and adjustment. When a SASD indicates low confidence, the task will be to determine what one has learned already and what slight modification would shift the rating higher, and this is in line with the solution-focused focus on incremental progress. This method is especially applicable within SASD since it scales down all-or-nothing thinking and offers a systematic approach to perceiving effort and progress, even when external opportunities are limited. Support and reinforcement strategies comprise a central ecological dimension of career transitioning for SASD because transition outcomes are affected not only by individual capacity or planning but by the quality, consistency, and accessibility of social and institutional scaffolding surrounding the student (Lee & Carter, 2012; Nguyen et al., 2020; Scheef et al., 2019). In this study, support is the guidance, accommodation, advocacy, and opportunity provided by people and institutions during career transition. At the same time, reinforcement is the acknowledgement of the strengthening of effort, progress, and adaptive behaviour. These strategies are understood as mechanisms that assist engagement, buffer stress, and stabilise motivation across protracted and uncertain career transition periods. Support and reinforcement strategies are foundational for SASD, specifically those whose transition trajectories are constantly disrupted by social misconceptions and environmental inflexibility. Empirical evidence has demonstrated that SASD achieve better in post-school outcomes when career transitions are embedded with support from families, teachers, counsellors, and employers. For instance, meaningful collaboration between various agencies and family supports is an essential element of high-quality transition services (Lee & Carter, 2012). In addition, employment preparation programme support services that provide internships and collaboration between school and adult services (social and communication) for job skills to support competitive employment have proven impactful (Wehman et al., 2013). Counsellors fostering independence through activities like schedules, tactile prompting, and peer support interventions enhance task participation and reduce reliance on adult prompts (Hume et al., 2009; Milley & Machalicek, 2012). The role of reinforcement strategies is very critical in the career transition mechanism, especially by validating cumulative progress and opposing the cumulative discouragement that often accompanies repeated transition setbacks (Tomaszewski et al., 2022). This resonates with the social cognitive and self-determination framework that highlights that sustained participation depends on environments that reinforce effort and competence rather than focusing exclusively on outcomes (Ryan et al., 2023; Szulc-Kurpaska, 2023).

The educational system in Nigeria intensifies the significance of support and reinforcement strategies due to the limited and unevenly distribution of formal transition infrastructures. As a result, in secondary schools, career guidance services are often not well developed, and specialised transition planning for SASD is rare. Research evidence has shown that teachers have low levels of perception of SASD (Iwuji et al., 2024), and parents of SASD had poor knowledge of the condition, hence many internalising stigma (Oduyemi et al., 2021). In this environment, SASD constantly navigate complex transition requirements with minimal institutional guidance, and heavily relies on the family support and exposes inequalities associated with socioeconomic status. Therefore, family support becomes a major source of support for career transition mediators in Nigeria. Research evidence has also revealed that parents take advocacy roles like monitors, negotiators, supporters and advocates for their children's educational well-being (Stoner & Angell, 2006), as a result lack of educational professionals and insufficient institutional support (Razaq-Shuaib, 2025). Parents of SASD revealed to have experienced a lot of emotional distress due to a lack of understanding and acceptance from family and friends (Azubuike et al., 2024). Similarly, a huge amount of financial burden rests on the parents as services for children with developmental disorders are scarce and often expensive, limiting access to necessary support (Adeniyi & Adeniyi, 2020).

Consistent feedback and recognition are essential to avoid effort going unnoticed. Solution-focused and behavioural literature emphasise that reinforcement strengthens adaptive behaviour by making improvement visible and meaningful (Evans, 2015; Sugai & Simonsen, 2020). In the career transition context of SASD, reinforcement may encompass verbal validation, progress tracking, opportunities to generalise skills, and, in transition contexts, reinforcement may involve verbal validation, progress tracking, opportunities to generalise skills, or environmental adjustments that reward engagement. Qualitative research evidence has shown that higher education SASD constantly experience withdrawal of support after school leaving, leading to increased stress and disengagement (Sefotho & Onyishi, 2021). This indicates how fragile transition gains can be when reinforcement mechanisms are inconsistent.

Reinforcement processes are affected by the critical role of school-based support systems. Schools provide an avenue where teachers, counsellors, and administrators collaborate to recognise and respond to individual transition needs by comprehending and accurately using reinforcement to implement effective behaviour support plans that increase the likelihood of desired behaviour recurring (Sugai & Simonsen, 2020), which enables SASD to engage effectively in preparatory activities. The Nigerian educational system lacks a well-structured career transition team; hence, supports are implemented rarely, which limits opportunities for reinforcement that is timely and specific. Research evidence indicates that structure mentoring and supported internships offer powerful reinforcement by linking efforts to tangible outcomes and by modelling adaptive workplace behaviours (Ehsanian et al., 2025; Ramani & McHugh, 2024; Tobin & Rozek, 2025). Even though these programmes are scarce in Nigeria, emerging intervention studies have revealed their potential impacts. Victor-Aigbodion and Eseadi (2025) reported that purpose-based career coaching reported improved career transition self-efficacy among SASD, suggesting that structured support combined with consistent reinforcement can modify transition-related beliefs and behaviours.

There is a scarcity of empirical evidence concerning studies that examined solution-focused perspectives on career transition strategies for SASD, especially on these four dimensions within Nigerian schools. There is a lack of empirical studies that explored how SASD conceptualise their future careers, how strengths are identified and utilised within transition planning, how action planning and scaling can be operationalised in classrooms, and how support and reinforcement mechanisms function within Nigerian cultural and institutional settings.

Previous studies, mostly conducted outside Nigeria, examined these elements in isolation or to subsume them under broader discussions of inclusion, resulting in fragmented knowledge that limits theoretical coherence and practical applicability. There is evidence of a lack of robust frameworks that connect individual-level strategies with systemic variables like school policies, teacher practices, and community attitudes. As a result of insufficient empirical literature conducted in Nigerian schools that utilised a solution-focused lens also limited the Nigerian scholarly contributions on the global debates on the SASD and career transition strategies, perpetuating the marginalisation of African perspectives in international research. The present study is therefore situated within a critical gap at the intersection of solution-focused theory, career transition research, and SASD education in Nigeria. As this study examined Solution-Focused Perspectives on Career Transition Strategies for SASD, taking cognisance of strengths and exceptions, action planning and scaling, and support and reinforcement as career transition strategies, this study responds directly to documented shortcomings in both policy and practice. This study has provided a theoretical ground and an empirical informed understanding of how SASD can be supported to navigate career transitions more effectively.

RESEARCH OBJECTIVES

The main objective of this study is to examine teachers' and parents' solution-focused perspectives on career transition strategies for students with ASD. The specific objectives include:

1. To compare teachers and parents across the four solution-focused dimensions of career transition strategies for students with ASD.
2. To determine whether sociodemographic factors such as gender and location influence participants' solution-focused perspectives on career transition strategies.
3. To evaluate the predictive value and inclusion probabilities of participants' category, gender, location, and their interaction effects on solution-focused perspectives using Bayesian ANOVA evidence.

RESEARCH QUESTIONS

1. Do teachers and parents differ in their ratings across the solution-focused dimensions of career transition strategies for students with ASD?

2. To what extent do gender and location influence participants' solution-focused perspectives on career transition strategies for students with ASD?
3. Which sociodemographic factors and interactions provide the strongest evidence for inclusion in predicting solution-focused perspectives based on Bayesian ANOVA?

THEORETICAL FRAMEWORK

This chapter is anchored on the Hephapreneurship Theory, an employment and entrepreneurship theory for people with disability developed by Maximus Monaheng Sefotho in 2013 (Sefotho, 2013). Hephapreneurship is a process of promoting positive and meaningful existence anchored on subsistence entrepreneurship of differently abled individuals and disadvantaged individuals, which is founded on the ethos of career choice/construction, towards transformative social justice and change (Sefotho, 2013). Hephapreneurship emerged from Hephaestus and entrepreneurship: joining the prefix Hepha and the suffix -preneurship. Sefotho (2015) indicated that Hephapreneurship is premised on the ethos of self-reliance, independence and self-employment, and underpinned by principles of entrepreneurship in general, and disability entrepreneurship in particular.

Underpinning Hephapreneurship theory are two fundamental guiding values compatible with social constructivism and the transformative paradigm: Transformative social justice and social change. Hephapreneurship as a vehicle of lifelong career guidance for social justice (Hooley & Sultana, 2016). The need for social change is driven by the plight of disabled people for social justice in all spheres of their lives. SASD are among the disabled people who encounter several barriers to employment due to their disability. Hephapreneurship is directed at social justice and contemporary career guidance, in an era that has been coined as the age of accepting disabilities that might exist in ways that reward ability (Sefotho, 2015). Hephapreneurship is the anchor of social justice for disability and other marginalised groups for inclusion in the labour market for sustainable development.

This theory promotes career construction for individuals with disabilities, which focuses on the positive differences and abilities of differently abled persons rather than their disabilities (Sefotho, 2014). Hephapreneurship is conceptualised as an innovative theory of career development that emphasises the capabilities, agency, and purposeful engagement of individuals with disabilities in work and livelihood, moving beyond deficit-based understandings of disability. This theory is seen as an alternative model of career development that is beyond deficit-based understandings of disability by highlighting capability, agency, and purposeful participation with work and livelihood (Sefotho, 2014).

Hephapreneurship posits that work is a process of meaning-making, self-determination, and social participation, not only for economic activity. Therefore, Sefotho positions meaningful work as a fundamental human aspiration, especially for youth with disabilities who are systematically marginalised within formal markets (Ferrari et al., 2017). Therefore, this framework highlights the creation of an enabling environment where individuals can express their aspirations, develop capabilities, and engage in productive activity that aligns with their strengths and lived realities (Sefotho, 2014). The Hephapreneurship theory is significant to the current study due to the career transition of SASD that are constantly restrained by strict employment expectations, stigma, and restricted institutional support.

The principles of Hephapreneurship affirm the solution-focused perspectives based on privileging preferred futures, strengths, and small, actionable changes over problem-saturated narratives. The framework implicitly supports future-focused vision through encouraging individuals to articulate expected life and work outcomes grounded in meaning instead of deficit. It reinforces strengths and exceptions through its explicit emphasis on abilities over disabilities and its rejection of exclusionary labour norms. Action planning is reflected in its advocacy for self-employment, micro-enterprise, and context-responsive pathways that translate aspirations into feasible steps. Support and reinforcement are embedded through its call for multisectoral collaboration among education, career guidance, community structures, and social justice-oriented policy actors.

POLICY FRAMEWORK

This research paper is informed by the National Policy on Inclusive Education in Nigeria, which offers the major policy framework for handling career transition strategies to SASD in Nigerian schools (FRN, 2023). Umeh and Anyaele (2024) revealed that the policy affirms inclusion as a rights-based and system-wide duty that is not limited to access to schooling and encompasses meaningful participation, support, and positive outcomes of transition among SASD. In this context, career transition is implicitly identified as one of the critical educational outcomes, specifically in learners who struggle with structural, social, and attitudinal barriers to post-school participation. The National Policy on Inclusive Education focuses on equity, participation, individualised support and elimination of barriers to learning and development (FRN, 2023). These values are consistent with the solution-focused perspective that focuses on the future-oriented vision, strengths, and exceptions, plan of action and scaling, and support and reinforcement as the mechanisms of successful transitions of SASD. The future-oriented career transition strategies have a valid ground in the current policy of addressing SASD with a learner-centred planning since it enables the systematic directing of learners on realistic and meaningful post-school destinations as opposed to the mere flow of the education system.

Furthermore, the policy promotes the acknowledgement of learner diversity and the modification of educational practices to cater to individual requirements. This approach bolsters strengths and exceptions strategies by validating methods that recognise and enhance the skills, interests, and successful experiences of SASD, without categorising them by their limitations. The focus on differentiated support further reinforces action planning and scaling strategies, as these offer practical means for converting policy intentions into organised, measurable transition practices within educational institutions.

According to Barrio et al. (2019), the National Policy on Inclusive Education emphasises the importance of collaboration among schools, families, communities, and relevant agencies as crucial for achieving inclusive outcomes. This policy directly supports support and reinforcement strategies by framing transition as a collective responsibility that necessitates ongoing encouragement, guidance, and accommodation. By grounding this study in the National Policy on Inclusive Education, the research positions solution-focused career transition strategies for SASD within a recognised Nigerian policy framework that aims not only for inclusion in education but also for equitable preparation for life after school.

METHODOLOGY

Study Participants

A total of 102 participants took part in this study. The sample consisted of 37 teachers and 65 parents drawn from Akwa Ibom and Cross River States in the South-South Geopolitical Zone of Nigeria. These states were selected because they contain diverse urban and rural educational settings as well as rising numbers of families and schools seeking support for students with ASD. The gender distribution was 39 male and 63 female participants. With respect to location, 36 participants lived in urban areas, 46 in semi-urban areas, and 20 in rural communities. All participants met the criteria of having direct professional or parental involvement with students with ASD enrolled in schools within the study area.

In this research, the multi-stage sampling technique was utilised to identify study participants. First, local government areas where schools and parents' networks supporting SASD are based were identified. Second, schools and parent networks involved in inclusive and special education activities within these areas were selected. Finally, eligible teachers and parents were recruited from these institutions. This approach ensured broad representation across Akwa Ibom and Cross River States.

Study Context

Akwa Ibom and Cross River States form an important part of the South South Geopolitical Zone of Nigeria. These states have diverse linguistic and cultural communities along with urban and remote rural areas (Udoh & Okon, 2008). Schools in these states serve students with various neurodevelopmental learning needs, including those with ASD. Both states have a growing number of special educators and parent support networks. These characteristics made them ideal for this study. Conducting the study in these states provided access to a broad representation of teachers and parents who regularly support SASD.

Study Design

This research study followed a cross-sectional quantitative survey design (Greenleaf et al., 1977). All participants completed a paper-based questionnaire that assessed their perspectives on solution-focused career transition strategies for SASD. The independent variables were participant category, gender, and location. The dependent variables were scores on four solution-focused dimensions: future-focused vision, strengths and exceptions, action planning and scaling, and support and reinforcement. The design was appropriate for capturing the views of teachers and parents at a single point in time and for comparing these perspectives across groups.

Research Paradigm

The research was anchored on the positivist paradigm, which provided us with a clear foundation for examining solution-focused perspectives as measurable constructs (Park et al., 2020). Positivist paradigm supports the use of quantitative measures and quantitative analysis to investigate social phenomena systematically, and this aligns with our aim of assessing participants' views through numerical responses. Following this, we further aligned our research process with the ontological, epistemological, axiological and methodological assumptions.

Ontological Assumption

Using this philosophical lens, the positivist paradigm assumes that reality exists independently of individual interpretation. We applied this view by treating participants' ratings as reflections of an observable and documentable phenomenon related to career transition strategies for students with ASD.

Epistemological Assumption

Based on this philosophical stance, the positivist paradigm holds that objective knowledge is attainable through neutral and standardised procedures. We used a structured questionnaire to minimise personal influence and ensure that knowledge was generated from participants' responses rather than researcher interpretation.

Axiological Assumption

The positivist paradigm emphasises value neutrality. We upheld this by applying consistent procedures throughout the study so that the findings reflected participants' perspectives rather than our own.

Methodological Assumption

From a methodological stance, the positivist paradigm supports systematic and replicable methods. This guided our use of a quantitative design, a structured instrument, and Bayesian analysis. The paradigm also informed the choice of multi-stage sampling to achieve fair representation across participant groups.

Research Instrument

Questionnaire on Solution Focused Perspectives on Career Transition Strategies (QSPCTS) (see Table 5): The self-developed questionnaire consisted of 28 items that assessed four core dimensions derived from solution-focused practice. Seven items measured future-focused vision, seven measured strengths and exceptions, seven measured action planning and scaling, and seven measured support and reinforcement. Participants rated each item statement on a five-point scale (1 meant strongly disagree, and five meant strongly agree). Higher scores reflected stronger endorsement of solution-focused approaches. The reliability score for the QSPTCS was acceptable. The future-focused vision scale recorded an alpha of 0.88. The strengths and exceptions scale recorded an alpha of 0.82. The action planning and scaling scale recorded an alpha of 0.80 with an omega of 0.81. The support and reinforcement scale recorded an alpha of 0.81 with an omega of 0.80. The items demonstrated adequate factor loadings across the four dimensions.

Study Procedure

After receiving ethical clearance, we contacted selected schools and parent networks in both Akwa Ibom and Cross River States. Two trained postgraduate research assistants aided us in the administration of the questionnaire. The assistants had experience in special needs education and educational psychology and were briefed on all data collection procedures. Participants were informed about the aim of the research study, and they signed consent forms. They then completed the questionnaire individually. The research assistants stayed in contact with participants to clarify instructions; nevertheless, they did not determine participants' responses. The questionnaires were retrieved as soon as they were completed to ensure data integrity. No identifying information appeared on any questionnaire.

Data Analysis

Data analysis involved two stages. First, descriptive statistics were computed to summarise the distribution of scores for each of the four solution-focused dimensions and the demographic distribution of participants. These statistics included means, standard deviations, standard errors, and confidence intervals. They were used to examine the general pattern of responses among teachers and parents. Second, Bayesian ANOVA was done to determine the influence of participant category, gender, and location on the solution-focused dimensions. This analytic approach enabled us to evaluate the strength of evidence for each model and to compare the likelihood of sociodemographic effects relative to the null model. Bayesian analysis was chosen because it evaluates model evidence directly rather than relying on significance tests.

Ethical Considerations

Ethical clearance was received prior to the commencement of the study (University of Johannesburg Faculty of Education Research Ethics Committee, Sem-2-2020-057). Participation in this research study was voluntary, and no financial compensation was offered. Informed consent procedures were followed in order to ensure that participants comprehended the study's aim, their rights, as well as the confidential nature of the research. Questionnaires did not have any identifiers, and all completed forms were stored securely. All participants were made aware that the information provided would be used for research purposes only.

RESULTS

Table 1. Demographic characteristics of respondents

Variables	N	%
Participants Teachers Parents	37 65	36.3 63.7
Gender Male Female	39 63	38.2 61.8
Location Urban Semi-urban Rural	36 46 20	35.3 45.1 19.6

In Table 1, we present the demographic profile of the respondents in this study. A total of 102 respondents took part, consisting of 37 teachers (36.3 per cent) and 65 parents (63.7 per cent). The gender distribution shows that 39 participants (38.2 per cent) were male, and 63 participants (61.8 per cent) were female. In terms of location, 36 respondents (35.3 per cent) resided in urban areas, 46 (45.1 per cent) were from semi-urban settings, and 20 (19.6 per cent) were from rural communities. These demographic analyses show that the sample leaned toward a higher representation of parents and female participants. The results also reflect a stronger involvement from individuals situated in semi-urban environments.

Table 2. Descriptive statistics on solution-focused perspectives on career transition strategies for students with ASD

	Group	N	Mean	SD	SE	Coefficient of variation	95% Confidence Interval	
							Lower	Upper
Future-Focused Vision	Teacher	37	17.838	5.585	.918	.313	15.976	19.700
	Parents	65	18.646	5.716	.709	.307	17.230	20.062
Strengths and Exceptions	Teacher	37	20.676	5.864	.964	.284	18.720	22.631
	Parents	65	20.908	5.300	.657	.253	19.595	22.221
Action Planning and Scaling	Teacher	37	18.351	5.117	.841	.279	16.645	20.057
	Parents	65	18.692	4.667	.579	.250	17.536	19.849
Support and Reinforcement	Teacher	37	18.432	5.199	.855	.282	16.699	20.166
	Parents	65	18.738	4.463	.554	.238	17.633	19.844

Table 2 and Figure 1 present the descriptive findings comparing teachers and parents across the four solution-focused dimensions. Overall, both groups reported similar patterns, although parents consistently recorded slightly higher mean scores across the dimensions. For Future Focused Vision, teachers had a mean of 17.84, whereas parents had a mean of 18.65. A similar pattern was seen for Strengths and Exceptions, where teachers recorded a mean of 20.68 compared to 20.91 among parents. In Action Planning and Scaling, teachers recorded a mean of 18.35, and parents recorded 18.69. For Support and Reinforcement, teachers scored 18.43 compared with parents who scored 18.74. These differences were small, and the confidence intervals overlapped, which suggests that the ratings of teachers and parents were largely comparable.

The trends in Figure 1 further reinforce these findings. The plotted mean ratings of both groups moved in parallel across all four dimensions, indicating that teachers and parents generally perceive solution-focused career transition strategies in a similar way. Although parents gave slightly higher ratings across most areas, the differences do not seem substantial. These results suggest that both teachers and parents share similar expectations and experiences regarding the use of solution-focused strategies to support students with ASD during career transition.

Figure 1. Means ratings of teachers and parents on solution-focused perspectives on career transition strategies for students with ASD

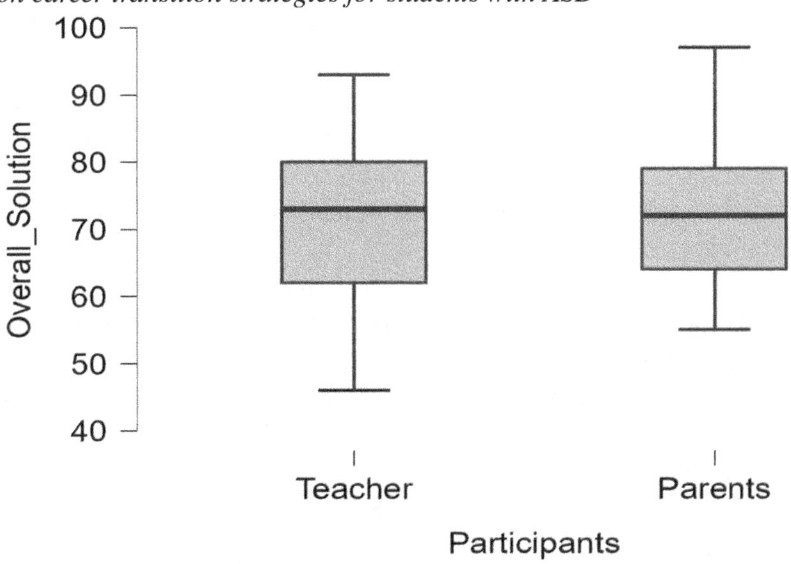

Figure 2. Means ratings of participants on solution-focused perspectives on career transition strategies for SASD based on gender

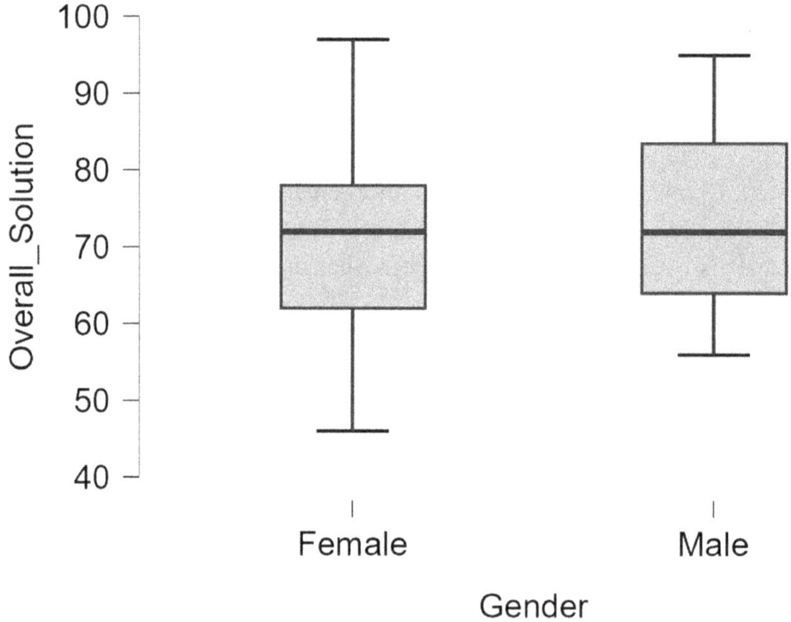

Figure 2 and Figure 3 illustrate the influences of gender and location. In Figure 2, the mean ratings for males and females are relatively close across the four solution-focused dimensions. Although females appear to rate the strategies slightly higher in some areas, the visual patterns suggest minimal gender-based differences overall. This result shows that both male and female participants hold similar views regarding future-focused vision, strengths and exceptions, action planning, and support and reinforcement.

Figure 3 shows ratings based on urban, semi-urban, and rural locations. Although participants from semi-urban locations tended to report slightly higher ratings than those in urban and rural settings, the difference was not large. Participants living in rural settings appear to score slightly lower across some dimensions, yet the overall pattern remains consistent across all groups. This result implies that location does not exert a strong influence on solution-focused perspectives of teachers and parents concerning the career transition of students with ASD. The consistency across gender and location suggests that the perceived usefulness of solution-focused strategies is stable across different demographic groups.

Figure 3. Means ratings of participants on solution-focused perspectives on career transition strategies for SASD based on location

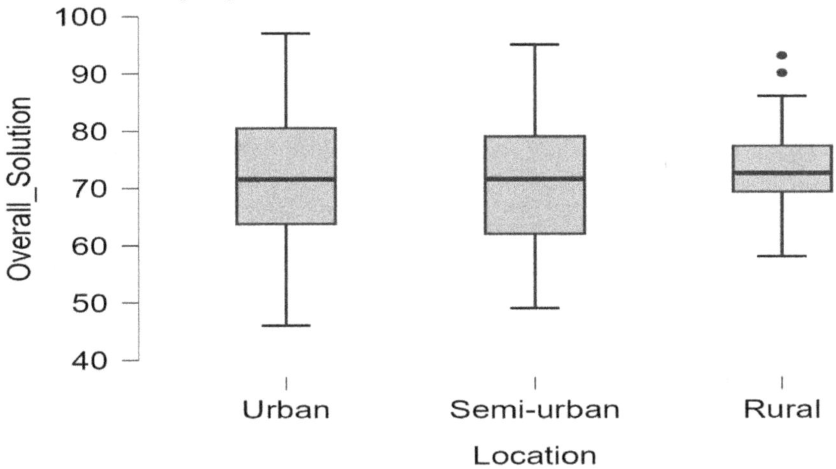

Table 3. Bayesian ANOVA results on solution-focused perspectives of teachers and parents on career transition strategies for SASD

Models	P(M)	P(M|data)	BF_M	BF_{10}	error %
Null model	**0.053**	**0.508**	**18.563**	**1.000**	
Gender	0.053	0.196	4.374	0.385	0.019
Participants	0.053	0.117	2.389	0.231	0.023
Location	0.053	0.059	1.130	0.116	0.026
Participants + Gender	0.053	0.047	0.883	0.092	1.024
Gender + Location	0.053	0.021	0.387	0.042	1.157
Participants + Gender + Participants Gender	0.053	0.019	0.346	0.037	1.306
Participants + Location	0.053	0.013	0.243	0.026	1.513
Participants + Gender + Location	0.053	0.005	0.088	0.010	1.711
Gender + Location + Gender Location	0.053	0.005	0.083	0.009	4.145

In Table 3, the null model received the strongest support, with a posterior probability of 0.508, indicating that the data did not strongly favour any model that included sociodemographic variables. Gender had the next highest model probability of 0.196, while participants' category (teacher or parent) had a probability of 0.117.

Location had even weaker support with a probability of 0.059. All the interaction models had even smaller posterior probabilities. These findings suggest that none of the sociodemographic predictors substantially improved the model when compared with the null model.

Table 4. Analysis of the influences of sociodemographic factors on solution-focused perspectives on career transition strategies for students with ASD

Effects	P(incl)	P(excl)	P(incl|data)	P(excl|data)	BF_{Incl}
Participants	**0.737**	**0.263**	**0.211**	**0.789**	**0.096**
Gender	0.737	0.263	0.298	0.702	0.152
Location	0.737	0.263	0.114	0.886	0.046
Participants Gender	0.316	0.684	0.022	0.978	0.048
Participants Location	0.316	0.684	0.008	0.992	0.017
Gender Location	0.316	0.684	0.007	0.993	0.015
Participants Gender Location	0.053	0.947	1.280	1.000	0.002

Table 4 provides further clarity through the inclusion probabilities. Gender had the highest inclusion probability at 0.298, followed by participants' category at 0.211. Location had a lower inclusion probability of 0.114. The interaction terms all showed very low inclusion probabilities, suggesting that interaction effects did not influence participants' ratings. Taken together, the evidence indicates that sociodemographic factors, and especially their interactions, do not substantially explain variation in solution-focused perspectives. Although gender showed the strongest evidence among the factors, the strength of evidence remains weak overall. This result reinforces those of Table 3 that participants across different demographic backgrounds largely share similar views regarding solution-focused career transition strategies for SASD.

DISCUSSION

This study examined the solution-focused career transition strategies for SASD in Nigerian secondary schools, focusing on future-focused vision, strengths and exceptions, action planning and scaling, and support and reinforcement strategies. The results of this study unveiled how teachers and parents prioritised career transition strategies for SASD. The results revealed a coherent and convergent perception among teachers and parents, suggesting a shared recognition of what comprises career transition strategies for SASD. These findings are interpreted through the lens of Hephapreneurship to enable a deeper comprehension of why certain strategies appear as more salient than others and what this implies for transforming career transition practice for SASD.

This study revealed that teachers and parents consistently rated strengths and exceptions career transition strategies as one of the viable strategies. This dimension of career transition strategy scored highest among the participants, showing that recognition and mobilisation of abilities as the most feasible leverage points for career transition among SASD. The findings of this study align with the empirical reports from literature which revealed that tailoring transition services such as personalised career development plans and early work experiences to the individual strengths and needs of the SASD is very significant (Hatfield et al., 2021; Lee & Carter, 2012; Reis et al., 2024). Empirical research findings have shown that with transition process strategies that emphasises competence, interest alignment, and prior success experiences, SASD demonstrate enhanced self-determination (Cadondon et al., 2023; Dean et al., 2022). The finding supports a recent research report in Nigeria, which revealed that purpose-based career strategies can boost SASD self-efficacy when personal purpose and strengths are integrated into career planning (Victor-Aigbodion & Eseadi, 2025).

This research finding is consistent with the Hephapreneurer framework, which objects disability through the lens of capability, meaning and contribution, and which opposes exclusionary labour norms that equate productivity to conformity (Sefotho, 2014). This model suggests that the primary sources of developing purposeful work paths include strengths and exceptions. Teachers and parents perceived this dimension as important since effective strategies imply an implicit correspondence between the perceptions of the stakeholders and the Hephapreneurial values. This finding signals readiness for a paradigm shift towards capability-centred transition models in Nigeria, where deficit narratives around disability remain pervasive.

Nevertheless, a structural tension can also be seen in the feature of strengths and exceptions dominating. Although stakeholders value ability recognition, the school systems in Nigeria often lack a formal mechanism for translating strengths into potential career opportunities. Curricula based on exams, slim vocational diversification and inflexible certification systems inhibit the institutionalisation of strengths that fall outside conventional academic metrics. Consequently, strengths can receive recognition on a rhetoric level but are not used in practice, which reflects external criticisms of strengths-based practices that warn of thin-slicing implementation unless it is aligned systemically. The current results, hence, highlight the necessity of structural aids that enable the conversion of strengths into opportunities, which can be acted upon, and is a central theme in Hephapreneurship (Sefotho, 2014).

This study found that the future-focused career transition strategy was rated the least among other strategy dimensions. This finding literally deviates from literature which has affirmed future-focused approaches as an essential driver of active participation, persistence, perseverance, and adaptive decision making among SASD. Empirical evidence shows that future orientation assists autistic youth manoeuvre uncertainties by providing a sense of direction and purpose (Chun et al., 2025; Cui et al., 2020). Articulating desired plans by SASD is associated with the likelihood of participating meaningfully in transition planning and sustaining effort through uncertainty. The lower rating of the future-focused vision career transition strategy indicates that Nigerian SASD have lower chances of being supported to construct credible occupational futures. This finding can be attributed to a lack of exposure, scaffolding, and legitimised pathways through which future images can be formed.

This finding could be attributed to the shortcomings of the Nigerian education system, which is characterised by uneven distribution of career guidance services, rare disability transition planning, and constant societal stigma, which limits what adults consider realistic futures for SASD (Eze et al., 2025; Otu, 2025). These have resulted in making future-focused vision a weak and underdeveloped strategy. From a Hephapreneurial standpoint, this reflects a deeper social injustice. Hephapreneurship posits that the capacity to imagine a meaningful working life is socially produced instead of individually owned (Sefotho, 2014). In a weak opportunity structure, preferred futures become hard to communicate, no matter how well an individual can do it. The current results, therefore, emphasise future-focused vision as a vital intervention target for SASD.

This study revealed that action and scaling strategies were rated moderately by parents and teachers, which indicates the significance of translating aspiration into concrete steps as well as revealing limitations in implementation. This finding could be attributed to reliance on informal planning processes, which are prevalence in Nigeria. Previous studies have shown that SASD benefits from structured career transition planning practice that reduces cognitive load and externalises organisations (Esposito et al., 2025; Milley & Machalicek, 2012; Panganiban et al., 2022). Furthermore, a study revealed that joint action routine has shown immediate and significant improvement in the social behaviour of students (Alwahbi, 2023). The alignment of the current findings with the previous reports indicates that transition success for SASD is highly sensitive to the availability of structured planning supports.

In the Nigerian context, families initiate action planning more times than institutional design, especially when they possess the required resources for networking and advocacy. As a result, this undermines sustainability and creates inequalities. The present findings resonate with literature highlighting that transition success for SASD is highly sensitive to the availability of structured planning supports (Essex & Melham, 2019; Roitsch, 2024). A corrective measure to this situation is within the Hephapreneurship model, which proposes context-responsive paths such as entrepreneurship and self-employment, which can be strategised in small steps within local realities (Sefotho, 2014). Action planning and scaling, therefore, becomes a means by which Hephapreneurial futures can be realised so long as schools are in a position to support them.

This study revealed that support and reinforcement were moderately acknowledged as the career transition strategy for SASD in Nigerian schools. The moderate approval of this strategy reflects the teachers' and parents' recognition of its importance and constraints on delivery. This finding could be attributed to the nature of support SASD receives in Nigeria, which is constantly fragmented, as families bear most of the burden, which is disproportionate. Support strategy has been widely acknowledged strategy for enhancing SASD career transition. Informal social supports are important resources for families, which indirectly support the SASD's active participation in career transitions. Furthermore, holistic support approaches that encompass guidance from autistic role models and tailored support for SASD in rural areas, which assist them in navigating multiple pathways and acquiring the skills needed for the labour market (White et al., 2024).

Reinforcement when available is often inconsistent and informal. Empirical evidence has shown that reinforcement is extremely significant for sustaining active engagement during transition, especially for SASD, which encountered repeated setbacks. For instance, Noel and Rubow (2018) revealed that noncontingent reinforcement has been found effective in reducing perseverative speech and increasing engagement in social skills training for SASD. Also, activity schedule and tactile prompting assist to improve task engagement and reduce reliance on adult prompts, and foster greater independent in SASD (Milley & Machalicek, 2012). The present findings suggest that stakeholders recognise this need but operate within systems that limit coordinated support provision.

From the perspective of Hephapreneurship, support and reinforcement are social justice approaches. Sefotho (2014) stated that Hephapreneurship focuses on multisectoral teamwork, community-embedded support, and provision of enabling conditions in which effort and contribution are acknowledged. Based on this model, moderate approval of this dimension is a systemic failure. It highlights the necessity of policy and practice frameworks that emphasizes sharing of support responsibilities between schools, families, communities, and economic actors.

This study revealed that there is no significant difference based on the participants' type, gender, and location on the perceived career transition strategies for SASD. This finding clearly means that career transition strategies for SASD are broadly shared across stakeholders irrespective of gender and location. In cases where the gender and place of the respondents do not affect their perceptions, it implies that urban and rural, males and females are all constrained by the same structural restraints. From the perspective of the Hephapreneurship framework, this is a shift from individual difference to systemic conditions. The framework points out that it is the social organisation that creates exclusion of meaningful work and not individual characteristics (Sefotho, 2014). The current results support this and indicate that to ensure better career transition results among SASD in Nigeria, system-level transformation is required rather than demographic targeting. Strategies that rely on individual motivation or family resources alone are unlikely to produce equitable outcomes.

The current study provides a significant theoretical value by incorporating solution-focused career transition strategies and Hephapreneurship as a transformative framework that redefines career development within the context of SASD among schools in Nigeria. It builds upon current theory by showing that stakeholder disagreement is not central to the limitations faced in the career transition of SASD, but structural conditions that limit the translation of shared values into practice. As an interdependent system of strategy, the empirical operationalisation of future-focused vision, strengths and exceptions, action planning and scaling, and support and reinforcement has been extended to the school-based and policy-relevant settings of solution-focused perspectives. The integration of Hephapreneurship reframes career transition into a social justice concern, which focuses on capability, meaning-making, and context-relevant directions as opposed to normative labour market fit. Theoretically, the study challenges deficit-oriented transition models and contributes an integrated, capability-centred lens that is transferable to other low and middle-income educational contexts.

Regarding practical importance, this chapter provides a diagnostic perspective on the reason why well-intentioned inclusion policies frequently do not yield any significant transitions. It proves that the alignment of stakeholders is a sufficient condition of change. Solution-focused strategies cannot achieve their transformative potential without structures that facilitate future building, operationalise planning and provide support. This observation has a consequence in terms of teacher training, curriculum development, and policy execution in the Nigerian education system.

CONCLUSIONS

The current chapter contributes to the knowledge of career transition strategies among the SASD by incorporating solution-oriented views with Hephapreneurship as an innovative concept. The results of this study revealed a convergent perception among teachers and parents, indicating a shared recognition of what comprises effective career transition strategies for SASD. The study contends deficit-based descriptions of career transition by foregrounding capability, meaning, and social justice. It proposes a way through more equitable and sustainable career outcomes in Nigeria by developing an informed strategy to support SASD.

REFERENCES

Abdulla, A., & Woods, R. (2023). The Effect of Solution-Focused Scaling and Solution-Focused Questions on Expectancy and Commitment. *School Psychology Review, 52*(6), 709–720. DOI: 10.1080/2372966X.2021.1942196

Adeniyi, Y. C., & Adeniyi, A. F. (2020). Development of a community-based, one-stop service centre for children with developmental disorders: Changing the narrative of developmental disorders in sub-saharan africa. *The Pan African Medical Journal, 36*, 1–10. DOI: 10.11604/pamj.2020.36.164.23402 PMID: 32952808

Ahmad, S., & Khairuddin, K. F. (2025). Transition to career for students with disability: Lecturers' readiness. *International Journal of Evaluation and Research in Education, 14*(4), 2869–2877. DOI: 10.11591/ijere.v14i4.31798

Akbar, A. A., Rameli, M. F. P., Nor, A. R. M., & Rohana, N. A. M. (2024). Empowering Career Pathways for Asnaf Faqir (Poor People). *Global Journal Al-Thaqafah, JULY2024*(SPECIALISSUE), 155–170. DOI: 10.7187/GJATSI072024-11

Alwahbi, A. A. (2023). Effects of Joint Action Routine on Improving Social Behavior of a Student with ASD. *Education and Training in Autism and Developmental Disabilities, 58*(1), 62–73. DOI: 10.1177/215416472305800106

Awe, E. M., Stephenson, P., & Griffith, A. (2009). An assessment of education and training needs of skilled operatives within the Nigerian construction industry. *Assoc. Res. Constr. Manage., ARCOM - Proc. Annu. Conf.*, 685–694.

Azubuike, A. O., Azubuike, P. C., Onyekachi, E. L., Enyam, M. O., Akinreni, T., Abuo, J., Ogbonna, C. K., Timothy, P. N., Uchegbu, E. R., & Adai, G. S. (2024). Experiences and unmet needs among caregivers of children living with autism spectrum disorder in Nigeria: A qualitative study using the socio-ecological model. *Discover Social Science and Health, 4*(1), 77. Advance online publication. DOI: 10.1007/s44155-024-00141-w

Barrio, B. L., Miller, D., Ojeme, C., & Tamakloe, D. (2019). Teachers' and Parents' Knowledge about Disabilities and Inclusion in Nigeria. *Journal of International Special Needs Education, 22*(1), 14–24. DOI: 10.9782/17-00010

Blokker, R., Akkermans, J., Nguyen, Y. N. N., Khapova, S., & Jansen, P. (2025). Beyond one-size-fits-all in school-to-work transition success: The role of career competency profiles. *Journal of Vocational Behavior, 161*, 104158. Advance online publication. DOI: 10.1016/j.jvb.2025.104158

Cadondon, S., Dawson, M., Carriere, J. A., Griffiths, A. J., & Gehricke, J.-G. (2023). Short report: Initial pilot of a brief career development program for autistic young adults. *Research in Developmental Disabilities*, *143*, 104634. Advance online publication. DOI: 10.1016/j.ridd.2023.104634 PMID: 37939494

Childre, A., & Chambers, C. R. (2005). Family perceptions of student centered planning and IEP meetings. *Education and Training in Developmental Disabilities*, *40*(3), 217–233. DOI: 10.1177/215416470504000304

Chun, J., Curtiss, S. L., Richard, C., Zhou, K., Rios, Y. C., Park, S., Kim, J., & Koc, M. (2025). Where Does Hope Lie? The Dialectical Tensions Between Hopes and Expectations of Vocational Transition Planning from the Perspectives of Autistic Young Adults, Parents, and Practitioners. *Journal of Autism and Developmental Disorders*, *55*(5), 1857–1875. DOI: 10.1007/s10803-024-06348-9 PMID: 38635131

Coppola, P. J., & Young, A. F. (2022). Making the difficult career transition: Writing the next chapter during the great resignation or in the future. *Frontiers in Psychology*, *13*, 905813. Advance online publication. DOI: 10.3389/fpsyg.2022.905813 PMID: 36389592

Cui, Z., Oshri, A., Liu, S., Smith, E. P., & Kogan, S. M. (2020). Child Maltreatment and Resilience: The Promotive and Protective Role of Future Orientation. *Journal of Youth and Adolescence*, *49*(10), 2075–2089. DOI: 10.1007/s10964-020-01227-9 PMID: 32236791

Cumming, T. M., Strnadová, I., & Danker, J. (2020). Transitions of Students with Autism and Intellectual Disabilities in Inclusive Settings: The Nexus Between Recommended and Actual Practice. *Australasian Journal of Special and Inclusive Education*, *44*(1), 28–45. DOI: 10.1017/jsi.2020.1

Dean, E. E., Hagiwara, M., Shogren, K. A., Wehmeyer, M. L., & Shrum, J. (2022). Promoting Career Design in Youth and Young Adults with ASD: A Feasibility Study. *Journal of Autism and Developmental Disorders*, *52*(6), 2689–2700. DOI: 10.1007/s10803-021-05146-x PMID: 34184143

Dermer, S. B. (2014). On a scale from one to ten…. In T. S. Nelson & T. S. Trepper (Eds.), *101 More Interventions in Family Therapy* (pp. 266–268). Taylor and Francis. https://doi.org/DOI: 10.4324/9781315810072-65

Ehsanian, V., Derijani, F., Khorraminia, M., & Eiliaei, S. (2025). Implementation and evaluation of a mentoring and counseling program for medical students at Shahid Beheshti University of Medical Sciences. *BMC Medical Education*, *25*(1), 940. Advance online publication. DOI: 10.1186/s12909-025-07488-x PMID: 40598190

Esposito, M., Caputi, M., Fadda, R., Ricciardi, O., Pagano, E., Bove, D., Mazza, M., & Valenti, M. (2025). Group Physical Activity and Behavioral Practices in Adolescents with Autism: A Case Series on Integrated Educational Interventions. *Education Sciences, 15*(11), 1491. Advance online publication. DOI: 10.3390/educsci15111491

Essex, J., & Melham, P. (2019). Experiences of educational transition: Young women with ASD, and the staff supporting them, speak. *Support for Learning, 34*(1), 86–111. DOI: 10.1111/1467-9604.12235

Evans, I. M. (2015). Reinforcement, Principle of. In Wright, J. D. (Ed.), *International Encyclopedia of the Social & Behavioral Sciences* (2nd ed., pp. 207–210). Elsevier Inc., DOI: 10.1016/B978-0-08-097086-8.21051-9

Eze, P., Alabi, A., & Osunbunmi, I. (2025). AI-driven career guidance: Comparing Nigerian undergraduate and postgraduate perceptions. *Discover Education, 4*(1), 543. Advance online publication. DOI: 10.1007/s44217-025-00900-0

Ferrari, L., Sgaramella, T. M., Santilli, S., & Di Maggio, I. (2017). Career adaptability and career resilience: The roadmap to work inclusion for individuals experiencing disability. In Maree, K. (Ed.), *Psychology of Career Adaptability, Employability and Resilience* (pp. 415–431). Springer International Publishing., DOI: 10.1007/978-3-319-66954-0_24

Fisher, M. H., Englehart, V., Kam, C., Norwine, L., Patino, K., Patterson, A., Rodríguez, M., Bouck, E., Sung, C., & Taylor, J. C. (2025). Successful Transition Planning for Students with Intellectual Disability and Extensive Support Needs. In *Springer International Handbooks of Education: Vol. Part F910* (pp. 371–391). Springer Nature. DOI: 10.1007/978-3-031-60258-0_18

FRN. (2023). National Policy on Inclusive Education. In *Nigeria*. Federal Republic of Nigeria.

Gentil-Gutiérrez, A., Santamaría-Peláez, M., Mínguez-Mínguez, L. A., Fernández-Solana, J., González-Bernal, J. J., González-Santos, J., & Obregón-Cuesta, A. I. (2022). Executive Functions in Children and Adolescents with Autism Spectrum Disorder in Family and School Environment. *International Journal of Environmental Research and Public Health, 19*(13), 7834. DOI: 10.3390/ijerph19137834 PMID: 35805490

Greenleaf, J. F., Johnson, S. A., Bahn, R. C., & Rajagopalan, B. (1977). *QUANTITATIVE CROSS-SECTIONAL IMAGING OF ULTRASOUND PARAMETERS.: Ultrason Symp Proc*. 989–995. https://www.scopus.com/pages/publications/0017791518

Greer, T. W., & Minnis, S. E. (2022). Using Developmental Relationships to Navigate Career Transitions: Implications for Diverse Populations. In Ghosh, R., & Hutchins, H. M. (Eds.), *HRD Perspectives on Developmental Relationships: Connecting and Relating at Work* (pp. 15–39). Springer International Publishing., DOI: 10.1007/978-3-030-85033-3_2

Griffiths, A. J., Cosier, M. E., Wiegand, R., Mathur, S. K., & Morgan, S. (2021). Developing strong transition-focused IEPS using labour market data. *Support for Learning*, *36*(4), 608–629. DOI: 10.1111/1467-9604.12383

Harrison, J. R., State, T. M., Wills, H. P., Custer, B. A., & Miller, E. (2017). Transition goals for youth with social, emotional, and behavioral problems: Parent and student knowledge. *Preventing School Failure*, *61*(3), 248–257. DOI: 10.1080/1045988X.2016.1266596

Hatfield, M., Ciccarelli, M., Mangan, C., & Whelan, M. (2021). Boosting post-school outcomes: Supporting adolescents on the autism spectrum to feel ready for life after school. In Carrington, S., Saggers, B., Harper-Hill, K., & Whelan, M. (Eds.), *Supporting Students on the Autism Spectrum in Inclusive Schools: A Practical Guide to Implementing Evidence-Based Approaches* (pp. 118–132). Taylor and Francis. DOI: 10.4324/9781003049036-13

Hazan-Liran, B., & Walter, O. (2025). Psychological Capital, Self-Advocacy, and Future Orientation among Adults on the Autism Spectrum. *Journal of Autism and Developmental Disorders*, *55*(11), 3986–3997. DOI: 10.1007/s10803-024-06493-1 PMID: 39080049

Hill, D. A., Fayemi, A., & Ostrowski, S. (2024). The Evolution of Services for Children with Autism and Developmental Disabilities in Nigeria. *International Journal of Disability Development and Education*, *71*(7), 1116–1132. DOI: 10.1080/1034912X.2023.2291570

Hume, K., Loftin, R., & Lantz, J. (2009). Increasing independence in autism spectrum disorders: A review of three focused interventions. *Journal of Autism and Developmental Disorders*, *39*(9), 1329–1338. DOI: 10.1007/s10803-009-0751-2 PMID: 19430897

Iwuji, U., Hamrick, J., Wheeler, K., Ihenagwam, C., Hixson, J., Kelly, D., Duru, H., Ademulegun, T., Banda, D., & Hilbert, S. (2024). Educators' knowledge of and perceptions towards students with autism in Nigeria. *International Journal of Developmental Disabilities*, 1–11. Advance online publication. DOI: 10.1080/20473869.2024.2359137

Kim, S.-I., Jo, E., Ryu, M., Cha, I., Kim, Y.-H., Yoo, H., & Hong, H. (2019). Toward becoming a better self: Understanding self-tracking experiences of adolescents with autism spectrum disorder using custom trackers. *PervasiveHealth: Pervasive Computing Technol Healthc.*, 169–178. DOI: 10.1145/3329189.3329209

Lam, G. Y. H., Timmons, J., & Zalewska, A. (2023). Program logic model and impacts perceived by stakeholders in a post-school transition program for autistic young adults. *Research in Autism Spectrum Disorders, 107*, 102220. Advance online publication. DOI: 10.1016/j.rasd.2023.102220

Lee, G. K., & Carter, E. W. (2012). Preparing Transition-Age Students with High-Functioning Autism Spectrum Disorders for Meaningful Work. *Psychology in the Schools, 49*(10), 988–1000. DOI: 10.1002/pits.21651

Luft, P., & Reynolds, M. (2023). Optimising transition outcomes for dhh students: A case study analysis. In Neild, N. R., & Graham, P. J. (Eds.), *Cases on Teacher Preparation in Deaf Education* (pp. 165–226). IGI Global., DOI: 10.4018/978-1-6684-5834-1.ch007

Maggin, D. M., & Bruhn, A. (2018). Evidence-Based Assessment and Single-Case Research: A Commentary for the Special Issue on Direct Behavior Ratings. *Assessment for Effective Intervention, 43*(2), 71–78. DOI: 10.1177/1534508417738722

Malekpour, S. (2019). Models as scenario tools for developing robust transformative plans. In Moallemi, E. A., & de Haan, F. J. (Eds.), *Modelling Transitions: Virtues, Vices, Visions of the Future* (pp. 165–181). Taylor and Francis., DOI: 10.4324/9780429056574-10

Malta, C., Damo, C., & Meirinhos, V. (2025). Career Transitions: Insights from a Narrative Approach. In *Lecture Notes on Multidisciplinary Industrial Engineering: Vol. Part F528* (pp. 243–271). Springer Nature. DOI: 10.1007/978-3-031-89948-5_11

McCook, L., Del Vecchio, M. L., & Crosland, K. (2025). Using Progressive Muscle Relaxation to Increase Academic Engagement for Elementary School Students with Autism Spectrum Disorder. *Behavioral Sciences (Basel, Switzerland), 15*(11), 1516. Advance online publication. DOI: 10.3390/bs15111516 PMID: 41301318

Milley, A., & Machalicek, W. (2012). Decreasing Students' Reliance on Adults: A Strategic Guide for Teachers of Students With Autism Spectrum Disorders. *Intervention in School and Clinic, 48*(2), 67–75. DOI: 10.1177/1053451212449739

Monteiro, E. M. (2022). An ecologically valid understanding of executive functioning. *Psychology in the Schools, 59*(7), 1390–1401. DOI: 10.1002/pits.22627

Nguyen, L., Jack, S., Ketelaar, M., Di Rezze, B., Soper, A. K., & Gorter, J. W. (2020). Understanding the essential components and experiences of youth with autism spectrum disorders in peer mentorship programmes during the transition to adulthood: A qualitative meta-ethnography. *Child: Care, Health and Development, 46*(6), 667–681. DOI: 10.1111/cch.12804 PMID: 32840907

Noel, C. R., & Rubow, C. C. (2018). Using noncontingent reinforcement to reduce perseverative speech and increase engagement during social skills instruction. *Education & Treatment of Children, 41*(2), 157–168. DOI: 10.1353/etc.2018.0006

Nwosu, K. C., Letzel-Alt, V., & Pozas, M. (2025). From theory to practice: Exploring Nigerian student teachers' experiences of managing learners with special needs in inclusive classrooms. *British Journal of Special Education, 52*(4), 511–522. DOI: 10.1111/1467-8578.70042

Obadeji, A., Louw, A., & Couper, I. (2024). Medical students' perceptions of the learning environment and its implications on teaching and learning: A qualitative study in Nigeria. *Tehran University Medical Journal, 17*(56), 29–38. DOI: 10.61186/edcj.17.56.29

Oduyemi, A. Y., Okafor, I. P., Eze, U. T., Akodu, B. A., & Roberts, A. A. (2021). Internalisation of stigma among parents of children with autism spectrum disorder in Nigeria: A mixed method study. *BMC Psychology, 9*(1), 182. Advance online publication. DOI: 10.1186/s40359-021-00687-3 PMID: 34802470

Okolie, U. C., Nwajiuba, C. A., Binuomote, M. O., Osuji, C. U., Onajite, G. O., & Igwe, P. A. (2020). How careers advice and guidance can facilitate career development in technical, vocational education, and training graduates: The case in Nigeria. *Australian Journal of Career Development, 29*(2), 97–106. DOI: 10.1177/1038416220916814

Onalu, C., Chukwu, N., Nnama-Okechukwu, C. U., Iwuagwu, A., Agha, A., Anazonwu, N., Okah, P., & Okoye, U. O. (2024). An Exploratory Study of the Situation of Persons with Disabilities in Nigeria: Practice Consideration for Social Workers. *Journal of Evidence-Based Social Work, 21*(1), 90–103. DOI: 10.1080/26408066.2023.2265920 PMID: 37796793

Onyishi, C. N. (2022). Teachers' use of inclusive education practices for learners with neuro-developmental disorders in Enugu State, Nigeria. *Ikenga, 23*(3), 1–17. Advance online publication. DOI: 10.53836/ijia/2022/23/3/003

Otu, M. S. (2025). Exploration of career coaching programmes for employability skills acquisition. In Otu, M. S., & Sefotho, M. M. (Eds.), *Career Coaching and Employability Skills Acquisition* (pp. 257–283). IGI Global., DOI: 10.4018/979-8-3693-4014-1.ch010

Panganiban, J. L., Shire, S. Y., Williams, J., & Kasari, C. (2022). Supporting peer engagement for low-income preschool students with autism spectrum disorder during academic instruction: A pilot randomised trial. *Autism, 26*(8), 2175–2187. DOI: 10.1177/13623613221085339 PMID: 35420044

Park, Y. S., Konge, L., & Artino, A. R. J. (2020). The Positivism Paradigm of Research. *Academic Medicine, 95*(5), 690–694. DOI: 10.1097/ACM.0000000000003093 PMID: 31789841

Pugliese, C. E., Werner, M. A., Alexander, K. C., Cannon, L., Strang, J. F., Caplan, R., Klinger, L., Mandell, D., Dieckhaus, M., Handsman, R., Kenworthy, L., & Anthony, L. G. (2024). Development of a High School-Based Executive Function Intervention for Transition-Age Autistic Youth: Leveraging Multi-level Community Partnerships. *School Mental Health, 16*(3), 862–878. DOI: 10.1007/s12310-024-09661-x

Qian, X., Johnson, D., & Papay, C. (2021). Exploring Correlates of Paid Early Work Experiences for Youth With Autism Using NLTS2012 Data. *Focus on Autism and Other Developmental Disabilities, 36*(1), 14–24. DOI: 10.1177/1088357620956915

Ramani, R. S., & McHugh, P. P. (2024). Cultural influences on internship development value and job pursuit intention: An exploratory comparison of student experiences in France and the United States. *International Journal of Management Education, 22*(3), 101008. Advance online publication. DOI: 10.1016/j.ijme.2024.101008

Razaq-Shuaib, B. (2025). Understanding the Impact of Early Childhood and Primary Education for Children with Neurodevelopmental Disabilities on Parents in Nigeria. *BMJ Paediatrics Open, 9*(1), e003909. Advance online publication. DOI: 10.1136/bmjpo-2025-003909 PMID: 41125261

Reis, S. M., Madaus, J. W., Gelbar, N. W., & Miller, L. J. (2024). Strength-Based Strategies for Twice-Exceptional High School Students With Autism Spectrum Disorder. *Teaching Exceptional Children, 57*(1), 24–33. DOI: 10.1177/00400599221108899

Rochat, S., & Borgen, W. A. (2023). Career life as a game: An overlooked metaphor for successful career transitions. *British Journal of Guidance & Counselling, 51*(2), 298–309. DOI: 10.1080/03069885.2021.1940844 PMID: 37313007

Roitsch, J. (2024). Transitioning from High School to Adulthood: Optimising Outcomes for Students with Autism Spectrum Disorder. In Volkmar, F. R., Reichow, B., & McPartland, J. C. (Eds.), *Adolescents and Adults with Autism Spectrum Disorders* (2nd ed., pp. 55–74). Springer International Publishing., DOI: 10.1007/978-3-031-46463-8_3

Rumsa, S., Afsharnejad, B., Lim Lee, E. A., Bölte, S., Tan, T., & Girdler, S. (2025). A scoping review of current approaches to strengths-based transition practices for autistic adolescents. *Autism, 29*(11), 2644–2661. DOI: 10.1177/13623613251346336 PMID: 40559186

Ryan, R. M., Reeve, J., Kaplan, H., Matos, L., & Cheon, S. H. (2023). Education as Flourishing: Self-Determination Theory in Schools as They Are and as They Might Be. In Ryan, R. M. (Ed.), *The Oxford Handbook of Self-Determination Theory* (pp. 591–618). Oxford University Press., DOI: 10.1093/oxfordhb/9780197600047.013.60

Salmela-Aro, K., Mutanen, P., Koivisto, P., & Vuori, J. (2010). Adolescents' future education-related personal goals, concerns, and internal motivation during the "towards working life" group intervention. *European Journal of Developmental Psychology, 7*(4), 445–462. DOI: 10.1080/17405620802591628

Scheef, A. R., Hollingshead, A., & Voss, C. S. (2019). Peer Support Arrangements to Promote Positive Postschool Outcomes. *Intervention in School and Clinic, 54*(4), 219–224. DOI: 10.1177/1053451218782430

Sefotho, M., & Onyishi, C. (2020). Transition to Higher Education for Students with Autism: Challenges and Support Needs. *International Journal of Higher Education, 10*(1), 18808–18808. DOI: 10.5430/ijhe.v10n1p201

Sefotho, M. M. (2014). Career construction for hephapreneurship: Alternative framework for persons with disabilities. *Mediterranean Journal of Social Sciences, 5*(15), 303–312. DOI: 10.5901/mjss.2014.v5n15p303

Sefotho, M. M., & Onyishi, C. N. (2021). Transition to Higher Education for Students with Autism: Challenges and Support Needs. *International Journal of Higher Education, 10*(1), 201. https://EconPapers.repec.org/RePEc:jfr:ijhe11:v:10:y:2021:i:1:p:201. DOI: 10.5430/ijhe.v10n1p201

Sefotho, M. M. M. (2015). Mainstreaming disability in education beyond 2015. *South African Journal of Education, 35*(1), 1–8. Advance online publication. DOI: 10.15700/201503070007

Sefotho, (2013). *Narratives of differently abled persons: Informing career guidance policy* [University of Pretoria]. http://hdl.handle.net/2263/31652

Shepherd, J. (2022). Beyond tick-box transitions? Experiences of autistic students moving from special to further education. *International Journal of Inclusive Education, 26*(9), 878–892. DOI: 10.1080/13603116.2020.1743780

Snyman, C., Van Eeden, C., & Heyns, M. (2023). How character strengths of autistic learners aid primary school educators in the class: An exploratory study. *South African Journal of Childhood Education, 13*(1). Advance online publication. DOI: 10.4102/sajce.v13i1.1311

Stambulova, N. (2010). Counseling athletes in career transitions: The five-step career planning strategy. *Journal of Sport Psychology in Action, 1*(2), 95–105. DOI: 10.1080/21520704.2010.528829

Stark, M. D., & Lindo, E. J. (2023). Executive Functioning Supports for College Students with an Autism Spectrum Disorder. *Review Journal of Autism and Developmental Disorders, 10*(4), 604–614. DOI: 10.1007/s40489-022-00311-z

Stoner, J. B., & Angell, M. E. (2006). Parent Perspectives on Role Engagement: An Investigation of Parents of Children With ASD and Their Self-Reported Roles With Education Professionals. *Focus on Autism and Other Developmental Disabilities, 21*(3), 177–189. DOI: 10.1177/10883576060210030601

Sugai, G., & Simonsen, B. (2020). Reinforcement Foundations of a Function-Based Behavioral Approach for Students With Challenging Behavior. *Beyond Behavior, 29*(2), 78–85. DOI: 10.1177/1074295620902444

Szulc-Kurpaska, M. (2023). Exploring Teacher Engagement on the Example of Polish FL Teachers. In *English Language Education* (Vol. 32, pp. 87–108). Springer Science and Business Media B.V., DOI: 10.1007/978-3-031-28655-1_6

Taylor, E. R. (2019). Solution-focused therapy and integration with creative and tangible approaches. In Taylor, E. R. (Ed.), *Solution-Focused Therapy with Children and Adolescents: Creative and Play-Based Approaches* (pp. 46–58). Taylor and Francis., DOI: 10.4324/9781315166674-5

Thompson, J. R., Fulk, B. M., & Piercy, S. W. (2000). Do Individualised Transition Plans Match the Postschool Projections of Students with Learning Disabilities and Their Parents? *Career Development for Exceptional Individuals, 23*(1), 3–25. DOI: 10.1177/088572880002300102

Tobin, C. T., & Rozek, E. (2025). Enhancing undergraduate psychology internship by integrating professional core competencies. *Mentoring & Tutoring*. Advance online publication. DOI: 10.1080/13611267.2025.2571494

Tomaszewski, B., Klinger, L. G., & Pugliese, C. E. (2022). Self-Determination in Autistic Transition-Aged Youth without Intellectual Disability. *Journal of Autism and Developmental Disorders, 52*(9), 4067–4078. DOI: 10.1007/s10803-021-05280-6 PMID: 34536165

Tomaszewski, B., Kraemer, B., Steinbrenner, J. R., Smith DaWalt, L., Hall, L. J., Hume, K., & Odom, S. (2020). Student, Educator, and Parent Perspectives of Self-Determination in High School Students with Autism Spectrum Disorder. *Autism Research, 13*(12), 2164–2176. DOI: 10.1002/aur.2337 PMID: 32743977

Torres, R., Schroeder, M., & Griffiths, A. J. (2024). The Path to Success: Engaging and Preparing Autistic Youth for Entrepreneurship. In Markel, K. S., Hanson, M. E., Giannantonio, C. M., & Hurley-Hanson, A. E. (Eds.), *Neurodiversity and Entrepreneurship* (pp. 21–53). Emerald Publishing., DOI: 10.1108/978-1-83753-798-320241002

Tourais, P., & Videira, N. (2024). Sustainability transition strategies in a business context: A co-creation process in the Portuguese hospitality sector. *Corporate Social Responsibility and Environmental Management, 31*(1), 600–628. DOI: 10.1002/csr.2588

Udoh, I. I. L., & Okon, B. A. (2008). *The languages of the Niger Delta Region of Nigeria.*

Umeh, N. C., & Anyaele, D. O. (2024). Assessment of the Implementation of Inclusive Education Policy Among Stakeholders in Abia State, Nigeria. In *Ius Gentium* (Vol. 117, pp. 1–19). Springer Science and Business Media B.V., DOI: 10.1007/978-3-031-64549-5_1

Victor-Aigbodion, V., & Eseadi, C. (2025). Effect of purpose-based career coaching on career transition self-efficacy among college students with autism spectrum disorder. *EDULEARN25 Proceedings*, 8088–8101. *17th International Conference on Education and New Learning Technologies*. DOI: 10.21125/edulearn.2025.2059

Webster, A., Bruck, S., & Saggers, B. (2022). Supporting self-determination of autistic students in transitions. *Research in Developmental Disabilities, 128*, 104301. Advance online publication. DOI: 10.1016/j.ridd.2022.104301 PMID: 35797777

Wehman, P., Schall, C., McDonough, J., Molinelli, A., Riehle, E., Ham, W., & Thiss, W. R. (2013). Project SEARCH for Youth With Autism Spectrum Disorders: Increasing Competitive Employment On Transition From High School. *Journal of Positive Behavior Interventions, 15*(3), 144–155. DOI: 10.1177/1098300712459760

Wehmeyer, M., & Zhao, Y. (2020). *Teaching Students to Become Self-Determined Learners*. ASCD.

White, L. M., Simpson, K., Malone, S., & Adams, D. (2024). Autistic Adults' Reflections on What Supported Their Transitioning from Secondary School. *Education Sciences, 14*(6), 576. Advance online publication. DOI: 10.3390/educsci14060576

Wolffe, K. E., Ajuwon, P. M., & Kelly, S. M. (2013). Working with visual impairment in Nigeria: A qualitative look at employment status. *Journal of Visual Impairment & Blindness*, *107*(6), 425–436. DOI: 10.1177/0145482X1310700605

APPENDIX

Table 5. Questionnaire on Solution-focused Perspectives on Career Transition Strategies (QSPCTS)

S/No	Items	Factor Loading	Cronbach's α	Omega ω
	Future-Focused Vision			
1	Students imagine and describe their ideal career scenario.	0.774		
2	Miracle-style questions are used.	0.782		
3	We encourage students to articulate what success looks like one year from now.	0.795		
4	Insight on personal values and goals is emphasised in sessions.	0.658		0.88
5	Emphasis is placed on how the future will feel when career goals are met.	0.815		
6	Visualisation tools help students picture workplace success.	0.736		
7	Students are encouraged to reflect on the positive changes they'd like to see in their working lives.	0.827		
	Strengths and Exceptions			
8	Students recall past moments when career tasks were successful.	0.403		
9	Conversations focus on what worked, not what went wrong.	0.583		
10	We help students identify skills they have used effectively before.	0.541		
11	Exception questions are used.	0.712		0.82
12	Students note what resources or support made transitions easier in the past.	0.646		
13	Praise is given for small achievements in transition planning.	0.738		
14	Discussions highlight students' existing competencies and successes.	0.780		
	Action Planning and Scaling			

continued on following page

Table 5. Continued

S/No	Items	Factor Loading	Cronbach's α	Omega ω
	Future-Focused Vision			
15	Students set concrete, step-by-step goals for their transition.	0.579	0.80	0.81
16	We use scaling questions.	0.852		
17	Weekly progress check-ins are scheduled.	0.815		
18	Action steps are regularly reviewed and adjusted collaboratively.	0.799		
19	When obstacles occur, we explore questions.	0.779		
20	Students track their progress and reflect on growth.	0.844		
21	Contingency planning is part of strategy discussions.	0.515		
	Support and Reinforcement			
22	Students identify people who are helping them through the transition.	0.634	0.81	0.80
23	Regular encouragement is provided by counselors and mentors.	0.558		
24	Feedback is framed positively around "What's better since last time?" questions.	0.977		
25	Family or community members are included to celebrate milestones.	0.593		
26	Students receive recognition for early successes in transition.	0.500		
27	Counselors document and praise each small step forward.	0.459		
28	Students feel encouraged and understood when focus is on "what works."	0.473		

Conclusion

The findings presented in this volume highlight the following key messages regarding the career transition of students with ASD:

- Career transition outcomes for students with ASD are influenced primarily by systemic and contextual factors.
- Parents experience consistently high levels of transition-related stress, with service navigation stress emerging as the most pronounced dimension. Career planning uncertainty, financial demands, work–family balance pressures, and limited social support further intensify parental burden.
- Teachers and school-based professionals report moderate but persistent stress, driven predominantly by role overload. Transition responsibilities frequently exceed available resources, training, and institutional capacity, undermining long-term effectiveness.
- Theoretical orientation and reflective practice are more predictive of effective transition support than formal role definitions. Theory-informed reflective practice consistently emerged as a strong predictor of professional engagement in career transition activities.
- Structured counselling and intervention programmes produce significant and sustained improvements in work readiness, vocational confidence, independence in career planning, and long-term transition outcomes for students with ASD.
- Institutional support services are present but uneven in quality and accessibility. Their effectiveness appears shaped by broader system practices rather than by school type, location, or participant demographics.
- Career transition counselling services receive moderate overall evaluations, with stronger endorsement for counselling processes and personalisation, and weaker ratings for resource availability and accessibility, indicating a misalignment between professional intent and infrastructural capacity.

- Validated career transition assessment tools grounded in ecological frameworks provide valuable insights into students' readiness by capturing the interaction between personal strategies, self-related factors, support systems, and situational conditions.
- Barriers to career transition are perceived as predominantly institutional and structural. Parents consistently report higher barrier levels than teachers, reflecting greater exposure to post-school systems and labour market constraints.
- Solution-focused and strengths-based transition strategies are widely endorsed by parents and professionals, emphasising capability, meaning-making, and context-responsive pathways over deficit-based models.

Compilation of References

Aaen Maagaard, C. A., & Nielsen, A. S. (2025). Motivational interviewing and the reframing of identity: Small stories in first encounters between clients with alcohol use disorders and their therapists. *Text & Talk*, •••, 1–26. DOI: 10.1515/text-2024-0161

Abdulla, A., & Woods, R. (2023). The Effect of Solution-Focused Scaling and Solution-Focused Questions on Expectancy and Commitment. *School Psychology Review*, *52*(6), 709–720. DOI: 10.1080/2372966X.2021.1942196

Abidin, R. R., Smith, L. T., & Kim, H. (2022). Parenting Stress. *WikiJournal of Medicine*, *9*(1), 3. Advance online publication. DOI: 10.15347/WJM/2022.003

Accardo, A. L., Kuder, S. J., & Woodruff, J. (2019). Accommodations and support services preferred by college students with autism spectrum disorder. *Autism*, *23*(3), 574–583. DOI: 10.1177/1362361318760490 PMID: 29475372

Adachi, T. (2004). Career self-efficacy, career outcome expectations and vocational interests among Japanese university students. *Psychological Reports*, *95*(1), 89–100. DOI: 10.2466/pr0.95.1.89-100 PMID: 15460362

Adams, R., Bishop, S., & Taylor, J. L. (2017). Negative Peer Experiences in Adolescents With Autism Spectrum Disorders. *International Review of Research in Developmental Disabilities*, *52*, 75–107. DOI: 10.1016/bs.irrdd.2017.07.003

Adams, S. N., Dadabhay, A., & Neille, J. (2021). An Exploration into Mothers' Experiences of Feeding Children with Autism Spectrum Disorder in South Africa. *Folia Phoniatrica et Logopaedica*, *73*(3), 164–173. DOI: 10.1159/000507928 PMID: 32645696

Adeboye, T. A., & Obawole, A. (2019). Pay Satisfaction and Role Ambiguity as Predictors of Job Burnout Among Osun State Civil Servants, Nigeria. *European Scientific Journal*, *15*(8), 41–58. DOI: 10.19044/esj.2019.v15n8p41

Adekunle, A. N. (2021). United Nations sustainable development goal 4: Exploring inclusive education of students with developmental disabilities in Lagos State, Nigeria [University of British Columbia]. DOI: 10.14288/1.0406184

Adeniyi, Y. C., & Adeniyi, A. F. (2020). Development of a community-based, one-stop service centre for children with developmental disorders: Changing the narrative of developmental disorders in sub-saharan africa. *The Pan African Medical Journal*, *36*, 1–10. DOI: 10.11604/pamj.2020.36.164.23402 PMID: 32952808

Adewale, A. S., Ghavifekr, S., & Abdulsalam, I. (2017). Impact of stress on academic staff: Implication for higher education management and leadership. *Malaysian Online Journal of Educational Management*, *5*(2), 75–91. DOI: 10.22452/mojem.vol5no2.5

Adigun, O. T., Tijani, F. A., Nzima, D. R., & Vivekanantharasa, R. (2021). Perceived Stress of Special Education Teachers in the Context of the Person-Environment Relationship. *The Open Psychology Journal*, *14*(1), 300–309. DOI: 10.2174/1874350102114010300

Admiraal, W., Post, L., Kester, L., Louws, M., & Lockhorst, D. (2024). Learning labs in a secondary school in the Netherlands: Effects of teachers' autonomy support on student learning motivation and achievement. *Educational Studies*, *50*(5), 939–956. DOI: 10.1080/03055698.2021.2023473

Aduwa-Ogiegbaen, S. E. O., & Iyamu, E. O. S. (2010). Availability and utilization of classroom computers across urban and rural schools in Southwestern Nigeria. In Tomei, L. (Ed.), *Online Courses and ICT in Education: Emerging Practices and Applications* (pp. 189–202). IGI Global., DOI: 10.4018/978-1-60960-150-8.ch015

Aguilera Rodríguez, G., Márquez González, C. V., Villaseñor-Cabrera, T. J., & Valadez Sierra, M. (2024). University experiences of students and graduates with neurodiversity: Tools for creating a specialized mentoring program related to working life. *Frontiers in Education*, *9*, 1432930. Advance online publication. DOI: 10.3389/feduc.2024.1432930

Agunowei, D. I., & Mayombe, C. (2024). The fate of special needs children in the midst of inclusive education policy in Abuja, Nigeria. In Sánchez-Santamaría, J., & Cervantes, B. B. (Eds.), *Exploring Educational Equity at the Intersection of Policy and Practice* (pp. 264–286). IGI Global., DOI: 10.4018/979-8-3693-1614-6.ch015

Ahmad, S., & Khairuddin, K. F. (2025). Transition to career for students with disability: Lecturers' readiness. *International Journal of Evaluation and Research in Education*, *14*(4), 2869–2877. DOI: 10.11591/ijere.v14i4.31798

Ahmed, Y., Mesa, M. P., Zucker, T. A., Fumero, K., Clay, M., & Duran, S. O. (2025). The role of artificial intelligence in modernising multi-tiered systems of support. *Theory into Practice*, *64*(4), 448–464. DOI: 10.1080/00405841.2025.2528541

Ain, G. (2025). Parental involvement and barriers in transitional services for students with autism spectrum disorder in Saudi schools: A mixed-methods study. *Frontiers in Education*, *10*, 1647206. DOI: 10.3389/feduc.2025.1647206

Ajitoni, B. D. (2024). Ubuntu and the philosophy of community in African thought: An exploration of collective identity and social harmony. *Journal of African Studies and Sustainable Development*, *7*(3), 1–15.

Akanaeme, I. N., Ekwealor, F. N., Ifeluni, C. N., Onyishi, C. N., Obikwelu, C. L., Ohia, N. C., Obayi, L. N., Nwaoga, C. T., Okafor, A. E., Victor-Aigbodion, V., Ejiofor, T. E., Afiaenyi, I. C., Ekomaru, C. I., & Dike, I. C. (2021). Managing job stress among teachers of children with autism spectrum disorders: A randomised controlled trial of cognitive behavioral therapy with yoga. *Medicine*, *100*(46), E27312. Advance online publication. DOI: 10.1097/MD.0000000000027312 PMID: 34797272

Akande, O. O. (2024). *Exploring the Challenges Faced by Parents of Children With ASD in Rural Nigerian Communities: A Multidimensional Analysis of Support Systems and Intervention* [Ed.D., Houston Baptist University]. https://www.proquest.com/docview/3054424848/abstract/D177D505934E4DEBPQ/1

Akanle, O., & Nwaobiala, U. R. (2019). Changing but Fragile: Female Breadwinning and Family Stability in Nigeria. *Journal of Asian and African Studies*, *55*(3), 398–411. DOI: 10.1177/0021909619880283

Akbar, A. A., Rameli, M. F. P., Nor, A. R. M., & Rohana, N. A. M. (2024). Empowering Career Pathways for Asnaf Faqir (Poor People). *Global Journal Al-Thaqafah*, *JULY2024*(SPECIALISSUE), 155–170. DOI: 10.7187/GJATSI072024-11

Akin-Fakorede, O. O., Ironbar, V. E., Inaku, J. F., Ekpo, M. E., Umoh, M. S., Nakanda, E. V., Agbade, O. P., Bessong, C. D., Bessong, N. O., Ayiba, O. R., Odey, M. O., Odok, J. A., Arop, L. O., Eburu, O. S., Egbonyi, E. E., Undie, A. A., & Oko, B. A. (2025). Exploring the use of Assistive Digital Resources in Enhancing Learning for Students with Intellectual Disabilities in Cross River and Akwa Ibom States, Nigeria. *Journal of Intellectual Disability - Diagnosis and Treatment*, *13*(2), 161–177. DOI: 10.6000/2292-2598.2025.13.02.5

Akubo, J. (2025, October 30). Senator Natasha pushes autism bill. *The Guardian Nigeria*. https://guardian.ng/news/senator-natasha-pushes-autism-bill/

Alfawzan, S., & Almulhim, N. (2024). Barriers and facilitators to implementing transition services for students with intellectual disabilities in the kingdom of Saudi Arabia: A systematic review. *Journal of Intellectual Disabilities*, 17446295241301853. Advance online publication. DOI: 10.1177/17446295241301853

Ali, I. M. (2024). A guide for positivist research paradigm: From philosophy to methodology. *Idealogy Journal, 9*(2). https://www.idealogyjournal.com/ojs/index.php/idealogy/article/view/596

Alibekova, R., Kai Chan, C., Crape, B., Kadyrzhanuly, K., Gusmanov, A., An, S., Bulekbayeva, S., Akhmetzhanova, Z., Ainabekova, A., Yerubayev, Z., Yessimkulova, F., Bekisheva, A., Ospanova, Z., & Rakhimova, M. (2022). Stress, anxiety and depression in parents of children with autism spectrum disorders in Kazakhstan: Prevalence and associated factors. *Global Mental Health (Cambridge, England), 9*, 472–482. DOI: 10.1017/gmh.2022.51 PMID: 36618742

Ali, I. M. (2024). A Guide for positivist research paradigm: From philosophy to methodology. *Idealogy Journal*, *9*(2). Advance online publication. DOI: 10.24191/idealogy.v9i2.596

Almalky, H. A., & Alqahtani, S. S. (2021). Special education teachers' reflections on school transition practices that support partnerships with businesses to prepare students with disabilities for employment in Saudi Arabia. *Children and Youth Services Review*, *120*, 105813. Advance online publication. DOI: 10.1016/j.childyouth.2020.105813

Almughyiri, S. (2024). Saudi teachers 'knowledge and implementation of transitional skills and transition planning for students with autism spectrum disorder in Saudi Arabia. *International Journal of Developmental Disabilities*. Advance online publication. DOI: 10.1080/20473869.2024.2327783 PMID: 41624035

Alnuaimi, A., Opoku, M. P., & Nketsia, W. (2025). Assessment of school leadership and quality of inclusive practices in early childhood education in the United Arab Emirates. *Educational Management Administration & Leadership, 17411432251319999*, 17411432251319999. Advance online publication. DOI: 10.1177/17411432251319999

Alsarmi, A. M., & Al-Hemyari, Z. A. (2015). Quantitative and qualitative statistical indicators to assess the quality of teaching and learning in higher education institutions. *International Journal of Information and Decision Sciences*. https://www.inderscienceonline.com/doi/10.1504/IJIDS.2014.066631

Aluede, O., Iyamu, F., Adubale, A., & Oramah, E. U. (2017). Policy, Capacity Building and School-Based Counselling in Nigeria. In Carey, J. C., Harris, B., Lee, S. M., & Aluede, O. (Eds.), *International Handbook for Policy Research on School-Based Counseling* (pp. 239–253). Springer International Publishing., DOI: 10.1007/978-3-319-58179-8_16

Alwahbi, A. A. (2023). Effects of Joint Action Routine on Improving Social Behavior of a Student with ASD. *Education and Training in Autism and Developmental Disabilities, 58*(1), 62–73. DOI: 10.1177/215416472305800106

Alwell, M., & Cobb, B. (2009). Functional life skills curricular interventions for youth with disabilities: A systematic review. *Career Development for Exceptional Individuals, 32*(2), 82–93. DOI: 10.1177/0885728809336656

Americans with Disabilities Act. (1990). *Americans with Disabilities Act of 1990, As Amended.* https://www.ada.gov/law-and-regs/ada/

Amponteng, M., Tracey, D., & Nketsia, W. (2025). Exploring teachers' concerns and recommendations regarding inclusive education in Ghana: An application of the ecological systems theory. *International Journal of Inclusive Education*, 1–18. Advance online publication. DOI: 10.1080/13603116.2025.2541910

Amucheazi, C., & Nwankwo, C. M. (2020). Accessibility to infrastructure and disability rights in Nigeria: An analysis of the potential of the discrimination against persons with disability (prohibition) act 2018. *Commonwealth Law Bulletin, 46*(4), 689–710. DOI: 10.1080/03050718.2020.1781674

Amu, S. I., Answem, A. B., & Amu, M. M. (2025). Impact of stress on teacher's performance in business studies at junior secondary schools in Makurdi metropolis. *Open Journal of Educational Development, 6*(1), 29–42. DOI: 10.52417/ojed.v6i1.707

Anastasiou, S., & Belios, E. (2020). Effect of Age on Job Satisfaction and Emotional Exhaustion of Primary School Teachers in Greece. *European Journal of Investigation in Health, Psychology and Education, 10*(2), 644–655. DOI: 10.3390/ejihpe10020047 PMID: 34542525

Anazia, I. U., Skinner, B., & Woods, C. (2025). Home-school partnerships: Values and expectations of rural teachers and parents. *Educational Research, 67*(2), 170–189. DOI: 10.1080/00131881.2025.2492143

Andaluz-Delgado, S., Ordóñez-Olmedo, E., & Gutiérrez-Martín, N. (2025). The 5 Best Educational Apps to Enhance Learning for Students with ASD. *Siglo Cero, 56*(3), 99–114. DOI: 10.14201/scero.32119

Anderson, K. A., Sosnowy, C., Kuo, A. A., & Shattuck, P. T. (2018). Transition of individuals with autism to adulthood: A review of qualitative studies. *Pediatrics, 141*(Supplement_4), S318–S327. DOI: 10.1542/peds.2016-4300I PMID: 29610413

Anderson, L. L., Larson, S. A., & McDonald, S. (2013). Unmet needs and quality of support for parents of transition-aged youth: Differences by disability group, age, and household income. *Research in Social Science and Disability*, *7*, 63–95. DOI: 10.1108/S1479-3547(2013)0000007006

Angwaomaodoko, E. A. (2023). The Challenges and Opportunities of Inclusive Education in Nigeria. *Traektoriâ Nauki, 9*(07), 1001–1009. https://www.ceeol.com/search/article-detail?id=1264806

Angwaomaodoko, E. A. (2023a). A Critique of Inclusive Education Policy and the Extent of Its Implementation in Nigeria. *Traektoriâ Nauki*, *9*(11), 2001–2008. DOI: 10.22178/pos.98-4

Angwaomaodoko, E. A. (2023b). The challenges and opportunities of inclusive education in Nigeria. *Traektoriâ Nauki*, *9*(7), 1001–1009. DOI: 10.22178/pos.94-1

Anthony, C. S., Agbo, C. E., Ogieuhi, I. J., Ajekiigbe, V. O., Agu, M. C., Ayomide, J. H., Oyetola, E. O., Adejumo, T. P., Umenzeakor, K. H., Akinmeji, O., Ajimotokan, O. I., Matthew, O. A., & Ikekwere, J. C. (2025). Caregiving for children with autism in africa: A scoping review of socioeconomic impact with a call for intersectoral collaboration. *European Child & Adolescent Psychiatry*. Advance online publication. DOI: 10.1007/s00787-025-02843-1

Antoniou, A.-S., Polychroni, F., & Vlachakis, A.-N. (2006). Gender and age differences in occupational stress and professional burnout between primary and high-school teachers in Greece. *Journal of Managerial Psychology*, *21*(7), 682–690. DOI: 10.1108/02683940610690213

Anyanwu, J. I., Onuigbo, L. N., Obiyo, N. O., Eze, U. N., Akaneme, I. N., Aye, E. N., Enyi, C., Oforka, T. O., Chigbu, B. C., Ezenwaji, I. O., Ogbuabor, S. E., & Adimora, E. D. (2019). Parenting Stress in Families of Children With Autism Spectrum Disorder: The Roles of the Extended Family. *Global Journal of Health Science*, *11*(8), 51. DOI: 10.5539/gjhs.v11n8p51

Arar, K., Abu Nasra, M., & Alshafi, H. (2018). Arab teachers' perception of parent involvement (PI): Components and differences. *International Journal of Educational Management*, *32*(3), 326–341. DOI: 10.1108/IJEM-01-2016-0003

Arimoro, A. E. (2019). Are they not nigerians? The obligation of the state to end discriminatory practices against persons with disabilities. *International Journal of Discrimination and the Law, 19*(2), 89–109. DOI: 10.1177/1358229119846764

Arora, D., Berman, M., Snider, L. A., Segall, M., & South, M. (2025). Educators' knowledge about strategies and supports for autistic students in the transition from school to adulthood. *Research in Autism, 126*, 202648. Advance online publication. DOI: 10.1016/j.reia.2025.202648

Arubayi, D. O., & Akobo, L. A. (2018). The capability approach and national development in Nigeria: Towards a youth transition model. *Human Resource Development International, 21*(5), 463–492. DOI: 10.1080/13678868.2018.1468588

Asa, F. T., & Lasebikan, V. O. (2016). Mental health of teachers: Teachers' stress, anxiety and depression among secondary schools in Nigeria. *International Neuropsychiatric Disease Journal, 7*(4), 1–10. DOI: 10.9734/INDJ/2016/27039

Ashburner, J., Bennett, L., Rodger, S., & Ziviani, J. (2013). Understanding the sensory experiences of young people with autism spectrum disorder: A preliminary investigation. *Australian Occupational Therapy Journal, 60*(3), 171–180. DOI: 10.1111/1440-1630.12025 PMID: 23730782

Athamanah, L. S., & Cushing, L. S. (2019a). Implementing a peer-mediated intervention in a work-based learning setting for students with autism spectrum disorders. *Education and Training in Autism and Developmental Disabilities, 54*(2), 196–210. DOI: 10.1177/215416471905400209

Atkinson, G. (2014). Suitable for reframing: The myers-briggs type indicator in couples therapy. In Brothers, B. J. (Ed.), *Couples Therapy, Multiple Perspectives: In Search of Universal Threads* (pp. 121–132). Taylor and Francis., DOI: 10.4324/9781315801278

Australian Department of Education. (2022, July). *Milestones and transitions*. Australian Department of Education. https://www.education.gov.au/download/13621/milestones-and-transitions/28292/milestones-and-transitions/pdf

Autism New Zealand, & Ministry of Social Development. (2025). *Employment and Transition Services Support for gaining employment or to transition from school into work and general life.* AutismNZ. https://autismnz.org.nz/employment-transition-service

Awe, E. M., Stephenson, P., & Griffith, A. (2009). An assessment of education and training needs of skilled operatives within the Nigerian construction industry. *Assoc. Res. Constr. Manage., ARCOM - Proc. Annu. Conf.*, 685–694.

Ayala, K. (2023). LEADERS: A Psychoeducational support group for college-bound high school students with autism spectrum disorder (ASD). *Journal of Applied School Psychology*, *39*(4), 397–412. DOI: 10.1080/15377903.2023.2221201

Ayeni, A. J. (2017a). Teachers' Classroom management and Quality Assurance of Students' Learning Outcome in Secondary Schools in Ondo State, Nigeria. *Journal of Social and Administrative Sciences*, *4*(2), 166–180. DOI: 10.1453/jsas.v4i2.1312

Ayinla, I., Chang, H.-J., & Ayodele, K., & Olanrewaju. (2019). African Parents' Perceptions, Stress and Coping Strategy. *European Journal of Scientific Research*, *153*(4), 434–447.

Azad, G. F., Minton, K. E., Mandell, D. S., & Landa, R. J. (2021). Partners in School: An Implementation Strategy to Promote Alignment of Evidence-Based Practices Across Home and School for Children with Autism Spectrum Disorder. *Administration and Policy in Mental Health*, *48*(2), 266–278. DOI: 10.1007/s10488-020-01064-9 PMID: 32653973

Azubuike, A. O., Azubuike, P. C., Afape, A. O., Enyam, M. O., Akinreni, T., Imo, U. F., Nwadiche, M., Ogbonna, C. K., Timothy, P. N., Uchegbu, E. R., & Adai, G. S. (2025). Caregiving for autistic children in Nigeria: Experiences and challenges. *Discover Mental Health*, *5*(1), 32. DOI: 10.1007/s44192-025-00159-9 PMID: 40063222

Azubuike, A. O., Azubuike, P. C., Onyekachi, E. L., Enyam, M. O., Akinreni, T., Abuo, J., Ogbonna, C. K., Timothy, P. N., Uchegbu, E. R., & Adai, G. S. (2024). Experiences and unmet needs among caregivers of children living with autism spectrum disorder in Nigeria: A qualitative study using the socio-ecological model. *Discover Social Science and Health*, *4*(1), 77. Advance online publication. DOI: 10.1007/s44155-024-00141-w

Azubuike, P. C., Akinreni, T., Adai, S. G., Ogbonna, C. K., Abba, M. E., Udofia, M. D., Odo, O. J., Nwadiche, M., & Imo, U. F. (2025). Equity and social justice perspectives on disability inclusion in healthcare services in Nigeria. *Communications Medicine*, *5*(1), 1–7. DOI: 10.1038/s43856-025-01070-8

Bacakova, M., Veck, W., & Wharton, J. (Eds.). (2025). *Forced Migration, Disability and Education: Inclusion and Exclusion at the Intersection of Displacement and Disablement*. Routledge., DOI: 10.4324/9781003590422

Bakare, M. O., Ebigbo, P. O., Agomoh, A. O., Eaton, J., Onyeama, G. M., Okonkwo, K. O., Onwukwe, J. U., Igwe, M. N., Orovwigho, A. O., & Aguocha, C. M. (2009). Knowledge about childhood autism and opinion among healthcare workers on availability of facilities and law caring for the needs and rights of children with childhood autism and other developmental disorders in Nigeria. *BMC Pediatrics*, *9*(1), 12. DOI: 10.1186/1471-2431-9-12 PMID: 19216754

Bakare, M. O., Frazier, T. W., Karpur, A., Abubakar, A., Nyongesa, M. K., Mwangi, P. M., Dixon, P., Khaliq, I., Gase, N. K., Sandstrom, J., Okidegbe, N., Rosanoff, M., Munir, K. M., & Shih, A. (2022). Brief report: Validity and reliability of the Nigerian Autism Screening Questionnaire. *Autism*, *26*(6), 1581–1590. DOI: 10.1177/13623613221080250 PMID: 35261274

Bakare, M. O., Taiwo, O. G., Bello-Mojeed, M. A., & Munir, K. M. (2019). Autism Spectrum Disorders in Nigeria: A Scoping Review of Literature and Opinion on Future Research and Social Policy Directions. *Journal of Health Care for the Poor and Underserved*, *30*(3), 899–909. DOI: 10.1353/hpu.2019.0063 PMID: 31422978

Bakare, M. O., Tunde-Ayinmode, M. F., Adewuya, A. O., Bello-Mojeed, M. A., Sale, S., James, B. O., Yunusa, M. A., Obindo, J. T., Igwe, M. N., Odinka, P. C., Okafor, C. J., Oshodi, Y. O., Okonoda, K. M., Munir, K. M., & Orovwigho, A. O. (2015). Recognition of Autism Spectrum Disorder (ASD) symptoms and knowledge about some other aspects of ASD among final year medical students in Nigeria, Sub-Saharan Africa. *BMC Research Notes*, *8*(1), 1–8. DOI: 10.1186/s13104-015-1433-0

Balachandran, K. P., & Bhuvaneswari, M. (2024). 'I may have to give up on my career.' Breadwinners or caregivers? Exploring the complexities of work-family conflict among parents of children with neurodevelopmental disabilities. *International Journal of Developmental Disabilities*, *0*(0), 1–18. DOI: 10.1080/20473869.2024.2394733

Bambling, M. (2014). Creating positive outcomes in clinical supervision. In C. Edward Watkins & D. L. Milne (Eds.), *The Wiley International Handbook of Clinical Supervision* (pp. 445–457). wiley. DOI: 10.1002/9781118846360.ch21

Bansal, D., & Bhattacharya, N. (2025). Navigating Success: The Intersection of Emotional Intelligence and Career Development. In Dutta, P. K., Gupta, S., Kashyap, S., Gehlot, A., Karmakar, R., & Bhattacharya, P. (Eds.), *Emotional Intelligence in the Digital Era: Concepts, Frameworks, and Applications* (pp. 141–158). CRC Press., DOI: 10.1201/9781032715377-10

Barbi, K. B. S., Serralvo, E. R., Pavão, G. M., Bitencort, L. P., Messias, J. C. C., & Labarthe, J. (2024). Challenges of social interaction of people with autism in the job market. *Ciencias Psicológicas (Montevideo)*, *18*(1). Advance online publication. DOI: 10.22235/cp.v18i1.3283

Barrett, B., Byford, S., Sharac, J., Hudry, K., Leadbitter, K., Temple, K., Aldred, C., Slonims, V., Green, J., Bourne, K., Blazey, L., Holt, C., Kapadia, D., MacDonald, W., Pickles, A., White, L., Houghton, T., Taylor, C., Cutress, A., & Charman, T. (2012). Service and wider societal costs of very young children with autism in the UK. *Journal of Autism and Developmental Disorders*, *42*(5), 797–804. DOI: 10.1007/s10803-011-1306-x

Barrio, B. L., Miller, D., Ojeme, C., & Tamakloe, D. (2019). Teachers' and Parents' Knowledge about Disabilities and Inclusion in Nigeria. *Journal of International Special Needs Education*, *22*(1), 14–24. DOI: 10.9782/17-00010

Baum, A., Fleming, R., & Singer, J. E. (2020). Understanding environmental stress: Strategies for conceptual and methodological integration. In A. Baum & J. E. Singer (Eds.), *Advances in Environmental Psychology (Volume 5): Methods and Environmental Psychology* (pp. 185–205). Taylor and Francis. DOI: 10.4324/9781003052944-7

Baum, C. (2024). KITCHEN TASK ASSESSMENT (KTA). In Bortnick, K. (Ed.), *Occupational Therapy Assessments for Older Adults: 100 Instruments for Measuring Occupational Performance* (pp. 250–251). Taylor and Francis., DOI: 10.4324/9781003525288-103

Bellman, S., Burgstahler, S., & Ladner, R. (2014). Work-based learning experiences help students with disabilities transition to careers: A case study of University of Washington projects. *Work (Reading, Mass.)*, *48*(3), 399–405. DOI: 10.3233/WOR-131780 PMID: 24284672

Bello-Mojeed, M., Ani, C., Lagunju, I., & Omigbodun, O. (2016). Feasibility of parent-mediated behavioural intervention for behavioural problems in children with Autism Spectrum Disorder in Nigeria: A pilot study. *Child and Adolescent Psychiatry and Mental Health*, *10*(1), 1–8. DOI: 10.1186/s13034-016-0117-4

Benita, M., & Matos, L. (2021). Internalization of Mastery Goals: The Differential Effect of Teachers' Autonomy Support and Control. *Frontiers in Psychology*, *11*, 599303. DOI: 10.3389/fpsyg.2020.599303 PMID: 33613356

Bertrand-Ouellet, J., Vincent, C., Julien-Gauthier, F., Dumont, F., Desmarais, C., Lecours, A., Poulin, V., Kiss, J., Hu, T., & Blouin, L. (2025). Instructional Videos to Familiarize Young Autistic Adults With Grocery Tasks With a View to Vocational Integration: From Design to Practicability. *Journal of Vocational Rehabilitation*, *62*(3), 218–233. DOI: 10.1177/10522263251326017

Bhattacharya, S., Sethi, M., Behl, A., & Venkatesh, V. G. (2017). *12. Regression techniques and their application in the corporate social responsibility domain: An overview. Handbook of Research Methods in Corporate Social Responsibility*. Elgar Online., DOI: 10.4337/9781784710927.00019

Bialopotocki, R. N. (2006). *Recognition and Praise Relate to Teachers' Job Satisfaction* [Ph.D., The University of Nebraska - Lincoln]. https://www.proquest.com/docview/305291829/abstract/33DAF7ED8DE43FCPQ/1

Biddle, B. J. (1979). *Role Theory: Expectations, Identities, and Behaviors. Elsevier.* Academic Press., DOI: 10.1016/C2009-0-03121-3

Bitsika, V. (2008). Including an analysis of difficult behaviour in the assessment of children with an autism spectrum disorder: Implications for school psychologists. *Australian Journal of Guidance & Counselling*, *18*(1), 1–14. DOI: 10.1375/ajgc.18.1.1

Bitsika, V., & Sharpley, C. F. (2004). Stress, Anxiety and Depression Among Parents of Children With Autism Spectrum Disorder. *Australian Journal of Guidance & Counselling*, *14*(2), 151–161. DOI: 10.1017/S1037291100002466

Bitsika, V., Warren, A. C., & Sharpley, C. F. (2017). An evaluation of a professional development programme in functional behavior assessment for educators in Australia. *International Journal of Special Education*, *32*(3), 630–641.

Black, W. R., & Simon, M. D. (2014). Leadership for all students: Planning for more inclusive school practices. *The International Journal of Educational Leadership Preparation*, *9*(2), 153–172.

Blokker, R., Akkermans, J., Nguyen, Y. N. N., Khapova, S., & Jansen, P. (2025). Beyond one-size-fits-all in school-to-work transition success: The role of career competency profiles. *Journal of Vocational Behavior*, *161*, 104158. Advance online publication. DOI: 10.1016/j.jvb.2025.104158

Bochaver, A. A., Akhmedjanova, D. R., Bayramyan, R. M., & Fomicheva, E. V. (2023). Initial psychometric properties of the Parental Stress Scale examined using a sample of Russian mothers. *Frontiers in Psychology*, *14*, 1202401. Advance online publication. DOI: 10.3389/fpsyg.2023.1202401 PMID: 37731869

Boujut, E., Dean, A., Grouselle, A., & Cappe, E. (2016). Comparative Study of Teachers in Regular Schools and Teachers in Specialized Schools in France, Working with Students with an Autism Spectrum Disorder: Stress, Social Support, Coping Strategies and Burnout. *Journal of Autism and Developmental Disorders, 46*(9), 2874–2889. DOI: 10.1007/s10803-016-2833-2 PMID: 27282858

Bredeson, P. V. (1993). Letting Go of Outlived Professional Identities: A Study of Role Transition and Role Strain for Principals in Restructured Schools. *Educational Administration Quarterly, 29*(1), 34–68. DOI: 10.1177/0013161X93029001004

Bridges, S., & Searle, A. (2011). Changing workloads of primary school teachers: "I seem to live on the edge of chaos.". *School Leadership & Management, 31*(5), 413–433. DOI: 10.1080/13632434.2011.614943

Bright, J. E. H., & Pryor, R. G. L. (2015). Limitation and Creativity: A Chaos Theory of Careers Perspective. In Maree, K., & Di Fabio, A. (Eds.), *Exploring New Horizons in Career Counselling: Turning Challenge into Opportunities* (pp. 131–147). Sense Publishers., DOI: 10.1007/978-94-6300-154-0_8

Bronfenbrenner, U. (1994). Ecological models of human development. *International Encyclopedia of Education, 3*(2), 37–43.

Bronfenbrenner, U. (2000). *Ecological systems theory.* American Psychological Association. https://psycnet.apa.org/record/2004-12701-046

Brooke, V., Brooke, A. M., Schall, C., Wehman, P., McDonough, J., Thompson, K., & Smith, J. (2018). Employees with Autism Spectrum Disorder Achieving Long-Term Employment Success: A Retrospective Review of Employment Retention and Intervention. *Research and Practice for Persons with Severe Disabilities : the Journal of TASH, 43*(3), 181–193. DOI: 10.1177/1540796918783202

Brooks, F., Bunn, F., & Morgan, J. (2009). Transition for adolescents with long-term conditions: Event to process. *British Journal of Community Nursing, 14*(7), 301–304. DOI: 10.12968/bjcn.2009.14.7.43078 PMID: 19597382

Bross, L. A., Leko, M., Patry, M. B., & Travers, J. C. (2021). Barriers to competitive integrated employment of young adults with autism spectrum disorder. *Education and Training in Autism and Developmental Disabilities, 56*(4), 394–408. DOI: 10.1177/21541647210560040 3

Brown, H. K., Ouellette-Kuntz, H., Hunter, D., & Kelley, E. (2010). Assessing need in school-aged children with an autism spectrum disorder. *Research in Autism Spectrum Disorders, 4*(4), 539–547. DOI: 10.1016/j.rasd.2009.12.009

Bruck, S., Webster, A. A., & Clark, T. (2022). Transition support for students on the autism spectrum: A multiple stakeholder perspective. *Journal of Research in Special Educational Needs*, *22*(1), 3–17. DOI: 10.1111/1471-3802.12509

Buchholz, S. W. (2021). Quantitative designs for practice scholarship. In B. A. Staffileno, M. P. Murphy, & S. W. Buchholz (Eds.), *Research for Advanced Practice Nurses, Fourth Edition: From Evidence to Practice* (pp. 143–172). Springer Publishing Company. DOI: 10.1891/9780826151339.0009

Buhari, A. M., Sultan Ibrahim, S. A., & Radhil, N. I. M. (2025). Exploring Factors Influencing Employment Opportunities Among People With Disabilities: A Scoping Review. *Malaysian Journal of Medicine and Health Sciences*, *21*, 253–264. DOI: 10.47836/mjmhs.21.s7.29

Bukhori, I., Nora, E., & Suputra, I. N. (2020). Role conflict, training, and participative leadership on teachers' performance: Lesson from junior high school in Mojokerto of Indonesia. *International Journal of Scientific and Technology Research*, *9*(3), 3264–3266.

Buntinx, W. (2008). The logic of relations and the logic of management. *Journal of Intellectual Disability Research*, *52*(7), 588–597. DOI: 10.1111/j.1365-2788.2008.01067.x PMID: 18557861

Busack, J., Payton, C., & Hudson, C. (2021). Harnessing Community Resources to Enhance Student Learning and Development. In Cox, T., Fitzgerald, T., & Alvarez, M. E. (Eds.), *The Art of Becoming Indispensable: What School Social Workers Need to Know in Their First Three Years of Practice* (pp. 75–84). Oxford University Press., DOI: 10.1093/oso/9780197585160.003.0008

Cadondon, S., Dawson, M., Carriere, J. A., Griffiths, A. J., & Gehricke, J.-G. (2023). Short report: Initial pilot of a brief career development program for autistic young adults. *Research in Developmental Disabilities*, *143*, 104634. Advance online publication. DOI: 10.1016/j.ridd.2023.104634 PMID: 37939494

Calderwood, C., Breaux, R., ten Brummelhuis, L. L., Mitropoulos, T., & Swanson, C. S. (2022). When daily challenges become too much during COVID-19: Implications of family and work demands for work–life balance among parents of children with special needs. *Journal of Occupational Health Psychology*, *27*(5), 516–527. DOI: 10.1037/ocp0000333 PMID: 35901404

Cappe, É., Despax, J., Ridremont, D., & Boujut, E. (2025). Are Stress and Burnout Specific to French Teachers of Autistic Students? A Comparative Study With Attention-Deficit/Hyperactivity Disorder and Conduct Disorder. *Psychology in the Schools*, *62*(5), 1397–1409. DOI: 10.1002/pits.23409

Carden, J. (2025). Self-Awareness. In Laker, B., Soga, L. R., & Bolade-Ogunfodun, Y. (Eds.), *Elgar Encyclopedia of Leadership* (pp. 284–285). Edward Elgar Publishing Ltd., DOI: 10.4337/9781035307074.000123

Carolan, M., & Slattery, Ó. M. (2025). The nature of collaboration in transition planning for autistic students moving into further education and training from the perspectives of post-primary teachers in Ireland. *Irish Educational Studies*, 1–23. Advance online publication. DOI: 10.1080/03323315.2025.2509522

Carter, E. W., Harvey, M. N., Taylor, J. L., & Gotham, K. (2013). Connecting Youth and Young Adults with Autism Spectrum Disorders to Community Life. *Psychology in the Schools*, *50*(9), 888–898. DOI: 10.1002/pits.21716 PMID: 26236045

Carter, E. W., & Schutz, M. A. (2022). Addressing Transition Preparation in Middle and High Schools. In Viezel, K. D., Wilczynski, S. M., & Davis, A. S. (Eds.), *Postsecondary Transition for College- or Career-Bound Autistic Students* (pp. 179–200). Springer International Publishing., DOI: 10.1007/978-3-030-93947-2_9

Challenger, C. D., Lombardi, A. R., Duquette, K., Espositio, C., & DeJesus, J. (2025). Strategies to Increase Collaboration Between School Counselors and Transition Specialists: A Multi-Tiered Approach to College and Career Readiness. *Journal of Education*, *205*(2), 153–165. DOI: 10.1177/00220574241309103

Chan, C.-C., Chen, S.-C., Lin, Y.-W., Liao, T.-Y., & Lin, Y.-E. (2018). Social Cognitive Perspective on Factors Influencing Taiwanese Sport Management Students' Career Intentions. *Journal of Career Development*, *45*(3), 239–252. DOI: 10.1177/0894845316681643

Chancel, R., Miot, S., Dellapiazza, F., & Baghdadli, A. (2022). Group-based educational interventions in adolescents and young adults with ASD without ID: A systematic review focusing on the transition to adulthood. *European Child & Adolescent Psychiatry*, *31*(7), 1–21. DOI: 10.1007/s00787-020-01609-1 PMID: 32889578

Chandra, S. (Ed.). (2024). *Universal Design for Learning: Addressing the Barriers.* IP Innovative Publication., DOI: 10.18231/978-93-91208-76-9

Chandroo, R., Strnadová, I., & Cumming, T. M. (2018). A systematic review of the involvement of students with autism spectrum disorder in the transition planning process: Need for voice and empowerment. *Research in Developmental Disabilities*, *83*, 8–17. DOI: 10.1016/j.ridd.2018.07.011 PMID: 30086472

Chan, V., Moore, J., Derenne, J., & Fuchs, D. C. (2019). Transitional age youth and college mental health. *Child and Adolescent Psychiatric Clinics of North America*, *28*(3), 363–375. DOI: 10.1016/j.chc.2019.02.008 PMID: 31076114

Chapados, P., Provencher, S., Aramideh, J., Dumont, É., Lugasi, T., Laverdière, C., Sultan, S., & Desjardins, L. (2023). Transition Readiness Assessment Questionnaire: Skill gaps and psychosocial predictors of transition readiness among adolescents and young adults with chronic medical conditions. *Child: Care, Health and Development, 50*(1).1-10. e13156. DOI: 10.1111/cch.13156

Charles, O. O. (2019). Cultural factors currently affecting inclusive practice—Africa. In Heck, S., & Block, M. E. (Eds.), *Inclusive Physical Education Around the World: Origins, Cultures, Practices* (pp. 205–213). Taylor and Francis., DOI: 10.4324/9780429026294-14

Chauvet, G. (2015). Coupling methods for multistage sampling. *Annals of Statistics, 43*(6), 2484–2506. DOI: 10.1214/15-AOS1348

Chen, B. B., & Yakubova, G. (2023). Evaluating the Effects of Video-Based Intervention to Teach Vocational Skills to Transition-Age Youth with Autism Spectrum Disorder: An Evidence-Based Systematic Review. *Review Journal of Autism and Developmental Disorders, 10*(1), 22–37. DOI: 10.1007/s40489-021-00282-7

Chen, J. L., Leader, G., Sung, C., & Leahy, M. (2015). Trends in Employment for Individuals with Autism Spectrum Disorder: A Review of the Research Literature. *Review Journal of Autism and Developmental Disorders, 2*(2), 115–127. DOI: 10.1007/s40489-014-0041-6

Chen, J., Cohn, E. S., & Orsmond, G. I. (2019). Parents' future visions for their autistic transition-age youth: Hopes and expectations. *Autism, 23*(6), 1363–1372. DOI: 10.1177/1362361318812141 PMID: 30445828

Chen, S., Haziza, D., & Mashreghi, Z. (2022). A Comparison of Existing Bootstrap Algorithms for Multi-Stage Sampling Designs. *Stats, 5*(2), 521–537. DOI: 10.3390/stats5020031 PMID: 38737922

Chen, X., Yu, Q., Yu, F., Huang, Y., & Zhang, L. (2019). Psychometric evaluation of the Chinese version of the Snizek-revised Hall's Professionalism Inventory Scale. *The Journal of International Medical Research, 47*(3), 1154–1168. DOI: 10.1177/0300060518817401 PMID: 30614338

Cherewick, M., & Matergia, M. (2024). Neurodiversity in Practice: A Conceptual Model of Autistic Strengths and Potential Mechanisms of Change to Support Positive Mental Health and Wellbeing in Autistic Children and Adolescents. *Advances in Neurodevelopmental Disorders, 8*(3), 408–422. DOI: 10.1007/s41252-023-00348-z

Chigangaidze, R. K., & Chinyenze, P. (2022). What it means to say, 'a person is a person through other persons': Ubuntu through humanistic-existential lenses of transactional analysis. *Journal of Religion & Spirituality in Social Work, 41*(3), 280–295. DOI: 10.1080/15426432.2022.2039341

Childre, A., & Chambers, C. R. (2005). Family perceptions of student centered planning and IEP meetings. *Education and Training in Developmental Disabilities, 40*(3), 217–233. DOI: 10.1177/215416470504000304

Chitiyo, J., Simone, K., Taole, M., & Motitswe, J. M. (2026). An examination of South African teachers' competency in inclusive education: A case of Limpopo. *Journal of Research in Special Educational Needs, 26*(1), e70046. Advance online publication. DOI: 10.1111/1471-3802.70046

Chong, K., Neo, P. H., Sing, S. H., Krishnan, T., & Choo, K. W. (2021). Enhancing workplace learning through structured internship. *Proc. Int. CDIO. Conf.*, 273–282.

Chow, C., & Cooper, K. (2024). What Are the Lived Experiences of Strengths in Autistic Individuals? A Systematic Review and Thematic Synthesis. *Autism in Adulthood: Challenges and Management*, aut.2023.0172. Advance online publication. DOI: 10.1089/aut.2023.0172

Chung, I. (2006). The use of reframing in clinical practice with Chinese immigrants. *Journal of Immigrant and Refugee Services, 3*(3–4), 1–14. DOI: 10.1300/J191v03n03_01

Chun, J., Curtiss, S. L., Richard, C., Zhou, K., Rios, Y. C., Park, S., Kim, J., & Koc, M. (2025). Where Does Hope Lie? The Dialectical Tensions Between Hopes and Expectations of Vocational Transition Planning from the Perspectives of Autistic Young Adults, Parents, and Practitioners. *Journal of Autism and Developmental Disorders, 55*(5), 1857–1875. DOI: 10.1007/s10803-024-06348-9 PMID: 38635131

Chun, J., Kuo, H. J., Curtiss, S. L., Lee, G. K., Lee, H., & Awadu, J. (2023). The interplay of supports and barriers during the transition to adulthood for youth on the autism spectrum. *Disability and Rehabilitation, 45*(18), 2879–2889. DOI: 10.1080/09638288.2022.2112097

Cimera, R. E., Burgess, S., & Wiley, A. (2013). Does Providing Transition Services Early Enable Students with ASD to Achieve Better Vocational Outcomes as Adults? *Research and Practice for Persons with Severe Disabilities : the Journal of TASH, 38*(2), 88–93. DOI: 10.2511/027494813807714474

Clarà, M., Mauri, T., Colomina, R., & Onrubia, J. (2019). Supporting collaborative reflection in teacher education: A case study. *European Journal of Teacher Education, 42*(2), 175–191. DOI: 10.1080/02619768.2019.1576626

Clark, M., & Adams, D. (2020). The self-identified positive attributes and favourite activities of children on the autism spectrum. *Research in Autism Spectrum Disorders, 72*, 101512. Advance online publication. DOI: 10.1016/j.rasd.2020.101512

Cleary, M., West, S., McLean, L., Johnston-Devin, C., Kornhaber, R., & Hungerford, C. (2024). When the Education System and Autism Collide: An Australian Qualitative Study Exploring School Exclusion and the Impact on Parent Mental Health. *Issues in Mental Health Nursing, 45*(5), 468–476. DOI: 10.1080/01612840.2024.2328251

Cohen, R., Katz, I., Aelterman, N., & Vansteenkiste, M. (2022). Understanding shifts in students' academic motivation across a school year: The role of teachers' motivating styles and need-based experiences. *European Journal of Psychology of Education*, •••, 1–26. DOI: 10.1007/s10212-022-00635-8 PMID: 40479431

Conger, R. D., Conger, K. J., & Martin, M. J. (2010). Socioeconomic Status, Family Processes,and Individual Development. *Journal of Marriage and Family, 72*(3), 685–704. DOI: 10.1111/j.1741-3737.2010.00725.x PMID: 20676350

Connor, A., Fabrizi, S. E., Nasamran, A., & Sung, C. (2022). Near-Peer Facilitation of a Soft Skills Program for Young Adults With Autism. *The American Journal of Occupational Therapy, 76*(4), 7604345020. Advance online publication. DOI: 10.5014/ajot.2022.048207 PMID: 35759360

Coombs, E. C., Vincent, J., McMorris, C. A., & Ames, M. E. (2023). Barriers and facilitators to supporting Canadian autistic postsecondary students: Experiences of accessible learning staff and administrators. *Research in Autism Spectrum Disorders, 109*, 102260. Advance online publication. DOI: 10.1016/j.rasd.2023.102260

Coppola, P. J., & Young, A. F. (2022). Making the difficult career transition: Writing the next chapter during the great resignation or in the future. *Frontiers in Psychology, 13*, 905813. Advance online publication. DOI: 10.3389/fpsyg.2022.905813 PMID: 36389592

Corby-Edwards, A. K. (2014). The Combating Autism Act: Overview and funding. In D. Harlow (Ed.), *The Combating Autism Act: Elements, Funding and Analyses* (pp. 1–18). Nova Science Publishers, Inc.

Córdova, A., Caballero-García, A., Drobnic, F., Roche, E., & Noriega, D. C. (2023). Influence of Stress and Emotions in the Learning Process: The Example of COVID-19 on University Students: A Narrative Review. *Health Care, 11*(12), 1787. DOI: 10.3390/healthcare11121787 PMID: 37372905

Cornelius-Ukpepi, B. U., & Opuwari, O. S. (2019). Determinants of effective implementation of inclusive education at the basic education level in Nigeria. *Brock Journal of Education, 7*(8), 34–44.

Corona, L. L., Christodulu, K. V., & Rinaldi, M. L. (2017). Investigation of School Professionals' Self-Efficacy for Working With Students With ASD: Impact of Prior Experience, Knowledge, and Training. *Journal of Positive Behavior Interventions, 19*(2), 90–101. DOI: 10.1177/1098300716667604

Courchesne, V., Langlois, V., Gregoire, P., St-Denis, A., Bouvet, L., Ostrolenk, A., & Mottron, L. (2020). Interests and Strengths in Autism, Useful but Misunderstood: A Pragmatic Case-Study. *Frontiers in Psychology, 11*, 569339. Advance online publication. DOI: 10.3389/fpsyg.2020.569339 PMID: 33123051

Craig, F., Operto, F. F., De Giacomo, A., Margari, L., Frolli, A., Conson, M., Ivagnes, S., Monaco, M., & Margari, F. (2016). Parenting stress among parents of children with Neurodevelopmental Disorders. *Psychiatry Research, 242*, 121–129. DOI: 10.1016/j.psychres.2016.05.016 PMID: 27280521

Crosbie, J., Wilson, E., Davis, H., & Campain, R. (2024). *School to work transition for young people with disability, the current ecosystem, and the Ticket to Work approach.* https://figshare.swinburne.edu.au/articles/report/School_to_work_transition_for_young_people_with_disability_the_current_ecosystem_and_the_Ticket_to_Work_approach/28646756

Crowell, J. A., Keluskar, J., & Gorecki, A. (2019). Parenting behavior and the development of children with autism spectrum disorder. *Comprehensive Psychiatry, 90*, 21–29. DOI: 10.1016/j.comppsych.2018.11.007 PMID: 30658339

Cui, Z., Oshri, A., Liu, S., Smith, E. P., & Kogan, S. M. (2020). Child Maltreatment and Resilience: The Promotive and Protective Role of Future Orientation. *Journal of Youth and Adolescence, 49*(10), 2075–2089. DOI: 10.1007/s10964-020-01227-9 PMID: 32236791

Cumming, T. M., Strnadová, I., & Danker, J. (2020). Transitions of Students with Autism and Intellectual Disabilities in Inclusive Settings: The Nexus Between Recommended and Actual Practice. *Australasian Journal of Special and Inclusive Education, 44*(1), 28–45. DOI: 10.1017/jsi.2020.1

Dada, J. A., Adesina, S., Obaseki, B. E., Dada, G. O., & Adesina, J. A. (2025). Can Role Ambiguity and Role Conflict Affect Employee's Job Performance in Christian Faith-based University in Nigeria. *Journal of Arts and Sociological Research.* DOI: 10.70382/ajasr.v8i6.033

Dale, B. A., Ogle, L. N., Ruble, L. A., & Azad, G. F. (2025). Dyadic mechanisms of effect in home–school consultation: Evidence from two school-based consultation models. *School Psychology International, 46*(2), 115–134. DOI: 10.1177/01430343241283025

Dallas, B., Ramisch, J., & Ashmore, A. (2018). How Involved should they be? Students with ASD in postsecondary settings and their family members. *The Qualitative Report, 23*(5), 1208–1222. DOI: 10.46743/2160-3715/2018.3149

Dankade, U., Bello, H., & Deba, A. (2016). Analysis of job stress affecting the performance of secondary schools' vocational technical teachers in north east, Nigeria. *Journal of Technical Education and Training, 8*(1), 43–51.

Darpatova-Hruzewicz, D., Marek, P., & Kaminski, K. (2025). An Ecological Investigation of Polish Olympic Coaches' Career Pathways and Their Experiences of Career Transition to Olympic Coaching Roles. *International Sport Coaching Journal, 12*(1), 79–92. DOI: 10.1123/iscj.2023-0109

David, L. T., Tru a, C., Cazan, A.-M., Albisser, S., & Keller-Schneider, M. (2022). Exploring the impact of a career guidance intervention program in schools: Effects on knowledge and skills as self-assessed by students. *Current Psychology (New Brunswick, N.J.), 41*(7), 4545–4556. DOI: 10.1007/s12144-020-00973-0

Davis, M. T., Watts, G. W., & López, E. J. (2021). A systematic review of firsthand experiences and supports for students with autism spectrum disorder in higher education. *Research in Autism Spectrum Disorders, 84*, 101769. Advance online publication. DOI: 10.1016/j.rasd.2021.101769

de Oliveira Bernardo, N. (2025). *Promoting a Fully Inclusive School Culture* [PhD Thesis, Grand Canyon University]. https://search.proquest.com/openview/0ac571050860c1d08c2899c64c92cf6c/1?pq-origsite=gscholar&cbl=18750&diss=y

Dean, E. E., Hagiwara, M., Shogren, K. A., Wehmeyer, M. L., & Shrum, J. (2022). Promoting Career Design in Youth and Young Adults with ASD: A Feasibility Study. *Journal of Autism and Developmental Disorders, 52*(6), 2689–2700. DOI: 10.1007/s10803-021-05146-x PMID: 34184143

Deardorff, M. E., Peltier, C., Choiseul-Praslin, B., Williams-Diehm, K., & Wicker, M. (2021). Teacher Knowledge in Transition Planning: Does Locale Matter? *Rural Special Education Quarterly, 40*(3), 132–142. DOI: 10.1177/87568705211027982

DeMatteo, F., & Arter, P. S. (2015). When Job Skills Are Not Enough: Transitioning Young Adults with Autism Spectrum Disorder. *Electronic Journal for Inclusive Education, 3*(3), 6.

Deng, Y., Zeng, H., Xu, A., & Chen, Y. (2022). Based on Role Expectation to Discuss Role Ambiguity and Practice of University Teachers in Business Administration. *Frontiers in Psychology, 13*, 789806. DOI: 10.3389/fpsyg.2022.789806 PMID: 36478930

Dente, C. L., & Parkinson Coles, K. (2012). Ecological approaches to transition planning for students with autism and asperger's syndrome. *Children & Schools, 34*(1), 27–36. DOI: 10.1093/cs/cdr002

Department of Education. (2001, July). *Education White Paper 6, Special Needs Education: Building an inclusive education and training system*. Department of Education, South Africa. https://www.gov.za/sites/default/files/gcis_document/201409/educ61.pdf

Dermer, S. B. (2014). On a scale from one to ten…. In T. S. Nelson & T. S. Trepper (Eds.), *101 More Interventions in Family Therapy* (pp. 266–268). Taylor and Francis. https://doi.org/DOI: 10.4324/9781315810072-65

DesChamps, T. D., Ibañez, L. V., Edmunds, S. R., Dick, C. C., & Stone, W. L. (2020). Parenting stress in caregivers of young children with ASD concerns prior to a formal diagnosis. *Autism Research, 13*(1), 82–92. DOI: 10.1002/aur.2213 PMID: 31593362

Devi, B., Lepcha, N., & Basnet, S. (2022). Application of correlational research design in nursing and medical research. *Journal of Xi'an Shiyou University, Natural Sciences Edition, 65*(11), 60-69. https://doi.org/DOI: 10.17605/OSF.IO/YRZ68

Devi, B., Lepcha, N., & Basnet, S. (2022). Application of correlational research design in nursing and medical research. *Journal of Xi'an Shiyou University. Natural Sciences Education, 65*(11), 60–69.

Dhai, A., & Kurihara, C. (2025). Ubuntu Principles: Solidarity to Include Vulnerable Communities for Equitable Access. In C. Kurihara, D. Greco, & A. Dhai (Eds.), *The 2024 Declaration of Helsinki: Global Efforts Towards the Highest Ethical Standards* (pp. 23–32). Springer Science+Business Media. DOI: 10.1007/978-981-96-9294-1_2

Dhungana, P., Joshi, A., Chalise, A., & Paudel, S. (2025). Psychological well-being and occupational stress among public secondary school teachers in Beni Municipality, Nepal: A cross-sectional study. *BMC Public Health*, *25*(1), 3372. DOI: 10.1186/s12889-025-24677-x PMID: 41057805

Di Rezze, B., O'Connor, I., Georgiades, S., Brennan, R., Honeyman, S., DiFazio, A., Hall, G. B., Chan, L., Steele, R., Fallowfield, E., & Bennett, T. (2023). The Development and Evaluation of a Cross-Context Employment Program for Autistic Adolescents. *Autism in Adulthood: Challenges and Management*, *5*(4), 457–467. DOI: 10.1089/aut.2022.0010 PMID: 38116048

Diale, B. M., & Eseadi, C. (2024). *Perspectives on Career Transitioning of Students with Attention Deficit Hyperactivity Disorder (ADHD)*. IGI Global., DOI: 10.4018/979-8-3693-2635-0

Diale, B. M., & Eseadi, C. (2025). *Perspectives on career transitioning of students with attention deficit hyperactivity disorder (ADHD)*. IGI Global.

Dietrich, J., & Salmela-Aro, K. (2013). Parental involvement and adolescents' career goal pursuit during the post-school transition. *Journal of Adolescence*, *36*(1), 121–128. DOI: 10.1016/j.adolescence.2012.10.009 PMID: 23190942

Dijkstra-de Neijs, L., Boeke, D. B., Van Berckelaer-Onnes, I. A., Swaab, H., & Ester, W. A. (2024). Parental Stress and Quality of Life in Parents of Young Children with Autism. *Child Psychiatry and Human Development*. Advance online publication. DOI: 10.1007/s10578-024-01693-3 PMID: 38724870

Dike, I. C., Onyishi, C. N., Adimora, D. E., Ugodulunwa, C. A., Adama, G. N., Ugwu, G. C., Eze, U. N., Eze, A., Ogba, F. N., Obiwluozo, P. E., Onu, J. C., Onu, A. O., Omenma, Z. O., Nwaeze, V. C., Ani, C., Ngwu, C. N., Uzodinma, U. E., & Iremeka, F. U. (2021). Yoga complemented cognitive behavioral therapy on job burnout among teachers of children with autism spectrum disorders. *Medicine*, *100*(22), E25801. Advance online publication. DOI: 10.1097/MD.0000000000025801 PMID: 34087823

Dike, N., D'Ambruoso, L., Morgan, H. M., Skea, Z. C., & Ekpenyong, B. N. (2025). How does the Nigerian health system serve people living with disabilities? A socio-ecological analysis on people living with visual impairment. *Global Health Action*, *18*(1), 1–23. DOI: 10.1080/16549716.2025.2581456

Dillenburger, K., McKerr, L., Jordan, J.-A., & Keenan, M. (2016). Staff training in autism: The one-eyed wo/man.... *International Journal of Environmental Research and Public Health*, *13*(7), 716. DOI: 10.3390/ijerph13070716

Dinamarca-Aravena, K. A. (2024). Professional training of health professionals to work in schools with school integration programmes in Chile: A mixed-methods analysis. *Professional Development in Education, 50*(2), 263–278. DOI: 10.1080/19415257.2023.2203721

Dipeolu, A. O., Storlie, C., & Johnson, C. (2015). College Students with High-Functioning Autism Spectrum Disorder: Best Practices for Successful Transition to the World of Work. *Journal of College Counseling, 18*(2), 175–190. DOI: 10.1002/jocc.12013

Disability Standards for Education. (2005). *Disability Standards for Education 2005*. Attorney-General's Department Australia. https://www.legislation.gov.au/F2005L00767/latest/text

Ditchman, N. M., Miller, J. L., & Easton, A. B. (2018). Vocational Rehabilitation Service Patterns: An Application of Social Network Analysis to Examine Employment Outcomes of Transition-Age Individuals With Autism. *Rehabilitation Counseling Bulletin, 61*(3), 143–153. DOI: 10.1177/0034355217709455

Doda, V., Kennedy, C., & Kaur, M. (2024). Policies for Individuals With Autism: Gaps, Research, and Recommendations. *Cureus, 16*(1), e51875. DOI: 10.7759/cureus.51875 PMID: 38327931

Donnell, C. M., Lustig, D. C., & Strauser, D. R. (2004). The working alliance: Rehabilitation outcomes for persons with severe mental illness. *Journal of Rehabilitation, 70*(2), 12–18.

Dörffer, N., & Bernhard, N. (2025). Overcoming Obstacles? Institutional Support for the Pathways to Higher Education at German Vocational Schools. *Social Inclusion (Lisboa), 13*, 8771. Advance online publication. DOI: 10.17645/si.8771

Dorney, K. E., & Erickson, K. (2019). Transactions within a classroom-based AAC intervention targeting preschool students with autism spectrum disorders: A mixed-methods investigation. *Exceptionality Education International, 29*(2), 42–58. DOI: 10.5206/eei.v29i2.9401

dos Santos, P. M., & Cirillo, M. Â. (2023). Construction of the average variance extracted index for construct validation in structural equation models with adaptive regressions. *Communications in Statistics. Simulation and Computation, 52*(4), 1639–1650. DOI: 10.1080/03610918.2021.1888122

Duvenage, A. (2025). Realising Pedagogical Love Through Ubuntu: Cultivating Inclusion and Undoing Coloniality for Pluriversity. In E. Vanderheiden, C.-H. Mayer, & A. M. F. Barcelos (Eds.), *Pedagogical Love in Adult Education: New Perspectives in Nurturing, Growth and Transformation* (pp. 247–262). Springer Science+Business Media. DOI: 10.1007/978-3-031-82046-5_13

Eastman, K., Zahn, G., Ahnupkana, W., & Havumaki, B. (2021a). Small Town Transition Services Model: Postsecondary Planning for Students With Autism Spectrum Disorder. *Rural Special Education Quarterly*, *40*(3), 157–166. DOI: 10.1177/87568705211027978

Economic and Social Commission for Asia and the Pacific United Nations. (2023). *Harmonization of national laws with the convention on the rights of persons with disabilities: Country case study Republic of Korea*. United Nations Bangkok. https://www.unescap.org/sites/default/d8files/2023-07/ESCAP-2023-RP-Harmonization-National-Laws-Convention-Rights-Person-Disability-korea-Case-study.pdf

Ehsanian, V., Derijani, F., Khorraminia, M., & Eiliaei, S. (2025). Implementation and evaluation of a mentoring and counseling program for medical students at Shahid Beheshti University of Medical Sciences. *BMC Medical Education*, *25*(1), 940. Advance online publication. DOI: 10.1186/s12909-025-07488-x PMID: 40598190

Eilenberg, J. S., Paff, M., Harrison, A. J., & Long, K. A. (2019). Disparities Based on Race, Ethnicity, and Socioeconomic Status Over the Transition to Adulthood Among Adolescents and Young Adults on the Autism Spectrum: A Systematic Review. *Current Psychiatry Reports*, *21*(5), 32. Advance online publication. DOI: 10.1007/s11920-019-1016-1

El Zaatari, W., & Maalouf, I. (2022). How the Bronfenbrenner Bio-ecological System Theory Explains the Development of Students' Sense of Belonging to School? *SAGE Open*, *12*(4), 21582440221134089. Advance online publication. DOI: 10.1177/21582440221134089

Elias, R., Muskett, A. E., & White, S. W. (2019). Educator perspectives on the post-secondary transition difficulties of students with autism. *Autism*, *23*(1), 260–264. DOI: 10.1177/1362361317726246 PMID: 29034690

ElSayary, A., Karaki, S., & Ahmed, R. (2025). Exploring Reflective Practices In Blended Learning: A Deep Dive Into Educators' In-Action And On-Action Perspectives In Interdisciplinary Courses. *Journal of Information Technology Education*, *24*, 019. Advance online publication. DOI: 10.28945/5553

Eltantawy, M. M., & Fouad, B. O. E. (2025). The Effectiveness of a Training Program in Equipping Teachers of Students with Intellectual Disabilities with Competencies for Implementing Transition Plans and Enhancing Their Teaching Self-Efficacy. Journal of Intellectual Disability - Diagnosis and Treatment, 13(2), 108–119. DOI: 10.6000/2292-2598.2025.13.02.1

Elwyn, G., O'Connor, A. M., Bennett, C., Newcombe, R. G., Politi, M., Durand, M.-A., Drake, E., Joseph-Williams, N., Khangura, S., Saarimaki, A., Sivell, S., Stiel, M., Bernstein, S. J., Col, N., Coulter, A., Eden, K., Härter, M., Rovner, M. H., Moumjid, N., & Edwards, A. (2009). Assessing the quality of decision support technologies using the International Patient Decision Aid Standards instrument (IPDASi). *PLoS One*, *4*(3), e4705. Advance online publication. DOI: 10.1371/journal.pone.0004705 PMID: 19259269

Employment and Training Administration U.S. Department of Labour. (2016). Workforce Innovation and Opportunity Act. *Federal Register*, *81*(161), 56072–56469.

Enabling Guide. (2025). *School-To-Work (S2W) Transition Programme*. SG Enable. https://www.enablingguide.sg/im-looking-for-disability-support/training-employment/school-to-work-%28s2w%29-transition-programme

England, A. (2022). Quantitative and qualitative research methods. In E. Seeram, R. Davidson, A. England, & M. F. McEntee (Eds.), *Research for Medical Imaging and Radiation Sciences* (pp. 71–96). Springer International Publishing. DOI: 10.1007/978-3-030-79956-4_5

Epp, A. (2023). Relations between Professional Action and Biographical Transition Experiences of Teachers' – Dealing with Uncer-tainty as an Intertwined Connection. *Historia Scholastica*, *9*(1), 55–81. DOI: 10.15240/tul/006/2023-1-003

Eseadi, C. (2023b). Interventions for Supporting Career Transition among Students with Visual Impairments. *Psikoislamika: Jurnal Psikologi dan Psikologi Islam,* 20(2), 698-715.

Eseadi, C. (2023a). Assessing Theories and Strategies Regarding Career Transition for Students with Visual Impairments. *Didaktika: Jurnal Kependidikan*, *12*(4), 803–818.

Eseadi, C., & Diale, B. M. (2025). *Perspectives on Career Transitioning of Students with Hearing Impairments*. IGI Global.

Eseadi, C., & Diale, B. M. (2025). *Perspectives on career transitioning of students with hearing impairments*. IGI Global., DOI: 10.4018/979-8-3693-2631-2

Espinoza, J. G. R. (2018). *Workfare Factors in the US: An Analysis of Employment Attainment by TANF Job Seekers in the US Workforce Development System* [PhD Thesis, California Baptist University].

Esposito, M., Caputi, M., Fadda, R., Ricciardi, O., Pagano, E., Bove, D., Mazza, M., & Valenti, M. (2025). Group Physical Activity and Behavioral Practices in Adolescents with Autism: A Case Series on Integrated Educational Interventions. *Education Sciences*, *15*(11), 1491. Advance online publication. DOI: 10.3390/educsci15111491

Essex, J., & Melham, P. (2019). Experiences of educational transition: Young women with ASD, and the staff supporting them, speak. *Support for Learning*, *34*(1), 86–111. DOI: 10.1111/1467-9604.12235

European Agency for Special Needs and Inclusive Education. (2019, November 27). *Country information for Netherlands—Legislation and policy*. European Agency for Special Needs and Inclusive Education. https://www.european-agency.org/country-information/netherlands/legislation-and-policy

European Agency for Special Needs and Inclusive Education. (2021, April 5). *Country information for Italy—Legislation and policy*. European Agency for Special Needs and Inclusive Education. https://www.european-agency.org/country-information/italy/legislation-and-policy

European Agency for Special Needs and Inclusive Education. (2023, March 13). *Country information for Sweden—Legislation and policy*. European Agency for Special Needs and Inclusive Education. https://www.european-agency.org/country-information/sweden/legislation-and-policy

European Agency for Special Needs and Inclusive Education. (2024). *Country Policy Development Support – Framework*. https://www.european-agency.org/resources/publications/CPDS-framework

European Agency for Special Needs and Inclusive Education. (2025, May 4). *Country information for Denmark—Legislation and policy*. European Agency for Special Needs and Inclusive Education. https://www.european-agency.org/country-information/denmark/legislation-and-policy

European Centre for the Development of Vocational Training. (2025, May 2). *Sweden: Reformed VET curricula for learners with intellectual disabilities*. European Centre for the Development of Vocational Training. https://www.cedefop.europa.eu/en/news/sweden-reformed-vet-curricula-learners-intellectual-disabilities

European Commission. (2023, August 30). *Together for inclusive education and work opportunities*. European Commission. https://employment-social-affairs.ec.europa.eu/together-inclusive-education-and-work-opportunities_en

European Union. (2000). *Council Directive 2000/78/EC of 27 November 2000 establishing a general framework for equal treatment in employment and occupation*. EUR-Lex: Official Journal of the European Union, L 303/16-L 303/22. https://eur-lex.europa.eu/legal-content/EN/TXT/PDF/?uri=CELEX:32000L0078

European Union. (2012). *Charter of Fundamental Rights of the European Union*. EUR-Lex: Official Journal of the European Union, C 326/391-C 326/407. https://eur-lex.europa.eu/legal-content/EN/TXT/PDF/?uri=CELEX:12012P/TXT

Evans, I. M. (2015). Reinforcement, Principle of. In Wright, J. D. (Ed.), *International Encyclopedia of the Social & Behavioral Sciences* (2nd ed., pp. 207–210). Elsevier Inc., DOI: 10.1016/B978-0-08-097086-8.21051-9

Evans, T. M., & Raines, L. (2017). Career Planning Quick Guide. In Evans, T. M., Lundsteen, N., & Vanderford, N. L. (Eds.), *ReSearch* (pp. 249–254). Elsevier., DOI: 10.1016/B978-0-12-804297-7.00018-5

Eze, P., Alabi, A., & Osunbunmi, I. (2025). AI-driven career guidance: Comparing Nigerian undergraduate and postgraduate perceptions. *Discover Education*, *4*(1), 543. Advance online publication. DOI: 10.1007/s44217-025-00900-0

Ezewuzie, S. O. Patricia Amaka Udeogu, & Okoli, H. N. (2025). Assessment of educational policies and reforms in nigeria: challenges and prospects. Chukwuemeka odumegwu ojukwu university journal of arts and social science education, 4(1). https://cooujoasse.org/index.php/cooujoasse/article/view/32

Ezewuzie, S. O. Patricia Amaka Udeogu, & Okoli, H. N. (2025). Assessment of educational policies and reforms in Nigeria: Challenges and prospects. *Chukwuemeka Odumegwu Ojukwu University Journal of Arts and Social Science Education, 4*(1). https://cooujoasse.org/index.php/cooujoasse/article/view/32

Fabris, C., Coscia, A., Bertino, E., Prete, M., Occhi, L., Giuliani, F., & Quadrino, S. (2009). Counselling in Neonatal Intensive Care Unit (NICU). *Early Human Development*, *85*(10, SUPPL.), S47–S48. DOI: 10.1016/j.earlhumdev.2009.08.014 PMID: 19833463

Fabris, C., Coscia, A., Tonetto, P., Bertino, E., & Quadrino, S. (2010). Counselling in neonatal intensive care unit. *Minerva Pediatrica*, *62*(3, Suppl 1), 109–111. PMID: 21089730

Fadele, A. A., & Rocha, A. (2025). The Art and Science of Quantitative Research. In Studies in Systems, Decision and Control (Vol. 599, pp. 1–188). Springer Science and Business Media Deutschland GmbH. DOI: 10.1007/978-3-031-91431-7

Faelasofi, R., Nisa, K., Usman, M., & Yunarti, T. (2025). Application of Confirmatory Factor Analysis and Latent Growth Model to Examines the Goal-Setting Behavior of Students. *Asian Journal of Interdisciplinary Research*, *8*(4), 13–25. DOI: 10.54392/ajir2542

Fagan, C., Lyonette, C., Smith, M., & Saldaña-Tejeda, A. (2012). *The influence of working time arrangements on work-life integration or 'balance': A review of the international evidence*. International Labour Organization. https://research.manchester.ac.uk/en/publications/the-influence-of-working-time-arrangements-on-work-life-integrati/

Fairchild, L. A., Powell, M. B., Gadke, D. L., Spencer, J. C., & Stratton, K. K. (2020). Increasing social engagement among college students with autism. *Advances in Autism*, *6*(2), 83–93. DOI: 10.1108/AIA-09-2019-0030

Farmer, S., Ward, C. S., & Cusumano, D. (2023). Implementation science: Foundations and applied practice in educational settings. In Fenning, P. A., & Nellis, L. M. (Eds.), *Systems Consultation and Change in Schools: Integrating Implementation Science into Practice* (pp. 13–34). Springer International Publishing., DOI: 10.1007/978-3-031-21381-6_2

Fasching, H. (2014). Career counselling at school for placement in sheltered workshops? *British Journal of Learning Disabilities*, *42*(1), 50–57. DOI: 10.1111/bld.12009

Feather, K. A., Dahl-Jacinto, H., & Clark, M. (2025). Exploring Mental Health Professionals' Experiences With Using Humanistic Counseling for Children With ASD. *The Journal of Humanistic Counseling*, *64*(3), 184–192. DOI: 10.1002/johc.70004

Federal Ministry of Education. (2015). *National Policy on Special Needs Education in Nigeria*. Federal Ministry of Education Abuja. https://www.rodra.co.za/images/countries/nigeria/policy/National%20Policy%20on%20Special%20Needs%20Education.pdf

Federal Ministry of Education. (2023). Revised National Policy on Inclusive Education in Nigeria. Federal Ministry of Education Abuja. https://tafafrica.co/publication/Inclusive%20Education.pdf

Federal Republic of Brazil. (2015, July 6). *The Brazilian Law for the Inclusion of Persons with Disabilities (Statute of Persons with Disabilities). Law No. 13,146, of July 6, 2015.* https://planalto.gov.br/ccivil_03/_Ato2015-2018/2015/Lei/L13146.htm

Federal Republic of Nigeria. (2015). *National Policy on Special Needs Education in Nigeria*. 1–44.

Federal Republic of Nigeria. (2015). *National Policy on Special Needs Education in Nigeria*. Federal Ministry of Education Abuja.

Federal Republic of Nigeria. (2018). *Discrimination Against Persons with Disabilities (Prohibition) Act, 2018.*

Federal Republic of Nigeria. (2018). *Discrimination Against Persons with Disabilities Prohibition Act, 2018.* https://www.un.org/development/desa/disabilities/wp-content/uploads/sites/15/2019/11/Nigeria_Discrimination-Against-Persons-with-Disabilities-Prohibition-Act-2018.pdf

Fegert, J. M., Hauth, I., Banaschewski, T., & Freyberger, H. J. (2016, June 23). Transition From Adolescence to Adulthood: The Challenges to Establish "Transition Psychiatry.". In *Key Issues Paper by DGKJP and DGPPN.* https://www.escap.eu/events/past-escap-congresses/geneva/duplicate-of-madrid-keynote-and-symposiums/transitions-from-adolescence-to-adulthood-key-issue-paper

Fernández-Batanero, J. M., Fernández-Cerero, J., & Montenegro-Rueda, M. (2025). Technological accessibility and Autism. Level of Training of Secondary Education, Baccalaureate and Vocational Training Teachers. *International Journal of Technology and Educational Innovation*, *11*(2), 42–58. DOI: 10.24310/ijtei.112.2025.21437

Fischer, H. E., Boone, W. J., & Neumann, K. (2023). Quantitative Research Designs and Approaches. In *Handbook of Research on Science Education*. Routledge. DOI: 10.4324/9780367855758-3

Fisher, M. H., Englehart, V., Kam, C., Norwine, L., Patino, K., Patterson, A., Rodríguez, M., Bouck, E., Sung, C., & Taylor, J. C. (2025). Successful Transition Planning for Students with Intellectual Disability and Extensive Support Needs. In *Springer International Handbooks of Education: Vol. Part F910* (pp. 371–391). Springer Nature. DOI: 10.1007/978-3-031-60258-0_18

Fisher, M. H., & Taylor, J. L. (2016). Let's talk about it: Peer victimization experiences as reported by adolescents with autism spectrum disorder. *Autism*, *20*(4), 402–411. DOI: 10.1177/1362361315585948

Folorunsho-Francis, A. (2025, October 31). Senate pushes for regional autism centres. *The Punch Newspaper.* https://punchng.com/senate-pushes-for-regional-autism-centres/

Folorunso, A. D. (2025). *Autism Spectrum Disorder Among Nigerian Children Ages 2-17: Prevalence, Awareness, Advocacy and Legislative Action Scoping Review. Research Square.* DOI: 10.21203/rs.3.rs-6735926/v1

Fong, C. J., Taylor, J., Berdyyeva, A., McClelland, A. M., Murphy, K. M., & Westbrook, J. D. (2021). Interventions for improving employment outcomes for persons with autism spectrum disorders: A systematic review update. *Campbell Systematic Reviews, 17*(3), e1185. DOI: 10.1002/cl2.1185 PMID: 37052419

Fong, V., Gardiner, E., & Iarocci, G. (2021). Satisfaction with informal supports predicts resilience in families of children with autism spectrum disorder. *Autism, 25*(2), 452–463. DOI: 10.1177/1362361320962677 PMID: 33106025

Frank, F., Jablotschkin, M., Arthen, T., Riedel, A., Fangmeier, T., Hölzel, L. P., & Tebartz van Elst, L. (2018). Education and employment status of adults with autism spectrum disorders in Germany – a cross-sectional-survey. *BMC Psychiatry, 18*(1), 75. DOI: 10.1186/s12888-018-1645-7 PMID: 29580218

Frazier, T. W., Crowley, E., Shih, A., Vasudevan, V., Karpur, A., Uljarevic, M., & Cai, R. Y. (2022). Associations between executive functioning, challenging behavior, and quality of life in children and adolescents with and without neurodevelopmental conditions. *Frontiers in Psychology, 13*, 1022700. DOI: 10.3389/fpsyg.2022.1022700

Frempong, G., & Kadam, R. (2025). The Ubuntu Mindset: Learning to Manage and Lead Better Together, the Africentric Way. In Williams, K. S., Mills, A. J., & Weigand, H. (Eds.), *Management Education in Canada: Historical Reflections* (pp. 156–175). Taylor and Francis., DOI: 10.4324/9781003612612-8

FRN. (2023). National Policy on Inclusive Education. In *Nigeria.* Federal Republic of Nigeria.

Furey, J., & Loftus-Rattan, S. M. (2022). Actively Involving Students With Learning Disabilities in Progress Monitoring Practices. *Intervention in School and Clinic, 57*(5), 329–337. DOI: 10.1177/10534512211032618

Gabio, J. A., & Cajandig, A. J. S. (2025). College of Teacher Education Students' Mastery of Statistical Concepts: Basis for Proposed Enhancement Program. *International Journal of Research and Innovation in Social Science, 9*(3), 2269–2284. DOI: 10.47772/IJRISS.2025.90300179

Galdames-Calderón, M. (2023). Distributed Leadership: School Principals' Practices to Promote Teachers' Professional Development for School Improvement. *Education Sciences, 13*(7), 715. DOI: 10.3390/educsci13070715

Gantman, A., Kapp, S. K., Orenski, K., & Laugeson, E. A. (2012). Social skills training for young adults with high-functioning autism spectrum disorders: A randomized controlled pilot study. *Journal of Autism and Developmental Disorders, 42*(6), 1094–1103. DOI: 10.1007/s10803-011-1350-6 PMID: 21915740

Garbacz, S. A., McIntyre, L. L., & Santiago, R. T. (2016). Family involvement and parent-teacher relationships for students with autism spectrum disorders. *School Psychology Quarterly, 31*(4), 478–490. DOI: 10.1037/spq0000157 PMID: 27929318

Garcia, N. A., & Campbell, S. E. (2023). Co-creating spaces for reflective practice in teacher education. In Adams, S. R., & Breidenstein, A. (Eds.), *Exploring Meaningful and Sustainable Intentional Learning Communities for P-20 Educators* (pp. 94–119). IGI Global., DOI: 10.4018/978-1-6684-7270-5.ch005

Gard, A. M., McLoyd, V. C., Mitchell, C., & Hyde, L. W. (2020). Evaluation of a longitudinal family stress model in a population-based cohort. *Social Development, 29*(4), 1155–1175. DOI: 10.1111/sode.12446 PMID: 33953492

Garuba, A. (2003). Inclusive education in the 21st century: Challenges and opportunities for Nigeria. *Asia Pacific Disability Rehabilitation Journal, 14*(2), 191–200.

Genova, H. M., Kallen, M. A., Sherwood, K. L., DaWalt, L., Bishop, L., Telfer, D., Brown, C., Sanchez, B., & Smith, M. J. (2023). Development and psychometric properties of self-reported job interview skills and job interview anxiety for autistic transition-age youth. *Journal of Vocational Rehabilitation, 58*(2), 199–217. DOI: 10.3233/JVR-230009 PMID: 38974409

Gentil-Gutiérrez, A., Santamaría-Peláez, M., Mínguez-Mínguez, L. A., Fernández-Solana, J., González-Bernal, J. J., González-Santos, J., & Obregón-Cuesta, A. I. (2022). Executive Functions in Children and Adolescents with Autism Spectrum Disorder in Family and School Environment. *International Journal of Environmental Research and Public Health, 19*(13), 7834. DOI: 10.3390/ijerph19137834 PMID: 35805490

George, L. K. (1993). Sociological Perspectives on Life Transitions. *Annual Review of Sociology, 19*(1), 353–373. DOI: 10.1146/annurev.so.19.080193.002033

Gillespie-Lynch, K., Bublitz, D., Donachie, A., Wong, V., Brooks, P. J., & D'Onofrio, J. (2017). "For a Long Time Our Voices have been Hushed": Using Student Perspectives to Develop Supports for Neurodiverse College Students. *Frontiers in Psychology, 8*, 544. DOI: 10.3389/fpsyg.2017.00544 PMID: 28458645

Gillies, A. (2024). *Healthcare Management: Global Perspectives*. Routledge., DOI: 10.4324/9781003478874

Giri, M., Pathak, S., Srivastava, S., & Mukherjee, S. (2024). Exploring the Psychosocial Challenges and Strengths of Indigent Adolescents: A Reflexive Thematic Analysis of Counsellor's Insights. *Journal of Research and Health, 14*(5), 439–448. DOI: 10.32598/JRH.14.5.2424.1

Gómez-Marí, I., Sanz-Cervera, P., & Tárraga-Mínguez, R. (2021). Teachers' Knowledge Regarding Autism Spectrum Disorder (ASD): A Systematic Review. *Sustainability (Basel), 13*(9), 5097. DOI: 10.3390/su13095097

Gonzales, G., Costan, F., Suladay, D., Gonzales, R., Enriquez, L., Costan, E., Atibing, N. M., Aro, J. L., Evangelista, S. S., Maturan, F., Selerio, E.Jr, & Ocampo, L. (2022). Fermatean Fuzzy DEMATEL and MMDE Algorithm for Modelling the Barriers of Implementing Education 4.0: Insights from the Philippines. *Applied Sciences (Basel, Switzerland), 12*(2), 689. Advance online publication. DOI: 10.3390/app12020689

Goodman, J., Schlossberg, N. K., & Anderson, M. L. (2006). *Counseling adults in transition: Linking practice with theory, 3rd ed* (pp. xvii, 334). Springer Publishing Company.

Goodson, I. F., & Ümarik, M. (2019). Changing policy contexts and teachers' work-life narratives: The case of Estonian vocational teachers. *Teachers and Teaching, 25*(5), 589–602. DOI: 10.1080/13540602.2019.1664300

Goodyear, V. A. (2017). Sustained Professional Development on Cooperative Learning: Impact on Six Teachers' Practices and Students' Learning. *Research Quarterly for Exercise and Sport, 88*(1), 83–94. DOI: 10.1080/02701367.2016.1263381 PMID: 28001911

Gorenstein, M., Giserman-Kiss, I., Feldman, E., Isenstein, E. L., Donnelly, L., Wang, A. T., & Foss-Feig, J. H. (2020). Brief Report: A Job-Based Social Skills Program (JOBSS) for Adults with Autism Spectrum Disorder: A Pilot Randomized Controlled Trial. *Journal of Autism and Developmental Disorders, 50*(12), 4527–4534. DOI: 10.1007/s10803-020-04482-8 PMID: 32297122

Gore, O. T. (2023). Disability and inclusion in South African higher education: An Ubuntu philosophical perspective. In Mutanga, O. (Ed.), *Ubuntu Philosophy and Disabilities in Sub-Saharan Africa* (pp. 30–47). Taylor and Francis., DOI: 10.4324/9781003343684-3

Government of Canada. (2022). *Canada's Disability Inclusion Action Plan, 2022.* Government of Canada. https://www.canada.ca/en/employment-social-development/programs/disability-inclusion-action-plan/action-plan-2022.html

Government of Canada. (2023). *Services and Supports to Promote the Social Inclusion of Persons with Developmental Disabilities Act, 2008.* https://www.ontario.ca/laws/statute/08s14

Government of India. (2016). *The Rights of Persons with Disabilities Act 2016.* https://www.indiacode.nic.in/bitstream/123456789/15939/1/the_rights_of_persons_with_disabilities_act%2C_2016.pdf

Greenleaf, J. F., Johnson, S. A., Bahn, R. C., & Rajagopalan, B. (1977). *QUANTITATIVE CROSS-SECTIONAL IMAGING OF ULTRASOUND PARAMETERS.: Ultrason Symp Proc.* 989–995. https://www.scopus.com/pages/publications/0017791518

Greer, T. W., & Minnis, S. E. (2022). Using Developmental Relationships to Navigate Career Transitions: Implications for Diverse Populations. In Ghosh, R., & Hutchins, H. M. (Eds.), *HRD Perspectives on Developmental Relationships: Connecting and Relating at Work* (pp. 15–39). Springer International Publishing., DOI: 10.1007/978-3-030-85033-3_2

Griffiths, A. J., Cosier, M. E., Wiegand, R., Mathur, S. K., & Morgan, S. (2021). Developing strong transition-focused IEPS using labour market data. *Support for Learning, 36*(4), 608–629. DOI: 10.1111/1467-9604.12383

Griffiths, A. J., Hurley-Hanson, A. E., Giannantonio, C. M., Hyde, K., Linstead, E., Wiegand, R., & Brady, J. (2023). Enhancing employment outcomes for autistic youth: Using machine learning to identify strategies for success. *Journal of Vocational Rehabilitation, 59*(2), 153–168. DOI: 10.3233/JVR-230034

Groce, N. E. (2004). Adolescents and youth with disability: Issues and challenges. *Asia Pacific Disability Rehabilitation Journal, 15*(2), 13–32.

Grothaus, T., McAuliffe, G., & Craigen, L. (2012). Infusing cultural competence and advocacy into strength-based counseling. *The Journal of Humanistic Counseling, 51*(1), 51–65. DOI: 10.1002/j.2161-1939.2012.00005.x

Grover, J. M. (2017). Bonding with your hard of hearing or late-deafened VR client. *Journal of Vocational Rehabilitation, 47*(1), 47–64. DOI: 10.3233/JVR-170882

Guldberg, K. (2010). Educating children on the autism spectrum: Preconditions for inclusion and notions of "best autism practice" in the early years. *British Journal of Special Education, 37*(4), 168–174. DOI: 10.1111/j.1467-8578.2010.00482.x

Güleç-Aslan, Y. (2013). A training programme for a teacher working with a student with ASD: An action research. *Educational Sciences: Theory & Practice, 13*(4), 2229–2246. DOI: 10.12738/estp.2013.4.1738

Hagiwara, M., Dean, E. E., & Shogren, K. A. (2019). The Self-determined Career Design Model: Supporting Young People with Developmental Disabilities and Their Families in Home and Community Settings. In *Promoting Social Inclusion: Co-Creating Environments that Foster Equity and Belonging* (13, p. 201-220). Emerald Publishing Limited. DOI: 10.1108/S1479-363620190000013016

Hagner, D., Kurtz, A., Cloutier, H., Arakelian, C., Brucker, D. L., & May, J. (2012). Outcomes of a family-centered transition process for students with autism spectrum disorders. *Focus on Autism and Other Developmental Disabilities, 27*(1), 42–50. DOI: 10.1177/1088357611430841

Hagner, D., Kurtz, A., May, J., & Cloutier, H. (2014). Person-centered planning for transition-aged youth with autism spectrum disorders. *Journal of Rehabilitation, 80*(1), 4–10.

Hajra, A., Ghosh, B., & Bhowmik, S. (2025). Cross-sectional studies. In Eltorai, A. E. M., Bakal, J. A., & Gibson, C. M. (Eds.), *Translational Cardiology* (pp. 221–225). Elsevier., DOI: 10.1016/B978-0-323-91790-2.00099-X

Hamidon, N. A., Anuar, N. I. S. M., Sharoni, S. K. A., & Isa, N. A. M. (2024). Parental Stress among Family Caregivers of Children with Autism in a Teaching Hospital. [MJN]. *The Malaysian Journal of Nursing, 15*(4), 139–149. DOI: 10.31674/mjn.2024.v15i04.016

Hamrick, J., Prueitt, N., & Favela, A. (2025). Supporting Special Education Practice for Students with ASD in Rural Districts. In *Springer International Handbooks of Education: Vol. Part F910* (pp. 89–124). Springer Nature. DOI: 10.1007/978-3-031-60258-0_5

Hanif, S., Peters, H., McDougall, C., & Lindsay, S. (2017). A systematic review of vocational interventions for youth with physical disabilities. *Factors in studying employment for persons with disability: How the picture can change*, 181-202.: DOI: 10.1108/S1479-354720170000010008

Hannah, E. F., & Topping, K. J. (2013). The transition from primary to secondary school: Perspectives of students with autism spectrum disorder and their parents. *International Journal of Special Education, 28*(1), 145–157.

Harris, A. H. S., Thoresen, C. E., & Lopez, S. J. (2007). Integrating positive psychology into counseling: Why and (when appropriate) how. *Journal of Counseling and Development*, *85*(1), 3–13. DOI: 10.1002/j.1556-6678.2007.tb00438.x

Harrison, J. R., State, T. M., Wills, H. P., Custer, B. A., & Miller, E. (2017). Transition goals for youth with social, emotional, and behavioral problems: Parent and student knowledge. *Preventing School Failure*, *61*(3), 248–257. DOI: 10.1080/1045988X.2016.1266596

Hartini, S., Simanjuntak, S. R., & Sutomo, R. (2021). Factors correlating with parenting stress among mothers of children with Autistic Spectrum Disorder (ASD). *Enfermeria Clinica*, *31*, 505–510. DOI: 10.1016/j.enfcli.2020.10.042

Hart, L. C., Pollock, M., Hill, S., & Maslow, G. (2017). Association of Transition Readiness to Intentional Self-Regulation and Hopeful Future Expectations in Youth With Illness. *Academic Pediatrics*, *17*(4), 450–455. DOI: 10.1016/j.acap.2016.12.004 PMID: 27979748

Haruna, H. H., Iftikhar, S., Isa, S. M., & Hasan, M. (2025). Effect of Professional Development, Collaborative Learning, and Technology Integration on Teachers' Self-Access Support Competence. *SiSal Journal*, *16*(3), 526–565. DOI: 10.37237/160304

Hassan, M., Azmat, U., Sarwar, S., Adil, I. H., & Gillani, S. H. M. (2020). Impact of job satisfaction, job stress and motivation on job performance: A case from private universities of karachi. [Kuwait Chapter]. *Arabian Journal of Business and Management Review*, *9*(2), 76–86.

Hasselbusch, A., & Baumgarten, A. (2014). Including children with autism in everyday life. *Ergotherapie und Rehabilitation*, *53*(1), 14–18.

Hatendi, C. M. (2025). Ubuntu, Diversity and Inclusiveness: Afro-descendants in the United States. In E. Chitando, B. Okyere-Manu, S. Chirongoma, & M. W. Dube (Eds.), *The Palgrave Handbook of Ubuntu, Inequality and Sustainable Development* (pp. 633–646). Springer Science+Business Media. DOI: 10.1007/978-3-031-69573-5_39

Hatfield, M., Ciccarelli, M., Mangan, C., & Whelan, M. (2021). Boosting post-school outcomes: Supporting adolescents on the autism spectrum to feel ready for life after school. In Carrington, S., Saggers, B., Harper-Hill, K., & Whelan, M. (Eds.), *Supporting Students on the Autism Spectrum in Inclusive Schools: A Practical Guide to Implementing Evidence-Based Approaches* (pp. 118–132). Taylor and Francis. DOI: 10.4324/9781003049036-13

Hatfield, M., Falkmer, M., Falkmer, T., & Ciccarelli, M. (2017). Effectiveness of the BOOST-A™ online transition planning program for adolescents on the autism spectrum: A quasi-randomized controlled trial. *Child and Adolescent Psychiatry and Mental Health, 11*(1), 54. Advance online publication. DOI: 10.1186/s13034-017-0191-2 PMID: 29051774

Hazan-Liran, B., & Walter, O. (2025). Psychological Capital, Self-Advocacy, and Future Orientation among Adults on the Autism Spectrum. *Journal of Autism and Developmental Disorders, 55*(11), 3986–3997. DOI: 10.1007/s10803-024-06493-1 PMID: 39080049

Hendricks, D. (2010). Employment and adults with autism spectrum disorders: Challenges and strategies for success. *Journal of Vocational Rehabilitation, 32*(2), 125–134. DOI: 10.3233/JVR-2010-0502

Hendricks, D. R., & Wehman, P. (2009). Transition from school to adulthood for youth with autism spectrum disorders: Review and recommendations. *Focus on Autism and Other Developmental Disabilities, 24*(2), 77–88. DOI: 10.1177/1088357608329827

Hendrickson, J. M., Woods-Groves, S., Rodgers, D. B., & Datchuk, S. (2017). Perceptions of students with Autism and their parents: The college experience. *Education & Treatment of Children, 40*(4), 571–596. DOI: 10.1353/etc.2017.0025

Henriques, C. G. P., Rosa, E. M., & Merçon-Vargas, E. A. (2025). Emotional Violence as an Inverse Proximal Process Under the Perspective of the Bioecological Theory. In L. F. Habigzang, A. S. G. Pessoa, & S. R. Lordello (Eds.), *Violence Against Children: Contributions of the Bioecological Theory of Human Development to Research and Intervention* (pp. 45–63). Springer Science+Business Media. DOI: 10.1007/978-3-031-91786-8_4

Herrick, S. J., Lu, W., Oursler, J., Beninato, J., Gbadamosi, S., Durante, A., & Meyers, E. (2022). Soft skills for success for job seekers with autism spectrum disorder. *Journal of Vocational Rehabilitation, 57*(2), 113–126. DOI: 10.3233/JVR-221203

Hervie, V. M. (2023). Social inclusion of children with intellectual disabilities in Accra, Ghana: Views of parents/guardians and teachers. *Children and Youth Services Review, 147*, 106845. Advance online publication. DOI: 10.1016/j.childyouth.2023.106845

Hetherington, S. A., Durant-Jones, L., Johnson, K., Nolan, K., Smith, E., Taylor-Brown, S., & Tuttle, J. (2010). The lived experiences of adolescents with disabilities and their parents in transition planning. *Focus on Autism and Other Developmental Disabilities, 25*(3), 163–172. DOI: 10.1177/1088357610373760

Hill, D. A., Fayemi, A., & Ostrowski, S. (2024). The Evolution of Services for Children with Autism and Developmental Disabilities in Nigeria. *International Journal of Disability Development and Education*, *71*(7), 1116–1132. DOI: 10.1080/1034912X.2023.2291570

Hofmeyr, B. (2025). Reading Ubuntu relationality through a Levinasian lens. *Acta Academica*, *57*(1), 53–71. DOI: 10.38140/aa.v57i1.9072

Holingue, C., Jang, Y., Azad, G., & Landa, R. (2022). Key Stakeholder Perspectives on Obstacles to an Autism-Specific Medicaid Waiver Service Delivery Model. *Journal of Applied Research in Intellectual Disabilities*, *35*(1), 205–216. DOI: 10.1111/jar.12940

Holton, E. F., & Burnett, M. F. (2005). The basics of quantitative research. *Research in Organizations: Foundations and Methods of Inquiry*, 29–44.

Honsberger, T. J., Brady, M. P., Honsberger, C. F., & Kearney, K. B. (2019a). Peer-Mediated Literacy-Based Behavioral Interventions: A Job Coaching Strategy for Secondary Students With ASD. *Career Development and Transition for Exceptional Individuals*, *42*(2), 99–110. DOI: 10.1177/2165143418808508

Horn, A. L., Gable, R. A., Bobzien, J. L., Tonelson, S. W., & Rock, M. L. (2020). Teaching Young Adults Job Skills Using a Constant Time Delay and eCoaching Intervention Package. *Career Development and Transition for Exceptional Individuals*, *43*(1), 29–39. DOI: 10.1177/2165143419828983

Hossan, D., Mansor, Z. D., & Jaharuddin, N. S. (2023). Research Population and Sampling in Quantitative Study. [IJBT]. *International Journal of Business and Technopreneurship*, *13*(3), 209–222. DOI: 10.58915/ijbt.v13i3.263

Hotez, E., Shane-Simpson, C., Obeid, R., DeNigris, D., Siller, M., Costikas, C., Pickens, J., Massa, A., Giannola, M., D'Onofrio, J., & Gillespie-Lynch, K. (2018). Designing a summer transition program for incoming and current college students on the autism spectrum: A participatory approach. *Frontiers in Psychology*, *9*(FEB), 46. Advance online publication. DOI: 10.3389/fpsyg.2018.00046 PMID: 29487547

Hsueh, N.-L., Chu, P.-H., & Chu, W. (2008). A quantitative approach for evaluating the quality of design patterns. *Journal of Systems and Software*, *81*(8), 1430–1439. DOI: 10.1016/j.jss.2007.11.724

Hughes, C. E. (2025). MTSS and Twice-Exceptional Learners: Problem-Solving and Possibility-Finding. *Gifted Child Today*, *48*(3), 190–197. DOI: 10.1177/10762175251330325

Hu, L., & Bentler, P. M. (1999). Cutoff criteria for fit indexes in covariance structure analysis: Conventional criteria versus new alternatives. *Structural Equation Modeling*, *6*(1), 1–55. DOI: 10.1080/10705519909540118

Hume, K., Dykstra Steinbrenner, J., Sideris, J., Smith, L., Kucharczyk, S., & Szidon, K. (2018). Multi-informant assessment of transition-related skills and skill importance in adolescents with autism spectrum disorder. *Autism*, *22*(1), 40–50. DOI: 10.1177/1362361317722029 PMID: 29020804

Hume, K., Loftin, R., & Lantz, J. (2009). Increasing independence in autism spectrum disorders: A review of three focused interventions. *Journal of Autism and Developmental Disorders*, *39*(9), 1329–1338. DOI: 10.1007/s10803-009-0751-2 PMID: 19430897

Hunter, S. T., & Hunter, M. D. (2022). PERFORMANCE MANAGEMENT AND CAREER DEVELOPMENT FOR EMPLOYEES WITH AUTISM: Uncovering Hidden Requirements. In Bruyère, S. M., & Colella, A. (Eds.), *Neurodiversity in the Workplace: Interests, Issues, and Opportunities* (pp. 211–240). Taylor and Francis., DOI: 10.4324/9781003023616-9

Hunziker, S., & Blankenagel, M. (2024). Cross-Sectional Research Design. In S. Hunziker & M. Blankenagel, *Research Design in Business and Management* (pp. 187–199). Springer Fachmedien Wiesbaden. DOI: 10.1007/978-3-658-42739-9_10

Hurwich-Reiss, E., & Watamura, S. E. (2019). Family processes among Latino Early Head Start families: Understanding the role of caregiver acculturation. *Journal of Community Psychology*, *47*(6), 1433–1448. DOI: 10.1002/jcop.22198 PMID: 31066922

Iannuzzi, D., Rissmiller, P., Duty, S. M., Feeney, S., Sullivan, M., & Curtin, C. (2019). Addressing a Gap in Healthcare Access for Transition-Age Youth with Autism: A Pilot Educational Intervention for Family Nurse Practitioner Students. *Journal of Autism and Developmental Disorders*, *49*(4), 1493–1504. DOI: 10.1007/s10803-018-3846-9 PMID: 30536218

Igwe, M. N., Bakare, M. O., Agomoh, A. O., Onyeama, G. M., & Okonkwo, K. O. (2010). Factors influencing knowledge about childhood autism among final year undergraduate Medical, Nursing and Psychology students of University of Nigeria, Enugu State, Nigeria. *Italian Journal of Pediatrics*, *36*(1), 44. DOI: 10.1186/1824-7288-36-44

Ihenagwam, C., Hamrick, J., Wheeler, K., Iwuji, U., Duru, H., & Banda, D. (2024). Parental Perceptions Upon Receiving Diagnosis of Autism Spectrum Disorder and/or Intellectual Developmental Disability for their Child in Nigeria. *International Journal of Special Education*, *39*(1), 73–87. DOI: 10.52291/ijse.2024.39.8

Ilesanmi, O. (2016). Stepping up Agenda 2030 for the Attainment of Gender Parity and Sustainable Development in Nigerian Tertiary Institutions: A Case Study. *Asian Research Journal of Arts & Social Sciences*, *1*(1), 1–18. DOI: 10.9734/ARJASS/2016/26525

ILO. (2022). *ILO Disability Inclusion Policy and Strategy 2020-23*. https://share.google/B8SQei7sNRjjDkpTR

Ineland, J., Karhina, K., & Vikström, L. (2021). School-to-work Transitions for Students with Intellectual Disabilities: Teachers' Perceptions and Experiences of a Recent Workplace-Based Reform in Sweden. *Journal of the International Special Needs Education*, *24*(2), 86–96. DOI: 10.9782/JISNE-D-20-00012

Iwuji, U., Hamrick, J., Wheeler, K., Ihenagwam, C., Hixson, J., Kelly, D., Duru, H., Ademulegun, T., Banda, D., & Hilbert, S. (2024). Educators' knowledge of and perceptions towards students with autism in Nigeria. *International Journal of Developmental Disabilities*, 1–11. Advance online publication. DOI: 10.1080/20473869.2024.2359137

Izuno-Garcia, A. K., & Pagán, A. F. (2024). Neurodiversity-Affirming Entrepreneurship: Improving Work Experiences for Young Adults on the Spectrum. In Markel, K. S., Hanson, M. E., Giannantonio, C. M., & Hurley-Hanson, A. E. (Eds.), *Neurodiversity and Entrepreneurship* (pp. 123–132). Emerald Publishing., DOI: 10.1108/978-1-83753-798-320241006

Jaipaeng, W., Payakkaraung, S., & Witoonsakul, P. (2025). Factors Predicting Transition Readiness in Adolescents with Kidney or Urinary Tract Diseases: A Cross-Sectional Study. *Pacific Rim International Journal of Nursing Research*, *29*(4), 748–762. DOI: 10.60099/prijnr.2025.273831

Jamison, J. M., Fourie, E., Siper, P. M., Trelles, M. P., George-Jones, J., Buxbaum Grice, A., Krata, J., Holl, E., Shaoul, J., Hernandez, B., Mitchell, L., McKay, M. M., Buxbaum, J. D., & Kolevzon, A. (2017). Examining the Efficacy of a Family Peer Advocate Model for Black and Hispanic Caregivers of Children with Autism Spectrum Disorder. *Journal of Autism and Developmental Disorders*, *47*(5), 1314–1322. DOI: 10.1007/s10803-017-3045-0 PMID: 28168677

Jellicoe, M., & Forsythe, A. (2024). Goal-setting practices that connect feedback with action in higher education. In Evans, C., & Waring, M. (Eds.), *Research Handbook on Innovations in Assessment and Feedback in Higher Education: Implications for Teaching and Learning* (pp. 38–52). Edward Elgar Publishing Ltd., DOI: 10.4337/9781800881600.00010

Jing, J. (2024). Perspectives on the concept of "neurodiversity" in autism spectrum disorder and related evaluation. *Zhongguo Ertong Baojian Zazhi, 32*(7), 709-712and745. DOI: 10.11852/zgetbjzz2024-0645

John, B. (2024). Parental Perceptions and Experiences of Children with Autism and their Educational Needs in Nigeria: An Interpretative Phenomenological Analysis [PhD Thesis, Leeds Beckett University]. https://figshare.leedsbeckett.ac.uk/articles/thesis/Parental_Perceptions_and_Experiences_of_Children_with_Autism_and_their_Educational_Needs_in_Nigeria_An_Interpretative_Phenomenological_Analysis/26370169/1

Johnson, N. L., & Simpson, P. M. (2013). Lack of father involvement in research on children with autism spectrum disorder: Maternal parenting stress and family functioning. *Issues in Mental Health Nursing, 34*(4), 220–228. DOI: 10.3109/01612840.2012.745177 PMID: 23566184

Johnson, N., Frenn, M., Feetham, S., & Simpson, P. (2011). Autism Spectrum Disorder: Parenting Stress, Family Functioning and Health-Related Quality of Life. *Families, Systems & Health, 29*(3), 232–252. DOI: 10.1037/a0025341 PMID: 21928891

Jones, E. K., Hanley, M., & Riby, D. M. (2020). Distraction, distress and diversity: Exploring the impact of sensory processing differences on learning and school life for pupils with autism spectrum disorders. *Research in Autism Spectrum Disorders, 72*, 101515. Advance online publication. DOI: 10.1016/j.rasd.2020.101515

Jose, B., & Muthulakshmi, S. (2022). Institutional Framework for the Rehabilitation of Differently Abled Persons in India. *Cuestiones de Fisioterapia, 51*(3), 280–287. DOI: 10.48047/qvyrpp57

Josilowski, C. S., & Morris, W. A. (2019). A Qualitative Exploration of Teachers' Experiences with Students with Autism Spectrum Disorder Transitioning and Adjusting to Inclusion: Impacts of the Home and School Collaboration. *The Qualitative Report, 24*(6), 1275–1286. DOI: 10.46743/2160-3715/2019.3757

Jung, S. B., & Sheldon, S. (2020). Connecting Dimensions of School Leadership for Partnerships with School and Teacher Practices of Family Engagement. *School Community Journal, 30*(1), 9–32.

Kahn, R. L., Wolfe, D. M., Quinn, R. P., Snoek, J. D., & Rosenthal, R. A. (1964). Organizational stress: Studies in role conflict and ambiguity.

Kahng, S., Butler, C., Kronfli, F. R., Zaki-Scarpa, C., Boragi, B., & Scott, J. (2023). An individualized approach to teaching adults with autism to successfully navigate job interviews via remote instruction. *Journal of Applied Behavior Analysis*, *56*(2), 352–364. DOI: 10.1002/jaba.977 PMID: 36759340

Karahan, S., Parlak, Ş. Y., & Hacıfazlıoğlu, Ö. (2022). The Experiences of Mothers of Children with Autism Spectrum Disorder in Searching for Balance Between Work and Family Life. *Education in Science*, *47*(212), 103–120. DOI: 10.15390/EB.2022.10970

Karim, K., Cook, L., & O'Reilly, M. (2014a). Diagnosing autistic spectrum disorder in the age of austerity. *Child: Care, Health and Development*, *40*(1), 115–123. DOI: 10.1111/j.1365-2214.2012.01410.x PMID: 22712808

Kariuki, L. W., Njoka, J. N., & Mbugua, Z. K. (2019). Influence of Teachers Preparedness on Performance of Pupils in Mathematics in Lower Primary Schools in Aberdares Region of Kenya. *European Journal of STEM Education*, *4*(1). Advance online publication. DOI: 10.20897/ejsteme/3931

Karkkola, P., Kuittinen, M., & Hintsa, T. (2019). Role clarity, role conflict, and vitality at work: The role of the basic needs. *Scandinavian Journal of Psychology*, *60*(5), 456–463. DOI: 10.1111/sjop.12550 PMID: 31124156

Karola, D., Julie-Ann, J., & Lyn, M. (2016). School's out Forever: Postsecondary Educational Trajectories of Students with Autism. *Australian Psychologist*, *51*(4), 304–315. DOI: 10.1111/ap.12228

Karpetis, G. (2016). Evaluating the Effectiveness of the Reframing Technique in Psychodynamic Social Work Practice. *Australian Social Work*, *69*(2), 194–205. DOI: 10.1080/0312407X.2015.1069865

Karst, J. S., & Van Hecke, A. V. (2012). Parent and family impact of autism spectrum disorders: A review and proposed model for intervention evaluation. *Clinical Child and Family Psychology Review*, *15*(3), 247–277. DOI: 10.1007/s10567-012-0119-6 PMID: 22869324

Karupiah, P. (2022). Positivism. In Islam, M. R., Khan, N. A., & Baikady, R. (Eds.), *Principles of Social Research Methodology* (pp. 73–82). Springer Nature., DOI: 10.1007/978-981-19-5441-2_6

Kaya, C., Chan, F., Rumrill, P., Hartman, E., Wehman, P., Iwanaga, K., Pai, C.-H., & Avellone, L. (2016). Vocational rehabilitation services and competitive employment for transition-age youth with autism spectrum disorders. *Journal of Vocational Rehabilitation, 45*(1), 73–83. DOI: 10.3233/JVR-160812

Kaya, C., Hanley-Maxwell, C., Chan, F., & Tansey, T. (2018). Differential vocational rehabilitation service patterns and outcomes for transition-age youth with autism. *Journal of Applied Research in Intellectual Disabilities, 31*(5), 862–872. DOI: 10.1111/jar.12443 PMID: 29441662

Kearney, K., & Bookspan, S. (2023). Increasing family engagement in transition planning. In Musyoka, M. M., & Shen, G. (Eds.), *Meaningful and Active Family Engagement: IEP, Transition and Technology Integration in Special Education* (pp. 222–238). IGI Global., DOI: 10.4018/979-8-3693-1384-8.ch012

Kehinde, O. A., Lindly, O. J., Ntombela, B., & Hermann, C. (2023). Brief Report: Gender-Based Stereotypical Roles of Parents Caring for Autistic Children in Nigeria and South Africa. *Journal of Autism and Developmental Disorders, 53*(12), 4917–4928. DOI: 10.1007/s10803-022-05582-3 PMID: 35581506

Kelly, J., Mckenzie, J., Watermeyer, B., Vergunst, R., Karisa, A., & Samuels, C. (2024). 'We Need to Go Back to Our Schools, and We Need to Make that Change We Wish to See': Empowering Teachers for Disability Inclusion. *International Journal of Disability Development and Education, 71*(4), 633–649. DOI: 10.1080/1034912X.2022.2141696

Kempen, M., & Steyn, G. M. (2016). Proposing a continuous professional development model to support and enhance professional learning of teachers in special schools in South Africa. *International Journal of Special Education, 31*(1), 32–45.

Kester, J., Beveridge, S., Flanagan, M., & Stella, J. (2019). Interdisciplinary professional development needs of transition professionals serving youth with autism spectrum disorders. *Journal of Rehabilitation, 85*(1), 53–63.

Khaleel, N., Alhosani, M., & Duyar, I. (2021). The Role of School Principals in Promoting Inclusive Schools: A Teachers' Perspective. *Frontiers in Education, 6*, 603241. Advance online publication. DOI: 10.3389/feduc.2021.603241

Khetarpal, S. K., Auster, L. S., Miller, E., & Goldstein, T. R. (2022). Transition age youth mental health: Addressing the gap with telemedicine. *Child and Adolescent Psychiatry and Mental Health, 16*(1), 8. DOI: 10.1186/s13034-022-00444-3 PMID: 35109881

Kim, S.-I., Jo, E., Ryu, M., Cha, I., Kim, Y.-H., Yoo, H., & Hong, H. (2019). Toward becoming a better self: Understanding self-tracking experiences of adolescents with autism spectrum disorder using custom trackers. *PervasiveHealth: Pervasive Computing Technol Healthc.*, 169–178. DOI: 10.1145/3329189.3329209

Kim, H., Molina, C. E., Watkinson, J. S., Leigh-Osroosh, K. T., & Li, D. (2024). Theory-informed school counseling: Increasing efficacy through prevention-focused practice and outcome research. *Journal of Counseling and Development*, *102*(2), 226–238. DOI: 10.1002/jcad.12507

Kim, H., Ruppar, A. L., Baker, D., Kim, S., & Yu, B. (2023). Interweaving disentangled: Korean American students with autism go to college. *Race, Ethnicity and Education*, *26*(7), 892–913. DOI: 10.1080/13613324.2020.1842349

Kim, S., Bochatay, N., Relyea-Chew, A., Buttrick, E., Amdahl, C., Kim, L., Frans, E., Mossanen, M., Khandekar, A., Fehr, R., & Lee, Y.-M. (2017). Individual, interpersonal, and organisational factors of healthcare conflict: A scoping review. *Journal of Interprofessional Care*, *31*(3), 282–290. DOI: 10.1080/13561820.2016.1272558 PMID: 28276847

King, L. A., & King, D. W. (1990). Role conflict and role ambiguity: A critical assessment of construct validity. *Psychological Bulletin*, *107*(1), 48–64. DOI: 10.1037/0033-2909.107.1.48

Kirby, A. V., Feldman, K. J. C., Himle, M. B., Diener, M. L., Wright, C. A., & Hoffman, J. M. (2021). Pilot test of the maximizing adolescent post-secondary-success(mapss) intervention: Supporting parents of autistic youth. *The American Journal of Occupational Therapy*, *75*(3), 7503180070. Advance online publication. DOI: 10.5014/ajot.2021.045815 PMID: 34781348

Klefbeck, K. (2023). Navigating Self-Reflection for Aspiring Special Education Teachers: A Scoping Review on Inclusive Educational Practices and Their Insights for Autism Education. *Education Sciences*, *13*(12), 1182. Advance online publication. DOI: 10.3390/educsci13121182

Knudson, S. (2024). Transition planning and perceptions of support in an autism spectrum disorder resource program. *Preventing School Failure*, *68*(3), 220–230. DOI: 10.1080/1045988X.2023.2207482

Kodama, M. (2017). Functions of Career Resilience Against Reality Shock, Focusing on Full-time Employees During Their First Year of Work. *The Japanese Psychological Research*, *59*(4), 255–265. DOI: 10.1111/jpr.12161

Korea Employment Agency for Persons with Disabilities. (2023). *Employment Support Service for PWDs*. KEAD. https://www.kead.or.kr/en/empsus/cntntsPage.do?menuId=MENU1461

Kossewska, J., Bombińska-Domżał, A., Cierpiałowska, T., Lubińska-Kościółek, E., Niemiec, S., Płoszaj, M., & Preece, D. R. (2021). Towards inclusive education of children with Autism Spectrum Disorder. The impact of teachers' autism-specific professional development on their confidence in their professional competences. *International Journal of Special Education*, *36*(2), 27–35. DOI: 10.52291/ijse.2021.36.15

Kristofik, A., & Johnson, K. (2024). Opportunities to support the caregivers of children and young adults with ASD as they transition into the workforce and university. In Papaneophytou, N. L., & Das, U. N. (Eds.), *Understanding Autism: Perspectives, Assessment, Interventions, and the Journey Towards Inclusion* (pp. 365–371). Elsevier., DOI: 10.1016/B978-0-443-27366-7.00021-3

Kucharczyk, S., Szidon, K., & Hall, L. J. (2022). Coaching in Complexity: Lessons Learned Investigating Implementation of Interventions in High Schools. *Career Development and Transition for Exceptional Individuals*, *45*(2), 99–113. DOI: 10.1177/21651434211041909

Kumari, K. (2025). *Employee Retention Strategies in Ireland's Hospitality Industry* [PhD Thesis, Dublin, National College of Ireland]. https://norma.ncirl.ie/8996/

Kumazaki, H., Muramatsu, T., Yoshikawa, Y., Corbett, B. A., Matsumoto, Y., Higashida, H., Yuhi, T., Ishiguro, H., Mimura, M., & Kikuchi, M. (2019). Job interview training targeting nonverbal communication using an android robot for individuals with autism spectrum disorder. *Autism*, *23*(6), 1586–1595. DOI: 10.1177/1362361319827134

Kuo, A. A., Crapnell, T., Lau, L., Anderson, K. A., & Shattuck, P. (2018). Stakeholder perspectives on research and practice in autism and transition. *Pediatrics*, *141*(Supplement_4), S293–S299. DOI: 10.1542/peds.2016-4300F

Kwembeya, M., Munasirei, P., Mutongoreni, N. A., Mandoga, E., & Kwembeya, L. (2025). Ubuntu Philosophical Framework for Inclusive Sustainable Development Goals. In Ro ca, A.-E. (Ed.), *Exploring Multicultural Dimensions of Literary, Linguistic, and Educational Frontiers* (pp. 207–231). IGI Global., DOI: 10.4018/979-8-3693-8196-0.ch009

Laghi, F., & Trimarco, B. (2020). Individual planning starts at school. Tools and practices promoting autonomy and supporting transition to work for adolescents with autism spectrum disorder. *Annali dell'Istituto Superiore di Sanita*, *56*(2), 222–229. DOI: 10.4415/ANN_20_02_12 PMID: 32567572

Lahza, H. F., Demartini, G., Noroozi, O., Gašević, D., Sadiq, S., & Khosravi, H. (2025). Enhancing peer feedback provision through user interface scaffolding: A comparative examination of scripting and self-monitoring techniques. *Computers & Education*, *230*, 105260. Advance online publication. DOI: 10.1016/j.compedu.2025.105260

Lairson, J. D. (2022). Educator and Community Transition-Service Provider Beliefs Regarding Student Outcomes as a Result of Participation in Work-Readiness Training Opportunities: A Qualitative Study [Ed.D., Northcentral University]. https://www.proquest.com/docview/2729063995/abstract/73074ECD5FC14611PQ/1

Lambert, A., McKelvey, S., Getzel, E. E., Belluscio, T., & Parthemos, C. (2023). Perspectives on the implementation of pre-ETS services: Identification of barriers and facilitators to early career planning for youth with disabilities. *Journal of Vocational Rehabilitation*, *58*(2), 103–114. DOI: 10.3233/JVR-230001

Lam, G. Y. H., Timmons, J., & Zalewska, A. (2023). Program logic model and impacts perceived by stakeholders in a post-school transition program for autistic young adults. *Research in Autism Spectrum Disorders*, *107*, 102220. Advance online publication. DOI: 10.1016/j.rasd.2023.102220

Landis, J. R., & Koch, G. G. (1977). An application of hierarchical kappa-type statistics in the assessment of majority agreement among multiple observers. *Biometrics*, *33*(2), 363–374. DOI: 10.2307/2529786 PMID: 884196

Lang, H. M. (2025). History of the Autism Diagnosis– How the Perspectives Have Changed. *Health Care Analysis*, *33*(4), 337–348. DOI: 10.1007/s10728-025-00527-0 PMID: 40439995

Lanou, A., Hough, L., & Powell, E. (2012). Case studies on using strengths and interests to address the needs of students with autism spectrum disorders. *Intervention in School and Clinic*, *47*(3), 175–182. DOI: 10.1177/1053451211423819

LaPoint, S. C., Kim, S. Y., & Bottema-Beutel, K. (2025). Barriers to Providing Transitional Supports for Autistic Students: Insights of School Professionals. *Journal of Autism and Developmental Disorders*, *55*(8), 2807–2819. DOI: 10.1007/s10803-024-06375-6 PMID: 38773033

LaRue, R. H., Pepa, L., Delmolino, L., Sloman, K. N., Fiske, K., Hansford, A., Liebross, S., & Weiss, M. J. (2016). A brief assessment for selecting communication modalities for individuals with Autism Spectrum Disorders. *Evidence-Based Communication Assessment and Intervention*, *10*(1), 32–43. DOI: 10.1080/17489539.2016.1204767

Lau, F. (2017). Methods for Correlational Studies. In *Handbook of eHealth Evaluation: An Evidence-based Approach* [Internet]. University of Victoria., https://www.ncbi.nlm.nih.gov/books/NBK481614/

Lavigna, A., & La Torre, G. (2024). Validation of the Self Awareness Outcome Questionnaire (SAOQ) in the Italian framework. *La Clinica Terapeutica, 175*(4), 234–238. DOI: 10.7417/CT.2024.5069 PMID: 39010807

Lazaraton, A. (2005). Quantitative Research Methods. In *Handbook of Research in Second Language Teaching and Learning*. Routledge.

Lee, S. (2025, May 15). *Multi-Stage Sampling: Principles & Methods*. NumberAnalytics. https://www.numberanalytics.com/blog/multi-stage-sampling-principles-methods

Lee, E. A. L., Black, M. H., Tan, T., Falkmer, T., & Girdler, S. (2019). "I'm Destined to Ace This": Work Experience Placement During High School for Individuals with Autism Spectrum Disorder. *Journal of Autism and Developmental Disorders, 49*(8), 3089–3101. DOI: 10.1007/s10803-019-04024-x PMID: 31049789

Lee, G. K., & Carter, E. W. (2012). Preparing Transition-Age Students with High-Functioning Autism Spectrum Disorders for Meaningful Work. *Psychology in the Schools, 49*(10), 988–1000. DOI: 10.1002/pits.21651

Lee, H. (2022). Family economic hardship and children's behavioral and socio-emotional outcomes in middle childhood: Direct and indirect pathways. *Children and Youth Services Review, 138*, 106527. Advance online publication. DOI: 10.1016/j.childyouth.2022.106527

Lee, H., Lee, G. K., Chun, J., Kuo, H.-J., Curtiss, S. L., & Okyere, C. (2023). Perspectives of Autistic Emerging Adults, Parents, and Practitioners on the Transition to Adulthood. *Journal of Child and Family Studies, 32*(3), 938–950. DOI: 10.1007/s10826-022-02430-x

Lee, H., & Park, K.-O. (2020). Analysis of experiences of secondary special educators on interagency collaboration in transition education. Korean Journal of Physical. *Multiple and Health Disabilities, 63*(4), 75–100. DOI: 10.20971/kcpmd.2020.63.4.75

Lee, J., & Barger, B. (2024). Factors Predicting Poor Mental and Physical Health in Parents of Children with Autism Spectrum Disorder: Results from 2016 to 2019 National Survey of Children's Health. *Journal of Autism and Developmental Disorders, 54*(3), 915–930. DOI: 10.1007/s10803-022-05870-y PMID: 36562931

Lee, N. R., McQuaid, G. A., Grosman, H. E., Jayaram, S., & Wallace, G. L. (2022). Vocational Outcomes in ASD: An Examination of Work Readiness Skills as well as Barriers and Facilitators to Employment Identified by Autistic Adults. *Journal of Autism and Developmental Disorders*, •••, 1–14. DOI: 10.1007/s10803-022-05804-8 PMID: 36394783

Lengelle, R., Van der Heijden, B. I. J. M., & Meijers, F. (2017). The foundations of career resilience. In Maree, K. (Ed.), *Psychology of Career Adaptability, Employability and Resilience* (pp. 29–47). Springer International Publishing., DOI: 10.1007/978-3-319-66954-0_3

Lent, R. W., & Brown, S. D. (2013). Social cognitive model of career self-management: Toward a unifying view of adaptive career behavior across the life span. *Journal of Counseling Psychology*, *60*(4), 557–568. DOI: 10.1037/a0033446 PMID: 23815631

Lent, R. W., Hackett, G., & Brown, S. D. (1999). A Social Cognitive View of School-to-Work Transition. *The Career Development Quarterly*, *47*(4), 297–311. DOI: 10.1002/j.2161-0045.1999.tb00739.x

Leonard, K. M., Coyne, M. D., Oldham, A. C., Burns, D., & Gillis, M. B. (2019). Implementing MTSS in Beginning Reading: Tools and Systems to Support Schools and Teachers. *Learning Disabilities Research & Practice*, *34*(2), 110–117. DOI: 10.1111/ldrp.12192

Lesnykh, K. A., & Zangieva, I. K. (2025). Factors Determining the Perceptions and Attitudes of People with Autism Spectrum Disorder in Russia. *Mir Rossii*, *34*(3), 146–166. DOI: 10.17323/1811-038X-2025-34-3-146-166

Lien, K., Lashewicz, B., Mitchell, J., & Boettcher, N. (2021). Blending Traditional and Nurturing Fathering: Fathers of Children With Autism Managing Work and Family. *Family Relations*, *70*(1), 264–281. DOI: 10.1111/fare.12472

Ligon, K., & McKelvey, S. (2025). Effects of a Paid Internship Model on Postschool Outcomes of At-risk Youth with Disabilities. *Journal of Vocational Rehabilitation*, *62*(3), 279–285. DOI: 10.1177/10522263251326495

Li, H. (2025). Reflective Practice for Pre-Service Teachers' Professional Development. *SAGE Open*, *15*(3), 21582440251363136. Advance online publication. DOI: 10.1177/21582440251363136

Lindley, L. D. (2005). Perceived barriers to career development in the context of social cognitive career theory. *Journal of Career Assessment*, *13*(3), 271–287. DOI: 10.1177/1069072705274953

Lindner, K.-T., Nusser, L., Gehrer, K., & Schwab, S. (2021). Differentiation and Grouping Practices as a Response to Heterogeneity – Teachers' Implementation of Inclusive Teaching Approaches in Regular, Inclusive and Special Classrooms. *Frontiers in Psychology, 12*, 676482. Advance online publication. DOI: 10.3389/fpsyg.2021.676482 PMID: 34566756

Lindsay, S., Cagliostro, E., & Osten, V. (2023). Exploring autistic workplace disability disclosure: Youth and employer perspectives. In Barret, S. B. (Ed.), *People with Disabilities: Perceptions, Stigmas and Stereotypes* (pp. 145–170). Nova Science Publishers, Inc.

Lindsay, S., Duncanson, M., Niles-Campbell, N., McDougall, C., Diederichs, S., & Menna-Dack, D. (2018). Applying an ecological framework to understand transition pathways to postsecondary education for youth with physical disabilities. *Disability and Rehabilitation, 40*(3), 277–286. DOI: 10.1080/09638288.2016.1250171 PMID: 27868448

Lindsay, S., Osten, V., Rezai, M., & Bui, S. (2021). Disclosure and workplace accommodations for people with autism: A systematic review. *Disability and Rehabilitation, 43*(5), 597–610. DOI: 10.1080/09638288.2019.1635658

Lingo, M. E., Deardorff, M. E., & Williams-Diehm, K. (2024). Using Applied Behavior Analysis Methodology to Improve Transition to Postsecondary Education and Employment. In Carr, R. N. (Ed.), *Applied Behavior Analysis in Schools: Realistic Implementation of Evidence-Based Interventions by Teachers* (pp. 237–254). Taylor and Francis., DOI: 10.4324/9781003522584-13

Li, P., Fu, N., Li, Q., Wang, G., Gao, L., & Zhang, X. (2020). The Griffiths Development Scales-Chinese (GDS-C): A reliable and valid neurodevelopmental assessment tool in children with ASD aged 3–8 years old in Tianjin, China. *Asian Journal of Psychiatry, 52*, 102144. Advance online publication. DOI: 10.1016/j.ajp.2020.102144 PMID: 32417746

Lippold, M. A., Powers, C. J., Syvertsen, A. K., Feinberg, M. E., & Greenberg, M. T. (2013). The Timing of School Transitions and Early Adolescent Problem Behavior. *The Journal of Early Adolescence, 33*(6), 821–844. DOI: 10.1177/0272431612468317 PMID: 24089584

Loubser, D. (2025). Lecturers as redemptive change agents supporting students with autism spectrum disorder (ASD) at higher educational institutions. *Koers, 90*(1), 2626. Advance online publication. DOI: 10.19108/KOERS.90.1.2626

Louis, M. R. (1980). Career Transitions: Varieties and Commonalities. *Academy of Management Review, 5*(3), 329–340. DOI: 10.5465/amr.1980.4288836

Lovett, B. J. (2021). Educational Accommodations for Students With Disabilities: Two Equity-Related Concerns. *Frontiers in Education*, *6*, 795266. Advance online publication. DOI: 10.3389/feduc.2021.795266

Lucas, R., & James, A. I. (2018). An Evaluation of Specialist Mentoring for University Students with Autism Spectrum Disorders and Mental Health Conditions. *Journal of Autism and Developmental Disorders*, *48*(3), 694–707. DOI: 10.1007/s10803-017-3303-1 PMID: 28918532

Luft, P., & Reynolds, M. (2023). Optimising transition outcomes for dhh students: A case study analysis. In Neild, N. R., & Graham, P. J. (Eds.), *Cases on Teacher Preparation in Deaf Education* (pp. 165–226). IGI Global., DOI: 10.4018/978-1-6684-5834-1.ch007

Lukianova, N. N., Fell, E. V., & Shavlokhova, A. A. (2022). Environmental barriers as a factor affecting the ways in which students with disabilities construct their career design. *Perspektivy Nauki i Obrazovania*, *58*(4), 425–439. DOI: 10.32744/pse.2022.4.25

Luwei, W., & Huimin, M. (2024). From jobs to careers: Drivers and barriers to career development in emerging labor markets. *Frontiers in Sociology*, *9*, 1486871. DOI: 10.3389/fsoc.2024.1486871

Lyne, K. D., Barrett, P. T., Williams, C., & Coaley, K. (2000). A psychometric evaluation of the Occupational Stress Indicator. *Journal of Occupational and Organizational Psychology*, *73*(2), 195–220. DOI: 10.1348/096317900166985

Maas, C. J. M., & Hox, J. J. (2004). Robustness issues in multilevel regression analysis. *Statistica Neerlandica*, *58*(2), 127–137. DOI: 10.1046/j.0039-0402.2003.00252.x

MacNaughton, K., Chreim, S., & Bourgeault, I. L. (2013). Role construction and boundaries in interprofessional primary health care teams: A qualitative study. *BMC Health Services Research*, *13*(1), 486. DOI: 10.1186/1472-6963-13-486 PMID: 24267663

Maggin, D. M. (2022). Group Experimental and Quasi-Experimental Research Designs for Special Education Intervention Validation. In *Handbook of Special Education Research* (Vol. I). Routledge. DOI: 10.4324/9781003156857-10

Maggin, D. M., & Bruhn, A. (2018). Evidence-Based Assessment and Single-Case Research: A Commentary for the Special Issue on Direct Behavior Ratings. *Assessment for Effective Intervention*, *43*(2), 71–78. DOI: 10.1177/1534508417738722

Maietta, H. (2023). CAREER DEVELOPMENT NEEDS OF FIRST-GENERATION COLLEGE STUDENTS. In Longwell-Grice, R., & Longwell-Grice, H. (Eds.), *At the Intersection: Understanding and Supporting First-Generation Students* (pp. 244–259). Taylor and Francis., DOI: 10.4324/9781003443131-29

Makhanya, T. B. (2022). Azibuyele emasisweni: Exploring the discourse of Ubuntu philosophy in social work education and practice. *African Journal of Social Work, 12*(6), 136–143.

Malekpour, S. (2019). Models as scenario tools for developing robust transformative plans. In Moallemi, E. A., & de Haan, F. J. (Eds.), *Modelling Transitions: Virtues, Vices, Visions of the Future* (pp. 165–181). Taylor and Francis., DOI: 10.4324/9780429056574-10

Malta, C., Damo, C., & Meirinhos, V. (2025). Career Transitions: Insights from a Narrative Approach. In *Lecture Notes on Multidisciplinary Industrial Engineering: Vol. Part F528* (pp. 243–271). Springer Nature. DOI: 10.1007/978-3-031-89948-5_11

Manthalu, C. H. (2023). An Ubuntu Philosophy of Higher Education as Justice. In *African Higher Education: Developments and Perspectives* (15, pp. 58–72). Brill Academic Publishers. DOI: 10.1163/9789004543805_005

Maphal, M. C. (2014). The manifestation of occupational stress in the teaching profession: The unheeded voices of teachers. *Mediterranean Journal of Social Sciences, 5*(1), 77–88. DOI: 10.5901/mjss.2014.v5n1p77

Margeviča-Grinberga, I., & Kalēja, A. (2025). Job shadowing adults' non-formal education programme through social-emotional learning. *Frontiers in Sociology, 10*, 1524922. DOI: 10.3389/fsoc.2025.1524922 PMID: 40933785

Marsack-Topolewski, C. N. (2020). A Snapshot of Social Support Networks Among Parental Caregivers of Adults with Autism. *Journal of Autism and Developmental Disorders, 50*(4), 1111–1122. DOI: 10.1007/s10803-019-04285-6 PMID: 31848797

Martinez, V. C., & Turnage, D. (2022). Social Support and Parenting Stress in Hispanic Parents of Children with Autism Spectrum Disorder. *Issues in Mental Health Nursing, 43*(11), 1030–1040. DOI: 10.1080/01612840.2022.2100949 PMID: 35849744

Martin, J. E., & Williams-Diehm, K. (2013). Student Engagement and Leadership of the Transition Planning Process. *Career Development and Transition for Exceptional Individuals, 36*(1), 43–50. DOI: 10.1177/2165143413476545

Martin, T., Dixon, R., Verenikina, I., & Costley, D. (2021). Transitioning primary school students with Autism Spectrum Disorder from a special education setting to a mainstream classroom: Successes and difficulties. *International Journal of Inclusive Education*, *25*(5), 640–655. DOI: 10.1080/13603116.2019.1568597

Masarik, A. S., & Conger, R. D. (2017). Stress and child development: A review of the Family Stress Model. *Current Opinion in Psychology*, *13*, 85–90. DOI: 10.1016/j.copsyc.2016.05.008 PMID: 28813301

Masicampo, E. J., & Baumeister, R. F. (2012). Committed but closed-minded: When making a specific plan for a goal hinders succes. *Social Cognition*, *30*(1), 37–55. DOI: 10.1521/soco.2012.30.1.37

Mason, S. (2019). Teachers, twitter and tackling overwork in Japan. *Issues in Educational Research*, *29*(3), 881–898.

Matthews, N. L., Laflin, J., Orr, B. C., Warriner, K., DeCarlo, M., & Smith, C. J. (2020). Brief Report: Effectiveness of an Accelerated Version of the PEERS® Social Skills Intervention for Adolescents. *Journal of Autism and Developmental Disorders*, *50*(6), 2201–2207. DOI: 10.1007/s10803-019-03939-9 PMID: 30825083

Matthews, R. A., Booth, S. M., Taylor, C. F., & Martin, T. (2011). A qualitative examination of the work–family interface: Parents of children with autism spectrum disorder. *Journal of Vocational Behavior*, *79*(3), 625–639. DOI: 10.1016/j.jvb.2011.04.010

Mauri, A. J., & Neiva de Figueiredo, J. (2025). Multi-stage Team Projects in the Management Classroom: Using a Double-loop Peer Presentation Feedback to Cultivate Reflective Learning. *Journal of Management Education*, *49*(2), 236–268. DOI: 10.1177/10525629241313196

Mavuso, M. F. (2022). Exploring Senior Phase teachers' competencies in supporting learners with specific learning difficulties: Implications for inclusive education. *African Journal of Disability*, *11*. Advance online publication. DOI: 10.4102/ajod.v11i0.901 PMID: 36092477

Ma, Z., Dhir, P., Perrier, L., Bayley, M., & Munce, S. (2020). The impact of vocational interventions on vocational outcomes, quality of life, and community integration in adults with childhood onset disabilities: A systematic review. *Journal of Occupational Rehabilitation*, *30*(1), 1–21. DOI: 10.1007/s10926-019-09854-1 PMID: 31535267

Mazzotti, V. L., Rowe, D. A., Kwiatek, S., Voggt, A., Chang, W.-H., Fowler, C. H., Poppen, M., Sinclair, J., & Test, D. W. (2021). Secondary Transition Predictors of Postschool Success: An Update to the Research Base. *Career Development and Transition for Exceptional Individuals*, *44*(1), 47–64. DOI: 10.1177/2165143420959793

McCook, L., Del Vecchio, M. L., & Crosland, K. (2025). Using Progressive Muscle Relaxation to Increase Academic Engagement for Elementary School Students with Autism Spectrum Disorder. *Behavioral Sciences (Basel, Switzerland)*, *15*(11), 1516. Advance online publication. DOI: 10.3390/bs15111516 PMID: 41301318

McDonough, J. T., & Revell, G. (2010). Accessing employment supports in the adult system for transitioning youth with autism spectrum disorders. *Journal of Vocational Rehabilitation*, *32*(2), 89–100. DOI: 10.3233/JVR-2010-0498

McGuinness, C., & Shankar, K. (2019). Supporting reflection in the MLIS through a Professionally-Oriented capstone module. *Education for Information*, *35*(2), 173–178. DOI: 10.3233/EFI-190256

McKnight-Lizotte, M. (2018). Work-Related Communication Barriers for Individuals with Autism: A Pilot Qualitative Study. *Australian Journal of Rehabilitation Counselling*, *24*(1), 12–26. DOI: 10.1017/jrc.2018.4

McLaren, J., Lichtenstein, J. D., Lynch, D., Becker, D., & Drake, R. (2017). Individual Placement and Support for People with Autism Spectrum Disorders: A Pilot Program. *Administration and Policy in Mental Health*, *44*(3), 365–373. DOI: 10.1007/s10488-017-0792-3 PMID: 28176032

McLucas, A. S., & Gonçalves, B. F. (2025). Using Practitioner-Implemented Video Models to Teach Vocational Social Skills in a Rural Public School. *Career Development and Transition for Exceptional Individuals*, 21651434251328271. Advance online publication. DOI: 10.1177/21651434251328271

McMahon, J., & Cullinan, V. (2016). Exploring Eclecticism: The impact of educational theory on the development and implementation of comprehensive education programmes (CEP's) for young children with Autism Spectrum Disorder (ASD). *Research in Autism Spectrum Disorders*, *32*, 1–12. DOI: 10.1016/j.rasd.2016.07.005

McStay, R. L., Dissanayake, C., Scheeren, A., Koot, H. M., & Begeer, S. (2014). Parenting stress and autism: The role of age, autism severity, quality of life and problem behaviour of children and adolescents with autism. *Autism*, *18*(5), 502–510. DOI: 10.1177/1362361313485163 PMID: 24104515

Meethal, S. V. K., & Thomas, A. (2024). Construction of a Scale to Measure Correlates of Adoption of Sustainable Domains in On-Farm Testing Interventions. *Indian Journal of Extension Education*, *60*(4), 112–117. DOI: 10.48165/IJEE.2024.604RT1

Meiring, M., Seabi, J., Amod, Z., Vorster, A., & Kern, A. (2016). Transition for adolescents with autism spectrum disorder: South African parent and professional perspectives. *Frontiers in Psychiatry*, *7*(JUN). Advance online publication. DOI: 10.3389/fpsyt.2016.00093 PMID: 27375502

Michaels, C. A., & Orentlicher, M. L. (2004). The role of occupational therapy in providing person-centred transition services: Implications for school-based practice. *Occupational Therapy International*, *11*(4), 209–228. DOI: 10.1002/oti.212 PMID: 15771211

Milen, M. T., & Nicholas, D. B. (2017). Examining transitions from youth to adult services for young persons with autism. *Social Work in Health Care*, *56*(7), 636–648. DOI: 10.1080/00981389.2017.1318800

Milley, A., & Machalicek, W. (2012). Decreasing Students' Reliance on Adults: A Strategic Guide for Teachers of Students With Autism Spectrum Disorders. *Intervention in School and Clinic*, *48*(2), 67–75. DOI: 10.1177/1053451212449739

Ministry of Community and Social Services. Ontario & Ministry of Children and Youth Services, Ontario. (2011, May). *Provincial Transition Planning Framework for Young People with Developmental Disabilities*. https://coordinatedaccess.ca/wp-content/uploads/2015/07/Transition-Planning-Framework-Final-English.pdf?

Ministry of Disabled People. (2025, May 12). *Strategic Intentions Tauākī Whakamaunga Atu: 1 July 2025 to 30 June 2028*. Ministry of Disabled People. https://www.strategicintentions.whaikaha.govt.nz/

Ministry of Education and Research Sweden. (2010). *Skollag (2010:800) [Swedish Education Act, 2010)*. https://www.riksdagen.se/sv/dokument-och-lagar/dokument/svensk-forfattningssamling/skollag-2010800_sfs-2010-800/

Ministry of Education Chile. (2015, May 29). *LEY NÚM. 20.845 De inclusión escolar que regula la admisión de los y las estudiantes, elimina el financiamiento compartido y prohíbe el lucro en establecimientos educacionales que reciben aportes del estado*. Ministry of Education Chile. https://www.bcn.cl/leychile/navegar?idNorma=1078172

Ministry of Education Government of Ghana. (2015). *Inclusive Education Policy*. Ministry of Education Government of Ghana. https://sapghana.com/data/documents/Inclusive-Education-Policy-official-document.pdf

Ministry of Education Government of India. (2025, April 2). *Ministry of Education reaffirms its commitment to inclusive education by strengthening support systems for children with autism spectrum disorder in schools*. https://dsel.education.gov.in/sites/default/files/update/PIB2117857.pdf

Ministry of Education Government of New Zealand. (2016, November 25). *New Zealand Disability Strategy 2016-2026*. Ministry of Education Government of New Zealand. https://ieag.org.nz/assets/Uploads/NZ-Disability-Strategy.pdf

Ministry of Education, Culture and Science, Government of the Netherlands. (2014, August). *Appropriate Education Act, 2014*. Ministry of Education, Culture and Science. https://www.government.nl/topics/appropriate-education

Ministry of Education. (2003, October 21). *The Folkeskole (Consolidation) Act*. https://media.unesco.org/sites/default/files/webform/r2e002/db4e18f1f260d4ef8ea9ca6e1d4e08d4532fc083.pdf

Ministry of Health and Welfare Republic of Korea. (1989). *A. The Welfare Law for Persons with Disabilities (Amended as Law No. 4179, Promulgated on December 30th 1989)*. Ministry of Health and Welfare Republic of Korea. https://www.dinf.ne.jp/doc/english/intl/z15/z15007le/z1500746.html

Ministry of Justice Japan. (2019). *Act to Facilitate the Employment of Persons with Disabilities(Act No. 123 of July 25, 1960). Updated Act No. 36 of 2019*. https://www.japaneselawtranslation.go.jp/en/laws/view/3845/en

Ministry of Labour and Social Protection. Kenya. (2024, May). *Persons with Disabilities National Policy*. Ministry of Labour and Social Protection, Kenya. https://socialprotection.go.ke/sites/default/files/Downloads/FINAL%20PERSONS%20WITH%20DISABILITIES%20NATIONAL%20POLICY%20-%20LAKE%20NAIVASHA%20RESORT%20v2-%2030TH%20APRIL%202024.pdf

Ministry of Labour. Immigration, Training and Skills Development. (2018, February 7). *Supported Employment Program Guidelines*. Ministry of Labour, Immigration, Training and Skills Development, Ontario. https://eopg.labour.gov.on.ca/wp-content/uploads/2025/04/se-guidelines-program-en.pdf?

Ministry of Planning Chile. (2010, February 3). *LEY NÚM. 20.422 Establece normas sobre igualdad de oportunidades e inclusión social de personas con discapacidad*. https://www.bcn.cl/leychile/navegar?idNorma=1010903

Ministry of Social and Family Development Singapore. (2021). *Enabling Masterplan 2030*. https://www.msf.gov.sg/docs/default-source/enabling-masterplan/emp2030-report-%28final2%29.pdf

Mitra, G., & Dominik, G. (2023). United Nations Disability Inclusion Strategy: A framework to accelerate transformative change for persons with disabilities in the peace and security pillar. *International Review of the Red Cross*, *105*(922), 459–464. DOI: 10.1017/S1816383122001096

Mohammed, A. S., & Hlalele, D. (2025). Inclusion in Early Childhood Education in Ghana. In Sustainable Development Goals Series: Vol. Part F1175 (pp. 255–271). Springer. DOI: 10.1007/978-3-032-05453-1_18

Mohammed, O. O., Ayeni, V. O., & Fowowe, A. I. (2025). A Comparative Analysis of the Discrimination Against Persons with Disabilities (Prohibition) Act 2018, and The United Kingdom Equality Act 2010: Prospects and Challenges. *East African Journal of Law, Policy and Globalization, 2*(1), 24–43. https://journal.kiut.ac.tz/index.php/eajlpg/article/view/192

Molloy, E., & Keating, J. (2011). Targeted Preparation for Clinical Practice. In Professional and Practice-based Learning (Vol. 7, pp. 59–82). Springer Nature. DOI: 10.1007/978-90-481-3937-8_4

Montallana, K. L., Gard, B. M., Lotfizadeh, A. D., & Poling, A. (2019). Inter-Rater Agreement for the Milestones and Barriers Assessments of the Verbal Behavior Milestones Assessment and Placement Program (VB-MAPP). *Journal of Autism and Developmental Disorders*, *49*(5), 2015–2023. DOI: 10.1007/s10803-019-03879-4 PMID: 30661147

Monteiro, E. M. (2022). An ecologically valid understanding of executive functioning. *Psychology in the Schools*, *59*(7), 1390–1401. DOI: 10.1002/pits.22627

Moody, E. J., Kaiser, K., Sharp, D., Kubicek, L. F., Rigles, B., Davis, J., McSwegin, S., D'Abreu, L. C., & Rosenberg, C. R. (2019). Improving Family Functioning Following Diagnosis of ASD: A Randomized Trial of a Parent Mentorship Program. *Journal of Child and Family Studies*, *28*(2), 424–435. DOI: 10.1007/s10826-018-1293-z

Mori, Y., Downs, J., Wong, K., Heyworth, J., & Leonard, H. (2018). Comparing Parental Well-Being and Its Determinants Across Three Different Genetic Disorders Causing Intellectual Disability. *Journal of Autism and Developmental Disorders*, *48*(5), 1651–1665. DOI: 10.1007/s10803-017-3420-x PMID: 29192378

Morris, P., Weglarz-Ward, J. M., & Love, H. R. (2021). Preparing Families of Young Children With Autism Spectrum Disorder for Formal School Settings. *Intervention in School and Clinic*, *57*(2), 126–131. DOI: 10.1177/1053451220928968

Mosala, M. (2025). Promoting Inclusivity Through Ubuntu Philosophy. In Dhakal, R., Davis, W. G., & Heske, K. (Eds.), *Building Collaborative Learning Communities to Drive Student Success* (pp. 237–288). IGI Global., DOI: 10.4018/979-8-3373-0796-1.ch008

Moss, C. (2015). Role Conflict and Role Ambiguity as Predictors of Burnout in Special and General Education Co-teachers [Ph.D., Walden University]. https://www.proquest.com/docview/1637727036/abstract/FE142CB37B154B8FPQ/1

Mpofu, E., Tansey, T., Mpofu, N., Tu, W.-M., & Li, Q. (2019). Employment practices with people with autism spectrum disorder in the digital age. In Potgieter, I. L., Ferreira, N., & Coetzee, M. (Eds.), *Theory, Research and Dynamics of Career Wellbeing: Becoming Fit for the Future* (pp. 309–326). Springer International Publishing., DOI: 10.1007/978-3-030-28180-9_15

Mpofu, J., & Sefotho, M. M. (2025). Embracing Ubuntu: Promoting Inclusion of Learners With Autism Spectrum Disorders in Education. In Phasha, N. T. (Ed.), *Mental Health, Disability, and Combating Marginalization in Education* (pp. 117–144). IGI Global., DOI: 10.4018/979-8-3373-7163-4.ch005

Munandar, V. D., Morningstar, M. E., & Carlson, S. R. (2020). A systematic literature review of video-based interventions to improve integrated competitive employment skills among youth and adults with Autism Spectrum Disorder. *Journal of Vocational Rehabilitation, 53*(1), 29–41. DOI: 10.3233/JVR-201083

Munsell, E. G. S., Orsmond, G. I., Fulford, D., & Coster, W. J. (2022). Metacognition Mediates the Effect of Social Communication and Internalizing Behaviors on Self-management of Daily Life Tasks for Diploma-Track Autistic Youth. *Journal of Autism and Developmental Disorders, 52*(10), 4274–4285. DOI: 10.1007/s10803-021-05306-z PMID: 34611837

Murray, C., & Doren, B. (2013). The effects of working at gaining employment skills on the social and vocational skills of adolescents with disabilities: A school-based intervention. *Rehabilitation Counseling Bulletin, 56*(2), 96–107. DOI: 10.1177/0034355212452614

Murtadlo, M., Albana, H., Nisa, Y. F., Izazy, N. Q., Sumiati, N. T., Dewi, M. S., Abdullah, H., & Henry, C. (2025). Inclusive education in Africa: Transforming higher education in low-income countries. *Scientific African, 28*, e02708. Advance online publication. DOI: 10.1016/j.sciaf.2025.e02708

Mushambi, C., Diale, B., Sefotho, M. M., & Eseadi, C. (2024). Exploring obstacles experienced by learners with high-functioning autism in pursuing careers in sports. *Bulletin of Counseling and Psychotherapy*, *6*(1). Advance online publication. https://journal.kurasinstitute.com/index.php/bocp/article/view/630. DOI: 10.51214/00202406630000

Mutema, G. (2025). Confronting Inequalities in Education: The Symbiosis of Ubuntu and the Nordic Model. In E. Chitando, B. Okyere-Manu, S. Chirongoma, & M. W. Dube (Eds.), *The Palgrave Handbook of Ubuntu, Inequality and Sustainable Development* (pp. 473–482). Springer Science+Business Media. DOI: 10.1007/978-3-031-69573-5_30

Myburgh, S., & van der Vyver, C. P. (2022). Role conflict and role ambiguity in mid-level management in primary schools: Challenges and expectations. In L. van Jaarsveld, C. C. Wolhuter, & C. P. van der Vyver (Eds.), *Education leadership: Scoping, perspectives and future trajectory* (pp. 139–159). AOSIS (pty) Ltd. DOI: 10.4102/aosis.2022.BK383.08

Nachman, B. R. (2024). "A little too helicoptery": Reconciling parental involvement during autistic students' transitions into college. *Teachers College Record*, *126*(11-12), 32–58. DOI: 10.1177/01614681241311637

Nadeem, N. J., Afzal, S., Dogar, I. A., Smith, J. G., Shah, T., Noreen, M., & Ali, A. (2024). The impact of having an autisTic child on parental mental health and well-being in pakistan. *Research in Autism Spectrum Disorders*, *115*, 102423. Advance online publication. DOI: 10.1016/j.rasd.2024.102423

Nakpodia, E. D., & James, U. (2012). Gender Discrimination in Nigerian School System. *International Journal of Development and Management Review*, *7*(1). https://www.ajol.info/index.php/ijdmr/article/view/79287

National Agency for Special Needs Education and Schools. (2019, November 13). *Our mission and role*. National Agency for Special Needs Education and Schools (SPSM in Sweden). https://www.spsm.se/om-oss/other-languages/english/our-mission/

National Disability Insurance Scheme Act. (2013). *National Disability Insurance Scheme Act 2013*. Department of Health, Disability and Ageing Department of the Treasury. https://www.legislation.gov.au/C2013A00020/latest/text

Navarro, J. L., & Tudge, J. R. H. (2025). *Understanding and Teaching Bronfenbrenner's Bioecological Theory*. Taylor & Francis. DOI: 10.4324/9781003464860

Neale, M., & Griffin, M. A. (2006). A model of self-held work roles and role transitions. *Human Performance*, *19*(1), 23–41. DOI: 10.1207/s15327043hup1901_2

Nelson, J. R., & Lund, E. M. (2017). Bronfenbrenner's theoretical framework adapted to women with disabilities experiencing intimate partner violence. In Johnson, A. J., Nelson, J. R., & Lund, E. M. (Eds.), *Religion, Disability, and Interpersonal Violence* (pp. 11–23). Springer International Publishing., DOI: 10.1007/978-3-319-56901-7_2

Nestorowich, D. L., Lupien, S. P., & Madaus Knapp, V. (2022). Perceptions of Behaviors Associated with ASD in Others: Knowledge of the Diagnosis Increases Empathy and Improves Perceptions of Warmth and Competence. *European Journal of Investigation in Health, Psychology and Education, 12*(11), 1594–1606. DOI: 10.3390/ejihpe12110112

Ng, C. S. M., Fang, Y., Wang, Z., & Zhang, M. (2021). Potential Factors of Parenting Stress in Chinese Parents of Children With Autism Spectrum Disorder: A Systematic Review. *Focus on Autism and Other Developmental Disabilities, 36*(4), 237–248. DOI: 10.1177/10883576211012599

Ngubane, N. I., & Makua, M. (2021). Intersection of ubuntu pedagogy and social justice: Transforming south african higher education. *Transformation in Higher Education, 6*, 113. DOI: 10.4102/the.v6i0.113

Nguyen, L., Jack, S., Ketelaar, M., Di Rezze, B., Soper, A. K., & Gorter, J. W. (2020). Understanding the essential components and experiences of youth with autism spectrum disorders in peer mentorship programmes during the transition to adulthood: A qualitative meta-ethnography. *Child: Care, Health and Development, 46*(6), 667–681. DOI: 10.1111/cch.12804 PMID: 32840907

Nguyen, T. M. H., Khuu, D. T., Nguyen, T. A. N., & Nguyen, T. P. (2025). Understanding the link between parental stress and child autism spectrum disorder symptoms: Insights from Vietnam. *Research in Autism, 125*, 202627. Advance online publication. DOI: 10.1016/j.reia.2025.202627

Nicholas, D. B., Attridge, M., Zwaigenbaum, L., & Clarke, M. (2015). Vocational support approaches in autism spectrum disorder: A synthesis review of the literature. *Autism, 19*(2), 235–245. DOI: 10.1177/1362361313516548 PMID: 24449603

Nicholas, D. B., Mitchell, W., Zulla, R., Solomatin, E., & Qi, S. (2019). A Review of CommunityWorks Canada®: Toward Employability Among High School–Age Youth With Autism Spectrum Disorder. *Global Pediatric Health, 6*, 2333794X19885542. Advance online publication. DOI: 10.1177/2333794X19885542 PMID: 31700949

Nicholas, D. B., Zwaigenbaum, L., Zwicker, J., Clarke, M. E., Lamsal, R., Stoddart, K. P., Carroll, C., Muskat, B., Spoelstra, M., & Lowe, K. (2018). Evaluation of employment-support services for adults with autism spectrum disorder. *Autism, 22*(6), 693–702. DOI: 10.1177/1362361317702507 PMID: 28637355

Nigerian Educational Research and Development Council. (2013). *National Policy on Education (6th Edition)*. Nigerian Educational Research and Development Council. https://education.gov.ng/wp-content/uploads/2020/06/NATIONAL-POLICY-ON-EDUCATION.pdf

Nikmat, A. W., Ahmad, M., Oon, N. L., & Razali, S. (2008). Stress and psychological wellbeing among parents of children with autism spectrum disorder. *ASEAN Journal of Psychiatry*, *9*(2), 65–72.

Nir, A. E., & Eyal, O. (2003). School-based management and the role conflict of the school superintendent. *Journal of Educational Administration*, *41*(5), 547–564. DOI: 10.1108/09578230310489362

Nnah, M. O., & George, A. (2025). *Tackling Teacher Burnout and Low Morale in Nigerian Secondary Schools through Effective Leadership Strategies. 18(2b)*, 313–333.

Nnubia, U. I., Ibeanu, V. N., & Okechukwu, F. O. (2020). Characterizing female breadwinners among Nigerian primary school teachers. *Community Work & Family*, *25*(4), 508–522. DOI: 10.1080/13668803.2020.1797634

Nnubia, U. I., Ibeanu, V. N., & Okechukwu, F. O. (2023). Marital structure and domestic gender role practice: Implications for subjective well-being of working mothers teaching in Nigerian primary schools. *Community Work & Family*, *28*(2), 209–232. DOI: 10.1080/13668803.2023.2230347

Nnubia, U. I., Ibeanu, V. N., & Okechukwu, F. O. (2024). Gender role shift: Implications for balancing work and family responsibilities among female primary school teachers in Nigeria. *Journal of Family Studies*, *31*(1), 35–53. DOI: 10.1080/13229400.2024.2405106

Nnubia, U., Ibeanu, V., & Okechukwu, F. (2022). Socio-economic and household characteristics associated with work-family conflict among female primary school teachers in Enugu State, Nigeria. *African Journal of Teacher Education*, *11*(1), 143–165. DOI: 10.21083/ajote.v11i1.6995

Noel, C. R., & Rubow, C. C. (2018). Using noncontingent reinforcement to reduce perseverative speech and increase engagement during social skills instruction. *Education & Treatment of Children*, *41*(2), 157–168. DOI: 10.1353/etc.2018.0006

Nthibeli, M., Griffiths, D., & Bekker, T. (2022). Teaching learners with autism in the South African inclusive classroom: Pedagogic strategies and possibilities. *African Journal of Disability*, *11*(0), 12. DOI: 10.4102/ajod.v11i0.979 PMID: 35812767

Numisi, S., Themane, M., Nel, K., & Govender, I. (2020). Parent-teacher collaboration in children with autism spectrum disorder in Limpopo Province, South Africa. *Journal of Human Ecology (Delhi, India)*, *69*(1–3), 117–126. DOI: 10.31901/24566608.2020/69.1-3.3208

Nuske, H. J., McGhee Hassrick, E., Bronstein, B., Hauptman, L., Aponte, C., Levato, L., Stahmer, A., Mandell, D. S., Mundy, P., Kasari, C., & Smith, T. (2019). Broken bridges—new school transitions for students with autism spectrum disorder: A systematic review on difficulties and strategies for success. *Autism*, *23*(2), 306–325. DOI: 10.1177/1362361318754529 PMID: 29458258

Nwagwu, C. C.NWAGWU. (1997). The Environment of Crises in the Nigerian Education System. *Comparative Education*, *33*(1), 87–96. DOI: 10.1080/03050069728659

Nwamara, E. N., & Nwakacha, C. I. (2025). National Policy on Education: An examination of policy provisions and implications. *Beyond Babel: BU Journal of Language. Literature and Humanities*, *9*(1), 352–360. DOI: 10.5281/zenodo.16273925

Nwoko, J. C., Anderson, E., Adegboye, O., Malau-Aduli, A. E. O., & Malau-Aduli, B. S. (2024). Navigating Teachers' Occupational Well-Being in the Tides of Classroom Processes and School Structures. *Education Sciences*, *14*(11), 1225. DOI: 10.3390/educsci14111225

Nwokolo, E. U. (2023). Screening for Autism and Intellectual Disabilities Amongst the Nigerian Adolescent Population [Ph.D., University of Kent (United Kingdom)]. DOI: 10.22024/UniKent/01.02.102390

Nwosu, K. C., Letzel-Alt, V., & Pozas, M. (2025). From theory to practice: Exploring Nigerian student teachers' experiences of managing learners with special needs in inclusive classrooms. *British Journal of Special Education*, *52*(4), 511–522. DOI: 10.1111/1467-8578.70042

Nye-Lengerman, K. (2017). Vocational rehabilitation service usage and outcomes for individuals with Autism Spectrum Disorder. *Research in Autism Spectrum Disorders*, *41–42*, 39–50. DOI: 10.1016/j.rasd.2017.08.003

Nzimande, N. G. (2025). Exploring the Impact of Formal Continuous Professional Development Activities on Foundation Phase Mathematics Teachers' Instructional Quality. International Journal of Learning. *Teaching and Educational Research*, *24*(5), 497–516. DOI: 10.26803/ijlter.24.5.26

O'Hara, S., Bookmyer, J., Martin, R., & Newton, R. (2019). Theory of action for resourcing professional growth. *Journal of Professional Capital and Community*, *4*(1), 52–65. DOI: 10.1108/JPCC-02-2018-0006

Obadeji, A., Louw, A., & Couper, I. (2024). Medical students' perceptions of the learning environment and its implications on teaching and learning: A qualitative study in Nigeria. *Tehran University Medical Journal*, *17*(56), 29–38. DOI: 10.61186/edcj.17.56.29

Obasa, A. E. (2024). Large language models through the lens of ubuntu for health research in sub-Saharan Africa. *South African Journal of Science*, *120*(5/6). Advance online publication. DOI: 10.17159/sajs.2024/16814

Obasi, C. C., Ishola, A. A., & Fashola, T. M. (2019). Perceived social support as a predictor of parenting stress among parents of children with autism in Lagos, Nigeria. *African Journal for the Psychological Study of Social Issues*, *22*(1), 58–66.

Obimakinde, A. M., Balogun, M. O., Adeleye, J., Oloruntoba, E., Popoola, O., Adedokun, B., & Omokhodion, F. (2022). Work-related psychological distress among teachers in southwest Nigeria: A rural and urban comparison. *Occupational Health Southern Africa*, *28*(3), 95–100. DOI: 10.10520/ejc-ohsa_v28_n3_a4

Odoh, J. N. (2020). Comparative analysis of school climate and teachers' commitment in public and private secondary schools in Ebonyi state. *National Journal Of Educational Leadership*, *5*(1). https://ezenwaohaetorc.org/journals/index.php/NJOEL/article/view/1373

Odunsi, R., Preece, D., & Garner, P. (2017a). Nigerian teachers' understanding of autism spectrum disorder: A comparative study of teachers from urban and rural areas of Lagos state. *Disability, CBR and Inclusive Development*, *28*(3), 98–114. DOI: 10.5463/dcid.v28i3.637

Oduyemi, A. Y., Okafor, I. P., Eze, U. T., Akodu, B. A., & Roberts, A. A. (2021). Internalization of stigma among parents of children with autism spectrum disorder in Nigeria: A mixed method study. *BMC Psychology*, *9*(1), 182. Advance online publication. DOI: 10.1186/s40359-021-00687-3 PMID: 34802470

Oertle, K. M., & Trach, J. S. (2007). Interagency collaboration: The importance of rehabilitation professionals' involvement in transition. *Journal of Rehabilitation*, *73*(3), 36–44.

Office of Special Education and Rehabilitative Services U.S. Department of Education. (2000, July). *A Guide to the Individualized Education Program*. Office of Special Education and Rehabilitative Services U.S. Department of Education. https://www.ed.gov/sites/ed/files/parents/needs/speced/iepguide/iepguide.pdf

Ogba, O. (2025, October 30). Senate Moves to Establish National Autism Centers across Nigeria [Government]. *National Assembly Library Trust Fund.* https://naltf.gov.ng/senate-moves-to-establish-national-autism-centers-across-nigeria/

Ogba, F. N., Onyishi, C. N., Victor-Aigbodion, V., Abada, I. M., Eze, U. N., Obi-weluozo, P. E., Ugodulunwa, C. N., Igu, N. C. N., Okorie, C. O., Onu, J. C., Eze, A., Ezeani, E. O., Ebizie, E. N., & Onwu, A. O. (2020). Managing job stress in teachers of children with autism: A rational emotive occupational health coaching control trial. *Medicine, 99*(36), e21651. DOI: 10.1097/MD.0000000000021651 PMID: 32898998

Ogharen, B. B., Egbule, E. O., & Joy, A. C. (2022). Management of Interpersonal Conflict Involving Principals and Teachers of Selected Public Secondary Schools in Nigeria. *Journal of Educational and Social Research, 12*(3), 320–336. DOI: 10.36941/jesr-2022-0090

Ogu, E. N., & Chike, O. G. -. (2025). Curriculum Management in Nigerian Secondary School for Sustainable Development: Challenges and Opportunities. *International Journal of Educational Management, Rivers State University., 1*(2), 118–129. https://ijedm.com/index.php/ijedm/article/view/49

Ogundeji, Y. K., Tinuoye, O., Bharali, I., Mao, W., Ohiri, K., Ogbuoji, O., Orji, N., & Yamey, G. (2023). Is Nigeria on course to achieve universal health coverage in the context of its epidemiological and financing transition? A knowledge, capacity and policy gap analysis (a qualitative study). *BMJ Open, 13*(3), e064710. Advance online publication. DOI: 10.1136/bmjopen-2022-064710 PMID: 36898742

Ojionuka, A. N. (2016). *Nigerian Educators' Attention Deficit Hyperactivity Disorder Knowledge and Classroom Behavior Management Practices* [Ph.D., Walden University]. https://www.proquest.com/docview/1783595516/abstract/2FAA5256A138461EPQ/1

Okolie, U. C., Nwajiuba, C. A., Binuomote, M. O., Osuji, C. U., Onajite, G. O., & Igwe, P. A. (2020). How careers advice and guidance can facilitate career development in technical, vocational education, and training graduates: The case in Nigeria. *Australian Journal of Career Development, 29*(2), 97–106. DOI: 10.1177/1038416220916814

Okpaka, O., & Ajayi, O. (2025). *Inclusive Strategies for Students with Autism Spectrum Disorder Within the Framework of Evidence-Based Practices—A Scoping Review* (SSRN Scholarly Paper No. 5119762). Social Science Research Network. DOI: 10.2139/ssrn.5119762

Okpilike Felix, M. E. (2010). Towards coping with the major contemporary challenges of the classroom teacher in Nigeria. *Social Sciences*, *5*(6), 565–569. DOI: 10.3923/sscience.2010.565.569

Okurame, D. E. (2007). Perceived mentoring functions: Does mentor's gender matter? *Women in Management Review*, *22*(5), 418–427. DOI: 10.1108/09649420710761473

Okwaraji, F. E., & Aguwa, E. N. (2015). Burnout, psychological distress and job satisfaction among secondary school teachers in Enugu, south east Nigeria. *African Journal of Psychiatry (Johannesburg)*, *18*(1). Advance online publication. DOI: 10.4172/Psychiatry.1000198

Olagunju, A. T., Akinola, M. A., Fadipe, B., Jagun, O. O., Olagunju, T. O., Akinola, O. O., Ogunnubi, O. P., Olusile, O. J., Oluyemi, O. Y., & Chaimowitz, G. A. (2021). Psychosocial Wellbeing of Nigerian Teachers in Special Education Schools. *Journal of Autism and Developmental Disorders*, *51*(4), 1131–1141. DOI: 10.1007/s10803-020-04606-0 PMID: 32666197

Oleribe, O. O., & Taylor-Robinson, S. D. (2016). Before Sustainable Development Goals (SDG): Why Nigeria failed to achieve the Millennium Development Goals (MDGs). *The Pan African Medical Journal*, *24*, 156. DOI: 10.11604/pamj.2016.24.156.8447 PMID: 27795754

Ololube, N. P. (2013). The problems and approaches to educational planning in Nigeria: A theoretical observation. *Mediterranean Journal of Social Sciences*, *4*(12), 37–48. DOI: 10.5901/mjss.2013.v4n12p37

Olubiyi, S. (2022). Psychosocial Burden of Mothers' Care of Children with Autism Attending Federal Neuro-Psychiatric Hospital Yaba Nigeria. *TEXILA INTERNATIONAL JOURNAL OF NURSING*, *8*(1), 9–17. DOI: 10.21522/TIJNR.2015.08.01.Art002

Onalu, C., Chukwu, N., Nnama-Okechukwu, C. U., Iwuagwu, A., Agha, A., Anazonwu, N., Okah, P., & Okoye, U. O. (2024). An Exploratory Study of the Situation of Persons with Disabilities in Nigeria: Practice Consideration for Social Workers. *Journal of Evidence-Based Social Work*, *21*(1), 90–103. DOI: 10.1080/26408066.2023.2265920 PMID: 37796793

Onyishi, C. N. (2022). Teachers' use of inclusive education practices for learners with neuro-developmental disorders in Enugu State, Nigeria. *Ikenga*, *23*(3), 1–16. DOI: 10.53836/ijia/2022/23/3/003

Onyishi, C. N., Okpoko, C. C., & Victor-Aigbodion, V. (2025). Teachers' awareness and perceptions of inclusive education for learners with autism: Implications for the campaign against stigma. *Ikenga*, *26*(1), 51–80. DOI: 10.53836/ijia/2025/26/1/004

Onyishi, C. N., Sefotho, M. M., & Victor-Aibodion, V. (2023). Psychological distress among parents of children with autism spectrum disorders: A randomized control trial of cognitive behavioural therapy. *Research in Autism Spectrum Disorders, 100*, 102070. Advance online publication. DOI: 10.1016/j.rasd.2022.102070

Ookeditse, G. B., Habulezi, J., Batsalelwang, K. J. P., & Molemane, N. J. (2024). Postsecondary transition barriers for students with disabilities in two neighboring school regions in Botswana. *Preventing School Failure, 68*(1), 37–49. DOI: 10.1080/1045988X.2022.2153784

Opara, C. J. (2024). Workplace Stress: A comparison of public and private school teachers in Port Harcourt, Rivers State, Nigeria. *The Nigerian Health Journal, 24*(2), 1211–1219. DOI: 10.60787/tnhj.v24i2.798

Opelusi, O. I., & Omoruyi, O. L. (2021). Adoptable coping strategies of parents with autistic school children in tender brain remedial centre, Oredo local government area, Benin city, Edo state. *Sapientia Global Journal of Arts, Humanities and Development Studies, 4*(1). https://www.sgojahds.com/index.php/SGOJAHDS/article/view/160

Orhero, A. E., Okereka, O. P., & Okolie, U. C. (2023). Role Stressor and Work Adjustment of University Lecturers in Delta State. *Ianna Journal of Interdisciplinary Studies, 5*(1), 124–135.

Orlunga, B. G., & Alikor, O. (2023). Inclusive education and policy implementation in Nigeria: An implication for educational development in the 21st century. *European Journal of Education Studies, 10*(11). Advance online publication. DOI: 10.46827/ejes.v10i11.5076

Osagiobare, E. O., & Ekwukoma, V. (2025). Perceived Challenges of Implementing the National Policy on Inclusive Education in Nigeria. *Revue Plurilingue: Études Des Langues. Littératures et Cultures, 9*(1), 79–88. DOI: 10.46325/ellic.v9i1.164

Otegbeye, C. U. (2021). Rethinking Teacher Professionalism and Policy Reforms in the Nigerian Educational Context [Doctoral, UCL (University College London)]. In *Doctoral thesis, UCL (University College London).* UCL (University College London. https://discovery.ucl.ac.uk/id/eprint/10136626/

Otu, M. S. (2025). Exploration of career coaching programmes for employability skills acquisition. In Otu, M. S., & Sefotho, M. M. (Eds.), *Career Coaching and Employability Skills Acquisition* (pp. 257–283). IGI Global., DOI: 10.4018/979-8-3693-4014-1.ch010

Otu, M., & Sefotho, M. M. (2024). Relationship between employability skills and career transition among neurodivergent individuals. *The International Journal of Interdisciplinary Social and Community Studies, 19*(2), 237–255. DOI: 10.18848/2324-7576/CGP/v19i02/237-255

Ozdemir, N. K., & Koç, M. (2023). Career adaptability of parents of children with autism spectrum disorder. *Current Psychology (New Brunswick, N.J.), 42*(17), 14320–14333. DOI: 10.1007/s12144-021-02649-9 PMID: 35103038

Ozoemena, E. L., Agbaje, O. S., Ogundu, L., Ononuju, A. H., Umoke, P. C. I., Iweama, C. N., Kato, G. U., Isabu, A. C., & Obute, A. J. (2021). Psychological distress, burnout, and coping strategies among Nigerian primary school teachers: A school-based cross-sectional study. *BMC Public Health, 21*(1), 2327. DOI: 10.1186/s12889-021-12397-x PMID: 34969391

Pagano, G., Kiwior, M., Gross, J., Reyes, A., Ramos, E., Cumberbatch, I., Latimore, J., Hu-Au, E., Robila, S., & Tuininga, A. R. (2026). Greens Do Good: A Hydroponic Vertical Farm Augmented and Virtual Reality Training Prototype for Autistic Trainees. *Commun. Comput. Info. Sci., 2598 CCIS*, 287–303. DOI: 10.1007/978-3-031-98080-0_18

Pandey, S., & Agarwal, S. (2013). Transition to adulthood for youth with disability: Issues for the disabled child and family. *IOSR Journal of Humanities and Social Science (IOSR-JHSS), 17*(3), 41–45.

Panganiban, J. L., Shire, S. Y., Williams, J., & Kasari, C. (2022). Supporting peer engagement for low-income preschool students with autism spectrum disorder during academic instruction: A pilot randomised trial. *Autism, 26*(8), 2175–2187. DOI: 10.1177/13623613221085339 PMID: 35420044

Panichelli, C. (2013). Humor, Joining, and Reframing in Psychotherapy: Resolving the Auto-Double-Bind. *The American Journal of Family Therapy, 41*(5), 437–451. DOI: 10.1080/01926187.2012.755393

Park, J., Lu, F.-C., & Hedgcock, W. M. (2017). Relative Effects of Forward and Backward Planning on Goal Pursuit. *Psychological Science, 28*(11), 1620–1630. DOI: 10.1177/0956797617715510 PMID: 28910234

Park, Y. S., Konge, L., & Artino, A. R. J. (2020). The Positivism Paradigm of Research. *Academic Medicine, 95*(5), 690–694. DOI: 10.1097/ACM.0000000000003093 PMID: 31789841

Patel, T. R. (2019). Confidence and Its Impact on Your Aspiring Career. In M. M. Shoja, A. Arynchyna, M. Loukas, A. V. D'Antoni, S. M. Buerger, M. Karl, & R. S. Tubbs (Eds.), *A Guide to the Scientific Career: Virtues, Communication, Research, and Academic Writing* (pp. 33–44). wiley. DOI: 10.1002/9781118907283.ch5

Pearson, C., Watson, N., Gangneux, J., & Norberg, I. (2021). Transition to where and to what? Exploring the experiences of transitions to adulthood for young disabled people. *Journal of Youth Studies*, *24*(10), 1291–1307. DOI: 10.1080/13676261.2020.1820972

Peretomode, V. F. (2006a). Decisional deprivation, equilibrium and saturation as variables in teacher motivation, job satisfaction and morale in Nigeria. *Academic Leadership*, *4*(1), 111–126.

Pérez, E. G. S., Medina, D. E. M., & Caraveo, M. del C. S. (. (2017). Indications of role ambiguity in university teachers. *Revista Electrónica de Investigación Educativa*, *19*(1), 73–83. DOI: 10.24320/redie.2017.19.1.889

Perryman, T., Ricks, L., & Cash-Baskett, L. (2020). Meaningful transitions: Enhancing clinician roles in transition planning for adolescents with autism spectrum disorders. *Language, Speech, and Hearing Services in Schools*, *51*(4), 899–913. DOI: 10.1044/2020_LSHSS-19-00048 PMID: 32585119

Pettey, A. (2015). *Examining work-family conflict and parenting stress for parents of children with autism spectrum disorder through the lens of boundary and conservations of resources theories* [Master's Thesis, California State University]. https://scholarworks.lib.csusb.edu/etd/231

Phelps, L. A., & Hanley-Maxwell, C. (1997). School-to-Work Transitions for Youth With Disabilities: A Review of Outcomes and Practices. *Review of Educational Research*, *67*(2), 197–226. DOI: 10.3102/00346543067002197

Pinder-Amaker, S. (2014). Identifying the unmet needs of college students on the autism spectrum. *Harvard Review of Psychiatry*, *22*(2), 125–137. DOI: 10.1097/HRP.0000000000000032 PMID: 24614767

Plesa Skwerer, D., Jordan, S. E., Brukilacchio, B. H., & Tager-Flusberg, H. (2016). Comparing methods for assessing receptive language skills in minimally verbal children and adolescents with autism spectrum disorders. *Autism*, *20*(5), 591–604. DOI: 10.1177/1362361315600146 PMID: 26408635

Plotner, A. J., Trach, J. S., & Strauser, D. R. (2012). Vocational Rehabilitation Counselors' Identified Transition Competencies: Perceived Importance, Frequency, and Preparedness. *Rehabilitation Counseling Bulletin*, *55*(3), 135–143. DOI: 10.1177/0034355211427950

Poirier, S.-È., St-Pierre, M.-C., Julien-Gauthier, F., Flamand, V., Martin-Roy, S., & Desmarais, C. (2022). Inter-Agency Collaboration in the Transition from School to Adulthood of Students with Disabilities: A Narrative Review of the Literature. *International Journal of Disability Development and Education*, *69*(4), 1249–1256. DOI: 10.1080/1034912X.2020.1779915

Polovina, N. (2010). General beliefs of teachers and students about working and living environment: Implications for mutual cooperation. *Zbornik Instituta za Pedagoska Istrazivanja*, *42*(1), 74–91. DOI: 10.2298/ZIPI1001074P

Pongsaksri, M., Lersilp, S., & Suchart, S. (2017). Development and Reliability of the Basic Skill Assessment Tool for Adolescents with Autism Spectrum Disorder. *TheScientificWorldJournal*, *2403943*, 1–7. Advance online publication. DOI: 10.1155/2017/2403943 PMID: 28280769

Ponnet, K. (2014). Financial Stress, Parent Functioning and Adolescent Problem Behavior: An Actor–Partner Interdependence Approach to Family Stress Processes in Low-, Middle-, and High-Income Families. *Journal of Youth and Adolescence*, *43*(10), 1752–1769. DOI: 10.1007/s10964-014-0159-y PMID: 25053382

Popov, D., Tyumeneva, Y., & Larina, G. (2013). Life after 9th grade: How do personal achievements of students and their family resources influence life trajectories. *Voprosy Obrazovaniya / Educational Studies Moscow*, *2013*(4), 310–334. DOI: 10.17323/1814-9545-2013-4-310-334

Popovic, N., & Jinks, D. (Eds.). (2013). *Personal consultancy: A model for integrating counselling and coaching*. Taylor and Francis., DOI: 10.4324/9781315882550

Porter, S. G. (2021). It takes a well-organised village: Implementing RTI/MTSS models in secondary schools. In *Research Anthology on Inclusive Practices for Educators and Administrators in Special Education* (pp. 339–368). IGI Global., DOI: 10.4018/978-1-6684-3670-7.ch020

Puerta, P., Ciannelli, L., & Johnson, B. (2019). A simulation framework for evaluating multi-stage sampling designs in populations with spatially structured traits. PeerJ, 2019(2). DOI: 10.7717/peerj.6471

Pugliese, C. E., Werner, M. A., Alexander, K. C., Cannon, L., Strang, J. F., Caplan, R., Klinger, L., Mandell, D., Dieckhaus, M., Handsman, R., Kenworthy, L., & Anthony, L. G. (2024). Development of a High School-Based Executive Function Intervention for Transition-Age Autistic Youth: Leveraging Multi-level Community Partnerships. *School Mental Health*, *16*(3), 862–878. DOI: 10.1007/s12310-024-09661-x

Qian, X., Johnson, D., & Papay, C. (2021). Exploring Correlates of Paid Early Work Experiences for Youth With Autism Using NLTS2012 Data. *Focus on Autism and Other Developmental Disabilities, 36*(1), 14–24. DOI: 10.1177/1088357620956915

Quick, J., & Hall, S. (2015). Part Three: The Quantitative Approach. *Journal of Perioperative Practice, 25*(10), 192–196. DOI: 10.1177/175045891502501002 PMID: 26717587

Ramani, R. S., & McHugh, P. P. (2024). Cultural influences on internship development value and job pursuit intention: An exploratory comparison of student experiences in France and the United States. *International Journal of Management Education, 22*(3), 101008. Advance online publication. DOI: 10.1016/j.ijme.2024.101008

Ramos, A. de S., & Alves, L. M. (2008). Speech therapy in the interaction between regular primary schools and special education schools in the process of inclusion. *Revista Brasileira de Educação Especial, 14*(2), 235–250. DOI: 10.1590/S1413-65382008000200007

Rashid, T., & Ostermann, R. F. (2009). Strength-based assessment in clinical practice. *Journal of Clinical Psychology, 65*(5), 488–498. DOI: 10.1002/jclp.20595 PMID: 19294732

Raudeliūnaitė, R., & Steponėnienė, E. (2020). Challenges for primary school teachers in ensuring inclusive education for children with autism spectrum disorders. *Pedagogika, 138*(2), 209–225. DOI: 10.15823/p.2020.138.12

Razaq-Shuaib, B. (2025). Understanding the Impact of Early Childhood and Primary Education for Children with Neurodevelopmental Disabilities on Parents in Nigeria. *BMJ Paediatrics Open, 9*(1), 1–9. DOI: 10.1136/bmjpo-2025-003909

Read, C., & Szokolszky, A. (2025). Developmental Ecological Psychology meets organicist biology: The example of the ecological self. *Frontiers in Psychology, 16*, 1569356. Advance online publication. DOI: 10.3389/fpsyg.2025.1569356 PMID: 40667396

Reichow, B., Doehring, P., & Volkmar, F. R. (Eds.). (2025). *Handbook of Evidence-Based Practices in Autism Spectrum Disorder*. Springer Nature., DOI: 10.1007/978-3-031-78143-8

Reis, S. M., Madaus, J. W., Gelbar, N. W., & Miller, L. J. (2024). Strength-Based Strategies for Twice-Exceptional High School Students With Autism Spectrum Disorder. *Teaching Exceptional Children, 57*(1), 24–33. DOI: 10.1177/00400599221108899

Republic of Kenya. (2025, May 13). *The Persons With Disabilities Act, 2025*. Kenya Gazette Supplement No 69 (Acts No 4). Government Printer, Nairobi. https://ncpwd.go.ke/download/personswithdisabilitiesact-pdf/?ind=1747986120993&filename=The%20Persons%20with%20Disabilities%20Act%202025.pdf&wpdmdl=640&refresh=693557689954e1765103464

Rindfleisch, A., Malter, A. J., Ganesan, S., & Moorman, C. (2008). Cross-Sectional versus Longitudinal Survey Research: Concepts, Findings, and Guidelines. *JMR, Journal of Marketing Research*, *45*(3), 261–279. DOI: 10.1509/jmkr.45.3.261

Ríos, M., Zekri, S., Alonso-Esteban, Y., & Navarro-Pardo, E. (2022). Parental stress assessment with the parenting stress index (PSI): A systematic review of its psychometric properties. *Children (Basel, Switzerland)*, *9*(11), 1649. DOI: 10.3390/children9111649 PMID: 36360377

Rivard, M., Terroux, A., Parent-Boursier, C., & Mercier, C. (2014). Determinants of stress in parents of children with autism spectrum disorders. *Journal of Autism and Developmental Disorders*, *44*(7), 1609–1620. DOI: 10.1007/s10803-013-2028-z PMID: 24384673

Roberts, K. D. (2010). Topic areas to consider when planning transition from high school to postsecondary education for students with autism spectrum disorders. *Focus on Autism and Other Developmental Disabilities*, *25*(3), 158–162. DOI: 10.1177/1088357610371476

Robinson, S., & Fisher, K. R. (2023). *Research handbook on disability policy*. Edward Elgar Publishing. DOI: 10.4337/9781800373655

Rochat, S., & Borgen, W. A. (2023). Career life as a game: An overlooked metaphor for successful career transitions. *British Journal of Guidance & Counselling*, *51*(2), 298–309. DOI: 10.1080/03069885.2021.1940844 PMID: 37313007

Rodil, M. S. P. (2024). Gearing towards Efficient Problem Solving: Exploring the Determinants That Influence Success. *Journal of Interdisciplinary Studies in Education*, *13*(2), 120–151. DOI: 10.32674/thv32d10

Rodríguez, Y. Y. (2024). Autism: An Interdisciplinary Analysis from Neuroscience. *Seminars in Medical Writing and Education*, *3*, 615. Advance online publication. DOI: 10.56294/mw2024615

Roitsch, J. (2024). Transitioning from High School to Adulthood: Optimising Outcomes for Students with Autism Spectrum Disorder. In Volkmar, F. R., Reichow, B., & McPartland, J. C. (Eds.), *Adolescents and Adults with Autism Spectrum Disorders* (2nd ed., pp. 55–74). Springer International Publishing., DOI: 10.1007/978-3-031-46463-8_3

Romasanta, J. M. (2025). Integrating Organizational Culture and Leadership Competence for Effective School-Based Management: Inputs for School Improvement Plan. *International Journal of Multidisciplinary Research and Publications, 8*(1), 519–542.

Rosa, R. A., Correa, M. V. P., & Bulgacov, S. (2025). RESOURCES IN ACTION: THE DYNAMICS OF RESOURCING IN AN EDUCATIONAL ORGANIZATION. *RAE Revista de Administracao de Empresas, 65*(5). https://doi.org/DOI: 10.1590/S0034-759020250504x

Rosenkoetter, S. E., Hains, A. H., & Dogaru, C. (2007). Successful transitions for young children with disabilities and their families: Roles of school social workers. *Children & Schools, 29*(1), 25–34. DOI: 10.1093/cs/29.1.25

Roux, A. M., Rast, J. E., Anderson, K. A., Garfield, T., & Shattuck, P. T. (2021a). Vocational Rehabilitation Service Utilization and Employment Outcomes Among Secondary Students on the Autism Spectrum. *Journal of Autism and Developmental Disorders, 51*(1), 212–226. DOI: 10.1007/s10803-020-04533-0 PMID: 32399821

Roux, A. M., Rast, J. E., & Shattuck, P. T. (2020). State-Level Variation in Vocational Rehabilitation Service Use and Related Outcomes Among Transition-Age Youth on the Autism Spectrum. *Journal of Autism and Developmental Disorders, 50*(7), 2449–2461. DOI: 10.1007/s10803-018-3793-5 PMID: 30357645

Roux, A. M., Shattuck, P. T., Cooper, B. P., Anderson, K. A., Wagner, M., & Narendorf, S. C. (2013). Postsecondary Employment Experiences Among Young Adults With an Autism Spectrum Disorder RH: Employment in Young Adults With Autism. *Journal of the American Academy of Child and Adolescent Psychiatry, 52*(9), 931–939. DOI: 10.1016/j.jaac.2013.05.019 PMID: 23972695

Ruble, L. A., Parsons, B. M., McGrew, J. H., & Hoffman, B. (2013). COMPASS Across Settings. In Ruble, L. A., & McGrew, J. H. (Eds.), *Compass and Innovative Education for Students with Autism* (pp. 191–205). Springer International Publishing., DOI: 10.1007/978-3-031-31395-0_9

Rumsa, S., Afsharnejad, B., Lim Lee, E. A., Bölte, S., Tan, T., & Girdler, S. (2025). A scoping review of current approaches to strengths-based transition practices for autistic adolescents. *Autism, 29*(11), 2644–2661. DOI: 10.1177/13623613251346336 PMID: 40559186

Rumsey, M. G. (2020). Personality and interests for selection: Theoretical perspectives. *Military Psychology : the Official Journal of the Division of Military Psychology, American Psychological Association, 32*(1), 7–23. DOI: 10.1080/08995605.2019.1652478 PMID: 38536247

Russ, S., Arora, S., Wharton, R., Wheelock, A., Hull, L., Sharma, E., Darzi, A., Vincent, C., & Sevdalis, N. (2013). Measuring safety and efficiency in the operating room: Development and validation of a metric for evaluating task execution in the operating room. *Journal of the American College of Surgeons, 216*(3), 472–481. DOI: 10.1016/j.jamcollsurg.2012.12.013 PMID: 23357728

Ryan, G., Bhatti, K., Duncan, C., McGinnis, S., Elliott, R., & Cooper, M. (2023). Reliability and validity of an auditing tool for person-centred psychotherapy and counselling for young people: The PCEPS-YP. *Counselling & Psychotherapy Research, 23*(2), 563–576. DOI: 10.1002/capr.12505

Ryan, R. M., Reeve, J., Kaplan, H., Matos, L., & Cheon, S. H. (2023). Education as Flourishing: Self-Determination Theory in Schools as They Are and as They Might Be. In Ryan, R. M. (Ed.), *The Oxford Handbook of Self-Determination Theory* (pp. 591–618). Oxford University Press., DOI: 10.1093/oxfordhb/9780197600047.013.60

Sabela, P. T. (2023). Inclusive education: Challenging barriers, claiming human rights and social justice. In Maguvhe, M. O., & Masuku, M. M. (Eds.), *Using African Epistemologies in Shaping Inclusive Education Knowledge* (pp. 259–284). Springer., DOI: 10.1007/978-3-031-31115-4_15

Salahu, M. O. (2020). *Assessment of Educational Policy in Nigeria: A Study of State and Non-state Provision of Basic Education in Kwara State (2009-2019)* [Ph.D., Kwara State University (Nigeria)]. https://www.proquest.com/docview/2447051198/abstract/82A9E457504CB7PQ/1

Sales, B. D., & Folkman, S. E. (2000). *Ethics in research with human participants.* American Psychological Association. https://psycnet.apa.org/record/2000-07971-000

Salmela-Aro, K., Mutanen, P., Koivisto, P., & Vuori, J. (2010). Adolescents' future education-related personal goals, concerns, and internal motivation during the "towards working life" group intervention. *European Journal of Developmental Psychology, 7*(4), 445–462. DOI: 10.1080/17405620802591628

Sánchez Amate, J. J., & Luque De La Rosa, A. (2025). Research on the Inclusion of Students with Autism Spectrum Disorder: Educational Strategies, Attitudes, and Resources from an Integrative Systematic Review. *Journal of Cultural Analysis and Social Change*, *10*(2), 2006–2016. DOI: 10.64753/jcasc.v10i2.1899

Sánchez-Blanchart, J., Sánchez-Oliva, A., Pastor-Vicedo, J. C., & Martínez-Martínez, J. (2019). Teacher training in the face of the austism spectrum. *Sport TK*, *8*(2), 59–66. DOI: 10.6018/sportk.401121

Sanders, S., Rollins, L. H., & McFall, A. (2023). Aiming High: Applying Goal Setting to Social and Emotional Learning Skills in the Elementary Classroom. *Beyond Behavior*, *32*(1), 4–14. DOI: 10.1177/10742956221145692

Sansosti, F. J., Merchant, D., Koch, L. C., Rumrill, P., & Herrera, A. (2017). Providing supportive transition services to individuals with autism spectrum disorder: Considerations for vocational rehabilitation professionals. *Journal of Vocational Rehabilitation*, *47*(2), 207–222. DOI: 10.3233/JVR-170896

Sansosti, F. J., & Sansosti, J. M. (2013). Effective School-Based Service Delivery For Students With Autism Spectrum Disorders: Where We Are And Where We Need To Go. *Psychology in the Schools*, *50*(3), 229–244. DOI: 10.1002/pits.21669

Santhanam, S. P., & Wilson, K. (2024). A Comparison of Autistic and Non-Autistic College Students' Perceived Challenges and Engagement in Self-Advocacy. *American Journal of Speech-Language Pathology*, *33*(3), 1471–1484. DOI: 10.1044/2024_AJSLP-22-00381

Santosa, I., Sakya, K. A., Junaidy, D. W., Rahma, M. S., Mawali, L., & Rangga, S. (2025). Associative Concept Network Analysis-Driven Insights for Developing Adaptive Seating Solutions for Children with Autism Spectrum Disorder. *International Journal of Designed Objects*, *19*(2), 21–45. DOI: 10.18848/2325-1379/CGP/v19i02/21-45

Sasere, O. B. (2023). *Leadership roles of school administrators in teachers' professional development in Nigeria* [University of the Free State]. http://hdl.handle.net/11660/12404

Sasere, O. B., & Makhasane, S. D. (2023). School-Based Teacher Professional Development Framework (SBTPDF): A Blueprint for School Principals in Nigeria. International Journal of Learning. *Teaching and Educational Research*, *22*(8), 391–414. DOI: 10.26803/ijlter.22.8.21

Schall, C., Wehman, P., & McDonough, J. L. (2012). Transition from School to Work for Students with Autism Spectrum Disorders: Understanding the Process and Achieving Better Outcomes. *Pediatric Clinics of North America*, *59*(1), 189–202. DOI: 10.1016/j.pcl.2011.10.009 PMID: 22284802

Scheef, A. R., Hollingshead, A., & Voss, C. S. (2019). Peer Support Arrangements to Promote Positive Postschool Outcomes. *Intervention in School and Clinic*, *54*(4), 219–224. DOI: 10.1177/1053451218782430

Scheef, A., & Mahfouz, J. (2020). Supporting the post-school goals of youth with disabilities through use of a transition coordinator. *Research in Educational Administration and Leadership*, *5*(1), 43–69. DOI: 10.30828/real/2020.1.2

Schiamberg, L. B., Paulson, S., & Zawacki, K. (2019). An ecological perspective for teaching about the adolescent. In Paul McKinney, J., Schiamberg, L. B., & Shelton, L. G. (Eds.), *Teaching About Adolescence: An Ecological Approach* (pp. 15–38). Taylor and Francis., DOI: 10.4324/9781315861500-2

Schoen, S. A., & Valdez, A. (2023). Preliminary efficacy of a transition training program for autistic adolescents. *Research in Autism Spectrum Disorders*, *109*, 102281. Advance online publication. DOI: 10.1016/j.rasd.2023.102281

Schutz, M. A., & Carter, E. W. (2022). Employment interventions for youth with disabilities: A review of transition practices and partners. *Career Development and Transition for Exceptional Individuals*, *45*(3), 154–169. DOI: 10.1177/21651434221075810

Schwab, R. L., & Iwanicki, E. F. (1982). Perceived Role Conflict, Role Ambiguity, and Teacher Burnout. *Educational Administration Quarterly*, *18*(1), 60–74. DOI: 10.1177/0013161X82018001005

Schweizer, T., Endres, D., Dziobek, I., & Tebartz van Elst, L. (2024). Psychosocial therapeutic approaches for high-functioning autistic adults. *Frontiers in Psychiatry*, *14*, 1265066. DOI: 10.3389/fpsyt.2023.1265066 PMID: 38274434

Scott, R. D. (2014). The treatment barrier. In Walrond-Skinner, S. (Ed.), *Developments in Family Therapy: Theories and Applications since 1948* (pp. 30–59). Taylor and Francis., DOI: 10.4324/9781315814742-13

Sefotho, (2013). *Narratives of differently abled persons: Informing career guidance policy* [University of Pretoria]. http://hdl.handle.net/2263/31652

Sefotho, M. M. (2014). Career construction for hephapreneurship: Alternative framework for persons with disabilities. *Mediterranean Journal of Social Sciences*, *5*(15), 303–312. DOI: 10.5901/mjss.2014.v5n15p303

Sefotho, M. M. M. (2015). Mainstreaming disability in education beyond 2015. *South African Journal of Education, 35*(1), 1–8. Advance online publication. DOI: 10.15700/201503070007

Sefotho, M. M., & Onyishi, C. N. (2021). Transition to Higher Education for Students with Autism: Challenges and Support Needs. *International Journal of Higher Education, 10*(1), 201. https://EconPapers.repec.org/RePEc:jfr:ijhe11:v:10:y:2021:i:1:p:201. DOI: 10.5430/ijhe.v10n1p201

Segev, E., Gadot, L., & Fine, M. (2025). Between a "ball and chain" and a "half-full glass": Work–family balance experiences of fathers to children with disabilities. *The American Journal of Orthopsychiatry*. Advance online publication. DOI: 10.1037/ort0000868 PMID: 40587314

Senate and House of Representatives of the United States of America in Congress. (2016, January 7). *Rehabilitation Act of 1973 [As Amended Through P.L. 114–95, Enacted December 10, 2015]*. https://assets.section508.gov/assets/files/rehabilitation-act-of-1973-amended-by-wioa.pdf

Setia, M. S. (2016). Methodology series module 3: Cross-sectional studies. *Indian Journal of Dermatology, 61*(3), 261–264. DOI: 10.4103/0019-5154.182410 PMID: 27293245

Sharma, A. (2025). Positivism. In Jahn, B., & Schindler, S. (Eds.), *Elgar Encyclopedia of International Relations* (pp. 302–303). Edward Elgar Publishing Ltd., DOI: 10.4337/9781035312283.000138

Sharma, U., Furlonger, B., & Forlin, C. (2019). The Impact of Funding Models on the Education of Students With Autism Spectrum Disorder. *Australasian Journal of Special and Inclusive Education, 43*(1), 1–11. DOI: 10.1017/jsi.2019.1

Sharpe, M., Hutchinson, C., & Alexander, J. (2022). The Lived Experiences and Perspectives of People with Autism Spectrum Disorder in Mainstream Employment in Australia. *Disabilities, 2*(2), 164–177. DOI: 10.3390/disabilities2020013

Shattuck, P. T., Narendorf, S. C., Cooper, B., Sterzing, P. R., Wagner, M., & Taylor, J. L. (2012). Postsecondary Education and Employment Among Youth With an Autism Spectrum Disorder. *Pediatrics, 129*(6), 1042–1049. DOI: 10.1542/peds.2011-2864 PMID: 22585766

Sheftel, A., Lindstrom, L., & McWhirter, B. (2014). Motivational enhancement career intervention for youth with disabilities. *Advances in School Mental Health Promotion, 7*(4), 208–224. DOI: 10.1080/1754730X.2014.949061

Shen, L., & Zhang, L. (2025). Linking Healthcare, Family, and Work Systems: The Roles of Family-Centered Care, Family Resilience, and Caregiving-to-Work Conflict in Psychological Well-being among Parents of Children with Autism Spectrum Disorder. *Applied Research in Quality of Life*, *20*(5), 2099–2117. Advance online publication. DOI: 10.1007/s11482-025-10515-0

Shepherd, J. (2022). Beyond tick-box transitions? Experiences of autistic students moving from special to further education. *International Journal of Inclusive Education*, *26*(9), 878–892. DOI: 10.1080/13603116.2020.1743780

Sher, J. P. (2019). Education in the countryside: Overview of conditions and some conclusions. In Sher, J. P. (Ed.), *Rural Education In Urbanized Nations: Issues and Innovations* (pp. 21–90). Taylor and Francis., DOI: 10.4324/9780429305054-2

Shernoff, E. S., Mehta, T. G., Atkins, M. S., Torf, R., & Spencer, J. (2011). A Qualitative Study of the Sources and Impact of Stress Among Urban Teachers. *School Mental Health*, *3*(2), 59–69. DOI: 10.1007/s12310-011-9051-z

Sherwood, K., Smith, M. J., Ross, B., Johnson, J., Harrington, M., Blajeski, S., DaWalt, L., Bishop, L., & Smith, J. D. (2023). Mixed methods implementation evaluation of virtual interview training for transition-age autistic youth in pre-employment transition services. *Journal of Vocational Rehabilitation*, *58*(2), 139–154. DOI: 10.3233/JVR-230004 PMID: 38881791

Shikuku, D. N., Mohammed, H., Mwanzia, L., Ladur, A. N., Nandikove, P., Uyara, A., Waigwe, C., Nyaga, L., Bashir, I., Ndirangu, E., Bedwell, C., Bar-Zeev, S., & Ameh, C. (2024). Evaluation of the feasibility of a midwifery educator continuous professional development (CPD) programme in Kenya and Nigeria: A mixed methods study. *BMC Medical Education*, *24*(1), 534. Advance online publication. DOI: 10.1186/s12909-024-05524-w PMID: 38745243

Shogren, K. A., & Plotner, A. J. (2012). Transition planning for students with intellectual disability, autism, or other disabilities: Data from the national longitudinal transition study-2. *Intellectual and Developmental Disabilities*, *50*(1), 16–30. DOI: 10.1352/1934-9556-50.1.16 PMID: 22316223

Shrepnek, G. K. (2005). Regression methods in the empiric analysis of health care data. *Journal of Managed Care Pharmacy : JMCP*, *11*(3), 240–251. DOI: 10.18553/jmcp.2005.11.3.240 PMID: 15804208

Shrout, P. E., & Fleiss, J. L. (1979). Intraclass correlations: Uses in assessing rater reliability. *Psychological Bulletin*, *86*(2), 420–428. DOI: 10.1037/0033-2909.86.2.420 PMID: 18839484

Shumbamhini, M., & Chirongoma, S. (2025). Ubuntu, Gender Equality and Sustainable Development in Africa: An African Feminist Perspective. In E. Chitando, B. Okyere-Manu, S. Chirongoma, & M. W. Dube (Eds.), *The Palgrave Handbook of Ubuntu, Inequality and Sustainable Development* (pp. 781–798). Springer Science+Business Media. DOI: 10.1007/978-3-031-69573-5_47

Siew, C. T., Mazzucchelli, T. G., Rooney, R., & Girdler, S. (2017). A specialist peer mentoring program for university students on the autism spectrum: A pilot study. *PLoS One*, *12*(7), e0180854. Advance online publication. DOI: 10.1371/journal.pone.0180854 PMID: 28704446

Sigurðardóttir, Á. (2017). *Stress, anxiety, depression and social constraints in parents of children with autism* [BSc Thesis, Reykjavik University]. https://skemman.is/handle/1946/28355

Šilc, M., & Krajnc, M. S. (2022). Challenges in Educational Inclusion of Students with Autism Disorders in Primary Schools. *Journal of Elementary Education*, *15*(2), 181–198. DOI: 10.18690/rei.15.2.181-198.2022

Silva, R. C., Corona, C. C., & Galdeano, J. L. V. (2014). Solving regression analysis by fuzzy quadratic programming. *Studies in Computational Intelligence*, *537*, 139–147. DOI: 10.1007/978-3-642-53737-0_9

Silvia, M., Hadi, S., & Kurniawan, I. S. (2025). The role of role overload, role conflict, and role ambiguity in job stress. *The Fourth International Conference on Government Education Management and Tourism*, *4*, 094–094. https://www.conference.loupiasconference.org/index.php/ICoGEMT-4/article/view/616

Simelane, A. P. (2020). Understanding daily parenting stresses in caring for children with autism spectrum disorders. *SAJCH : the South African Journal of Child Health*, *14*(3), 115. DOI: 10.7196/SAJCH.2020.v14i3.1596

Simon, D. J., Cruise, T. K., Huber, B. J., Swerdlik, M. E., & Newman, D. S. (2014). Supervision in school psychology: The developmental/ecological/problem-solving model. *Psychology in the Schools*, *51*(6), 636–646. DOI: 10.1002/pits.21772

Singer, J. (1998). *Odd people. The Birth of Community Amongst People on the" Autistic Spectrum.* University of Technology.

Singha, R. (2024). Cultivating holistic learning environments in higher education: Mindfulness, compassion, and ubuntu philosophies. In Omona, K., & O'dama, M. K. (Eds.), *Global Perspectives on Micro-Learning and Micro-Credentials in Higher Education* (pp. 174–194). IGI Global., DOI: 10.4018/979-8-3693-0343-6.ch011

Siraj, I., & Huang, R. (2020). Operationalizing Bronfenbrenner's PPCT Model in Researching Human Development: Commentary on Xia, Li, and Tudge. *Human Development, 64*(1), 21–25. https://www.jstor.org/stable/27139590. DOI: 10.1159/000508341

Sitimin, S. A., Fikry, A., Ismail, Z., & Hussein, N. (2017). Work-family conflict among working parents of children with autism in Malaysia. *Procedia Computer Science, 105*, 345–352. DOI: 10.1016/j.procs.2017.01.232

Smith, E. J. (2006). The Strength-Based Counseling Model. *The Counseling Psychologist, 34*(1), 13–79. DOI: 10.1177/0011000005277018

Smith, M. J., Merle, J. L., Baker-Ericzén, M., Sherwood, K., Bornheimer, L. A., Ross, B., Harrington, M., Sharma, A., Brown, C., Gordon, T., Telfer, D., Reese, J., Hirst, J., Oulvey, E. A., Dignadice, V., Williams, E.-D., Magaña, S., Hume, K., Sung, C., & Smith, J. D. (2024). A type 1 hybrid multi-site randomized controlled trial protocol for evaluating virtual interview training among autistic transition-age youth. *Contemporary Clinical Trials Communications, 42*, 101384. Advance online publication. DOI: 10.1016/j.conctc.2024.101384 PMID: 39525564

Smith, M. J., Sherwood, K. L., Genova, H. M., Ross, B., DaWalt, L. S., Bishop, L., Telfer, D., Brown, C., Sanchez, B., & Kallen, M. A. (2023). Psychometric properties of the mock interview rating scale for autistic transition-age youth. *Frontiers in Psychiatry, 14*, 1235056. Advance online publication. DOI: 10.3389/fpsyt.2023.1235056 PMID: 38025460

Smith, M. J., Sherwood, K., Ross, B., Smith, J. D., DaWalt, L., Bishop, L., Humm, L., Elkins, J., & Steacy, C. (2021). Virtual interview training for autistic transition age youth: A randomized controlled feasibility and effectiveness trial. *Autism, 25*(6), 1536–1552. DOI: 10.1177/1362361321989928 PMID: 33567883

Smith, T. E., Reinke, W. M., Herman, K. C., & Sebastian, J. (2021). Exploring the link between principal leadership and family engagement across elementary and middle school. *Journal of School Psychology, 84*, 49–62. DOI: 10.1016/j.jsp.2020.12.006 PMID: 33581770

Smyth, S., Mc Laughlin, N., Egan, C., Gurrin, C., Quinn, K., McGarrell, M., & Devlin, S. (2021). Study protocol for autism specific transition resources (T-Res Study): Developing a flexible resource package for dealing with the loosening and/or lifting of COVID-19 related restrictions. *HRB Open Research, 4*. https://doi.org/ DOI: 10.12688/hrbopenres.13155.1

Snell-Rood, C., Ruble, L., Kleinert, H., McGrew, J. H., Adams, M., Rodgers, A., Odom, J., Wong, W. H., & Yu, Y. (2020). Stakeholder perspectives on transition planning, implementation, and outcomes for students with autism spectrum disorder. *Autism, 24*(5), 1164–1176. DOI: 10.1177/1362361319894827 PMID: 31957461

Snyman, C., Van Eeden, C., & Heyns, M. (2023). How character strengths of autistic learners aid primary school educators in the class: An exploratory study. *South African Journal of Childhood Education, 13*(1). Advance online publication. DOI: 10.4102/sajce.v13i1.1311

Soeker, M. S. (2020). A descriptive, qualitative study of the challenges that individuals with Autism Spectrum Disorder experience when transitioning from skills training programs into the open labor market in Cape Town, South Africa. *Work (Reading, Mass.), 65*(4), 733–747. DOI: 10.3233/WOR-203127

Sokratous, S., Merkouris, A., Middleton, N., & Karanikola, M. (2013). The association between stressful life events and depressive symptoms among Cypriot university students: A cross-sectional descriptive correlational study. *BMC Public Health, 13*(1), 1121. DOI: 10.1186/1471-2458-13-1121 PMID: 24304515

Soltanifar, A., Akbarzadeh, F., Moharreri, F., Soltanifar, A., Ebrahimi, A., Mokhber, N., Minoocherhr, A., & Naqvi, S. S. A. (2015). Comparison of parental stress among mothers and fathers of children with autistic spectrum disorder in Iran. *Iranian Journal of Nursing and Midwifery Research, 20*(1), 93–98. PMID: 25709697

Söner, O., & Yılmaz, O. (2025). Exploring the associations of career transition components with adolescents' career decision-making self-efficacy and anxiety. *BMC Psychology, 13*(1), 1115. DOI: 10.1186/s40359-025-03479-1

Southall, C. (2013). Use of Technology to Accommodate Differences Associated with Autism Spectrum Disorder in the General Curriculum and Environment. *Journal of Special Education Technology, 28*(1), 23–34. DOI: 10.1177/016264341302800103

Spelman, D. B. (2025). Routine Disruption in Autism. *Private Therapy Clinic.* https://theprivatetherapyclinic.co.uk/blog/autism-and-routine-disruption/

Sraboni, S. A. (2023). *Experience of Child Rearing in Balance with Work-Life of Employed Parents who have a Child with Autism Spectrum Disorder* [PhD Thesis, Bangladesh Health Professions Institute, Faculty of Medicine, the University …]. http://library.crp-bangladesh.org:8080/xmlui/handle/123456789/1060

Sreckovic, M. A., Hume, K. A., & Regan, T. E. (2020). Use of Work Systems to Increase the Independence of Adolescents With Autism Spectrum Disorder. *Career Development and Transition for Exceptional Individuals*, *43*(4), 240–256. DOI: 10.1177/2165143420948766

Stambulova, N. (2010). Counseling athletes in career transitions: The five-step career planning strategy. *Journal of Sport Psychology in Action*, *1*(2), 95–105. DOI: 10.1080/21520704.2010.528829

Stampoltzis, A., Peristeri, E., & Kalouri, R. (2025). Career counselors' attitudes about employment-related skills of individuals with autism spectrum disorders in Greece. *Frontiers in Education*, *10*, 1662929. Advance online publication. DOI: 10.3389/feduc.2025.1662929

Stanton, A. L. (2012). Regulating Emotions during Stressful Experiences: The Adaptive Utility of Coping through Emotional Approach. In Folkman, S. (Ed.), *The Oxford Handbook of Stress, Health, and Coping*. Oxford University Press., DOI: 10.1093/oxfordhb/9780195375343.013.0018

Stark, M. D., & Lindo, E. J. (2023). Executive Functioning Supports for College Students with an Autism Spectrum Disorder. *Review Journal of Autism and Developmental Disorders*, *10*(4), 604–614. DOI: 10.1007/s40489-022-00311-z

Stavrou, K. (2024). Independent Living for Individuals With Autism. In Dimitriadou, I., Vasileiadis, I., & Koutras, S. (Eds.), *Tools for Promoting Independent Living Skills in Individuals with Disabilities* (pp. 151–170). IGI Global., DOI: 10.4018/979-8-3693-6026-2.ch008

Stephenson, J., Browne, L., Carter, M., Clark, T., Costley, D., Martin, J., Williams, K., Bruck, S., Davies, L., & Sweller, N. (2021). Facilitators and Barriers to Inclusion of Students With Autism Spectrum Disorder: Parent, Teacher, and Principal Perspectives. *Australasian Journal of Special and Inclusive Education*, *45*(1), 1–17. DOI: 10.1017/jsi.2020.12

Stone-MacDonald, A., Cihak, D. F., & Zager, D. (Eds.). (2016). *Autism Spectrum Disorders: Identification, Education, and Treatment* (4th ed.). Routledge., DOI: 10.4324/9781315794181

Stoner, C. R., & Stoner, J. B. (2014). How can we make this work? Understanding and responding to working parents of children with autism. *Business Horizons*, *57*(1), 85–95. DOI: 10.1016/j.bushor.2013.10.002

Stoner, J. B., & Angell, M. E. (2006). Parent Perspectives on Role Engagement: An Investigation of Parents of Children With ASD and Their Self-Reported Roles With Education Professionals. *Focus on Autism and Other Developmental Disabilities, 21*(3), 177–189. DOI: 10.1177/10883576060210030601

Strachan, L., Fraser-Thomas, J., & Nelson-Ferguson, K. (2016). An ecological perspective on high performance sport and positive youth development. In N. L. Holt (Ed.), *Positive Youth Development through Sport: Second edition* (pp. 57–68). Taylor and Francis. DOI: 10.4324/9781315709499-6

Strnadová, I., Cumming, T. M., & Danker, J. (2016). Transitions for Students with Intellectual Disability and/or Autism Spectrum Disorder: Carer and Teacher Perspectives. *Australasian Journal of Special Education, 40*(2), 141–156. DOI: 10.1017/jse.2016.2

Sugai, G., & Simonsen, B. (2020). Reinforcement Foundations of a Function-Based Behavioral Approach for Students With Challenging Behavior. *Beyond Behavior, 29*(2), 78–85. DOI: 10.1177/1074295620902444

Sung, C., Sánchez, J., Kuo, H.-J., Wang, C.-C., & Leahy, M. J. (2015). Gender Differences in Vocational Rehabilitation Service Predictors of Successful Competitive Employment for Transition-Aged Individuals with Autism. *Journal of Autism and Developmental Disorders, 45*(10), 3204–3218. DOI: 10.1007/s10803-015-2480-z PMID: 26060047

Sweden Sverige, & Swedish Institute. (2025, November 3). *The Swedish school system*. https://sweden.se/life/society/the-swedish-school-system

Szechy, K. A., & O'Donnell, L. A. (2025). Autism Knowledge Matters: Perceptions of an Autistic Employee's Competency and Attitudes Toward Workplace Social Inclusion. *Autism in Adulthood: Challenges and Management*, aut.2024.0261. Advance online publication. DOI: 10.1089/aut.2024.0261

Szulc-Kurpaska, M. (2023). Exploring Teacher Engagement on the Example of Polish FL Teachers. In *English Language Education* (Vol. 32, pp. 87–108). Springer Science and Business Media B.V., DOI: 10.1007/978-3-031-28655-1_6

Tabancalı, E., & Su, Y. (2021). Role ambiguity of school principals. *Eğitimde Nitel Araştırmalar Dergisi, 9*(1), 335–359.

Taber, B. J. (2019). Career Counselling Interventions to Enhance Career Adaptabilities for Sustainable Employment. In Maree, J. G. (Ed.), *Handbook of Innovative Career Counselling* (pp. 103–115). Springer International Publishing., DOI: 10.1007/978-3-030-22799-9_7

ăpuru, I. A. (2023). KNOWLEDGE SHARING THROUGH INFORMAL COMMUNICATION. *eLearning Softw. Educ. Conf., 1*, 433–444. DOI: 10.12753/2066-026X-23-041

Taylor, D. F. P. (2014). Defining ubuntu for business ethics- A deontological approach. *South African Journal of Philosophy, 33*(3), 331–345. DOI: 10.1080/02580136.2014.948328

Taylor, E. R. (2019). Solution-focused therapy and integration with creative and tangible approaches. In Taylor, E. R. (Ed.), *Solution-Focused Therapy with Children and Adolescents: Creative and Play-Based Approaches* (pp. 46–58). Taylor and Francis., DOI: 10.4324/9781315166674-5

Taylor, J. L., & Mailick, M. R. (2014). A longitudinal examination of 10-year change in vocational and educational activities for adults with autism spectrum disorders. *Developmental Psychology, 50*(3), 699–708. DOI: 10.1037/a0034297 PMID: 24001150

Taylor, J. L., McPheeters, M. L., Sathe, N. A., Dove, D., Veenstra-VanderWeele, J., & Warren, Z. (2012a). A Systematic Review of Vocational Interventions for Young Adults With Autism Spectrum Disorders. *Pediatrics, 130*(3), 531–538. DOI: 10.1542/peds.2012-0682 PMID: 22926170

Taylor, J. L., Smith, L. E., & Mailick, M. R. (2014). Engagement in Vocational Activities Promotes Behavioral Development for Adults with Autism Spectrum Disorders. *Journal of Autism and Developmental Disorders, 44*(6), 1447–1460. DOI: 10.1007/s10803-013-2010-9 PMID: 24287880

Teachers Institute. (2023, December 27). *Advancing Inclusive Education for Children with Disabilities in India*. https://teachers.institute/alternative-education/inclusive-education-children-disabilities-india/

Teresa Rani, V. S., Mpm, P. K., & Kareem, J. (2025). Understanding the disconnect: A study on competency of special educators in autism education in India. *Support for Learning, 40*(4), 334–342. DOI: 10.1111/1467-9604.70013

Test, D. W., Smith, L. E., & Carter, E. W. (2014). Equipping Youth With Autism Spectrum Disorders for Adulthood: Promoting Rigor, Relevance, and Relationships. *Remedial and Special Education, 35*(2), 80–90. DOI: 10.1177/0741932513514857

Thiem, K. C., & Dasgupta, N. (2022). From Precollege to Career: Barriers Facing Historically Marginalized Students and Evidence-Based Solutions. *Social Issues and Policy Review, 16*(1), 212–251. DOI: 10.1111/sipr.12085

Thompson, C., Falkmer, T., Evans, K., Bölte, S., & Girdler, S. (2018). A realist evaluation of peer mentoring support for university students with autism. *British Journal of Special Education, 45*(4), 412–434. DOI: 10.1111/1467-8578.12241

Thompson, J. R., Fulk, B. M., & Piercy, S. W. (2000). Do Individualised Transition Plans Match the Postschool Projections of Students with Learning Disabilities and Their Parents? *Career Development for Exceptional Individuals, 23*(1), 3–25. DOI: 10.1177/088572880002300102

Thuy, V. T. T., & Duong, D. P. N. (2026). Can internship experiences bridge the gap between university training and work readiness? Evidence from vietnamese economics students. *Multidisciplinary Science Journal, 8*(4), 2026265. Advance online publication. DOI: 10.31893/multiscience.2026265

Tobin, C. T., & Rozek, E. (2025). Enhancing undergraduate psychology internship by integrating professional core competencies. *Mentoring and Tutoring: Partnership in Learning*. 1-25https://DOI: 10.1080/13611267.2025.2571494

Tomaszewski, B., Klinger, L., & Pugliese, C. E. (2022). Self-Determination in Autistic Transition-Aged Youth without Intellectual Disability. *Journal of Autism and Developmental Disorders, 52*(9), 4067–4078. DOI: 10.1007/s10803-021-05280-6 PMID: 34536165

Tomaszewski, B., Kraemer, B., Steinbrenner, J. R., Smith DaWalt, L., Hall, L. J., Hume, K., & Odom, S. (2020). Student, Educator, and Parent Perspectives of Self-Determination in High School Students with Autism Spectrum Disorder. *Autism Research, 13*(12), 2164–2176. DOI: 10.1002/aur.2337 PMID: 32743977

Tomfohrde, O., Hudock, R. L., Kremer, K. B., Fatiha, N., & Weiler, L. (2023). Fostering social connectedness among adolescents and adults with autism: A qualitative analysis. *Psychology in the Schools, 60*(1), 23–39. DOI: 10.1002/pits.22759

Tomlinson, J., Baird, M., Berg, P., & Cooper, R. (2018). Flexible careers across the life course: Advancing theory, research and practice. *Human Relations, 71*(1), 4–22. DOI: 10.1177/0018726717733313

Tong, P., & An, I. S. (2023). Review of studies applying Bronfenbrenner's bioecological theory in international and intercultural education research. *Frontiers in Psychology, 14*, 1233925. Advance online publication. DOI: 10.3389/fpsyg.2023.1233925 PMID: 38259539

Tonnsen, B. L., & Hahn, E. R. (2016). Middle School Students' Attitudes Toward a Peer with Autism Spectrum Disorder. *Focus on Autism and Other Developmental Disabilities, 31*(4), 262–274. DOI: 10.1177/1088357614559213

Torgbenu, E. L., Oginni, O. S., Opoku, M. P., Nketsia, W., & Agyei-Okyere, E. (2021). Inclusive education in Nigeria: Exploring parental attitude, knowledge and perceived social norms influencing implementation. *International Journal of Inclusive Education*, *25*(3), 377–393. DOI: 10.1080/13603116.2018.1554715

Tourais, P., & Videira, N. (2024). Sustainability transition strategies in a business context: A co-creation process in the Portuguese hospitality sector. *Corporate Social Responsibility and Environmental Management*, *31*(1), 600–628. DOI: 10.1002/csr.2588

Trede, F., & Smith, M. (2012). Teaching reflective practice in practice settings: Students' perceptions of their clinical educators. *Teaching in Higher Education*, *17*(5), 615–627. DOI: 10.1080/13562517.2012.658558

Trembath, D., & Iacono, T. (2016). Standardized Assessment of Prelinguistic Communication. In Keen, D., Meadan, H., Brady, N. C., & Halle, J. W. (Eds.), *Prelinguistic and Minimally Verbal Communicators on the Autism Spectrum* (pp. 75–100). Springer., DOI: 10.1007/978-981-10-0713-2_5

Tsiopela, D., & Jimoyiannis, A. (2017). Using a Web-Based Environment to Enhance Vocational Skills of Students with Autism Spectrum Disorder. In Mikropoulos, T. A. (Ed.), *Research on e-Learning and ICT in Education: Technological, Pedagogical and Instructional Perspectives* (pp. 381–395). Springer International Publishing., DOI: 10.1007/978-3-319-95059-4_23

Turcan, C., Delamain, H., Loke, A., Pender, R., Mandy, W., & Saunders, R. (2024). Measurement invariance of the parent-reported Strengths and Difficulties Questionnaire in autistic adolescents. *Autism*, *28*(10), 2623–2636. DOI: 10.1177/13623613241236805 PMID: 38481018

Tyrrell, B., & Woods, K. (2018). Gathering the views of children and young people with ASD: A systematic literature review. *British Journal of Special Education*, *45*(3), 302–328. DOI: 10.1111/1467-8578.12235

U.S. Equal Employment Opportunity Commission. (2023). *Employment protections under the Rehabilitation Act of 1973: 50 years of protecting Americans with disabilities in the workplace*. https://www.eeoc.gov/employment-protections-under-rehabilitation-act-1973-50-years-protecting-americans-disabilities

Uba-Mbibi, F. O. (2013). Decision making and job satisfaction as correlates of teachers' job performance in junior secondary schools in Abia state, Nigeria. *Mediterranean Journal of Social Sciences*, *4*(8), 107–112. DOI: 10.5901/mjss.2013.v4n8p107

Udah, H., Tusasiirwe, S., Mugumbate, R., & Gatwiri, K. (2025). Ubuntu philosophy, values, and principles: An opportunity to do social work differently. *Journal of Social Work : JSW, 25*(4), 433–451. DOI: 10.1177/14680173241312749

Udoh, I. I. L., & Okon, B. A. (2008). *The languages of the Niger Delta Region of Nigeria.*

Ugwu, J. (2025, October 30). Senate begins consideration of bill to establish autism centres nationwide. *The Cable*. https://www.thecable.ng/senate-advances-bill-to-set-up-autism-centres-for-early-diagnosis-care/

Ulofoshio, J. I. (2017). *Lived experiences of mothers raising children with autism spectrum disorder in Nigeria* [Doctoral dissertation]. Walden University. https://scholarworks.waldenu.edu/cgi/viewcontent.cgi?article=5982&context=dissertations

Umeh, N. C. (2024). Access to Inclusive Education for Learners with Disabilities in Nigeria: Discursive Interpretation of Findings. In *Ius Gentium* (Vol. 117, pp. 47–71). Springer Science and Business Media B.V. DOI: 10.1007/978-3-031-64549-5_3

Umeh, N. C., & Anyaele, D. O. (2024a). Assessment of the Implementation of Inclusive Education Policy Among Stakeholders in Abia State, Nigeria. In *Ius Gentium* (Vol. 117, pp. 1–19). Springer Science and Business Media B.V., DOI: 10.1007/978-3-031-64549-5_1

Underhill, J. C., Ledford, V., & Adams, H. (2019). Autism stigma in communication classrooms: Exploring peer attitudes and motivations toward interacting with atypical students. *Communication Education, 68*(2), 175–192. DOI: 10.1080/03634523.2019.1569247

United Nations. (2008, May 3). *Convention on the Rights of Persons with Disabilities*. United Nations Human Rights Office of the High Commissioner. https://www.ohchr.org/en/instruments-mechanisms/instruments/convention-rights-persons-disabilities

Uttayotha, S., & Scheef, A. R. (2021). Partnerships to promote inclusive education for students with disabilities in Thailand. *Journal of Global Education and Research, 5*(1), 85–95. DOI: 10.5038/2577-509X.5.1.1102

Uzodinma, U. E., & Onyishi, N, C., Ngwoke, A. N., Ugwu, J. I., Okorie, C. O., A. Amujiri, B., ... & Akanaeme, I. N. (. (2022). Effectiveness of rational emotive occupational health coaching in reducing burnout symptoms among teachers of children with autism. *Science Progress, 105*(2), 00368504221100907. DOI: 10.1177/00368504221100907 PMID: 35619571

Van der Stede, W. A. (2014). A manipulationist view of causality in cross-sectional survey research. *Accounting, Organizations and Society, 39*(7), 567–574. DOI: 10.1016/j.aos.2013.12.001

Van Hees, V., Moyson, T., & Roeyers, H. (2015). Higher Education Experiences of Students with Autism Spectrum Disorder: Challenges, Benefits and Support Needs. *Journal of Autism and Developmental Disorders, 45*(6), 1673–1688. DOI: 10.1007/s10803-014-2324-2 PMID: 25448918

Vargo, K. K., & Loflin, L. J. (2022). Assessing Preference for Activities and Instructional Contexts. *Intervention in School and Clinic, 58*(1), 31–38. DOI: 10.1177/10534512211047575

Vázquez-Cano, E., & Holgueras-González, A. I. (2019). Teacher stress factors and performance in high schools in Ecuador. *KEDI Journal of Educational Policy, 16*(2), 21–41.

Velec, M., & Huang, S. H. (2014). Quantitative methodologies and analysis. In Gillan, C., Di Prospero, L., Harnett, N., & Holden, L. (Eds.), *Research for the Radiation Therapist: From Question to Culture* (pp. 87–126). Apple Academic Press. DOI: 10.1201/b16449-8

Victor-Aigbodion, V., & Eseadi, C. (2025). Effect of purpose-based career coaching on career transition self-efficacy among college students with autism spectrum disorder. *EDULEARN25 Proceedings*, 8088–8101. https://library.iated.org/view/VICTORAIGBODION2025EFF

Victor-Aigbodion, V., & Eseadi, C. (2025). Effect of purpose-based career coaching on career transition self-efficacy among college students with autism spectrum disorder. *EDULEARN25 Proceedings*, 8088–8101. *17th International Conference on Education and New Learning Technologies*. DOI: 10.21125/edulearn.2025.2059

Vinson, D., Nixon, S., Walsh, B., Walker, C., Mitchell, E., & Zaitseva, E. (2010). Investigating the relationship between student engagement and transition. *Active Learning in Higher Education, 11*(2), 131–143. DOI: 10.1177/1469787410365658

Von Holzen, A. V., Skoning, S. N., Fisher, T. A., Clark, D. M., & Cook, J. A. (2024). Factors of Career Development Impacting Transition for Young Adults with Autism Spectrum Disorder. *Exceptionality Education International, 34*(2), 91–114. DOI: 10.5206/eei.v34i2.17529

Wagacha, N., Mutisya, A., & Ounoi, I. (2025, October 15). *A landmark shift in rights, compliance and inclusion with Kenya's new Persons with Disabilities Act*. CDH. https://www.cliffedekkerhofmeyr.com/en/news/publications/2025/Practice/Corporate-Commercial/corporate-and-commercial-alert-15-october-A-landmark-shift-in-rights-compliance-and-inclusion-with-Kenyas-new-Persons-with-Disabilities-Act

Wahab, R., Fahmy, K. A. M. F. M., Ibrahim, S. A. S., & Philip, W. (2022). Social support and stress among parents with autism spectrum disorder children. *Environment-Behaviour Proceedings Journal*, *7*(20), 449–454. DOI: 10.21834/ebpj.v7i20.3409

Waisman-Nitzan, M., Gal, E., & Schreuer, N. (2021). "It's like a ramp for a person in a wheelchair": Workplace accessibility for employees with autism. *Research in Developmental Disabilities*, *114*, 103959. Advance online publication. DOI: 10.1016/j.ridd.2021.103959

Waisman, T., Alba, L. A., & Green, S. A. (2022). Barriers to Inclusive Learning for Autistic Individuals. *Pediatrics*, *149*(Suppl 4), e2020049437Q. DOI: 10.1542/peds.2020-049437Q

Wang, A., Yu, S., Wang, M., Wu, L., Wang, D., & Huang, L. (2023). Promoting meaningful peer feedback among in-service Chinese language teachers in an online lesson study. *System*, *115*, 103055. Advance online publication. DOI: 10.1016/j.system.2023.103055

Wang, D., Liu, X., & Deng, H. (2022). The perspectives of social cognitive career theory approach in current times. *Frontiers in Psychology*, *13*, 1023994. DOI: 10.3389/fpsyg.2022.1023994 PMID: 36533045

Wang, J., Hu, Y., Wang, Y., Qin, X., Xia, W., Sun, C., Wu, L., & Wang, J. (2013). Parenting stress in Chinese mothers of children with autism spectrum disorders. *Social Psychiatry and Psychiatric Epidemiology*, *48*(4), 575–582. DOI: 10.1007/s00127-012-0569-7 PMID: 22968576

Wang, J., Zhou, X., Xia, W., Sun, C.-H., Wu, L.-J., Wang, J.-L., & Tomoda, A. (2012). Parent-reported health care expenditures associated with autism spectrum disorders in Heilongjiang province, China. *BMC Health Services Research*, *12*(1), 1–7. DOI: 10.1186/1472-6963-12-7

Wawire, B. A. (2021). Promoting effective early grade reading: The case study of primary teachers' preparation programmes in Kenya. *Curriculum Journal*, *32*(2), 247–268. DOI: 10.1002/curj.69

Webster, A., Bruck, S., & Saggers, B. (2022). Supporting self-determination of autistic students in transitions. *Research in Developmental Disabilities, 128*, 104301. Advance online publication. DOI: 10.1016/j.ridd.2022.104301 PMID: 35797777

Wehman, P., Schall, C., Carr, S., Targett, P., West, M., & Cifu, G. (2014). Transition From School to Adulthood for Youth With Autism Spectrum Disorder: What We Know and What We Need to Know. *Journal of Disability Policy Studies, 25*(1), 30–40. DOI: 10.1177/1044207313518071

Wehman, P., Schall, C., McDonough, J., Molinelli, A., Riehle, E., Ham, W., & Thiss, W. R. (2013). Project SEARCH for Youth With Autism Spectrum Disorders: Increasing Competitive Employment On Transition From High School. *Journal of Positive Behavior Interventions, 15*(3), 144–155. DOI: 10.1177/1098300712459760

Wehmeyer, M., & Zhao, Y. (2020). *Teaching Students to Become Self-Determined Learners*. ASCD.

Welch, K. C., Pennington, R., Vanaparthy, S., Do, H. M., Narayanan, R., Popa, D., Barnes, G., & Kuravackel, G. (2023). Using Physiological Signals and Machine Learning Algorithms to Measure Attentiveness During Robot-Assisted Social Skills Intervention: A Case Study of Two Children with Autism Spectrum Disorder. *IEEE Instrumentation & Measurement Magazine, 26*(3), 39–45. DOI: 10.1109/MIM.2023.10121412

Wendling, E., & Sagas, M. (2020). An Application of the Social Cognitive Career Theory Model of Career Self-Management to College Athletes' Career Planning for Life After Sport. *Frontiers in Psychology, 11*, 9. Advance online publication. DOI: 10.3389/fpsyg.2020.00009 PMID: 32038437

Westbrook, J. D., Fong, C. J., Nye, C., Williams, A., Wendt, O., & Cortopassi, T. (2013). Pre-Graduation Transition Services for Improving Employment Outcomes among Persons with Autism Spectrum Disorders: A Systematic Review. *Campbell Systematic Reviews, 9*(1), 1–70. DOI: 10.4073/csr.2013.11

Westheimer, J. (1998). *Among School Teachers: Community, Autonomy and Ideology in Teachers' Work*. Teachers College Press.

White, J., McGarry, S., Williams, P. J., & Black, H., M. (. (2025). 'We think differently, we learn differently, but at the end of the day we're not that different': Strengths-based approaches in high school from the perspectives of autistic adolescents. *Autism, 29*(11), 2804–2817. DOI: 10.1177/13623613251348557 PMID: 40567122

White, L. M., Simpson, K., Malone, S., & Adams, D. (2024). Autistic Adults' Reflections on What Supported Their Transitioning from Secondary School. *Education Sciences, 14*(6), 576. Advance online publication. DOI: 10.3390/educsci14060576

White, S. W., Brewe, A. M., & Powell, N. (2025). Stepped Transition to Employment and Postsecondary Education Success (STEPS) for Adolescents and Adults with Autism: Community Implementation Pilot Trial. *JMIR Formative Research, 9*, v9i4e70137. Advance online publication. DOI: 10.2196/70137 PMID: 40882612

White, S. W., Koenig, K., & Scahill, L. (2010). Group social skills instruction for adolescents with high-functioning autism spectrum disorders. *Focus on Autism and Other Developmental Disabilities, 25*(4), 209–219. DOI: 10.1177/1088357610380595

Wiedman, C. (2023). Navigating role conflict: One professional's journey as a new clinician leader. *BMJ Leader, 8*(1), 6–8. DOI: 10.1136/leader-2022-000715 PMID: 37339846

Williams Harryman, E. (2025). Elementary Teachers' Experiences Supporting the Academic Growth and Development of Students on the Autism Spectrum in Inclusion Classrooms. *Walden Dissertations and Doctoral Studies*. https://scholarworks.waldenu.edu/dissertations/16909

Winn, S., & Hay, I. (2009). Transition from school for youths with a disability: Issues and challenges. *Disability & Society, 24*(1), 103–115. DOI: 10.1080/09687590802535725

Wisner-Carlson, R., Uram, S., & Flis, T. (2020). The Transition to Adulthood for Young People with Autism Spectrum Disorder. *The Psychiatric Clinics of North America, 43*(4), 673–686. DOI: 10.1016/j.psc.2020.08.005

Wolffe, K. E., Ajuwon, P. M., & Kelly, S. M. (2013). Working with visual impairment in Nigeria: A qualitative look at employment status. *Journal of Visual Impairment & Blindness, 107*(6), 425–436. DOI: 10.1177/0145482X1310700605

Wong, J., Coster, W. J., Cohn, E. S., & Orsmond, G. I. (2021). Identifying School-Based Factors that Predict Employment Outcomes for Transition-Age Youth with Autism Spectrum Disorder. *Journal of Autism and Developmental Disorders, 51*(1), 60–74. DOI: 10.1007/s10803-020-04515-2 PMID: 32356081

Wong, L. H. G. (2023). Sensory-Based Interventions for Managing Difficulties of Children with Autism Spectrum Disorder at School. *Current Developmental Disorders Reports, 10*(4), 240–249. DOI: 10.1007/s40474-023-00288-2

Wong, V. W., Ruble, L. A., Yu, Y., & McGrew, J. H. (2017). Too stressed to teach? Teaching quality, student engagement, and IEP outcomes. *Exceptional Children, 83*(4), 412–427. DOI: 10.1177/0014402917690729 PMID: 30555178

Wong, V., McGrew, J., & Ruble, L. (2020). Predicting the Outcomes of Parents of Transition-Age Youth or Young Adults with ASD. *Journal of Autism and Developmental Disorders, 50*(8), 2723–2739. DOI: 10.1007/s10803-020-04362-1 PMID: 32030578

Yakubova, G., & Zeleke, W. A. (2016). A Problem-Solving Intervention Using iPads to Improve Transition-Related Task Performance of Students With Autism Spectrum Disorder. *Journal of Special Education Technology, 31*(2), 77–86. DOI: 10.1177/0162643416650023

Yamamoto, S. H., & Alverson, C. Y. (2022). From high school to postsecondary education, training, and employment: Predicting outcomes for young adults with autism spectrum disorder. *Autism & Developmental Language Impairments, 7*, 23969415221095019. Advance online publication. DOI: 10.1177/23969415221095019 PMID: 36382083

Yang, J., Yang, L., Quan, H., & Zeng, Y. (2021). Implementation Barriers: A TASKS Framework. *Journal of Integrated Design & Process Science, 25*(3–4), 134–147. DOI: 10.3233/JID-210011

Yang, J., & Zhang, R. (2025). Melodic bridges: Music intervention as a catalyst for social skills development in preschool children with autism. *Frontiers in Psychology, 16*, 1542662. DOI: 10.3389/fpsyg.2025.1542662 PMID: 40636053

Yang, L., Pang, F., & Sin, K.-F. (2023). Assessing the Psychometric Properties of the Practice and Product Inventory of Supporting Students with ASD (PPI-SSA): A Concise Assessment Tool for Teachers in Inclusive Classrooms. *Sustainability (Basel), 15*(19), 14576. Advance online publication. DOI: 10.3390/su151914576

Yarrow, E., Tereshko, L. M., Weiss, M. J., Gerhardt, P., & Magrauth, M. (2024). Interventions targeting work-related skills in adults with autism spectrum disorders: A comprehensive literature review. *Journal of Vocational Rehabilitation, 61*(3), 348–370. Advance online publication. DOI: 10.1177/10522263241285204

Yibakuro, E. A. (2025). The Role of Education Law in Supporting Special Needs Students in Nigerian Tertiary Institutions. *International Journal of Educational Management, Rivers State University., 1*(2), 372–385. https://ijedm.com/index.php/ijedm/article/view/67

Yi, T., Hu, Y., Xia, L., Zhang, Y., Chen, X., & Dong, C. (2025). Instruments to Assess Transition Readiness Among Adolescents With Chronic Disease: A COSMIN Systematic Review of Measurement Properties. *Child: Care, Health and Development, 51*(1), e70017. DOI: 10.1111/cch.70017 PMID: 39629862

Yokota, S., & Tanaka, M. (2024). Less Negative Implicit Attitudes Toward Autism Spectrum Disorder in University Students: A Comparison with Physical Disabilities. *Journal of Autism and Developmental Disorders*, *54*(1), 182–192. DOI: 10.1007/s10803-022-05749-y

Young, R. A. (1983). Career development of adolescents: An ecological perspective. *Journal of Youth and Adolescence*, *12*(5), 401–417. DOI: 10.1007/BF02088723 PMID: 24306360

Yuliawati, L., & Ardyan, E. (2022). The Role of Life Planning in Finding Purpose and Living Out One's Career Calling Among Indonesian Emerging Adults. *Journal of Career Development*, *49*(3), 538–550. DOI: 10.1177/0894845320950834

Zainal, M. S., & Zainodin, N. N. A. W. (2025). Educational and Psychosocial Challenges Among Individuals with High-Functioning Autism: A Systematic Literature Review. *International Journal of Learning. Teaching and Educational Research*, *24*(8), 1024–1040. DOI: 10.26803/ijlter.24.8.45

Zemrani, C., Vincent, C., Dumont, F. S., Julien-Gauthier, F., Caouette, M., Jolicoeur, E., Letscher, S., Boucher, N., & Mercure, F. (2025). The 'Work Rehabilitation and Adaptation Profile' for Adults with Autism, a Validated French-Canadian Observation Grid. *Journal of Vocational Rehabilitation*, *63*(3), 282–298. DOI: 10.1177/10522263251376329

Zhao, Y., Luo, Y., Zhang, R., & Zheng, X. (2023). Direct and indirect costs for families of children with autism spectrum disorder in China. *Autism*, *27*(8), 2337–2347. DOI: 10.1177/13623613231158862

Zhong, N. H., Grimm, R. P., Kanne, S. M., & Mazurek, M. O. (2023). Measurement invariance of the Autism Impact Measure (AIM) across sex in children with autism spectrum disorder. *Autism Research*, *16*(1), 154–163. DOI: 10.1002/aur.2845 PMID: 36341720

Zincirli, M., & Polat, E. (2025). Development of the Digital Transformation Scale: Assessment of Measurement Invariance. *SAGE Open*, *15*(3), 21582440251378827. Advance online publication. DOI: 10.1177/21582440251378827

Zovko, M., Šimleša, S., & Olujić Tomazin, M. (2024). Parenting stress, coping strategies and social support for mothers of preschool children with autism spectrum disorder in the Republic of Croatia. *Clinical Child Psychology and Psychiatry*, *29*(2), 674–686. DOI: 10.1177/13591045231191802 PMID: 37491211

Zulkifli, N. R., & Zin, H. M. (2024). The Performance of Regularization Technique in Assessing Reliability and Validity of the Constructs in Structural Equation Modeling: Application in Breast Cancer Awareness Research. *Malaysian Journal of Medicine and Health Sciences*, *20*, 112–118. DOI: 10.47836/mjmhs.20.s8.15

About the Authors

Boitumelo Molebogeng Diale is a Professor and Dean of Education at Sol Plaatje University, Kimberley, South Africa. She is a registered Educational Psychologist with the Health Professions Council of South Africa and a certified Employee Wellness Practitioner. Her work advances career development across the lifespan through a life design orientation, with a strong emphasis on youth and neurodiverse populations. She currently serves as a Visiting Professor at the University of Nigeria, Nsukka, and previously co-coordinated the Centre for Neurodiversity at the University of Johannesburg, Soweto Campus, where she led community-focused initiatives supporting career transitions for individuals with neurodiverse needs.

Chiedu Eseadi is a Senior Lecturer in the Department of Educational Psychology at the University of Johannesburg, South Africa. His professional expertise spans career guidance, mental health, and rehabilitation counselling. His scholarship centres on mental health across clinical and educational contexts, neurodiversity, and the development of evidence-informed frameworks for career transition and career counselling.

Index

A

C

D

E

P

Q

R

S

T

V